MICROECONOMIC
POLICY
ANALYSIS

Economics Handbook Series

Anderson: National Income Theory and Its Price Theoretic Foundations
Atkinson and Stiglitz: Lectures on Public Economics
Carlson: Economic Security in the United States
Chacholiades: International Monetary Theory and Policy
Chacholiades: International Trade Theory and Policy
Chow: Econometrics
Friedman: Microeconomic Policy Analysis
Gapinski: Macroeconomic Theory: Statics, Dynamics, and Policy
Hansen: A Survey of General Equilibrium Systems
Hansen: The American Economy
Harris: The Economics of Harvard
Harris: Monetary Theory
Harrod: The British Economy
Henderson and Quandt: Microeconomic Theory: A Mathematical Approach
Herrick and Kindleberger: Economic Development
Hirsch: The Economics of State and Local Government
Hirsch: Urban Economic Analysis
Jones: An Introduction to Modern Theories of Economic Growth
Kendrick: Stochastic Control for Economic Models
Maddala: Econometrics
Ott, Ott, and Yoo: Macroeconomic Theory
Quirk and Saposnik: Introduction to General Equilibrium Theory
    and Welfare Economics
Taylor: A History of Economic Thought
Theil, Boot, and Kloek: Operations Research and Quantitative Economics
Walton and McKersie: A Behavioral Theory of Labor Negotiations

MICROECONOMIC POLICY ANALYSIS

Lee S. Friedman

Graduate School of Public Policy
University of California, Berkeley

McGRAW-HILL BOOK COMPANY

New York   St. Louis   San Francisco   Auckland   Bogotá
Hamburg   Johannesburg   London   Madrid   Mexico   Montreal   New Delhi
Panama   Paris   São Paulo   Singapore   Sydney   Tokyo   Toronto

This book was set in Times Roman by Santype-Byrd.
The editors were Patricia A. Mitchell and Frances Koblin;
the production supervisor was Leroy A. Young.
The drawings were done by ECL Art.
Halliday Lithograph Corporation was printer and binder.

MICROECONOMIC POLICY ANALYSIS

1 2 3 4 5 6 7 8 9 0   HALHAL   8 9 8 7 6 5 4

ISBN 0-07-022408-0

Library of Congress Cataloging in Publication Data

Friedman, Lee S.
    Microeconomic policy analysis.

    (Economics handbook series)
    Includes indexes.
    1. Macroeconomics.   2. Economic policy.   I. Title.
II. Series: Economics handbook series (McGraw-Hill Book
Company)
HB172.5.F74   1984   338.5   X 83-19602
ISBN 0-07-022408-0

To My Parents
Beverly and Oliver

CONTENTS

PREFACE   xiii

**PART 1   RESOURCE ALLOCATION DECISIONS AND
           THE PUBLIC SECTOR**

1   Introduction to Microeconomic Policy Analysis   3

POLICY ANALYSIS AND RESOURCE ALLOCATION   3
THE DIVERSE ECONOMIC ACTIVITIES OF GOVERNMENTS   5
POLICY MAKING AND THE ROLES OF
    MICROECONOMIC POLICY ANALYSIS   8
ORGANIZATION OF THE BOOK   13
CONCLUSION   15

2   An Introduction to Modeling, Efficiency, and Equity   16

MODELING: A BASIC TOOL OF MICROECONOMIC POLICY
    ANALYSIS   17
A MODEL OF INDIVIDUAL RESOURCE ALLOCATION
    DECISIONS   21
EFFICIENCY   26
        The General Concept / Efficiency with an
        Individualistic Interpretation / Efficiency in a
        Model of an Exchange Economy / A Geometric
        Representation of the Model / Relative Efficiency
EQUITY   40
        Equality of Outcome Is One Concept of Equity /
        Equality of Opportunity Is Another Concept of
        Equity / Integrating Equity-Efficiency Evaluation in
        a Social Welfare Function

SUMMARY   47
EXERCISES   49
∇ APPENDIX: CALCULUS MODELS OF CONSUMER
   EXCHANGE   50

PART 2   USING MODELS OF INDIVIDUAL CHOICE
          MAKING IN POLICY ANALYSIS

3   The Specification of Individual Choice Models
     for the Analysis of Welfare Programs   59

STANDARD ARGUMENT: IN-KIND WELFARE TRANSFERS
   ARE INEFFICIENT   60
INTERDEPENDENT PREFERENCE ARGUMENT: IN-KIND
   TRANSFERS MAY BE EFFICIENT   64
CHOICE RESTRICTIONS IMPOSED BY POLICY   70
   Food Stamp Choice Restrictions / Public Housing
   Choice Restrictions / The Design of an Income
   Maintenance Plan
SUMMARY   86
EXERCISES   87
APPENDIX: INCOME AND SUBSTITUTION EFFECTS   88
∇ THE MATHEMATICS OF INCOME AND
   SUBSTITUTION EFFECTS   94

4   Utility Maximization and Intergovernmental Grants:
     Analyzing Equity Consequences   97

INTERGOVERNMENTAL GRANTS   98
DESIGN FEATURES OF A GRANT PROGRAM   99
   Income Effects and Nonmatching Grants / Price
   Effects and Matching Grants / The Role of
   Choice Restrictions / Alternative Specifications of
   Recipient Choice Making
EQUITY STANDARDS WITH APPLICATION TO SCHOOL
   GRANTS   109
   Equity Objectives / Equity in School Finance
SUMMARY   137
EXERCISES   139

5   A Fundamental Test for Relative Efficiency:
     The Compensation Principle   141

THE EFFECTS OF A POLICY CHANGE ON ONE
   INDIVIDUAL'S WELFARE   143

∇Denotes an optional section using calculus.

Three Measures of Individual Welfare Change /
∇Duality: The Cobb-Douglas Expenditure Function
and Measures of Individual Welfare

THE COMPENSATION PRINCIPLE OF RELATIVE
   EFFICIENCY   160
   The Purpose of a Relative Efficiency Standard /
   The Hicks-Kaldor Compensation Principle /
   Controversy over the Use of the Compensation
   Principle

AGGREGATE CONSUMER SURPLUS AND MARKET
   STATISTICS   175
SUMMARY   187
EXERCISES   189

6   Uncertainty and Public Policy   191

EXPECTED VALUE AND EXPECTED UTILITY   193
RISK CONTROL AND RISK-SHIFTING MECHANISMS   206
   Risk Pooling and Risk Spreading / Policy Aspects
   of Risk Shifting and Risk Control

ALTERNATIVE MODELS OF INDIVIDUAL BEHAVIOR UNDER
   UNCERTAINTY   217
   The Slumlord's Dilemma and Strategic Behavior /
   Bounded Rationality

MORAL HAZARD AND MEDICAL CARE INSURANCE   225
∇ ASSESSING THE COSTS OF UNCERTAINTY   232
SUMMARY   236
EXERCISES   239

**PART 3   POLICY ASPECTS OF PRODUCTION, COST,
           AND ORGANIZATIONAL DECISION MAKING**

7   Technical Possibilities and Costs in Policy Analysis   243

TECHNICAL POSSIBILITIES AND THE PRODUCTION
   FUNCTION   246
COSTS   259
   Social Opportunity Cost and Benefit-Cost
   Analysis / Accounting Cost and Private
   Opportunity Cost / An Application in a Benefit-
   Cost Analysis / Cost-Output Relations /
   ∇Duality: Some Mathematical Relations between
   Production and Cost Functions

SUMMARY   289
EXERCISES   290

**8 Private Profit-Making Organizations: Objectives,
Capabilities, and Policy Implications** 292

THE CONCEPT OF A FIRM 294
THE PRIVATE PROFIT-MAXIMIZING FIRM 296
    Profit Maximization Requires that Marginal
    Revenue Equal Marginal Cost / The Profit-
    Maximizing Monopolist / Types of Monopolistic
    Price Discrimination / Normative Consequences
    of Price Discrimination / The Robinson-Patman
    Act of 1936 / Predicting Price Discrimination
ALTERNATIVE MODELS OF ORGANIZATIONAL
    OBJECTIVES AND CAPABILITIES 316
    Objectives Other than Profit Maximization /
    Limited Maximization Capabilities
SUMMARY 330
EXERCISES 332

**9 Public and Nonprofit Organizations: Objectives,
Capabilities, and Policy Implications** 334

NONPROFIT ORGANIZATIONS: MODELS OF HOSPITAL
    RESOURCE ALLOCATION 336
PUBLIC BUREAUS AND ENTERPRISES 345
EMPIRICAL PREDICTION OF PUBLIC ENTERPRISE
    BEHAVIOR: THE PRICING DECISIONS OF BART 348
A NORMATIVE MODEL OF PUBLIC ENTERPRISE PRICING:
    THE EFFICIENT FARE STRUCTURE 356
∇ THE MATHEMATICS OF RAMSEY PRICING 364
SUMMARY 369
EXERCISES 371

**PART 4 POLICY EFFECTS ON THE INTERACTION OF
SUPPLY AND DEMAND**

**10 General Competitive Analysis of Market
Organization, with Application to Taxation** 375

COMPETITIVE EQUILIBRIUM IN ONE INDUSTRY 376
ECONOMIC EFFICIENCY AND GENERAL COMPETITIVE
    EQUILIBRIUM 382
GENERAL COMPETITIVE ANALYSIS WITH A TAX
    INCIDENCE ILLUSTRATION 388
    Partial Equilibrium Analysis: The Excise Tax /
    General Equilibrium Analysis: Perfect Competition,
    No Taxation / General Equilibrium Analysis: The
    Excise Tax / Comparing Partial and General

Equilibrium Analysis / Lump-Sum Taxes Are
Efficient and Real Taxes Are Inefficient

SUMMARY   406
EXERCISES   406

11   Market Allocation in an Imperfect World   408

PERFECT COMPETITION IN AN IMPERFECT WORLD   410
The Theorem of the Second Best / The Second-
Best Solution Involves Policy Intervention in the
Market / Piecemeal Policy Analysis May Not
Reveal Efficiency Consequences / Identifying the
Second-Best Solution May Be beyond Current
Analytic Abilities / Some Responses to the
Second-Best Dilemma

THE MARKET AS AN IMPERFECT COORDINATING
    ORGANIZATION   424
Increasing Returns to Scale over the Relevant
Range of Demand / Public Goods / Externalities /
Imperfect Information

SUMMARY   434
EXERCISES   435

**12   The Control of Prices and Profits to Achieve Equity
in Specific Markets**   436

DISSATISFACTION WITH MARKET PRICING DURING
    TEMPORARY SHORTAGE OF A NECESSITY   438
A STANDARD EXPLANATION OF THE INEFFICIENCY
    OF RENT CONTROL   440
RENT CONTROL AS THE CONTROL OF LONG-RUN
    ECONOMIC RENT   446
THE RELATION BETWEEN RENT CONTROL AND
    CAPITALIZED PROPERTY VALUES   449
THE SUPPLY RESPONSE TO RENT CONTROL   452
THE EFFECTS OF RENT CONTROL ON APARTMENT
    EXCHANGE   457
A WINDFALL PROFITS TAX AS RENT CONTROL   461
SUMMARY   466
EXERCISES   468

13   Distributional Control with Rations and Vouchers   471

RATION COUPONS   472
VOUCHERS AND RATION-VOUCHERS   477
RATIONING GASOLINE DURING A SHORTAGE   480
SUMMARY   496
EXERCISES   499

14   Policy Problems of Allocating Resources over Time   501

INTERTEMPORAL ALLOCATION AND CAPITAL MARKETS   503
Individual Consumption Choice with Savings
Opportunities / Individual Consumption Choice
with Borrowing and Savings Opportunities / The
Separation Theorem of Individual Investment and
Consumption Choices / Capital Market
Equilibrium / Investment and Equilibrium in
Multiperiod Models
EDUCATION AS A CAPITAL INVESTMENT   518
Income-Contingent Loan Plans for Financing
Higher Education / Higher Education Subsidies:
Proposals for Grants and Tax Credits
THE ALLOCATION OF NATURAL RESOURCES   525
Renewable Resources: Tree Models / A Note on
Investment Time and Interest Rates: Switching
and Reswitching / The Allocation of Exhaustible
Resources: Oil and the Windfall Profits Tax
Revisited
SUMMARY   537
EXERCISES   540
APPENDIX ONE: UNCERTAIN FUTURE PRICES AND INDEX
CONSTRUCTION   541
APPENDIX TWO: DISCOUNTING OVER DISCRETE OR
CONTINUOUS INTERVALS   550

**PART 5   THE FRONTIERS OF MICROECONOMIC
POLICY ANALYSIS: ORGANIZATIONAL
PROCESS AND INSTITUTIONAL CHOICE**

**15   Designing Governance Structures for Economic
Activities**   561

EFFICIENT ORGANIZATIONAL DESIGN AND THE DEGREE
OF CENTRALIZED DECISION MAKING   563
ORGANIZING AIR POLLUTION CONTROL EFFORTS   569
REGULATING A NATURAL MONOPOLY   577
NONPROFIT ORGANIZATIONS AND THE DELIVERY
OF DAY-CARE SERVICES   591
SUMMARY   600
EXERCISES   604

INDEXES   I-1
Name Index
Subject Index

PREFACE

This book is for those who wish to learn how to apply microeconomic theory to the analysis of public sector issues. It builds systematically upon intermediate-level theory to develop the skills of microeconomic modeling and the principles of welfare economics used in policy analysis. A typical chapter begins with a few principles familiar from intermediate-level theory and uses them to develop more advanced principles and models that are applied, in some depth, to one or more policy issues. The issues selected are diverse, and they cut across the traditional applied fields of public finance, urban economics, industrial organization, and labor economics.

The book contains material suitable for a one- or two-semester course. The one-semester course would normally have intermediate microeconomic theory as a prerequisite; the book contains some review of that theory in each of its chapters, but the expositions are terse. With this prerequisite, I have used the book as the primary text in one-semester courses offered both to undergraduates (primarily economics majors) and to graduate students (from diverse disciplinary and professional fields).

In the two-semester course this book would typically be used in conjunction with the study of microeconomic theory. The chapters of *Microeconomic Policy Analysis* are sequenced to draw upon microeconomic principles in the same order that they are developed in most theory textbooks. In a two-semester sequence of the core program at the Graduate School of Public Policy, I alternate teaching a chapter or two of microeconomic theory and then a chapter or two of microeconomic policy analysis. When policy analysis is not the main focus, the instructor may use the book as a course supplement and emphasize the particular substantive applications in it.

The book has no mathematical prerequisite, although it has considerable empirical illustration of the models discussed. The illustrations have been kept numerically simple. There are substantial *optional* sections in many chapters (denoted by the symbol ∇) in which differential calculus is used freely. These optional sections are for those who expect to perform microeconomic policy analysis at a professional level. The students in the Graduate School of Public Policy, for example, are required to master most of the optional sections; the Berkeley undergraduates, however, are not required to. Other than in the optional sections, calculus is relegated to footnotes.

Exercises are included at the end of Chapters 2 through 15. Use of them is recommended as a means to develop, practice, and test analytic skills.

ACKNOWLEDGMENTS

Without continuing encouragement from former students, I would not have begun or continued with this project. My primary aim has been to improve instruction for others like them, and I am grateful for the support they have offered during this undertaking.

Many colleagues have given generous portions of their time to read and comment on the drafts of this book. I have benefited greatly from their good advice. Phillip Cook (Duke University), Richard C. Porter (University of Michigan), Richard Murnane (Yale University), and Jeffrey Wolcowitz (Harvard University) provided detailed comments from start to finish. I cannot overestimate the value of their thorough and thoughtful efforts. They helped to clarify and correct individual sections, as well as to shape the book as a whole.

Substantial portions of the manuscript were read and commented upon by Eric Hanushek (University of Rochester), Julian Le Grand (London School of Economics), C. B. McGuire (University of California, Berkeley) and Richard Nelson (Yale University). Many other colleagues made helpful comments on various chapters of the manuscript: Eugene Bardach, Henry Brady, David Kirp, Arnold Meltsner, and John Quigley (all of the Graduate School of Public Policy), P. D. Henderson (University College, London), Keith Hinman (Environmental Protection Agency), Fritzie Reisner (Department of Justice), and Dorothy Robyn (M.I.T.). I am indebted to all these colleagues, and I am deeply appreciative of their advice and encouragement throughout this enterprise.

With so much good advice, I have little excuse for the errors that inevitably will remain. Perhaps I can claim that they are typographical or editorial errors. But with the excellent typing assistance I have received from Deirdre Kessner, Shirly Thatcher, Kathy Tryhorn, Michelle Dethke, and Liz Keyser, that would indeed be a lame excuse. Furthermore, my editors at McGraw-Hill have provided nothing but first-rate, prompt, and professional assistance (and unending patience). Therefore, the only honest path is simply to shoulder the responsibility for remaining errors. I can only hope that those who find the errors will think enough of the overall effort to inform me about them.

Lee S. Friedman

MICROECONOMIC
POLICY
ANALYSIS

RESOURCE ALLOCATION DECISIONS AND THE PUBLIC SECTOR

INTRODUCTION TO MICROECONOMIC POLICY ANALYSIS

POLICY ANALYSIS AND RESOURCE ALLOCATION

Policy analysis involves the application of social science to matters of public policy. The specific tasks of an analysis depend importantly on which aspects of policy are to be understood, who wants to know, and how quickly the analysis is needed. For many, the excitement of this discipline is in its often turbulent political application: the undertaking and use of policy analysis as a part of actual government decision making. In that application the analysis is undertaken in order to advise; it is for the use of specific decision makers whose actions will depend on the analytic results. For others, the excitement is in rising to a more purely intellectual challenge: to create a more general understanding about how public policy is, and ought to be, made. The latter effort represents the more academic side of policy analysis. However, the same basic intellectual skills are used to conduct analysis of both types.

Microeconomic analysis is one of the fundamental skills of this discipline. It provides a critical foundation for both the design and evaluation of policies. This is hardly surprising: *Most public policy involves resource allocation.* To carry out virtually any government policy either requires the direct use of significant resources or severely constrains the use of resources by economic agents (i.e., individuals, firms, or government agencies). These resources—labor, buildings, and machinery and natural resources like water, oil, and land—are scarce, and different people will have different ideas about what to do

3

with them. A proposed dam may mean economic survival for farmers needing water to grow crops, but at the same time it may threaten destruction of a unique white-water river and canyon irreplaceable to lovers of nature. A town may, through its powers of zoning, declare certain or all areas within it for residential use only—to the chagrin of a company which wants to build a small factory (which would employ some of the town residents and provide local tax revenues) and to the delight of estate owners adjacent to the restricted area (who fear plummeting property values). As in these examples, public policy making typically forces tough choices. *Microeconomics is the study of resource allocation choices, and microeconomic policy analysis is the study of those special choices involving government.*

Proficiency in policy analysis requires more microeconomics than that usually conveyed in a basic microeconomic theory course. Typically, most of the basic course is devoted to explaining and evaluating the operation of a private market system. By a private market we refer to the voluntary trading offers and exchanges made by independent, private, economic agents acting as buyers or sellers of resources, goods, or services. Public policy involves, by contrast, a *collective* decision to influence or control behavior which would otherwise be shaped completely by the individual decisions of the private agents in a market. This does not imply, however, that public policy is antithetical to the use of markets. As we will see, much of the task of public policy analysis is to help create a proper blending of collective and market controls over resource allocation decisions. Thus microeconomic policy analysis requires a thorough understanding of the conditions which favor collective over individual action and the alternative collective or policy actions which might be taken, and it requires a means of evaluating the alternatives in order to choose among them.

To offer a brief preview of analytic thinking, consider the following hypothetical and informal conversation:

Official: We have got to do something about the traffic congestion and pollution caused by commuting into the city. Why don't we make a toll-free lane for automobiles carrying four or more passengers?

Analyst: That's an interesting idea, and it has worked with some success in a few other areas. But may I offer an alternative suggestion? The four-for-free plan has two important disadvantages. One, it reduces revenues that we sorely need. Two, it provides no incentive for commuters to form car pools of two and three, nor does it encourage the use of our mass transit systems.

Suppose instead that we raise the tolls during the peak commuting hours. The peak-toll plan would help solve our deficit problem. Furthermore, it would increase commuter incentives to form car pools of all sizes, to take mass transit rather than drive, and even to drive at off-peak hours for those who have that discretion.

In the above conversation, the analyst recognizes immediately that pollution and congestion are what economists call external effects (side effects of allocating resources to the activity of commuting). The analyst knows that economic efficiency requires a solution which "internalizes" the externalities and that the four-for-free plan deviates substantially from this idea. These same economic principles influenced the design of the alternative peak-toll plan.

In an actual setting, this conversation might lead to further consideration of alternative plans: the design of new alternatives, careful estimation of the consequences of the alternatives to be evaluated (e.g., the effect on the city's budget), and evaluation by a set of criteria wider than efficiency (e.g., fairness or equity, legality, and political and administrative feasibility). This book focuses on developing the microeconomic skills essential to applying this kind of analysis to a wide range of public policy problems.

THE DIVERSE ECONOMIC ACTIVITIES OF GOVERNMENTS

To illustrate more concretely the specific subject matters of microeconomic policy analysis, let us take a brief tour of the many economic activities of government. This tour will serve the additional purpose of indicating the extensiveness of public controls over resource allocation. While we have already asserted that most public policy involves resource allocation, the reverse relation is just as important to understand: *All resource allocation decisions are shaped by public policy*. This shaping occurs in different ways: through direct government purchase or supply of particular activities, the regulation of market activities, the development and maintenance of a legal system, and the undertaking of redistributive programs. Let us consider each of these in turn.

In 1981 the total value of all measured goods and services produced in this country—called the gross national product, or GNP—was about $3.0 trillion.[1] Roughly 21 percent of the total GNP, valued at $616 billion, consisted of purchases by governments to provide various goods and services to citizens. The governments include federal, state, and local governments and regional authorities acting as collective agents for the citizens. These different governments operate schools, hospitals, and parks, provide refuse collection, fire protection, and national defense, build dams, maintain the roads, sponsor research to fight cancer, and purchase a host of other goods and services which are intended to benefit the citizenry. What explains why these goods are provided through governments instead of markets? Why not let individual consumers seek them through the marketplace as they seek movies and food? What do we know about the economic advantages of doing it one way or the other?

Such questions are still quite general. Of the 21 percent of goods and services purchased by governments, approximately 12 percent was supplied directly through government agencies and enterprises (e.g., the Post Office) and the other 9 percent was provided through contracts and grants (e.g., a local government may tax its citizens to provide refuse collection and contract with a

---

[1] *Economic Report of the President,* January 1982 (U.S. Government Printing Office, 1982), p. 233, table B-1.

private firm to actually do the work).[2] When is it that a government should actually supply the goods, and when should it contract with private firms to supply them? If it does the latter, how should the contract be written to protect the economic interests of the citizens footing the bill? If a government actually produces the good or service itself, what mechanisms are there to encourage economy in production?

To purchase all these services, governments must raise revenues. The overwhelming bulk of the revenues comes from taxes; a smaller portion comes from individual user fees (e.g., park admission charges). When should user fees be used, and to what extent? If taxes must be collected, who should pay them and how much should each taxpayer be assessed?

The economic policy issues illustrated so far arise when governments have taken primary responsibility for providing goods and services. However, governments have great influence over a much wider range of goods and services through their regulatory mechanisms. In these cases, individual economic agents acting in the market still retain considerable decision-making power over what and how much to buy or sell of different commodities, although the available choices are conditioned by the regulations. Government regulatory mechanisms influence prices, qualities, and quantities of goods and services traded in the market as well as the information available to consumers about them.

Many industries are subject to price controls on their products. The form that such controls take varies. For example, some industries have their prices controlled indirectly through limits set by regulatory commissions on the return that producers are allowed to earn on their investments. Natural gas, electricity, truck and rail shipping, air travel, and telephone services have historically been subject to these controls. Occasionally, rental housing prices are regulated through rent control policies; over the last decade, domestic oil prices have been controlled. Another form of price control operates through taxes and subsidies. Alcohol and tobacco products are taxed to raise their prices and thus discourage their use; disaster insurance and loans for small businesses and college educations are subsidized to encourage their use. Although it is difficult to give precise figures on the amount of economic activity subject to some form of price regulation, a reasonable estimate is that at least an additional 20 to 25 percent of GNP is affected by this type of public policy.

Price regulation may be the least common form of regulation. Product regulations controlling quantities and qualities are widely used, generally to provide certain environmental and consumer protection. Some of these regulations are highly visible; examples are automobile safety standards and the prescription requirements for the sale of medicines and drugs. Other regulatory activities, such as public health standards in food-handling institutions (restau-

---

[2] Ibid, p. 244, table B-10. In 1980, $303.4 billion of GNP was produced by government and government enterprises. Since, in 1980, all government purchases were $534.7 billion (table B-1), government produced directly 303.4 ÷ 534.7 = 57 percent of all its purchases. The 12 percent in the text is approximately 0.57 of 21 percent.

rants, supermarkets, frozen food factories, etc.) and antiflammability requirements for children's clothing, are less visible. There are standards for clean air and water, worker health and safety, and housing construction; there are licensing requirements for physicians and auto repair shops; and there is restricted entry into the industries providing taxi service and radio broadcasting. There are age restrictions on the sale of certain goods or services, notably the alcoholic beverages. Product regulations of one kind or another affect virtually every industry.

In addition to the product and price regulations, information about products is regulated. The Securities and Exchange Commission requires that certain information be provided to prospective buyers of new stock and bond offerings; lending institutions are subject to truth-in-lending laws; the Environmental Protection Agency tests new model automobiles for their fuel consumption rates each year and publishes the results; tobacco products must be labeled "dangerous to your health."

What are the economic circumstances that might make these regulatory public policies desirable, and are such circumstances present in the industries now regulated? How does one know when to recommend price, product, or information controls, and what form they should take? The social objectives or benefits of these policies may be readily apparent, but their costs are often less obvious. For example, when electricity production must be undertaken with nonpolluting production techniques, the cost of electricity production, and therefore its price, typically rises. Thus a decision to regulate pollution by utility companies is paid for through higher electricity prices. One task of microeconomic policy analysis is to consider costs and to design pollution control policies which achieve pollution reduction goals at the least total cost.

Another important area of public policy which greatly affects resource allocation is the activity of developing the law. The legal system defines property rights and responsibilities which shape all exchanges among economic agents. If there were no law establishing your ownership, you might have a hard time selling a good or preventing others from taking it. Without a patent system to establish the inventor's ownership rights, less effort would be devoted to inventing. Whether or not the existing patent system can be improved is a fair question for analysis. An example of a policy change involving property responsibilities is the spread of no-fault automobile accident liability. Under the old system, the driver at fault was liable for damages done to the injured party. The cost of insurance reflected both the damage and the transaction costs of legal battles to determine which driver was at fault. These transaction costs amounted to a significant proportion of the total insurance costs. The idea behind the no-fault concept is to reduce the transaction costs by eliminating in some cases the need to determine who is at fault. To the extent that this system works, consumers benefit from lower automobile insurance premiums. These examples should illustrate that analysis of the law is another public policy area in which microeconomic policy analysis can be applied.

There is another very important function of government activity which can be put through the filter of microeconomic analysis: Governments undertake redistributive programs to influence the distribution of goods and services among citizens. Of course, all resource allocation decisions affect the distribution of well-being among citizens, and the fairness of the distribution is always a concern of good policy analysis; here the interest is in the many programs undertaken with that equity objective as the central concern. Government redistributive programs include welfare, food stamps, Medicaid, farm subsidies, and Social Security, just to name a few. These programs generally transfer resources to the poorest groups in society from those better off. However, some programs might be seen as forcing individuals to redistribute their own spending from one time period to another: Social Security takes away some of our income while we work and gives back income when we retire. Other public policies, such as farm subsidies, grants to students for higher education, and oil depletion allowances, may redistribute resources from poorer to richer groups. Because the success of redistributive programs generally depends heavily on the resource allocation decisions made by the affected economic agents, microeconomic policy analysis provides tools for both the design and evaluation of such programs.

By now it should be clear that all resource allocation decisions are influenced, at least to some degree, by public policy. Governments shape resource allocations through their direct purchase and supply of goods and services, their regulation of specific economic activities, their development and maintenance of the legal system, and their redistributive programs. All the activities mentioned above illustrate the set of public policy actions which can be analyzed by the methods presented in this book. In undertaking such studies, it is important to consider the roles of analysis in a policy-making process and how the process influences the objectives of the analysis. The next section contains a general discussion of these issues.

POLICY MAKING AND THE ROLES OF MICROECONOMIC POLICY ANALYSIS

Public policy making is a complex process. Policy is the outcome of a series of decisions and actions by people with varying motivations and differing information. Policy analysis, when not done for purely academic purposes, may be used to aid any of these people—be they elected officials or candidates for elected office, bureaucrats, members of various interest groups (including those attempting to represent the "public" interest), or the electorate. Not surprisingly, these different people may not agree on the merits of particular policies, even if perfectly informed about them, because of differing values. Policy analysis cannot resolve these basic conflicts; for better or for worse, the political process is itself the mechanism of resolution.

It is important to recognize that the political process heavily influences the type of policy analysis that is done and the extent to which it is used. For that reason, anyone interested in learning the skills of analysis for the purpose of advising should try to understand the process. Such understanding yields a better perspective of the possibilities for contributions through analytic work and the limitations as well. We offer below the barest introduction (bordering shamelessly on caricature) to some of the rich thinking which has been done on this subject, and we strongly encourage a full reading of the source material.

Lindblom, in 1965, put forth an optimistic model of a democratic political process.[3] He described a system like ours as one of partisan mutual adjustment among the various interest groups (e.g., unions, bureaucracies, corporations, consumer groups, professional associations) in the society. In his view, the political pulling and hauling by diverse groups (from both within and outside government) in pursuit of self-interest leads to appropriate compromises and workable solutions.

No one in this pluralist process ever sets national goals or identifies the alternative means available to achieve them.[4] Rather, progress is made by sequential adaptation, or trial and error. Legislation proposed by one group, for example, has its design modified frequently as it wends its way through legislative subcommittees, committees, the full legislative bodies, and executive branch considerations. At each stage, the modifications reflect the compromises that arise in response to strengths and weaknesses identified by the affected interest groups and the changes they propose.

After enactment and during implementation, the diverse interest groups continue to influence the specific ways in which the new legislation is carried out. These groups will also monitor the resulting government operating procedures. The procedures may not lead to the intended results, or someone may think of a better set of procedures. If enough support can be mustered for program modification, the groups can force renewed legislative consideration.

Lindblom argued that muddling through is better than any alternative process designed to solve problems in a synoptic or comprehensive way. For example, an attempt to specify goals in a clear way may permit a sharper evaluation of the alternative means, but it will also increase the political difficulty of achieving a majority coalition. Interest groups are diverse precisely because they have real differences in goals, and they are unlikely to put those differences aside. Instead, they will agree only to statements of goals which are virtually meaningless in content (e.g., "This legislation is designed to promote the national security and the national welfare.") and do not really guide efforts at evaluation. The groups affected by proposed legislation are concerned about the end result. It is easier politically to build a coalition around a specific alternative and worry later about how to describe (in a sufficiently bland way) the purposes it fulfills.[5]

---

[3] Charles E. Lindblom, *The Intelligence of Democracy* (New York: The Free Press, 1965).

[4] We refer to "national goals" for illustrative simplicity; the same logic applies to state, local, or other polities which use representative or direct democratic forms of government.

[5] This general view is also shared by Wildavsky. See Aaron Wildavsky, "The Political Economy of Efficiency: Cost-Benefit Analysis, Systems Analysis, and Program Budgeting," *Public Administration Review, 26,* No. 4, December 1966, pp. 292–310. See also D. Braybrooke and C. Lindblom, *A Strategy of Decision: Policy Evaluation as a Social Process* (New York: The Free Press, 1963).

Optimistic views of the "intelligence" of actual pluralistic processes are not widely held. Many people argue that the actual processes differ significantly (and perhaps inevitably) from the view Lindblom offered in 1965. For example, one obvious concern is whether an actual process is weighted unduly toward the "haves" (e.g., who can afford to employ high-powered lobbyists and analysts) and away from the "have nots." In a more recent book, Lindblom himself writes that "business privilege" in the United States causes "a skewed pattern of mutual adjustment."[6]

Another important source of "skewness," argues Schultze, is that efficiency and effectiveness considerations are not brought into the political arena.[7] Schultze accepts the value of having a pluralist process and the inevitability that it will be characterized by special interest advocacy and political bargaining "in the context of conflicting and vaguely known values."[8] But he argues that *there is a crucial role for policy analysis in this process*. It improves the "intelligence" of it. Analysis can identify the links between general values (in particular, efficiency and effectiveness) and specific program characteristics— links that are by no means obvious to anyone. Thus he offers this view of policy analysis:[9]

> It is not really important that the analysis be fully accepted by all the participants in the bargaining process. We can hardly expect . . . that a good analysis can be equated with a generally accepted one. But analysis can help focus debate upon matters about which there are real differences of value, where political judgments are necessary. It can suggest superior alternatives, eliminating, or at least minimizing, the number of inferior solutions. Thus by sharpening the debate, systematic analysis can enormously improve it.

Viewing a political process as a whole helps us to understand the inevitability of *analytic suboptimization:* the problem worked on by any single analyst is inevitably only a partial view of the problem considered by the system as a whole, and thus a single analyst's proposed solution is not necessarily optimal from the larger perspective. For example, during the Carter administration the president directed two independent analytic teams from the Departments of Labor and Health and Human Services to develop welfare reform proposals. Not surprisingly, the team from the Labor Department proposed a reform emphasizing a work component of the welfare system, while the team from Health and Human Services emphasized the cash assistance components. This not only reflects bureaucratic interests; it is a natural consequence of the expertise of each team. Similarly, other analysts on congressional committees or for other interest groups would be expected to perceive the welfare problem slightly differently.

---

[6] Charles E. Lindblom, *Politics and Markets* (New York: Basic Books, Inc., 1977), p. 348.
[7] See Charles L. Schultze, *The Politics and Economics of Public Spending* (Washington, D.C.: The Brookings Institution, 1968), particularly chaps. 3 and 4.
[8] Ibid., p. 74.
[9] Ibid., p. 75.

The inevitability of suboptimization has important consequences. It becomes clear that the intelligence of the process as a whole depends not only on how well each analyst does the task assigned but also on the total analytic effort and on how cleverly the analytic tasks are parceled out. A certain amount of analytic overlap provides checks and balances, for example. However, excessive duplication of efforts may leave an important part of the problem unattended. Another pitfall is to rely too heavily on analysis when the "true" social objectives are difficult to operationalize. For example, the problem of identifying an efficient national defense is not really soluble by analytic techniques (although certain important insights can be generated). If, however, it is decided that we should have the capability to gather a certain number of troops near the Alaskan oil pipeline within a certain number of days, then analysts may be able to reject alternative methods which are too costly and help identify lower-cost methods.[10]

The line of thought concerning analytic contributions in a pluralist political process can be carried further. Nelson suggests that analysts can and should play important roles in clarifying the nature of the problem, the values that are at stake, and an appropriate weighting of those values to identify a recommended solution.[11] The idea is that the political process, without analysis, operates largely in the "intellectual dark" about efficiency and equity consequences. Thus both Nelson and Schultze appreciate the value of muddling through but think we can do it somewhat better with substantial analytic input to the pluralistic process.

Nelson goes on to suggest that it is also important for substantial analysis to go on *outside* the constraints of whatever is the current political environment. The industry of government, like any other industry, continually needs research and development to improve its products. Analysis from within the thick of government tends to concentrate on identifying incremental improvements to existing activities. Achieving those improvements is important. In addition, however, analytic efforts in an environment which offers more freedom to reexamine fundamental assumptions and methods may be a crucial source of important new ideas.

The above general thoughts about the political process help us to understand the roles of public policy analysis. We have mentioned that (1) *analysis may help define a problem that is only dimly perceived or vaguely understood* by participants in the policy-making process. We have also mentioned that (2) *a crucial role of analysis is in identifying or designing new policy proposals.* In addition, policy analysis has these two important functions: (3) *identification of the consequences of proposed policies and* (4) *normative evaluation of those*

---

[10] An excellent exposition of suboptimization with application to national defense is contained in C. Hitch and R. McKean, *The Economics of Defense in the Nuclear Age* (New York: Athenum, 1967).

[11] See Richard R. Nelson, *The Moon and the Ghetto: An Essay on Public Policy Analysis* (New York: W. W. Norton & Co., Inc., 1977).

consequences in terms of certain broad social goals. Let us distinguish these latter two analytic objectives.

The third objective, identification of consequences, is a *positive* or factual task. It involves answering questions such as these: "If the bridge toll is raised from $0.25 to $1.00, by how much will that reduce congestion?" (Presumably, fewer automobile trips will be taken across the bridge.) "If we combine the two local schools into one larger one, how will that affect education costs?" "If we guarantee all adults an income of $3000 per year, how will that affect the amount of work adults are willing to undertake?" These questions can rarely be answered with absolute certainty, but analysis can frequently provide reasonable estimates. With improved estimates of the consequences of proposed policies, policy makers can make better decisions about whether to support them.

The fourth objective, evaluation, is a *normative* or judgmental task. It involves the "should" questions: "Should the bridge toll be raised from $0.25 to $1.00?" "Should the nation have a policy that guarantees all adults $3000 per year?" The answers to these questions always depend on values. *There is no single, well-defined set of values which analysts must use in attempting to evaluate policies; the choice of criteria is discretionary.*[12] Nevertheless, in practice certain criteria are generally common to all analyses: efficiency, equity or fairness, and political feasibility. Efficiency and equity are commonly used criteria because almost all people care about them; since the insights of microeconomic analysis apply directly to these concepts, this book will emphasize them. A beginning discussion of them is the subject of the next chapter.

Political feasibility is a common evaluative criterion because specific users of analyses are rarely interested in pursuing proposed policies, however efficient and equitable, if the policies cannot gain the necessary approval in the political process. In the author's personal view, this criterion differs from the others in that it makes no sense to pursue it for its own sake; it is a constraint rather than an objective. While it may be naive to recommend a policy that fosters certain social objectives without considering political feasibility, it is irresponsible to recommend a policy that is politically feasible without considering its effects on social objectives.

Although different individuals will have concern for political feasibility in accordance with their personal judgments, it should be made clear that analytic attention to political feasibility is very rational. If one is considering a policy which would need approval of the United Nations Security Council, but it is known that the Soviet Union is adamantly opposed to the policy and would exercise its veto power, then the only purpose of raising the issue would be to garner its symbolic value. At times, symbolism may be important; it may lay the groundwork for future action. Alternatively, one might make better use of

---

[12] That is why this task is described as normative. If analysts did not have to rely partially upon their own values to choose criteria and did not have any discretion about how to operationalize them, then we could describe the evaluative task as positive from the perspective of the analyst.

the time by seeking policies which are both socially beneficial and politically feasible.

The point to emphasize here is that good policy analysis will generally include a diagnosis of the political prospects for the policies analyzed. Other examples of political analysis might question the prospects for passage in key legislative committees, whether any powerful lobbyist will work to pass or oppose the proposed policy, and whether the policy's potential backers will gain votes for such a stand in the next election. General analysis of political feasibility is beyond the scope of this book, but a number of occasions on which microeconomic analysis provides political insight will be discussed. However, the reader interested in the use of policy analysis for other than academic purposes should undertake more complete study in this area.[13]

In addition to the general criteria mentioned so far, other criteria may be important for particular issues. Some policies might be intended to enhance individual freedom or develop community spirit. Policies must comform to existing law (though in the long run, the law should conform to good policy!). Good analyses of these policies will, at a minimum, make these considerations clear to the users of the analyses. Because the treatment of these aspects is at best a poorly understood and rough form of art, little will be said here other than to be on the alert for them and to remain open-minded about their importance.

ORGANIZATION OF THE BOOK

The task of this book is to show how to extend and relate microeconomic theory to the design and analysis of public policies. A theme that will be emphasized throughout is that a solid understanding of the actual behavior of economic agents is essential to the task. Part of the understanding comes from learning about the individual economic agents: their motivations and capabilities and the effects of public policies on their economic opportunities. Once behavior at the individual level is understood, it is easier to consider questions of organization: how to design and evaluate alternative systems which influence the interaction among economic agents. Thus the book focuses on individual behavior first and the organizational behavior second. It consists of five interrelated parts.

Part I, the introductory section, contains this chapter as well as a conceptual chapter on the evaluative criteria commonly used in analysis. These chapters are intended to give an overview of the subject matter and methods of microeconomic policy analysis.

Part II focuses on the resource allocation decisions of individuals. Different aspects of the theory of individual choice are developed to show their uses and importance in policy analysis. We begin with familiar aspects of price theory—

---

[13] See, for example, Aaron Wildavsky, *Speaking Truth to Power: The Art and Craft of Policy Analysis* (Boston: Little, Brown, and Co., 1979), and Arnold Meltsner, "Political Feasibility and Policy Analysis," *Public Administration Review, 32,* November–December 1972, pp. 859–867.

budget constraints, income and substitution effects—and relate those concepts to the design of specific policies: welfare programs and intergovernmental grants. This involves some extension of ordinary theory to include models with interdependent preferences and a variety of restrictions on individual choices. The relation between consumer demand functions and public policy benefit estimation—the *consumer surplus*—is explored. Finally, the connections between uncertainty, individual choice, and public policy are investigated by extending the ordinary model of rational decision making as well as considering the implications of *bounded rationality*. Policy examples like national health insurance and disaster insurance subsidies are used to illustrate these points. All of the topics covered in Part II relate to individual behavior in pursuit of personal satisfaction or utility.

Part III concerns the efforts of economic agents to convert scarce resources into goods and services: the production task in an economy. The effectiveness of many public policies depends on the response of private profit-seeking firms to them; an example is the deregulation of the trucking industry. Other public policies succeed or fail depending on the behavior of public agencies or private nonprofit agencies; an example is the effect of the pricing decisions of a public mass transit system on the number of people who will use the system.

The performance of an economic agent undertaking production is limited by the available technology, and policy analysis often has the task of uncovering technological limits through estimation of production possibilities and their associated costs. Potential performance can then be compared with actual practice or predicted behavior under a particular policy design. One must be careful in extending the ordinary method of production and cost analysis to the public sector, because of poor output measures and the possible lack of the usual duality relation between production choices and cost. Several examples of analyses involving these problems will be given.

Not only must the technological realities be understood, but predicting an agency's or a firm's response to a public policy requires an understanding of its motivations and capabilities. Different models used for these purposes are explained in Part III. For the most part, economic theory treats each production entity as an individual decision-making unit; e.g., a firm may maximize its profits. However, this treatment ignores the fact that firms and agencies are generally organizations consisting of many diverse individuals. A discussion of the firm as an organizational means to coordinate individual decision making helps to connect the analysis presented in Parts II and III with the organizational policy issues that are the focus of Parts IV and V.

Part IV focuses on the interaction of supply and demand forces, emphasizing both efficiency and equity consequences. Primary attention is devoted to the operation of markets, since extensive use of them is made throughout the world. The corresponding policy emphasis is on the degree of public control of markets thought desirable and the policy instruments that can be used to achieve varying degrees of control.

We begin Part IV with a review of the conditions for market efficiency, and then apply the conditions in a general equilibrium framework. We use that framework to illustrate how the effects of taxation can be predicted and evaluated. We demonstrate that taxation generally causes "market failure" or inefficiency and review other reasons for market failure. Then we examine a number of more specific markets. By using extended examples of apartment rent control, gasoline rationing, student loans for higher education, and the windfall profits tax on domestic oil, we examine a variety of ways to make the markets for specific goods more equitable and efficient. In these examples, the details of the institutional structure to administer and enforce policies bear importantly on the success of the policies.

Although certain strengths and weaknesses of alternatives for dealing with the problems raised in Part IV are readily grasped, the methods available for comparing and evaluating them in a specific policy area are largely undeveloped. Part V examines the frontiers of microeconomic policy analysis by considering recently introduced methods of organizational process analysis which have been used to compare organizational alternatives. Three case studies using process analysis will be considered: examination of the implications of information and transaction costs for the choice of methods to control air pollution and regulate local cable television franchises and the use of the concepts of "exit, voice, and loyalty" as a way of considering the likely tensions between consumer sovereignty and public control in the provision of day care services.

CONCLUSION

In this chapter we have had an overview of the relation between public policy analysis and the study of microeconomics. Public policy can often be analyzed and understood as a collective involvement in the resource allocation process. The intervention takes place to some degree in virtually all areas of the economy. Microeconomic policy analysis attempts to predict and evaluate the consequences of collective actions, and it can be used in the design of those actions and to identify areas in which public policy can be improved. Although there is no single well-defined set of evaluative criteria which must be used in policy analysis, this book will emphasize two criteria that are commonly used: efficiency and equity. By using and extending ordinary principles of microeconomic analysis, we will attempt to impart skills sufficient for the analysis of a wide range of public policies by those criteria.

AN INTRODUCTION TO MODELING, EFFICIENCY, AND EQUITY

Two of the primary tasks of microeconomic policy analysis are prediction and evaluation. This chapter illustrates, at a rudimentary level, how *models* constructed from microeconomic theory are used to help accomplish these tasks. To do so, we consider a standard theoretical model of consumer choices in an economy in which the only activity is the exchange of goods. The evaluative concepts of *efficiency* and *equity* (fairness) are introduced, and we discuss the linkages between the predicted consumer behavior and its efficiency and equity consequences.

In actual practice, considerable skill is required to predict and evaluate the consequences of specific policy alternatives. The successive chapters build upon microeconomic theory to develop more sophisticated modeling skills and illustrate their use in specific policy contexts. However, even when the predictions and evaluations are derived from the best practicable analytic methods, the possibility remains that the judgments are wrong. In this chapter we try to clarify why analytic efforts are important despite the persistence of uncertainty about the conclusions.

The chapter begins with a general discussion of modeling. Then we review a standard model of consumer choice, sometimes referred to as the model of *economic man* or *utility maximization*. We next introduce the concept of an efficient allocation of resources in an economy and illustrate how inferences about efficiency can be drawn from models of the exchange of goods among "economic men." In the last substantive section we introduce several concepts of equitable resource allocation and illustrate their relevance to evaluating the exchanges previously discussed. In a brief appendix a calculus version of the model of economic man and the conditions which characterize exchange efficiency is explained.

MODELING: A BASIC TOOL OF MICROECONOMIC POLICY ANALYSIS

A powerful technique used to predict the consequences of policies is *modeling*. A model is an abstraction intended to convey the essence of some particular aspect of the real world. A child can get a pretty good idea of what an airplane is by looking at a plastic model of one. A science student can predict how gravity will affect a wide variety of objects, falling from any number of different heights, simply by using the mathematical equations which model gravity's effects. In the latter case the model equations represent assumptions based on a theory of gravity, and their implications can be tested against reality.

But can microeconomic theory be used to model resource allocation decisions accurately enough to help determine the consequences of proposed policies? The answer is a qualified yes. Economists have developed models with assumptions which seem plausible in a wide range of circumstances and whose predictions are frequently borne out by actual consumer behavior. Of course, predictions can be more or less ambitious. A qualitative prediction that "consumers will use less home heating oil as its price increases" is less ambitious than "consumers will reduce home heating oil consumption by 5 percent in the year following a price increase of 20 percent." The latter is less ambitious than one that adds to it: "And this will cause an efficiency decrease valued at $2 billion." Since the more precise predictions generally come from models that are more difficult to construct and require more detailed information to operate, the analyst must think about the precision required to resolve a particular policy question.

Although there is analytic choice about the degree of precision to seek in modeling, it is important to recognize from the start that all models only approximate reality. In general, the usefulness of a model to its users depends on the extent to which it increases knowledge or understanding (and not on how much it leaves unexplained). The plastic display model of an airplane is not considered a failure because it does not fly. Or consider the scientific models which represent the laws of aerodynamics. Earlier in this century, the models of those laws were used for airplane design, even though the same models predicted that bumblebees must be unable to fly! Without any loss of respect for science over this apparent model failure, airplanes (as well as bumblebees) flew successfully.

The perception that there is "something wrong" with a model does not necessarily deter us from using the model, as the above example illustrates. Analytically, we do not replace a partial success with nothing. Before replacing the earlier models of aerodynamic laws as applied to bumblebees, we required "something better."[1] And the same is true of economic models: "Good" models predict well enough to increase our understanding of certain situations, even though they may not predict them perfectly and there may be related situations in which the same models do not predict as well as expected. The unexplained imperfections in the predictions remain as "puzzles" which stimulate new research that leads (with luck) to better models. As in science, the process of improvement is continual.

Although all models are imperfect, not all are imperfect in the same way. Models vary in the variety of phenomena they can explain, as well as the accuracy of explaining any particular phenomenon. In the economic example of the consumer response to a price increase for home heating oil, we suggested that alternative models can be constructed, models which attempt both increasingly precise estimates of the magnitude of the response (e.g., the specific percentage reduction in home heating oil usage) as well as broader implications of the response (e.g., the value of an efficiency increase or decrease associated with it). Even the simplest prediction illustrated—that consumers will purchase less home heating oil if its price rises—might be all that is necessary to resolve a particular issue.

For example, suppose the consumer price of heating oil has been increased by a tax in order to induce greater conservation of the supply. Imagine the problem now is to alleviate the increased financial burden of the tax on low-income families. It is not unusual to hear some policy proposals to reduce the price for these families only (e.g., exempt them from the tax). But this works in opposition to the primary objective.

The next chapter shows that such proposals are likely to be inferior to alternatives designed to provide the same amount of aid without reducing the price of heating oil.[2] This conclusion is derived from the model making the least ambitious predictions; it depends primarily on the qualitative prediction that consumers purchase less home heating oil at higher prices and more at lower prices. This model also is constructed without using any numerical data; it is based entirely on microeconomic theory.

On the other hand, suppose the policy problem is how to achieve a primary objective of reducing home heating oil consumption by 5 percent within a definite time period. We know from the simplest model that one way to do so is

---

[1] According to one expert: "It used to be thought that insect flight could be understood on the basis of fixed-wing aerodynamics, when in fact the wings of many insects, including bumblebees, operate more on the principle of helicopter aerodynamics." See Bernd Heinrich, *Bumblebee Economics* (Cambridge, Mass.: Harvard University Press, 1979), p. 39. Even this more refined model is imperfect: ". . . when the wings flap, fluctuating or *unsteady* flow pattern must occur . . . but we are only beginning to understand the nature of the problem and how animals make use of such unsteady flow." See Torkel Weis-Fogh, "Energetics and Aerodynamics of Flapping Flight: A Synthesis," in R. Rainey (ed.), *Insect Flight* (Oxford: Blackwell Scientific Publications, 1976), pp. 48–72.

[2] Inferior in this case means that less conservation will be achieved for a given amount of tax relief. The conclusion is qualified for several important reasons explained in the next chapter. For example, it is based on a model which does not consider the informational problems of identifying the tax burden on each family.

to raise the price, but by how much?[3] This question is easy to ask but difficult to answer. To resolve it, a model that makes specific numerical predictions is required.

Building this type of model requires empirical skills beyond the scope of this text; they are best acquired in courses on quantitative methods like statistics and econometrics.[4] However, careful use of the empirical skills requires knowledge of the microtheoretic modeling skills that we do cover. Furthermore, models constructed from theory can often be applied directly to available empirical evidence (from past studies), as examples later on in the text will illustrate.

Each of the above two examples assumes that a policy objective is to reduce the consumption of heating oil. But suppose one wanted to consider whether that should be an objective at all. That is, suppose we asked a more basic question: Does the nation have an appropriate amount of heating oil relative to all other goods, or by how much should the price be changed (possibly increased or decreased) to remedy the situation?[5] Even if the only criterion is to choose a quantity which is efficient, the model is required to explain *two* phenomena: the price to charge which would lead to each possible quantity of heating oil, and whether that quantity is efficient or not. Accurate predictions of the price-quantity combinations would be of little help if that information could not be linked to the efficiency consequences. It is like needing the plastic model of the airplane to be of the proper scale and to fly as well.

One of the themes we shall emphasize throughout is the importance of *model specification:* the choice of a particular set of abstractions from reality used to construct the model. These building blocks are the model *assumptions*. For the plastic model of an airplane, the assumptions consist of the physical components included in the unassembled kit and the assembly instructions, as well as the way the model builder interprets or modifies them. In microeconomic policy analysis this set typically includes some representation of the policy objectives, the alternative policies under consideration, the motivations or objectives of the economic agents (people and organizations) affected by the policies, and the constraints on the agents' resource allocation decisions.

An important factor in model specification is the use of what has been learned previously about the phenomenon being modeled. This explains why

---

[3] There are other policy alternatives for achieving this objective than simply raising the price. A fuller discussion of rationing methods is contained in Chapter 13, with application to gasoline rationing.

[4] See, for example, Eric Hanushek and John Jackson, *Statistical Methods for Social Scientists* (New York: Academic Press, 1977) or Robert Pindyck and Daniel Rubinfeld, *Econometric Models and Economic Forecasts* (New York: McGraw-Hill Book Company, 1976). For a brief overview of econometric methodology as it applies in one policy context, see Lee S. Friedman, "The Use of Multiple Regression Analysis to Test for a Deterrent Effect of Capital Punishment: Prospects and Problems," in S. Messinger and E. Bittner (eds.), *Criminology Review Yearbook*, vol. I (Beverly Hills, Calif.: Sage Publications, 1979), pp. 61–87.

[5] To keep this example simple, we continue to assume that the only policy *instrument* is to determine the price. A policy instrument is a particular method that government can use to influence behavior, in this case the quantity of heating oil made available to consumers.

many of the specific assumptions used in policy analysis are a part of conventional or neoclassical microeconomic theory. Models based on that theory have been very successful in predicting the direction of allocative changes made by economic agents in response to a wide variety of economic stimuli. Furthermore, they do not require inordinate amounts of information to predict the changes; the models are parsimonious. Therefore, a reasonable strategy for microeconomic policy analysis is to rely generally on conventional theory as a starting point and adapt it to account for the circumstances specific to each problem.

On the other hand, conventional theory is not so powerful that all of its implications deserve to be accepted uncritically. To get a sense of the limits of any theory, let us look at an example suggested by Milton Friedman.[6] He notes that an expert billiard player shoots *as if* he or she has an expert knowledge of physics. Therefore, by using calculations based on the laws of physics as the model, one can predict accurately the shots of the expert. This illustrates Friedman's proposition that a theory should be judged by the empirical validity of its predictions, not of its assumptions.

As long as the only purpose of this theory is to predict how an expert at billiards will direct the ball (or how a novice will fail to direct it), it does not matter that the assumptions are clearly inaccurate. However, theories are generally used to predict or explain a variety of phenomena. For example, suppose one proposed, based on the above theory, to evaluate applicants for jobs as physicists by their billiard scores (i.e., high billiard scores can be achieved only by individuals with an expert knowledge of physics). This method of predicting job success is not likely to do very well.[7] In other words, the substantial inaccuracy of the assumptions severely limits the variety of phenomena which can be successfully explained or predicted by the theory.

Few analysts think that the assumptions used in conventional microeconomic theory, which attribute a high degree of rationality to each economic agent, are highly accurate themselves. Sometimes an "as if" logic is used to justify the assumptions. For example, firms do not really know how to maximize profits (their assumed objective), but those which survive in competitive markets must behave *as if* they maximize profits.[8] Since the directional predictions made with the theory have been borne out over a wide range of phenomena, the assumptions seem quite acceptable for this purpose (at least until a better set of assumptions is discovered). However, other uses of the theory may require more "faith" in the assumptions themselves.

For example, let us refer to the evaluative concept of efficiency. In order to

---

[6] See M. Friedman, "The Methodology of Positive Economics," in *Essays in Positive Economics* (Chicago: University of Chicago Press, 1953), pp. 3–46.

[7] The problem we are referring to is that those hired are not likely to perform well on the job. There is another problem: Some perfectly good physicists will be found unqualified for the job. However, the latter problem is not caused by the model assumptions. The model assumes that all experts at billiards are expert physicists, and not that all expert physicists are experts at billiards.

[8] Firm behavior is discussed in Chapter 8.

have an efficient allocation, consumers must make the most rational choices available to them. (We review this shortly.) Conventional theory assumes that people make choices in this manner. But to interpret an allocation resulting from consumer choices as efficient, one must "believe" the assumption is accurate.

However, consider the following analogy: Assume all billiard players are experts at the game; justify the assumption because it accurately predicts the direction in which players shoot; and interpret the poor shots of novices as misses on purpose. It may be that, for many types of choices, consumers rarely "miss." But surely there are some decisions which are harder to make than others (e.g., the purchase of complex insurance contracts, legal services, or used cars), and one should recognize that inefficiency can occur as a consequence of poor choice.

It is not enough to develop a sense of the strengths and weaknesses of any particular assumption. A fundamental analytic skill is to be able to identify plausible alternative specifications relevant to a particular policy analysis. The point is to understand how heavily a *policy* conclusion depends on specific assumptions. For example, the same conclusion may be reached over a wide range of reasonable specifications, in which case confidence in the policy conclusion is enhanced.

To build skill in model specification, each of the later chapters contains examples of alternative specifications relevant to the particular policy context. Two general points arise repeatedly, and it may be useful to state them in advance. First, *policy conclusions are often quite sensitive to variations in the way the policy itself is modeled.* Therefore, the analyst must take care to understand the details of any specific proposal before deciding how to model it (or evaluating another's model of it). Second, *the reexamination of assumptions which are standard and appropriate in many contexts often becomes the central focus in a particular policy context.*

The importance of model specification will become clearer as the models used in microeconomic policy analysis become more familiar. To begin, let us construct a simple economic model and illustrate how conclusions about efficiency consequences can be drawn from it. Even though this first model is a very simple one, it is an appropriate way to review and clarify some basic aspects of microeconomic reasoning.

A MODEL OF INDIVIDUAL RESOURCE ALLOCATION DECISIONS

Let us review here the most conventional and general assumptions about individual resource allocation choices. These assumptions form a model of decision making sometimes referred to as *economic man,* where each individual is portrayed as a *utility maximizer.* In later chapters, we will consider alternatives to the economic man model, like the model of bounded rationality (Chapter 6), and show that policy recommendations can depend in critical ways on which of the models is more accurate for the situation being studied. However, since the utility-maximizing behavior of economic man has so far been found to have the most general use, we will review it first.

The model of economic man can be described in terms of four assumptions. First, *each consumer is assumed to have a preference ordering*. This means two things. One is that the consumer can compare any two possible bundles or collections of goods and services and will prefer one to the other or be indifferent. (This rules out responses like ''I don't know'' or ''I can't decide.'') The other is that the consumer is consistent: if bundle A is preferred or equal to bundle B, and B is preferred or equal to C, then A must be preferred or equal to C.

Second, *each consumer is nonsatiable*. Roughly speaking, this means that a property of the consumer's ordering is that more goods are preferred to less, other things equal. The consumer is, of course, the judge of what things are ''goods'' as opposed to ''bads.'' If a consumer does not like air pollution or street crime, then the corresponding good is clean air or safe streets. The consumer may consider charity to others as a good, and thus is by no means assumed to be selfish.

But is it not true that the consumer can be sated? Consider rare (but not raw) hamburgers as goods. You may like only one, and I may prefer two, and we both may know people who prefer more, but doesn't everyone have a limit? The answer is yes, of course: Consumers may commonly have limits for specific goods within any particular time period.[9] A precise way to state the assumption of nonsatiation which allows for these limits is as follows: There is always at least one good for which the consumer is not yet sated.

Practically speaking, individuals are constrained by their limited budgets from having consumption bundles which contain everything they could possibly want. Even very rich people might prefer more leisure time, an extra summer home, or making more philanthropic donations (if they did not have to give up something they already have). And, of course, most people would prefer to be able to afford more (in terms of quantity or better quality) of most goods they are currently consuming. A convenient generalization is to treat consumers as not sated with any of the specific goods in alternative consumption bundles under discussion. We often use this version of the nonsatiation assumption (sometimes referred to as *strong monotonicity* in the professional literature), but it should be kept in mind that it is not appropriate if the focus is to be on some good such that satiation is an empirical likelihood (e.g., microeconomic policy analysis courses per semester).

The third assumption is that *each consumer has strictly convex preferences or, stated informally, prefers diversity in consumption bundles*. Suppose we

---

[9] Obviously, the limit depends on the time period. The example is for hamburgers per meal; the limit would presumably be much higher for hamburgers per year. In general, economic activities must include a time dimension to be well defined. Since no particular period is required for many of our illustrations, the activities can simply be thought of as per period.

know one consumer is indifferent between two bundles: one with much housing but little entertainment; the other with little housing but much entertainment. The third assumption asserts that the consumer would strictly prefer a third bundle formed by using any proportional combination (weighted average) of the housing and entertainment in the first two. For example, a bundle made up of one-third of the housing and entertainment in the first bundle plus two-thirds of the housing and entertainment in the second would be a proportional combination.

The idea is that the consumer would prefer a more "balanced" bundle to either of the extremes. This tries to capture the empirical reality that most people consume a diversity of goods rather than extreme quantities of only one or two items. Since nothing stops them from choosing less balanced bundles, it must be that the less balanced ones are not considered as desirable as the more balanced ones. Like the second assumption, this is simply an empirical generalization thought to be true in most circumstances but for which there are exceptions. (For example, someone might be indifferent to spending a one-week vacation in either of two places but think that half a week in each is strictly worse.)

The fourth assumption is that *each consumer makes resource allocation choices in accordance with his or her ordering.* This implies that the consumer is both self-interested and informed (in terms of knowing which choice is the best one to make). Together, these four assumptions form the most common model of rational consumer decision making. The first and fourth assumptions model rationality; the second and third assumptions are generalizations about preferences.

The first three assumptions of this model are often theoretically represented by an ordinal *utility function,* and the fourth assumption is equivalent to the consumer acting to *maximize* utility. Imagine that the consumer mentally considers all possible bundles of goods and lines them up in sequence from best to worst. Further imagine that some number (the utility level) is assigned to each of the bundles in accordance with this rule: More preferred bundles get higher numbers than less preferred bundles, and equally preferred bundles get the same number assigned to them. This is an ordinal ranking because the numbers indicate nothing besides the consumer's ordering.[10] Mathematically, we can write the utility function as

$$U(X_1, X_2, \ldots, X_n)$$

[10] The ranking tells us which of two bundles is preferred, but not by how much. The distance between the numbers in an ordinal ranking has no meaning. A cardinal ranking, by contrast, reveals both the order and the distance between bundles (like temperature scales). However, to construct a cardinal ranking of an individual's preference would require more knowledge about the consumer than that postulated in the four assumptions discussed. In particular, it would require a measure of the magnitude of the psychological change in utility or pleasure that an individual derives from consuming any specific bundle of goods relative to some comparison bundle. Since we do not know how to do that reliably, it is fortunate (and a notable achievement) that most economic models do not require the information in order to fulfill their purposes.

where there are n goods or services which can be in a bundle, X_i tells us how much of the ith good or service is in a bundle, and the value of the function tells us what utility level has been assigned to any particular bundle consisting of X_1, $X_2, \ldots, X_n$.

We can also represent the consumer's preferences graphically by using *indifference curves*. Assume that consumption bundles consist only of two goods, meat M and tomatoes T, and therefore that the utility level is a function only of them: $U(M, T)$. Any amount of meat and tomatoes can be represented by a single point in Figure 2-1. For example, point A represents 5 pounds of M and 4 pounds of T, and point B represents 4 pounds of M and 3 pounds of T. Define an indifference curve as the locus of points representing all consumption bundles which are equally preferred to each other (or equivalently, have the same utility level). In Figure 2-1, U_A shows all consumption bundles which have the same utility level as at point A, and U_B shows all bundles with the same utility level as at point B.

Through every point on the diagram, one (and only one) indifference curve must pass. The indifference curves are negatively sloped (they go downward from left to right). This is a consequence of the nonsatiation assumption. If the consumer begins at A, and some meat is taken away, he or she is worse off. If we were to take away some tomatoes as well, the consumer would be still worse off. To bring the consumer back to U_A, we must *increase* the amount of tomatoes to compensate for the meat loss. This results in the negative slope.

The *marginal rate of substitution* of a good M for another good T, represented by $\mathrm{MRS}_{M,T}$, is the maximum number of units of T a consumer is willing to give up in return for getting one more unit of M. This is the number

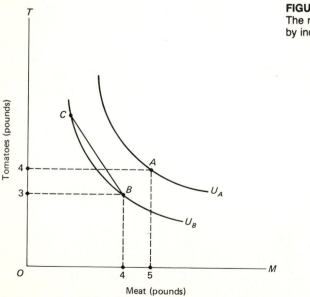

FIGURE 2-1
The representation of preferences by indifference curves.

which keeps the consumer just indifferent, by his or her own judgment, between the initial position and the proposed trade. Note that, unlike the utility level, the $MRS_{M,T}$ is a measurable number which can be compared for different consumers. (We will make use of this aspect shortly.) Formally, the $MRS_{M,T}$ is defined as the negative of the slope of the indifference curve (since the slope is itself negative, the MRS is positive).

Note in Figure 2-1 that the indifference curves are drawn to become *less steep* from left to right. The MRS is *diminishing:* along an indifference curve, the more tomatoes a consumer has, the less meat he or she will be willing to give up for still another pound of tomatoes. This is a consequence of the strict convexity assumption.

To see this consider any two equally preferred bundles, like *B* and *C* in Figure 2-1. The set of bundles which represent proportional combinations of *B* and *C* correspond to the points on the straight line between them.[11] By the strict convexity assumption, each of the bundles in this set is strictly preferred to *B* and *C*. Therefore, the indifference curve that connects any two equally preferred bundles, like *B* and *C*, must lie *below* the straight line that connects them. This is possible only if the slope of the indifference curve becomes less steep from *B* to *C*.

The four assumptions described in this section form the model of economic man: an individual who has a utility function and acts to maximize it. We wish to show (in a very simple setting) how this model can be used to make inferences about efficiency. To do so, we must first explain the concept of efficiency.

---

[11] Represent *B* as the bundle (M_B, T_B) and *C* as (M_C, T_C). A proportional combination of *B* and *C* is defined, letting α $(0 < \alpha < 1)$ be the proportion of *B* and $1 - \alpha$ the proportion of *C*, as follows:

$$M_\alpha = \alpha M_B + (1 - \alpha)M_C = M_C + \alpha(M_B - M_C)$$

and

$$T_\alpha = \alpha T_B + (1 - \alpha)T_C = T_C + \alpha(T_B - T_C)$$

We can show that the point (M_α, T_α) must lie on the line connecting *B* and *C*. The slope of the line connecting *B* and *C* is

$$\frac{\Delta T}{\Delta M} = \frac{T_B - T_C}{M_B - M_C}$$

The slope of the line connecting (M_α, T_α) and *C* is

$$\frac{\Delta T}{\Delta M} = \frac{T_\alpha - T_C}{M_\alpha - M_C}$$

Substituting the definitions of T_α and M_α in the equation directly above gives us

$$\frac{\Delta T}{\Delta M} = \frac{T_C + \alpha(T_B - T_C) - T_C}{M_C + \alpha(M_B - M_C) - M_C}$$
$$= \frac{\alpha(T_B - T_C)}{\alpha(M_B - M_C)} = \frac{T_B - T_C}{M_B - M_C}$$

Since both (M_α, T_α) and *B* lie on a line through *C* with slope $(T_B - T_C)/(M_B - M_C)$, they must lie on the same line.

EFFICIENCY

The General Concept

Society is endowed with a limited supply of a wide variety of resources: people, land, air, water, minerals, time, etc. A fundamental economic problem faced by society is how to use the resources. If the resources were not scarce, there would be no economic problem; everything that anyone wanted could be provided today, and an infinite amount of resources would still be left to meet the desires of tomorrow. But although human wants or desires may be insatiable, resource scarcity limits our ability to satisfy them. Scarcity implies that any specific resource allocation involves opportunity costs; e.g., if more resources are allocated to education, fewer resources will remain to be allocated to health care, food production, road construction, and other goods and services.

People differ in terms of their specific ideas for the use of scarce resources. However, we all generally agree that resources are too precious to waste. If it is possible, by a change in the allocation of resources, to improve the lot of one person without doing harm to any other person, then resources are currently being wasted. All efficiency means is that there is no waste of this kind: *An efficient allocation of resources is one from which no person can be made better off without making another person worse off.* Sometimes efficiency is referred to as *Pareto optimality* after the Italian economist Vilfredo Pareto (1848–1923), who first developed the formulation. Any allocation of resources which is not efficient is called, not surprisingly, *inefficient*.

To demonstrate the practical import of efficiency for policy, consider the resources devoted to national defense by the world's people.[12] In order to keep the illustration simple, let us assume that each nation, acting for its citizens, seeks only to produce "security" from military aggression by others. Then the efficient defense policy would be for the world to have no military resources at all: no person anywhere would face a military threat, and the freed-up resources could be devoted to increasing supplies of food, shelter, clothing, or other important goods and services.[13]

However, each nation is mistrustful of the others and allocates some

---

[12] For example, by a conservative definition the United States in 1980 spent about 5 percent of the GNP on defense. The federal government spent $136 billion on national defense out of total federal spending of $580 billion and total GNP of $2627 billion. The $136 billion figure does not include all spending that is part of national defense; e.g., it does not include $21 billion spent on veterans' benefits and services. Source: *Economic Report of the President*, January 1981 (U.S. Government Printing Office, 1981), p. 233, table B-1 and p. 315, table B-70.

[13] The efficient level of national defense is substantially above zero for at least two important reasons that our illustration rules out: (1) some nations may in fact wish to initiate aggressive military activities for offensive rather than defensive reasons, and (2) some nations may consider a military response appropriate to a nonmilitary threat (e.g., to enforce a claim to ownership of a natural resource like land). Each possibility leads every nation to allocate some resources for national defense. Nevertheless, the reasons cited do not affect the point of our example, which is that defense expenditures can be significantly higher than necessary in order to produce the desired level of protection.

resources to defense as a form of insurance. But that increases the threat perceived by each nation and leads to increases in national defense spending, which further increases the perceived threats, leads to more defense increases, and so on. In short, defense policies become the runners in an inefficient arms race.[14] Furthermore, efficiency is not achieved by a unilateral withdrawal: If the United States dropped out of the arms race but no other nation did, many U.S. citizens would feel worse off, not better off. *This illustrates not only that efficiency is an important objective but that its achievement typically requires coordination among the different economic agents* (countries, in this example). This is the primary objective of negotiations like the Strategic Arms Limitation Treaty (SALT) agreements between the United States and the Soviet Union.

Efficiency with an Individualistic Interpretation

The definition of efficiency refers to individuals being either better off or worse off. To apply the definition to any practical problem, there must be a method of deciding whether someone's well-being has improved or deteriorated. One way to develop such a method is by using the *principle of consumer sovereignty,* which means that *each person is the sole judge of his or her own welfare.*[15] Based on that principle, economists have devised numerous analytic techniques for making inferences about whether individuals consider themselves better off or worse off under alternative allocations of resources.

Although the above principle is commonly used in the economic analysis of most western societies, it is not the only logical way of constructing a concept of efficiency that meets the definition given earlier. An alternative route is to let some other person (e.g., a philosopher-king) or perhaps a political process (e.g., democratic socialism or communism) be the judge of each person's welfare. Then efficiency would be evaluated by the values and standards of judges, rather than by those of the individuals affected.

In this text, we will always mean efficiency as judged under consumer sovereignty unless it is explicitly stated otherwise. If efficiency is not judged by that principle, one jeopardizes its acceptance in domestic policy analysis as representing a value most people share. It is worth mentioning, however, that there are a number of situations in which deviations from the concept are commonly thought appropriate. Typically, they are those in which individuals have incomplete or erroneous information or are unable to process the available information.

One obvious example of such a deviation concerns children: Parents generally substitute their own judgments for those of their young children.

---

[14] The behavior described here may be thought of as a version of the Slumlord's Dilemma or Prisoner's Dilemma analyzed in Chapter 6. In that chapter, applications involving urban renewal and health insurance are discussed.

[15] The term ''consumer'' in ''consumer sovereignty'' is a slight misnomer. The principle is intended to apply to all resource allocation decisions which affect an individual's welfare: the supply of inputs (e.g., the value of holding a particular job) as well as the consumption of outputs.

Another example, and this one a matter of public policy, is that we do not allow suppliers to sell thalidomide, even though some consumers might purchase it if they were allowed to do so. Certain medicinal drugs are legal to sell, but consumers can purchase them only by presenting physicians' prescriptions. In each of these cases, some social mechanism is used to try to protect consumers from the inadequacies of their own judgments.[16]

In using the consumer sovereignty principle, it is important to distinguish between consumer *judgments* and consumer *actions*. It is only the sovereignty of the judgments which we rely upon for this definition of efficiency. Indeed, there will be many illustrations throughout this book of inefficient allocations which result from sovereign actions of well-informed consumers. The defense example given earlier is of this nature: The people of each nation can recognize the inefficiency of an arms race; but when each nation acts alone, the inefficiency is difficult to avoid. The problem is not with the judgments of people about how to value security, but with the mechanisms of coordination available to achieve it.

Efficiency in a Model of an Exchange Economy

To illustrate the analysis of efficiency, we will utilize a model of a highly simplified economy: a pure exchange economy in which there are only two utility-maximizing consumers and two different goods. By assuming that the goods are already produced, we suppress the very important problems of how much of each good to produce and by what technical processes. Nevertheless, the basic principle of efficiency developed here holds for the more complicated economy as well. Furthermore, it highlights the critical connection between efficiency and the consumer sovereignty definition of human satisfaction.

The principle to be established is this: *The allocation of resources in an economy is efficient in exchange if and only if the marginal rate of substitution of one good for another is the same for each person consuming both of the goods.* To see the truth of the principle, imagine any initial allocation of resources between two people, Smith and Jones, each of whom has a different $MRS_{M,T}$ and some of each of the two goods. Let us say that Smith has an $MRS_{M,T}^S = 3$ (that is, $3T$ for $1M$), and Jones has an $MRS_{M,T}^J = 2$. Then imagine taking away 1 pound of meat from Jones and giving it to Smith and taking away 3 pounds of tomatoes from Smith. Smith's utility level is thus unchanged. We still have 3 pounds of tomatoes to allocate; let us give 2 pounds to Jones. Jones is now back to the initial utility level. Both have the same level of utility as when they started, but there is still 1 pound of tomatoes left to allocate between them. No matter how the last pound is allocated, at least one will be made better off than initially and the other will be no worse off (in terms of their own judgments). Therefore, the initial allocation was inefficient.

---

[16] The fact that individuals may be imperfect judges of their own welfare does not necessarily imply that there is any better way to make the judgments. In later chapters we discuss several information problems such as these and analyze alternative responses to them.

Any time that two consumers of each good have different values for the MRS, there is "room for a deal" as illustrated above. On the other hand, if both consumers have the same value for the MRS, then it is impossible to make one of them better off without making the other worse off. Although the illustration involved only Smith and Jones, the same reasoning would apply to any pair of consumers picked randomly from the economy. Therefore, efficiency requires that *all* consumers of the two goods have the same $MRS_{M,T}$. Furthermore, there is nothing special about meat and tomatoes in this example; meat and fruit would work just as well, and so would fruit and clothing. Therefore, efficiency requires that the MRS between *any* two goods in the economy must be the same for all consumers of the two goods.

Now that we know what is required for efficiency in this pure exchange economy, recall that we have said absolutely nothing so far about any mechanisms which a society might utilize to allow its citizens to achieve an efficient allocation. If there are only two consumers, they could achieve an efficient allocation by bartering or trading.[17] Since trading can increase the utility level of each person, we predict the two consumers will trade. Note that the value of the MRS depends on (all) the specific goods in a consumer's bundle, and it changes as the bundle changes through trading. We know that an "equilibrium" position of efficiency will be reached because of diminishing marginal rates of substitution. This is illustrated below.

In the example with Smith and Jones, Smith is gaining meat and losing tomatoes (and Jones the opposite). Smith will offer less than 3 pounds of tomatoes to get still more meat *after* the first trade, since tomatoes are becoming relatively more dear. Jones, with less meat than initially, will now demand more than two pounds of tomatoes to part with still another pound of meat. As they trade, Smith's $MRS_{M,T}^{S}$ continues to diminish from 3 while Jones' $MRS_{M,T}^{J}$ rises from 2 (or equivalently, $MRS_{T,M}^{J}$ diminishes).[18] At some point each will have precisely the same $MRS_{M,T}$ and then the two will be unable to mutually agree upon any additional trades. They will have reached an efficient allocation.

Note that knowledge of the marginal rate of substitution allows us to predict the direction of trade in the model. We have not had to decide whether Smith is more of a meat lover than Jones in terms of abstract utility.[19] All we compare is a relative and measurable value: the pounds of tomatoes each is willing to give up for additional meat *at the margin*. At the initial point, meat will be traded to Smith because Smith is willing to give up more tomatoes than Jones in order to get an additional pound of meat. Smith may not like meat more than Jones in an absolute sense. Alternatively, for example, Smith may like tomatoes less than (and meat as much as) Jones in the absolute sense. Or they could both have

---

[17] We must also assume that there are negligible *transaction costs:* neither incurs any significant expense in arranging and conducting the trading. In more realistic problems of policy, transaction costs are often significant and may play a major role in determining efficiency.

[18] At any point on a normal indifference curve $MRS_{M,T} = 1/MRS_{T,M}$.

[19] This would require not only a cardinal utility measure for each but also a method of making the interpersonal comparison between Smith utils and Jones utils.

identical absolute preferences but Smith might have an initial allocation with a great many tomatoes and little meat compared to Jones. Fortunately, efficiency requires only that we equate the comparable MRS values of each consumer at the margin; we do not have to know individual preferences in an absolute sense.

Efficiency may be achieved through a barter process when there are only two consumers and two goods, but what about the actual world which consists of a great many consumers and a very large number of different goods and services? What mechanisms exist to facilitate communication and coordination among the diverse economic agents? That general problem of organization will be the focus of Parts IV and V, but it is useful to introduce at this very early stage the idea of *price* as one simple coordinating mechanism which can help with the task.

If each good has one price which all consumers either pay to buy the good or receive when they sell it, then each consumer can be thought of as having a *budget constraint* derived by multiplying the quantity of each good in the initial endowment by its price and summing over all the goods in the endowment. The consumer will then try to allocate his or her budget such that, for any two goods X and Y that are bought,

$$\text{MRS}_{X,Y} = \frac{P_X}{P_Y}$$

To show this, suppose the price of meat P_M is \$4.00 per pound and the price of tomatoes P_T is \$1.00 per pound. We assume that each consumer acts to maximize his or her utility. But if $\text{MRS}_{M,T} \neq \$4.00 \div \$1.00$, the consumer is not at a utility maximum. Suppose the consumer has $\text{MRS}_{M,T} = 3$, for example: indifferent between the current allocation and one with 3 pounds more of tomatoes and 1 pound less of meat. The consumer can sell 1 pound of meat for \$4.00, buy 3 pounds of tomatoes for \$3.00, and have \$1.00 left over to spend and thus increase utility over the initial allocation. For utility to be maximized, any consumer of both goods must have $\text{MRS}_{M,T} = 4$. Since all consumers face the same prices, all try to achieve the same $\text{MRS}_{M,T}$. If they are successful, the resulting allocation is efficient. Prices thus can be a very powerful coordinating device.

Note that if consumers faced different prices for the same good and could buy the amounts of it they wished, they would end up with different values for the MRS. This suggests a generalization (with exceptions to be uncovered elsewhere in the book) relevant to policy design: *If a policy results in at least one consumer of a good being charged a price different from the price charged other consumers of the good, the policy will generally be inefficient.*[20]

---

[20] The exceptions are typically based on one of three considerations: (1) It is only the price of the marginal unit purchased which must be the same for all consumers. (2) The consumer is unable or unwilling to alter the quantity purchased. (3) The price discrimination offsets an inefficiency that arises elsewhere in the economy.

Are there policies for which this principle is relevant? One is the Robinson-Patman Act of 1936, which prohibits firms from engaging in price discrimination among their customers. However, many policies cause different consumers to be faced with different prices. We will consider one such policy in the next chapter when we discuss food stamps. Since food stamps reduce the price of food for the recipients and only some people receive them, we might expect the result to be inefficient resource allocation. This proposition turns out to be more complicated under plausible alternative model specifications. Of course, one purpose of food stamps is to help the poor and it is possible that achieving the equity objective is worth some efficiency cost. Similar questions can be raised about other benefits that only some people receive, e.g., housing subsidies, education benefits for veterans, Medicare, and Medicaid.

The main point of raising these issues here, even without resolving them, is to demonstrate the earlier claim that considerable insight into the efficiency consequences of policies can be achieved through modeling. We did not have to go around asking every (or even any) consumer how he or she would be affected by price discrimination. The conclusion that price discrimination is inefficient comes from applying the utility-maximizing model of behavior to the definition of efficiency. This type of reasoning, displayed in very elementary form here, can be extended to quite sophisticated forms of analysis.

All such analysis is subject to the same type of criticism: If the underlying model of consumer behavior is erroneous, then the analytic conclusion may be wrong. If some individuals are not utility maximizers, then making all individuals face the same prices will not necessarily result in each having the same MRS for any two goods. Finally, recall that models cannot be expected to be perfectly accurate. The relevant question, which is not addressed in this example, is whether the model is accurate enough. The answer depends, in part, on the alternative means of analysis with which it is compared.

The theoretical example of coordination through prices illustrates only part of the coordinating potential of a price system. It does not consider the problem of how to ensure that the total amount people wish to buy of one good, given its price, equals the total amount that other people will be willing to sell. (The only goods available are those in the initial endowments of the consumers.) If the price of one good is too low, for example, then the quantity demanded will exceed the quantity supplied. But prices can solve that problem as well: Raise the price of the goods in excess demand and lower the price of those in excess supply until the prices which exactly balance the demand and supply for each good are found. The *equilibrium prices* are the ones which will allow the consumers in the above example actually to achieve efficiency; any other

---

When applying this generalization, it is important to make sure that the prices compared are for truly identical goods. For example, the price for a television with installation provided by the dealer need not be the same as the price for the same television at a cash-and-carry outlet. Differences in times of delivery, shipping costs, and guarantees also are common reasons for distinguishing otherwise identical goods.

prices will result in some consumers not being able to buy the quantities necessary to maximize their utility.[21]

A Geometric Representation of the Model

The concept of efficiency in exchange can also be explained geometrically through the use of an Edgeworth box diagram. In our simple example with Smith and Jones, let $\overline{M}$ be the total amount of meat between them and $\overline{T}$ be the total amount of tomatoes. These amounts determine the dimensions of the Edgeworth box shown in Figure 2-2.

Let the bottom left corner O_S represent the origin of a graph showing Smith's consumption. Point A shows Smith's initial endowment of meat M_S^E and tomatoes T_S^E. Let the upper right corner O_J represent the origin of a graph showing Jones' consumption. The amount of meat consumed is measured by

---

[21] We should also note an important difference between two coordinating mechanisms mentioned: prices and SALT agreements. The price mechanism allows *decentralized* coordination: Consumers do not have to consult with one another about how much each plans to buy. SALT agreements are a *centralized* way of coordinating: Each country will agree only to "not buy" certain arms based on knowledge of what the other country promises to not buy. Thus, efficiency can be sought with both decentralized and centralized institutional procedures. One of the more interesting and subtle questions of policy design concerns the choice of centralized versus decentralized procedures. We focus on that choice in Part V.

FIGURE 2-2
The Edgeworth box.

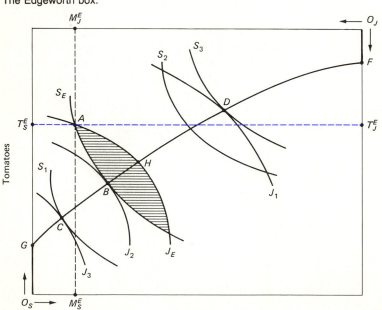

the horizontal distance to the left of O_J, and tomato consumption is measured by the vertical distance below O_J. Then, given the way the box is constructed, point A also represents Jones' initial endowment. Since the total quantities available are $\overline{M}$ and $\overline{T}$ and Smith starts with M_S^E and T_S^E, Smith must have the rest:

$$M_J^E = \overline{M} - M_S^E$$
$$T_J^E = \overline{T} - T_S^E$$

and

In fact, every possible allocation of the two goods between Smith and Jones is represented by one point in the Edgeworth box. At O_S, for example, Smith has nothing and Jones has everything. At O_J, Jones has nothing and Smith has everything. Every conceivable trade between Smith and Jones can thus be represented as a movement from A to another point in the Edgeworth box.

We can also draw in the indifference curves to show each person's satisfaction level. Let S_E be the indifference curve reflecting Smith's level of satisfaction at the initial endowment (and thus point A lies on it). Higher levels of utility for Smith are shown by curves S_2 and S_3; a lower level of satisfaction is shown by S_1. The curves drawn are only illustrative, of course; for every point in the box, Smith has an indifference curve that passes through it.

The indifference curves for Jones are drawn bowed in the opposite direction because of the way the box is constructed, with Jones having more consumption at points away from O_J and toward O_S. Let J_E be the indifference curve showing Jones' utility level at the initial endowment (and thus point A lies on it). J_2 and J_3 represent increasing levels of satisfaction; J_1 shows a lower amount of satisfaction.

Thus the Edgeworth box combines two indifference curve diagrams, each like Figure 2-1. Smith's preferences are represented like those in Figure 2-1: origin at the bottom left, tomatoes on the vertical axis, meat on the horizontal axis, and higher utility levels upward and to the right. The same is true for Jones if the Edgeworth box is turned upside down.

Notice that the shaded area between S_E and J_E represents all allocations of meat and tomatoes whereby *both* Smith and Jones would consider themselves better off than at the initial allocation. If we include the points *on* as well as those strictly between the indifference curves S_E and J_E, they represent the set of all possible trades which would make at least one person better off and no one worse off.

Consider the possibility that we could start the exchange economy (choose feasible initial endowments for each person) from any point in the Edgeworth box. From most points, there will be some trades which could make each person better off. For every point like A, through which the indifference curves *intersect,* improvements by trading are possible. But there are some points, like point B, where the indifference curves do not intersect but are just tangent to one another. Note that every single point which improves Jones' satisfaction over the level at B lies below the J_2 indifference curve. At each of these points

Smith would be worse off than at *B* and so would not agree to any of the proposed trades. Similarly, Jones would not agree to move to any of the points which would make Smith better off. *Thus B is an efficient allocation: from it, it is impossible to find a trade which will make one person better off without making the other person worse off.* And, as was claimed earlier, the $MRS_{M,T}$ is the same for Smith and Jones at *B* because the indifference curves are tangent there.

There are a few other efficient points, like *C* and *D,* illustrated in Figure 2-2. (Although the $MRS_{M,T}$ may be different at *B, C,* and *D,* at any one of the points the two consumers will have the same $MRS_{M,T}$.) Imagine finding each of the efficient points. Define this set of points as the *contract curve;* the curve is drawn as the line through the Edgeworth box connecting O_S and O_J. The contract curve illustrates that there are many possible resource allocations which are efficient.

Of course, if Smith and Jones are initially at point *A* and can trade with one another, utility maximization implies they will trade within the shaded area. Their trading will continue until they reach a point on the *BH* segment of the contract curve. (We cannot predict which point without further assumptions.) Furthermore, we can see that Smith will be gaining meat and losing tomatoes, while Jones does the opposite.[22] In other words, the behavior that we described previously can be seen in the Edgeworth box diagram.

Note that some of the points from the entire contract curve lie on the boundaries of the box. These segments, O_SG and O_JF, do not meet the same tangency conditions as the efficient points interior to the boundaries. Although the latter points are just as efficient, Smith and Jones are not each consuming both of the goods. Careful examination of these points is interesting because it suggests why consumers do not purchase some goods at all, although they have strictly convex preferences. The reason is simply that the price is considered too high.

In Figure 2-3 the left corner of the Edgeworth box is blown up a bit to see this more clearly. At *G,* Smith has utility level *S'* and Jones *J'.* The solid portions of each indifference curve are in the feasible trading region (within the boundaries of the box). The dashed extension of *J'* shows the consumption bundles which would give Jones the same utility level as at *G,* but there is not enough total meat in the economy to create these bundles. (Also, the points on this dashed segment do not exist from Smith's perspective, since they would involve negative quantities of meat!)

Although the indifference curves *J'* and *S'* are clearly not tangent at *G,* there are no mutually satisfactory trades which can be made from that point. Smith has only tomatoes to trade, and $MRS^S_{M,T} < MRS^J_{M,T}$. This means Jones will only part with another pound of meat for more tomatoes than Smith is willing to offer. Smith considers the meat price (in terms of tomatoes) demanded by Jones to be too high, and Jones feels similarly about the price (in terms of meat) for

---

[22] The slopes of the indifference curves at point *A* reveal that $MRS^S_{M,T} > MRS^J_{M,T}$.

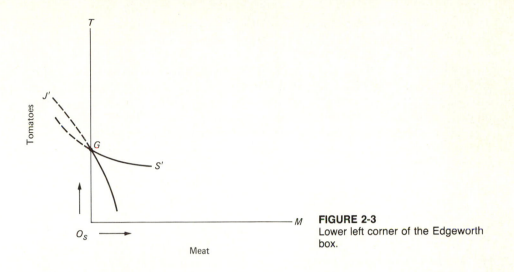

FIGURE 2-3
Lower left corner of the Edgeworth box.

tomatoes. As with the other points on the contract curve, every point which makes Jones better off (those below J') makes Smith worse off, and vice versa. Thus G is efficient, although the tangency conditions are not met. This is explained by the limits imposed by the boundaries (along which at least one of the consumers is consuming only one of the two goods).

This analysis, of two consumers and two goods, generalizes to the many goods, many consumers economy just as before. Efficiency requires every pair of consumers to be on their contract curves for every pair of goods. Thus, we may use the Edgeworth diagram to represent metaphorically exchange efficiency for the entire society.

Let us digress for a moment to comment on a general modeling issue. An economic model has now been constructed in two forms: verbal description and geometric representation. Examples were given earlier of other forms that models might take: the plastic model of an airplane, and the mathematical model of gravity's effects. Models may appear in the form of short stories or other abstractions. What should determine the form that the model builder chooses? In each of the two forms of the economic model, the essence of the consumer behavior (utility maximization) is the same. What purpose is served by presenting it in different ways?

We wish to note this distinction: Modeling is a way for the model builder to learn, but it is also a way to communicate with (or to teach) others. The main point of doing policy analysis is to learn: The analyst does not know the conclusion at the start and seeks to come to one by a logical procedure which can be subjected to evaluation by professional standards. Yet the form of a model used for learning is not necessarily appropriate as a form for communication. The latter depends upon the audience. If policy analysis is to influence policy, it is particularly important to communicate it effectively.

As a general rule, policy analysis is done in a more technical format than that used to communicate it to decision makers. Analysts communicate their work to each other quite fully and efficiently through the presentation of technical models (like those in professional journals). However, most public officials, administrators, and politicians with interest in a specific analysis prefer it to be presented in a concise, clear, jargon-free form.[23] The material presented here goes somewhat in the reverse direction; we expand and build upon technical concepts in order to see how microeconomic theory is used in policy analysis. Presenting two different forms of an elementary economic model (as a first step) makes it easier to understand the analytic process that connects consumer choices to their efficiency consequences. A third common form of this model, using mathematical equations and calculus, is contained in the appendix to Chapter 2.[24]

Relative Efficiency

The Pareto concept of efficiency is an absolute one: Each possible allocation is either efficient or inefficient. It is often useful, however, to compare the efficiency of one allocation with that of another. That is, we wish to know whether one allocation is *relatively* more efficient than another or whether an allocative change *increases* efficiency.

Measures of relative efficiency have been devised and are frequently used in policy analysis. They are controversial and more complex than the absolute standard of Pareto optimality, and we defer most formal exposition of them until Chapter 5. Below, we briefly introduce the general ideas that underlie measures of relative efficiency.

There is a natural extension of the Pareto rule which can be used to make some judgments about relative efficiency. *One allocation is defined as Pareto-superior to another if and only if it makes at least one person better off and no one worse off.* In Figure 2-4, the axes show utility levels for Smith and Jones. Point A in Figure 2-4 shows Smith with a utility level of S_E and Jones with a utility level of J_E (chosen to correspond with the utility levels of their indifference curves through point A in Figure 2-2). The shaded quadrant

---

[23] The form of the analysis may be tailored for a specific user. An extreme example is offered by Richard Neustadt, who was asked by President Kennedy to analyze the decision-making process leading to a controversial decision in 1962 to cancel the Skybolt missile. The decision had unexpected and embarrassing foreign relations consequences, and the President hoped Neustadt could draw some lessons to improve future policy making.

Neustadt felt that to understand the lessons from his analysis, Kennedy would have to read a lengthy document. (That would have violated Washington's KISS rule: Keep it short and simple). But presidential schedules generally do not allow time for reading lengthy documents. This president was known to be a fan of Ian Fleming novels, and Neustadt therefore put his lengthy analysis in a format designed to appeal to such a fan. He sent the report to the President on November 15, 1963, and Kennedy finished it on November 17, 1963, suggesting Neustadt's strategy was successful. Unfortunately the report itself is confidential; some of the lessons from Skybolt are discussed in Richard E. Neustadt, *Alliance Politics* (New York: Columbia University Press, 1970).

[24] Recommended for graduate students.

represents the set of all utility levels which are Pareto-superior to those at point *A*.

For reference, we also draw in Figure 2-4 the *utility-possibilities frontier: the locus of utility levels associated with the Pareto-optimal allocations of the economy*. These levels correspond to the levels of the indifference curves passing through each point on the contract curve of Figure 2-2. The part of the shaded area *ABH* in Figure 2-4 corresponds to the utility levels of the allocations in the shaded area of Figure 2-2. These are the Pareto-superior points which are feasible in the economy. Point *R* in Figure 2-4 is Pareto-superior to point *A*, but it is not feasible if the amounts of meat and tomatoes available only equal the dimensions of the Edgeworth box in Figure 2-2. Given the resources of the economy, the efficient allocations are those from which no Pareto-superior change can be made.

The concept of Pareto superiority is not itself controversial. It can become controversial if one proposes to use it normatively as a criterion for policy making. For example, suppose one thought that all policy changes should be required to be Pareto-superior. That would restrict the pursuit of efficiency from point *A* to the allocations in the shaded area of Figure 2-4.

The problem with this proposed rule is that it eliminates all the changes whereby some people are better off (perhaps many people are much better off) and some are worse off (perhaps a few are slightly worse off). But in an actual economy most allocative changes, and especially those caused by public policy, are characterized precisely by these mixed effects. Inevitably, evaluating these changes involves interpersonal comparisons which the concepts of Pareto optimality and superiority try to avoid.

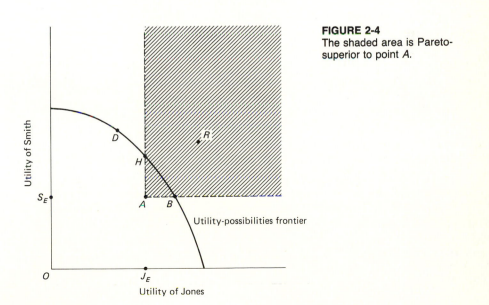

FIGURE 2-4
The shaded area is Pareto-superior to point *A*.

Utility of Smith

Utility-possibilities frontier

Utility of Jones

For example, the government may be considering building a new highway which bypasses a small town in order to increase the ease of traveling and the conduct of commerce between two or more cities. Benefits or gains will accrue to the users of the new highway and to those who own land adjacent to it which may be used to service the new traffic. But the owners, employees, and local customers of the service stations, restaurants, and motels in the small town may well experience losses because of the traffic reduction. However, if the gains to the gainers are great enough and the losses to the losers are small enough, collectively the society might think the change justified.

Allocative changes whereby some people gain and others lose certainly raise questions of equity or fairness. Suppose, however, we try to put these questions aside for the moment and consider whether some objective statements about relative efficiency can be made in these circumstances. Consider, for example, a change like the one from point A to point D in Figure 2-4. This clearly moves the economy from an inefficient allocation to an efficient one, and we might think that any objective measure of relative efficiency should indicate that the change is an efficiency improvement.

Note that the test for efficiency or Pareto optimality does not depend on whether someone *has* been made worse off (Jones in the above example); it depends only on whether it is *possible* to make someone better off without making anyone else worse off. Efficiency is a matter of whether there is room for improvement, and one might wish that measures of efficiency indicated only the scarcity of the available room for improvement (e.g., closeness to the utility-possibilities frontier). Then we would say that one allocation is more efficient than another if relatively less room for improvement is possible from it. For any given initial allocation the set of more efficient allocations would include not only the Pareto-superior ones but others as well.

An example of a measure which avoids the restrictiveness of the Pareto-superiority criterion is the aggregate (or sum) of utilities.[25] In Figure 2-5, the line through point A with a slope of -1 is the locus of points with constant aggregate utility equal to the level at point A. Any point above this line has higher aggregate utility and by that measure would be considered relatively more efficient. All allocations which are Pareto-superior to point A have a higher aggregate utility level (since at least one person's utility level is higher and no one's utility level is lower), and thus are considered more efficient by this test. We can see that point D, which is efficient but not Pareto-superior, also is considered more efficient than point A. Therefore, this test is less restrictive than the test of Pareto superiority.

However, there are also problems with this measure. As we have pointed out before, utility is neither measurable nor comparable among persons. Therefore, the measure is not very pragmatic. Later in the text, we shall review

---

[25] This somewhat unusual example is chosen because it is easy to explain and because the most common measures (based on the Hicks-Kaldor compensation principle) can be seen as simple variations upon it.

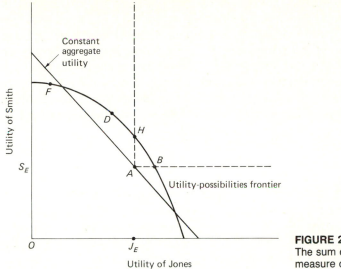

FIGURE 2-5
The sum of utilities at point *A* as a measure of its relative efficiency.

methods of constructing related indices which solve the measurability problem.[26] Then we must face the remaining problem: The implicit interpersonal judgments in this measure (and the related measures discussed later) are arbitrary from an ethical viewpoint.

Consider, for example, point *F* in Figure 2-5. Like point *D*, point *F* is Pareto-optimal, but it is considered relatively *less* efficient than point *A* by the sum-of-utilities test. Why? One reason is that the test is defined independently of the utility-possibilities frontier. Unless the shape of the test line is geometrically identical to the shape of the utility-possibilities frontier, the different Pareto-optimal points will not receive the same relative efficiency ranking. Rather than an attempt to measure the distance *to* the frontier, the aggregate utilities test is better thought of as measuring distance *from* the origin; how far we have come, rather than how much farther there is to go. Since better use of resources does move us farther from the origin, a measure of this distance can be interpreted as an index of efficiency.

If we accept the notion of measuring distance from the origin, the aggregate utilities test still imposes an interpersonal judgment: To hold relative efficiency constant, a 1-util loss to someone is just offset by a 1-util gain to another. But why should this judgment be accepted? Why can't the social judgment be something else, e.g., that losses are more serious than gains, so that perhaps 2 utils of gain should be required to offset each util of loss? Then a quite different set of allocations would be considered relatively more efficient than point *A*.

---

[26] A *weighted* sum of utilities, where the weights are the inverses of each individual's marginal utility of income, is equivalent to the Hicks-Kaldor compensation test (measurable in monetary units). This is demonstrated and explained in Chapter 5.

The point of this last illustration is to suggest that, normatively, measures of relative efficiency can be controversial if one does not agree with the implicit ethical judgment in them. Rather than leave such judgments implicit, the strategy recommended here is to make equity or fairness an explicit criterion in policy analysis and evaluate policies on both efficiency and equity grounds. Standardized measures of relative efficiency can then be very useful, but they take on normative significance only when looked at in conjunction with some explicit ethical perspective. To illustrate that, we must introduce the criterion of equity or fairness.

EQUITY

It is clear from the earlier Edgeworth analysis that there are many efficient allocations of resources. These allocations, represented by the points on the contract curve, *dominate* all other possible allocations. That is, for any allocation not on the contract curve, there is at least one point on the contract curve which makes one or more persons better off and no one worse off. Thus if a society could choose any allocation for its economy, it would certainly be one from the contract curve. But which one?

Recall that efficiency is but one social objective. Another important objective is equity: *fairness in the distribution of goods and services among the people in an economy*. However, no unique concept of equity is widely regarded as definitive for public policy making. We shall use the term to refer collectively to all the various concepts of fair distribution, and later in the text we shall introduce specific concepts (e.g., strict equality or a universal minimum) to compare and contrast their implications in the analyses of particular issues.[27] At this stage we wish primarily to make the point that diverse concepts of equity deserve analytic consideration.

Equality of Outcome Is One Concept of Equity

Although all the points on the contract curve of Figure 2-6 are efficient, they differ in the distribution of well-being. In fact, the contract curve offers a continuum of distributional possibilities. As we move along it from O_S to O_J, Smith is getting an increasing share of the total goods and services and is becoming better off relative to Jones. One way in which equity is sometimes considered is in terms of these relative shares. Intuitively, distributions in the "middle" of the contract curve represent more equal outcomes than those at the extremes, and for that reason they might be considered preferable on equity grounds. According to this interpretation, *equality* of relative shares is the most equitable allocation.

Using the equality of relative shares as a standard, the question "shares of

---

[27] Most of the specific concepts are introduced in Chapter 4. The concept of a *just price* is not introduced until Chapter 12, in order to permit prior development of the workings of price systems.

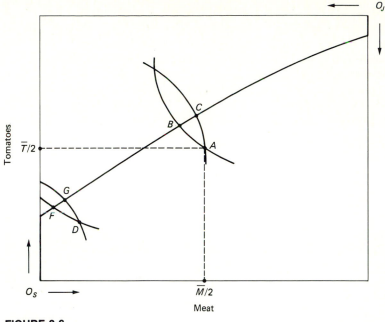

FIGURE 2-6
Equity versus efficiency.

what?'' must still be confronted. If equality of well-being or satisfaction is the objective, then it is the shares of *utility* which should be of equal size. But since utility is neither measurable nor interpersonally comparable, in practice we usually fall back on proxy measures like income or wealth.

For example, point *A* in Figure 2-6 is the allocation which gives each person exactly one-half of the available wealth (meat and tomatoes). Without being able to measure or compare utility, making this the initial endowment may be the best we can do to ensure equal relative shares. This necessarily ignores the possibility that one of the two people, say Smith, simply does not like meat or tomatoes very much, and might require twice the quantity given to Jones in order to reach a comparable utility level. Furthermore, it would be difficult to distinguish on equity grounds any of the efficient allocations which the two might then reach by voluntary trading from point *A*: the *BC* segment of the contract curve. Some objective standard for weighing the equity of the meat and tomato exchange between Smith and Jones would be necessary.[28]

[28] To understand why such a voluntary exchange might change the equity of the distribution, consider the move from point *A* to point *B*. Since the allocations at point *A* are perfectly equal by definition and at point *B* Jones' welfare has increased but Smith's welfare is the same, we must conclude that Jones is now better off than Smith. Obviously there must be some point on the *BC* segment which has the same equity as at point *A*, but the problem is whether it can be identified in any objective sense.

One possible method is to use prices as weights. If the trading were done through a price system

Equality of Opportunity Is Another Concept of Equity

Some people do not feel that equality of outcomes should be a social goal of great importance. An alternative view is that only the process must be fair. One specific principle of this type, for example, is that all persons should have equal opportunity. We illustrate this view below.

The equal endowments at point A might be considered equitable if we were starting an economy from scratch, but in reality we always start from some given initial allocation such as that at point D. Let us say that at point D it is obvious that Jones is richer (having a bundle that contains much highly valued meat, whereas Smith's bundle consists mostly of tomatoes). Consider whether your own sense of equity is affected by why we are starting at point D.

Suppose that Smith and Jones have equal abilities, opportunities, knowledge, and luck but that point D is the result of different efforts at production. That is, Jones obtained the initial endowment by working very hard to produce it, whereas Smith was lazy. Then you might think that the distribution at D is perfectly fair and that some allocation on FG reached through voluntary trading is equally fair. Furthermore, you might think that any policies aimed at redistribution toward equality (point A) are inequitable.

Alternatively, suppose you feel that we started at point D because of past discrimination against Smith. Jones was sent to the best agricultural schools, but Smith's family was too poor to afford the tuition and no loans were made available. Or the best schools excluded minorities or women, or there was some other reason for denying this opportunity to Smith that you think is unfair. While both worked equally hard at production, Jones knew all the best ways to produce and Smith did not. In this case, you might think that some redistribution away from point D and toward point A improves equity. Your sense of the fairest distribution depends on how responsible you think Jones should be for the past discrimination.[29]

These two examples of different principles of equity (equality of outcome and equality of opportunity) are by no means intended to exhaust the list of equity concepts thought relevant to public policy and its analysis. They are intended to illustrate that diverse concepts of equity can be used as standards and that quite different conclusions about the fairness of policies can be reached as a result. They reflect real problems of equity which any society must confront. To be influential, analytic evaluation of equity consequences must be sensitive to the different principles of equity that will be applied by

---

using the equilibrium prices, the market values of the endowments and the final consumption bundles would be equal (since no one can spend more than his or her endowment, and anyone spending less would not be maximizing utility). Thus we might define these equilibrium final-consumption bundles as the ones which keep the equity of the allocations identical with those at point A and use the equilibrium prices to evaluate the relative values of *any* allocations in the Edgeworth diagram. The important feature of these prices is that they are the ones which achieve an efficient equilibrium when starting from a perfectly equal allocation of the goods available in the economy.

[29] This example provides another illustration of why allocative changes should not be restricted to those which are Pareto-superior to the starting point.

those involved in the policy-making process. Methodology for doing this will be illustrated later in the book in the context of specific cases.

Integrating Equity-Efficiency Evaluation in a Social Welfare Function

Suppose that we are currently at the efficient allocation point G (Figure 2-6) but the allocations near point A are considered more equitable. Suppose also that some constraints in the economy prevent us from achieving any of the efficient allocations on BC but point A itself can be achieved.[30] Which of the two is preferable? To decide, a trade-off must be made between efficiency and equity.

Making such a trade-off of course requires a social judgment; it is not a factual matter to resolve by policy analysis. However, analytic work can clarify the consequences of alternative ways of making the trade-off. One approach for doing so, which we introduce here, rests on the concept of a *social welfare function: a relation between a distribution of utility levels among society's members and a judgment about the overall social satisfaction (the level of social welfare) achieved by that distribution.* Mathematically, we denote such a function by

$$W = W(U^1, U^2, \ldots, U^m)$$

where U^i = the utility level of the ith individual
$i = 1,2, \ldots, m$ individuals in the economy

To clarify the meaning of a social welfare function, consider the Smith-Jones two-person economy. Social welfare is then a function of the utility level of each:

$$W = W(U^S, U^J)$$

Figure 2-7 displays three *social indifference* curves. The axes show the utility levels for Smith and Jones; assume for illustrative purposes that we can measure them in comparable units. The social indifference curves represent social welfare functions with differing ethical choices about how to trade off the aggregate of utilities (used here as a measure of relative efficiency) versus the equality of their distribution (used as a measure of equity). Each curve illustrates a different conception of the set of Smith-Jones utility combinations which yield the same level of social welfare as that at point A.

W^B comes from a social welfare function which considers relative efficiency but is indifferent to the degree of equality. The representative social indiffer-

---

[30] This approximates the situation when considering programs of income maintenance: Every method for transferring resources to the worst-off members of society causes at least some inefficiency. Income maintenance is discussed in Chapter 3. The inefficiency of taxes, used to finance income maintenance as well as other public expenditures, is discussed in Chapter 10.

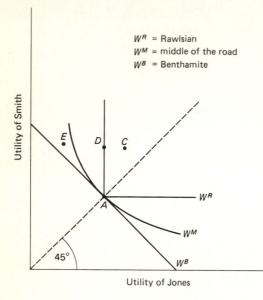

W^R = Rawlsian
W^M = middle of the road
W^B = Benthamite

Utility of Smith

Utility of Jones

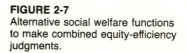

FIGURE 2-7
Alternative social welfare functions
to make combined equity-efficiency
judgments.

ence curve is a straight line with a slope of -1. The shape implies that the transfer of units of utility between Smith and Jones (thus holding the aggregate utility level constant) does not affect the level of social welfare, whether or not the transfer increases or decreases the equality of the distribution. Any increase in the aggregate sum of utility would improve social welfare by the same amount no matter who received it. This is sometimes called a Benthamite social welfare function after Jeremy Bentham. In 1789 Bentham proposed maximizing the sum of satisfactions as a social objective.[31] Mathematically, the Benthamite social welfare function is simply $W = U^S + U^J$. A move from point A to point E, for example, would increase social welfare (lie on a higher social indifference curve, not drawn) by this function.

W^R is a very egalitarian function. The representative social indifference curve is in the shape of a right angle with its corner on the 45° line. Starting from the equal distribution at point A, social welfare cannot be increased by giving more utility to just one person. The only way to increase social welfare is by raising the utility level of both people (e.g., point C). Starting from any unequal distribution (like point D), social welfare can be increased only by raising the utility level of the worst-off person (Jones).

W^R is sometimes called a Rawlsian function after the philosopher John Rawls. It was Rawls who suggested that inequalities in a society should be tolerated only to the extent that they improve the welfare of the worst-off

---

[31] Jeremy Bentham, *An Introduction to the Principle of Morals and Legislation* (London: Oxford University Press, 1907).

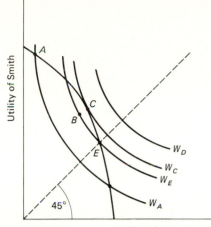

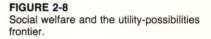

FIGURE 2-8
Social welfare and the utility-possibilities frontier.

person.[32] Mathematically, the Rawlsian social welfare function is $W = \min(U^S,$ $U^J)$.[33] Note that a change like the one from point A to point E improves welfare by the Benthamite function, but decreases it by Rawlsian standards because the minimum utility level, that of the worst-off person, declines.

W^M represents a middle-of-the-road function that lies between the Benthamite and Rawlsian ideals. The social indifference curve has the shape of an ordinary indifference curve, and its changing slope takes on the value of -1 at the point on the 45° line. It implies that, for any given level of aggregate utility, social welfare increases with greater equality.[34] However, a big enough increase in aggregate utility can increase social welfare even if it makes the distribution less equal. The change from point A to point C illustrates the latter. However, the change from point A to point E is a social welfare decrease by this function; the increase in aggregate utility is not big enough to offset the reduction in equality.

To see how a social welfare function makes a combined equity-efficiency judgment, let us examine Figure 2-8. It is a graph of a utility-possibilities frontier representing the Pareto-optimal utility levels possible in the economy. Now let us return to the question posed in the beginning of this section: How do we choose an allocation from among them?

In Figure 2-8 we have also drawn some social indifference curves, each

---

[32] John Rawls, *A Theory of Justice* (New York: Oxford University Press, 1971).

[33] The function min $(X_1, X_2, \ldots, X_n)$ has a value equal to the minimum level of any of its arguments $X_1, X_2, \ldots, X_n$. For example, min(30,40) = 30 and min(50, 40) = 40.

[34] The locus of points with constant aggregate utility is a straight line with slope of -1. The maximum social welfare on this locus is where the social indifference curve is tangent to it, which by construction is on the 45° line.

representing a different level of social welfare according to one underlying middle-of-the-road welfare function. The level of social welfare rises as we move upward and to the right on the graph. For example, if the economy is at the efficient point A, the level of social welfare is W_A. However, the inefficient point B is one of greater social welfare than point A: this reflects the social importance of the greater equality at B. The maximum social welfare that can be achieved is shown as point C, where the social indifference curve is just tangent to the utility-possibilities frontier. Higher levels of social welfare, like W_D, are not feasible with the limited resources available in the economy.

Note that, as drawn, the maximum possible social welfare is not at a point of equality, i.e., it is not on the 45° line. This happens even though, other things equal, the society prefers (by this welfare function) more equality to less. The explanation lies in the shape of the utility-possibilities frontier. For illustrative purposes, we chose one that has this characteristic: With the available resources and the preferences of Smith and Jones, it is easier for the economy to increase Smith's happiness than that of Jones (e.g., Jones may not like meat or tomatoes very much). The best attainable point of equality is the allocation at point E, but society considers the gain in aggregate utility at point C to more than compensate for the loss in equality.

There are important limitations to the use of social welfare functions in policy analysis. One obvious problem is that since utility is neither measurable nor interpersonally comparable, it is not possible to identify empirically the relative satisfaction levels of each individual. However, there are some situations in which the construction of social welfare functions is useful anyway. Typically they are those in which policy affects individuals on the basis of some observable characteristic (e.g., income level). All individuals with the same characteristic are to be treated alike, regardless of their individual preferences (e.g., all pay the same tax). We provide an illustrative example in Chapter 4 as part of the analysis of school finance policies.

A second problem, more conceptual than empirical, is that there is no agreement or consensus on what the "proper" social welfare function is: Each individual in the society may have his or her own view of what is proper. We have already illustrated that there are many possible social welfare functions (e.g., Rawlsian and Benthamite) concerning how society should trade off aggregate utility and equality. But other efficiency and equity concepts are not reflected by those formulations of social welfare, and they deserve attention as well.

For example, note the independence of the social welfare function and the utility-possibilities frontier. In Figure 2-8 it is apparent that the level of social welfare associated with an allocation does not depend on the location of the utility-possibilities frontier (i.e., the social indifference curves are drawn without knowledge of the frontier). But it is only the latter which represents the efficient or Pareto-optimal allocations (corresponding to the contract curve of an Edgeworth diagram). Thus the level of social welfare does not reveal whether there is room for more improvement (i.e., if we are interior to the utility-possibilities frontier). However, knowing whether an alternative is or is not Pareto-optimal is important because it may raise the possibility that a new and superior alternative can be found.

Similarly, the equity concept of equal opportunity is not reflected in the social welfare functions we illustrated. Indeed, it is a practical impossibility to have it otherwise. Knowledge of the utility level outcomes is not enough: One must decide the fairness of the process which determined the starting point as well as the fairness of the processes associated with each way of making a specific change in outcome levels. That is, a change may make Smith better off relative to Jones for quite different reasons. Perhaps, for example, Smith worked harder than Jones and earned an extra reward or Jones was unfairly denied an opportunity which by default then went to Smith. One needs to know both the outcomes and the fairness of the process which explains them in order to incorporate an equal opportunity standard of equity into a social welfare function.

These problems illustrate that despite the appealing neatness of integrating social values in one social welfare function, the approach will not generally substitute for explicit evaluation by the general criteria of efficiency and equity separately. The diversity of specific concepts of efficiency and equity should receive attention. Given the lack of any predetermined social consensus about which of them apply and how to integrate those that do apply, policy analysis can usually best help users reach informed normative conclusions by clearly laying out its predictions and evaluating them by the different normative elements (e.g., efficiency, relative efficiency, equality, equal opportunity). Certainly, nontechnical users will find each of the elements more familiar or at least easier to understand than the concept of a social welfare function. Thus only occasionally will it be useful to combine some of the elements in the form of a social welfare function.

In the following chapters, we will build more thoroughly upon the general concepts introduced here in order to develop skills of application in specific policy contexts.

SUMMARY

In this chapter we have introduced, at a simplified level, the elements of prediction and evaluation in policy analysis. The most common analytic method for predicting the consequences of proposed policies is modeling. A model is an abstraction intended to convey the essence of some particular aspect of the real world; it is inherently unreal and its usefulness depends on the extent to which it increases knowledge or understanding. The accuracy and breadth of a model's predictions depend on its specification: the choice of a particular set of abstractions or assumptions used to construct the model. A fundamental skill of policy analysis is to be able to identify the alternative plausible specifications relevant to a particular policy analysis and to understand how analytic conclusions depend upon them.

The predictions of policy analyses typically involve both positive and normative elements. Positive predictions concern factual consequences: e.g., if the price of gasoline is increased by a 10-cent excise tax, by how many gallons will consumption be reduced? Normative predictions involve value judgments; e.g., if the gasoline tax reduces consumption by 2 percent, is that good or bad? The value judgments of individuals in a society about public policies are diverse and usually depend upon multiple criteria. Microeconomic policy analysis is able to generate considerable insight into the consequences of policies in terms of two of these criteria: efficiency and equity.

Efficiency, or Pareto optimality, is defined as an allocation of resources from which no person can be made better off without making another person worse off. Equity refers to the relative distribution of well-being among the people in an economy. Both concepts involve predicting how policies will affect each individual's well-being, or overall satisfaction, or utility level. To make these evaluative predictions, we typically follow the principle of consumer sovereignty: Each person judges his or her own well-being. On the basis of those predictions the analyst tries to infer whether existing or proposed policies are efficient and equitable.

Because of the limits on obtainable data, a central task of the economics profession is to develop tools which allow the analyst to infer efficiency and equity consequences accurately and with a minimum of data required. The construct of the utility function, combined with a behavioral model of how individuals make decisions, forms an important part of these analytic techniques. In this chapter we combined the idea of an ordinal utility function with a utility maximization model of rational decision making (economic man) to begin to demonstrate how models can be used to make inferences about efficiency and equity. The assumptions used in the model are not intended to be literally true; they are intended to yield accurate predictions of many decisions. The analyst always retains discretionary judgment about whether the model works well for the particular decisions a policy might affect.

The principal result of the assumption of utility-maximizing behavior derived in this chapter is that efficiency (in exchange) requires that all consumers of any two goods in the economy must have the same MRS for those two goods. We illustrated that two individuals in a barter economy, starting from an inefficient allocation, can reach an efficient allocation by the voluntary trading of goods; this happens as a result of each individual attempting to maximize utility and the property of diminishing MRS. We also showed that, with a price system, each utility-maximizing individual will equate his or her MRS for any two goods consumed to the ratio of the prices for those two goods. Thus, it may be possible, by having one set of prices which apply to all individuals, to achieve efficiency in a complex economy with many individuals and many goods.

Whether this is desirable depends on whether equity can be simultaneously achieved. By using the Edgeworth box diagram, it becomes clear that an infinite number of efficient allocations are possible; each point on the contract curve is efficient. These efficient allocations differ from one another in equity: The relative well-being of each individual can vary from extremes at which one person has everything and the others nothing to more "balanced" allocations in which the goods are more evenly distributed among individuals. If one can pick any allocation within the Edgeworth box, it is at least theoretically possible to achieve both efficiency and equity.

A source of analytic difficulty is that there are no universally agreed upon principles which allow one to draw the inference that one allocation is more equitable than another: different individuals, with full and identical information about an allocation, may disagree about its "fairness." This becomes apparent when we recognize that an economy is always currently at some particular point in the Edgeworth box and that a policy change is equivalent to a proposal to move from that point to another one. What is considered fair may depend not only on where the initial location is but also on why it is the initial location; e.g., to what extent does it represent a past characterized by "just rewards" or plain luck or unfair discrimination? We illustrated how two different principles of equity, equality of outcomes and equal opportunity, can lead to conflicting judgments about the fairness of a change.

The definition of efficiency as Pareto optimality is not very controversial because the set of efficient allocations spans a very wide distributional range and thus causes little conflict with notions of equitable allocations. However, public policy changes inevitably involve making some people better off and others worse off. Measures of relative efficiency and the construction of social welfare functions are analytic techniques which have been developed to help clarify some normative consequences of those changes, but they do involve equity judgments at some level. Although there may be some policy issues in which equity does not play a major role in the analysis, the analyst must be sensitive to equity's potential importance as a social goal and its impact on political feasibility.

EXERCISES

2-1 Consider an economy of two people who consume just two goods X and Y. Person 1 has an endowment of $X_1 = 30$ and $Y_1 = 120$. Person 2 has an endowment of $X_2 = 180$ and $Y_2 = 90$. Their utility functions are respectively

$$U_1 = X_1 Y_1 \quad \text{and} \quad U_2 = X_2 Y_2$$

a Graph the Edgeworth box corresponding to this economy.
b What are the equations for the indifference curves of persons 1 and 2 that go through the initial endowments? Plot the curves. *Hint:* How does total utility change along an indifference curve?
c Shade in the locus of points which are Pareto-superior to the initial endowments.
d What is the equation of the contract curve in this economy? Graph it. *Hint:* Recall that a marginal rate of substitution can be expressed as a ratio of marginal utilities. (Answer: $Y_1 = X_1$)

    e Identify the boundaries of points on the contract curve which are Pareto-superior to the initial endowments. (Answer: $X_1 = Y_1 = 60$, $X_1 = Y_1 = 82.7$)

    f ▽Suppose a secretary of the market announces that all trading must take place at $P_X = \$1$ and $P_Y = \$2$. Furthermore, the secretary takes away each person's initial endowment and replaces it with its cash value. The secretary instructs each person to order the quantities of X and Y which maximize utility subject to the budget constraint.

        1 What quantities will persons 1 and 2 order? Can the secretary fill these orders with the endowments collected? (Answer: No)

        2 Go through the same exercise with $P_X = \$2$ and explain why the outcome is feasible and efficient.

▽APPENDIX: Calculus Models of Consumer Exchange

It is useful to see the exchange principles covered so far in a mathematical form. Actual empirical application often involves mathematics, so that the ability to consume, criticize, and conduct analysis requires some facility with mathematical procedures. However, some prior background in calculus is necessary in order to understand the mathematical material presented.[35]

Let $U(X_1, X_2, \ldots, X_n)$ represent a utility function for a consumer in an economy with n goods. For mathematical ease, we assume this function is smooth and continuous and the goods are infinitely divisible. The assumption that more is better (strong monotonicity) can be expressed as follows:

$$\frac{\partial U}{\partial X_i} > 0 \qquad \text{for all } i$$

The left-hand term is a partial derivative. It represents the marginal utility from a small increment of good X_i to the bundle, holding all the other X's constant. The expression says that the marginal utility of this increment is positive or, equivalently, that total utility increases as X_i consumption becomes greater.

We have defined an indifference set (a curve if there are only two goods and a surface if there are more than two goods) as the locus of all consumption bundles which provide the consumer with the same level of utility. If $\overline{U}$ represents some constant level of utility, then as the goods $X_1, X_2, \ldots, X_n$ change along the $\overline{U}$ indifference surface, it must always be true that

$$\overline{U} = U(X_1, X_2, \ldots, X_n)$$

---

[35] It is strongly recommended that graduate students obtain this background. Basic courses in calculus which cover derivatives, partial derivatives, and techniques of maximization and minimization are usually sufficient background for understanding the optional material presented in this book. Two compact expositions of the most relevant aspects of calculus for economics are (1) W. Baumol, *Economic Theory and Operations Analysis*, 4th ed. (Englewood Cliffs, N.J.: Prentice-Hall, Inc., 1977), chaps. 1–4, pp. 1–71, and (2) W. Nicholson, *Microeconomic Theory* (Hinsdale, Ill.: The Dryden Press, 1978), chap. 2, pp. 17–52.

As the X's are varied slightly, the total differential of the utility function tells us by how much utility changes. If we consider only changes in the X's along an indifference surface, then total utility doesn't change at all. Suppose the only changes we consider are of X_1 and X_2; all the other X's are being held constant. Then as we move along an indifference curve,

$$dU = 0 = \frac{\partial U}{\partial X_1} dX_1 + \frac{\partial U}{\partial X_2} dX_2$$

or

$$-\frac{dX_1}{dX_2}\bigg|_{U=\bar{U}} = \frac{\partial U/\partial X_2}{\partial U/\partial X_1}$$

The term on the left-hand side of this equation is simply the negative of the slope of the indifference curve; we have defined it as the marginal rate of substitution MRS_{X_2,X_1}. The term on the right-hand side is the ratio of the marginal utilities for each good. Therefore, the MRS_{X_i,X_j} at any point can be thought of as the ratio of the marginal utilities MU_{X_i}/MU_{X_j}.

Efficiency requires that each consumer of two goods have the same MRS for the two goods. Here we wish to show that this condition can be mathematically derived.

Consider Smith and Jones, who have utility functions for meat and tomatoes $U^S(M_S,T_S)$ and $U^J(M_J,T_J)$. Let $\bar{M}$ be the total amount of meat in the economy and $\bar{T}$ be the total amount of tomatoes. We will be efficient (on the contract curve) if, for any given utility level $\bar{U}^S$ of Smith, Jones is getting the maximum possible utility. To achieve this maximum, we are free to allocate the available goods any way we want to between Smith and Jones, as long as we keep Smith at $\bar{U}^S$. We will find this maximum mathematically, and show that the equations which identify it also imply that Smith and Jones must have the identical MRS.

Note that, in the two-person economy, knowledge of Jones' consumption of one good allows us to infer Smith's consumption of that good; for example, $M_S = \bar{M} - M_J$. Thus we know that an increase in Jones' meat consumption (and similarly for tomatoes) causes the following change in Smith's:

$$\frac{\partial M_S}{\partial M_J} = \frac{\partial(\bar{M} - M_J)}{\partial M_J} = -1$$

We use this fact in the derivation of the efficiency proposition below.

The mathematical problem is to choose the levels of two variables, meat and tomato consumption, which maximize the utility level of Jones, which we denote as follows:

$$\max_{M_J,T_J} U^J(M_J,T_J)$$

With no other constraints and the assumption of nonsatiation, the solution to the problem is to choose infinite amounts of meat and tomatoes. But, of course, the real problem is to maximize subject to the constraints that total real resources are limited to $\overline{M}$ and $\overline{T}$ and that Smith must get enough of those resources to yield a utility level of $\overline{U}^S$:

$$\overline{U}^S = U^S(M_S, T_S)$$

The total resource constraints can be incorporated directly into the above equation by substituting for M_S and T_S as follows:

$$M_S = \overline{M} - M_J \qquad T_S = \overline{T} - T_J$$

Then all these constraints can be represented in one equation:

$$\overline{U}^S = U^S[(\overline{M} - M_J), (\overline{T} - T_J)]$$

To solve the maximization problem with a constraint, we use the technique of Lagrange multipliers. We formulate the Lagrange expression $L(M_J, T_J, \lambda)$:

$$L(M_J, T_J, \lambda) = U^J(M_J, T_J) + \lambda\{\overline{U}^S - U^S[(\overline{M} - M_J), (\overline{T} - T_J)]\}$$

The first term on the right is simply the function we wish to maximize. The second term always consists of λ, the Lagrange multiplier, multiplied by the constraint in its implicit form.[36] Note that, when the constraint holds, the second term is zero and the value of L equals the value of U^J. Thus from among the (M_J, T_J) combinations which satisfy the constraint, the one that maximizes U^J will also maximize L.

In addition to the two variables that we started with, M_J and T_J, we make λ a third variable. How do we find the values of the variables which maximize the original function subject to the constraint? The solution requires taking the partial derivatives of the Lagrange expression with respect to all three variables, equating each to zero (thus forming one equation for each unknown

---

[36] The implicit form of an equation is found by rewriting the equation so that zero is on one side of it. If we have a constraint that says $F(X, Y) = Z$, we can always rewrite the equation as

$$Z - F(X, Y) = 0$$

and define the implicit function $G(X, Y)$:

$$G(X, Y) = Z - F(X, Y)$$

Then the constraint in its implicit form is

$$G(X, Y) = 0$$

This is mathematically equivalent to the original expression $F(X, Y) = Z$. That is, $G(X, Y) = 0$ if and only if $F(X, Y) = Z$.

variable), and solving the equations simultaneously.[37] We do the first two parts below, making use of the chain rule in taking the partial derivatives:[38]

$$\frac{\partial L}{\partial M_J} = \frac{\partial U^J}{\partial M_J} - \lambda \frac{\partial U^S}{\partial (\overline{M} - M_J)} \frac{\partial (\overline{M} - M_J)}{\partial M_J} = 0 \tag{i}$$

$$\frac{\partial L}{\partial T_J} = \frac{\partial U^J}{\partial T_J} - \lambda \frac{\partial U^S}{\partial (\overline{T} - T_J)} \frac{\partial (\overline{T} - T_J)}{\partial T_J} = 0 \tag{ii}$$

$$\frac{\partial L}{\partial \lambda} = \overline{U}^S - U^S[(\overline{M} - M_J), (\overline{T} - T_J)] = 0 \tag{iii}$$

Note that equation (iii) requires that the constraint be satisfied, or that Smith end up with a utility level of $\overline{U}^S$. This always happens with the Lagrange method; the form in which the constraint enters the Lagrange expression ensures it. Thus, when the equations are solved simultaneously, the value of $L(M_J, T_J, \lambda)$ will equal $U^J(M_J, T_J)$.

We can think of equation (iii) in terms of the Edgeworth box. It requires that the solution be one of the points on the indifference curve all along which Smith has utility level $\overline{U}^S$. With this equation, the first two equations will identify the point on the indifference curve which maximizes the utility of Jones. To see this, recall that $M_S = \overline{M} - M_J$, $T_S = \overline{T} - T_J$ and that we pointed out earlier:

---

[37] We try to explain this intuitively. Imagine a hill in front of you. Your object is to maximize your altitude, and the variable is the number of (uniform) steps you walk in a straight line. Naturally, you walk in a line that goes over the top of the hill. As long as your altitude increases with an additional step, you will choose to take it. This is like saying the derivative of altitude with respect to steps is positive, and it characterizes each step up the hill. If you go too far, the altitude will decrease with an additional step: the derivative will be negative and you will be descending the hill. If the altitude is increasing as you go up, and decreasing as you go down, it must be neither increasing nor decreasing exactly at the top. Thus at the maximum, the derivative is zero.

This extends to the many-variable case, in which the variables might represent steps in specific directions. Exactly at the top of the hill, the partial derivative of altitude with respect to a step in *each* direction must be zero. This analogy is intended to suggest why the maximum utility above can be identified by finding the points where all the partial derivatives equal zero.

Technically, we have only discussed the first-order or necessary conditions; they identify the interior critical points of the Lagrange expression. However, not all critical points are maxima; all the partial derivatives are zero at function minima also, for example. Most functions we use will only have the one critical point we seek. Some functions, however, have both maxima and minima (as if, in our analogy, there were a valley between the start of our straight walk and the top of the hill). The second-order conditions to ensure that the identified values of M_J and T_J maximize L are more complicated. For a review of the second-order conditions, see J. Henderson and R. Quandt, *Microeconomic Theory*, 2d ed. (New York: McGraw-Hill Book Company, 1971), pp. 404–407.

[38] The chain rule for derivatives is this: If $Z = G(Y)$ and $Y = F(X)$, then

$$\frac{dZ}{dX} = \frac{dZ}{dY} \frac{dY}{dX}$$

The same rule applies for partial derivatives when $G(\ )$ and $F(\ )$ are functions of variables in addition to Y and X. In the economic problem above, the function $U^S(\ )$ plays the role of $G(\ )$ and the functions $(M - M_J)$ and $(\overline{T} - T_J)$ play the role of $F(\ )$ in equations (i) and (ii), respectively.

$$\frac{\partial(\overline{M} - M_J)}{\partial M_J} = \frac{\partial(\overline{T} - T_J)}{\partial T_J} = -1$$

Then equations (i) and (ii) can be simplified as follows:

$$\frac{\partial L}{\partial M_J} = \frac{\partial U^J}{\partial M_J} + \lambda\frac{\partial U^S}{\partial M_S} = 0 \qquad\qquad \text{(i')}$$

$$\frac{\partial L}{\partial T_J} = \frac{\partial U^J}{\partial T_J} + \lambda\frac{\partial U^S}{\partial T_S} = 0 \qquad\qquad \text{(ii')}$$

Subtract the terms with λ in them from both sides of each equation and then divide (i') by (ii'):

$$\frac{\partial U^J/\partial M_J}{\partial U^J/\partial T_J} = \frac{-\lambda(\partial U^S/\partial M_S)}{-\lambda(\partial U^S/\partial T_S)} = \frac{\partial U^S/\partial M^S}{\partial U^S/\partial T_S}$$

or
$$\text{MRS}^J_{M,T} = \text{MRS}^S_{M,T}$$

That is, the first two equations require that Smith and Jones have the same MRS, or that their indifference curves be tangent. This is precisely the efficiency condition we sought to derive. We can also think of the first two equations as identifying the contract curve, and then with them the third equation identifies the point on the contract curve where Smith has utility level $\overline{U}^S$.

We also showed in the text that when a pricing system is used, each consumer will allocate his or her budget in such a way that the MRS of any two goods X_i and X_j equals the price ratio of those two goods P_i/P_j. This can be seen mathematically as follows, letting I represent the consumer's total budget to be allocated.[39] The consumer wants to choose goods $X_1, X_2, \ldots, X_n$ which maximize utility subject to the following budget constraint:

$$I = P_1X_1 + P_2X_2 + \cdots + P_nX_n$$

We formulate the Lagrange expression with $n + 1$ variables λ and $X_1, X_2, \ldots, X_n$:

$$L = U(X_1, X_2, \ldots, X_n) + \lambda(I - P_1X_1 - P_2X_2 - \cdots - P_nX_n)$$

To find the X's which maximize utility, all of the $n + 1$ partial derivative

---

[39] If a consumer starts with an initial endowment of $X_1^E, X_2^E, \ldots, X_n^E$, then the total budget

$$I = \sum_{i=1}^{n} P_iX_i^E$$

equations must be formed. Taking only the ith and jth of these equations for illustrative purposes, we have

$$\frac{\partial L}{\partial X_i} = \frac{\partial U}{\partial X_i} - \lambda P_i = 0 \qquad \text{or} \qquad \frac{\partial U}{\partial X_i} = \lambda P_i \qquad (i)$$

$$\frac{\partial L}{\partial X_j} = \frac{\partial U}{\partial X_j} - \lambda P_j = 0 \qquad \text{or} \qquad \frac{\partial U}{\partial X_j} = \lambda P_j \qquad (j)$$

and upon dividing the top equation by the bottom one we see that

$$\frac{\partial U/\partial X_i}{\partial U/\partial X_j} = \frac{P_i}{P_j}$$

We have not yet noted any significance to the value of λ which comes from solving constrained maximization problems. However, from the above equations we can see that

$$\lambda = \frac{\partial U/\partial X_i}{P_i} \qquad \text{for all } i = 1, 2, \ldots, n$$

This can be interpreted approximately as follows:

$$\lambda = \frac{\text{marginal utility per unit of } X_i}{\text{dollars per unit of } X_i} = \text{marginal utility per dollar}$$

That is, λ can be interpreted as the amount of marginal utility this consumer would receive from increasing the budget constraint by one extra dollar. In general, the value of λ signifies the marginal benefit in terms of the objective (utility in the example) of relaxing the constraint by one increment (increasing the budget by one dollar in the example). This is sometimes referred to as the *shadow price* of the resource causing the constraint, and it can be a useful way to estimate the value of that resource to its user.

A numerical example may help clarify the mechanics of constrained maximization. Suppose a consumer has a utility function $U = M \cdot T$. Suppose also that the budget constraint is 100, $P_M = \$5.00$ per pound, and $P_T = \$1.00$ per pound. How many pounds of meat and tomatoes should this consumer buy in order to maximize utility? The consumer wants to maximize $M \cdot T$, subject to $100 = 5.00M + 1.00T$. We formulate the Lagrange expression $L(M, T, \lambda)$:

$$L = M \cdot T + \lambda(100 - 5.00M - 1.00T)$$

Taking the partial derivatives and setting each to zero, we have

$$\frac{\partial L}{\partial M} = T - 5.00\lambda = 0 \qquad \text{or} \qquad T = 5.00\lambda \qquad (i)$$

$$\frac{\partial L}{\partial T} = M - 1.00\lambda = 0 \qquad \text{or} \qquad M = 1.00\lambda \tag{ii}$$

$$\frac{\partial L}{\partial \lambda} = 100 - 5.00M - 1.00T = 0 \tag{iii}$$

On substituting 5λ for T and λ for M in equation (iii), we get

$$100 - 5.00\lambda - 5.00\lambda = 0$$

from which
$$\lambda = 10 \qquad M = 10$$
$$T = 50 \qquad U = 500$$

That is, the consumer achieves the maximum utility of 500 by purchasing 10 pounds of meat and 50 pounds of tomatoes. According to this solution, the shadow price of the budget is 10 utils. This means that increasing the budget by $1.00 would allow the consumer to gain approximately 10 more utils, or achieve a utility level of 510. Let us check this. Suppose the budget is $101 and we maximize utility according to this constraint. Equations (i) and (ii) are unaffected, so we can make the same substitution in the new equation (iii):

$$101 - 5.00\lambda - 5.00\lambda = 0$$

from which
$$\lambda = 10.1 \qquad M = 10.1$$
$$T = 50.5 \qquad U = 510.05$$

As we can see, the utility level has indeed increased by approximately 10 utils. As one last check on our original solution, it should be that

$$\text{MRS}_{M,T} = \frac{P_M}{P_T} = 5$$

From the utility function,

$$\frac{\partial U}{\partial M} = T = 50$$

$$\frac{\partial U}{\partial T} = M = 10$$

and therefore

$$\text{MRS}_{M,T} = \frac{\partial U/\partial M}{\partial U/\partial T} = 5$$

PART **TWO**

USING MODELS OF INDIVIDUAL CHOICE MAKING IN POLICY ANALYSIS

THE SPECIFICATION OF INDIVIDUAL CHOICE MODELS FOR THE ANALYSIS OF WELFARE PROGRAMS

In the introductory chapters we reviewed general predictive and evaluative aspects of microeconomic modeling. Now we wish to be specific. In this chapter, we develop skills of model specification useful for policy applications. The problems posed can be analyzed with models of individual consumer choice. The series of problems—chosen to be similar in some ways but different in others—is intended to create a facility with modeling which carries over to the analysis of new problems in new settings.

All the analyses in the chapter are drawn from one policy context: government programs which provide welfare grants to individual families or households. Welfare assistance is an important function of governments at all levels. It is important to those who receive it and to those who pay for it. Welfare is extensive and expensive. In 1980 a total of 21 million low-income individuals (just under 10 percent of the population) participated in the federal Food Stamp Program. In the same year taxpayers spent $43.3 billion on the five main federal welfare programs (Medicaid, Food and Nutrition Assistance, Aid to Families with Dependent Children, Supplemental Security Income, and Low-Income Energy Assistance). Clearly, it is worthwhile to make welfare policies as efficient as possible. The skills developed here can be used to make a contribution to that goal.

Each of the analyses presented involves thinking about different elements of consumer choice models and how to put them together. The elements consist of the utility function and the nature of the constraints which limit the utility attainable. We consider two general types of utility functions and various alterations in budget constraints due to public policies. We use these different specifications to make predictions about the responses of individuals to the policies and to evaluate the efficiency of the predicted responses.

The particular variations in the specifications we explore relate to two common phenomena. One is the existence of external effects or spillovers. These arise whenever the actions of one economic agent affect another agent directly (not through priced transactions). Common examples of external effects are the hazardous pollution from some factories and automobiles and the loud radio next door. However, we analyze only a particular type of externality here: the *interdependent preference*. This occurs whenever one person cares about some aspect of another person's well-being (e.g., when my utility depends on whether you receive at least some minimum amount of food to eat). In a model, interdependent preferences show up as a variant of the utility function. We will show that the efficiency of in-kind welfare programs like food stamps and that the usefulness of enforcing certain welfare rules depend upon the extent of interdependent preferences.

The second phenomenon is the existence of segmented or discontinuous budget constraints caused by various policy-imposed restrictions on individual choice. Sometimes these restrictions are an explicit part of the details of a policy design: e.g., a limit on the number of food stamps a family receives, a take-it-or-leave it offer to live in a subsidized public housing unit, or a rule that says welfare benefits are to be reduced by the amount of household earnings. Other times the restrictions arise from the information and transaction costs involved in the operation of the policy: e.g., the enforcement efforts to prevent illegal resale of food stamps. These restrictions can have significant effects on the response of individuals to policy; we shall show how to analyze a number of them.

Throughout this chapter, we focus primarily on how to spend a given amount of welfare funds efficiently. We begin with a standard analysis of food stamps which demonstrates that such transfers in kind are inefficient. We reconsider this conclusion after examining a model with interdependent preferences. We then adapt the standard model to incorporate choice restrictions in the food stamp and public housing programs and examine the changes in predicted responses and their efficiency. Finally, we examine aspects of an income maintenance proposal known as the Negative Income Tax and focus on how it affects the individual's choice between labor and leisure.

STANDARD ARGUMENT: IN-KIND WELFARE TRANSFERS ARE INEFFICIENT

In the U.S. economy all levels of government are involved in providing welfare payments (through a variety of programs) to eligible low-income persons. These payments are transfers in the sense that they take away purchasing power from taxpayers and transfer it to welfare recipients. Some of the

TABLE 3-1
FEDERAL EXPENDITURES FOR SELECTED WELFARE PROGRAMS, 1971–1981
(Dollars in Billions)

Fiscal year	Food and nutrition assistance	Housing assistance	Public assistance and related programs
1971	1.6	0.7	7.8
1972	1.9	1.1	9.1
1973	2.2	1.6	8.5
1974	2.8	1.8	10.2
1975	6.2	2.1	12.6
1976	7.5	2.5	14.6
1977	8.2	2.9	15.7
1978	8.2	3.6	16.6
1979	9.8	4.2	16.4
1980*	12.1	5.1	18.9
1981*	13.3	6.3	20.2

* Estimated.
Source: The Budget of the United States Government, Fiscal Year 1981, p. 598, table 17.

programs, like Aid to Families with Dependent Children, provide cash payments; other programs, like food stamps, Medicaid, and housing allowances, provide transfers in kind (i.e., transfers that can be used only for the purchase of specific goods). Although all welfare expenditures grew dramatically during the 1970s, the in-kind transfers accounted for the bulk of the growth.[1] Table 3-1 shows that, from 1971 to 1981, in-kind federal expenditures for food and housing assistance grew from 29 to 97 percent of the federally funded level of general public assistance programs (primarily consisting of cash assistance from the Aid to Dependent Families Program and Supplemental Security Income). Yet the conventional wisdom among economists has always been that transfers of this type are inefficient.

The proof of this proposition usually follows one of two closely related patterns: (1) For a given amount of tax dollars to be transferred to the poor, the utility level of recipients will be higher if the transfers are in cash rather than in kind or (2) to achieve given utility level increases among the recipients, fewer taxpayer dollars will be required if the transfers are in cash rather than in kind. Either argument suffices to demonstrate the inefficiency of in-kind transfers, since each shows the possibility of making one group better off with all others no worse off. We will demonstrate the proof by using the second of the two patterns.

In Figure 3-1 let the line *AB* represent the budget constraint of a low-income individual with no welfare program. Note that to represent consumer choice with a budget constraint on a diagram properly, all the available spending

---

[1] For an interesting discussion that combines economic and political analysis of the issue, see F. Doolittle, F. Levy, and M. Wiseman, "The Mirage of Welfare Reform," *The Public Interest,* No. 47, Spring 1977, pp. 62–87.

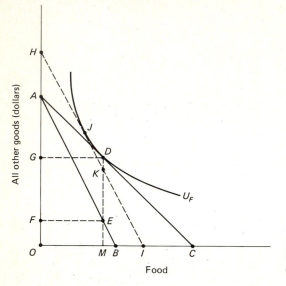

FIGURE 3-1
Standard argument: The inefficiency of "in-kind" transfers.

choices must be represented. That is why the axes are labeled "food" and "all other goods"; we measure the amount of all other goods by the total dollar cost of the items selected. The implicit assumption of the everything-else axis is that the consumer spends the dollar amount selected for the other goods in a way that maximizes utility. If the consumer spends the whole budget on food, he or she can buy *OB* quantity of food. If the whole budget is used to buy other things, then *OA* dollars worth of everything else can be bought. Thus we also know that *OA* dollars is the total size of the consumer's budget.

Now suppose we introduce a food stamp program which allows eligible recipients to buy for their own use any quantity they wish of $1 stamps at a price of $0.50 per stamp. Grocers must accept the food stamps at face value for food purchases, and the government gives the grocer cash reimbursement for the stamps collected. From the individual's perspective, this changes the budget constraint from *AB* to *AC*. That is, the consumer eligible for food stamps could take the whole budget, buy food stamps with it, and consume *OC* units of food—exactly twice as much as *OB*. However, if the consumer buys only other things, the maximum that can be purchased is *OA*, as before. Thus, the program, from the perspective of the eligible consumer, is equivalent to a price reduction for food.

To maximize utility, let us say the consumer chooses the quantities shown at *D*, where an indifference curve is just tangent to the new budget constraint.[2]

---

[2] The slope of a budget constraint is equal to minus the ratio of the prices of the goods on each axis. If a consumer has a budget of I to spend on only two goods X and Y, with prices P_X and P_Y, the budget constraint equation is

$$I = P_X X + P_Y Y$$

The market price of the *OM* food purchased at *D* must be *FA*, since that is the amount of budget the consumer would have been required to give up to purchase the same quantity if there were no Food Stamp Program. (Total budget *OA* minus *OF* spent on other things means *FA* spent on food.) But under the Food Stamp Program, the individual pays only *GA* for the food quantity *OM*. (Total budget *OA* minus *OG* spent on other things means the consumer spent *GA* on food.) Therefore, the government must be paying *FG*, the difference between the market cost *FA* and the individual's contribution *GA*. Taxpayers pay *FG* dollars to bring this consumer to the indifference curve U_F.

To prove this is inefficient, we must show that it is possible to make someone better off and no one worse off. Let us ask how many taxpayer dollars it would take to bring the consumer to utility level U_F with a cash welfare grant. With this type of grant, the recipient does not face any price changes. The slope of the budget constraint remains at the original slope of *AB*, but it is "pushed out" until it reaches *HI*, where it becomes just tangent to U_F. *AH* is the dollar amount of the cash grant.

Now we will show that *AH* is less than *FG*. First note that *EK* = *AH* and *ED* = *FG* (because the vertical distance between two parallel lines is constant). On the diagram, it is obvious that *EK* is less than *ED*, or therefore that the cash subsidy *AH* is smaller than the food stamp subsidy *FG*. But why does it come out this way? Note that the original budget constraint *AB* is steeper than the food stamp constraint *AC*. All points on U_F with steeper slopes than *AC* lie to the left of *D*; therefore, the tangency with *HI* (which has the same slope as *AB*) occurs to the left of *D*. But then *HI* must go through the line segment *DE*—if it

---

If we represented this constraint on a diagram with *Y* on the vertical axis and *X* on the horizontal axis, the same equation would be rewritten (to solve for *Y* in terms of *X*):

$$Y = \frac{I}{P_Y} - \frac{P_X}{P_Y} X$$

The first term on the right-hand side is the *Y* intercept, and $-P_X/P_Y$ is the slope.

For the particular illustration we are using in the text, *Y* represents the expenditures on all other goods and the "price" of another expenditure is $1. That is, if we let $X_1, \ldots, X_n$ represent all goods including food X_F with prices $P_1, \ldots, P_n$, the budget constraint equation for *AB* is

$$\sum_{i \neq F} P_i X_i = I - P_F X_F$$

where we can think of *I* and P_F as being divided by the $1 price of an additional expenditure.

Given the budget constraint, the consumer chooses the quantities of each good that maximize utility. This optimum will never be interior to the budget constraint (below *AC*) because of the more-is-better assumption. That is, from any interior point it is possible to get more of one good with no less of the other. But this increases utility, so the interior point could not have been the maximum. Therefore, one of the points on *AC* must be the maximum. We know from the preceding chapter that the consumer will choose quantities such that the MRS equals the ratio of the prices. Since the slope of an indifference curve is the negative of the MRS and the slope of the budget constraint is the negative of the price ratio, the slopes must be equal at the utility-maximizing point. But equal slopes at the same point is the definition of tangency: The consumer will choose the point on *AC* where the indifference curve is just tangent to it.

crossed above *D,* it would violate the tangency condition. This completes the proof: Since a cash welfare program could achieve U_F at a lower cost to taxpayers than food stamps, the food stamp program is inefficient.

It is useful to note a few characteristics of this result. First, it causes the individual to consume more food and less of other things compared to the lower-cost cash welfare program yielding the same utility. Second, we know the food stamp recipient is indifferent to a cash grant of *EK* or a food stamp subsidy costing the taxpayer *ED*. Therefore, we can say that the recipient values each taxpayer dollar spent on food stamps at *EK/ED* cents, or that the waste per taxpayer dollar spent on food stamps is 100 − *EK/ED* cents, or *KD/ED* cents. According to one study conducted in the early 1970s (before certain changes in the program discussed later), recipients on average valued each $1 of food stamp subsidy at $0.82.[3]

The basic result of inefficiency should not be very surprising. Consider the MRS of food for "everything else." The recipient chooses a consumption point such that the MRS equals minus the slope of *AC*. But every consumer not eligible for the program chooses an MRS equal to the ratio of the prices in the market, or minus the slope of *AB*. Therefore, the condition for exchange efficiency is violated, and we know there is room for a deal. The proof above simply illustrates one possible deal which would make some people (taxpayers) better off and all other people (food stamp eligibles) no worse off. The cash welfare program leaves all consumers (taxpayers and welfare recipients) facing the same market prices and thus, under the assumption of utility-maximizing behavior, leaves no room for a deal. By this reasoning, all in-kind welfare pograms which cause recipients and nonrecipients to face different prices for the same good are inefficient.

INTERDEPENDENT PREFERENCE ARGUMENT: IN-KIND TRANSFERS MAY BE EFFICIENT

One possible specification error in utility maximization models concerns the sources of utility: the arguments or variables of the utility function. The model of behavior as it is specified above has an implicit assumption of "selfish" preferences: The only sources of utility to individuals are from the goods and services they consume directly. There is nothing in the model of rational behavior which implies that people are selfish. It is perfectly plausible that one individual can derive satisfaction through another person's consumption; this is an example of an *interdependent preference.* You might feel better if you gave some food to a neighbor whose kitchen had just been destroyed by a fire. This

---

[3] See K. Clarkson, *Food Stamps and Nutrition,* Evaluative Studies No. 18 (Washington, D.C.: The American Enterprise Institute for Public Policy Research, 1975). One reviewer of this study argues that this waste estimate is exaggerated because of failure to measure recipient income correctly. See J. Barmack, "The Case Against In-Kind Transfers: The Food Stamp Program," *Policy Analysis, 3,* No. 4, Fall 1977, pp. 509–530.

act might please you more than if you gave the neighbor the cash equivalent of the food. People in a community might donate money to an organization created for the purpose of giving basic necessities to families who are the victims of "hard luck." This organization might be a church or a charity. It might also, however, be a government whose voters approved collection of the "donations" through taxes paid by both supporters and opponents of the proposal.

The use of government as the organization to make these transfers does raise an equity issue: What is the nature of the entitlement, if any, of the recipients to the funds being transferred? From the examples above, one might assume too quickly that initial entitlements rest fully with the donors and certain resources of their choice are granted to the recipients. The government is then used to effect these transfers as a mere organizational convenience. But the fact that some people are made to contribute involuntarily suggests that the transfer is enforced as part of a preexisting social contract. This latter interpretation affects the way we think about the extent of interdependent preferences.

In a social contract interpretation, all members of the society have contingent claims on their wealth (e.g., taxes) and contingent entitlements to wealth (e.g., transfers). A claim or entitlement is contingent upon an individual's future economic circumstances (e.g., tax payments if rich and transfers if poor). The magnitudes of entitlements and liabilities depend upon the rules of the social contract. These specifications are not necessarily reflected in the preferences expressed by citizens *after* they know their own levels of economic success. In fact, one might think that there is a specific bias after the "future" is revealed: The vast majority of people who end up with liabilities rather than entitlements would prefer to give less at the time of transfer than they would agree to be liable for before knowing who will be transferring to whom.[4] This helps explain why a legal system is sometimes necessary to be the "social umpire": to interpret contracts, to judge their validity, and to enforce them. Under the social contract interpretation, the appropriate interdependent preferences are those revealed when the valid contract is specified. This is presumably closer (compared to the pure donation interpretation) to the preferences that would be expressed when everyone is in the dark about who will end up "needy" and who will not.[5]

While the size of the transfer is definitely affected by whichever of the above two situations is thought closer to the truth, interdependent preferences may exist in both cases. *If there are interdependent preferences involving the consumption of specific goods, then it is no longer efficient for each consumer*

---

[4] This is like asking people how much they are willing to pay for automobile insurance after they know whether they will be involved in any accidents.

[5] The legal problems of interpreting the contract vary with the policy area. For the provision of food stamps, congressional legislation like the original Food Stamp Act of 1964 may be the document of primary interest. For another in-kind good, the provision of legal defense counsel, the courts have ruled that important entitlements are contained in the Sixth Amendment to the Constitution of the United States.

to have the same MRS for any two goods consumed.[6] Suppose we go back to our example with Smith and Jones (as two of many consumers) consuming meat and tomatoes. For purposes here, let us assume that Jones is quite poor relative to Smith and that Smith would derive some satisfaction (other things being equal) from an increase in Jones' meat consumption. This is equivalent to saying that Smith has a utility function

$$U^S = U^S(M_S, T_S, M_J)$$

where Smith's utility level increases as Jones' meat consumption rises.

Initially, suppose consumption of meat and tomatoes is such that each person has an $\text{MRS}_{M,T} = 4$ (4 pounds of tomatoes for 1 pound of meat). Smith, however, would also be willing to give up 1 pound of tomatoes in order to increase Jones' meat consumption by 1 pound ($\text{MRS}^S_{M_J,T_S} = 1$). After telling this to Jones, Smith and Jones approach a third consumer. They give the third consumer 4 pounds of tomatoes, 3 pounds from Jones and 1 from Smith, in exchange for 1 pound of meat. The third consumer is indifferent. Jones keeps the meat, so Smith is indifferent. But Jones is strictly better off, having given up only 3 pounds of tomatoes to get 1 extra pound of meat. Thus the initial position

---

[6] If the interdependent preferences are for general well-being, rather than for specific goods like food or housing consumption, then no subsidization is required to sustain an efficient allocation. Ordinary prices will do. This result can be derived mathematically by following the format used in the appendix to Chapter 2. An efficient allocation can be thought of as one that maximizes the utility of Jones subject to keeping Smith at some given constant level of utility $\overline{U}^S$. We formulate the Lagrange expression as in the appendix to Chapter 2, noting the slight change in Smith's utility function due to the interdependent preference:

$$L(M_J, T_J) = U^J(M_J, T_J) + \lambda[\overline{U}^S - U^S(M_S, T_S, U^J)]$$

Recall that $M_S = \overline{M} - M_J$ and therefore $\partial M_S/\partial M_J = -1$, and similarly $T_S = \overline{T} - T_J$ and therefore $\partial T_S/\partial T_J = -1$. To find the values of M_J and T_J which maximize L requires the same procedure as before: taking the partial derivatives of L with respect to M_J, T_J, and λ, setting them all equal to zero, and solving them simultaneously. However, writing down only the first two of these equations will suffice to show the efficiency condition:

$$\frac{\partial L}{\partial M_J} = \frac{\partial U^J}{\partial M_J} - \lambda \frac{\partial U^S}{\partial U^J}\frac{\partial U^J}{\partial M_J} - \lambda \frac{\partial U^S}{\partial M_S}\frac{\partial M_S}{\partial M_J} = 0 \qquad \text{(i)}$$

$$\frac{\partial L}{\partial T_J} = \frac{\partial U^J}{\partial T_J} - \lambda \frac{\partial U^S}{\partial U^J}\frac{\partial U^J}{\partial T_J} - \lambda \frac{\partial U^S}{\partial T_S}\frac{\partial T_S}{\partial T_J} = 0 \qquad \text{(ii)}$$

By moving the last term in each equation (after simplifying) to the other side and dividing (i) by (ii), we get

$$\frac{(\partial U^J/\partial M_J)\,(1 - \lambda \partial U^S/\partial U^J)}{(\partial U^J/\partial T_J)\,(1 - \lambda \partial U^S/\partial U^J)} = \frac{-\lambda \partial U^S/\partial M_S}{-\lambda \partial U^S/\partial T_S}$$

On canceling like terms in numerator and denominator and recalling the definition of MRS, we have

$$\text{MRS}^J_{M_J,T_J} = \text{MRS}^S_{M_S,T_S}$$

This is the usual requirement for exchange efficiency.

cannot be efficient, despite the fact that all consumers have the same $\text{MRS}_{M,T}$ in terms of their own consumption.[7]

Exchange efficiency requires, in this case, that the total amount of tomatoes consumers will give up to increase Smith's meat consumption by 1 pound equals the total amount of tomatoes consumers will give up to increase Jones' meat consumption by 1 pound. We can express this more generally if we think of M as any good for which there are interdependent preferences and T as any good for which there are none. Then for every pair of consumers i and j in an economy of m consumers:

$$\sum_{k=1}^{m} \text{MRS}^k_{M_i, T_k} = \sum_{k=1}^{m} \text{MRS}^k_{M_j, T_k}$$

That is, the sum of tomatoes all m consumers will give up to increase i's meat consumption by 1 pound must equal the sum of tomatoes all m consumers will give up to increase j's meat consumption by 1 pound. In our specific example, in which the only interdependent preference among all m consumers is Smith's concern for Jones' consumption of meat M,

$$\text{MRS}^k_{M_S, T_k} = 0 \qquad \text{whenever } k \neq S$$
$$\text{and} \qquad \text{MRS}^k_{M_J, T_k} = 0 \qquad \text{whenever } k \neq S \text{ or } J$$

Then the above efficiency condition collapses to

$$\text{MRS}^S_{M_S, T_S} = \text{MRS}^J_{M_J, T_J} + \text{MRS}^S_{M_J, T_S}$$

where the last term reflects Smith's willingness to give up tomatoes in order to increase Jones' meat consumption.[8] The initial position can be seen to violate this condition:

$$4 \neq 4 + 1$$

---

[7] Note that the existence of interdependent preferences does *not* interfere with consumer sovereignty. Each consumer is still attempting to use the initial resources to arrange voluntary trades that lead to maximum satisfaction by the consumer's own judgment. The claim that interdependent preference interferes with consumer sovereignty, sometimes seen in the literature, may mistake the equity issue for the efficiency one. If both parties believe they have the initial entitlement to the transfer, then each will feel the other has no authority to direct its allocation.

[8] To see this, let us use the model from the prior note but substitute M_J for U^J in Smith's utility function:

$$L(M_J, T_J, \lambda) = U^J(M_J, T_J) + \lambda[\bar{U}^S - U^S(M_S, T_S, M_J)]$$

Writing down the first two equations for optimization as before, we get:

$$\frac{\partial L}{\partial M_J} = \frac{\partial U^J}{\partial M_J} - \lambda \left(\frac{\partial U^S}{\partial M_S} \frac{\partial M_S}{\partial M_J} + \frac{\partial U^S}{\partial M_J} \right) = 0 \qquad \text{(i)}$$

$$\frac{\partial L}{\partial T_J} = \frac{\partial U^J}{\partial T_J} - \lambda \left(\frac{\partial U^S}{\partial T_S} \frac{\partial T_S}{\partial T_J} \right) = 0 \qquad \text{(ii)}$$

This violation created the room for a deal that we illustrated.

It should be noted that this illustration is of a *positive consumption externality:* Smith derives pleasure or external benefits from an increase in Jones' meat consumption. In other situations the externality may be *negative:* For example, some people experience reduced pleasure or external costs when others consume tobacco products in their presence.[9] The "standard" case can thus be seen as the middle or neutral ground between positive and negative externalities. In all cases of externalities, the key characteristic is that some agents cause costs or benefits to others as a side effect of their own actions.

In order to relate interdependent preferences to in-kind welfare programs, let us first consider whether efficiency can be achieved if all consumers independently buy and sell at the same market prices. With no mechanism for Smith to influence Jones' consumption, efficiency will not be achieved. Each will choose a consumption pattern that equates the MRS in terms of personal consumption to the ratio of the market prices, and thus each MRS will be the same and the interdependent efficiency condition above will be violated (since $\mathrm{MRS}^{S}_{M_J, T_S} > 0$). This violation would continue even if a mechanism were created to transfer cash from Smith to Jones, since both would spend their new budgets in light of the market prices.

However, suppose we could create a situation in which Smith and Jones faced different prices. In particular, suppose P_M and P_T represent the market prices but that Jones gets a subsidy of S_M for every pound of meat consumed. Then the real price to Jones per unit of meat is $P_M - S_M$ and the chosen consumption pattern will be such that

$$\mathrm{MRS}^{J}_{M_J, T_J} = \frac{P_M - S_M}{P_T} = \frac{P_M}{P_T} - \frac{S_M}{P_T}$$

Since Smith will so arrange purchases that $P_M/P_T = \mathrm{MRS}^{S}_{M_S, T_S}$, the above equation implies

$$\mathrm{MRS}^{J}_{M_J, T_J} = \mathrm{MRS}^{S}_{M_S, T_S} - \frac{S_M}{P_T}$$

This simplifies to:

$$\frac{\partial U^J}{\partial M_J} = \lambda \left(\frac{-\partial U^S}{\partial M_S} + \frac{\partial U^S}{\partial M_J} \right) \tag{i'}$$

$$\frac{\partial U^J}{\partial T_J} = \lambda \left(\frac{-\partial U^S}{\partial T_S} \right) \tag{ii'}$$

By dividing (i') by (ii') and recalling the definition of MRS, we get the result in the text:

$$\mathrm{MRS}^{J}_{M_J, T_J} = \mathrm{MRS}^{S}_{M_S, T_S} - \mathrm{MRS}^{S}_{M_J, T_S}$$

[9] Interdependent preferences may also be negative externalities. For example, you may feel angry if your neighbor washes a car during a severe water shortage. Or you may simply be envious of someone else's good fortune.

If S_M is so chosen that $S_M = P_T \, \text{MRS}^S_{M_J, T_S}$,

$$\text{MRS}^J_{M_J, T_J} = \text{MRS}^S_{M_S, T_S} - \text{MRS}^S_{M_J, T_J}$$

which is the interdependent efficiency requirement. This illustrates the possibility that in-kind transfer programs like food stamps can be efficient if the subsidy rate is chosen correctly.

The correct subsidy rate in the example equals the dollar value of the tomatoes Smith will forego in return for increasing Jones' meat consumption by one unit (from the efficient allocation). This is necessary for the efficient allocation to be an equilibrium: At the real relative price each faces, neither has incentive to alter the consumption bundle.[10]

This example suggests that, in the presence of interdependent preferences for the consumption of specific goods (rather than general well-being), in-kind transfers may be efficient. Furthermore, cash transfers will generally be inefficient. Thus the standard argument depends on a particular specification of the factors which give individuals utility, namely, that no one has a utility function with arguments representing the consumption of specific goods by others.[11]

The above analysis raises several questions. First, do interdependencies involving specific consumption goods exist, and if so, how large are they? This is an unresolved empirical issue, although several analysts have suggested methods for estimating such external benefits.[12] Second, given the extent of interdependencies relevant to a specific good, do the actual subsidies involved in provision of the good induce the efficient amount of consumption? We consider several aspects of this second question in the following section.

---

[10] In this example we are ignoring the problem of how to finance the subsidy. If we had to put a tax on Smith, it might alter the (after-tax) prices Smith faces and mess up the equilibrium. We discuss these and other effects of taxation in a general equilibrium framework in Chapters 10 and 11.

In a more general case with many "caring" consumers the correct subsidy rate to the ith consumer equals the sum of the dollars each other consumer is willing to forego in return for increasing the ith consumer's meat consumption by one more unit. That is, to make an efficient allocation be a market equilibrium, the subsidy to the ith consumer must be as follows:

$$S^i_M = P_T \sum_{k \neq i} \text{MRS}^k_{M_i, T_k}$$

Of course, there may be other needy individuals besides the ith consumer, and presumably the willingness to donate to (or subsidize) one consumer depends on how many other needy individuals there are.

[11] For more general reading on this subject, see H. Hochman and J. Rodgers, "Pareto Optimal Redistribution," *The American Economic Review*, 59, No. 4, September 1969, and G. Daly and F. Giertz, "Welfare Economics and Welfare Reform," *The American Economic Review*, 62, No. 1, March 1972, pp. 131–138.

[12] See Henry Aaron and Martin McGuire, "Public Goods and Income Distribution," *Econometrica*, 38, November 1970, pp. 907–920; Joseph DeSalvo, "Housing Subsidies: Do We Know What We Are Doing?" *Policy Analysis*, 2, No. 1, Winter 1976, pp. 39–60; and Henry Aaron and George von Furstenberg, "The Inefficiency of Transfers in Kind: The Case of Housing Assistance," *Western Economic Journal*, 9, June 1971, pp. 184–191.

Finally, note that the use of theory in this section has not resolved an issue. It has raised empirical questions which otherwise would not have been asked at all. Sometimes this is one of the most important functions of analysis: to clarify and question the assumptions underlying a judgment about a policy.

CHOICE RESTRICTIONS IMPOSED BY POLICY

The preceding section demonstrates, by using the particular example of interdependent preferences, that model inferences about a policy's effects can depend upon specific assumptions concerning the nature of utility functions. In this section we shift the focus from the utility function to the budget constraint, which determines the opportunity set, or feasible choices available to an individual. That is, we wish to show how alternative model specifications of the budget constraint can affect inferences about policy made with the model. Consideration of these alternative specifications can lead to important suggestions for improving the policy.

More specifically, we wish to highlight two general factors important to the design and evaluation of a policy: (1) the actual details of the policy design and (2) the information and transaction costs necessary for the policy's operation and enforcement. Both factors can have important effects on the actual opportunity sets that individuals face, and thus they should be considered when model assumptions about the opportunity sets are chosen. We illustrate these factors with examples concerning the Food Stamp Program, public housing, and income maintenance programs.[13]

Food Stamp Choice Restrictions

The driving force of the standard model is the change in the price of food to food stamp recipients (but not others). This is what creates the room for a deal. But as presented, the model assumed that eligible individuals could buy all the stamps they desired. A policy like that could easily lead to serious black-market problems—some individuals buying more stamps than they will use in order to sell them (at a profit) to others not legitimately eligible to obtain them. One way to try to minimize this problem is simply to limit the quantity of stamps any eligible individual can buy to an amount thought reasonable given the family size. In fact, the actual Food Stamp Program sets a limit based on Department of Agriculture estimates for a low-cost nutritious diet. But then this changes the budget constraint in an important way.

In Figure 3-2 several budget constraints are shown. AB represents the budget constraint with no program; AC represents the unrestricted food stamp program as before; and ARS represents the restricted budget constraint. Under

---

[13] Because in these and later analyses we will refer to income and substitution effects, this chapter contains an appendix which reviews those concepts and illustrates their application. The reader who wants to brush up on the material should do so now.

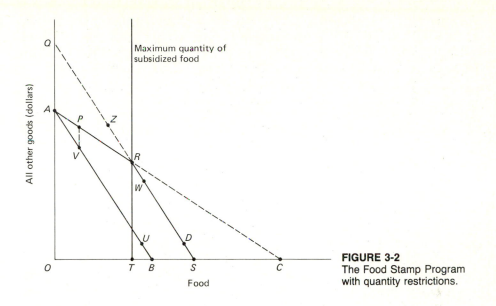

FIGURE 3-2
The Food Stamp Program
with quantity restrictions.

the latter program, the individual can buy up to OT quantity of food with food stamps but above that limit must pay the regular market price for additional food. Thus from A to R the slope of the budget constraint reflects the food stamp subsidy, and from R to S the slope is identical with that of AB. The kink in the budget constraint occurs at the food stamp limit.

How does the individual respond to a restricted food stamp program? The answer depends on where the individual started (on AB) in relation to the limit OT. Suppose the individual was initially at point U, consuming over the program limit for food subsidy. Then the program has only an income effect. That is, given the quantity of food being consumed at U, there is no change in the price of additional food at the margin. Under the highly plausible assumption that food and everything else are normal goods, the individual's new utility-maximizing point must lie between W and D. In that case, if there are no interdependent preferences, no inefficiency arises because of the food stamp program. The behavior is the same as if a cash transfer program with constraint QRS were implemented, the amount of the cash being QA, the size of the subsidy for the maximum allotment.

Suppose, however, that the individual was initially under the subsidy limit at a point like V. The new utility optimum must then be on the PR segment of ARS.[14] We explain this prediction below in two parts: first, that the individual prefers P to other points on AP and, second, that the individual prefers R to

[14] This argument is affected by the choice of V, where the quantity of everything else is greater than at R. A related argument could be made for an initial point where the quantity of everything else is less than that at R; in that case the argument is that the optimal quantity of everything else on ARS must be at least as great as at the initial point.

other points on *RS*. Together, these imply that the individual's optimum point on *ARS* is on the remaining segment *PR*.

The first part is relatively easy. Since the price of additional food from *V* has been reduced, the substitution effect works to increase food consumption. Since food is a normal good, the positive income effect also works to increase food consumption. Both effects push in the same direction, so food consumption will increase from the level at *V*. Therefore, the individual will choose a point on *ARS* that has more food than at *V* or is to the right of *P*. (The points to the left of *P* on *AP* are ruled out because they contain less food than at *V*.)

The second part is slightly trickier. The income effect on everything else is to increase it from *V*, since it also is a normal good. But the substitution effect is to decrease it. The effects go in opposite directions, and we do not know if the quantity of everything else will increase or decrease. However, even if it does decrease, it will not be less than the quantity at point *R*. This deduction follows from knowing the initial position *V* and that both goods are normal.

To see this, imagine that the individual had *QRS* as a budget constraint: a pure income increase compared to *AB*. Then, by the normality property, the utility-maximizing consumption choice would be some point on *QR* with more of both goods than at *V*, like *Z*. As we move downward and to the right from *Z* along *QRS*, the individual's utility level is steadily decreasing (Figure 3-3). Therefore, *R* must yield greater utility than any other point on *RS*. Since the segment *RS* is feasible with the actual food stamp budget constraint *ARS*, the individual will be at *R* if on this segment at all.

Note also, in Figure 3-3, that the kink point *R* will be a popular choice among utility-maximizing individuals with budget constraint *ARS*. We have drawn the

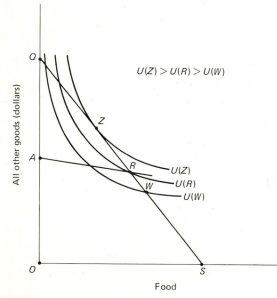

FIGURE 3-3
Utility levels along an ordinary budget constraint decrease with distance from the utility-maximizing point.

indifference curves to show R as the maximum utility for an individual with this constraint. It is not a point of tangency; it is a "corner" solution. R will be the utility maximum whenever the slope of the indifference curve at it equals or falls between the slopes of the segments AR and RS. It is like a trap. The individual, when considering choices moving upward from S, wishes to go past R (to Z) but is unable to do so. The same individual, when considering choices moving rightward from A, wishes to continue past R but cannot do so. From either direction, things get worse when the corner is turned. Thus R will be the utility-maximizing point for a number of individuals (all those with an MRS at R equal to the absolute value of the slope of AR or RS or between the two absolute values).

To sum up the general argument, the individual who starts at V and has a new budget constraint ARS will choose a point on the PR segment. The choices on AP yield less utility than P itself, and the choices on RS yield less utility than R itself. Therefore, the utility-maximizing point must be one from the remainder, the PR segment.

These examples imply that the efficiency of a food stamp program, if we ignore the possibility of interdependent preferences, is higher when a limit is put on the quantity of stamps available to a household. We explain this below. A household consuming a low quantity of food initially—meaning a quantity less than the limit—may choose a consumption point like the ones illustrated by line segment PR of Figure 3-2. For this household, inefficiency arises exactly as in the standard analysis: a cash grant smaller than the food stamp subsidy would allow the household to achieve the same utility level by purchasing less food and more of other things.

However, a household consuming a high quantity of food initially—meaning a quantity greater than the limit—treats the subsidy exactly like a cash transfer. For this latter household, the resulting allocation is efficient: There is no cheaper way for taxpayers to bring the household to the same utility level. Thus the total impact of putting a limit on the food stamp subsidy is to increase efficiency overall: Low-food-consumption households are unaffected by the limit, and efficiency with respect to high-food-consumption households increases. The program is still not as efficient as a pure cash grant, but it is closer to being so.

Let us reflect on this conclusion for a moment. If the only change in the program is a limit on the subsidy per recipient, the total taxpayer cost must be reduced. Recipients with low food consumption levels end up with the same subsidy and same utility levels as without the limit. Therefore, high-food-consumption households must have reduced subsidies. True, the value to them of each subsidy dollar is higher. But these households must end up with lower utility levels than they would have without the limit. Without a limit they could choose the same consumption levels as with the limit; since they do not do so, it must be that the without-limit choices yield more utility than the limited choices. (This is clear in Figure 3-2, where the household initially at U would prefer some point on RC to any of the points on WD.)

How then do we make the statement about increased efficiency, if some people lose because of the limits (eligible households with high food consumption) and others gain (taxpayers)? Recall the discussion in Chapter 2 about relative efficiency. We have simply pointed out that the limits result in fewer potential deals among the members of the economy. (All potential deals are unaffected by the limits except those between taxpayers and high-food-consumption food stamp recipients, which are reduced.)[15] Whether one thinks such a change is desirable depends as well on views of the equity of the change. In the latter regard, note that the high-food-consumption family still receives a greater subsidy than the low-food-consumption family.

But the desirability of such a change is not really the issue here. The issue is how to model the effects of food stamps. The actual Food Stamp Program does include limits on the subsidy available to any recipient family. Thus the model which takes account of these limits, and moves one step closer to reality, is more accurate. So far, it leads to a higher efficiency rating compared to the less realistic standard model.

Let us juxtapose this analysis of the effect of limits with the interdependent preferences argument. In the actual Food Stamp Program, a standard limit is set in accordance with family size and income. But, as our examples suggest, preferences for food relative to other things will vary even among families of the same size and income. Some families will place greater priority on such nonfood uses of money as education, dental work, clothing, and recreation. While we are uncertain about the extent of interdependent preferences for food consumption, they are surely greatest for households with the least food consumption.

Thus the "inefficiency" of food stamps from the perspective of the low-food-consuming household is offset to an unknown degree by the willingness of others to pay for increasing the household's food consumption. Furthermore, the high-food-consuming households who make efficient use of food stamp subsidies from their own perspectives are also the households of least concern to those with interdependent preferences. Thus the limits not only increase efficiency for the reasons mentioned above but could also increase efficiency by concentrating subsidy funds on families for whom interdependent preferences are likely to be highest.[16]

This examination of the effect of subsidy limits illustrates that good analytic

[15] Limiting the maximum allotment to each eligible family can provide gains to taxpayers (dollar reduction in food stamp expenditures) which exceed the losses to food stamp recipients (the dollar amount recipients would be willing to pay to prevent the imposition of the limit). This is a version of the Hicks-Kaldor test for relative efficiency explained in Chapter 5.

[16] In our earlier analysis, we simply had taxpayers pocket the reduction in subsidies caused by the limits. With interdependent preferences, the use of the extra funds would be different. Assume that the original (prelimit) program funding level was based on taxpayer willingness to pay for increased food consumption only up to the limit and that the use of those funds to subsidize some consumption above the limit was an unintended leakage. Then the price of food to stamp recipients in the original plan was too high (not the optimal price subsidy), and the extra funds from imposing the limit should be used to reduce the price of food. In both cases, the imposition of limits allows resources to be channeled from less valuable to more valuable uses.

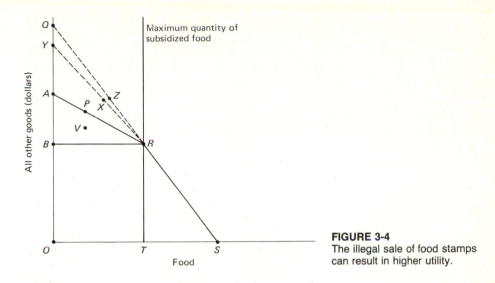

FIGURE 3-4
The illegal sale of food stamps
can result in higher utility.

use of microeconomic theory requires consideration of the specific features of a
policy's design. Because the subsidy limits for food stamps have important
effects on the recipient's opportunity set, or budget constraint, they affect the
efficiency of the program. The standard model ignores this feature; it is
misspecified.

Another source of specification concern involves the information and
transaction costs necessary for the policy's operation and enforcement. The
standard model does not explicitly consider them. Implicitly it is assumed, for
example, that recipients obey the rules of the program. But recipients may not
obey the rules; they have incentive to participate in the illegal resale of the
stamps. Accounting for this results in another change in the budget constraint.
We illustrate this below.

In Figure 3-4 we draw the food stamp budget constraint *ARS* as before.
Suppose the recipient is at *V* before food stamps and has maximum utility on
PR if the stamps are used only by the eligible household. Consider what this
household would do if food stamps were freely exchangeable among individuals.

To maximize utility, the household would always buy the maximum
subsidized allotment of stamps. Then any stamp not used for the household's
food consumption could be profitably converted into cash through resale at its
face value (to any food shopper or, for that matter, any food store). Thus each
stamp is equivalent to a cash grant of value equal to the difference between the
face value and the household's subsidized cost. In Figure 3-4 this makes *QRS*
the effective budget constraint.[17] The household, initially at *V*, would end up at

---

[17] For example, *OQ* can be obtained by selling the full allotment of stamps. The sale price will
equal *BQ*, the market value of the food which can be obtained with the stamps. When added to *OB*,
the amount the household has left after purchasing the stamps (= *OA* − *BA*), the total is *OQ*.

a point like Z (more of both goods). This is financed by selling the unused portion of the food stamp allotment.

Of course, food stamps are not freely exchangeable. It is, in fact, illegal for food stamp recipients to sell their stamps to others and for noneligible households to use them. Most people obey the rules out of respect for the law, but some will be tempted by the room for a deal. The food stamp recipient is tempted by any offer to purchase unused stamps for an amount greater than cost. A potential purchaser will not offer the full market value because of the risk of being caught but may well offer an amount greater than the seller's cost. Thus the effective budget constraint for the recipient will not be QRS but will by like YRS in Figure 3-4: a black-market price for food stamps having a slope between the slope with the subsidy AR and the slope at the market value QR.

How do information and transaction costs enter the analysis? The slope of the budget constraint YRS is determined in part by the resources allocated to governmental enforcement efforts to prevent the illegal transactions. At one extreme, vigorous enforcement efforts lead to an effective constraint closer to AR. (A high probability of being punished or an inability to use illegally purchased stamps dries up the black market.) At the other extreme, little or no enforcement efforts lead to a constraint closer to QR. (Easy use of the stamps by ineligibles raises the black-market price of the stamps.)

What are the implications of illegal trading possibilities? The eligible high-food-consumption household is unaffected: It prefers to use the maximum allotment for its own consumption, as before. However, the eligible low-food-consumption household may alter its behavior. Suppose it does engage in illegal trading and ends up with a point like X on YRS. Obviously, the buyer and seller consider themselves better off. Let us ignore the possibility of interdependent preferences for the moment. Then we can say that the closer X is to Z the more the exchange inefficiency between taxpayers and eligible households is reduced. Why then should this be prevented?

One reason might be because of increased taxpayer cost, but on reflection that does not seem to be a very persuasive argument. If the eligible household could be at R without any trading, the resales to reach X occur at *no* additional taxpayer cost. (The full subsidy would be used even without illegal trading.) If the eligible household would be elsewhere on PR without any trading, it increases its subsidized stamp purchases and therefore taxpayer cost in order to reach X. But recall that other households, no different in terms of eligibility, are receiving the full subsidy because they happen to have high food consumption. If there is no special concern about the low-food-consumption choice, why shouldn't the subsidies to each household be the same?

This returns us to interdependent preferences. That is, a clear reason for prohibiting resale and enforcing the prohibition might be if the household's level of food consumption is of concern and is reduced by the resales. The household that would otherwise be at R certainly reduces food consumption in order to reach X. Some households, however, might actually increase food consumption: If a household would otherwise be near P, the choice of X

implies the income effect of the resales outweighs the substitution effect of a higher food price (equal to the subsidized stamp cost plus the profit foregone by not selling it on the black market). Therefore, it is an empirical matter whether the resales of stamps lead to higher or lower food consumption among eligible families.

A recent change in the Food Stamp Program allows the inference that illegal resales of stamps must reduce food consumption. The Food Stamp Act of 1977 eliminated (as of 1979) the purchase requirement for participating households. That is, each household is given a free monthly allotment of food stamps based on its income and family size. The effect of this on a household is illustrated in Figure 3-5. In the diagram *AB* is the original budget constraint, *ARS* is the budget constraint under the old Food Stamp Program, and *AJK* is the budget constraint under the revised Food Stamp Program with no purchase requirement.

With *AJK* as the constraint, the household will always be on the *JK* segment. Starting from *A*, the household gives up nothing to increase its food consumption to *OT* at *J*. Since additional food increases utility, the household will always move at least to *J*. Thus all eligible households will always use the full allotment of stamps.

Think of the constraint *NJK* as an unrestricted cash grant. If the household prefers a point below *J* on the constraint, its behavior with respect to illegal trading of food stamps will be identical to that of the high-food-consumption household we analyzed previously. That is, it will prefer to use the full allotment for its own food consumption. But if the household has low preferences for food and prefers a point above *J* on *NJ*, then *J* is the best it can do under food stamps without illegal trading. If *LJ* represents the black-market

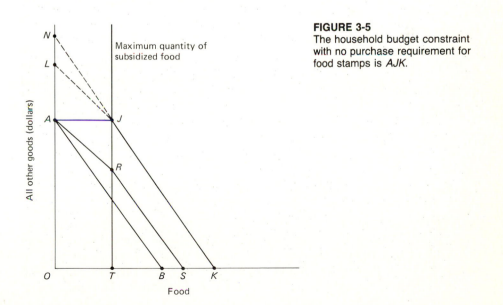

FIGURE 3-5
The household budget constraint with no purchase requirement for food stamps is *AJK*.

opportunities, this household might take advantage of them and thereby reduce its food consumption. Under the revised Food Stamp Program, since all families use their full allotment, any family engaging in illegal selling of stamps must be reducing its food consumption. However, there is no extra subsidy cost to the government from this trading.

Let us summarize this analysis. The standard model suggests that food stamps are inefficient relative to a cash grant. The interdependent preference model suggests the opposite. We do not have the empirical information to determine the specification of preferences. Nevertheless, the imposition of maximum limits on the number of food stamps per household is an important source of efficiency gain under either preference specification. The limits make food stamps more like a cash grant (i.e., for high-food-consumption house-holds), and they allow for better targeting of available funds (i.e., to low-food-consumption households, if desired because of interdependent preferences). Another area of policy concern is the prohibition of resales of food stamps and its enforcement. Under the current food stamp program rules, such resales inevitably reduce the food consumption of the selling households. With no interdependent preferences, these transactions are pure efficiency gains and it is difficult to see why they should be prohibited. If they were not prohibited, food stamps would effectively be cash grants. In order to be efficient, prohibition and enforcement efforts should increase with the extent of interde-pendent preferences.

There are other questions we could raise about food stamps; examples are the administrative costs and the difference between increasing food consump-tion and increasing nutritional intake. But keep in mind that our primary purpose is to develop skills in microeconomic policy analysis. We have used the food stamp issue to illustrate how alternative specifications of models of consumer behavior bear on policy analysis. Different model assumptions (about the arguments of consumer utility functions, the specific design features of a policy, and the information and transaction costs relevant to a policy's operation) have been used to generate insight about how consumers will respond to the Food Stamp Program and how to evaluate that response. Now let us see if we can use these skills, and build on them, in other settings.

Public Housing Choice Restrictions

Another type of choice restriction can be seen in certain public housing programs. In these a family may be given a take-it-or-leave-it choice. In Figure 3-6a, we illustrate how such a choice affects the budget constraint. Let the original budget constraint, with no program, be *AB* and assume the family initially maximizes utility at *C*, thereby consuming *OG* of housing. (Think of each consumption unit of housing in terms of a standardized quality, so higher-quality housing is measured as more of the standardized units.) The public housing authority then tells the family that it may have an apartment which is of the same size as their current one but of better quality (thus more housing) and

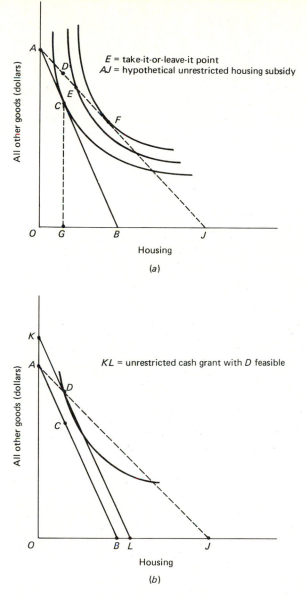

E = take-it-or-leave-it point
AJ = hypothetical unrestricted housing subsidy

Housing

(a)

KL = unrestricted cash grant with D feasible

Housing

(b)

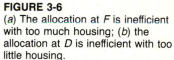

FIGURE 3-6
(a) The allocation at F is inefficient with too much housing; (b) the allocation at D is inefficient with too little housing.

furthermore that the rent is less than it currently pays (because the housing is subsidized). Thus the family's new budget constraint is simply the old one plus the single point E. (Note that the family can consume more of "other things" at E because of the reduction in rent.) By the more-is-better logic, the family must prefer E to C, and it will accept the public housing offer (remember that, by assumption, the quality really is better). Is this efficient or inefficient?

The argument we will make is that the take-it-or-leave-it choice is not necessarily inefficient. We will show the possibility that the indifference curve through E has a slope identical to the slope of AB, or (equivalently) that the individual at E could have an MRS equal to the ratio of the market prices. If that is so, there is no room for a deal and the public housing program is efficient.[18]

To make this argument, let us construct a hypothetical budget constraint AJ to represent an unrestricted housing subsidy program with the same percentage subsidy as at E. We will identify two points on AJ: one inefficient because it has too much housing (the slope of the indifference curve at it is flatter than AB, the market trade-off rate), and the other inefficient because it has too little housing (the slope of the indifference curve at it is steeper than AB). As one moves along AJ from one of those points to the other, the slope of the isoquants through them is gradually changing. Therefore, there must be some point between them where the slope equals AB, and at that point there is neither too much nor too little housing. The point is efficient, and it could be E.

First, let us show there is a point on AJ which is inefficient because it has too much housing. This point is an old friend by now: It is the utility-maximizing choice of the household free to choose any point on AJ. We label this F in Figure 3-6a, where the indifference curve is tangent to AJ. This case is identical with the standard model of food stamps examined earlier. There is room for a deal because the household's MRS of other things for housing (the absolute value of the slope of the indifference curve) is *less* than that of ordinary consumers who buy at market (unsubsidized) prices. This household would be willing to give up housing for cash (other things) at a rate attractive to the nonsubsidized household; both could be made better off by trading. The point F is inefficient because the household has "too much" housing relative to other things, given the market prices.

Now let us examine another point. Suppose the housing authority simply offers to subsidize the current apartment (at the same rate as along AJ), which on the diagram is shown at point D. This point also is inefficient, but because it results in too little housing. To see this, in Figure 3-6b we have added a cash transfer program KL through D. Since the family started at C, it would choose a point from those on KL to the right and below D as long as both goods are normal.[19] Therefore, D is not the utility maximum on KL. Since it lies above the KL maximum, the slope of the indifference curve through D must be *steeper* than the slope of KL (it equals the slope of AB, the market trade-off rate). The household at D would trade cash (other things) for housing at a rate

---

[18] For purposes of this illustration, we will ignore the possibility of interdependent preferences for housing.

[19] A slightly weaker version of this argument can be made without relying on the normality of the goods. Find the point at which the indifference curve through C intersects AJ (this will be to the left of D). At that point, too little housing is being consumed (the slope of the indifference curve is steeper than at C and therefore steeper than the cash transfer constraint KL). The rest of the argument is the same as above.

attractive to nonsubsidized households; both could be made better off. Thus D is inefficient because it has too little housing relative to other things, given the market prices.

We have shown that the slope of the indifference curve through F at AJ is too flat for it to be efficient and that the slope of the indifference curve through D on AJ is too steep for it to be efficient. But as we move upward along AJ from F to D, the slopes of the indifference curves are gradually changing from the flat slope at F to the steep slope at D. Therefore, there must be some point between F and D where the slope of the indifference curve precisely equals the slope of AB, the market trade-off. This point is an efficient allocation. If the public housing authorities offer it as the take-it-or-leave-it choice, the public housing program is efficient.

Whether actual public housing programs are or are not efficient is a matter for empirical determination. The analysis we presented serves the function of raising the issue. According to one study of federal housing programs, the degree of inefficiency is probably less than 5 percent (the average public housing recipient would require a cash grant of at least $0.95 to forego a $1.00 housing subsidy).[20] As with food stamps, any inefficiency from too much housing might be offset by interdependent preferences. Meanwhile, we have seen that microeconomic theory can be used to analyze the take-it-or-leave-it choice, another type of budget constraint that is sometimes created by public policy.

The Design of an Income Maintenance Plan

The standard analysis with which we began has another source of oversimplification in its *partial equilibrium* nature. This means, roughly, that analytic attention is focused on only one of the resource allocation choices that is affected by a program. We have been focusing so far only on the analysis of exchange efficiency. Of course, the other questions of efficiency—whether the right goods are being produced and right resources are being used to produce them—are equally important. *General equilibrium analysis* requires that all the resource allocation choices affected by a program be considered. Although we shall continue to defer general discussion of these other efficiency issues until later chapters, it is convenient to introduce one element of them through analysis of the *labor-leisure choice* of recipients. All transfer programs affect this choice and can cause inefficiency through it.[21]

The primary purpose of this section is to reinforce the usefulness of theory as a guide to policy design and evaluation. In particular, we build up to the idea

---

[20] For further discussion of this issue along with some empirical work, see H. Aaron and G. Von Furstenberg, "The Inefficiency of Transfers in Kind: The Case of Housing Assistance," *Western Economic Journal*, June 1971, pp. 184–191.

[21] We note that taxpayer choices also are affected by transfer programs, because all methods of taxation cause distortions in prices that might be efficient otherwise. This is discussed in Chapters 10 and 11.

of using a Negative Income Tax (NIT) as a method of income maintenance. First, we review the general labor-leisure decision that all individuals face. Then we will show how current welfare programs discourage work. Finally, we will show how the NIT can reduce the work disincentives of current programs.

The Labor-Leisure Choice   To this point we have referred to individuals having a budget constraint or an initial endowment without being very specific about where it comes from. The basic sources of individual wealth are gifts: material things, like inheritances; childhood upbringing, like schooling received; and natural endowments, like intelligence. Individuals use these gifts over time to alter their wealth further, increasing it through labor or capital investments (the latter includes skill development or "human capital" investments, like advanced schooling),[22] and decreasing it through consumption.

For now, we shall focus only on the labor market decisions of individuals as if they were the only source of wealth. One constraint individuals face in earning labor income is the wage offered to them, but the more important constraint is *time*. There is only so much time available, and a decision to use it to work means not using it for other things we will refer to here simply as *leisure*. Presumably every individual has preferences about how much to work, given the income that can be derived from it and the *opportunity costs* of foregone leisure.[23]

We represent the labor-leisure choice in Figure 3-7a by using a diagram virtually identical with those we have been using all along. Leisure is measured on the horizontal axis, and dollars for everything else on the vertical axis. The budget constraint is shown as *AB*, and its slope equals minus the wage rate. (Since more work is shown on the diagram as a movement to the *left*, the budget size goes up in accordance with the wage rate as the individual works more.) Thus the price per unit of leisure equals the wage. The location of the constraint depends upon the time framework selected by the analyst. If we select a one-year period, the maximum leisure must be one year, represented by *OB*. The dashed vertical line at *B* indicates that it is impossible to choose a point to the right of it. Point *C*, let us say, represents the utility-maximizing choice of some individual.

Consider the response of an individual to a change in the wage rate, say an increase. This changes the budget constraint to one like *DB*. How will the

---

[22] This is discussed further in Chapter 14.

[23] For those of you thinking that individuals have little choice about how much to work (e.g., most jobs are 40 hours per week, and an individual can only take it or leave it), consider the many sources of flexibility. Many people work only in part-time jobs, and others hold two jobs simultaneously. Some jobs have more paid vacation than others. Sometimes the decision to pursue certain careers is heavily influenced by the time dimension, e.g., most teaching jobs are for 9 or 10 months (and pay correspondingly). If one thinks broadly about work during an individual's lifetime, there are important decisions about when to begin and when to retire. There are decisions about how hard to seek new employment during a spell of unemployment. There are very subtle decisions such as how hard to work when working; some people prefer to take it easy on the job in full knowledge that this usually slows down promotions or raises that come from working more. In short, there is a great deal of choice between labor and leisure.

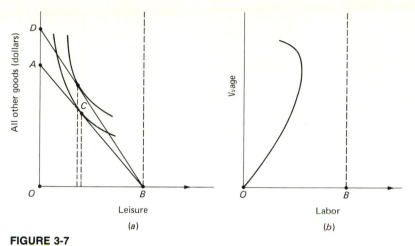

FIGURE 3-7
(a) The labor-leisure choice; (b) backward-bending labor supply curve.

individual respond? This is clearly a price change involving both income and substitution effects. The rise in wages is a rise in the price of leisure (relative to all other things), and thus the substitution effect works to decrease leisure (or increase work). Real income increases because of the wage rise; if leisure is a normal good, the income effect acts to increase its consumption (or reduce work).[24] Thus the income and substitution effects work in opposite directions, and the net effect cannot be predicted on purely theoretical grounds.

Empirically, the labor supply curve of an individual (the locus of points relating the choice of hours worked to each possible wage rate) is often thought to be "backward-bending" as in Figure 3-7b. That is, as the wage increases from a low initial rate, the substitution effect outweighs the income effect: The individual finds it more important to earn income for basic necessities than to reduce work effort and live on almost nothing. But as the wage rises past some point, the income effect begins to outweigh the substitution effect: The individual may feel that he or she has earned the right to spend more time relaxing and enjoying the fruits of a big paycheck.

Work Disincentives of Current Welfare Programs   Let us now consider the population of low-income and low-wealth individuals who are, or might be, eligible for the various welfare programs we have mentioned: AFDC, Food Stamps, Medicaid, local housing assistance programs, etc. Historically, many of these programs were designed in such a way that benefits available to recipients were reduced dollar for dollar in response to any increases in the recipient's earned income. This created some bizarre incentives for the recipients.

---

[24] Leisure is generally considered a normal good because it is a complement to a highly aggregated (and undoubtedly normal) good: consumption. More simply, it often takes more time to consume more (e.g., theater, restaurants, shopping, vacation trips, reading).

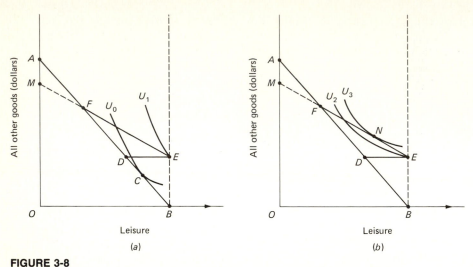

FIGURE 3-8
(a) The labor supply response to welfare policies; (b) NIT can increase work efforts.

For example, consider a family receiving under the old system both AFDC payments and local housing assistance. If a part-time job were offered to one of the family members, not only would AFDC payments be reduced by the amount of the earnings, but so would the housing assistance; by accepting the job, the family could lose twice as much money as the amount earned! Needless to say, welfare recipients were hardly enthused by the moral encouragement of some to increase ''self-reliance.'' While most of the programs have been modified individually to allow some net increases in family income through earnings, as a group they still have close to a ''100 percent tax'' (i.e., for families eligible for several of them).

We can see the effects of this situation on a labor-leisure diagram. Figure 3-8a shows an ordinary budget constraint AB for a low-income family. With no welfare programs, the family might choose a point like C—where, say, the mother and young teenage son work part time but spend most of their time taking care of the preschool children and being in school, respectively. Let's say the current amalgam of programs can be represented by the line segment DE. This means that the family members receive total benefits of BE if they don't work at all; and as their work effort increases from E (i.e., moving to the left along DE), their total ability to purchase goods remains constant (their net welfare benefits are reduced dollar for dollar by any earnings) until D. At that point, their welfare benefits have been reduced to zero and they go off welfare, thus retaining the full earnings from additional work efforts (along DA).

It is hardly surprising that this family maximizes utility by completely withdrawing from the labor force, at E. Both the income and the substitution effects act to increase leisure. (Higher real income works to increase leisure; the lowered effective wage reduces the price of leisure, which acts to increase its consumption.) We thus know the family will choose a point on the new effective constraint *ADE* with greater leisure than at *C*; this means it is on the *DE* segment. But although the slopes of indifference curves approach zero (the slope of *DE*) to the right because of diminishing MRS, they will not reach it if the nonsatiation assumption holds. The utility level increases as the family moves to the right along *DE*, but it never reaches a tangency position; instead, it runs into the boundary condition at *E*, which is the maximum attainable utility.[25]

The NIT Proposal   The NIT has been proposed as a federal response to a variety of difficulties in welfare programs, including some not previously mentioned. One of these other problems has been the disparity in payments to equally needy eligible families caused by differences in the generosity of state and local programs; another problem has been disparity in eligibility, particularly in regard to the eligibility of two-parent, so-called intact, families. One version of the NIT plan would replace most existing welfare programs (Medicaid is the notable exception), guarantee a certain minimum income level (dependent on family size), and tax any earnings at a rate of the order of 50 percent until the family preferred to no longer participate in NIT and went off welfare. All this could be done through the Internal Revenue Service, just as tax collection is, and that would also reduce the stigma associated with current welfare policies.

The NIT budget constraint is shown as *MFE* in Figure 3-8*a*. *BE* represents the guaranteed minimum. Then for each unit of work at wage *w*, the family pays taxes of *tw*, where *t* is the tax rate, and supplements its net income by $(1 - t)w$. Thus the line *MFE* rises to the left at a slope less steep than that of *AB*. At *F* the family would go off welfare because, for any additional work, its net income is higher without NIT. Thus *AFE* becomes the effective budget constraint. Note that one could think of the old welfare system constraint *ADE* as an NIT plan with a 100 percent tax rate ($t = 1$).

The particular family shown at point *E* under the old welfare system would not be affected by the NIT program; its utility-maximizing point would still be at *E*. However, the family shown in Figure 3-8*b*, which also began at *E*, will increase its work effort under the new system and choose a point like *N*. The difference is in the slope of the respective indifference curves at the boundary *E*. Families with slopes less steep than *MFE* will perceive a substitution effect sufficiently powerful to induce them to work; those with slopes greater than MFE will not perceive an effective substitution effect.[26]

Thus, when families are already covered by welfare, the NIT plan should on

---

[25] We note also that some families initially working with income *above* the welfare minimum will withdraw if the welfare plan becomes available to them. This will occur whenever the initial indifference curve crosses the welfare minimum height to the left of point *E*: If the family is indifferent to the initial position and the minimum income with *some* work effort, it must strictly prefer the minimum income and *no* work effort.

[26] In the normal case of initial tangency, a new steeper budget constraint always implies a substitution effect. But along the boundary the slope of the indifference curve is initially steeper than the original constraint. To some extent, the constraint can become steeper without triggering a substitution effect.

the average increase work efforts. On the other hand, when families not previously eligible for welfare are eligible for NIT, theory predicts a reduction in work effort. Consider the family in Figure 3-8a shown initially at C and now eligible for the NIT plan. The income effect acts to increase leisure (higher real income increases consumption of normal goods), and the substitution effect (a reduction in net wage rate due to the NIT tax) also acts to increase leisure.

It was this latter group of families who were of great concern to policy makers. Few wanted to reform welfare if it led to serious reductions in work effort. The concern led to the undertaking of several social experiments to estimate the magnitude of the effect. The general findings from these experiments is that, among intact families, adult males decreased their work efforts by an average of 1 or 2 hours per week, or about a 7 percent reduction in total. Only about 16 percent of wives were participating in the labor force, but their reduction in work effort was more pronounced (about 33 percent).[27] Those effects, of course, would be offset to some extent by groups that might work more. Probably the safest interpretations to offer are that the experiments did lay to rest fears of massive labor market withdrawal and did yield enormous practical learning about how to operate such a program.[28]

Note that throughout this discussion of labor market effects of policies, little attention was focused on resolving the efficiency issue. Rather, it was suggested that there was a problem with the current welfare system, and one alternative to alleviate the problem was explored. The problem was identified as poor work incentives, and we simply used knowledge about income and substitution effects to understand it and theoretically develop an idea which might mitigate it. If it is impossible to determine efficiency effects precisely (recall all the other determinants of efficiency we have discussed in regard to the same set of policies), the next best thing to do may be to suboptimize: take one piece of the larger issue where there seems to be consensus that it is a problem and try to do something about it.

SUMMARY

This chapter uses models of individual choice for the analysis of government welfare programs. Each of the models assumes utility-maximizing behavior, although the models vary in details of their specification. The predictions and efficiency conclusions drawn from these models depend on the particular specifications. The analyses presented are intended primarily to develop a facility with these types of models in order to be able to adapt and use them in other settings.

---

[27] Note that the public may favor a program which allows mothers or fathers with child-rearing responsibilities more time at home.

[28] See H. Watts and A. Rees (eds.), *The New Jersey Income-Maintenance Experiment*, vol. 2: *Labor Supply Responses* (New York: Academic Press, 1977); J. Pechman and P. Timpane (eds.), *Work Incentives and Income Guarantees* (Washington, D.C.: Brookings Institution, 1975); J. Hausman and D. Wise, "Social Experimentation, Truncated Distributions, and Efficient Estimation," *Econometrica, 45,* pp. 919–938.

We began with a standard argument used to demonstrate the inefficiency of in-kind welfare programs involving price subsidies, like the Food Stamp Program from 1964 to 1978. Such subsidies create differences in the prices faced by program eligibles and noneligibles. In the standard model these price differences leave room for a deal and thus cause inefficiency. A cash grant, on the other hand, is efficient by this model. However, the model of interdependent preferences involving food consumption indicates exactly the opposite result: Price subsidies for food are required for efficiency, and cash transfers are inefficient. This raises an important and unresolved empirical issue about the extent of interdependent preferences for food and other necessities.

The standard argument does not account for certain choice restrictions typically imposed by in-kind welfare programs. These restrictions can have important effects, and they deserve analytic attention. We showed that some of them can prevent or reduce the inefficiency identified by the standard analysis. That is a characteristic of the food stamp allotment limits and the take-it-or-leave-it choice in public housing. We also analyzed the prohibition against black-market food stamp transactions, and we suggested that any harm from the sales depends on the extent of interdependent preferences. It follows that enforcement efforts to prevent such sales also ought to depend on the extent of interdependent preferences.

In the final section we reconsidered the partial-equilibrium nature of the standard result. Such analysis can be misleading because it fails to call attention to other important effects of welfare programs, like the impact on the labor market. We constructed a simple model of the labor-leisure choice which suggests that the work disincentive effects of the current mix of welfare programs may be unnecessarily high. We analyzed the Negative Income Tax proposal for welfare reform, which improves the work incentives for current welfare recipients but reduces work incentives for others who would be eligible for it. This last example suggests another purpose that is served by the analysis of various details of policy: It increases skills of policy design.

EXERCISES

3-1 Sally is a representative member of the "working poor." She has a job which pays $4 per hour. She chooses to work 8 hours per day, although her employer would hire her to work any number of hours per day. Assume, because of her large family, that she would not be required to pay any income taxes even if she worked 24 hours per day.

    a Draw Sally's budget constraint on a graph on which income per day is measured on the vertical axis and leisure per day on the horizontal axis (with 24 hours per day the maximum possible leisure). Label her current income-leisure choice as point A. What is Sally's MRS of leisure for income at this point?

    b Under a new negative income tax plan, Sally is told she will qualify for a basic allowance of $20 per day but must pay 50 percent of her earnings in taxes. She is free to participate or not participate in the NIT plan. Draw Sally's budget constraint assuming participation in the plan. Above what daily earnings should

Sally decide to forego participation in the plan? (Answer: $40) Label this as point *C*, the *break-even point.*

c Can you predict how the NIT plan will affect Sally's working hours? (Answer: It will reduce them.) Is it possible, assuming leisure is a normal good, that Sally will choose a point at which the MRS of leisure for income is *not* equal to $2? (Answer: Yes)

d The secretary of the Department of Health and Human Services, in a rough draft of a speech on the NIT plan, says it has been calculated that Sally's income will be increased by $4 per day. Furthermore, with 10 million individuals exactly like Sally, the daily cost to the government will be $40 million. The subsidy cost is based on Sally's current working hours. Is this a good estimate of Sally's daily subsidy? Explain. Assuming that leisure is a normal good, what is the range of possible daily costs to the government? (Answer: $40 to $200 million)

e In order to get a better estimate of the cost to the government of the NIT plan, a social experiment was undertaken. The experiment consisted of varying the amount of basic allowance given to each family unit while the tax rate on earnings was held at 50 percent. The first thing learned was that, when utility was held constant at the pre-NIT level, each individual chose to work 6 hours per day. The basic allowance for the plan was $16 per day. The second thing learned was that, for these individuals, leisure is a necessity. Under the utility-constant NIT plan, what portion of real income is spent on leisure? Measure real income as the level of the budget constraint when covered by the experimental NIT: Its dollar value is shown at the intercept of the constraint with the vertical axis. (Answer: 0.5625)

Using this new information, what is the range of possible daily cost to the government of the proposed NIT plan with a $20 basic allowance? *Hint:* Explain why each individual will work at least 4.875 hours but no more than 6 hours. (Answer: $80 to $102.5 million)

APPENDIX: Income and Substitution Effects

In Figure 3A-1*a* we show an individual's utility-maximizing choice for each of several different budget constraints. The constraints differ only by the total budget size (income level); the identical slopes reflect the assumption that prices are constant. Imagine considering every possible budget size (at the given prices) and asking what quantity of the good *X* the individual would purchase. In Figure 3A-1*b* that relation is drawn. The horizontal axis shows each possible budget size; the vertical axis measures quantity of *X*; and the curve shows the quantity of *X* which would be purchased for each possible budget constraint. This relation is called an *Engel curve.*[29] The one illustrated slopes upward; as income increases, the individual increases the quantity of the good purchased. Goods of this type are called *normal;* they have a positive

---

[29] Sometimes it is more convenient to define the vertical axis as $P_X X$, the expenditure on *X*. This relation is called the Engel-expenditure curve.

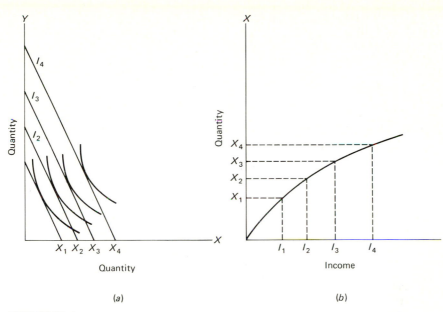

FIGURE 3A-1
Consumption response to income change. (a) Utility-maximizing choices; (b) Engel curve.

income elasticity.[30] Some goods, like spaghetti and potatoes, may have downward-sloping Engel curves (at least over a broad range of budget levels). These are called *inferior goods;* the individual buys less of them as income increases.

Among normal goods, sometimes distinctions are made between *necessities* and *luxuries*. A necessity is a normal good whose income elasticity is less than 1: the proportion of income spent on it declines as income rises. Individuals often treat food and medical services as necessities. To say that food is a necessity means operationally that an individual spends a decreasing proportion of income on it as income increases (everything else held constant).[31] A luxury good, on the other hand, is a normal good whose income elasticity is greater than 1. For many people, sports cars and yachts are considered luxuries. One interesting good to mention is "everything"; it is normal with an income elasticity of 1, since the same proportion of the budget (100 percent) is

---

[30] Elasticity is defined as the percentage change in a variable X associated with a 1 percent change in another variable Z. The income elasticity measures the percentage change in the quantity demanded of a good X in response to a 1 percent change in income (the budget level).

[31] Sometimes it is useful to speak of aggregates of certain goods; in fact, we have already done so several times. "Food" is not a single good but refers to an aggregate category of goods. How do we know whether an individual consumes more food? Typically, we measure the expenditures on food and calculate an Engel-expenditure curve.

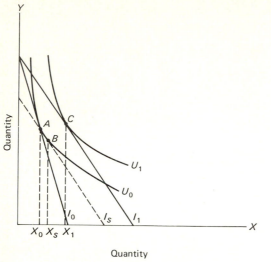

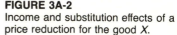

Quantity

FIGURE 3A-2
Income and substitution effects of a
price reduction for the good X.

always spent on it.[32] The reason for mentioning this is to suggest that the broader the aggregate of goods considered, the more likely it is to be normal with elasticity close to 1.

Once the effects of income changes on consumption patterns are understood at a conceptual level, it is relatively easy to deduce the effects of price changes. A price change can be understood as stimulating two different responses: a substitution effect and an income effect. In Figure 3A-2, assume an individual is initially at A, with budget constraint I_0 and consuming X_0 of the good X. Then say that the price of X falls, which changes the budget constraint to I_1. The individual's new utility-maximizing point is shown at C with increased consumption of X (now at level X_1).

Does this model always predict that consumption of a good will increase if its price falls? The answer is no, and the reasoning can be seen more clearly if we break the response into two effects. To do so, we *pretend* that the individual moves from A to C in two steps: first from A to B and then from B to C.

The first step, from A to B, shows the change in consumption ($X_S - X_0$) which would occur in response to the new price *if* the individual were required to remain on the *initial* indifference curve. The quantity $X_S - X_0$ is referred to as the *substitution effect,* the *pure price effect,* or the *compensated price effect* (because real income, or utility, is held constant). It is found by finding the budget constraint which has the same *slope* as I_1 (reflecting the new price) but is just *tangent* to U_0. This is shown as the dashed line I_S, and thus the hypothetical compensation required to keep utility at the initial level is to take $I_1 - I_S$ dollars away from the budget.

---

[32] Saving is, of course, a legitimate possibility. It can be thought of as spending on *future-consumption goods*.

The substitution effect of a price reduction for a good is always positive; the quantity of that good consumed increases. To show this, observe on the diagram that a price reduction for the good X always makes the slope of the new budget constraint less steep than the original one. This means that the tangency of the "compensating" budget I_S to U_0 must occur to the right of A (consumption of X increases), since all points on U_0 with less steep slopes than at A lie to the right of it (because of diminishing MRS). By analogous reasoning, the substitution effect of a price increase is always negative: The quantity of that good consumed decreases. *Thus the substitution effect on quantity is always in the opposite direction of a change in price for that good.*

The change in consumption associated with the second step, from B to C, is shown as $X_1 - X_S$. This is referred to as the income effect, since the source of the change is the changing budget level (from I_S to I_1). Observe that we have already analyzed changes like this in deriving the Engel curve. The income effect (of a price reduction) will be positive if X is a normal good and negative if it is an inferior good. Since the change drawn on the diagram is positive, we have assumed that X is a normal good.

Thus the total effect of the price change, including both the income and the substitution effects, is not clearly predictable without information about the good being analyzed. If we know the good is normal, the income and substitution effects work in the same direction: Quantity consumed will change in the direction opposite that of the change in price. If the good is inferior, however, the substitution and income effects work in *opposite* directions. In these cases it is typical for the substitution effect to outweigh the income effect, and thus price and quantity will still move in opposite directions. But there may be a few goods, known as Giffen goods, such that the income effect predominates and we get the unusual result that price and quantity move in the same direction.[33]

At this point, a simple extension is to consider how an individual would respond to various possible price changes. The analogous question for pure income changes is used to derive the Engel curve; for price changes, one derives the demand curve. The *ordinary demand curve* shows the quantity of a good an individual will consume at each possible price. Except for Giffen goods, the ordinary price elasticity of demand is negative; e.g., a 1 percent increase in price will reduce the quantity demanded. The *compensated demand curve* is derived analogously except that it is based only on the substitution effect. The compensated price elasticity of demand is always negative. We shall consider the use of demand curves more fully in Chapter 5; for now we shall focus primarily on the workings of the income and substitution effects themselves.

Understanding individual responses to a price change by the hypothetical two-step procedure is important because it aids in predicting the effects of

---

[33] Sir Robert Giffen was an English economist (1837–1910) who observed that a rise in the price of potatoes in Ireland caused an increase in the quantity demanded.

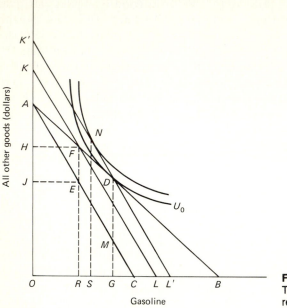

FIGURE 3A-3
The gasoline tax with rebate will
reduce gasoline consumption.

policies. We demonstrate this with a theoretical analysis and some rough empirical calculations relevant to a proposed gasoline tax considered by President Carter in December 1979. For a variety of reasons, such as fears of dependence on foreign oil and a general desire to conserve nonrenewable resources, the president considered imposing a $0.50 excise tax on top of the price (then about $1.00 per gallon) of gasoline. The tax would be rebated to the public in the form of lower Social Security taxes (thus, in a sense compensating us). To what extent should we expect this policy to reduce gasoline consumption?

On theoretical grounds, such a compensated tax change should reduce gasoline consumption, as we illustrate in Figure 3A-3. Assume the individual is initially at D. If the tax is imposed without any rebate, the budget constraint rotates inward (say from AB to AC). Gasoline consumption will clearly be reduced: The substitution effect reduces it; and since gasoline is a normal good, the income effect reduces it. Call E the new equilibrium. The only characteristic of E that matters for this example is that there is less gasoline consumption at E than at the initial position D.

At E the individual is making tax payments of FE. To see this, note that $FE = HJ$. If the individual starting with OA dollars has OJ dollars left for other things after purchasing gas, the total gasoline expenditure is $OA - OJ = AJ$. But before the tax, that same quantity of gasoline cost only $AH = OA - OH$. The difference between the two amounts, $AJ - AH$, is the tax HJ.

Each individual will not receive a rebate exactly equal to his or her own tax payment. (If that were guaranteed, there would be no real price change.) Nevertheless, the average tax payment equals the average rebate, since all taxes collected are rebated.[34] In order to predict whether average (or total) gasoline consumption drops after the combined tax and rebate plan, we treat this individual as an average: tax rebate equal to tax payment. This makes the compensated budget constraint *KL* (the line through *F* with slope *AC*). The move from *E* on *AC* to some point on *KL* is a pure income effect. Now we shall argue that this income effect cannot be strong enough to cause the individual to consume more than the initial quantity of gasoline *OG*.

The key to the argument is that the average tax rebate *FE* is less than *DM* (as long as gasoline is not a Giffen good, and therefore *E* has less gasoline than *D*). For suppose that we gave the average individual a rebate of as much as *DM*. Gasoline consumption must still be less than at the initial position. A rebate of *DM* would lead to a compensated budget constraint of *K'L'* (the line through *D* with slope *AC*). At *D* the slope of the indifference curve U_0 is "too flat" to be tangent to *K'L'*: We know its slope equals that of *AB*, because it is the original (pretax) equilibrium point. To get to the utility maximum on *K'L'*, the consumer has to move upward and to the left from *D* (shown as *N*). But then the income effect on gasoline consumption of the change from *AC* to *K'L'* is only *RS*, and gasoline consumption *OS* is less than the initial level *OG*. Therefore, the smaller income change from *AC* to *KL* will result in gas consumption less than *OS*, a reduction from the initial pretax level.

Although it is important to know that some reduction in gasoline consumption should be caused by the tax-rebate plan, it is also important to try to estimate the magnitude of the expected change. For that task we make use of available elasticity estimates and the Slutsky relation to separate income and substitution effects.[35] The latter allows us to take account of the rebate effect of the tax-rebate plan.

The ordinary price elasticity of gasoline ϵ_{X,P_X} is currently thought to be inelastic (i.e., a 1 percent change in price causes less than 1 percent change in gasoline consumption) in the range of -0.2 to -0.3, and the income elasticity $\epsilon_{X,I}$ is thought to be 1 to 1.1. (Both are in the short run, where the time to respond is within 1 year. Elasticities are always greater the longer the response period.)[36] A rough approximation of the expected response without accounting for the rebate is a demand reduction of 10 to 15 percent:[37]

---

[34] The fact that some of the rebates would go to individuals who do not consume gasoline only strengthens the argument we are constructing.

[35] This is described further in the optional section of this appendix.

[36] These numbers, and those given below, although chosen to be realistic, should be considered illustrative only. In careful analysis one must give serious attention to the range of parameter estimates utilized.

Note also that we are using theory about individual behavior and applying it to a group. The elasticities used refer to the whole market of consumers, some of whom have high elasticities and some low. In Chapter 5 we consider this aggregation of consumers more carefully.

[37] Recall that elasticities are not necessarily constant. Empirical estimates of elasticities are usually derived from observations containing only small price changes; they may not be applicable for large price changes. Our example, for simplicity, assumes the elasticities apply for the large price change discussed here.

$$\text{Percent reduction} = \epsilon_{X,P_X}(\% \text{ price increase})$$
$$10\% \text{ reduction} = -0.2(50\% \text{ price increase}) \quad \text{lower bound}$$
$$15\% \text{ reduction} = -0.3(50\% \text{ price increase}) \quad \text{upper bound}$$

However, this estimates the uncompensated effect of the \$0.50 tax. The reduction would be smaller because of the rebate. Since the average annual expenditure per family on gasoline was about \$1000, or about 7 percent of average family income, the compensated elasticity ϵ_{X,P_X}^S can be approximated from the ordinary price and income elasticities by using the Slutsky relation derived in the optional section of the appendix:

$$\epsilon_{X,P_X}^S = \epsilon_{X,P_X} + \frac{P_X X}{I} \epsilon_{X,I}$$
$$= -0.2 + 0.07(1.1) = -0.123 \quad \text{lower bound}$$
$$= -0.3 + 0.07(1) \quad\; = -0.230 \quad \text{upper bound}$$

and the expected percent reduction in demand is

$$\text{Percent reduction} = \epsilon_{X,P_X}^S(50\% \text{ price increase})$$
$$6.15\% \text{ percent reduction} = -0.123(50\%)$$
$$11.50\% \text{ percent reduction} = -0.230(50\%)$$

The above example illustrates the importance of being able to separate the income and substitution effects of a price change.

▽THE MATHEMATICS OF INCOME AND SUBSTITUTION EFFECTS

For a given utility function we need to know the prices of all goods and the budget level in order to calculate the utility-maximizing choice. We know that individuals change their demands for a certain good X in response to changes in any of the parameters, e.g., a change in price or income level as discussed above. The responses are summarized in an ordinary demand function:

$$X = D_X(P_1, P_2, \ldots, P_X, \ldots, P_n, I)$$

where the P_i represent the prices of each good (including X) and I represents the income or budget level. The shape of the demand function depends, of course, on the individual's preferences. However, certain aspects of a demand function will appear for anyone who maximizes utility, independently of the particular preferences. It is those general aspects which we attempt to describe by the income and substitution effects.

The response to a unit increase in income is found by taking the partial derivative of the demand equation with respect to income $\partial X/\partial I$. We call a good "normal" if this partial derivative is positive, and "inferior" if it is negative. (Note that it is possible for the same good to be normal to one individual but inferior to another.)

The income elasticity is defined as

$$\epsilon_{X,I} = \frac{\partial X}{\partial I} \cdot \frac{I}{X}$$

where $\epsilon_{X,I}$ denotes the elasticity of the variable X with respect to the variable I. Since I and X are positive quantities, the income elasticity has the same sign as the partial derivative $\partial X/\partial I$. Within the class of normal goods, a good is a luxury if $\epsilon_{X,I} > 1$ and a necessity if $\epsilon_{X,I} < 1$. If X is an inferior good, $\epsilon_{X,I} < 0$. Note that the magnitude of the elasticity does not have to be constant; it depends on the consumption point from which it is measured. As an obvious example, a good which is inferior at one income level must have been normal at some lower income level. (Otherwise, there would not be a positive quantity of it to reduce.)

The response to a unit increase in price is found by taking the partial derivative of the demand equation with respect to price $\partial X/\partial P_X$. The decomposition of this total effect of a price change into its component income and substitution effects is described by the Slutsky equation:

$$\frac{\partial X}{\partial P_X} = \frac{\partial X}{\partial P_X}\bigg|_{U=U_0} - X\frac{\partial X}{\partial I}$$

where the first term is the substitution effect (the utility level is held constant at its initial level U_0) and the second term is the income effect.[38]

The price elasticity of demand is defined as

$$\epsilon_{X,P_X} = \frac{\partial X}{\partial P_X}\frac{P_X}{X}$$

Except for a Giffen good, the price elasticity is negative (P_X and X are positive; $\partial X/\partial P_X$ is negative). If $\epsilon_{X,P_X} < -1$ (for example, -2), the good is considered *price-elastic,* which means the percent change in quantity will exceed the percent change in price. If $-1 < \epsilon_{X,P_X} < 0$, the good is considered *price-inelastic,* which means the percent change in quantity will be less than the percent change in price.

It is often easier, when doing empirical analysis, to work with elasticities because they are thought to be more "constant" than the partial derivatives

---

[38] Eugen E. Slutsky (1880–1948) was the Russian economist who first derived this equation. The derivation is too complicated to be duplicated here, but it can be found in P. Samuelson, *Foundations of Economic Analysis* (Cambridge, Mass.: Harvard University Press, 1947), chap. 5.

over the changes in prices or income considered. The Slutsky equation can be rewritten in terms of price and income elasticities. Multiply both sides of it by P_X/X and the last term by I/I:

$$\frac{\partial X}{\partial P_X}\frac{P_X}{X} = \left.\frac{\partial X}{\partial P_X}\right|_{U=U_0}\frac{P_X}{X} - X\frac{\partial X}{\partial I}\frac{P_X}{X}\frac{I}{I}$$

or

$$\epsilon_{X,P_X} = \epsilon_{X,P_X}^S - \frac{P_X X}{I}\frac{\partial X}{\partial I}\frac{I}{X}$$

where ϵ_{X,P_X}^S is the "substitution" elasticity, or

$$\epsilon_{X,P_X} = \epsilon_{X,P_X}^S - \frac{P_X X}{I}\epsilon_{X,I}$$

Note that $P_X X/I$ is the proportion of income spent on the good X.

UTILITY MAXIMIZATION AND INTERGOVERNMENTAL GRANTS: ANALYZING EQUITY CONSEQUENCES

This chapter is intended to develop further the skills of model specification and to show how to use those skills to understand the equity consequences of proposed or actual policies. The equity or fairness of a policy is often difficult to evaluate because of lack of social consensus on the appropriate standard. However, that does not mean that the analysis of equity consequences is left to the whims of the analyst. A number of competing concepts of equity are commonly used as the basis for evaluative judgments, and a part of analytic skill is to utilize the concepts which policy makers and others will think important. In this chapter we will introduce several equity standards and apply them in a discussion of school finance policy. It should be emphasized that these standards can be and are applied routinely to the analysis of a broad range of policies.

Before presenting these standards, it will be useful to extend the utility maximization framework we have been using to the analysis of intergovernmental grant programs (of which school finance is an example). In most applications, utility maximization models are used to represent an individual's choice making. However, sometimes the decisions of a large group or team of people can be modeled with the same analytic apparatus. In fact, considerable insight into a locality's response to a grant program can be drawn from analysis paralleling that of the preceding chapter. However, several new sources of specification concern suggest that these results be interpreted cautiously.

The chapter is organized as follows. First, some general information about intergovernmental grants is provided. Then alternative design features of grants are compared by using a community utility maximization framework. Two specifications which do not use the framework are briefly described: the Tiebout theory of individual locational decisions and a bureaucratic theory of grant allocative effects.

With that as background we turn to the problem of choosing equity standards with which to evaluate policies. A number of principles of equity are described: strict equality, a universal minimum, equal opportunity, and simple and conditional neutrality. Some of these characterize the *outcomes* of a resource allocation process, and others characterize the fairness of the *process* itself. Then we review school finance policies to see which of the standards appear to be of current public concern. Finally, we consider how intergovernmental grant programs can be designed to achieve these standards. In an optional section we present an exercise to illustrate the use of social welfare functions in evaluating school finance policies.

INTERGOVERNMENTAL GRANTS

In the 1981 fiscal year approximately $90 billion was provided through grants-in-aid from the federal government to state and local governments.[1] These funds were provided through a wide variety of programs, such as general revenue sharing, urban mass transit assistance, and community development block grants. States also fund grant-in-aid programs to local governments, most notably for school financing.

Although these grants have diverse purposes, most economic rationales for them depend on either externalities or equity arguments. An example of an externality argument might be as follows. School districts do not have sufficient incentive to bear the costs of devising innovative educational techniques, because the benefits of success will accrue primarily to schools external to the district boundaries (who will imitate for free). Thus, although the social benefits of research and development for the education sector might outweigh the costs, the private benefits to any single district may not justify the expense to the taxpayers within it.[2] As an attempt to ameliorate this problem, the federal government sponsors Title IV of the Elementary and Secondary Education Act which provides grant funds to pay for innovative demonstration projects.[3]

In the last part of this chapter we will consider the design of a grant program

---

[1] *Economic Report of the President,* February 1982 (Washington, D.C.: U.S. Government Printing Office, 1982), p. 321, table B-76.

[2] Under a private market system, these social benefits can often be captured by the innovating unit through the patent system, which "internalizes" the externality.

[3] For more description and an analysis of this program, see P. Berman and M. McLaughlin, *Federal Programs Supporting Educational Change: The Findings in Review, 4,* R-1589/4-HEW (Santa Monica, Calif.: The Rand Corp., 1975).

to achieve an equity goal: the "neutralization" of the influence of local wealth on local school finance decisions required by the California Supreme Court in the *Serrano v. Priest* decision. Another grant program with a possible justification on equity grounds is the federal general revenue-sharing program for cities. No single city can impose too progressive a tax system on its own, or those faced with high taxes might simply move outside the city boundaries. The federal government, on the other hand, has less need to be concerned about tax avoidance through locational choice. Thus the federal government might play the role of tax collector and, through revenue sharing, fund given services in a more progressive manner.

Aside from strict economic rationales for intergovernmental grants, political rationales may also be relevant. For example, some people feel that individual liberties are threatened when too much decision-making power is left in the hands of the central government; they might favor more local control of spending even if revenue were raised by the central government.

DESIGN FEATURES OF A GRANT PROGRAM

In this section we will go over economically relevant design features of an intergovernmental grant program. They can generally be classified into three categories: income effects, price effects, and choice restrictions. Knowledge of these three features can then be combined with a model of the decision-making behavior of the recipient to predict the effects of the grant. Initially we will assume that the recipient community can be treated like a utility-maximizing individual; from that perspective, the analysis of intergovernmental grants is identical with the welfare policies analyzed in the preceding chapter. (Welfare payments also are grants, but to individuals rather than collectivities.) Then we will consider model variants of the decision-making process, which challenge the "community utility–maximization" perspective.

Income Effects and Nonmatching Grants

Nonmatching grants, or block grants, affect the recipient primarily by altering the amount of funds available to spend on anything—a pure income effect. This can be seen in Figure 4-1, which shows the trade-offs faced by a community allocating its budget between government and private goods. Here government goods are goods and services provided through the local government and financed by taxes. Private goods are goods and services which community members buy as individuals in the marketplace with their after-tax incomes. Both government and private goods are measured by the dollar expenditures on them; the sum of expenditures on them equals the community budget level.

Let *AB* represent the pregrant budget constraint, and say the community initially is at a point like *C*. Then let the central government provide general revenue-sharing funds to the community to be used for any local government

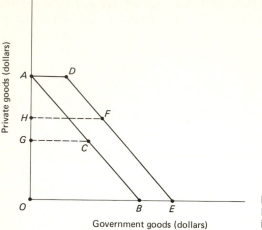

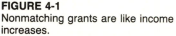

FIGURE 4-1
Nonmatching grants are like income increases.

goods or services.[4] The new budget constraint is then *ADE*. That is, the community still cannot obtain more than *OA* in private goods, can have government goods up to the amount at *D* (*AD* is the size of the grant) without sacrifice of private goods, and past *D* must sacrifice private goods to consume additional government goods. Since the grant does not alter the prices of either government or private goods, the *DE* segment is parallel to *AB* (as a pure income increase would be). Assuming that both government and private goods are normal, the community will increase its purchases of both; it will move to a point like *F* on the new budget constraint.

Note that the grant described above, restricted to use for purchasing government goods only, has the effect of increasing the community's consumption of private goods. Observe on the diagram the dollar amount of expenditure on private goods *OG* at *C* and *OH* at *F*. The ratio *GA/OA* is the tax rate that the community used before the grant program, i.e., the proportion of private wealth given up to have government goods. The ratio *HA/OA* is the tax rate after the grant program is introduced; it is *lower* than the initial rate. Thus the community meets the legal terms of the grant by using it for government goods, but it reduces the amount of its local wealth previously allocated to government goods.

To make sure the resulting allocation is clear, think of the community response as follows. Imagine that the immediate response to the grant is to reduce the tax rate so that exactly the same amount of government goods is being provided as before the grant. This meets the terms of the grant. But now the community can have the same private consumption as before and still have

---

[4] Throughout this chapter, we will not consider the sources of central government revenues used to fund the grant program. The pregrant budget level of the local community is measured *after* central government taxes have been collected.

resources left over to spend on anything. The extra resources are just like extra income, and the community behaves as an individual would: It buys a little more of everything normal including government goods. Thus, the revenue-sharing grant to the community has allocative effects identical with those of a tax cut of the same size by the central government. Its net effect is to increase spending on government goods, but not nearly by the amount of the grant.

In this example the restriction that the grant be used to purchase only government goods did not play an important role; the grant size is small relative to the funds the community would provide for government goods without any restriction. Figure 4-2 gives an illustration of a *binding constraint:* The size of the grant is greater than the amount the community would freely choose to spend on government goods. This occurs when the grant size (measured along *AD*) is large enough to cross the income-expansion path *OCK*.[5] If *ADE* is the budget constraint with the grant, the community will choose *D* as its optimal point: More of the covered goods than it would choose if the grant were a pure income supplement.[6] This is unlikely to occur with general revenue sharing, but it becomes more likely (for a given grant size) as the allowable uses of the grant are narrowed, as for new fire-fighting equipment. Grants that restrict the recipient to spend it on only certain types of goods are called *categorical* or *selective grants*.

---

[5] The income-expansion path is defined as the locus of utility-maximizing consumption choices at each possible income level when all prices are held constant.

[6] Note that the MRS at *D* must be less steep than at *J* (the preferred point if the categorical constraint is removed). Starting from the utility-maximizing point along an ordinary budget constraint, the slopes of the indifference curves passing through the budget constraint become progressively less steep to the right and more steep to the left. The utility level becomes progressively lower as we move away from *J* in either direction. Thus *D* is the maximum attainable utility, and fewer grant goods are purchased than if the categorical restriction were relaxed.

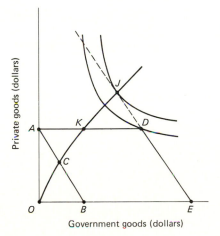

FIGURE 4-2
Nonmatching grant: The categorical constraint can be "binding."

Price Effects and Matching Grants

Analysis of the effect of *matching requirements* in a grant system is identical with the analysis of the Food Stamp Program. A matching grant offers the recipient unit a certain number of dollars for each dollar that the recipient unit provides out of its own resources (for the goods covered by the grant). For example, under a program to develop mass transit facilities, the federal government will provide $9 for every $1 that is raised by a local jurisdiction for mass transit in that jurisdiction. The program has a matching rate m of 9 to 1. In other grant programs the matching rate may not be as generous; perhaps the donor government might offer only $0.10 for $1 raised by the recipient ($m = 0.1$). It is also possible for the matching rate to be negative, which is a matter of taxing the local community for its expenditures on the specified good.[7]

To see how the matching grant affects the price of the covered goods from the recipient's perspective, imagine the recipient purchasing one additional unit. If the market price is P_0, the recipient provides the amount P_S (the subsidized price) which makes the following equation hold:

$$P_S + mP_S = P_0$$

or   Local funds + matching funds = total funds

Then it is easy to see that P_S, the price per unit as perceived by the recipient, is as follows:

$$P_S = \frac{P_0}{1 + m}$$

Thus a matching grant changes the terms of trade by which a community can exchange the good covered by the grant for other goods. In the example used for food stamps in the preceding chapter, the program provided a match of $1 for every $1 provided by the recipient. Thus the matching rate was 1, which translates into a price reduction of 50 percent. The recipient had to give up only $0.50 instead of $1 worth of other things for *each* $1.00 worth of food.

Matching grants may either be *open-ended* or *closed-ended*. In an open-ended grant there is no limit on the quantity the donor government is willing to subsidize. An open-ended grant is shown in Figure 4-3 by AC; the pregrant budget constraint is AB. In a closed-ended grant arrangement, on the other hand, the donor government will subsidize purchases only up to a certain amount. In Figure 4-3 this is illustrated as budget constraint AFG, where the limit is reached at F. These two cases can be seen to correspond exactly with the food stamp analyses of the preceding chapter (Figure 3-2). The effect of closing the grant is either to reduce purchases of the grant good and the total subsidy (if the community prefers a point on FC, no longer attainable because

---

[7] The district power-equalizing proposal for financing local schools has this feature; it is discussed later in the chapter.

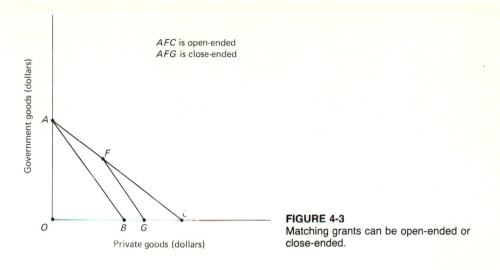

FIGURE 4-3
Matching grants can be open-ended or
close-ended.

of the restriction) or to have no effect (if the community prefers a point on *AF*,
which can still be attained).

To see the effect of the matching provision, let us compare an open-ended
matching grant with a nonmatching grant of equivalent total subsidy. In Figure
4-4 the open-ended matching grant is *AC,* and let us assume the community
chooses a point like *F*. Then we construct an equivalent subsidy nonmatching
grant, shown as *ADE*. Note that point *D* must lie to the left of point *F* (*DE* must
be parallel with *AB* and pass through point *F*).

We know, by "revealed preferences" reasoning, that the utility-maximizing

FIGURE 4-4
An open-ended matching grant
compared with a nonmatching grant.

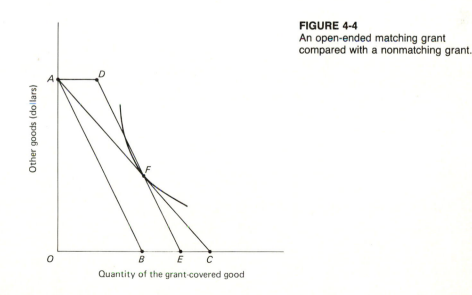

choice from *ADE* cannot be on the segment *FE*. That is, if the community preferred a point on *FE* to *F*, it could have chosen it under the open-ended plan. Since it did not, *F* must yield more utility than anything on *FE*. But point *F* is not itself a tangency point of an indifference curve with *DE*. Thus there are points on *ADE* which have greater utility than at *F*, and they must be to the left of *F*. If the categorical restriction is binding, *D* is the point of maximum utility; but since *D* is always to the left of *F*, it always implies a lower quantity of the grant-covered good than does the open-ended matching grant. Thus *the open-ended matching grant induces greater consumption of the covered good than an equivalent subsidy nonmatching grant*. Therefore, there is also a matching grant with lower cost to the central government that induces the same consumption of the covered good as the nonmatching grant.

The above result suggests that matching grants have an advantage when the program's objective is to alter the allocation of some specific good. This objective characterizes grants to correct for externalities. Matching grants are generally considered appropriate for these cases because the matching rate alters the price to recipients and, if chosen correctly, internalizes the external costs or benefits of the recipient's allocative choice. (An example is the optimal food-stamp subsidy when there are interdependent preferences, discussed in Chapter 3.) Equity objectives may concern the relative distribution of a specific good, like the school financing issue discussed later in the chapter, and matching grants can be appropriate for those policy objectives as well. Nonmatching grants, on the other hand, are most appropriate for general redistributive goals, like those of general revenue sharing.[8]

The Role of Choice Restrictions

We have already introduced several forms of choice restriction common to intergovernmental grants: the expanse of goods covered and the maximum quantity for which matching subsidies are available. Their importance depends not only on the allocative effects of the type we have been examining but also on institutional effects in terms of the information and transaction costs of grant administration and enforcement. We illustrate this by introducing another common restriction: maintenance of effort. This means that the recipient community is eligible only for grant funds to supplement its prior spending on the covered goods.

In Figure 4-5 is shown an example of how a nonmatching grant with *maintenance-of-effort* requirement achieves an increase in the government good at lower subsidy cost than an open-ended matching grant. The community initially has budget constraint *AB* and chooses *C*. Then a matching grant changes the budget constraint to *AD*, where the community chooses *E* (more of

---

[8] For a more detailed review of general economic policy issues concerning grants, see George F. Break, *Financing Government in a Federal System* (Washington, D.C.: The Brookings Institution, 1980).

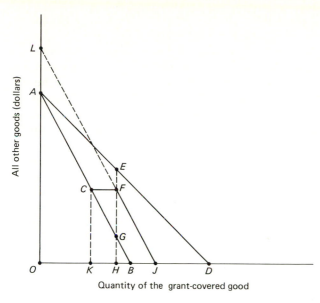

FIGURE 4-5
Maintenance-of-effort restriction.

Quantity of the grant-covered good

the grant good than if a cash-equivalent transfer had been made) at subsidy cost
EG. The same quantity *OH* of the grant good can be stimulated with the less
costly nonmatching grant with maintenance of effort represented by the budget
constraint *ACFJ*.

The shape of *ACFJ* can be explained as follows. Imagine the community
starting from point *A*. As it purchases units of the grant-covered good, it pays
the ordinary market price and proceeds down the *AB* line until it reaches point
C. At this point the quantity of the grant-covered good is *OK*, the amount
which maintains the effort of the community in terms of its past expenditure on
this good. Additional units of the grant-covered good can then be had without
sacrifice of other goods, because the community now qualifies for the grant and
the grant funds fully pay for them. Thus the community proceeds horizontally
and to the right from point *C* until it has spent the entire grant.

We have deliberately selected the grant which allows a maximum free
purchase of *CF*, which would bring the community to *OH* consumption of the
grant-covered good (the same quantity as would be chosen with the matching
grant *AD*). The dollar cost of this grant is *FG*: less than the cost *EG* of the
matching grant. Beyond point *F*, the community must sacrifice other goods at
the market rate in order to further increase consumption of the grant-covered
good; thus, the slope of *FJ* is the same as that of *AC*.

With budget constraint *ACFJ*, the theory of individual choice predicts the
community will choose point *F*. Given that it chooses point *C* with constraint
AB, point *F* is clearly preferable because it has more of one good and no less of
any other good. How do we know that some point on *FJ* is not even better?
Since the goods on each axis are normal, the community should increase the

purchase of both goods as income increases. That is, the income-expansion path would cross *LJ* (the extension of *FJ*) to the left of *FJ*. Thus, point *F* is closer to the optimal point on *LJ* than any other point on *FJ* and therefore must be preferred. The community chooses *F*; its consumption is *OH* of the grant-covered good (as with the matching grant); and the cost to the donor government is less than the cost with the matching grant (*FG* < *EG*).

This highlights the strong impact of the restriction. However, it does not change our prior results about the greater inducement of matching requirements per subsidy dollar. That result holds, as long as other things are kept equal (including the restrictions).[9] It does suggest that empirically one should not necessarily expect to find that matching grants have a more stimulative effect unless the restrictions are similar. However, it has been pointed out in the literature that the effectiveness of intergovernmental grant restrictions cannot be assumed; it depends upon the ability and effort made to administer and enforce the restrictions.[10] This caveat deserves further discussion.

In the chapter on efficiency we saw that whenever one consumer has an MRS for two goods different from that of another consumer, there is room for a deal. When economic agents make consumption (and production) choices, they usually do so in light of the prevailing market prices. However, a grant recipient subject to matching provisions or certain restrictions will typically have an MRS that is not equal to the prevailing market price ratio. Correspondingly, this creates incentives for deals. That is precisely what we saw in Chapter 3 in the discussion of individual food stamp grants and the illegal market for stamp resales. The recipient could increase utility by exchanging the food stamps at prevailing market prices. The income could then be used to purchase whatever goods generate the maximum utility in light of the recipient's preferences.

The desire to exploit divergences in the MRS can be applied to communities as well as individuals. Any intergovernmental grant program which contains provisions causing divergences of this nature may fail to achieve its inducement objectives if the recipient community can find ways of making the potential deals. Thus the success of a grant program depends not only upon the allocative effects we have described so far but also on the administration and enforcement capabilities.

Consider a community offered a grant which requires maintenance of effort. It may keep its local budget size constant but change the composition of what is purchased with that budget. For example, a community may feel a pressing need to obtain more medical equipment for its local hospital but the only grant offered to it is for criminal justice with maintenance of effort required. It therefore decides to make its hospital security guards part of the police force. The grant funds are then used to maintain police services exactly as they were

---

[9] To see this, it is left to the reader to compare the effects of matching versus nonmatching terms when both grants require maintenance of effort.

[10] See, for example, Martin McGuire, "A Method for Estimating the Effect of a Subsidy on the Receiver's Resource Constraint: With an Application to U.S. Local Governments 1964–71," *Journal of Public Economics, 10,* 1978, pp. 25–44.

plus the hospital security guards, and the hospital finds its revenues unchanged but its costs decreased by the cost of the security guards. Thus the hospital buys the additional medical equipment with the grant, even though that is not the way it appears on the record.

If a grant program continues for several years, it may become harder to enforce choice restrictions. For example the maintenance-of-effort requirements may be clear in the initial year, but no one can know for certain what the community would have spent without any grants in successive years. That is particularly true in times of high inflation, when nominal dollar increases in budgets may reflect an actual decline in services. Thus, over time, one would expect such a grant program to have effects more like those of an unrestricted block grant.

The point of these examples is to demonstrate the importance of recognizing the incentives created by any particular grant design. Part of any policy analysis of these programs is to consider whether the administration and enforcement of the grant provisions can be accomplished pragmatically; otherwise, the overall objectives of the program can be jeopardized. There is no standard answer to whether enforcement is easy or difficult; it depends upon the nature of the good. Black markets may arise readily with food stamps because illegal exchanges of the stamps are hard to prevent or detect; highways, on the other hand, are another matter.

Alternative Specifications of Recipient Choice Making

To this point in the chapter we have assumed that it is reasonable to treat a community as if it were an individual, as in having preferences or choosing a consumption bundle. But a community is not an individual. It is an aggregate of individual residents who have chosen to live in the area and may relocate if they wish. It also generally contains public and private agencies which may employ nonresidents and be owned by nonresidents; these people as well as the residents will be concerned about and affected by grant programs available to the community.

The community choice perspective we have been using is often given some theoretical justification by appeal to the idea of the median voter, according to which local decisions reflect the median voter's tastes and preferences. Imagine, for example, successive voting on school expenditures: After each level approved, a new and slightly higher level is voted on and the level selected is the last one to muster a majority. If the voters are then lined up in the order of the maximum school expenditures they have approved, it becomes apparent that the median voter determines the total expenditure. In short, the community preferences can be represented by those of the median voter.[11]

---

[11] This is offered only as a justification for why the community choice theory might predict collective decisions accurately. It is not intended to suggest that the choices are efficient; in fact, there is good reason to believe that no democratic voting procedure can be used to attain an efficient allocation of resources. See Kenneth Arrow, *Social Choice and Individual Values* (New Haven: Yale University Press, 1951).

Applied to local choices, the theory has been shown to be useful empirically in a number of studies.[12] However, it is important to recognize that over a period of time individuals and firms can choose their locations from among alternative communities in a given area. Charles Tiebout hypothesized that the ability to vote with their feet creates pressure on the community to provide the most attractive possible bundle of public services (including taxes) lest its occupants go elsewhere.[13] Of course, as people gradually relocate, this changes the characteristics of the median voter in any particular community. Thus, competition among communities is thought to be an important additional determinant of community decisions; its influence is undoubtedly greater in the long run than in the short run.

A second reason for tempering faith in the community choice perspective comes from theories of bureaucratic behavior. The idea is that any particular grant-receiving bureau is like flypaper: The grant will stick where it hits. Let us go back to our earlier example of the community seeking funds for new medical equipment but offered only a criminal justice grant with maintenance of effort required. We suggested that the hospital security guards would be added to the police budget in order to meet the legal terms of the grant and the allocative effect would be to use the extra hospital funds (once used to pay for guards) to buy the new equipment.

However, what happens if the police chief does not like this idea? In particular, what happens when the police insist they need to use the grant funds to purchase helicopters? There may be no effective political mechanism to prevent the police from doing just that. It depends, of course, on the political power of the police department relative to other officials (who may or may not sympathize) and the public. Perhaps the public view will receive greater weight over a longer period of time (e.g., through new elections of officials who have the power to hire and fire the police chief). Thus the grant may in the short run, because of local bureaucratic support, have the effect its designers intended; in the long run there is more chance that the income conversion effect will predominate.

In fact, empirical research on the effect of grants offers strong support that something like the flypaper effect occurs and persists. According to Gramlich, a pure income effect in almost all of the grant programs he reviewed would be to increase spending on the covered goods in the long run by $0.05 to $0.10 for each $1 of a nonmatching grant. (The figures correspond to an income elasticity near unity.) But the actual estimated income effects are always substantially larger, between $0.25 and $1.00.[14]

---

[12] See Edward Gramlich, "Intergovernmental Grants: A Review of the Empirical Literature," in Wallace Oates (ed.), *The Political Economy of Fiscal Federalism* (Lexington, Mass.: Lexington Books, 1977).

[13] See Charles Tiebout, "A Pure Theory of Local Expenditure," *Journal of Political Economy,* 64, No. 5, October 1956, pp. 416–424. For a recent test of this hypothesis and that of the median voter, see Edward Gramlich and Daniel Rubinfeld, "Micro Estimates of Public Spending Demand Functions and Test of the Tiebout and Median-Voter Hypotheses," *Journal of Political Economy,* 90, No. 3, June 1982, pp. 536–560.

[14] See Gramlich, op. cit.

Thus it seems that political and bureaucratic effects on grants can be significant and should be accounted for in making empirical predictions of a grant program's effects. The evidence, for example, contradicts the assertion based on individual choice theory made earlier that a nonmatching grant has the same effect on a community as a tax cut equal in size. The evidence suggests a nonmatching grant stimulates greater expenditure on the covered good than an equivalent tax cut would stimulate.

EQUITY STANDARDS WITH APPLICATION TO SCHOOL GRANTS[15]

In this section we build upon the introductory discussion of equity in Chapter 2 to consider some equity objectives that public policies might seek to achieve. Then we connect them to intergovernmental grants by reviewing their application to school finance policies, with particular attention to the requirements of the California Supreme Court in its *Serrano v. Priest* decision of 1976.

Equity Objectives

In general, *equity* or *fairness* refers to the relative distribution of well-being among the people in an economy. But although this identifies the topic clearly, it provides no guidance to what is equitable. There are a number of shared principles of equity which can serve as analytic guides, but in any particular situation the analyst must recognize that there may be no consensus about which one is most applicable. Nevertheless, analysts can describe the effects of proposed or actual policies in terms of the particular equity concepts thought most relevant.

The use of well-defined concepts of equity not only helps users of the analysis to understand policy consequences of concern to them but avoids arbitrariness in the analytic methodology. Even if the analyst feels that none of the better known principles are applicable to a particular policy, those principles can still serve as a context for the analysis. By having to argue that some other concept is more appropriate than the better known ones, this helps to produce a clarity of reasoning that otherwise might be absent.

It is useful to distinguish two broad categories of equity concepts: those that relate to outcomes and those that relate to process. Outcome concepts of equity are concerned with the existence in the aggregate of variation in the shares that individuals receive. Process concepts of equity are concerned with whether the rules and methods for distributing the shares among individuals are fair. Keep in mind that these are different standards by which to judge a system of resource allocation; a system can do well by one of these two broad concepts

---

[15] Much of the material in this section is explained in more detail in Lee Friedman, "The Ambiguity of Serrano: Two Concepts of Wealth Neutrality," *Hastings Constitutional Law Quarterly, 4,* 1977, pp. 97–108, and Lee Friedman and Michael Wiseman, "Understanding the Equity Consequences of School Finance Reform," *Harvard Educational Review, 48,* No. 2, May 1978, pp. 193–226.

and poorly by the other. Furthermore, changes made to improve the system in one equity dimension can cause deterioration as judged by the other (and, of course, can affect efficiency as well). We will illustrate this for school finances shortly.

It should also be noted that there is an issue concerning the type of shares that should be scrutinized in the light of an equity norm. One position is that we are interested in *general distribution:* how policies affect the overall distribution of utility in the economy, or measurable proxies for utility like income or wealth. A different position is that we are interested in the equity of the distribution of particular goods and services. James Tobin has called this latter concern *specific egalitarianism.*[16] The underlying philosophy of specific egalitarianism is that although it might be fine to allow most goods to be allocated and distributed purely as the rewards of market forces, different rules should apply to a limited category of goods and services. The basic necessities of living (e.g., food, shelter, clothing, essential medical care) should be guaranteed to all, and civic rights and obligations (e.g., voting, the military draft, jury duty) should not be allocated purely by the forces of the market.[17] Most of the equity concepts discussed below can be applied either to the general redistributive effects or to the distribution of a specific good or service of concern.

There are two outcome concepts of equity which are commonly used: strict equality and a universal minimum. The norm of strict equality means that all people should receive equal shares. There are numerous ways of measuring the degree to which a system attains that standard.

One common method is to graph the Lorenz curve and calculate its associated Gini coefficient. To illustrate, Figure 4-6 shows a hypothetical *Lorenz curve* for yearly jury duty. The percent of total population (eligible for jury duty) is measured along the horizontal axis and the percent of total annual jury service is measured along the vertical axis (in terms of person-days spent on jury duty). Imagine ordering the population from those with the least jury service to those with the most and plotting the percent of total service supplied by the xth percent of population who have served the least. As it is drawn, 25 percent of the population provided no service, the next 25 percent provided 10 percent of jury service, the next 25 percent provided 15 percent of jury service, and the last 25 percent provided the remaining 75 percent of jury service.[18]

---

[16] James Tobin, ''On Limiting the Domain of Inequality,'' *Journal of Law and Economics, 13,* October 1970, pp. 263–278.

[17] Note that this can imply a rejection of utilitarianism. For example, we can imagine allowing the buying and selling of votes, which would increase individual welfare. Yet the laws prohibiting the transfer of voting rights suggest that the underlying norm of one person, one vote applies to the distribution of the voting right itself and not the individual utility that might be derived from it.

[18] Note that the shape of the Lorenz curve in this example might shift dramatically if we redefined the period of time considered, e.g., 2 years instead of 1 year. Obviously this does not imply that the longer period is fairer; both are pictures of the same distribution and must represent equal fairness. The analyst must be careful to recognize the effect of choosing a particular definition of the units being distributed and to keep the units constant when making comparisons.

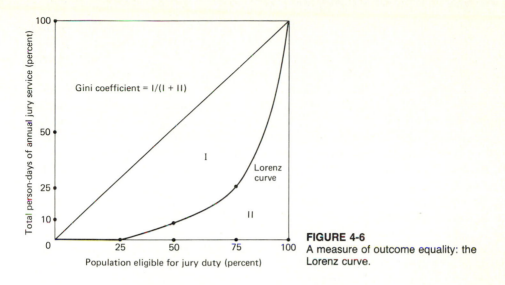

FIGURE 4-6
A measure of outcome equality: the Lorenz curve.

The Gini coefficient is defined as the ratio of area I to area I + II.[19] If each person in the population provided the same jury service, the Lorenz curve would coincide with the 45° line, area I would shrink to zero, and the Gini coefficient would be zero. At the other extreme, if one person provided all the jury service, the Lorenz curve would coincide with the outer bounds of area II and the Gini coefficient would be 1. Thus the Gini coefficient is a measure of the degree to which strict equality is attained: zero if it is attained exactly, positive if there is any inequality, and increasing to a maximum of 1 as the inequality

[19] Mathematically, if $d_1, d_2, \ldots, d_n$ represent the days served as juror by each of the n people in the eligible population, the Gini coefficient equals

$$\frac{\sum\limits_{i=1}^{n} \sum\limits_{j=1}^{n} \left| d_i - d_j \right|}{2n^2 \bar{d}}$$

where $\bar{d}$ is the mean of the d_i.

As an illustrative example, suppose there are only four people and the jury days served by each (ordered from highest to lowest) are 75, 15, 10, and 0. Then there are a total of 100 days of jury service, and the average number of days per person is $\bar{d} = 100/4 = 25$. The denominator of the formula for the Gini coefficient is $2n^2\bar{d} = 2(4^2)(25) = 800$. The numerator is:

$$
\begin{aligned}
\sum_{i=1}^{n} \sum_{j=1}^{n} |d_i - d_j| = & \, |75 - 75| + |75 - 15| + |75 - 10| + |75 - 0| + |15 - 75| + |15 - 15| \\
& + |15 - 10| + |15 - 0| + |10 - 75| + |10 - 15| + |10 - 10| + |10 - 0| \\
& + |0 - 75| + |0 - 15| + |0 - 10| + |0 - 0| \\
= & \, 460
\end{aligned}
$$

The Gini coefficient is then .575 = 460/800.

worsens. If the Lorenz curve for one policy alternative lies strictly within the Lorenz curve for another policy alternative, the first is unambiguously more equal and will have a lower Gini coefficient.

Like all single-parameter measures of the degree of equality, the Gini coefficient does not always reflect legitimate concerns about the location of the inequality.[20] For example, two Lorenz curves that cross can each have the same Gini coefficient: One curve will have greater inequality among the people in the lower end and the other greater inequality among those in the upper end. Thus, one must be cautious about comparing two very different distributions by this or any other single-parameter measure. A simple technique for helping to reveal this potential difficulty is to display on the same graph the Lorenz curves of the distributions being compared or, similarly, to construct a chart which shows what each decile of the population receives under the alternative distributions.

The other outcome standard of equity is the universal minimum, which means that each person should receive a share that is at least the size of the minimum standard. Unlike strict equality, application of this norm requires that a particular minimum standard be selected. During the Nixon administration, a Negative Income Tax proposal was debated by the Congress and did not pass, although a majority favored such a plan. One part of the majority insisted upon a higher minimum guarantee than the other part would agree to support, so the majority became two minorities.

Once a minimum standard is selected, one can count the number or proportion of individuals below the minimum and the total quantity required to bring all those below up to the minimum. Often the analyst will pose several alternative minimum standards to discover the "equity cost" of increases in the standard. However, this latter exercise can be much trickier than one might suspect.

One issue is whether the source of supplementation to those below the standard must come from those above it or whether other goods or services can be converted into the good or service of concern. For example, if minimum educational resources per child are the issue, one need not take educational resources away from those who have them in abundance. More educational services can be produced by doing with less of all other goods. On the other hand, a shortage of water in an emergency might require the redistribution of water from those who usually consume larger quantities (e.g., owners of swimming pools) to others. That is, the supply of water during the relevant time period may be fixed, or perfectly inelastic. When the good in question has positive elasticity of supply, it need not be directly redistributed. In the elastic case, it is not hard to show that the efficiency cost of achieving the minimum is

---

[20] Another common measure is the coefficient of variation, which is defined as the standard deviation divided by the mean. It is zero at perfect equality and increases as the distribution becomes more unequal. For a general discussion of inequality measurement, see A. B. Atkinson, "On Measurement of Inequality," *Journal of Economic Theory, 2,* 1970, pp. 244–263.

lower by expanding production than by direct redistribution of the existing quantities.[21]

Not only does the cost bear on the method of achieving the minimum; it also bears on whether a minimum is more desirable than strict equality. For example, consider whether it might be appropriate to ensure strict equality in the distribution of the entire privately produced GNP. If all potential suppliers of resources (labor and nonlabor) to the market knew that they would end up with the average share independently of their individual decisions (each having a negligible effect on the total), all would choose to supply very little and the GNP would plummet drastically. The achievement of strict equality does not seem to be a very pragmatic objective for a market-oriented economy. That is not to say that moving closer toward it is an unreasonable objective. Rather, past some point, the reduction in equality would not be worth its efficiency cost.[22] On the other hand, a reasonable universal minimum might be attainable well before the economy reached its "most equal" overall distribution. Thus cost considerations might influence the choice of equity standards to emphasize.

Of course, the choice of standards still comes down to a moral judgment about which is best. In the education example given above, a universal minimum was posited as the objective. But many people feel that is just not the relevant standard; they might insist that all children be educated equally. The responsibility of the analyst in this situation is to make clear that there are competing conceptions and to try to clarify the consequences of achieving the alternative standards.

Having discussed some issues relevant to the selection of an outcome standard of equity, let us turn to the process standards of equity. Process standards become applicable when inequality of share sizes is explicitly permitted. The concern here is not with how much aggregate inequality exists but with whether the share that each person ends up with has resulted from a fair process. There may be only one winner and many losers of a lottery, but if the entry conditions are the same for all and each entrant has an equal chance of winning, we might think the distribution to be perfectly equitable.

The economic agents in an economy might be viewed in an analogous way. When individuals make resource allocation decisions in an economic system, there is often uncertainty about what the outcome will be. For example, consider the sequence of decisions to invest in higher education by attending college, to choose a major subject, and to select a job from the jobs offered after

---

[21] Imagine assigning a tax to each person having more than the minimum standard so that the total tax will provide enough resources to bring all up to the minimum. Then give each taxpayer the choice of paying the tax directly from his or her existing stock of the good or by its cash equivalent. All the taxpayers will prefer to give cash, which is then used to produce additional units of the good. Thus it is more efficient to expand production (when it is elastic) than to redistribute directly.

[22] Recall the discussion in Chapter 3 about the Negative Income Tax, which illustrated that welfare guarantees reduced work effort more or less depending on the design.

graduation. These represent a series of contingent decisions which affect but do not completely determine the income streams of particular individuals. After all the decisions are made, we observe that, on average, those with college degrees have higher incomes than those without, those with certain majors have higher incomes than other college graduates, and those who accepted jobs in certain industries earn higher incomes than similarly educated people who entered other industries. Whether this whole process is thought fair depends on the entry conditions to colleges, major subjects, and industries, as well as on how the payoffs are distributed within each part of the whole sequence. If, because of their sex, women are denied entrance to the best schools or are not considered for promotion within a particular industry, then one might think that this process of resource allocation is unfair.

There are several standards by which an attempt is made to capture the ideal of process equity. A fundamental one is *equal opportunity:* Each person should have the same chance of obtaining a share of a given size. However, in practice it is virtually impossible to tell whether a particular person has been given equal opportunity. For example, periodically the government has a lottery, which any citizen can enter for a minimal fee, to award oil leasing rights on federally owned land. If a loser in the government lottery claims that his or her number did not have the same chance of being drawn as every other number, how can one tell after the fact? Because it is often the case that each person makes a specific decision only rarely (e.g., to enter the lottery), it may be impossible to know whether the outcome is explained by chance or by denial of equal opportunity. On the other hand, if a person made many sequential bets on the same roulette wheel, it would be possible by using statistical laws to tell whether the game had been rigged against the person.

Suppose that the oil lease lottery really was rigged to favor certain entrants. Could that be discovered through an examination of the results? If some identifiable group of entrants (e.g., private citizens as opposed to oil companies) does not win its fair share of leases, it may be taken as a strong indication of rigging.[23] But without group evidence of this kind, the rigging may go unnoticed. Thus, it may be necessary to fall back on tests involving a group of participants to substitute for the lack of multiple tests involving a single participant. If there really is equal opportunity for each person and if we divided the participants into two groups, each group ought to receive a similar distribution of share sizes.[24]

In fact, sometimes we simply substitute the concept of neutrality for particular groups instead of the more stringent concept of equal opportunity for

---

[23] The lottery for oil and gas leasing was temporarily suspended on February 29, 1980, by Interior Secretary Cecil Andrus. The government charged that some oil companies had cheated by submitting multiple entries for individual parcels, in violation of federal rules. See the articles in *The Wall Street Journal* on April 8, 1980 (p. 12, col. 2) and October 6, 1980 (p. 29, cols. 4–6). Unfortunately, the articles do not make clear how the government detected the apparent rigging.

[24] In this manner, we use knowledge about the outcomes for the purpose of judging the process. Note this is quite different from judgment by the outcome standards themselves.

each individual. That is, we may accept a resource allocation process as fair if it does not discriminate against selected groups of particular social concern. These groups usually become identified by suspicions that they have been discriminated against in the past. The courts, for example, often apply "strict scrutiny" in cases in which the alleged denial of equal opportunity or equal treatment arises by classifying people into groups by race or wealth.[25] This scrutiny was relevant to the findings that poll taxes are unconstitutional and that states must provide counsel to poor individuals accused of serious crimes. In both rulings, a key part of the arguments was that wealth was a suspect means of classification and that state action prevented poor people from having opportunity equal to that of others. Let us refer more loosely to the groupings thought to be of particular social concern as the *suspect groupings* and define *simple neutrality:* The distribution of shares within a suspect group should be identical to the distribution of shares among all others.

Whenever there is equal opportunity, there will be simple neutrality. If each person has the same chance as other persons of receiving a share of any given size, then any large groupings will be characterized by simple neutrality. Each group will receive approximately the same proportions of any given share size, and the average share size in each group will therefore be approximately the same.

However, simple neutrality with respect to one suspect group does not mean there is equal opportunity. Overweight people, for example, can be systematic victims of discrimination and thus are denied equal opportunity. The discrimination will not affect neutrality with respect to race (the suspect group in this example) as long as each race has the same proportion of overweight people in it. Thus simple racial neutrality can hold while, at the same time, equal opportunity is not available to all. Simple neutrality is therefore a less stringent standard than equal opportunity.

One reasonable objection to the simple neutrality concept is that there may be legitimate reasons for group differences in share sizes. For example, excessive weight might be just cause for denial of employment as a police officer. If Caucasian applicants are more overweight than others and in all other respects the applicants grouped by race have identical characteristics, then simple neutrality would not be expected to hold because a smaller proportion of Caucasian applicants would be offered employment. To account for legitimate deviations from simple neutrality caused by these *exceptional characteristics,* we define the standard of *conditional neutrality:* If the members of a suspect group have exceptional characteristics identical with those of all others, the distribution of shares within each group should be identical.[26] Thus, suspect

---

[25] "Strict scrutiny" is a legal term for a particular type of judicial test for constitutionality. As the term suggests, it is more difficult for laws to withstand judicial examination with strict scrutiny than with other tests. For more information see David L. Kirp and Mark G. Yudof, *Educational Policy and the Law* (Berkeley, Calif.: McCutchan Publishing Corp., 1974), chap. 6, part IV.

[26] Exceptional characteristics can also be a reason for deviating from the equal opportunity principle, and we could define an analogous standard of conditional equality of opportunity.

factors are those which are not allowed to cause distributional differences, and the exceptional characteristics are factors which are allowed to cause those differences.

Whenever there are differences in exceptional characteristics across suspect groupings, simple and conditional neutrality offer different standards. (Both cannot be met by one system.) Conditional neutrality is less stringent than simple neutrality in the sense that it permits larger differences between the shares received by each group. Even if one finds that a system is conditionally neutral, it is wise to examine the effects of the exceptional characteristics. Exactly how much difference is to be allowed because of an exceptional characteristic depends upon the specific situation being analyzed.

Because the allowable difference due to an exceptional characteristic is a matter of judgment, it provides an obvious source of abuse. If a school wishes to discriminate covertly against women, and it happens that women receive lower SAT scores than men, it can reduce the proportion of women accepted by increasing the weight placed on SAT scores in admissions. An analyst reviewing this policy (e.g., as a condition for the school's eligibility for federal funds) has no special authority to decide what the correct weight is and must instead try to clarify the consequences of using alternative weights and offer arguments why some particular range is more reasonable than another.

Equity in School Finance

In this section we apply both the theory of grants and the equity concepts to the problem of public school financing. We shall focus primarily on the California system, which was declared unconstitutional by the state supreme court in its 1976 *Serrano v. Priest* decision. However, the general problems considered apply to many other states as well. First we will review the system found defective and the equity requirements enunciated by the court, and then we will consider what system might meet those requirements.

The Equity Defects Identified in *Serrano*   To illustrate the defective system, we can use diagrams similar to those we have been using so far. In Figure 4-7 we represent the budget constraints of a "rich" school district (subscript R) and a "poor" school district (subscript P). Along the horizontal axis public school expenditures per child E are measured, and along the vertical axis wealth for all other goods per child W is measured.[27] The dashed lines represent

[27] Note that two districts can have the same budget constraint in this diagram but different total wealth, caused by differences in the number of children each has in attendance at public schools. The "per child" units are convenient for the analysis presented here, but one must be careful in their use: A community will respond to changes in its total wealth as well as changes in the size of the school population, and accurate empirical prediction of the overall response may require more information than the proportion of the two. Consider two communities which are initially perfectly identical; one then experiences a doubling of real wealth while the other experiences a 50 percent drop in the public school population. Their new budget constraints on the diagram will continue to be identical, but there is no theoretical reason to expect them to choose the same point on it. The

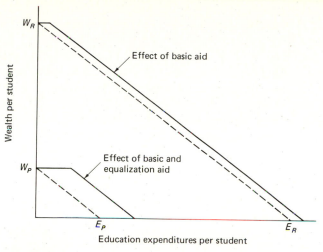

FIGURE 4-7
California foundation plan for school financing.

a hypothetical school financing system that is purely local; i.e., that in which the state contributes nothing to the local school district. Under such a system, it would hardly be surprising to find the rich district spending more on education per child than the poor district; that will happen as long as public education is a normal good.

The actual system declared unconstitutional was not purely local. California, like many other states, had been using a system of school finance known as a foundation plan. Under it, every school district was entitled to some state aid. The amount of state aid received was an inverse function of the district property wealth per child.[28] All districts received at least $125 per child, an amount referred to as *basic aid*. This was the only aid received by rich districts. Poor districts received additional funds in the form of *equalization aid,* the actual amount of which was determined by a somewhat complicated formula. For our purposes it is sufficient to note that poorer districts received greater amounts of equalization aid.

In Figure 4-7 the solid lines represent the budget constraints of the two representative districts including state aid. The grants are equivalent to nonmatching grants restricted to educational spending. The rich district is

---

choice depends on the respective wealth elasticities for spending on children versus other goods. For the purposes here, we are holding the number of children in the representative districts constant.

[28] Because the property tax is used almost universally to raise local funds for education, the measure of district wealth used by the courts and other government agencies is the total assessed valuation of property in the district. The appropriateness of this proxy measure is discussed later in the chapter.

shown as receiving a smaller grant than the poor district. This plan should make spending in the two districts more equal, since the larger grant will have a bigger income effect (assuming positive nonincreasing marginal effects of budget increases). However, there is no reason to think this system would lead to equal spending. The size of the grants received by poor districts would have to be very large to do so, since high-wealth California districts have been spending more than four times the amount spent by low-wealth districts.[29] Note that this system of grants has no price effects and that we showed earlier that expenditure inducements for particular goods can best be achieved by matching grants (which make use of price effects). However, we have not yet discussed what equity standard is relevant in this case.

Why might a court find, as in the *Serrano* decision, that the system we have described denies "equality of treatment" to the pupils in the state?[30] The fact that there are differences in expenditure levels from district to district is not what the court found offensive; the decision made it very clear that the court was not requiring strict equality. Nor did the court require a universal minimum, although it did express particular concern about the low expenditure levels typical for children attending school in low-wealth districts. Thus neither of the outcome standards was found applicable in this setting.

Instead, the court held that the state had created a system of school finance which violated wealth neutrality. Children living in low-wealth districts (the suspect class) had less money spent for their public education on average than children living in other districts had. The court held that the education a child receives (measured by school expenditure per child) should not be a function of the wealth of his or her parents and neighbors as measured by the school district property tax base per child.

It is interesting to consider briefly this choice of an equity standard. It is one which is concerned with the expenditure on a child in one district *relative* to a

[29] Grants of this magnitude would certainly cause recipient districts to select the consumption bundle where the restriction is binding. To see this, imagine a district which is very poor and is spending 10 percent of its wealth measured by property value (a very high proportion). If we gave the district a grant 3 times larger than its current expenditure, its wealth would be increased by 30 percent, i.e., 3 times 10 percent. How much of that increase the district would spend on education if unconstrained depends on the wealth elasticity. Empirical research suggests it is inelastic.

By a unitary elasticity estimate, the district would freely choose to spend 3 of the 30 percent wealth increase on education, for a total of 13 percent of the original wealth. But the grant restriction is that education expenditures must be at least 30 percent of original wealth (i.e., the size of the grant), so the restriction must be binding. The wealth elasticity would have to be something like 7 in this example for the constraint to be nonbinding. That is not plausible. It is more implausible given the unrealistically high proportion of spending on education assumed initially, and that a grant as small as 3 times the initial level would achieve equality if completely spent on education.

[30] It is important to note that the specific legal interpretation of phrases like "equality of treatment" and "equal opportunity" can be quite different from their general definitions as analytic concepts. I know few who would argue, for example, that the provision of a public defender ensures neutrality or equal opportunity as we have defined it. It may provide a universal minimum, but the court is satisfied that the public defender ensures "equal opportunity" by legal standards.

To maintain these definitional distinctions, reference to legal meanings will be indicated by quotation marks or distinct terminology.

child in another. In theory, violations of this standard can be removed either by raising the expected expenditure level for those initially low or lowering the expected level for those initially high or both. The average expenditure level for the population as a whole is not restricted (no minimum has been held to be required), and there is no restriction on the overall distribution in terms of how much deviation from strict equality is allowed. The requirement is only that children in property-poor districts as a group have educational opportunities like those of children in all other districts.

Why should a neutrality standard be required as a matter of general policy? If we think back to our discussion of equity concepts, it is plausible to argue that a basic education is a requirement for modern-day life much like food, clothing, and shelter. Argued more modestly, perhaps a basic education is one of those goods which we wish to guarantee to everybody. But this logic calls for a universal minimum; and since the supply of educational resources is elastic, there is no reason to be concerned about the *relative* educational expenditures on different children.[31]

Another reason for concern about equity in education is the belief that it affects the other opportunities available to an individual during the course of a lifetime and that there is a social responsibility to move toward process equality for those other opportunities. By this rationale education is seen as a means to an end; policies like compensatory education might be derived from it. This concern does involve the relative expenditure levels for education, but it does not imply strict equality, equal opportunity, or neutrality as a requirement for educational expenditures. Requirements like the latter can prevent the attainment of equal opportunity for other life opportunities (e.g., if compensatory education is necessary), although they may represent an improvement from the status quo.

A somewhat different rationale from the above focuses more on the importance of even-handedness by government, particularly when its actions bear on vital interests of the citizenry. That is, one could argue that education is a vital interest; and because the state influences the education provided by local governments within it, it must ensure that its influence is even-handed on all the children of it.[32] Since it is the state which defines local district boundaries and determines the financing rules that local districts face, it must choose the rules to ensure the same availability of educational opportunities to the children in each district.

Of course, the state may influence district behavior in many ways, and as a

---

[31] An important issue not discussed here is the extent to which there is a relation between educational expenditures, real educational resources, and education absorbed by children. Most researchers in this area think the linkages are very weak. See, for example, E. Hanushek, "Throwing Money at Schools," *Journal of Policy Analysis and Management, 1*, Fall 1981, pp. 19–41.

[32] Perhaps this could be interpreted with some flexibility. Certain circumstances might present sufficiently compelling reasons to allow exceptions to even-handedness, e.g., compensatory education.

value judgment one might wish to apply the even-handedness rationale to all of the state influences. But the court expressed only the narrower concern about the opportunities affected by the wealth classifications (i.e., district boundaries) made by the state. Thus a rationale for a neutrality standard can be derived from an underlying concern with state even-handedness in regard to vital interests when they involve suspect classifications. It is concern of this type which is manifested as a matter of law in the *Serrano* decision.

The Design of Wealth-Neutral Systems   Now let us turn to the problem of designing a school finance system which meets the wealth-neutrality standard. Any state system which ensures equal spending, like full-state financing, is wealth-neutral. However, local control of schools is an important value which makes that politically unattractive.[33] One could also redraw district boundaries so that each district had equal wealth. There are two serious disadvantages to that approach: (1) It is politically unpopular because it threatens the status of many of the employees of the school system (e.g., district superintendents) and upsets families that have made residential choices partly on the basis of the school district characteristics. (2) In districts comparable in size with those now existing, the wealth of one relative to that of another can change significantly in just a few years (which would necessitate almost continuous redistricting). One could redistrict into much larger units, but then there are disadvantages similar to full state control.

As an interesting aside, the choice of residential location mentioned above suggests a Tiebout approach to wealth neutrality: If families really have free choice about where to locate, the system is wealth-neutral no matter how the state draws district boundaries or what grants are given to different districts. Obviously the court did not accept that reasoning, or it would have found the system free of state constitutional defect. Although few people would argue that actual residential choices (in terms of school districts) are made independently of wealth (e.g., zoning restrictions which prevent construction of low-cost housing), another way to neutralize the influence of wealth is by open enrollment. That is, suppose each child had the option of choosing (at no additional cost) a school from alternatives in the area which represented a broad range of expenditure levels. Then one might consider such a system wealth-neutral. The option has not been seriously considered, to the author's knowledge.

We are left with alternatives that maintain the existing districts but attempt to neutralize the influence of wealth. At this point it is time to confront the issue of whether the required neutrality is simple or conditional. The court decision left the matter ambiguous, despite the fact that the differences between the

---

[33] Hawaii is the only state to have full-state financing. One can separate the financing and use of resource decisions, but most would still consider the move to state financing as a diminution of local control.

concepts as applied to the remaining alternatives are great.[34] We construct simple models of school expenditure decisions and the effects of grants primarily to illustrate the difference between the equity standards. We wish it to be clear that the actual design of grant systems to achieve either standard involves consideration of a number of important factors which are omitted from the simple models used here. In the following section, we will briefly note a number of those factors.

Simple wealth neutrality requires that there be no functional relation between the wealth of a school district and its public school expenditure level on a per student basis. This implies that the expected expenditure of a district in one wealth class equals the expected expenditure of a district in any other wealth class.[35]

In Figure 4-8 we illustrate the aim of simple neutrality. The dashed lines represent the opportunities available to two representative districts based solely upon their local wealth. The state can pick any average school expenditure level it wants as the target (call this $\overline{E}$), and then it must design a grant system which causes districts in each wealth class to choose an *average* school expenditure level $\overline{E}$.[36] With knowledge of the price elasticity of school expenditures for each wealth grouping, this can be achieved through a variable matching grant program (which is really equivalent to a variable price change program). Depending on the target level $\overline{E}$, this may involve negative matching rates for the higher-wealth districts.

To illustrate the calculation, let us hypothesize that the demand for educational expenditures per child has a simple form embodying constant elasticity with respect to price and wealth,[37] e.g.:

[34] The labels "simple" and "conditional" are simplifications used for convenience. There are a number of special sources of funds, like federal funds for handicapped children, which could be included as part of the total expenditures and analyzed for their appropriateness in terms of exceptional characteristics. For purposes of the analysis here, we simply remove them from the expenditure base under examination and consider only the equity of general-purpose funds. However, we could describe the same choice as between two alternative specifications of conditional neutrality by including the special-purpose funds in the base. The equity of special-purpose funds does deserve scrutiny; for some thoughts on the subject see Friedman and Wiseman, op. cit.

[35] The earlier examples of simple neutrality were illustrated with dichotomous groupings, but the principle applies to a suspect classification into multiple groupings. In this illustration of district wealth classification, we treat each wealth level as a separate and continuous classification. The assumption here is that the court would be equally offended if middle-wealth or upper-middle-wealth districts were systematically handicapped relative to all other districts.

[36] Note this is not the same as requiring every district in a given wealth class to have the same expenditure. Indeed, the point is to allow local discretion as long as its exercise is not a function of wealth. Thus some districts with wealth W_L might choose to consume more than the $\overline{E}$ chosen by the representative district of Figure 4-8, and others less. The requirement is that their average equal $\overline{E}$.

[37] These assumptions are made for ease of illustration. The price elasticity of $-.4$ is realistic, although estimates of it in the literature vary between 0 and -1. A realistic wealth elasticity, based on the estimates available in the literature, would be lower than unitary and probably between .25 and .50. See Edward Gramlich, op. cit., and R. P. Inman, "Optimal Fiscal Reform of Metropolitan Schools," *The American Economic Review, 68,* No. 1, March 1978, pp. 107–122.

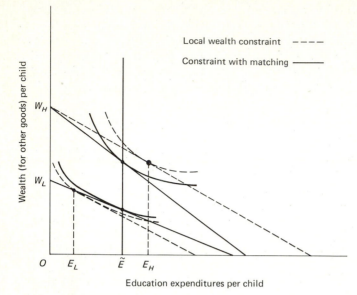

FIGURE 4-8
Matching grants can achieve simple wealth neutrality.

$$E = 0.03P_E^{-.4}W$$

Then a high-wealth district with assessed property value of $70,000 per student will spend (assuming no grants):

$$E_R = 0.03(1.00^{-.4})(70,000)$$
$$= 2100$$

Similarly, a lower-wealth district with only $20,000 per student will spend:

$$E_P = 0.03(1.00^{-.4})(20,000)$$
$$= 600$$

Suppose the state decides on a target spending level of $1600 to achieve by variable matching grants. Then it must make the rich district face a local price P_L such that

$$1600 = 0.03(P_L^{-.4})(70,000)$$
or
$$P_L \approx \$1.97$$

To make $P_L = \$1.97$, the state must set a matching rate m such that

$$P_L + mP_L = P_E$$

or
$$1.97 + m(1.97) = 1.00$$
and
$$m = -0.49$$

That is, the state can induce the higher-wealth district to spend $1600 by requiring that, for each dollar raised locally for education, 49 cents must be returned to the state. This illustrates how a negative matching rate may arise. This rate provides the state with revenues of $1537 per student in that district.[38]

For the lower-wealth district, the state must set a local price P_L such that

$$1600 = 0.03(P_L^{-.4})(20,000)$$
or
$$P_L \approx \$0.09$$

To make $P_L = \$0.09$, the matching rate must be set such that

$$0.09 + m(0.09) = 1.00$$
or
$$m = \$10.11$$

That is, the state offers this district $10.11 for every dollar raised locally. This positive matching rate will cost the state $1456 per student.

Naturally the state, in determining the target level, will consider how much funding it is willing to provide out of general revenues to pay for the matching grants as well as how much it can feasibly recapture through negative matching rates. Furthermore, to reduce the uncertainty about finding the correct matching rates to achieve neutrality (since the actual elasticities may be neither constant nor known), the state can use choice restrictions like those we have already discussed. As some indication that it is indeed possible to do that, let us examine the short-run effects of a school finance reform in Illinois.

Before 1973 the state of Illinois financed its schools with a system much like that illustrated for California in Figure 4-7. Because local financing provided the bulk of the school funds, the higher-property-wealth districts had on average higher school expenditures per child. The 1973 Hoffman-Fawell Reform introduced changes which substantially increased aid to lower-wealth districts. Its main component was a guarantee: Any district with assessed value per child of less than $42,000 would receive, from its own taxes and state aid, revenues equal to what its tax rate would raise if it did have a wealth of $42,000 per child. Other important provisions of the reform boosted enrollment figures of districts in proportion to the number of students in it from low-income families, ensured that no district was made worse off, and ensured that funding increases were introduced gradually.[39]

---

[38] Local revenues = 1600/0.51 = $3137. The state share is $3137 − $1600 = $1537.
[39] For more information about the reform, see Friedman and Wiseman, op. cit.

TABLE 4-1
EQUITY OF SCHOOL EXPENDITURES, ILLINOIS UNIT SCHOOL DISTRICTS

Decile*	Strict equality standard expenditure deciles			Simple wealth neutrality standard wealth deciles	
	1972–1973	1974–1975		1972–1973	1974–1975
1	$ 702	$ 791		$742	$ 958
2	750	850		779	966
3	775	880		843	944
4	798	912		815	962
5	824	952		862	1000
6	852	982		857	978
7	892	1016		886	988
8	916	1061		893	944
9	948	1120		892	968
10	1038	1201		920	1006
$\bar{E}$‡	849	973	R^2†	0.31	0.05
CV§	0.120	0.125			

* All decile figures are the mean expenditures per student in that decile.
† R^2 is the proportion of expenditure variation accounted for by a cubic wealth function.
‡ $\bar{E}$ is the expenditure mean for the full sample.
§ CV is the coefficient of variation.
Source: Lee Friedman and Michael Wiseman, "Understanding the Equity Consequences of School Finance Reform," *Harvard Educational Review, 48,* No. 2, May 1978, pp. 193–226.

Table 4-1 contains data from all unit school districts in Illinois except Chicago.[40] The 1972–1973 figures show the equity of the system before the 1973 Hoffman-Fawell finance reform act, and the 1974–1975 data indicate the short-run effects of the reform. Deviation from the strict equality standard can be examined by first classifying each student by the expenditure level per student in his or her district and then ordering the students by their classifications from lowest to highest. Table 4-1 shows the average expenditure level for each decile of students when ordered this way. Strict equality would result in identical average expenditures per decile, rather than the rising expenditure levels shown in the table. The greater the rise in average expenditure from decile to decile, the farther the distribution is from strict equality. Note that by a strict equality standard, there is more inequality after the reform than before: The coefficient of variation of expenditures per student increased from .120 to .125.

Deviations from simple wealth neutrality can be examined by first classifying each student by the property wealth level per student in his or her district and then ordering the students by this wealth classification from lowest to highest. The last two columns of Table 4-1 show the average expenditure level

---

[40] The data are taken from Friedman and Wiseman, op. cit., tables 6 and 7 and equations (1) and (6). Unit districts are those which comprise both elementary and secondary schools. Chicago was excluded because the data did not permit adjustment for differential input costs (a general problem mentioned in the following section). Only general-purpose funds were included in the calculations. For a full explanation of the technical assumptions and qualifications to the findings, see Friedman and Wiseman, op. cit.

for each decile of students ordered by the district property wealth level. Simple wealth neutrality would result in identical average expenditure levels in each of the deciles. The rise in average expenditure level from decile to decile in 1972–1973 indicates that the distribution deviates from simple wealth neutrality. However, there is a clear improvement by 1974–1975, and the 1974–1975 expenditures would pass the neutrality test required by the California *Serrano* court.[41] Note that this illustrates the possibility of a conflict between equity standards mentioned earlier: Greater neutrality can be associated with greater overall inequality.

To this point we have illustrated only the simple wealth neutrality interpretation of the Serrano decision. However, it is possible that the court intends to require conditional wealth neutrality with the district tax rate choice as the exceptional characteristic. That is, the court may define wealth neutrality to mean that those districts choosing the same tax rate should have the same expenditure level. This is equivalent to ensuring that an equal percentage sacrifice of district wealth buys the same amount of education everywhere. The interpretation is consistent with the court's indication that a system known as district power equalizing (DPE) would be acceptable.[42]

Under a DPE plan the state would publish a schedule associating each possible expenditure level with a property tax rate. Any district that wanted to spend, say, $1000 per child would have to tax itself at the rate associated with that expenditure level on the state schedule, e.g., 4 percent. If the district revenues collected at the 4 percent rate are not enough to provide $1000 per child, the state provides a subsidy to make up the difference. If the district revenues exceed the amount required to provide $1000 per child, the state recaptures the excess. But the only way a district can have an expenditure level of $1000 per child is to tax itself at the specified rate of 4 percent.

The advantage of the conditional neutrality interpretation is that it is relatively easy to design a system to meet the standard. As with the above illustration, no knowledge of district price or wealth elasticities is required. But there is a cost to this interpretation as well. One must ask why the district tax rate choice should be an exceptional characteristic.

One rationale might be to rely purely on a notion of taxpayer equity. However, wealthy districts that wish to spend a lot on education incur a substantial financial burden in the form of revenues recaptured by the state, whereas equally wealthy districts that do not wish to spend as much escape the burden. Why should equally wealthy districts provide differing contributions to state revenues? Taxpayers may not consider this very equitable.[43]

---

[41] The court indicated that wealth neutrality ruled out having wealth-related expenditure disparities of more than $100 per child, apart from all special funds like those for compensatory education. It is possible, however, that the court would not consider a decile breakdown fine enough.

[42] Another way to reconcile the court's acceptance of DPE as a possible solution is if it simply assumed (incorrectly) that simple wealth neutrality would result from using it. For more discussion of this issue, see Friedman and Wiseman, op. cit.

[43] The taxpayer equity issue will also depend on how district wealth is defined. We discuss this issue later.

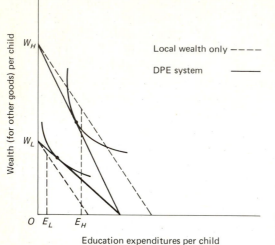

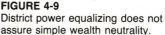

FIGURE 4-9
District power equalizing does not
assure simple wealth neutrality.

Perhaps more importantly, wealth will remain as an important determinant of educational spending. That is, one might reject the taxpayer equity rationale and argue instead that the burden on high-spending wealthier districts is intended to protect children by neutralizing the influence of wealth on education-spending decisions. But there can be no assurance that it will do so.

To show this, Figure 4-9 illustrates the budget constraints that result from using a DPE system. Observe that if all districts tax themselves at 100 percent, all must end up at the same point on the horizontal axis. As a matter of policy, the state can select any point on the horizontal axis as the common point; the farther to the right, the greater the total expenditure—and state aid—will be. Under the most commonly discussed DPE proposals, the new budget constraints can be represented as straight lines which intersect the vertical axis at the district's own wealth level. This is equivalent to the state selecting a common wealth base whereby educational expenditures in a district equal the district's tax rate choice times the common base.[44] The important characteristic for our purposes is that the state schedule determines the new budget constraints for all districts.

Let us see if the state can construct a DPE system to achieve the same result as in our earlier example: inducing districts of all wealth classes to average $1600 expenditure levels. We illustrated the procedure for two districts, one with a $70,000 wealth base and the other with a $20,000 base. Let us start with the $70,000 district. We know that to induce it to spend $1600 with our hypothetical demand curve, it must face a price of $1.97 for each $1.00 of education spending received. Geometrically, this is equivalent to choosing the

---

[44] The budget constraints need not be straight lines. For example, the state could increase the "common base" as the tax rate increases.

solid line from W_H in Figure 4-9. (The price determines the slope.) This means that the district would raise $3137 in revenues (see footnote 38 on p. 123) from its own base, or 4.481 percent of its wealth. ($1537 is recaptured by the state.) Thus to induce this district to spend $1600, the state schedule would have to associate the tax rate of 4.481 percent with a $1600 expenditure level.[45]

By the DPE principle, any district that has a $1600 education expenditure level must also sacrifice 4.481 percent of wealth. This means that the $20,000 district would be required to give up $896 ($= 0.04481 \times 20,000$) in order to have a $1600 expenditure level (the state provides $704 in aid); this in turn means that the price it faces is $0.56 ($= 896 \div 1600$) for every $1.00 of education spending. Geometrically, we observe that DPE requires the budget constraint for the low-wealth district of Figure 4-9 to go from W_L to the intersection point of the horizontal axis and the high-wealth budget constraint. The price of $0.56 is minus the slope of the W_L budget constraint. But at a price of $0.56, the district would demand

$$0.03(0.56^{-.4})(20,000) = \$757$$

In other words, associating the tax rate of 4.481 percent with a $1600 expenditure level ensures that the low-wealth district will *not* choose it: The implicit price it faces is still too high to induce it to choose a $1600 expenditure level. Thus this example illustrates the inconsistency of the simple and conditional neutrality standards as they apply to school finance.[46] Presumably the school finance system in California must meet one of these two standards eventually, although only time and the courts will determine which one.

Other Issues of School Finance Equity   When the *Serrano* issues are being explained, it is common to illustrate inequities by describing the plight of children in low-wealth districts. However, it is also important to recognize that many children from poor families do not live in low-wealth districts. In California, for example, the majority of such children live in districts that are property-rich; an example is San Francisco, which has property wealth more than twice the state average. Under a plan meeting either neutrality standard

---

[45] This DPE schedule is a linear function of the tax rate τ:

$$E = a + b(\tau)$$

To find the unknown constants a and b, note that $E = 0$ when $\tau = 0$, so $a = 0$. (If there are uniform nonmatching state grants, $a > 0$.) Then $E = b(\tau)$, and since $E = 1600$ when $\tau = 0.04481$, $b = \$35,706$. Then the state-determined schedule, which applies to all districts, is $E = \$35,706(\tau)$.

[46] It is important to note that the demand curve is hypothetical. In the example, DPE is weaker than simple neutrality requires. But if the demand for public education is price-elastic and wealth-inelastic, then DPE would induce lower-wealth districts to spend more than higher-wealth districts. Feldstein estimates that the latter is the case. (See M. Feldstein, "Wealth Neutrality and Local Choice in Public Education," *The American Economic Review, 65*, No. 1, March 1975, pp. 75–89.) However, there is considerable uncertainty about how districts would actually respond to such a plan.

and keeping average spending in the state at approximately the same level, these children could be made substantially worse off.

It is important for analysts to think carefully about how to avoid or minimize this or other unintended harms when implementing standards like those required in Serrano. Below are some suggested directions which an analyst working on the issue might explore; they are not intended to exhaust the range of equity issues that are encountered in school financing.

First, one dimension of a school finance plan which does not inherently interfere with neutrality is the proportion of funds derived from nonmatching revenues as opposed to matching grant arrangements. Earlier we suggested that full state financing meets both neutrality standards. It is possible to create a neutral system which maintains some degree of local choice but relies heavily on nonmatching revenues. For example, the state could provide $1200 to all students from general revenues and allow districts the option of adding up to $1000 to it by a matching grant system. This would reduce the stress due to recapture placed on city budgets (assuming the state general revenues are raised by broad-based taxes), at least as compared with a full matching grant system. Furthermore, by narrowing the range of expenditure variation which can occur due to local decision making, it would make control of the variation easier. That can be an absolutely critical design feature if one is trying to achieve simple wealth neutrality, given the uncertainty about actual district price and wealth elasticities.

Second, the analyst should think carefully about what measure to use of a district's fiscal capacity (i.e., ability to generate tax revenues). There is no law that requires the property tax base to be used as the measure of district wealth, nor is there any economic argument which maintains that total property value is the proper measure of a district's fiscal capacity. For example, most analysts think that the level of personal income in a district is an important determinant of true fiscal capacity. Thus, a wealth measure which depended on both property base and personal income could be constructed. It is no surprise that the hybrid measure would favor cities that have large low-income populations. One reason why the concern about them arises is the sense that property wealth alone does not give an accurate picture of fiscal capacity.

Another possibility is that commercial, industrial, and residential property should be weighted differently on the ground that the ability to tax different types of property is different. For example, it may be less possible to impose taxes on industrial wealth than on residential wealth if industry is more likely to relocate; many communities offer tax breaks to new industries as locational inducements.[47]

Third, the nominal dollar expenditures may not be the best measure of the

---

[47] See, for example, Helen F. Ladd, "State-wide Taxation of Commercial and Industry Property for Education," *National Tax Journal, 29,* 1976, pp. 143–153. It is interesting to think about the effects of a Serrano solution on the willingness of communities to have industry locate within them. To the extent that expenditure levels are determined by the "common base" of a DPE plan, every community has less incentive to attract industry to it.

educational opportunities being provided through the schools. Although that remark could stir up a hornet's nest (e.g., when is one educational opportunity better than another?), there are some cost differences from district to district in providing identical resources. For example, to provide a classroom of 65 to 68 degrees in northern California during the winter costs a great deal more than in other parts of the state. Similarly, to attract a person with high teaching ability to an inner city school might require a higher salary than a suburban school would have to offer to obtain comparable talent. Thus it might be appropriate to adjust the expenditure figures to reflect differences in the cost of obtaining educational resources. However, analysts who have considered the problem do not find it an easy one to solve.[48]

Fourth, the student populations of equally wealthy districts may differ substantially in regard to the educational resources appropriate to each. For example, some districts might be characterized by high proportions of children from non-English-speaking families or of children who are mentally or physically handicapped or of children who are in high school. Thus one has to think carefully about how to best account for these differences. One approach would be that of Illinois: to develop a pupil-weighting system which gives a higher measure of enrollment in districts with students who are relatively expensive to educate.

Fifth, it is important to keep in mind that the long-run effects of any school finance reform may be substantially different than those observed in the short run. Over time, residents and firms may change their locations because of the reform. The use of private schools rather than public schools may change as the reform causes changes in the attractiveness of public schools. All of these factors result in changes in a district's preferences for public education and its wealth base, and thus one expects its response to any particular grant system to change as well. A reform like that in Illinois, which achieves simple wealth neutrality in the short run, may itself set in motion forces which cause deviations from simple neutrality in the long run. Thus it is important to consider analytic models which account for the long-run effects.[49]

▽ **An Exercise in the Use of a Social Welfare Function as an Aid in Evaluating School Finance Policies**   The idea of using a social welfare function as a way of making evaluative judgments which combine equity and efficiency was introduced in Chapter 2. In this section we illustrate some of the mechanics of

[48] See, for example, W. Norton Grubb, "Cost of Education Indices: Issues and Methods," in J. Callahan and W. Wilken (eds.), *School Finance Reform: A Legislator's Handbook* (Washington, D.C.: National Conference of State Legislatures, 1976). See also Julian Le Grand, "Fiscal Equity and Central Government Grants to Local Authorities," *The Economic Journal, 85,* September 1975, pp. 531–547.

[49] Illustrating such models requires analytic methodology beyond our scope at this point. However, examples of them are in Ladd, op. cit.; Inman, op. cit., and Lee Friedman and Michael Wiseman, "Toward Understanding the Equity Consequences of School Finance Reform," in National Institute of Education, *School Finance and Governance: Research Perspectives for the Future* (Washington, D.C.: U.S. Government Printing Office 1980).

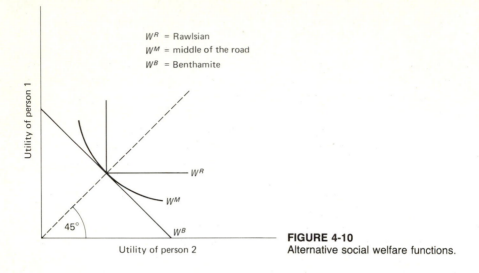

FIGURE 4-10
Alternative social welfare functions.

constructing a social welfare function for use in evaluating school finance grant systems. Realistic examples involve detailed empirical specification, and the hard analytic work of choosing parameters carefully and cogently is essential to the success of any such analysis. Here we wish to keep the mechanics as transparent as possible and thus greatly oversimplify by building on the illustrative example of the prior section. However, it is strongly recommended that several actual applications be studied before use of this technique is attempted.[50]

Figure 4-10, like Figure 2-7, displays three social indifference curves that represent different emphases on efficiency and equality (the Benthamite straight line W^B, the Rawlsian right angle W^R, and the middle of the road W^M). Although we know that there is no social consensus about an appropriate welfare function, it may be that individual politicians and interest group representatives have social preferences that are known to be closer to one function than another. Thus if policies could be evaluated with functions representing the interests of the decision makers, such an analysis could be helpful to those decision makers in deciding what policies to support.[51] This is

[50] The simple exercise presented here was actually inspired by a very thoughtful simulation study of school finance reform in New York. See R. P. Inman, op cit. An example using social welfare functions in another policy area is to be found in N. H. Stern, "On the Specification of Models of Optimum Income Taxation," *Journal of Public Economics*, 6, 1976, pp. 123–162.

[51] Policy conclusions from this type of analysis, and a defense of them, would have to be presented in a nontechnical way. For example, the analyst might learn that when the matching rate in a certain grant plan goes above $2 for every local dollar, the ranking by the Benthamite criterion declines rapidly. The analyst would have to realize that the Benthamite criterion is most relevant to the large middle class (because each person's utility level is weighted equally). Then one can state a conclusion and explain it in language understood by policy makers, e.g., "The matching rate should not be more than $2 for every local dollar. Otherwise, the state budget level would have to be raised and the crucial support of the Taxpayer's Association would be jeopardized."

most likely to be useful when the consequences of adopting policies are complex: gains and losses of varying sizes distributed over different interest groups in a non-obvious way.

Social welfare functions can be constructed to take the basic shape of any of the social indifference curves shown in Figure 4-10. For example, consider the family of social welfare functions represented by

$$W = \left(\sum_{i=1}^{n} U_i^{\delta} \right)^{1/\delta}$$

where $\delta \leq 1$. If we let $\delta = 1$, the social welfare function collapses to the Benthamite sum of utilities. As $\delta \to -\infty$, the function becomes more proequality and approaches the Rawlsian standard. Middle-of-the-road functions are generated by using values of δ between the extremes. The parameter δ simply specifies the weight to be given to each person; lower values of δ give greater weight to people with lower utility levels. Thus, once one knows the values of individual utility levels to enter as the arguments of the welfare function, one can see if a policy proposal ranks favorably over a broad range of values for δ. (If it does, a potentially broad range of support for the policy is implied.)

How does one know what values of individual utility levels to enter? After all, utility is nonmeasurable and noncomparable among different people. Here we deviate from consumer sovereignty and seek to identify a way of making utility comparisons which reflect the social judgments of potential users of the analysis.

Typically, the assumption is that policy makers will count people who are identical in terms of certain observable characteristics as having the same utility. For the case of school finance, we will assume that each household's utility level can be fairly represented by a function $U(E,B_T)$, where E is the amount of education consumed by the household (measured by the educational expenditures on its children) and B_T is the after-education tax wealth the household has available for all other goods (using the property tax base per child as a proxy variable adjusted for taxes paid). Both variables are observable, and households with the same E and B_T will be counted as having the same utility.

The specific functional form of the utility function is chosen to be common to all persons and to weight the observable characteristics in a manner that policy makers will judge reasonable. Here real-world statistics are important. For example, in the case of school finance for this exercise, we choose the form

$$U = B_T^{0.97} E^{0.03}$$

We will show in a moment that this form implies that households will choose to spend 3 percent of their wealth on education.[52] This percentage is precisely

---

[52] This form is a special case of the more general form $U = B_T^{\alpha} E^{1-\alpha}$, where α is the utility-maximizing proportion of the budget spent on B_T and $1 - \alpha$ for E. This function, called the Cobb-Douglas utility function, is discussed in Chapter 5.

what we "observed" in the hypothetical prereform districts in the preceding section. That is, the district with a $20,000 property tax base per child chose a $600 school expenditure level (per child), and the $70,000 district spent $2100 per child. In each case the ratio of expenditures to the tax base is 0.03 (= 600 ÷ 20,000 = 2100 ÷ 70,000). The policy maker aware of the equality might reasonably conclude that households prefer the proportion, and might wish the analysis to penalize deviations from it caused by policy.

Imagine that each district in our example is composed solely of homogeneous households with one child per household (this keeps the example as simple as possible). Then each household in a district will pay local taxes equal to the educational expenditure on its child (with no state intervention). If each of the households in one district has a pretax wealth of B_0, we now show that the utility function above implies it will spend 3 percent of B_0 on education. Each family wishes to choose B_T and E in order to maximize utility subject to the budget constraint $B_0 = B_T + E$. We form the Lagrangian

$$L = B_T^{0.97}E^{0.03} + \lambda(B_0 - B_T + E)$$

To maximize utility, we take the partial derivatives with respect to B_T, E, and λ, set them equal to zero, and solve the equations simultaneously:

$$\frac{\partial L}{\partial B_T} = 0.97B_T^{-0.03}\,E^{0.03} - \lambda = 0 \tag{i}$$

$$\frac{\partial L}{\partial E} = 0.03B_T^{0.97}\,E^{-0.97} - \lambda = 0 \tag{ii}$$

$$\frac{\partial L}{\partial \lambda} = B_0 - B_T - E = 0 \tag{iii}$$

In equations (i) and (ii) move the λ to the right-hand side and then divide (i) by (ii):

$$\frac{0.97B_T^{-0.03}E^{0.03}}{0.03B_T^{0.97}E^{-0.97}} = 1$$

or, simplifying

$$\frac{0.97E}{0.03B_T} = 1$$

$$\frac{E}{B_T} = \frac{0.03}{0.97}$$

The above equation shows that each household will wish to spend 3 percent of its wealth on education and 97 percent on other things, independently of its wealth level. Since within a district all the households in our example are assumed to be homogeneous, they will unanimously agree as local voters to spend $600 per child in the $20,000 district and $2100 per child in the $70,000 district.

Now we are almost ready to compare the three policies used in the preceding section's illustrations: do nothing, achieve simple wealth neutrality with target spending of $1600, and achieve conditional wealth neutrality with the high-wealth district spending $1600. First we must clarify some additional assumptions used in the calculations below.

We treat our two districts as if they were equal in population and comprised the state. The state treasury always breaks even. The surplus generated by each reform (recaptures exceed state aid) is assumed to be distributed in equal payments to each household in the state (e.g., a tax credit for households with children in school). The redistributions have small income effects which we ignore. We continue to rule out household locational changes or the substitution of private for public education, so that the district responses to the reform remain as calculated in the preceding section.

The effects of the three previously discussed policies on the households are summarized in Table 4-2. The positions of a low- and a high-wealth household with no reforms in effect are given in column 1. Since in this case a household's tax payment equals the district educational expenditure per child, B_T in the low-wealth district is $19,400 (= $20,000 − $600) and in the high-wealth district it is $67,900 (= $70,000 − $2100). The utility level U is calculated (here and in the other columns) by substituting the levels of B_T and E in the utility function chosen earlier. For example, the utility of each family in the low-wealth district is

$$U = 19,400^{0.97}(600^{0.03})$$
$$= 17,479$$

TABLE 4-2
SIMULATED EFFECTS OF SCHOOL FINANCE REFORMS ON HOUSEHOLDS

Districts		School finance policies		
	Pre-reform	Simple wealth neutrality (matching grants)	Conditional wealth neutrality (DPE)	Equal spending (full state financing)
Low-wealth district				
E	600	1,600	757	1,600
B_T	19,400	19,896	19,576	19,289
U	17,479	18,447	18,285	17,901
High-wealth district				
E	2,100	1,600	1,600	1,600
B_T	67,900	66,903	67,465	67,511
U	61,176	59,814	60,302	60,342

Columns 2 and 3 show similar calculations for the simple and conditional wealth neutrality proposals illustrated in the preceding section. The only entries that require explanation are those for B_T. Recall that the low-wealth district under simple wealth neutrality received $1456 in matching state aid and contributed only $144 of its own wealth to reach the $1600 expenditure level. The high-wealth district under this proposal raised $3137, of which the state recaptured $1537. Therefore, the state had net receipts of $81 (= $1537 − $1456) for every two households, or $40.50 per household. Under our assumption, the state rebates $40 (rounding off) to each household. Therefore, the after-tax wealth B_T of the household in the low-wealth district is

$$B_T = \$20,000 - \$144 + \$40$$
$$= \$19,896$$

Similarly for the high-wealth district

$$B_T = \$70,000 - \$3137 + \$40$$
$$= \$66,903$$

The after-tax wealth figures for the DPE proposal used to achieve conditional wealth neutrality are derived similarly. Note that in all cases the sum over both districts of educational expenditures and after-tax wealth for the two representative households is $90,000 (the joint budget constraint).

Column 4 of Table 4-2 contains a new policy alternative not previously discussed: equal spending per child achieved by full state financing of schools with a statewide property tax. A uniform expenditure of $1600 per child is made with state revenues. This level is chosen for comparability with the simple wealth neutrality proposal. This means that the state tax rate τ applied to both the low- and high-wealth districts must raise $3200 in revenues for every two households:

$$20,000\tau + 70,000\tau = 3200$$
$$90,000\tau = 3200$$
$$\tau = 3.556 \text{ percent}$$

The low-wealth district makes tax contributions to the state of $711 per household (= 0.03556 × 20,000), and the high-wealth district contributes $2489 (= 0.03556 × 70,000). These figures are used to determine the after-tax wealth in each district.

As we look across the columns, it becomes clear that no one of these proposals is obviously better than the others. Furthermore, their relative impacts on any single district are not obvious from the observable variables only. The DPE proposal, for example, barely increases educational spending in the low-wealth district compared to full state financing, but it is nevertheless ranked higher: The bigger after-tax wealth outweighs the lower educational spending.

The rankings are, of course, a consequence of the utility function chosen. Keep in mind that this choice has some justification: the observation that households across the wealth classes seem to prefer spending 3 percent of their wealth on education. The full-state-financing plan has the family in the low-wealth district spending 7.7 percent of its total after-tax wealth (20,889 = 1600 + 19,289) on education, whereas under the DPE plan the percentage is 3.72. Although the matching grant plan that achieves simple wealth neutrality also has the family spending a high percentage on education (7.44 percent), note that it must be ranked higher than the DPE plan because it gives the household more of both goods.

Table 4-3 shows the rankings of the four policy alternatives when evaluated by three different social welfare functions: Benthamite ($\delta = 1$), Rawlsian (the utility level of the worst-off household),[53] and a middle-of-the-road function ($\delta = 0.1$). Recall that the Benthamite function is simply the sum of the utility levels, and the middle-of-the-road function (using subscripts L and H for the households in the low-wealth and high-wealth districts) is

$$W^M = (U_L^{0.1} + U_H^{0.1})^{10}$$

On looking at the table, we see that a different alternative is ranked first by each of the social welfare functions. Although there is no consensus about what is best, note that the full-state-financing proposal is dominated by both the simple and conditional wealth neutrality proposals. (That is, the latter two are ranked higher than full state financing by all three evaluation rules.) Thus, unless policy makers have a very strong social preference for equal educational spending per se, we can eliminate this proposal from consideration.[54] Also, we can see that those with preferences other than Benthamite have some incentive to form a coalition and try to eliminate the prereform system. (They prefer any of the reform proposals to no reform at all.)

In a sense this exercise only begins to suggest how social welfare functions may be useful. A much more powerful use is in the design of the alternatives. We picked specific proposals rather arbitrarily: Why do we consider a full-state-financing proposal only at the $1600 expenditure level, for example, when some other level might rank much higher by one or more of the social welfare functions? It can be shown that the best full-state-financing plan by the Benthamite rule (indeed, any of the social welfare rules) is to set the expenditure level at $1350, with a statewide property tax rate of 3 percent,

---

[53] When handling large amounts of data, it can be convenient to approximate the Rawlsian function. Even though the Rawlsian function is the limit as $\delta \rightarrow -\infty$, it turns out that $\delta = -10$ is usually approximate enough. This approximation applied to the data in this example is typically within 0.00006 percent of the exact number.

[54] Recall that neutrality and educational equality are social values *in addition to* the social welfare criteria.

TABLE 4-3

SOCIAL WELFARE RANKINGS OF THE ALTERNATIVE SCHOOL FINANCE REFORMS

(1 = Best, 2 = Second Best, 3 = Third Best, 4 = Last)

		School finance policies		
	Prereform	Simple wealth neutrality (matching grants)	Conditional wealth neutrality (DPE)	Equal spending (full state financing)
Household utility levels*				
U_H	61,176	59,814	60,302	60,342
U_L	17,479	18,447	18,285	17,901
Social welfare functions†				
Benthamite	1 (78,655)	3 (78,261)	2 (78,587)	4 (78,243)
Middle of the road	4 (34,147,618)	2 (34,607,792)	1 (34,613,245)	3 (34,281,495)
Rawlsian	4 (17,479)	1 (18,447)	2 (18,285)	3 (17,901)

* H = high-wealth district; L = low-wealth district.

† The actual numerical scores for the alternatives are not comparable across the different welfare functions because the functional form changes. These numerical scores are presented in parentheses after the ranking of the policy alternative.

$U_L = 17,909$, $U_H = 60,370$, and $W^B = 78,279$.[55] With computer simulation one can identify the optimal financing plans of each type of reform according to various social welfare functions. When a simulation with actual data is undertaken, that is a way to begin to clarify the most promising alternatives for serious policy consideration.[56]

SUMMARY

In this chapter we have continued to rely primarily on the utility maximization model by using it to develop the theory of intergovernmental grants. Based upon the theory, a crucial distinction between grant types is whether there is a matching requirement: Grants with matching requirements have effects similar to those of price changes, whereas nonmatching or block grants have only income effects. However, this basic analysis must be modified to take account of the choice restrictions which are common design features of actual grant programs: the degree of selectiveness, whether the grant is open- or close-ended, and maintenance-of-effort requirements. The effectiveness of these restrictions depends upon their administration and enforcement; the analyst should be aware that grant recipients have incentive to convert a grant into its pure income equivalent.

One result that generally holds up within the context of these models is that a matching grant will induce greater spending on the covered goods than an equivalent subsidy nonmatching grant (other things being equal). This suggests that matching grants are more likely to be appropriate when the grant purpose is to correct an externality. Nonmatching grants are more likely to be appropriate when the purpose is general redistribution.

Other reasons for qualifying the predictions of these models are based upon the recognition that a community is not a single-minded maximizer. The

---

[55] For the full-state plan, the sum of taxes from one household in each district must equal twice the chosen expenditure level (in order for the treasury to break even):

$$20,000\tau + 70,000\tau = 2E$$

$$\tau = \frac{E}{45,000}$$

The household in the low-wealth district therefore always pays $\frac{4}{9}E$ in taxes ($= 20,000E/45,000$), and the high-wealth household pays $\frac{14}{9}E$. The best Benthamite plan requires choosing E to maximize U_L plus U_H:

$$\text{Maximize} \left(20,000 - \frac{4E}{9}\right)^{0.97} E^{0.03} + \left(70,000 - \frac{14E}{9}\right)^{0.97} E^{0.03}$$

The solution to this is $E = \$1350$; in fact, it is the level for a statewide plan preferred by each district independently and would therefore be preferred if any of the social welfare functions were used.

[56] Inman, op. cit., does precisely that. Similarly, Stern, op. cit., undertakes an exercise to determine optimal income tax rates.

Tiebout model makes us aware that individual locational choices influence community decision making by changing the make-up of the community; policy changes may induce changes in locational patterns and thus affect prediction of the policy effects. The bureaucratic model suggests that decision-making power does not rest exclusively with residents or voters; a grant may stick like flypaper to the bureau receiving it and thus prevent or slow down its conversion into an income effect.

Grants are often used to achieve equity goals. To strengthen understanding of grant uses as well as of equity in general policy analysis, a number of important and competing concepts of equity must become part of the analytic framework. One issue is the extent to which equity consequences refer *only* to effects on the general distribution of well-being (i.e., net effect on utility levels) or include specific egalitarian goals (e.g., equal distribution of jury service). In both cases, equity may be measured against outcome standards or process standards.

Outcome standards refer to the aggregate amount of variation in the shares (e.g., income, food) that individuals receive. Two common standards of this type are strict equality and a universal minimum. One factor besides moral feeling which influences the choice of the standards (as well as the methods for achieving them) is the elasticity of supply of the good(s) in question. The Lorenz curve and Gini coefficient illustrate methods of measuring the amount of outcome equality.

Process concepts of equity concern not the aggregate amount of variation but the rules and methods for assigning shares to individuals. These concepts become relevant once it is accepted that there will be inequality; the question is whether the share that each person ends up with has resulted from a fair process. A fundamental process standard is that of equal opportunity: Each person should have the same chance of obtaining a share of a given size. In practice it is often impossible to tell whether a particular individual had equal opportunity, and we sometimes try to test the implications of equal opportunity statistically by comparing the expected outcomes in a large group with the actual group outcomes.

In some instances, we substitute the less stringent concept of neutrality for particular groupings (the suspect ones) instead of equal opportunity for all. Simple neutrality means that the distribution of shares within a suspect group should be identical with the distribution of shares among all others. Often there will be exceptional characteristics which cause legitimate deviations from simple neutrality. (For example, the elderly will be overrepresented on juries if employment is a legitimate excuse from jury duty.) When deviations arise, the concept of conditional neutrality becomes appropriate: If the members of a suspect class have exceptional characteristics identical with those of all others, the distribution of shares within each group should be identical.

Armed with the theory of grants and some specific ideas about equity, an application to school finance is presented. The California foundation system of school finance, struck down as unconstitutional in the *Serrano* decision, is a nonmatching grant system which reduces aggregate inequality from the level that a purely local system would produce. However, the court was not concerned with the aggregate amount of inequality. It was offended because the state failed to provide a wealth-neutral system: Children in property-poor districts experienced much lower levels of school expenditures than did children in other districts.

The court was ambiguous as to requiring simple or conditional wealth neutrality; the ambiguity depends on whether the district tax rate choice is considered an exceptional characteristic. Several systems of school finance, e.g., full state financing, can achieve both simple and conditional neutrality, but for political reasons it is likely that the existing districts will continue to have at least some power over their individual expenditure levels. In that case, either (but not both) of the neutrality standards can be met by a system of matching grants. Simple neutrality is harder to achieve because it requires knowledge of each district's demand curve, but the Illinois experience suggests that, at least in the short run, it can be had. Conditional neutrality is easier to design but may result in substantial correlation between district wealth and expenditures. An optional section illustrates how social welfare functions can be used to aid in the evaluation of alternative policies.

A number of other issues must be considered in designing an equitable school finance policy. For example, a naive application of the neutrality principle in California could substantially and unintentionally worsen the position of children of lower-income families living in the large cities, since those cities are considered property-rich. Careful thinking about the degree of state general funding versus matching grant funds, the measurement of a district's true fiscal capacity, the district cost variation of providing equivalent educational resources, the measurement of pupil needs, and the long-run consequences of reform, can lead to a fairer system of finance and a reduction in unintended adverse consequences of seeking greater equity.

EXERCISES

4-1 Several years ago the Minnesota legislature was debating how to give financial relief to the poor from higher heating bills expected in the future. One suggestion was that any increase in expenditure per household compared with the expenditure of the prior year be billed directly to the state. A second suggestion was to give each household a heating voucher (a nonmatching grant to be used only for heating the household) of an amount equal to the difference between last year's expenditure and the cost of the same quantity at this year's higher prices. Both suggestions would give each household more utility than it had last year, but only one would help conserve energy. Explain.

4-2 Sometimes the political implications of grants may not be what they seem. At one time, members of the liberal caucus in Congress introduced legislation to provide increased funding for local social services. It came as a great surprise when the caucus was approached by several conservatives with an offer of bipartisan support. These same conservatives had long attacked spending on social services as wasteful; now, however, they found that their voters perceived them as "heart-less." Given the financial plight of local governments, they suggested dropping the matching requirement of the liberal version. This would allow them to take some credit for the legislation and to counteract their heartless image. The liberals readily agreed.

a Had these conservatives softened? Or can you offer an explanation for their behavior consistent with their long-standing objectives? *Hint:* Use diagrams and assume some local community choice under a matching plan; then construct an equally costly nonmatching plan.

b The answer to (*a*) was pointed out to one member of the liberal caucus. She chuckled softly, shook her head, and responded cryptically: "Never underesti-mate the tenacity of social service bureaucrats." What could the congresswoman be thinking?

4-3 The district demand for public education expenditures per child E is

$$E = 0.03P_E^{-0.4}W$$

where P_E = price per unit of E
      W = district property wealth per child

Suppose that there are only two districts in the state and that they have property wealth per child of $20,000 and $70,000. Currently, school finance is purely local and P_E = $1. If each district has the same number of children, identify a variable matching grant program that the state can introduce to make education spending equal with no net effect on the state treasury. *Hints:* Recaptured funds must equal state subsidies. Use a calculator. (Answer: Spending is equalized at $1618.92 per child with no net cost to the state when the state uses a matching rate of −$0.47818 for the $70,000 district and $10.95883 for the $20,000 district.)

A FUNDAMENTAL TEST FOR RELATIVE EFFICIENCY: THE COMPENSATION PRINCIPLE

One of the most important analytic tasks is to address questions of *relative efficiency*. For example, it was primarily analysts who argued for the deregulation of passenger air service because it was expected to *increase* efficiency. The analysts knew that some individuals would gain from the change and others would lose, but the analytic community was nevertheless virtually unanimous in advocating deregulation as an efficient change. The force of the analysts' arguments was largely responsible for the Airline Deregulation Act of 1978, which provided for the phasing out of the Civil Aeronautics Board by 1985 and return of the power to choose routes and set fares to the individual airlines. We consider in this chapter the shared concept of relative efficiency which led to this unusual degree of agreement.

We introduce the fundamental test of relative efficiency known as the *compensation principle*. Essentially, the principle is to consider whether it is possible for the gainers from a change to compensate the losers and still come out ahead. This principle not only helped lead to the substantial analytic agreement in the above example, but it is the guiding principle underlying common analytic techniques such as *benefit-cost analysis*. The latter technique is used extensively throughout government. It was required by the Flood Control Act of 1936 for use in estimating the economic value of proposed federal water resource projects such as dams. Since then its use has been spreading to all types of expenditure and regulatory decisions.

For example, many analysts argue that regulatory standards like those limiting water pollution or the use of hazardous substances were not originally designed with sufficient attention to relative efficiency. President Reagan issued an executive order in February 1981 directing regulatory agencies to use benefit-cost analysis when making new regulations and reviewing old ones. As the 1982 *Economic Report of the President* explains,[1]

> The motive for incorporating benefit-cost analysis into the regulatory decision-making process is to achieve a *more efficient* allocation of government resources by subjecting the public sector to the *same type* of efficiency tests used in the private sector. [Emphasis added.]

But what does it really mean to say that one allocation is more efficient than another or that an allocative change increases efficiency? Recall the introductory discussion of efficiency in Chapter 2. Efficiency or Pareto optimality is considered to be a neutral standard in terms of equity implications, in the sense that there are efficient allocations characterized by virtually any relative distribution of well-being among individuals. However, this is an absolute concept rather than a relative one: It is either possible or not possible to make someone better off without making another person worse off. To say whether one allocation is *more* efficient than another, a standard of relative efficiency is needed.

Most allocative changes caused by public policy involve situations in which some people are made better off and others are made worse off. Standards of relative efficiency used to decide if a change is an improvement in efficiency make interpersonal comparisons in a specific way and therefore may be controversial on equity grounds. In this chapter we explain the fundamental test of relative efficiency, the compensation principle, in a way which makes its equity implications explicit.

There is a second theme to this chapter, in addition to explaining the compensation principle. To this point the theory that we have been using to understand policy consequences consists primarily of principles of individual choice. But the data most commonly available (or most readily attainable) for policy analyses are usually market statistics: information about aggregations of individual choices rather than the individual decisions themselves. For example, we are more likely to have estimates of a market demand curve than of all the individual demand curves which shape it. To understand the inferences that can be made from market observations, one often has to rely upon additional logical bridges to connect individual decisions with market observations. Good use of these logical bridges requires skill in model specification. We consider this problem in the context of applying the compensation principle: How and when can one use knowledge of market demand curves to make inferences about relative efficiency?

We begin with a consideration of how one individual's utility level is affected

---

[1] *Economic Report of the President,* February 1982 (Washington, D.C.: U.S. Government Printing Office, 1982), p. 137.

by an economic change and derive monetary measures which reflect the size of the utility change. Three similar measures will be discussed: the compensating variation, the equivalent variation, and the change in the observed consumer surplus. All these are slightly different measures of a hypothetical change in the size of the individual's budget which would be needed to make him or her indifferent to the actual change. Then, on the basis of any one of those measures, we consider the *compensation principle:* If the hypothetical compensations associated with an economic change are such that the sum of gains to the gainers is greater than the sum of losses to the losers, the change is relatively efficient.

We examine rationales for the use of the compensation principle and some of the theoretical controversies about the desirability of its use. After reviewing them, we consider whether market observations can be used to estimate efficiency improvements by this standard. For some, but not all policy changes, the aggregate sum of hypothetical compensations can be deduced from the relevant market demand curves. We discuss the reasons for that and illustrate with several examples of policy changes: the imposition of an excise tax, a gasoline rationing strategy, and a change in regulatory policy concerning medicinal drugs.

THE EFFECTS OF A POLICY CHANGE ON ONE INDIVIDUAL'S WELFARE

Three Measures of Individual Welfare Change

Policy changes typically affect large numbers of individuals some of whom will be made better off and others worse off. Often a policy analyst will try to design a package of changes such that those who are made worse off by the main change are compensated by the secondary changes. For the moment we leave aside a discussion of the normative justifications for such a package. Let us just say that this may be required to achieve Pareto superiority which has been judged desirable or that it is necessary to make the policy politically feasible.

As an example from the late 1970s, many economists argued that domestic oil prices should be decontrolled to promote greater efficiency in the production of oil. However, the change by itself would cause a large redistribution of income in favor of those connected with oil-producing companies and against consumers in general. The passage of both decontrol and a windfall profits tax on oil companies as a secondary change was intended to mitigate the distributional consequences of decontrol.[2]

A second example is the federal Redwood Employee Protection Program. In 1978 the boundaries of Redwood National Park in northern California were extended to include an additional 48,000 acres. This *main change* reduced the

---

[2] Whether it will do so or not is a complicated issue. It depends both on the effects of the tax revenues on other government taxes and spending and on the effects of the tax on oil production. We discuss the tax further in Chapters 12 and 14.

job opportunities for lumberjacks in the area, and Congress attempted to compensate by providing special benefits (above normal state unemployment benefits) for those laid off. This *secondary change* allowed those eligible to receive benefits equaling their full salaries for up to five years.[3]

The question which we will consider in this section is what hypothetical compensation would be necessary to make a typical individual indifferent to a main policy change. We will review three different measures of this hypothetical compensation. (It is hypothetical unless it is actually provided.) In later sections we will discuss the use of these measures in policy analyses.

The exact nature of the main policy change is not important to a discussion of measuring the hypothetical compensation. Let us imagine that we are initially in a state of the world which we shall call S_0. The state of the world characterizes the economic opportunities and constraints faced by each individual. In S_0 there is a certain distribution of utility among the m people in the economy $U_0 [= (u_0^1, u_0^2, \ldots, u_0^m)]$. The people achieve it by spending their budgets B_0 on the n available goods X_0 with n associated prices P_0 and regulatory restrictions R_0.[4] The main policy change results in some new state of the world S_1 characterized by a new distribution of utility U_1 achieved by spending budgets B_1 on goods X_1 at prices P_1 with regulatory restrictions R_1.[5]

Let us focus on one individual who initially had utility level u_0 and has a lower utility level u_1 after the change. If we could measure utility, a perfect measure of the change in this individual's welfare is simply $u_0 - u_1$. Of course, we cannot do that, but we can estimate the monetary equivalent of the utility change. One plausible way to do so is to ask what the minimum income supplement to budget level b_1 would have to be in order to allow this individual to achieve utility level u_0 in state S_1. This amount is known as the *compensating variation: Given the state of the world at S_1, the compensating variation is the size of the budget change which would restore the individual to the initial utility level u_0 from the actual changed level of u_1.* Thus if we made the change to S_1 but in addition gave this individual the compensating variation, he or she would have the same utility level in each state and then be indifferent to the change. Note that the definition is unchanged when u_1 is greater than u_0; the budget change is simply of the opposite sign.

Consider a simple example. Suppose an individual has a budget constraint of $100 and consumes electricity and other things. The price of electricity rises, which changes the state of the world. Given the new higher price, the individual

---

[3] According to a newspaper report, the General Accounting Office has criticized this compensation program for being overly generous and poorly administered by the Department of Labor. See *The San Francisco Chronicle*, July 8, 1980, pp. 1 and 22.

[4] The regulatory restrictions take account of special constraints on choice. Examples that we have already seen include the choice restrictions of a food stamp program and the relation between the consumption of leisure (a good) and money income under income assistance programs like a Negative Income Tax.

[5] Explicit discussion of the private supply side effects are suppressed until later chapters; they are taken into account here through changes in the product-mix and individual budget levels.

may need a budget of, say, \$105 to reach the same utility level as before the change. Then \$5 (\$105 – \$100) would be the compensating variation.

There is a second way to determine the monetary equivalent, and it gives a slightly different answer. This method is to ask what is the maximum amount of the budget b_0 which the individual will give up in S_0 to prevent the change to S_1. This amount is referred to as the *equivalent variation: Given the state of the world at S_0, the equivalent variation is the size of the budget change which would move the individual from the initial utility level u_0 to the actual changed level of u_1.*

Using our example from above, the equivalent variation question is to ask how much money the electricity consumer would give up to prevent the price increase from occurring. The consumer might feel that a budget of \$95.50 with no price increase would yield the same utility as the \$100 budget but with higher electricity prices. Then the equivalent variation would be \$4.50.

In both cases we determine the budget change necessary to bring the consumer from the new utility level u_1 to the original utility level u_0. However, the compensating variation is measured under the conditions (i.e., uncompensated budget levels, prices, available goods, and regulatory restrictions) in the new state of the world S_1, whereas the equivalent variation is measured under the conditions of S_0. The two measures give slightly different answers because of differences in the way income effects are measured. To see this, we first illustrate the measures graphically and relate them to demand curves. We consider an increase in the price of residential electricity rates as the only change in the state of the world.

In Figure 5-1a we have drawn an ordinary demand curve of one individual for electricity, shown as AF. At the initial price p_0, the consumer buys q_0 and has utility level u_0. After the rate increase, the price is p_1 and the consumer buys q_1 and has a lower utility level u_1. Figure 5-1b is an indifference curve representation of the same consumer choices.

In Figure 5-1b it is easy to identify the compensating variation. Given the state of the world in which the consumer is at B (i.e., after the price change), how much extra income is needed to bring the consumer back to u_0? That is, keeping prices constant at the slope of DB, let us imagine adding income to move out the budget constraint until it just becomes tangent to u_0, which we have shown as the dashed line EC tangent to u_0 at C. The amount of income required is shown on the vertical axis as DE; this is the compensating variation. Note that it is the amount of income associated with the income effect $q_1 - q_1^c$ of the price increase.

To show the compensating variation in Figure 5-1a, we must first construct a compensated demand curve. It is simply an ordinary demand curve with the income effect removed. *A compensated demand curve is a locus of points which shows the quantity a consumer would purchase at any price if the income level were always adjusted to keep utility constant.* For example, let us construct the compensated demand curve associated with the utility level u_0 at

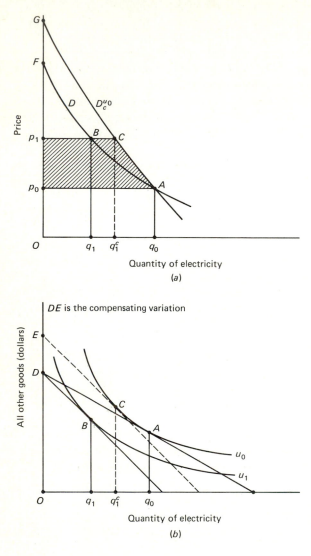

FIGURE 5-1
(a) The compensated demand curve and compensating variation (shaded) for a price change from p_0 to p_1; (b) the indifference curve representation of the same consumer choices.

point A. In Figure 5-1b, we have already located one other price-quantity combination which gives utility level u_0. It is at point C, where price is p_1 and quantity is q_1^c. We also show this as point C in Figure 5-1a.

In fact, all the price-quantity combinations for this compensated demand curve can be "read" from Figure 5-1b: For each point on the u_0 indifference curve, the quantity and associated price of electricity (known from the slope of the curve) are points on the compensated demand curve. We have shown this as $D_c^{u_0}$ in Figure 5-1a. For a normal good (which we have illustrated), the compensated demand curve is steeper than the ordinary demand curve. If the price increased above p_0, the uncompensated consumer would, of course, end up with less utility. Compensation requires that the consumer be given additional income which, for a normal good, results in greater consumption of it than without the compensation. For prices below p_0 we would have to take away income to keep the consumer at u_0 utility level, and therefore the consumer would buy less than without the (negative) compensation.

The height of a demand curve at any quantity has an interesting interpretation which is useful here. The height represents the maximum amount in dollars a consumer could give up, in exchange for receiving an incremental unit of the good, and just remain indifferent. For example, consider q_0 in Figure 5-1a and b. Utility maximization implies that at q_0 the consumer must have an MRS of a unit of q for other things equal to the price ratio of q relative to a \$1 unit of other things, which in this case is p_0. But the MRS is defined as the maximum amount of other things the consumer could give up for an incremental unit of q and still remain indifferent. Since that amount has a monetary value of p_0, we can say the marginal value of q at q_0 is p_0.

Similarly, if the price is p_1 and the consumer is compensated so that the demand curve is $D_c^{u_0}$, the consumer will buy q_1^c. This implies that the MRS at q_1^c is p_1, or that the marginal value of q at that point is p_1. (In fact, the negative slope or diminishing height of a compensated demand curve is a direct conseqyence of the diminishing MRS along an indifference curve.)

Suppose we added the marginal values for the q_1^c units consumed when price is p_1 and the demand curve is $D_c^{u_0}$. It gives us the total value to the consumer of all q_1^c units. It is the maximum amount of money a consumer is willing to pay to receive those units. Geometrically, it equals the area under the demand curve $OGCq_1^c$.

To see this, imagine breaking up the quantity q_1^c into infinitesimal increments Δq and adding the values of the increments starting from the origin (i.e., the heights of the demand curve over the increments). In Figure 5-2, we show this idea by drawing in a series of rectangles with common base Δq and declining heights. The sum of the areas of these rectangles approaches the area under the demand curve when the increment Δq is infinitesimal in size.

Of course, to receive the q_1^c units, the consumer pays $p_1 q_1^c$. That cost is shown geometrically in Figure 5-2 as $Op_1 C q_1^c$. For a given quantity, we *define the consumer surplus as the total amount a consumer is willing to pay minus the consumer cost*. Geometrically, it is the area under the demand curve up to the quantity consumed minus its cost; it is shown as the area $p_1 GC$.

Now let us return briefly to Figure 5-1a. The consumer surplus under a compensated demand curve (where utility is held constant) can be interpreted as a compensating variation.[6] For example, suppose we forbade the consumer

---

[6] The term *consumer surplus* is often used without explicit reference to a specific demand curve. Such usage has the ordinary (Marshallian) demand curve as the referent, and then the consumer surplus cannot be interpreted as a compensating variation. We explain this later in the chapter.

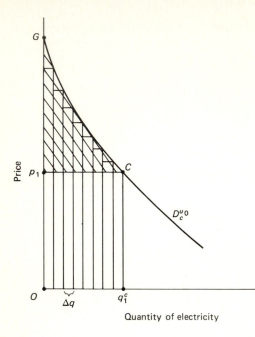

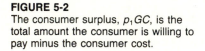

FIGURE 5-2
The consumer surplus, p_1GC, is the total amount the consumer is willing to pay minus the consumer cost.

from buying any electricity when its price is p_1. The consumer then does not spend $p_1q_1^c$ but loses the consumer surplus p_1GC. The amount of money which we would have to give this consumer to compensate for the rule change (i.e., to maintain utility at the u_0 level in the new state of the world) is p_1GC; thus this amount is the compensating variation.

Finally, what is the compensating variation for the price change from p_0 to p_1? Initially, the consumer surplus under the compensated demand curve is p_0GA. When restored to the initial utility level after the price increase, the consumer surplus is only p_1GC. Therefore, the amount of compensation necessary to restore the consumer to the initial utility level must be the *loss* in consumer surplus, the shaded area p_0p_1CA. This compensation plus the new consumer surplus equals the initial consumer surplus. Therefore, *the compensating variation for a price change is the area between the initial and new price lines bounded by the compensated demand curve for the* initial *utility level and the price axis*.

It is relatively easy at this point to explain the equivalent variation for the price change. When the price actually changes from p_0 to p_1, the hypothetical compensation is not made and the actual consumer behavior is shown by the ordinary demand curve. The consumer relocates to point B (in both Figure 5-1a and b), where the actual utility level is u_1. Now let us move to Figure 5-3a and b. In Figure 5-3b the equivalent variation is shown as DK. It is the amount of income that can be taken away, if price is kept at its initial level (i.e., the change is prevented), and the consumer will still be no worse off than if the

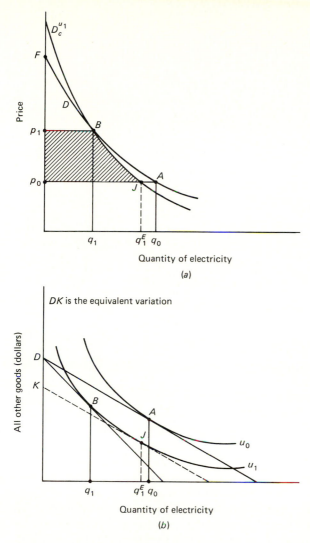

Quantity of electricity

(a)

DK is the equivalent variation

Quantity of electricity

(b)

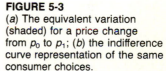

FIGURE 5-3
(a) The equivalent variation
(shaded) for a price change
from p_0 to p_1; (b) the indifference
curve representation of the same
consumer choices.

change were made. We find it by moving the budget constraint parallel to DA
and down until it is just tangent to u_1, shown at point J.

Note that DK is the income associated with the income effect $q_1^E - q_0$ of the
price increase when the substitution effect is measured along the new rather
than the original indifference curve. Recall that the compensating variation is
the income associated with the income effect measured in the usual way. This
explains why we stated earlier that the empirical difference between the
compensating and equivalent variations is due to the difference in the way
income effects are measured.

In Figure 5-3a we construct a compensated demand curve as before except

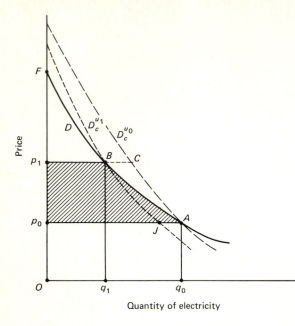

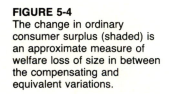

FIGURE 5-4
The change in ordinary consumer surplus (shaded) is an approximate measure of welfare loss of size in between the compensating and equivalent variations.

that this time the curve is associated with utility level u_1.[7] It goes through point B on the ordinary demand curve, and price p_0 is associated with quantity q_1^E (from point J in Figure 5-3b). It is steeper than the ordinary demand curve by the same reasoning as before. Its height at any point is the amount of income which, if given up for an additional unit of electricity, just allows the consumer to maintain u_1.

The equivalent variation is the reduction in the initial budget level which reduces the consumer's utility from u_0 to u_1 when the price is at its original level. But note that the price change does not change the consumer's budget level. The consumer's budget when at point B is the same as when at point A. Thus, we can just as well ask what budget change from point B is necessary to leave the consumer with u_1 utility if the price is reduced to p_0. But as we have already seen, this is the change in consumer surplus under the compensated demand curve (area $p_0 p_1 BJ$). Thus, *the equivalent variation for a price change is the area between the initial and new price lines bounded by the compensated demand curve for the* final *utility level and the price axis.*

In Figure 5-4 we have drawn the ordinary demand curve and both of the compensated demand curves. It is clear from the diagram that, for a price increase, the equivalent variation is smaller than the compensating variation in absolute size. That is true for normal goods; for inferior goods the size relation is reversed.

---

[7] Note that a whole family of compensated demand curves is associated with each ordinary demand curve (one for each utility level attainable).

Note that we have not given any reasons for preferring either the compensating variation or the equivalent variation. Both are exact measures of the welfare change; they just differ in whether the initial or final state of the world is used as the reference point. Sometimes it is argued that the compensating variation should be preferred because it is the amount that actually should be given if the change is made. (Nothing need be changed if the change is not made.) However, there is an implicit equity argument in this position which favors or accepts the status quo distribution, and one need not accept such reasoning. To actually calculate either of them requires knowledge of the (relevant) compensated demand curve. Since they are not observable in the actual uncompensated world, it can be difficult (but not impossible) to estimate them.

Fortunately, there is a third monetary measure which has two great virtues: It can be calculated directly from the ordinary demand curve, and it always has a value between the compensating and equivalent variations. It is simply the change in the consumer surplus under the ordinary demand curve (for short, the ordinary consumer surplus). The ordinary consumer surplus is the actual maximum amount of money a consumer would be willing to pay above cost in order to get the purchased goods. In Figure 5-4 the ordinary consumer surplus at price p_0 is the area of triangle p_0FA, and at price p_1 it is the area of triangle p_1FB. The loss in ordinary consumer surplus caused by the price increase is the difference in the areas, or p_0p_1BA. It is more than the equivalent variation, and it is less than the compensating variation.[8]

In practice, the change in ordinary consumer surplus is probably used more frequently than either of the other two measures. Exactly how close together the different measures are depends upon the nature of the change. In an interesting article, Willig demonstrates that the measures are quite close except when the change involves goods that make up a large proportion of the consumer's budget or for which the income elasticity is unusually large.[9] This is because it is the income effects which cause the differences in the measures; if the income effects were zero for a particular good, all the measures would be identical.

Another reason for variation in estimates of the change in individual welfare (other than the choice of measure) derives from analytic choice of the degree of comprehensiveness in tracing through the changes. Recall the brief discussion in Chapter 3 concerning the difference between partial and general equilibrium analysis. In our electricity example, we examined only the effect of the price change on residential electricity consumption. But that change may in turn increase the demand for natural gas, raise its price, and cause further changes in the consumer's welfare.

---

[8] Note that if we now consider a price decrease from p_1 to p_0, the compensating variation for the price increase becomes the equivalent variation for the price decrease, and similarly the equivalent variation for the increase becomes the compensating variation for the decrease. The change in consumer surplus is the same, and it remains the middle-size measure.

[9] R. D. Willig, "Consumer's Surplus without Apology," *The American Economic Review*, 66, No. 4, September 1976, pp. 589–597.

In most actual studies the analysis is limited to the most direct effects of the policy changes. Pragmatically, this may be the best that can be done, given available analytic methods and resource constraints. It also may be true that the "other" effects are very small compared to the ones included in an analysis. But if we had tools that allowed more comprehensiveness for the same effort, it would be desirable to take advantage of them.[10]

For a quick illustration of this concern about tools, suppose the price change for electricity applies to nonhousehold users as well. The primary effect which we have examined, by assuming that all other prices are constant, is on the consumer's own direct demand for electricity, presumably used for purposes like light, power, and heating in the residence. But this broader price change may affect the prices of other goods which the consumer buys (e.g., goods that are produced with electricity as an input), and thus have additional impact on the consumer's welfare. The information required to know all the effects of any single consumer probably exceeds analytic capacity. We will see later in the chapter that proper use of the market demand curve for electricity would capture those effects in the aggregate, but then we must deal with the controversy over the evaluative implications of such aggregate measures.

To sum up this section briefly, we have presented three measures that represent monetary equivalents of the effect of a policy change on one individual's welfare: the compensating variation, equivalent variation, and change in ordinary consumer surplus. Although they differ slightly from one another, each is an attempt to reveal the change in general purchasing power which would make the individual indifferent to the main change. In the following section, an illustrative calculation is presented.

▽Duality: The Cobb-Douglas Expenditure Function and Measures of Individual Welfare

The Cobb-Douglas function is a reasonably simple form of utility function which is often used in analytic work. For a two-good economy, its equation is

$$U = X_1^\alpha X_2^{1-\alpha}$$

where $0 < \alpha < 1$.[11] The ordinary demand curves derived from it are characterized by unitary price elasticity of demand, which is sometimes a good representation of actual behavior. The demand curves have the form

$$D(X_1) = \frac{\alpha B}{P_1}$$

---

[10] Furthermore, we might learn that the "other" effects are not as small as has been assumed.
[11] For an n-good economy, $U = X_1^{\alpha 1} X_1^{\alpha 2} \dots X_n^{\alpha n}$, where $0 < \alpha_i < 1$ and

$$\sum_{i=1}^{n} \alpha_i = 1$$

and
$$D(X_2) = \frac{(1 - \alpha)B}{P_2}$$

where B is the consumer's budget. The budget elasticity of demand is one. The proportion of this budget spent on $X_1 = \alpha$ and that on $X_2 = 1 - \alpha$. The demand curves can be derived by maximizing the utility function subject to a general budget constraint. We form the Lagrangian

$$L = X_1^\alpha X_2^{1-\alpha} + \lambda(B - P_1 X_1 - P_2 X_2)$$

To maximize utility subject to the constraint, we set the partial derivatives with respect to X_1, X_2, and λ equal to zero and solve the equations simultaneously:

$$\frac{\partial L}{\partial X_1} = \alpha X_1^{\alpha-1} X_2^{1-\alpha} - \lambda P_1 = 0 \qquad \text{(i)}$$

$$\frac{\partial L}{\partial X_2} = (1 - \alpha)X_1^\alpha X_2^{-\alpha} - \lambda P_2 = 0 \qquad \text{(ii)}$$

$$\frac{\partial L}{\partial \lambda} = B - P_1 X_1 - P_2 X_2 = 0 \qquad \text{(iii)}$$

To solve, first multiply both sides of equation (i) by X_1 and simplify:

$$\alpha X_1^\alpha X_2^{1-\alpha} - \lambda P_1 X_1 = 0$$
or
$$\alpha U - \lambda P_1 X_1 = 0$$

or
$$X_1 = \frac{\alpha U}{\lambda P_1} \qquad \text{(i')}$$

Similarly, multiply both sides of (ii) by X_2 and simplify:

$$(1 - \alpha)X_1^\alpha X_2^{1-\alpha} - \lambda P_2 X_2 = 0$$
or
$$(1 - \alpha)U - \lambda P_2 X_2 = 0$$

or
$$X_2 = \frac{(1 - \alpha)U}{\lambda P_2} \qquad \text{(ii')}$$

Now substitute (i') and (ii') in (iii):

$$B - \frac{P_1 \alpha U}{\lambda P_1} - \frac{P_2(1 - \alpha)U}{\lambda P_2} = 0$$
or
$$\lambda B = \alpha U + (1 - \alpha)U = U$$
or
$$\lambda = \frac{U}{B} \qquad \text{(iii')}$$

Finally, substituting (iii') back in (i') and (ii') gives us the demand functions:

$$X_1 = \frac{\alpha U}{P_1} \frac{B}{U} = \frac{\alpha B}{P_1}$$

$$X_2 = (1 - \alpha) \frac{U}{P_2} \frac{B}{U} = \frac{(1 - \alpha)B}{P_2}$$

The unitary price and budget elasticities may be derived by applying their definitions to these demand equations. Note that by multiplying each side of the demand equations by the price, we see that expenditures as a proportion of the budget equals a constant α and $1 - \alpha$ for X_1 and X_2, respectively.

In recent years, much research effort has been devoted to developing easier ways to relate the theory of utility-maximizing choice to observable phenomena like demand. One approach, which we introduce and use in this section, is based on the mathematics of *duality*. To convey the idea of the dual approach, note that we have formulated the consumer choice problem as maximizing utility subject to a budget constraint. An essentially equivalent way to formulate the problem is to minimize the expenditures necessary to achieve a certain utility level. In this dual problem we work with an expenditure function subject to a utility constraint, rather than a utility function subject to a budget constraint. Under certain fairly general conditions, knowledge of the expenditure function reveals the same information about the consumer as knowledge of the utility function would.[12]

To illustrate this dual approach, we define the concepts of an indirect utility function and an expenditure function. Then we use them in the Cobb-Douglas case to help calculate values of the welfare measures discussed in the preceding sections.

Sometimes it is convenient to express the maximum utility a consumer can achieve as a function of prices and the budget level. We call such a relation an *indirect utility function*. We will denote it by $U = U(B_1, P_1, P_2)$ for the two-good case. For the Cobb-Douglas function, we find the indirect utility function by substituting the demand equations for X_1 and X_2 in the ordinary utility function:

$$\begin{aligned}
U &= X_1^\alpha X_2^{1-\alpha} \\
&= \left(\frac{\alpha B}{P_1}\right)^\alpha \left[\frac{(1 - \alpha)B}{P_2}\right]^{1-\alpha} \\
&= \alpha^\alpha (1 - \alpha)^{1-\alpha} B P_1^{-\alpha} P_2^{\alpha-1}
\end{aligned}$$

---

[12] The dual approach applies to the supply side as well as the demand side. We introduce duality on the supply side in the optional section of Chapter 7. A good introductory reference to the use of duality in economics is Hal R. Varian, *Microeconomic Analysis* (New York: W. W. Norton Co., Inc., 1978). Additional references are contained in Chapter 7.

or, letting $\delta = \alpha^{\alpha}(1 - \alpha)^{1-\alpha}$, we have

$$U = \delta B P_1^{-\alpha} P_2^{\alpha-1}$$

The indirect utility function can be rewritten in a form generally referred to as the *expenditure function*. The expenditure function $B(U,P_1,P_2)$ shows the minimum budget or expenditure necessary to achieve any utility level U at prices P_1 and P_2. For the Cobb-Douglas function:

$$B = \frac{U P_1^{\alpha} P_2^{1-\alpha}}{\delta}$$

From the expenditure function it is easy to find the compensated demand curves. Recall that a compensated demand curve shows the quantity of a good that will be bought at each possible price when the utility is held constant at some level $\overline{U}$. *Shephard's lemma* states that this quantity equals the partial derivative of the expenditure function with respect to price:[13]

$$X_i = \frac{\partial B(U,P_1,P_2)}{\partial P_i} \qquad i = 1, 2$$

Applied to the Cobb-Douglas expenditure function:

$$X_1 = \frac{\partial B}{\partial P_1} = \frac{\alpha \overline{U} P_1^{\alpha-1} P_2^{1-\alpha}}{\delta}$$

$$X_2 = \frac{\partial B}{\partial P_2} = \frac{(1 - \alpha) \overline{U} P_1^{\alpha} P_2^{-\alpha}}{\delta}$$

We will use these equations for the compensated curves below. We also note that it is easier to derive the ordinary demand curves from an indirect utility function than from an ordinary utility function. That is because of *Roy's identity,* which states:[14]

$$X_i = \frac{-\partial U(B, P_1, P_2)/\partial P_i}{\partial U(B, P_1, P_2)/\partial B} \qquad i = 1, 2$$

---

[13] A proof of this is sketched in the optional section of Chapter 7.

[14] The following proof is from Varian, op. cit., p. 93. It is true by identity that a given utility level $\overline{U}$ can be expressed by the indirect utility function

$$\overline{U} = U[P_1,P_2,B(\overline{U},P_1,P_2)]$$

At any prices, that is, the consumer will achieve the $\overline{U}$ level if he or she is given the minimum expenditure necessary to achieve it. But then the derivative of this expression with respect to price must always equal zero:

$$\frac{\partial \overline{U}}{\partial P_i} = \frac{\partial U}{\partial P_i} + \frac{\partial U}{\partial B} \frac{\partial B}{\partial P_i} = 0$$

For the Cobb-Douglas function we find the ordinary demand curve for X_1:

$$\frac{\partial U(B, P_1, P_2)}{\partial P_1} = -\alpha\delta BP_1^{-\alpha-1}P_2^{\alpha-1}$$

$$\frac{\partial U(B, P_1, P_2)}{\partial B} = \delta P_1^{-\alpha}P_2^{\alpha-1}$$

and therefore, by Roy's identity,

$$X_1 = \frac{\alpha B}{P_1}$$

This is, of course, the same result we derived earlier by solving a system of simultaneous equations.

To illustrate some of the measures we have described, suppose an individual has this specific Cobb-Douglas utility function:

$$U = X_1^{0.1}X_2^{0.9}$$

and let us assume that the budget is $10,000, P_1 = $2.00, and P_2 = $1.00. Focusing on the first good, the consumer purchases

$$D(X_1) = \frac{0.1(10,000)}{2} = 500$$

Suppose the price of this good increases to $4.00. Then the consumer purchases

$$D(X_1) = \frac{0.1(10,000)}{4} = 250$$

We represent the initial situation and the change in Figure 5-5. Let us find the change in ordinary consumer surplus ΔCS, the compensating variation CV, and

---

We can write this

$$\frac{\partial B}{\partial P_i} = \frac{-\partial U/\partial P_i}{\partial U/\partial B}$$

But from Shephard's lemma we know the term on the left is X_i. This gives us Roy's identity:

$$X_i = \frac{-\partial U/\partial P_i}{\partial U/\partial B}$$

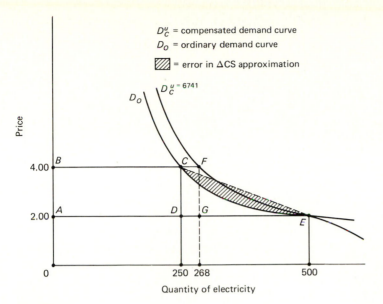

FIGURE 5-5
Calculating the compensating variation and the exact and the
approximate change in consumer surplus.

the equivalent variation EV. The change in consumer surplus is area $ABCE$. Its
exact area is[15]

$$\Delta CS = \int_{2.00}^{4.00} [X_1] \, dP_1$$

$$= \int_{2.00}^{4.00} \frac{0.1(10{,}000)}{P_1} \, dP_1$$

$$= 1000(\ln 4.00 - \ln 2.00)$$

$$= \$693.15$$

In practice, the demand curves are always estimated from actual observations, so the ΔCS also is an estimate. Sometimes the only information available
will be the initial and final prices and quantities. In that case, it is often assumed
that the demand curve is approximately linear "over the relevant range." This
assumption may be fine for small price changes, but it can lead to more serious
estimation errors as the change considered gets larger. If we make the linearity
assumption in the present case of a quite large price change (i.e., 100 percent),
the area we calculate is still $ABCE$ but we treat the CE boundary as the dashed

[15] Note that the area $ABCE$ can be calculated by integrating over either the price or the quantity
axis. Integrating over the price axis is more convenient in this case.

line shown in Figure 5-5. In this case, using subscript L for linearity assumption,

$$\Delta CS_L = ABCD + CDE$$
$$= 500 + \tfrac{1}{2}(2)(250)$$
$$= \$750$$

Thus we overestimate the change in ordinary consumer surplus by 8.2 percent—not bad for such a large price change. Think of this error as being caused by uncertainty about what the true demand curve is.

Now let us turn to calculating the CV. One method requires two steps: (1) Find the relevant compensated demand curve. (2) Calculate the area of the CV by the method of integration used for the ΔCS. The relevant compensated demand curve is the one through point E in Figure 5-5, where utility is held constant at its initial level. Since we know the utility function, we can find the initial utility level by plugging in the initial consumption amounts of X_1 and X_2 (or equivalently, by plugging in the budget level and initial prices in the indirect utility function). We know that X_1 is initially 500; X_2 is easily determined to be 9000 by substituting the known parameters $B = \$10,000$, $1 - \alpha = 0.9$, and $P_2 = 1.00$ into $D(X_2)$. Then

$$U_0 = 500^{0.1}(9000^{0.9})$$
$$\approx 6741$$

It is a simple matter to find the compensated demand curve associated with this utility level. We simply substitute in the compensated demand equation derived from the expenditure function:

$$X_1 = \frac{\alpha \overline{U} P_1^{\alpha - 1} P_2^{1 - \alpha}}{\delta}$$
$$= \frac{0.1(6741)P_1^{-0.9}(1^{0.9})}{0.1^{0.1}(0.9^{0.9})}$$
$$= 933.05 P_1^{-0.9}$$

This is the equation of the compensated demand curve through point E. When $P_1 = \$4.00$, $X_1 = 268$ if the consumer is compensated. This is shown as point F in Figure 5-5 and the compensating variation is area $ABFE$. To calculate it,

$$CV = \int_{2.00}^{4.00} 933.05(P_1^{-0.9})\, dP_1$$
$$= 933.05 \frac{P_1^{0.1}}{0.1} \Big|_{P_1 = 2.00}^{P_1 = 4.00}$$
$$= \$717.75$$

Thus, the CV is only 3.54 percent bigger than the ordinary consumer surplus in this case. Note that if we use the linear approximation here, the estimated CV_L is

$$CV_L = ABFG + FGE$$
$$= 2(268) + \tfrac{1}{2}(2)(232)$$
$$= \$768.00$$

This method might be used if nothing is known except the initial and final positions and there is an estimate of the income effect used to approximate the location of point F. These empirical examples should help illustrate why, in many situations, abstract debate about which of the different measures should be used may not be worth the fuss; uncertainty about the true demand curve is often the dominating source of potential evaluative error.

The exact method of calculating the CV used above illustrated how to identify the equation for a compensated demand curve. But a little thought about the meaning of an expenditure function leads to an interesting shortcut. When the change in the state of the world concerns prices, the CV can be simply expressed:

$$CV = B(P_1^1, P_1^2, U_0) - B(P_1^1, P_1^2, U_1)$$

where P_j^i = the price of the ith commodity in period j
U_j = the utility level in period j

The first term is the minimum budget necessary to achieve the original utility level at the new prices. The second term is the actual budget in the new state of the world (i.e., the minimum expenditure necessary to achieve the actual utility level at the actual prices). The difference between them is precisely what we have defined as the CV.

Note that since price changes do not affect the size of the consumer's budget, the second term is equivalent to the following:

$$B(P_1^1, P_1^2, U_1) = B(P_0^1, P_0^2, U_0)$$

That is, the actual budget in the new state of the world is the same as the initial budget. Then we can substitute this in the expression for the CV:

$$CV = B(P_1^1, P_1^2, U_0) - B(P_0^1, P_0^2, U_0)$$

In our example where $P_1^2 = P_0^2$, this expression corresponds exactly to the change in consumer surplus under the compensated demand curve for $U = U_0$ when price changes from P_0^1 to P_1^1. Rather than actually calculate this demand curve, one can compute the CV directly by using the Cobb-Douglas expenditure function and the above expression:

$$CV = \frac{U_0(P_1^1)^\alpha(P_1^2)^{1-\alpha}}{\delta} - \frac{U_0(P_0^1)^\alpha(P_0^2)^{1-\alpha}}{\delta}$$

On substituting the parameter values from our example, $\delta = 0.722467$, $U_0 = 6741$, $P_1^2 = P_0^2 = 1$, $P_1^1 = 4$, and $P_0^1 = 2$, we have

$$CV = \frac{6741}{0.722467}\ (4^{0.1} - 2^{0.1})$$
$$= \$717.75$$

Following the same reasoning, we can express the EV for price changes:

$$EV = B(P_0^1, P_0^2, U_0) - B(P_0^1, P_0^2, U_1)$$

The first term is the actual budget, and the second term is the minimum budget necessary to achieve the new utility level at the initial prices. The difference between the terms is what we have defined as the EV. Again, since price changes do not affect a consumer's budget, we substitute (this time for the first term):

$$EV = B(P_1^1, P_1^2, U_1) - B(P_0^1, P_0^2, U_1)$$

When $P_1^2 = P_0^2$, this expression corresponds to the change in consumer surplus under the compensated demand curve for $U = U_1$. For our example, we calculate $U_1 = 6289$ and by using the parameters above,

$$EV = \frac{6289}{0.722467}\ (4^{0.1} - 2^{0.1})$$
$$= \$669.62$$

As expected, this is less than the $693.15 loss in ordinary consumer surplus.

THE COMPENSATION PRINCIPLE OF RELATIVE EFFICIENCY

The Purpose of a Relative Efficiency Standard

In the preceding section we saw how a change in one individual's welfare can be measured. But as we know, public policy alternatives will cause changes in the welfare of many people. Furthermore, it is virtually inevitable that every policy change will improve the lot of some but worsen the lot of others. Recognizing that the decisions are made through a political process, the problem we address in this section is whether analytic input to the process can provide a useful judgment about the relative efficiency of each alternative. First, we try to convey what a measure of relative efficiency might reveal that other efficiency-related criteria do not.

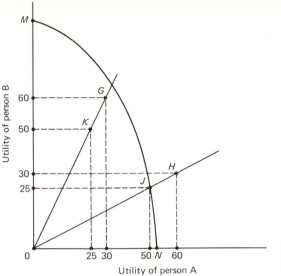

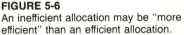

FIGURE 5-6
An inefficient allocation may be "more efficient" than an efficient allocation.

Put very simply, neither the criterion of Pareto superiority nor that of Pareto optimality reveals the extent to which the aggregate gains from a change exceed or fall short of the aggregate losses from the change. In Chapter 2 we saw that the criterion of Pareto superiority applies only to situations in which some gain but no one loses, or no one gains and some lose. As a practical matter, this does not characterize the effects of actual policy changes. As an ethical matter, there is no compelling justification for trying to restrict policy changes to Pareto-superior situations. Aside from the practical impossibility of doing so, equity considerations could lead to a social preference for making some better off at the expense of others—as when, for example, the status quo is a consequence of unfair discrimination in the past.

Why is the criterion of efficiency or Pareto optimality inadequate for the purpose here? In Chapter 2 we saw that this criterion is absolute rather than relative. Now we wish to make an additional point: The concept of relative efficiency we seek to develop is fundamentally different from the concept of Pareto optimality. The latter is a statement about the actual economic possibilities in an economy, and it is not the characteristic of social concern to be addressed by a relative efficiency standard.

To develop this point, turn to Figure 5-6. We assume for the moment that the utility levels of persons A and B, the axes on the diagram, are measurable and comparable. Consider first points *G* and *H*, where one person has 30 utils and the other has 60. We assume the society has symmetric equity preferences and that it judges these two allocations as equally desirable.

Suppose we are initially at point *G* and a proposed policy would lead to the utility outcomes at point *J*. Note that point *J* is Pareto-inferior to point *H* (i.e., both people are worse off), although the relative distribution of utility is constant (one person has twice as much as the other). A plausible social judgment would be that point *J* is less desirable than point *H because* it is relatively less efficient.

The inference that seems natural to make next is that point *J* is less desirable than point *G* for the same reason: it should be judged relatively less efficient. Indeed, we can buttress this logic by noting that point *K* is as desirable as point *J* by symmetry and point *G* is Pareto-superior to point *K*. Therefore, it seems that any reasonable method of judging relative efficiency ought to rank point *G* ahead of point *J*. Furthermore, this observation seems relevant to the social decision concerning the policy proposal.

To address the above issue we did not have to consider the full range of actual economic possibilities in the economy. They could be vast or meager, and depending on preferences and available resources, they could favor one person more than another. The utility-possibilities frontier that results from these possibilities could be, for example, more favorable to person B, like the locus *MN* shown in Figure 5-6.

It will be helpful to expand the discussion of the utility-possibilities frontier. For the purposes of this chapter we wish to use it with a model of the economy that is slightly more complex than the pure exchange model used in Chapter 2. Here we assume the economy starts with an endowment of factors like labor and capital rather than finished goods; the economic choice problem includes what to produce as well as how to allocate the total product among consumers. Thus, *MN* shows the maximum achievable utility level for person B (or person A) associated with each achievable utility level for person A (or person B), given freedom to achieve it with any combination of goods producible with the available factors. It is the locus of utility levels associated with the Pareto-optimal or efficient allocations of this economy.[16]

To explain the shape of *MN* in Figure 5-6, imagine that there are only two types of goods which can be produced with the available resources: meat and fruit. The economy is endowed with resources that make it easy to have fruit in abundance. However, these same resources happen not to be conducive to meat production. Furthermore, person B is a fruit-lover and person A has passion only for meat. Thus, it is possible in this economy for person B to attain much higher utility levels than person A. The utility-possibilities frontier intersects person B's utility axis at a much higher utility level than its intersection with person A's utility axis.

Now observe that point *J* (in Figure 5-6) represents an efficient allocation and point *G* represents an inefficient one. But we have just argued that any reasonable method of judging relative efficiency would rate point *G* more efficient than point *J*. That is, despite the Pareto optimality of point *J*, the

---

[16] Given the factor endowments, suppose one of the producible combinations is the initial endowment of goods in the Chapter 2 model of pure exchange. Then it should be obvious that the *MN* locus of Pareto-optimal points dominates the points on the contract curve in Chapter 2. We can always do as well as the pure exchange model by simply replicating it, but the extra degrees of freedom from the ability to vary the product mix allow us to improve the overall utility possibilities.

society may wish to judge Pareto-nonoptimal *G* as being relatively more efficient. This emphasizes the independence of the concepts of efficiency and relative efficiency.[17]

The example suggests that there is something desirable about point *G* as compared with point *J*, but that characteristic is not identified by our other criteria. We seek to define a criterion of relative efficiency which would identify this difference between the two points. In Chapter 2 we suggested that relative efficiency be thought of as a measure of distance from the (zero-utility) origin, like the sum of utilities. This is equivalent to making relative efficiency a measure of the size of the total utility pie, independently of how it is sliced. This measure of aggregate well-being would identify the difference between points *G* and *J* highlighted above. But it is not a practical measure; utility, other than in this example, is neither measurable nor comparable among persons. Therefore, we seek some other measure of aggregate well-being which also would identify differences like the one in this example.

Before turning to the more pragmatic measure commonly used in analysis, we offer some initial comments on questions of equity that might be raised by the use of a relative efficiency measure. Any comparative measure which rates two allocations like points *G* and *J* is inevitably weighing (in some manner) the gains to some against the losses to others. As with a social welfare function, one should not expect a social consensus about the value of achieving a high score by a particular relative efficiency measure. If losses are going to be imposed on some people, the rightness or wrongness remains a value judgment which may not be the same for everyone.

Nevertheless, if one is satisfied that a proposed change does no harm on equity grounds, it seems desirable to know whether it increases or decreases well-being in an aggregate sense (as in our example). More generally, those involved in decision making for public policy continually make tough trade-offs. When policies that benefit some at the expense of others are considered, it helps to know how big the gains are compared to the losses. There will be circumstances, for example, in which many feel that a net gain is too small to outweigh the perceived problems of equity. Thus, the analytic task is to develop a method of measuring the gains and losses which can be used consistently as an input to the policy process. The value of consistency is that it allows any particular application to be scrutinized for accuracy by any professional analyst. Furthermore, repeated use of the same measure helps users of analyses to understand the strengths and weaknesses of the measure.

The Hicks-Kaldor Compensation Principle

The standard of relative efficiency that has come to be widely utilized in analytic work was first developed by the British economists John Hicks and

---

[17] Note that this example does not detract from the fundamental importance of testing for efficiency. If it is recognized that point *G* is not Pareto-optimal, this indicates that there is another allocation which can make everyone better off. That provides motivation to look for it.

Nicholas Kaldor.[18] The underlying concept, called the compensation principle, builds on the notion of Pareto superiority. To introduce it, let us return to the more general notation used in the beginning of this chapter.

Imagine a policy (like building a new road) which would change the state of the world from S_0 to S_1. S_0 is characterized by the quantities of the n goods available $X_0 = [X_0^1, X_0^2, \ldots, X_0^n]$, all their prices P_0, regulatory restrictions R_0, the distribution of utility among the m people in the economy $U_0 = [u_0^1, u_0^2, \ldots, u_0^m]$, and their budgets B_0. S_1 is characterized analogously. If the policy results in a Pareto-superior allocation,

$$U_1 \geq U_0 \qquad \text{that is, } u_1^1 \geq u_0^1, \ u_1^2 \geq u_0^2, \ldots, \ u_1^m \geq u_0^m$$

and there is at least one person j where $u_1^j > u_0^j$.

Hicks and Kaldor generalized this concept and proposed that relative efficiency be decided by a compensation principle. Stated loosely, the principle is whether it is possible for the gainers from a change to compensate the losers and still come out ahead. The original version of the compensation principle is as follows:

> A policy change from S_0 to S_1 increases efficiency if it is *possible* to take the resulting goods X_1 in S_1 and distribute them in such a way that in the resulting *hypothetical* state of the world S_1^* (denoted by asterisks):
>
> $$U_1^* \geq U_0$$
>
> and there is at least one person j for whom $u_i^* > u_0^j$.

It is critically important to understand that the compensations are not in fact made. The actual distribution resulting from the policy is U_1, not U_1^*. If the necessary compensations were so made that the gainers in S_1 gave up some of their gains to the losers and the result really were U_1^*, then the policy would be Pareto-superior. *The compensation principle is a test for potential Pareto superiority.*

In Figure 5-7a suppose we are initially at point R with utility (u_0^A, u_0^B) achieved with goods X_0, and are considering the change to point T where utility is (u_1^A, u_1^B) achieved with goods X_1. The compensation test requires that we first find the contract curve associated with goods X_1 and then graph the feasible utility combinations on Figure 5-7a. This is shown as the locus $T_B T_A$; if T is itself an allocation that is efficient in exchange, it will be on the locus as drawn (otherwise, T is interior to the locus). The compensation test is to ask whether there are any points on $T_B T_A$ which are Pareto-superior to R. Since there obviously are (for example, Z), the move to T is considered an efficiency increase. That is, the gainer from the change (person B) *could* compensate the

[18] See J. R. Hicks, "The Valuation of the Social Income," *Economica, 7*, May 1940, pp. 105–124, and N. Kaldor, "Welfare Propositions of Economics and Interpersonal Comparisons of Utility," *Economic Journal, 49*, September 1939, pp. 549–551.

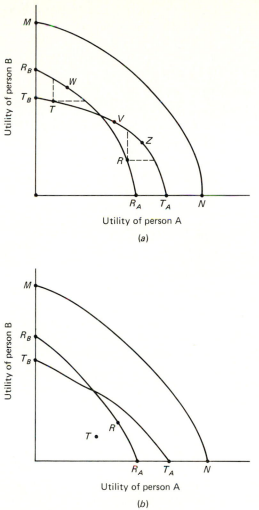

Utility of person A

(a)

Utility of person A

(b)

FIGURE 5-7
(a) The Hicks-Kaldor compensation
principle may give ambiguous results;
(b) the original compensation principle is
ill-suited for comparing allocations
which are inefficient in exchange.

loser (person A) by a redistribution of the goods X_1 and still come out ahead.

The original version of the compensation principle has a characteristic which most analysts consider undesirable: it ignores exchange inefficiencies. Consider the test when T is not efficient in exchange. In Figure 5-7b such a case is shown where T is actually Pareto-inferior to R but passes the original Hicks-Kaldor test anyway.[19] There are only losers from the actual change. The test ignores this and indicates that the new goods X_1 could be reallocated to make

[19] The return move, from T to R, also would pass the Hicks-Kaldor test. Thus, by the original compensation principle, it is ambiguous whether T or R is more efficient (despite the Pareto superiority of R).

both people better off than initially. The original test was intended to get at the "social preference" for alternative product mixes, and it did not pretend to address issues of exchange efficiency.

Modern usage extends the compensation test to include exchange efficiency considerations. The modified Hicks-Kaldor compensation principle is as follows:

> A policy change from S_0 to S_1 increases efficiency if the sum of the hypothetical compensations which would keep each person indifferent is positive (count the hypothetical compensations as positive for those gaining and negative for those losing).

This version ensures that an efficient change is one such that the actual gains are sufficient to enable the gainers to compensate the losers (even though the compensation is not made). If the actual change is to a "better" product mix (i.e., by the original version) but it also causes exchange inefficiency, the net gains will be measured as smaller than they would be without the exchange inefficiency. By this version of the compensation principle, the move from R to T in Figure 4-7b would be an unambiguous efficiency decrease. *The application of this modified compensation principle is referred to as benefit-cost analysis,* and we shall illustrate its use frequently throughout the book.

When there is exchange efficiency, the two versions of the compensation principle are equivalent. To see this, let us think of the hypothetical compensations for the modified version directly in terms of real goods rather than money. Using the two-person example, we illustrate the equivalent of the two versions in two steps: (1) Any change which passes the original Hicks-Kaldor test passes the modified test. (2) Any change which fails the original test also fails the modified test.

Consider a proposed change which passes the original Hicks-Kaldor test, which means that there is some way to redistribute the goods so that the gainer remains better off and the loser is indifferent.[20] This would fully compensate the loser, but the gainer could give up something more and still be ahead. Thus the compensation which would leave the gainer indifferent to the change is greater than the compensation necessary to make the loser indifferent. The modified compensation test also is satisfied.

The second step is to show that a change which fails the original Hicks-Kaldor test must fail the modified test also. Failing the original test means that there is no way to redistribute the goods to make both people better off. That means there is no way to redistribute the goods so that the loser is just compensated (kept indifferent) and the gainer remains ahead.[21] But then the compensation necessary to make the loser indifferent must be greater than the compensation necessary to make the gainer indifferent: The modified compensation test also is failed.

---

[20] If both people in fact gain, the change obviously passes the modified compensation test.
[21] If both people are losers, the change obviously fails the modified test.

One of the advantages of the modified compensation principle is that it can be understood in familiar monetary terms. To see this, consider how one might determine numerically whether a proposed change from state of the world S_0 to S_1 would pass the Hicks-Kaldor test. Ask each person what budgetary compensation would just make him or her indifferent to the change, assuming conditions are those in S_1. This is simply the compensating variation. All the test requires is that we add them up. That is, the Hicks-Kaldor compensation test of the change from S_0 to S_1 is equivalent to asking if [22]

$$\sum_{i=1}^{m} CV_i > 0$$

Now we can begin to see how the Hicks-Kaldor principle relates to the impractical sum-of-utilities test discussed earlier. The latter tries to do the impossible by testing whether a proposed change would increase the sum of utilities, or (equivalently) result in a positive sum of the changes in utility. The Hicks-Kaldor test is whether the sum of the monetary values the individuals place on their own utility changes is positive. For the nonmeasurable and noncomparable utility change, we substitute the measurable and commensurable monetary equivalents. Thus the Hicks-Kaldor test can also be thought of as a test to see if a proposed change increases the size of the total social pie. The pie size is simply measured in dollars rather than utility. Note that the test treats monetary transfers among individuals as neutral: The gain to the gainer is exactly offset by the loss to the giver.

The compensation principle is subject to some ambiguity. This can be seen readily in Figure 5-7a. We have already indicated that T is an improvement over R. Now let us ask how the move back, from T to R, fares by the Hicks-Kaldor test. Graphically, let $R_A R_B$ be the best feasible utility combinations given X_0. Clearly, there are points on $R_A R_B$ which are Pareto-superior to T (for example, W). Thus, the move back from T to R also is considered an improvement![23] This paradoxical result is explained by recognizing that the return move is measured by $\Sigma_i EV_i$, and thus the ambiguous result occurs only in the unusual case when $\Sigma_i CV_i$ and $\Sigma_i EV_i$ are opposite in sign.[24]

---

[22] Recall our sign convention, where we count the CV of a gainer as positive and the CV of a loser as negative, as if we were collecting the compensations.

[23] This possibility was first pointed out by Tibor Scitovsky, "A Note on Welfare Propositions in Economics," *The Review of Economic Studies*, 9, 1941, pp. 77–88.

[24] The paradoxical result is closely related to the alternative individual welfare change measures explained in the preceding section. To see this, consider how we numerically determine if the proposed change from R to T would pass the Hicks-Kaldor test. Take person B and consider the compensating variation question: If we move to T, how much income can we take away so that person B is left just indifferent to the change? Now ask the analogous question for person A: If we move to T, how much extra income will just make A indifferent to the change? If $CV_B + CV_A > 0$, the change is potentially Pareto-superior. Person B could compensate person A and still have something left over, which means $u_1^{B*} > u_0^B$ and $u_1^{A*} = u_0^A$.

Now consider the equivalent variation questions. How much would person A pay to prevent the change from R to T? And how much would person B demand in payment in return for not moving to

The compensation test may be described in explicit utility terms which help illuminate it as well as some aspects of its equity implications. To see this, let us denote λ_i as the marginal utility an individual would receive from one extra budgetary dollar in the ith state of the world. Consider how person B is affected by a change from state of the world S_0 to S_1. We already know this can be expressed as CV_B. It can be approximated for small changes as follows:[25]

$$CV_B = \frac{\Delta u_B}{\lambda_1^B}$$

That is, the numerator is the total change in utils, and the denominator is the util value per dollar in S_1. Therefore, the whole expression is the dollar

---

T? Note that these are the same calculations that one would make for a Hicks-Kaldor test of the move from S_1 to S_0 (with all signs reversed). That is, the response to the equivalent variation questions is that if $EV_A + EV_B < 0$, then we should not move from R to T. (Recalling our sign convention, EV_A is negative and EV_B is positive.) But since

and
$$EV_A^{R \rightarrow T} = -CV_A^{T \rightarrow R}$$
$$EV_B^{R \rightarrow T} = -CV_B^{T \rightarrow R}$$

then
$$\left(\sum_i EV_i\right)^{R \rightarrow T} = -\left(\sum_i CV_i\right)^{T \rightarrow R}$$

Thus the paradoxical result above occurs only when the sum of equivalent variations and the sum of compensating variations have opposite signs. In normal cases this is unlikely to arise: For any one person the CV and EV have the same signs; and if they are reasonably close to one another in absolute size, the sums over many people also will have the same signs.

To summarize, there are four possible outcomes of the Hicks-Kaldor compensation test. A proposed change is considered an efficiency improvement when $\Sigma_i CV_i > 0$ and $\Sigma_i EV_i > 0$. If both the signs are negative, the proposed change is considered an efficiency decrease. If the signs are opposite, the change in efficiency is ambiguous.

In Figure 5-7a all of the cases are illustrated. The move from R to V is an efficiency increase, and the move from V to R is an efficiency decrease. The move from R to T is ambiguous because $\Sigma_i CV_i$ is positive but $\Sigma_i EV_i$ is negative. (Starting from either R or T, the other point looks better.) The move from W to Z is ambiguous because ΣCV_i is negative and ΣEV_i is positive. (Starting from either point, it looks better to stay put.) For any one person, larger utility changes caused by an allocative change are more likely to cause bigger differences between the CV and EV measures. The larger the individual utility changes associated with a proposed policy that only some people prefer (i.e., one that affects people in opposite ways), the more likely it is that the compensation test will give an ambiguous result.

[25] This can be shown readily by using the duality relations introduced in the optional section. Let P_i characterize all prices in S_i, and let the only changes in the state of the world involve prices. Then the compensating variation can be defined exactly by the indirect utility function. The CV is the change in the budget level B which satisfies the following equation:

$$U(P_1, B + CV) = U(P_0, B) \tag{i}$$

For a small CV we can approximate the value of the indirect utility function on the left by a first-order Taylor series expansion:

$$U(P_1, B + CV) \approx U(P_1, B) + \frac{\partial U(P_1, B)}{\partial B} CV$$

or
$$U(P_1, B + CV) \approx U(P_1, B) + \lambda_1 CV \tag{ii}$$

equivalent of the utility change.[26] If, for example, the utility change is 50 utils and the marginal utility of a dollar in S_1 is 5 utils, the monetary compensation which would keep person B indifferent is approximately \$10.

Using a similar expression for CV_A, the compensation test for the move from S_0 to S_1 is to ask whether

$$\frac{\Delta u_B}{\lambda_1^B} + \frac{\Delta u_A}{\lambda_1^A} > 0$$

Consider the changes that are neutral:

$$\frac{\Delta u_B}{\lambda_1^B} + \frac{\Delta u_A}{\lambda_1^A} = 0$$

or

$$\Delta u_B = -\frac{\lambda_1^B}{\lambda_1^A} \Delta u_A$$

This expression has a direct geometric interpretation. In Figure 5-8a let R represent the initial position and T the final position. Then we draw the line through the initial point R with slope $-\lambda_1^B/\lambda_1^A$. If the final point T is on this line, the change is neutral. The compensation test is to ask whether the line with the same slope through the final point T is farther out or closer in. (If it is farther out, it is an improvement.) Note that any line that is farther out must have some points Pareto-superior to the initial point on it; thus it remains true that any change passing the compensation test is potentially Pareto-superior.

To evaluate the return move, we make the test analogous to that above by using as the slope the ratio of the marginal utilities of money in S_0: $-\lambda_0^B/\lambda_0^A$. In Figure 5-8a, we have drawn these in such a way that the test results are unambiguous: R is "more efficient." In Figure 5-8b is an illustration of an ambiguous test. It is clear from the diagram that the closer a change is to actually being Pareto-superior, the more likely it is to pass the test.

By the definition of the indirect utility function, the change in utility from S_0 to S_1 is

$$\Delta u \equiv U(P_0, B) - U(P_1, B) \tag{iii}$$

Substituting from (i) into (iii) gives us

$$\Delta u = U(P_1, B + CV) - U(P_1, B)$$

And on substituting from (ii) into the above, we have

$$\Delta u = \lambda_1 CV$$

or

$$CV = \frac{\Delta u}{\lambda_1}$$

[26] Similarly, $EV_B = \Delta u_B/\lambda_0^B$.

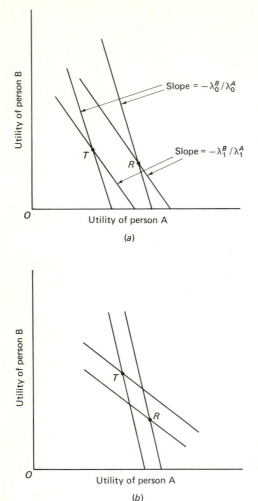

FIGURE 5-8
(a) The modified compensation test: R is more efficient than T; (b) the modified compensation test: ambiguous result.

Controversy over the Use of the Compensation Principle

Most of the controversy over the use of compensation tests concerns the equity judgments implicit in them. Some analysts would like to ignore equity altogether and use the compensation test as *the* decisive analytic test. One rationale is the hope that a separate set of policies can be designed to take account of and amend the overall distributional effects. However, this view may underestimate the process equity concerns with particular policy changes and overestimate the ability of policy makers to change the outcomes once they are "done."

A second rationale for relying solely on the compensation test is the belief that concern for equity is simply unfounded: If a large number of policy changes are made in accordance with the compensation rule, then everyone will end up with actual gains. Even if correct, this argument has an implicit equity judgment which restricts redistributive concerns. (For example, perhaps some people should gradually be made worse off to allow others to become better off.) Putting that aside, let us consider the argument directly.

Think of the payoff to an individual from a policy change as arising from the flip of a fair coin: \$2 if it is heads and $-\$1$ if it is tails. On any one flip the individual may lose, but in the long run the individual will be better off. However, this reasoning depends heavily on the debatable proposition that gains and losses from policy changes are distributed randomly. If they are not, what have the losers (gainers) done to deserve the losses (gains)? At least in the author's judgment, the compensation test cannot substitute for explicit consideration of equity effects.

Putting aside the arguments about whether to consider equity at all, some people argue that an implicit and unacceptable equity judgment is reflected in the slopes of the lines in Figure 5-8a and b. That is, why shouldn't the slopes be determined by an explicit ethical choice rather than by the marginal utilities of the initial (or final) position?

To clarify this argument, it may be helpful to think of the compensation principle as a proposal for a social welfare function. We have already seen that the sum of compensating variations may be expressed as follows:

$$CV_B + CV_A = \frac{\Delta u_B}{\lambda_1^B} + \frac{\Delta u_A}{\lambda_1^A}$$

Since $\Delta u_B \equiv U_1^B - U_0^B$ and $\Delta u_A \equiv U_1^A - U_0^A$, we can substitute and express this as

$$CV_B + CV_A = \frac{U_1^B}{\lambda_1^B} + \frac{U_1^A}{\lambda_1^A} - \left(\frac{U_0^B}{\lambda_1^B} + \frac{U_0^A}{\lambda_1^A} \right)$$

That is, the compensation test is equivalent to asking whether social welfare increases when the social welfare function is defined as the sum of the utility of each person weighted by the inverse of the marginal utility of money:

$$W = \sum_i \frac{U^i}{\lambda^i}$$

Viewed that way, objections to the compensation principle on equity grounds become clear. If there is declining marginal utility of wealth, a 1-util gain to a poor person will be judged socially *less* worthwhile than a 1-util gain to a rich person!

In Figure 5-9, we illustrate this in terms of social indifference curves. Imagine that persons A and B have identical utility functions, so that all differences in their utility levels are due solely to wealth differences. We saw in Chapter 2 that the Benthamite W^B and Rawlsian W^R social welfare functions

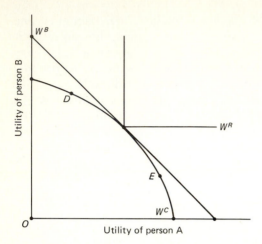

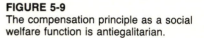

FIGURE 5-9
The compensation principle as a social
welfare function is antiegalitarian.

are usually considered the extremes of plausible social judgment. But the social
indifference curve corresponding to indifference by the compensation principle
W^C falls outside these extremes. It is bowed toward the origin. We explain this
below.

The slope of any social indifference curve is $\Delta u^B/\Delta u^A$, where Δu^B is the
change in person B's utility necessary to hold social welfare constant when
person A's utility changes by a small amount Δu^A. Indifference by the
compensation principle requires

$$\frac{\Delta u^B}{\lambda^B} + \frac{\Delta u^A}{\lambda^A} = 0$$

or

$$\frac{\Delta u^B}{\Delta u^A} = \frac{-\lambda^B}{\lambda^A}$$

At a point of equal utilities, $\lambda^B = \lambda^A$ and the slope of the social indifference
curve is -1. But as we move away from a point of equal utilities along the
social indifference curve, λ declines for the gainer and rises for the loser. At
point D, for example, $\lambda^B < \lambda^A$ and the slope of the indifference curve is flatter
or less negative $(-\lambda^B/\lambda^A > -1)$. At point E, where person A is relatively well
off, $\lambda^A < \lambda^B$ and the indifference curve is steeper or more negative $(-\lambda^B/\lambda^A < -1)$.

Thus, the social indifference curve associated with the compensation
principle is bowed toward the origin. If the Benthamite welfare function is
indifferent to equality, the compensation principle can be considered antiegalitarian. This explains why many analysts wish to assign different "ethical"
weights to the utility changes (or, more practically, weights to the compensating variations dependent on each individual's wealth or income level).[27]

---

[27] For examples of how to do this, see Edward M. Gramlich, *Benefit-Cost Analysis of
Government Programs* (Englewood Cliffs, N.J.: Prentice-Hall, Inc., 1981).

Of course, the equity objections to the compensation principle are primarily to proposals that the principle be used as a sufficient criterion for policy evaluation. We have suggested that it be used only in conjunction with other evaluative criteria of equity (and, indeed, Pareto optimality). Let us not forget that some consistent standard used to measure the size of the aggregate social pie is useful. To reinforce that statement, let us show that in an important sense the compensation test is at least as strict a test as asking if a change increases the value of the national product.

For purposes here, we define the value of the national product as the market value of all the goods in the economy. Actual measures of national product, like the gross national product (GNP), are flawed in the sense that they exclude important goods like leisure and bads like pollution. Nevertheless, it should be clear enough that even the flawed measures are of great concern to policy makers, and increases in them are generally considered desirable and decreases undesirable. For the case in which we can consider the national product to include all goods, we wish to show the following:

If a policy change from S_0 to S_1 passes the compensation test, then national product valued at current prices P_0 must be increased by the change. Mathematically:

$$\text{If} \quad \sum_i \text{CV}_i > 0 \quad \text{then} \quad P_0 X_1 > P_0 X_0$$

Thus, whatever one thinks about the desirability of using the compensation principle in policy analysis, it can be no more controversial than thinking that increases in national product are generally good.

Let us sketch the proof. If $\Sigma_i \text{CV}_i > 0$, there is some allocation of the aggregate bundle of goods X_1 among the consumers such that all consumers get at least as much utility as from the actual consumer allocations of X_0. Take the case in which X_1 is hypothetically so allocated that each person is strictly better off. Now consider the jth person. Since we assume utility maximization, it must be true that

$$P_0 X_1^{j^*} > P_0 X_0^{j}$$

That is, it must be that the jth person could not afford the bundle of goods $X_1^{j^*}$ in S_0; otherwise, the person could have increased utility by buying it.[28] Since the same is true for *every* person,

$$P_0 \sum_j X_1^{j^*} > P_0 \sum_j X_0^{j}$$

---

[28] Not *all* persons could buy their hypothetical allocations in S_0 because the goods were not available in the aggregate. But we are assuming that any *single* consumer would have no trouble finding the goods in his or her hypothetical allocation. Since *no* consumer chooses the hypothetical allocation, strictly preferred to the actual bundle, it must be that the hypothetical allocations are unaffordable.

But the sum of allocations to each person must add up to the appropriate aggregate allocation:

$$\sum_j X_1^{j*} = X_1 \qquad \text{and} \qquad \sum_j X_0^j = X_0$$

Therefore, we can substitute X_1 and X_0 in the above equation and get

$$P_0X_1 > P_0X_0$$

In short summary, the Hicks-Kaldor compensation principle has come to be widely utilized as a guide for making this comparison: A policy change is considered an efficiency improvement if it is *possible* for the gainers to compensate the losers and still have something left over for themselves. Although there can be no strong ethical justification for it, such a principle is an attempt to capture a sense of which alternative allocation is considered to be the biggest social pie. It is a more refined measure of efficiency change than simply looking at the change in national product, and we know that many people are willing to use the latter as an efficiency indicator. Therefore, looked at as an indicator to be considered along with equity effects, it provides useful information to policy makers.

In actual policy use, the compensation principle may play an even more defensible role than can be argued on theoretical grounds alone. That is because its most common use is in the form of benefit-cost studies to compare alternative programs for approximately the same target populations of gainers and losers. For example, the Department of Labor sponsors or has sponsored different public employment programs aimed at youth (e.g., Jobs Corps, Supported Work, Neighborhood Youth Corps) and has commissioned or undertaken major benefit-cost studies of each. In those situations, the studies are generally more important in their effects on which of these programs will survive or grow than on whether there will be any programs at all.

The relation between the policy process and policy analysis is very important to reflect upon. To the extent that policy alternatives must be carefully designed and their consequences analyzed, there can be an important role for policy experts. This depends on whether the experts can perform their tasks with the confidence and support of the other participants in the policy process. If analytic work either cannot clarify what participants in the decision process wish to know or does not add to what they already know, it is of little use. An analyst attempting to use the compensation principle as a way of deciding among very divergent allocative alternatives may find the work ignored (like it or not).

The problem of deciding what to do may be solved quite ''rationally'' by breaking the problem into pieces and giving policy analysts responsibility for the pieces with which they can deal least ambiguously. Since the policy significance of a compensation test becomes less clear as it is used to compare broader and more diverse allocations, perhaps the test should be relied upon less. The author knows of no instance, for example, in which a compensation test was actually used to decide between the mix of flood control projects and urban renewal. But analytic work of that type is used regularly to help sort out which programs seem better within each category. Other types of microeconomic policy analysis may influence the broader allocative decisions; but when they do so, it is likely that the analysts involved have been successful in addressing the concerns of the other participants in the policy process.

AGGREGATE CONSUMER SURPLUS AND MARKET STATISTICS

At this point we turn to the more pragmatic problem of carrying out a compensation test. For the rest of this discussion we will use the aggregate change in ordinary consumer surplus as the test; the same principles hold for the sum of compensating variations and the sum of equivalent variations. The problem, simply put, is how to find the magnitude of the aggregate change. A full exploration of this subject is not intended here. The particular source of information we focus upon is the market demand curve.

Let us begin by recalling that the market demand curve does indicate the sum of individual demands at any given price. Suppose we have a very simple two-person linear demand economy:

$$Q_1 = 10 - 2p$$

and
$$Q_2 = 20 - 4p$$

Then the market demand curve is the sum of the individual demands:

$$Q_m = 30 - 6p$$

All three demand curves are shown in Figure 5-10a. This is obviously a special case used for illustrative purposes; the generality of it will be considered shortly.

If the market price is $p = 2$, then $Q_1 = 6$, $Q_2 = 12$, and $Q_m = 18$. The consumer surplus from this good for each person, the area between the individual demand curve and the price line, is

$$CS_1 = \tfrac{1}{2}(5 - 2)(6) = \$9$$
$$CS_2 = \tfrac{1}{2}(5 - 2)(12) = \$18$$

Thus the actual total consumer surplus from this good (denoted CS) is $27 (= 9 + 18). Now let us see whether the consumer surplus under the market demand curve (denoted CS_m) does in fact equal $27:

$$CS_m = \tfrac{1}{2}(5 - 2)(18) = \$27$$

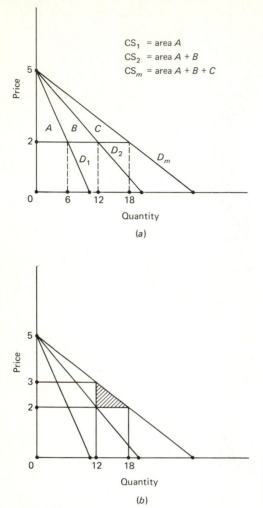

(a)

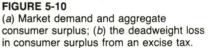

(b)

FIGURE 5-10
(a) Market demand and aggregate consumer surplus; (b) the deadweight loss in consumer surplus from an excise tax.

This illustrates the important result that the consumer surplus under the market demand curve, at least in some circumstances, equals the sum of the individual consumer surpluses.

Now suppose we consider this policy change: the imposition of a $1 excise tax on each unit of Q purchased. Then the price that consumers face would equal $3, and the quantity bought in the aggregate would equal 12.[29] This is illustrated in Figure 5-10b. How does this policy change fare by the compensa-

---

[29] For simplicity we are assuming that the supply of the good is infinitely elastic. Explicit discussion of the relevance of supply conditions to the compensation principle is deferred until Chapter 7. Explicit discussion of tax incidence is in Chapter 10.

tion principle? To answer that question correctly, one must take account of all the changes that arise. That is, we must add up the change in each individual's consumer surplus across *all* markets. However, many of these changes will cancel each other out, and under certain conditions everything we need to know is contained in the information about this one market. In this market, the new consumer surplus under the market demand curve (CS'_m) is

$$CS'_m = \tfrac{1}{2}(5 - 3)(12) = \$12$$

Thus the aggregate loss in consumer surplus *in this market* is $\$15 (= 27 - 12)$. It is hardly surprising that these consumers are losers, but are there no gainers? There are two more effects to consider: What happens to the tax receipts, and what happens to the real resources that used to be used in this industry when $Q_m = 18$ but are not used here now that Q_m is only 12?

We can see from Figure 5-10b that $12 in taxes is collected ($1 for each of the 12 units sold). Let us assume that the tax receipts are used entirely to provide cash welfare to the needy; then they are viewed as a *pure transfer*. The idea is that it is just like taking dollar bills out of one person's pocket (the taxpayer's) and stuffing them into another's. By itself the transfer is often assumed to have no significant effect on the aggregate amount or type of goods available; all real resources are still being used to produce essentially the same things. The $12 paid in taxes by the consumers in this market are given to some other people; the taxpayers would require $12 in compensation to be indifferent; and the recipients of the tax receipts would be indifferent if they received a compensating reduction of $12. So the sum of compensations is zero from this effect; $12 of the $15 loss in consumer surplus in this market is offset by the $12 gain to others from the tax receipts.

Now what about the remaining $3 loss? In Figure 5-10$b$, it is seen as the shaded triangle. This part of the loss in consumer surplus is referred to as *deadweight loss;* the idea is that it is a loss for which there are no offsetting gains.[30]

Under special assumptions, this is the end of the story. The resources that were used to produce units 13 to 18 have been released from this industry and are presumed in use elsewhere. The returns to the owners of the resources are assumed to be the same (their opportunity costs) in both cases, so no change arises in their budget constraints. Furthermore, the new products made with them generate no net change in aggregate consumer surplus; the assumption is that the released resources are spread evenly among the many other production activities. Then the change in quantity of each good is small and at the margin of its market where demand equals price. Thus the marginal change in the area between the demand curve and price is negligible in each of these other industries.

---

[30] The deadweight loss from a tax, sometimes referred to as its *excess burden,* can be defined as the difference between the tax revenues to the government and the loss the tax causes to others.

Thus, under these special assumptions, we are able to calculate that the change in aggregate consumer surplus is −$3. The remarkable aspect of this result is the parsimony of the calculation. The only pieces of information used are the price, tax, and market demand equation. Obviously, one is not required to make the assumptions that lead to this maximum economy in modeling. Indeed, it is completely irresponsible to do so if the analyst thinks an alternative model better. We will see in later chapters, for example, that the more common practice is to substitute the estimated supply curve for the assumption here that supply is at constant cost; this is easily incorporated into the compensation test through the concept of the producers' surplus.

However, not all of the assumptions made above are easily replaceable, and the accuracy of them is open to serious doubt. (This is discussed later on in the text under the "theory of the second best.") As always, the true art and skill of microeconomic policy analysis is in constructing a model that captures the particulars of the phenomenon being studied accurately enough to improve decision making. Thus one should by no means underestimate the difficulty of carrying out an analysis which pins the number down within a range relevant to decision making. The point of this parsimonious example is simply to dramatize that what might at first seem to be a totally hopeless quest (to discover all the necessary individual compensations) may be a useful endeavor after all.

To try to reinforce the preceding observations, let us point out an insight about taxation that follows directly from the illustration. One factor that determines the amount of deadweight loss is the elasticity of the demand curve: the more elastic it is, the greater the deadweight loss. Thus based on efficiency grounds, it may be preferable to tax goods which are more inelastic. On the other hand, goods that are characterized by inelastic demands are necessities. Since lower-income families spend greater portions of their budgets on necessities, such a tax is likely to be regressive in its incidence. Thus there can be a real tension between efficiency and equity in deciding how to raise taxes.

Now, putting aside other aspects of compensation testing, let us continue to focus on the information that can be extracted from the market demand curve. In the special case used before, we saw that the change in the sum of the individual consumer surpluses caused by an excise tax equals the change under the market demand curve. The more general principle is that this holds for a change in price levels applied uniformly to all. The easiest way to see this is to use the linear approximation to the change in consumer surplus experienced by one individual ΔCS_i in response to a price increase ΔP:

$$\Delta CS_i = \Delta P Q_i^1 + \tfrac{1}{2} \Delta P (Q_i^0 - Q_i^1)$$

where Q_i^0 = initial quantity purchased and Q_0^1 = quantity purchased after the price increase. The first term is the change in the consumer cost of the goods actually purchased after the price increase, and the second term is the deadweight loss. If we add this up for all r consumers,

$$\Delta CS = \sum_{i=1}^{r} [\Delta P Q_i^1 + \tfrac{1}{2} \Delta P(Q_i^0 - Q_i^1)]$$

$$= \Delta P \sum_{i=1}^{r} Q_1^1 + \tfrac{1}{2} \Delta P \sum_{i=1}^{r} (Q_i^0 - Q_i^1)$$

$$= \Delta P Q_m^1 + \tfrac{1}{2} \Delta P(Q_m^0 - Q_m^1)$$

These two terms are the areas under the *market* demand curve that are precisely analogous to the two relevant areas under each *individual's* demand curve. Thus, for a uniform price change applied to all, the relevant areas under the market demand curve tell us exactly what we want to know about the total change in consumer surplus.

If a policy change can be characterized by the *uniform price change* effect, as the imposition of an excise tax can be, the market demand curve can be used to identify the net direct change in consumer surplus. But many policy changes are not that simple. If a policy change causes a direct shift in individual demands (as opposed to movement along a demand curve) along with a price change, then the change in the area under the market demand curves does not reflect the information we seek. If there is inefficiency in exchange either before or after the change, the same lack of correspondence can arise.

For example, when the gasoline shortages of the 1970s occurred, it was common in many areas around the country to introduce various ration plans such as 10-gallon limits per fill-up, no Sunday sales, and odd-even rationing so that a motorist could make purchases only every other day.[31] At the same time, the price of gasoline was rising. The combination of effects served the purpose; short-run demand was reduced. From empirical observation of aggregate behavior during those periods, it is possible to estimate statistically the ordinary demand curve and even isolate the regulatory and price effects. But it is not possible, without disaggregated data, to make an unbiased estimate of the loss in consumer surplus.[32]

To see why this is so, let us use the same simple two-person linear demand system introduced at the beginning of this section. We interpret it as the market for gasoline, with a $2.00 initial price and a $1.00 gasoline tax slapped on by government in response to a shortage. Additionally, we add the regulatory constraint that no person can buy more than 4 gallons per time period. Because we know the individual demand equations, we know what quantity each person wishes to buy at the higher price:

$$Q_1 = 10 - 2(3) = 4$$
$$Q_2 = 20 - 4(3) = 8$$

---

[31] Rationing plans are the subject of Chapter 13.

[32] In this example the shortage will cause a loss in consumer surplus. The policy problem is to respond to the short-run shortage in a way which is fair and keeps losses at a minimum. The intention here is to illustrate only one aspect of evaluating a particular alternative.

But, because of the 4-gallon limit, person 2 can only buy 4 gallons. So the total quantity purchased in the market is 8 (= 4 + 4).

Figure 5-11 shows the demand curves that are discoverable from market statistics. The two market observations we have are the initial allocation ($p = 2$, $Q_m = 18$) and the final allocation ($p = 3$, $Q_m = 8$). One mistake to avoid is thinking that the change in quantity is due only to the change in price or, equivalently, that the ordinary demand curve passes through those points. If one made that mistake and estimated the change in consumer surplus by using the linear approximation to the erroneous demand curve (the dashed line), then

$$\Delta CS_M^L = 1(8) + \tfrac{1}{2}(1)(10)$$
$$= 13$$

A good analyst will realize that the dashed-line demand curve violates the usual *ceteris paribus* assumptions: Factors other than price are not being held constant; regulatory constraints have changed as well. After a bit of digging, suppose it is discovered that the ordinary demand curve has been estimated previously. Let us assume that the estimated equation is the true one, shown on Figure 5-11 as the solid line.[33]

The next analytic pitfall is to think that the change in consumer surplus can be estimated on the basis of this perfectly accurate market picture. That is, it appears plausible to assume that the loss in consumer surplus is the shaded area in Figure 5-11. The area seems to consist of the two usual components: the extra cost of purchased units and the foregone surplus on the unpurchased ones. It differs from our original analysis of the excise tax by triangle ABC. The extra triangle arises because of the regulatory constraint; without the constraint, four more units would be bought at a cost of $3 each (including the tax). To find the height at point A, we use the true market demand curve to find the price at which eight units would be bought:

$$8 = 30 - 6p$$
$$p = 3.667$$

Thus triangle ABC has the area

$$ABC = \tfrac{1}{2}(3.667 - 3.00)(12 - 8)$$
$$= 1.33$$

Adding this to the rest of the loss under the market curve, calculated in the beginning of this section as 15, we erroneously conclude that the loss in consumer surplus is $16.33.

The fallacy in the above analysis is that it assumes efficiency in exchange, but the regulatory constraint causes inefficiency in exchange. That is, the four-

---

[33] It is common in policy analysis to review the existing literature in order to make use of prior empirical research of this type.

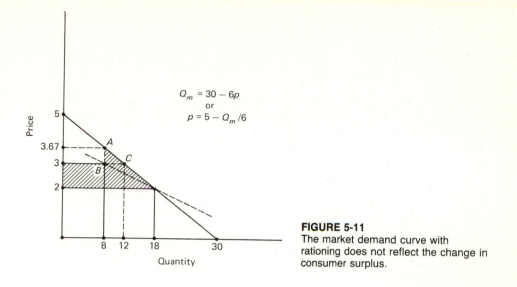

FIGURE 5-11
The market demand curve with rationing does not reflect the change in consumer surplus.

unit reduction due to the regulatory constraint is *not* accomplished by taking the four units valued the least by consumers. At a price to consumers of \$3.667 with no other constraints, $Q_1 = 2.67$ and $Q_2 = 5.33$ (and $Q_m = 8$). Since at a price of \$3, $Q_1 = 4$ and $Q_2 = 8$, the efficient reduction is to take 1.33 units from person 1 and 2.67 units from person 2. The extra loss in consumer surplus caused by *this* change is the one that triangle ABC measures.

But the actual change results in $Q_1 = 4$ and $Q_2 = 4$, and it has a larger loss associated with it. None of this information could be known on the basis of market statistics only. To calculate the actual losses, one needs information about the individual consumers. The actual individual losses are shown as the shaded areas in Figure 5-12*a* and *b*. Person 1, whose behavior is unaffected by the regulatory constraint, has the same loss as in the simple excise tax example:

$$\Delta CS_1 = 1(4) + \tfrac{1}{2}(1)(2) = 5$$

Person 2 loses more than in the simple excise tax case because the regulatory constraint is binding here; the extra loss is triangle EFG. The area of EFG is found analogously to the area of ABC in the above example; the height at point E must be 4, and thus the area of EFG is 2.

The loss in consumer surplus due to the tax alone (as in the original example) is 10 [= $(3 - 2)(8) + \tfrac{1}{2}(3 - 2)(12 - 8)$]. Therefore, $CS_2 = 12$ and the actual loss in aggregate consumer surplus is \$17 with \$8 as tax receipts and \$9 as deadweight loss. In this case one knows that the area under the market curve must underestimate the true loss. Do not be misled by the small size of the underestimate in this example; in actual situations the error could be quite substantial.

One researcher attempted to estimate the value of consumer protection

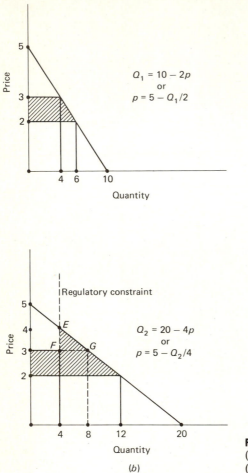

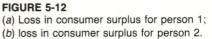

FIGURE 5-12
(a) Loss in consumer surplus for person 1;
(b) loss in consumer surplus for person 2.

legislation for prescription drugs by the general methods we have been discussing. A brief review of the methodology is quite instructive.[34] In 1962 the Kefauver-Harris amendments to the Food, Drug, and Cosmetics Act added (among other provisions) a proof-of-efficacy requirement to the existing legislation. The primary objective of the amendments was to reduce the harm and waste that consumers experienced because of poor knowledge about the actual effects of drugs. In congressional testimony, numerous examples of manufacturers' claims that could not be substantiated were offered. It was

[34] For a more detailed review of the methodology, the reader should refer to the debate in the professional literature. See S. Peltzman, "An Evaluation of Consumer Protection Legislation: The 1962 Drug Amendments," *Journal of Political Economy, 81,* No. 5, September/October 1973, pp. 1049–1091; McGuire, Nelson, and Spavins, "A Comment," and S. Peltzman, "A Reply," *Journal of Political Economy, 83,* No. 3, June 1975, pp. 655–667.

hoped that the new legislation would not only improve the use of drugs on the market but would deter the entry of new drugs which did not offer any real improvements over existing ones.

Figure 5-13*a* illustrates, at a greatly simplified level, the conceptual framework used in the study. There are two solid-line demand curves on the on the diagram: the *uninformed demand* D^U and the *informed demand* D^I. Think of these demand curves as representing the demands for a new drug of a physician for a particular patient. When uninformed, the physician-patient believes the drug will work miracles (perhaps like laetrile). Gradually the physician-patient learns (by trial and error, or from other physicians, or published reports, etc.)

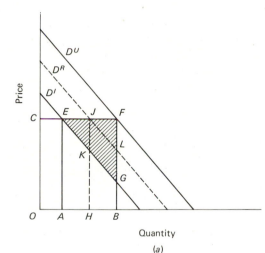

FIGURE 5-13
(*a*) The consumer overestimates the benefits of a drug; (*b*) the consumer underestimates the benefits of a drug.

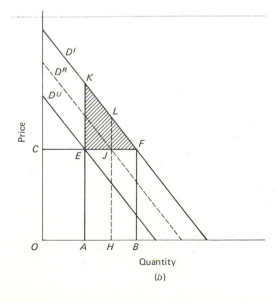

that the drug does not work as claimed. Thus, over time, as the physician-patient becomes informed, the demand curve shifts inward.[35] For simplicity, we assume there are only two time periods: the uninformed period, and the informed period.

Suppose we ask how much this consumer would value being perfectly informed from the start. In Figure 5-13a, the shaded area represents the value of the information. At price OC, the consumer buys OB units when uninformed. When informed, the consumer reduces the purchase by AB units to the quantity OA. The true benefits are always the area under the informed demand curve D^I, although the consumer is not aware of this when uninformed. (That is, when uninformed, the consumer misperceives the benefits.) Perfect information from the start would prevent the purchase of AB units; these units have costs (AEFB) greater than benefits (AEGB) by the amount EFG. Thus, if we ask what is the maximum amount of money this consumer would pay to be informed from the start, it is EFG. To find out what the aggregate value of perfect information is, we simply have to add up all these individual triangles.

Of course, the new drug regulation did not purport to make information perfect. The idea is that it would cause the initial period to be one of *improved* information, so the first-period demand curve would be shown as the dashed line D^R.[36] As drawn, the consumer would purchase OH in the initial period, overbuying by AH, and then buy OA when fully informed. Thus the effect of the regulation is to avoid the mistake of buying HB in the initial period, which has costs HJFB greater than benefits HKGB by the amount KJFG. Thus KJFG is the value to the consumer of the new drug regulations.

The study goes on to estimate the *market* demand curves corresponding to D^U, D^R, and D^I and report the area KJFG under the *market* curves as the aggregate value to consumers. This last step is flawed and misestimates the information value by an unknown but perhaps extremely high factor. To see that, let us turn to Figure 5-13b. The demand curves in this diagram are those of a second physician-patient. They have been chosen to be identical to those in Figure 5-13a with one crucial twist: The uninformed and informed demand curves are switched around. Upon a moment's reflection, the existence of this behavior is just as plausible as that previously described. In this case the physician-patient is simply a cynic and skeptic. Having been misled by false claims in the past, the physician-patient initially tries new drugs only with great reluctance. However, the drug works better than the skeptic expected and over time the demand shifts outward.

In Figure 5-13b, the consumer initially buys OA when uninformed and then

[35] There may be some situations in which the drug seems useful, so the demand curve does not necessarily disappear altogether.

[36] It could be argued, though probably not very plausibly, that the regulation actually worsens information. The idea would be that drug companies tell consumers what they really want to know and regulation prevents them from acting on the information. This argument does not affect the point of the discussion here: that information about shifts in the market demand curve does not include the information necessary to make a reasonable compensation test.

OB when perfectly informed. The true benefits are always the area under the informed demand curve for the quantity actually consumed. If perfectly informed from the start, this consumer would not make the mistake of underbuying *AB* units. These units have benefits of *AKFB* but cost only *AEFB*, so the net benefit from consuming them is *EKF,* the shaded area on the diagram. The maximum amount this consumer would pay to be perfectly informed from the start is *EKF*. As before, the drug legislation is not expected to achieve perfection. With improved information represented by the dashed demand curve D^R, the consumer initially buys *OH* and thus avoids underbuying quantity *AH*. The value of the drug legislation is *EKLJ*.

   If these are the only two consumers in the market, the aggregate value of the regulation is obviously *KJFG* in Figure 5-13*a* plus *EKLJ* in Figure 5-13*b*. But now let us consider how the *market* demand curve hides those benefits. The clearest example can be seen if we assume that *OH,* the initial quantity bought by each consumer after the regulation is introduced, halves the errors (i.e., *AH* = *HB* in both diagrams). In that case, the initial market quantity bought is

$$Q_m^U = OB + OA$$

After the regulation is passed, the initial market quantity bought is

$$Q_m^R = OH + OH$$

Since *AH* = *HB*, we can add and subtract them on the right-hand side:

$$Q_m^R = OH + HB + OH - AH$$
$$= OB + OA$$

That is, the initial market demand curve does not shift at all after the regulation is introduced! The reduction in overbuying by the first consumer exactly *offsets* the reduction in underbuying by the second consumer. The researcher finds that the drug regulation has had no impact on consumer purchasing and measures the information value as *zero,* whereas it is obviously much greater. If we had 100 million consumers divided into two camps like those drawn of 50 million skeptics and 50 million optimists, the market demand curve would still be unchanged by the regulation. That is why the flaw is so serious; savings in consumer surplus that should be adding up are being subtracted from one another.

   The seriousness of this flaw is not an artifact of the specific example chosen. The initial market demand curve will shift to the left if, preregulation, there are more optimistic purchases, to the right if there are more skeptical nonpurchases, and not at all should they happen to offset one another exactly. The point is that in all of these cases the shift in the market curve due to the regulation shows what is left *after* one subtracts one group of benefits from another. For that reason the market demand curves simply do not contain the information necessary to make this compensation test.

The alert reader may have noticed a second flaw: The use of the market curves here is subject to the same flaw discussed in the gasoline rationing case. To illustrate it, let us put aside the last flaw by assuming that no consumers underbuy. A remaining problem is that not all consumers make the same size mistake. Consider a very simple example with only two consumers who initially make mistakes but make none after the regulation is introduced. Now contrast these two situations: (1) Consumers 1 and 2 initially overbuy by *AH* in Figure 5-13*a*. (2) Consumer 1 initially overbuys by *AB,* and consumer 2 makes no mistakes at all. In both situations the amount of initial market overbuying is the same and the regulation prevents the errors, so the shift in the market curve due to the regulation is the same.

But the benefits of preventing those errors are not the same. The regulation is more valuable if it prevents the errors in the second situation. It is least valuable in the first situation; use of the market curves is equivalent to assuming that the starting point is the first situation. In Figure 5-13*a* think of situation 1 as each consumer overbuying *AH* and losing area *EJK*; preventing both these errors is worth twice area *EJK*. Situation 2 can be thought of as one consumer overbuying *AB* (twice *AH*). *But the second unit overbought, HB, hurts more than the first.* Thus the total loss in situation 2 is greater than twice the area *EJK*.[37]

Market demand curves are so constructed that, for any price, the most highly valued units will be purchased. If a good is priced too low, there will be overbuying but only of the next most highly valued units. This tends to minimize the aggregate error. But overbuying due to consumer ignorance hardly guarantees that the least serious mistakes will be the ones made. Thus this second flaw also causes misestimation, to an unknown degree, of the consumer benefits from the regulation.

The main point of this extended illustration is, as always, to emphasize the importance of model specification. Careful thought about this approach to evaluating the drug legislation suggests that the available market statistics cannot be used to bound the uncertainty about the true benefits within any reasonable range. In other uses, as for taxation or estimating the harm from monopoly, the market demand curves may contain precisely the information sought. An important part of analytic skill is learning to understand when the appropriate linkages are present.

Before concluding this section, it may be useful to speculate about the interpretation of an accurate compensation test for drug regulation. That is, suppose we had no regulation and knew (which we do not) that passing the drug regulation would comfortably pass the compensation test. What significance, if any, might this knowledge have to an analyst? The parties primarily affected by the legislation are the demanders and suppliers of drugs. The benefits to

---

[37] As drawn, with all demand curves the same slope, it is exactly 4 times the area *EJK*; the four triangles shown in *EFG* are equal in area. The actual error could be greater or smaller, depending on the shapes of the demand curves.

consumers are likely to be spread over a fairly large population: all the people who have occasion to use prescription drugs. This is not the kind of policy change in which one narrow segment of the population is gaining at the expense of another narrow segment. The losers, if there are any, might also be widely scattered consumers: the lovers of laetrile (and other drugs whose efficacy cannot be proved). On the assumption that the gains comfortably outweigh the losses, and with no special reason to favor laetrile lovers over other consumers, one might rely heavily on the test as a reason for recommending the regulation be passed.

An additional possibility is that the incomes of those on the supply side will be changed. Suppose the makers of laetrile will be forced to close down shop. Usually, such supply activities are geographically scattered and each is a small part of a local economy. If that is the case, the labor and capital resources may be quickly reemployed in other parts of the company or in other industries and suffer only small temporary losses (mitigated perhaps by unemployment insurance). Alternatively, all laetrile manufacturers might be geographically concentrated in one town the entire economy of which is dependent upon laetrile manufacture. In that case it is more likely that some form of secondary legislation, e.g., relocation assistance, would be passed to compensate the losers.

These speculative comments are intended only to suggest that an accurate compensation test could, in this case, have great significance to an analyst. Of course, actual analytic significance would require more detailed information and reasoning than can be provided here. Furthermore, most analysts would not wish to be restricted to a set of only two alternatives.

SUMMARY

In this chapter we have reviewed one of the most commonly utilized analytic principles in making evaluative judgments; the Hicks-Kaldor compensation criterion. The criterion is a test of *potential* Pareto superiority; it seeks to discover whether the gainers from a policy change *could* compensate the losers and still have enough left over to come out ahead. Because the compensations are only hypothetical, it is important to think carefully about whether, why, and when one might rely on such a principle. It is used because it seems to capture an important element of social reality and no better operational criterion to replace it has been found.

The two relatively uncontroversial criteria of Pareto optimality and Pareto superiority generally do not characterize actual states of the economy either before or after proposed policy changes; this renders them of little use in making policy choices from among alternatives which make some people better off and others worse off. Nevertheless, there are many alternative allocations of this latter type, and there can be wide (if not unanimous) consensus that some of them are better because there is more product to go around. Viewed that way, analytic use of the compensation principle takes on more appeal.

That is, we do not attempt to justify the principle as a rational decision rule that all reasonable people "should" follow. Consider it as an imperfect predictor of what informed social judgment on relative efficiency grounds would be. It does not purport to reflect equity judgments, and thus separate consideration of outcome and process equity issues would often be appropriate.

For changes involving only ordinary marketable goods, those which can pass the compensation test are a subset of those which would increase national product valued at the initial prices. This example suggests that the compensation test is no more controversial an indicator than measures of national product (which have flaws but are widely used). This comparison does not have much meaning if one is considering radically different resource allocations (so that prices also would be radically different), and thus the compensation principle should be expected to be of more use in comparing "smaller" changes. The most common use in practice is in comparing policy alternatives under the control of one agency that are similar in their target gainers and losers.

To carry out a compensation test, one must be able to measure the benefits to the gainers and the costs to the losers. Two exact monetary measures which do this are the compensating variation and the equivalent variation, both of which seek to identify the hypothetical change in general purchasing power (income) necessary to make the individual indifferent to the policy change. They differ only in the choice of a reference point.

In most cases these two measures are close to one another, but they cannot be calculated directly from knowledge of the ordinary demand curve. Fortunately, there is a third measure, the change in ordinary consumer surplus, which is easily calculated from ordinary demand curves and always has value between the two exact measures. Thus in practice, this latter measure is the one most commonly used.

The mathematical relations of utility functions, demand functions, and the above measures of individual welfare can be somewhat involved. In an optional section we derived them for the case of a utility function called the Cobb-Douglas function, and provided illustrative numerical calculations. A recent theoretical approach is to attempt to simplify some of these relations; it is based on the mathematics of duality. We introduced the concepts used in the dual theory of consumer choice, the expenditure function and indirect utility function, and illustrated how welfare measures can be derived from them.

The hardest part of most empirical analyses is to find the sum of the hypothetical compensations, but that is what is needed to make the compensation test: If the sum of compensations is positive, that implies the benefits to gainers are large enough that they could compensate the losers and still have something left over.

In this chapter no attempt was made to survey all the issues involved in carrying out a compensation test (or, as it is more commonly called, benefit-cost analysis). Instead, we focused on one important part of it: utilizing information available from market demand curves. We saw that, under certain conditions, the market demand curve can reveal virtually everything necessary to calculate the sum of compensations. Under other circumstances, knowledge of the market demand curves is essentially useless for those purposes.

The most important point from these examples is the one that is emphasized throughout the text: The development of analytic skill depends heavily on understanding the implications of alternative model specifications. Linkages which are assumed to be universal in the context of purely private markets may be nonexistent in the particular policy setting being analyzed. In this chapter, for example, we showed that the link between individual consumer surplus and the area under the market demand curve is broken when consumers are misinformed and thus make purchasing errors. But it is precisely in the areas in which consumer information is judged most seriously inadequate that public policy is likely to exist. The creators and users of policy analyses must be sensitive to the logical underpinnings of models in order to use the models and interpret them effectively.

EXERCISES

5-1 There are 40 consumers in an economy who purchase a drug to relieve the pain of arthritis. They think that the only effective drug is Namebrand. However, the same drug can be bought by its chemical name acethistestamine, or ace for short. The drug costs $2 to produce no matter what it is called; any quantity demanded can be supplied at that price. The company producing Namebrand exploits consumer ignorance by charging $6 for each unit; i.e., the consumers buy Namebrand at $6 per unit, not realizing that ace is a perfect substitute available for only $2.

The aggregate demand curve of the 40 uninformed consumers is

$$Q = 400 - 40P$$

a What would be the value to *consumers* of knowing that ace and Namebrand are identical? (Answer: $960)

b How much is the deadweight loss due to the consumers' lack of perfect information? (Answer: $320)

5-2 There are two and only two consumers, Smith and Jones, who buy a product of uncertain quality. When both are informed of the quality, they have the same demand curve:

$$P = 100 - \frac{Q}{4}$$

The market price is $P = \$50$. Suppose they are uninformed and have the following uninformed demand curves:

Smith	$P = 125 - Q/4$	overestimates value
Jones	$P = 80 - Q/4$	underestimates value

a Calculate the loss in consumer surplus to Smith from not having accurate information. Make a similar calculation for Jones.

b Calculate the uninformed market demand curve. Also calculate the informed market demand curve.

c What is the loss in consumer surplus as measured by the deadweight loss triangle between the market informed and uninformed curves? (Answer: $25)

d What is the actual loss in consumer surplus from having poor information? (Answer: $2050)

UNCERTAINTY AND PUBLIC POLICY

In this chapter we will introduce models that have been developed to explain the effect of uncertainty on individual economic behavior. Increasingly, analysts have come to recognize that uncertainty is not just a curious oddity that arises in a few isolated instances. It is a pervasive phenomenon which explains a great deal about individual behavior and can be a major factor in the design of policies.

Consider energy policy, for example. In the United States there continues to be much discussion about achieving "energy independence." This aim is antithetical to the elementary economic principle that free trade is desirable. If a consumer in the United States is willing to buy imported oil at a price acceptable to a world supplier, then both parties are made better off by trade and any public policy designed to prevent the trade would seem to be inefficient.

But the oil embargo of 1973 and 1974 made the nation aware of an additional cost of such trade. Large-scale dependence on foreign oil supplies makes much of the U.S. economy vulnerable to the vagaries of political events beyond our control. This introduces a large uncertainty about our future well-being, and *the uncertainty itself makes many people feel worse off.* The worthiness of such policies as stockpiling oil (e.g., in the Strategic Petroleum Reserve in Louisiana) or imposing an oil import tax depends in good part on how much people are willing to pay to avoid or reduce the uncertainty. This is one example of why analysts must be able to assess the importance of changes in the level and cost of uncertainty associated with proposed policies.

To accomplish the assessment, we must develop a more general understanding of how individuals respond to uncertainty. We begin by reviewing the concepts of expected value and expected utility, and we consider the proposition that individuals act to maximize expected utility. The latter proposition, known as the *expected utility theorem,* is helpful in understanding the economic costs of uncertainty.

However, there are many situations in which individual responses to uncertainty do not seem to be modeled well by the expected utility theorem. Some situations may be better modeled by concepts from the *theory of games against persons;* we illustrate this with an urban housing problem known as the *Slumlord's Dilemma.* Behavior in other situations may be better modeled by concepts of *bound rationality;* we consider this in the context of food-labeling requirements and federal policy to subsidize disaster insurance in areas which are highly flood-prone. These latter models are discussed in the section on alternative models of individual behavior under uncertainty, after consideration of some of the choice possibilities for responding to uncertainty introduced in the section on risk control and risk-shifting mechanisms.

That is, the response to uncertainty depends not only on how individuals think about it but also on the set of possible responses. The situations analyzed in this chapter are primarily those in which the individual cannot alter the amount of uncertainty, but may be able to reduce exposure to it.[1] An example is the uncertainty faced by the farmer planting now and concerned about crop price at harvest time. The farmer cannot change the price uncertainty, but he or she can reduce the risk from it by selling a futures contract (the sale of some portion of the expected future crop at a price agreed upon now).

A wide variety of social mechanisms are intended to reduce the costs of risk. We do not pretend in this chapter to give an exhaustive description of them, but we mention and explain many of them at points convenient to their development. *A fundamental principle* behind many of them *is to shift the risk to where it is less costly.* Two basic procedures, *risk pooling* and *risk spreading,* are often used by individuals to that end. Insurance, stock markets, and futures markets are examples of such mechanisms.

Some mechanisms of public policy, e.g., limited liability and the subsidized disaster insurance mentioned above, are used to alter the distribution of risk. Other public policies are adopted in an attempt to control risk more directly through such means as occupational licensing requirements, consumer product safety standards, and health standards in the workplace. The appropriateness of these policies is often a difficult question to resolve, in good part because of analytic uncertainty about how individuals respond to them relative to alternatives.

One interesting area of analysis involving uncertainty is health policy, particularly national health insurance or alternatives to it. In the section on

---

[1] There are also types of uncertainty which an individual may alter. For example, credit lenders and employers can use resources to gather information about credit and job applicants before responding to their respective applications. Examples which emphasize information are discussed throughout Parts IV and V. We defer these discussions until we have reviewed the functioning of markets and can develop perspective on the role of information within the markets.

medical care insurance later in this chapter the continuing cost spiral in the delivery of medical services is shown to be an unintended consequence of insurance coverage. The insurance coverage which reduces risk simultaneously distorts individual incentives to conserve scarce resources. The chapter concludes with an extended analysis of this *moral hazard* problem, including an optional section which illustrates an empirical method for estimating the value of risk savings from medical insurance.

EXPECTED VALUE AND EXPECTED UTILITY

When an individual makes an economic decision, we often assume that each of the alternatives is known and understood with certainty. But in many, perhaps most, cases there is uncertainty about what the individual will receive as a consequence of any specific choice. For example, the decision to allocate time to reading this textbook is a gamble; it may not pay off for any particular reader.[2] New cars may turn out to be lemons; a job may be offered that exposes the worker to risk injury. In each case the person making the decision simply does not know in advance what the outcome will be.

This type of uncertainty does not necessarily lead to any revisions in the ordinary theorems of demand and supply. For example, other things being equal, an increase in the price of a risky commodity would be expected to reduce the demand for the commodity. A reason for studying uncertainty on its own, however, is that we observe that the willingness to pay for a risky commodity depends upon the perceived likelihoods of possible outcomes. A potential buyer of a particular car will offer less as his or her subjective evaluation of the likelihood that it is a lemon increases. It is this phenomenon on which we wish to focus here: how individuals respond to changes in these perceived likelihoods and how social mechanisms can affect those perceptions.

Certain fundamental concepts must be clarified before we can consider alternative models of individual behavior under uncertainty. One is the set of alternative *states of the world,* of the different, mutually exclusive outcomes that may result from the process generating the uncertainty. For example, if a coin is flipped, two states of the world may result: It can come up heads, or it can come up tails. If a single die is thrown, there are six possible states, one corresponding to each face of the die. The definition of the states depends in part on the problem being considered. If you are betting that a three will come up on the die, then only two states are relevant to you: three and not three. An uncertain outcome of a university course may be any of the specific grades A−, B+, C+, and so on, for one student and pass or not pass for another, depending on which gamble has been chosen.

Another fundamental concept is the *probability* that a particular state will occur. If an evenly weighted coin is flipped, the probability that it will come up heads is $\frac{1}{2}$ and the probability that it will come up tails also is $\frac{1}{2}$. If the evenly

---

[2] Please note that the same thing is true of alternative textbooks.

weighted die is thrown, each face has a probability $\frac{1}{6}$ of being up. If you bet on three, then you have $\frac{1}{6}$ chance of getting three and a $\frac{5}{6}$ chance of getting not three.

The relation between an *objective conception* of the states of the world with their associated probabilities and an individual's *subjective perception* of them is a subject of considerable controversy in many applications. It is a philosophical issue whether any events are truly random. If a coin is flipped in exactly the same way every time (e.g., by machine), it will land with the same face up every time; under those conditions there is no uncertainty. Based on the laws of physics, and given perfect information on how a coin is flipped and time to calculate, one can predict with virtual certainty what the outcome will be. Put differently, in an objective sense there is no uncertainty.

Why then do we all agree, for the usual case like the coin toss at the start of a football game, that the outcomes heads and tails have equal probability? There are two parts to the answer. First, coins are not tossed exactly the same, and we lack the information and calculation time necessary to predict the outcome with a model based upon the laws of physics. Thus the *uncertainty is due to our own lack of information and/or information-processing ability.*

Second, we do have some information: historical evidence. We have observed that in a large number of these uncontrolled or irregular coin tosses, heads and tails appears with approximately equal frequency. We might say that when the actual determinants of the coin toss outcome are selected randomly (e.g., the force, speed, and distance of the flip), it is objectively true that the outcomes have equal probability. Furthermore, if we share the subjective perception that the football referee "chooses" the determinants of the toss randomly, we conclude that the probability of each outcome is $\frac{1}{2}$.

Recognizing that perceptions of probabilities depend heavily on the type of knowledge we possess, let us consider a distinction Frank Knight proposed be made between "risky" and "uncertain" situations.[3] *Risky situations,* in his terminology, are those in which each possible outcome has a known probability of occurring. *Uncertain situations,* again according to Knight, are those in which the probability of each outcome is not known. The coin toss is risky, but whether there will be a damaging nuclear accident next year is uncertain. There is some risk of particular medical problems arising during surgery, but the consequences of depleting the ozone layer in the earth's atmosphere are uncertain. It is clear that one of the factors which explains why we consider some situations uncertain is lack of experience with them; we do not have many trial depletions of the ozone layer, as we have with coin tossing.

Let us now recognize that knowledge differences may cause the same situation to be perceived differently by different people. Before you started this book, you may have been uncertain about whether you would enjoy it. I may

---

[3] In less formal usage common today, uncertainty is used to refer to all situations in which the outcome is unknown. Thus quotation marks are used to here to denote the meanings assigned by Knight. See F. H. Knight, *Risk, Uncertainty, and Profit* (Boston: Houghton Mifflin Company, 1921).

know the probability that you will enjoy it, based on surveys of past readers. But whether you will enjoy the rest of the book is perceived as risky by both of us. Furthermore, we will have different probability estimates, and yours will be based on better information (your own reactions so far) than mine. Thus our subjective perceptions of the probability will differ.

In most economic models *individual decision making depends upon the subjective perceptions about the possible states and their likelihoods.* We made two points about those perceptions above. First, doubts about which state will occur are due to lack of knowledge. Second, because there are knowledge differences among people, subjective perceptions will often be different.

At this point we might inquire further about how subjective perceptions are formed. For example, individuals can alter their perceptions by seeking additional information, and they might decide to do so in light of the perceived benefits and costs. Different analytic assumptions about the formation of subjective perceptions lead to different predictions about behavior and can lead to quite different policy recommendations. However, we avoid those complications in this section by sticking to situations like the coin toss: individuals perceive the world as "risky" and the subjective probability assessments coincide with the objective ones. Thus we can refer to "the" probability of an event in an unambiguous sense.

One other basic concept to be introduced is the *payoff* in each possible state of the world. Suppose when a coin is flipped, you will receive $2 if the coin turns up heads and −$1 if the coin turns up tails. These payments or prizes associated with each state are referred to as the payoffs. Then we can define the *expected value* of a risky situation: *The expected value is the sum of the payoff in each possible state of the world weighted by the probability that it will occur. If there are n possible states, and each state i has a payoff X_i and a probability of occurring Π_i, the expected value E(V) is*

$$E(V) = \sum_{i=1}^{n} \Pi_i X_i$$

In the coin toss game, the $E(V)$ is

$$E(V) = \tfrac{1}{2}(\$2) + \tfrac{1}{2}(-\$1) = \$0.50$$

If all the states are properly considered, it will always be true that $\sum_{i=1}^{n} \Pi_i = 1$; that is, it is certain that one of the states will occur. When we flip the coin, it must come up either heads or tails. (We do not count tosses in which the coin stays on its edge.)

If we agree to flip the coin 100 times with the same payoffs as above on each flip, then the $E(V)$ of this new game is $50 [100 times the $E(V)$ of one flip] because the result of any single flip is completely independent of the results of other flips in the game. Many people would be willing to pay some *entry price* to play this game. Suppose the entry price is $50, or $0.50 per flip. Then the entry price equals the $E(V)$ of playing the game, or the net expected gain is zero. Any risky situation in which the entry price equals the $E(V)$ is called a *fair game*.

It is common for individuals to refuse to play fair games. Let us go back to the simple game of a single coin toss with payoffs as above. For an entry price of $0.50, which makes the game fair, *risk-averse people* would not be willing to play. These people prefer the certainty of not playing, which has the same net expected value as playing, to the risky situation. However, some people would be willing to take the risk. But if the payoffs on a single toss were changed to be $200 on heads and $-$100 on tails and the entry price were raised to $50, fewer people would play. All three situations have the same net expected value, so it must be some other factor which explains why fewer people are willing to play as the stakes get raised. This other factor is the risk.

A common but somewhat incorrect example often used to illustrate this point (that expected value is not a sufficient predictor of decision-making behavior) is the St. Petersburg Paradox. Consider the game in which an evenly weighted coin is flipped until it comes up heads, which ends the game. Then the probability that the game will end on the ith flip is $(\frac{1}{2})^i$. If a head does not come up until the ith flip, then the payoff to the player is 2^i. Thus the game has the following expected payoffs:

Flip number	Probability	Payoff	Expected payoff
1	$\frac{1}{2}$	2	1
2	$\frac{1}{4}$	4	1
3	$\frac{1}{8}$	8	1
4	$\frac{1}{16}$	16	1
.			
.			
.			

Since theoretically the game can go on forever, its expected value is infinite. That is, $\sum_{i=1}^{\infty} \Pi_i X_i = 1 + 1 + 1 + \cdots = \infty$. But when people are asked what entry price they are willing to pay to play this game, the response is invariably a number below infinity; most people will not even pay a paltry million dollars to play this game. In fact, few people will offer more than $20 to play. This is the paradox: Why should people offer so little to play a game with such a high expected value?

A crucial insight was offered by Bernoulli, a mathematician of the eighteenth century, who suggested that individuals value not the expected *dollars*, but rather the expected *utility* that can be derived from them. If individual utility functions are characterized by a *diminishing marginal utility of money*, then the expected utility of a *gain* of, say, $100 will be less than the expected utility of a *loss* of $100. In the St. Petersburg Paradox, the expected utility payoff of successive tosses would diminish and could therefore have a finite sum. Then it is perfectly plausible that individuals would offer only finite amounts of money for the privilege of playing the game.

For example, suppose the utility value of the *i*th payoff is $(\frac{3}{2})^i$. Then the expected utility $E(U)$ from playing the game is[4]

$$E(U) = \sum_{i=1}^{\infty} (\tfrac{1}{2})^i(\tfrac{3}{2})^i = \sum_{i=1}^{\infty} (\tfrac{3}{4})^i = 3$$

We have not yet discussed the monetary value of an expected utility increase of 3 utils to this individual, but it should be clear that there is no reason why it could not be a low dollar amount.[5]

However, the above illustration does not explain why most individuals *in fact* will offer *low* dollar amounts to play the game, and in that sense Bernoulli's crucial insight does not really resolve the paradox. The answer actually has nothing to do with diminishing marginal utility. The real answer is that no game operator has the assets to be able to make the larger payoffs.

For example, suppose the U.S. government guaranteed to pay prizes up to $6.2 trillion—the approximate 1980 value of capital assets (excluding land) in the United States.[6] That would enable payment of the scheduled prizes if heads came up on any of the first 42 prizes, but beyond that the prize could get no larger than $6.2 trillion. Thus the expected value of this game would be only $43. Since no plausible game operator could guarantee payments anywhere near that size, the expected value of the game with realistic prize limits is considerably below $43. If the maximum prize is $1 million, for example, the expected value of the game is approximately $20.

---

[4] The sum of an infinite series $a, ar, ar^2, \ldots, ar^n, \ldots$ equals $a/(1 - r)$ for $r < 1$. In the above equation, $a = \frac{3}{4}$ and $r = \frac{3}{4}$.

[5] Since $X = 2^i$ and $U = (\frac{3}{2})^i$, we can take the logarithm of each equation and divide one by the other to deduce:

$$\ln U = \frac{(\ln X)\,(\ln \tfrac{3}{2})}{\ln 2}$$

or
$$U = X^{0.58496}$$

We interpret this equation as showing the utility increase from additional dollars. When $U = 3$, the equation implies $X = \$6.54$. If the individual behaves in accordance with the expected utility theorem to be discussed shortly, then $6.54 is the most this individual would offer to play the game.

[6] This rough estimate is made from data contained in E. F. Denison, *Accounting for Slower Economic Growth* (Washington, D.C.: The Brookings Institution, 1979) and the *Economic Report of the President, February 1982*. Table 4-1 of Denison (p. 51) indicates that the 1978 gross value of nonresidential structures, equipment, and inventories is $2055 billion (expressed in 1972 dollars). Table 6-4 of Denison (p. 89) indicates that the 1976 gross value of the housing stock is $1423.3 (again in 1972 dollars). Our $6.2 trillion estimate is made by converting those figures into 1980 dollars by using the implicit GNP price deflator of 1.7736 (*Economic Report*, p. 236, table B-3) and adding. This estimate excludes the value of government assets, which according to an estimate for 1980 in the *Economic Report* (p. 104, table 4-5) is $727 billion.

Nevertheless, Bernoulli's suggestion that behavior depends upon the expected utility of a risky situation has been shown to offer considerable insight into decision making of this type. We can define *expected utility* as follows: *The expected utility of a risky situation is the sum of the resulting utility level in each possible state of the world weighted by the probability that it will occur. If we let W_0 equal the initial wealth, E_0 equal the entry price, and $U(W)$ represent the utility function, the expected utility $E(U)$ may be expressed as*

$$E(U) = \sum_{i=1}^{n} \Pi_i U(W_0 - E_0 + X_i)$$

The *expected utility theorem* simply says that *individuals choose among alternatives in order to maximize expected utility.*[7]

As we discuss this theorem, let us keep in mind a distinction between positive and normative views of it. The positive question concerns the predictive power of the theory: the extent to which actual behavior is consistent with the implications of the theorem. The normative issue is whether people should behave in accordance with the theorem even if they don't. That is, perhaps individuals do not always understand the consequences of their choices under uncertainty and they would be better off if they did act to maximize expected utility. Unless stated otherwise, we will generally take the view that increases in expected utility are desirable.

To understand the behavior implied by the theorem, let us construct a diagram illustrating how an expected utility maximizer evaluates risky choices. Imagine for the moment that the individual can participate in a lottery with only two possible outcomes: winning $50,000 or nothing. Given a choice, naturally the individual would prefer a lottery with a higher rather than lower probability of winning the $50,000. The best lottery would be the one in which the probability of winning equaled 1, and the worst would have a probability of winning equal to 0. Let us arbitrarily assign a utility value of 1 to the best

---

[7] To derive the expected utility theorem from assumptions about behavior requires several assumptions about human decision making in addition to those introduced in Chapter 2. For a full review of them see K. Arrow, *Essays in the Theory of Risk-Bearing* (Chicago: Markham Publishing Co., 1971). The original derivation of a utility measure to include risky situations was made by John von Neumann and Oskar Morgenstern in their *Theory of Games and Economic Behavior* (Princeton, N.J.: Princeton University Press, 1944).

Probably the most controversial of the additional assumptions is one that implies that an individual is indifferent to two lotteries which are identical except in one state of the world; in that state the prizes are different but are ones to which the individual is indifferent. If a person is indifferent between A and B, then the assumption is that

$$\Pi_A U(A) + (1 - \Pi_A)U(C) = \Pi_A U(B) + (1 - \Pi_A)U(C)$$

However, it is commonly found in surveys and experiments that individuals are *not* indifferent between these two lotteries. See, for example, Jacques Dreze, "Axiomatic Theories of Choice, Cardinal Utility and Subjective Utility: A Review," in P. Diamond and M. Rothschild (eds.), *Uncertainty in Economics* (New York: Academic Press, 1978), pp. 37–57.

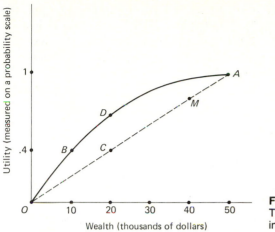

FIGURE 6-1
The Von Neumann–Morgenstern utility index for evaluating risky situations.

lottery (that is, $50,000 with certainty) and 0 to the worst lottery (that is, $0 with certainty).

In Figure 6-1 the horizontal axis shows the monetary payoff and the vertical axis shows the utility level. We graph the utility level and payoff of each of the two lotteries, shown as point *A* and the origin. Using these two lotteries as reference points, let us now construct a utility index specific to the individual. This index can be used to reveal the individual's preference ordering of all possible risky situations (with possible outcomes between the best and the worst), provided the individual is an expected utility maximizer.

Consider any amount of money between $0 and $50,000, like $10,000, which we offer to the individual with certainty. Obviously, the best lottery is preferred to a certain $10,000. Similarly, the certain $10,000 is preferred to the worst lottery. Therefore, there must be some lottery with a probability of winning between 0 and 1 which the individual considers exactly as desirable as the certain $10,000.

We ask the individual to identify the probability. Suppose it is .4. Then we define the .4 probability as the utility value to the individual of $10,000 with certainty. This is shown as point *B* in Figure 6-1. If we follow this procedure for all monetary amounts between $0 and $50,000, we have a relation showing the individual's utility level as a function of wealth.[8] This is shown as the solid curved line. The height of the curve, or the utility level, equals the probability of winning necessary to make the individual indifferent to the lottery and the level of certain wealth shown on the horizontal axis. This construct is referred to, after its creators, as the *Von Neumann–Morgenstern utility index*.[9]

---

[8] This is an *indirect* utility function; the utility comes not from wealth directly, but from the goods and services purchased with it.

[9] This index can be mistakenly interpreted as a cardinal utility scale. It is true that it is cardinal in the sense that it is unique up to a linear transformation. However, it does not measure preference intensity. For example, one cannot conclude that a risky situation with $E(U) = .2$ is twice as

The dashed straight line connecting the origin with point A shows the expected value of the lottery (on the horizontal axis) as a function of the probability of winning (on the vertical axis). For example, the $E(V)$ of the lottery with .4 chance of winning $50,000 is $20,000.

$$E(V) = .4 (\$50,000) + .6(\$0)$$
$$= \$20,000$$

This is shown as point C. The height at point C also equals the expected utility of the lottery:

$$E(U) = .4U (\$50,000) + .6U(\$0)$$
$$= .4(1) + .6(0)$$
$$= .4$$

This should not be surprising. The utility index was constructed in recognition of the individual's indifference between this lottery and the certain wealth ($10,000) assigned a utility level of .4. Of course, the lottery and its certain wealth equivalent should have the same utility level.

The utility index can now be used to rank-order risky situations because it allows their expected utilities to be calculated and compared. Suppose the individual actually has $20,000 with certainty; thus the current position is shown at point D. We then propose a fair game: We will allow the individual to take a chance on the above lottery with .4 probability of winning $50,000 in return for an entry price of $20,000 (the expected value of the lottery). The individual refuses; the expected utility from the gamble (the height at point C) is less than the utility of the certain $20,000 (the height of point D). *An individual who refuses a fair gamble is said to be risk-averse.*

Let us note that this does not imply that risk-averse individuals will refuse *any* gamble. Suppose, for the same $20,000 entry price, the individual could play a lottery which had a .8 probability of winning $50,000. This is shown as point M in Figure 6-1. It has expected value of $40,000, and we can see geometrically that the expected utility from the gamble (the .8 height of point M) exceeds the utility of the current position. Thus the risk-averse expected utility maximizer would accept this gamble. Its attraction is that it has an expected value sufficiently greater than the entry price (unlike a fair gamble). This suggests, for example, why even financially conservative people may invest in the stock market.

The risk aversion illustrated above is a consequence of the concavity of the utility function we drew. (That is, the curve lies above the straight line connecting any two of its points.) The concavity is equivalent to a diminishing

---

preferable as one in which $E(U) = .1$. All the index does is rank-order alternative risky situations. For a discussion of this, see William J. Baumol, *Economic Theory and Operations Analysis,* 4th ed. (Englewood Cliffs, N.J.: Prentice-Hall, Inc., 1977), pp. 431–432.

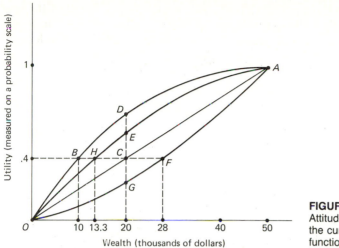

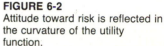

FIGURE 6-2
Attitude toward risk is reflected in the curvature of the utility function.

marginal utility of money or wealth. (That is, the slope of the curve diminishes.) Thus anyone with a diminishing marginal utility of wealth is risk-averse. The greater the degree of concavity of the utility function, the greater the risk aversion. (We will provide a measure of this shortly.) We illustrate in Figure 6-2 several different utility functions which vary in the degree of risk aversion.

Of course, it is possible that some individuals are not risk-averse. We also show in Figure 6-2 a utility function *OGFA* characterized by increasing marginal utility of wealth. This individual evaluates the utility of the fair gamble (the height at point *C*) as greater than the utility of a certain $20,000 (the height at point *G*). In other words, this individual would accept the fair gamble of participating in the lottery for an entry price of $20,000. *An individual who accepts a fair gamble is a risk lover.* Similarly, the individual with the straight-line utility function *OCA* (constant marginal utility of wealth) is indifferent to our proposal; *an individual who is indifferent to a fair gamble is said to be risk-neutral.*

One way to measure the strength of risk aversion to a gamble is to look at the pure risk cost. *The pure risk cost is defined as the difference between the expected value and the certain-value equivalent of a risky situation.* To illustrate, we look at Figure 6-2 in a different context.

Suppose each individual owns $50,000 in jewelry which has a .6 probability of being stolen. Think of the origin of the horizontal axis as an unspecified amount of wealth from other sources; the horizontal axis now measures the additional wealth from jewelry and is dependent upon which state occurs (stolen or not stolen). The expected wealth from jewelry is $20,000 [= .4($50,000) + .6($0)]. On the vertical axis the utility level is measured; the scale is from 0 for the worst outcome (stolen) to 1 for the best outcome (not stolen) as before.

Consider the individual with the utility curve *OHA*. This person is indifferent to the risky situation with a $20,000 expected value (point *C*) and having a certain $13,300 (point *H*). Thus the pure risk cost is $6700 (= $20,000 expected value − $13,300 certain-value equivalent). That is, this individual will pay up to $6700 in terms of reduced expected value in order to avoid the risk. *In general, risk-averse persons will pay to avoid gambles.* The willingness to pay to avoid risk is a fundamental reason for the existence of insurance and other risk-reducing mechanisms that we will consider shortly. For example, this individual will pay up to a $36,700 premium for full-coverage jewelry insurance; this ensures that the net wealth from jewelry (after insuring it) is $13,300 in both states of the world.

Recall that we stated earlier that the individual with the more concave utility function *OBDA* is more risk-averse. Now we can see that he or she evaluates the pure risk cost of the same risky situation at a greater amount than $6700; to be exact, $10,000 (= $20,000 expected value − $10,000 certain-value equivalent). The risk-neutral person has no risk cost and will take no reduction in expected value in order to avoid the risky situation. The risk lover has a negative risk cost of $8000, since the certain wealth equivalent (at point *F*) is $28,000. That is, because the latter enjoys the risk, the expected value would have to be increased by $8000 in order to persuade the individual to avoid the risk.

The above discussion shows that perceived risk cost is a function of risk preferences. Now we wish to illustrate the effect on one individual of varying the amount of risk. In Figure 6-3 we replicate the utility function *OBDA* from Figure 6-2. Point *C* shows the expected utility and expected value from the jewelry as discussed above.

Let us contrast this with another situation, one in which only $40,000 of jewelry is at risk and the other $10,000 of wealth is safe. Thus, the individual

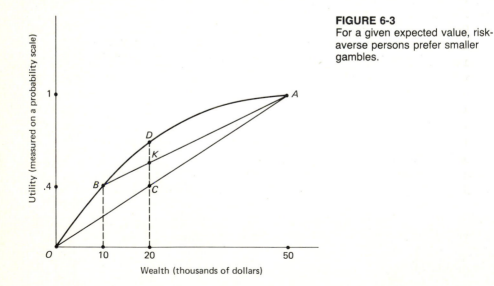

FIGURE 6-3
For a given expected value, risk-averse persons prefer smaller gambles.

will either end up at point *B* (the jewelry is stolen) or point *A* (not stolen). The straight line *BA* shows each possible combination of expected wealth (on the horizontal axis) and expected utility (on the vertical axis) that may result, depending on the probability of theft.[10] Suppose this probability is .75, chosen to keep the expected value at $20,000 as in the prior situation. That is, the *E(V)* of this new situation is

$$E(V) = .25(\$50,000) + .75(\$10,000)$$
$$= \$20,000$$

The expected utility can be calculated:

$$E(U) = .25U(\$50,000) + .75U(\$10,000)$$
$$= .25(1) + .75(.4)$$
$$= .55$$

This is shown as point *K* on line *BA*.

In Figure 6-3 we see that the expected utility of the new situation (the height at point *K*) is greater than that of the initial situation (the height at point *C*), even though the expected value is the same. Why? The risk is lower in the new situation; the likelihood of ending up in positions farther away from the expected value has been reduced. In the diagram this is reflected by the line *BA* being above the line *OA*: *For any expected wealth* (on the horizontal axis), *the smaller gambles are preferred by risk-averse persons.* This geometric illustration helps to clarify why, in our earlier examples of coin toss games with identical expected values but increasing stakes, individuals may become less inclined to play as the stakes become greater.[11]

The expected utility model allows for a diversity of risk preferences, as we have seen. But it is important to note that *empirically risk-averse behavior is predominant.* Probably the most important evidence of risk aversion is that virtually all individuals diversify their portfolios. That is, wealth is not stored all in one asset but is spread among various stocks, bonds, real estate, savings accounts, pension funds, and other assets. We show in the following section that such diversification has the primary purpose of reducing risk. An individual with risk-neutral or risk-loving preferences would not behave in this manner.

In addition, when individuals bear significant risk as a consequence of such factors as home ownership and automobile driving, they will usually offer others more than a fair price to bear the risk for them. Almost all insurance purchases are evidence of risk-averse behavior of this type, since the premiums

---

[10] Both the expected value and expected utility are weighted averages of their respective values at points *B* and *A*; the weights on each are the same and equal the probabilities of state *B* and state *A*.

[11] Recall that risk-averse people will gamble if the gamble has a sufficently high net positive expected value (i.e., is not fair).

are at least as great as the expected payout.[12] For example, most individuals who drive purchase more than the minimum insurance required by state regulations.

If risk aversion is so predominant, how do we explain the commonly observed willingness of individuals to participate in risky situations in which the odds are against them (i.e., the net expected value is negative)? For example, many people seem to enjoy an evening in Las Vegas or Atlantic City or a day at the race track. Apart from professional gamblers, this behavior is probably best understood for its direct consumption value. That is, people may receive utility directly from the process of gambling similarly to the consumption of any other good or service. The primary motivation for participation need not be the expected indirect utility from the wealth change associated with gambling.

Some individuals may engage in unfair gambles because of a limited preference for risk, even though they are primarily risk-averse. That is, it is possible to be risk-averse over some range of wealth while simultaneously being a risk lover over another range. In Figure 6-4a we illustrate one such possibility.[13]

An individual is currently at a wealth level of $50,000. However, this wealth includes a $25,000 home which has some possibility of being accidentally destroyed by fire or natural disaster. The individual also has a chance to invest $2000 in a new solar technology company which, if successful, will return $10,000. The preferences indicated by the utility function in Figure 6-4a suggest the individual is risk-averse concerning the bulk of wealth already in his or her possession but is willing to gamble small amounts "against the odds" if the prospects of wealth gains are large enough. As drawn, the individual will purchase actuarially fair insurance and may invest in the solar technology company even if the investment is less than a fair gamble.[14]

Athough the shape of the utility function in Figure 6-4a does seem to explain some behavior that we observe, it raises other questions. In particular, suppose the solar investment wins in the above example and the individual now has a wealth of $58,000. To remain consistent with the behavioral idea of preserving

---

[12] Private medical and dental insurance, when provided through an employer, is a form of nontaxable income. Roughly speaking, $50 of medical insurance provided in this way yields $50 of benefits to the individual in terms of expected medical services (ignoring risk costs). If the $50 is given to the individual as taxable income, after taxes there will be only $25 to $40 (depending on the individual's tax bracket) left for consumption purposes. Thus, the favorable tax treatment can result in expected medical care benefits (apart from risk reduction) which exceed the individual's cost of the insurance (in terms of foregone consumption of other things). Thus, we do not count employer-provided insurance of this type as evidence of risk aversion.

[13] This was first suggested in M. Friedman and L. Savage, "The Utility Analysis of Choices Involving Risk," *Journal of Political Economy, 56,* August 1948, pp. 279–304.

[14] We have not specified the probability of success of the solar technology. If it is a fair gamble, the individual will clearly invest because the expected utility exceeds the current utility. Therefore, the investment can be at least slightly less than fair and the individual will still invest. However, the probability of success may be so low that the expected utility falls below the current level, and then the individual will not invest despite the preference for risk.

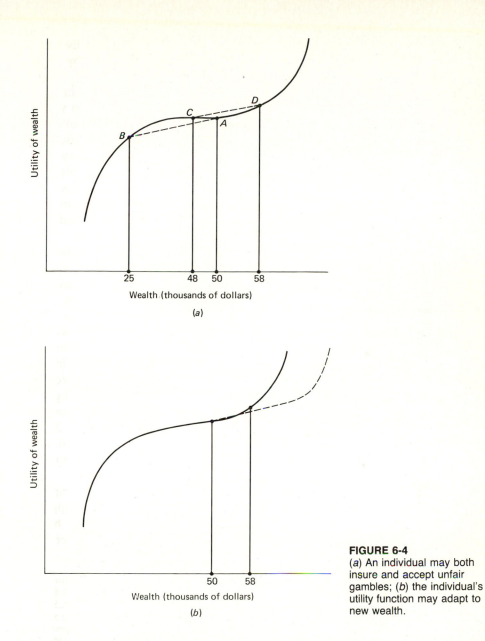

FIGURE 6-4
(*a*) An individual may both insure and accept unfair gambles; (*b*) the individual's utility function may adapt to new wealth.

wealth already possessed, the individual's utility function now has to shift to something like that illustrated by the dashed extension in Figure 6-4*b*. In most economic theory we typically assume that the utility function is fixed. But this example suggests that, for some situations, it may be important to consider the possibility of an *adaptive* utility function. (That is, the utility function depends on which state occurs.)

The above discussion is intended to suggest that, on balance, risk in our society is considered a social cost and not a social benefit. Thus, when public policy alternatives imply differing amounts of risk, those with more risk are disfavored unless other factors (e.g., sufficiently higher expected values) work in their favor. In the optional section later on in this chapter, an empirical method used to assess the risk costs of a change in policy (involving health insurance) is presented.

RISK CONTROL AND RISK-SHIFTING MECHANISMS

Recognizing that risk is generally considered costly, we consider in this section mechanisms used to affect its costs. Two fundamental mechanisms used to reduce risk costs are risk pooling and risk spreading. We discuss them below and then turn to a discussion of public policies which affect risk costs.

Risk Pooling and Risk Spreading

We begin by developing the idea of risk pooling informally. Imagine that each of many households has $5000 worth of property that is vulnerable to theft. Furthermore, suppose that each independently faces a .2 probability that the property will be stolen.[15] Let us consider what happens if an insurance company offers each household full-coverage insurance at an actuarially fair premium of $1000. (That is, the premium equals the expected loss.) Unlike each household, the insurance company doesn't care whose property is stolen; its concern is that the total premiums it collects will (at least) cover the total cost of replacing all the property that is stolen.

The statistical *law of large numbers* implies that, as the number of identical but independent random events increases, the likelihood that the actual *average* result will be close to the expected result increases. This is the same principle that applies to coin flips: The larger the number of flips, the more likely it is that the total proportion of heads will be close to $\frac{1}{2}$. For the insurance company it becomes a virtual certainty that approximately 20 percent of the insured households will have claims and that therefore it will face total claims approximately equal to the total premiums collected. Thus *by shifting the risk to the insurance company where it is pooled, the risk cost dissipates*. As long as the pool is large enough, the risk cost to the insurance company becomes negligible and premiums equal to expected losses will be sufficient to cover the claims.

Let us give a simple numerical example to illustrate how risk pooling reduces risk costs. Suppose we consider two identical risk-averse individuals. Each has $50,000 in wealth $5000 of which is subject to theft; each indepen-

---

[15] Independence implies that the probability of theft in one household is unrelated to whether theft has occurred in any other household.

dently faces a probability of theft equal to .2; and each has a utility function of wealth W:[16]

$$U(W) = -e^{-0.0002W}$$

Initially, the two bear the risks independently, or they *self-insure*. Then each has an expected utility of

$$E(U) = .2U(\$45,000) + .8U(\$50,000)$$
$$= .2(-e^{-9}) + .8(-e^{-10})$$

which, with the aid of a calculator, is found to be

$$E(U) = .2(-0.0001234098) + .8(-0.0000453999)$$
$$= -0.0000610019$$

We find the certain-wealth equivalent (W_c) by solving

$$-0.0000610019 = -e^{-0.0002W_c}$$
or
$$W_c = \$48,523.03$$

Since the expected wealth of each is $49,000 [= .2($45,000) + .8($50,000)], the risk cost is $476.97. In other words, each would forego as much as $476.97 of expected value in order to be rid of the risk from self-insurance.

Now suppose that these two individuals agree to pool their risk, so that any losses from theft will be evenly divided between them. Then there are three possible outcomes or states:

1 Neither individual has a loss from theft ($W = $50,000).
2 Both individuals have losses from theft ($W = $45,000).
3 One individual has a loss and the other does not ($W = $47,500).

The probability that the first case will arise is .64 = .8(.8); that of the second is .04 = .2(.2); and that of the third is .32 = .2(.8) + .8(.2).[17] We check this by noting that 1 = .64 + .04 + .32, or it is a certainty that one of the three outcomes will arise. Note what is happening as a consequence of this pooling arrangement: The probability of an extreme outcome of $45,000 or $50,000 is declining, compared with the self-insurance option, while the probability of an

---

[16] This utility function is one with diminishing marginal utility of wealth. It is characterized by mild risk aversion: The individual is indifferent to receiving $900 with certainty or accepting a 50 percent chance to win $2000. This is explained further in the optional section. The natural number e ≈ 2.71828.

[17] This case has two terms: There is a .16 probability that the first individual will suffer a loss and the second will not, and there is the same probability that the second will suffer a loss and the first will not.

outcome in the middle is increasing. The expected wealth, however, remains the same:

$$E(W) = .64(\$50,000) + .04(\$45,000) + .32(\$47,500)$$
$$= \$49,000$$

What happens to expected utility? With expected wealth the same and with the likelihood of ending up close to it greater, the risk is reduced and expected utility increases (i.e., is a smaller negative number):

$$E(U) = .64U(\$50,000) + .04U(\$45,000) + .32U(\$47,500)$$
$$= -0.0000579449$$

The certain-wealth equivalent is found by solving as follows:

$$-0.0000579449 = -e^{-W_c}$$

whence $\quad\quad W_c = \$48,780.09$

Thus, we can see that this simple risk-pooling arrangement increases expected utility because it reduces the risk cost per person from \$476.97 to only \$219.91. Another way to look at it is from the perspective of the compensation principle. That is, let us ask whether the change from self-insurance to risk pooling has benefits greater than costs. Each individual values the initial situation at \$48,523.03 and the risk-pooling situation at \$48,780.09. Therefore, each would be willing to pay up to the difference of \$257.06 in order to make the change. The net benefits from making the change are \$514.12, and, in this example, each person is strictly better off.

Now if we found more individuals to join this pool, we could reduce the risk costs even further. As the pool expands, the likelihood of outcomes near the expected value increases while the likelihood of extreme outcomes decreases. This is precisely what insurance is: a large pool of people who agree to divide any losses among themselves. The insurance company is only the intermediary: It organizes the pool, and it incurs the transaction costs of keeping track of membership and losses of insured property and making the necessary monetary transfers. A relatively simple way to do all this is to collect the expected loss plus a prorated share of the transaction costs from each member at the start and then pay out the losses as they arise. As the number of people in the pool gets large, the risk cost and often the transaction costs (both prorated) become smaller and in the limit may be negligible. Then the premium approaches the actuarially fair level (i.e., the expected loss).

When insurance is available at an actuarially fair premium, risk-averse individuals will of course purchase it. But for some items it may be that the transaction costs of operating the pool do not become negligible. Then the premium charged will be significantly higher than the expected loss to individuals, and many, depending on their degrees of risk aversion, will self-insure.

For example, low-cost items are rarely insured for the reason that the transaction costs of insuring them are large relative to the expected loss. Factors included in the transaction costs include determining the value of an item and the probability of its loss, verifying that an actual loss has occurred, and making sure that the loss did not arise through the negligence of the owner or someone else who might be held responsible. An interesting example of high transaction costs involves automobile insurance. When an accident involving more than one car occurs, substantial legal expenses are often incurred to determine if one party is at fault. (If there were no legal "fault," all premiums might be lower.[18])

Another reason why risk-averse individuals may self-insure is government tax policy. Uninsured casualty and theft losses (above a minimum) are deductible when calculated for federal income tax purposes, provided the taxpayer elects to itemize rather than take the standard deduction. If an individual's marginal tax bracket is 30 percent, a $1 deductible loss from theft reduces the tax bill by $0.30. With private insurance, the $1.00 is recovered, but the $0.30 in tax savings is lost. Thus the net expected payoff from insurance is only $0.70, which is substantially below the $1 fair premium. In other words, government insurance, with benefits that increase in proportion to income, encourages individuals to self-insure.

We will explore other aspects of insurance later in the chapter. Now, however, let us return to the main point: to understand how risk pooling and risk spreading reduce risk costs. We have shown that risk pooling is the essence of insurance. But it is just as important to recognize that the same principle operates in other institutional forms. For example, risk pooling is a factor when firms in unrelated businesses merge to become conglomerates. By pooling the independent risks that each firm takes, the likelihood that the average return on investments will be close to the expected return is greater. This has the effect of lowering the cost to the firm of obtaining investment funds (because it is "safer").

The general principle of diversification of assets can be seen as an example of risk pooling. That is, a portfolio of diverse investments which an individual holds is a pool much like the pool of theft insurance policies that an insurance company holds. Suppose that we compare the expected utility of a risk-averse individual under two alternative arrangements: one in which the individual invests in one firm, and the other in which the individual invests the same total amount spread equally among 10 *different* and *independent* firms similar to the first firm.

Let one strategy be to invest $1000 in a risky, high-technology firm with a probability .8 of being successful and returning $5000 and a probability .2 of failing and returning nothing. We assume the individual has $46,000 in wealth initially and the same utility function as before:

$$U(W) = -e^{-0.0002W}$$

---

[18] For an interesting analysis of this see Guido Calabresi, *The Cost of Accidents: A Legal and Economic Analysis* (New Haven, Conn.: Yale University Press, 1970).

When $W = \$46,000$;

$$U(\$46,000) = -e^{-9.2} = -0.0001010394$$

The proposed investment clearly has expected value greater than the entry cost:

$$.8(\$5000) + .2(0) = \$4000 > \$1000$$

We first check to see if making this investment would raise the individual's expected utility level (otherwise, the individual would not invest):

$$E(U) = .8U(\$50,000) + .2U(\$45,000)$$

This is the same expression we evaluated in the earlier example, where we found

$$E(U) = -0.0000610019$$

and the certain-wealth equivalent is

$$W_c = \$48,523.03$$

Thus the individual prefers this investment to no investment at all. The risk cost, as before, is $476.97.

Now we wish to see if diversification of assets can reduce the risk cost. The second strategy is to divide the $1000 into smaller investments of $100 in each of 10 different firms. We choose the firms to be similar in risk to the first: Each firm has a .8 chance of being successful and returning $500 and a .2 chance of losing the $100 investment. However, we also choose diverse firms, ones such that there are no linkages between the successes or failures of any of them.[19] The expected value of each investment is $400 [= .8($500) + .2(0)], and since the investments are independent, the total expected value is simply 10 times $400, or $4000.

The numbers used to calculate the expected utility are shown in Table 6-1. There are 11 possible outcomes, since the number of successful investments

---

[19] When there is interdependence among some of the investments in a portfolio, the diversification is reduced. As an extreme example, suppose the profitability of building supply firms is determined solely by whether interest rates are low (which increases the demand for new construction) or high (which reduces the demand). Making small investments in each of 10 building supply firms is then no different than investing the same total in any one: All 10 firms will either be profitable or will not be.

Calculating expected value and utility is more complicated when there is interdependence among the assets in a pool. For a discussion of this in the context of energy investments, see P. S. Dasgupta and G. M. Heal, *Economic Theory and Exhaustible Resources* (Oxford: James Nisbet & Co., Ltd. and Cambridge University Press, 1979), pp. 377–388 especially pp. 385–387.

TABLE 6-1
THE EXPECTED UTILITY OF A DIVERSIFIED PORTFOLIO

Number of successful investments	Probability Π	Wealth level W	Expected utility* $-\Pi U(W)$
0	.0000	45,000	.0
1	.0000	45,500	.0
2	.0001	46,000	.0000000101
3	.0008	46,500	.0000000731
4	.0055	47,000	.0000004550
5	.0264	47,500	.0000019761
6	.0881	48,000	.0000059669
7	.2013	48,500	.0000123364
8	.3020	49,000	.0000167464
9	.2684	49,500	.0000134669
10	.1074	50,000	.0000048760
Sums	1.0000		.0000559069

* $U(W) = -e^{-0.0002W}$

can be anywhere from 0 to 10. The probability that any given number of successes will arise, given that each firm has .8 chance of success, is provided by the binomial probability measure.[20] We follow the usual procedure for calculating expected utility; we multiply the probability of each possible outcome by the utility of that outcome and sum.

From Table 6-1 we see that the expected utility of the diversified portfolio is -0.0000559069, which is greater than that of the undiversified portfolio. The certain-wealth equivalent of this expected utility level is found by solving

$$-0.0000559069 = -e^{-0.0002W_c}$$

whence
$$W_c = \$48,959.11$$

Thus the risk cost has been reduced from $476.97 to only $40.89 by diversifying the portfolio. Again, this risk-pooling strategy works because it reduces the

---

[20] When there are n independent risky events each with probability of success Π, the probability Π_r that there are exactly r successes is given by the binomial probability measure

$$\Pi_r = \frac{n!}{r!(n-r)!} \Pi^r (1 - \Pi)^{n-r}$$

The notation $n!$ means $(n)(n-1)(n-2)\cdots(1)$. For example, $4! = 4(3)(2)(1) = 24$. To illustrate the calculations for Table 6-1, the probability that there are exactly 8 successes in the 10 investments is

$$\Pi = \frac{10!}{8!2!}(.8^8)(.2^2)$$

$$= \frac{10(9)(.00671)}{2}$$

$$= .30199$$

probability of extreme outcomes and increases the probability of an outcome near the expected value. In this example the individual has a 96.72 percent chance of ending up with wealth in the range from $48,000 to $50,000.

At this point it is a simple matter to illustrate the advantage of risk spreading: *Risk spreading occurs when different individuals share the returns from one risky situation.* An obvious example of this is the diversification of firm ownership through the stock market. Through the issuance of common stock a single firm can allow many individuals to bear only a small portion of the total risk, and the sum of the risk cost that each owner faces is considerably lower than if there were a sole owner. This reduction in total risk cost is the gain from risk spreading.

We can see the risk-spreading advantage easily through a reinterpretation of the empirical example we have just used. Suppose we characterize a risky high-technology firm by the $1000 investment with a .8 probability of returning $5000 and a .2 probability of returning nothing. Let us consider whether it is more efficient to have the firm owned by a single owner or by a partnership of 10. We assume for simplicity that potential owners are homogeneous and risk-averse and that each has preinvestment wealth of $46,000 and the same utility function we have been using.

We have already seen that a single owner would evaluate the certain-wealth equivalent of his or her position at $48,523. That is, an individual with the given preferences would be indifferent to receiving $2523 with certainty or owning the firm. Now let us show that a 10-person partnership would value the firm at a higher cash equivalency.

To raise the $1000 required to operate the firm, each partner would contribute $100, and so each would end up with either $45,900 (if unsuccessful) or $46,400 (if successful). The expected utility of this position is

$$E(U) = .8U(\$46,400) + .2U(\$45,900)$$
$$= -0.000095233$$

This has a certain-wealth equivalent of

$$-0.000095233 = e^{-0.0002W_c}$$

whence $$W_c = \$46,295.92$$

In other words, each partner would be indifferent to receiving $295.92 with certainty or owning the firm. But then in the aggregate the partnership values the firm at 10 times that, or $2959, compared with only $2523 for the single owner. By the compensation principle, a change from single ownership to the partnership would increase efficiency: The partners could buy out the single owner at a price that would make everyone better off. The "social profit" is $436; it consists totally of the reduction in risk cost from the $477 faced by a single owner to the $41 [$\approx$ 10($46,300 − $46,295.92)] total risk cost of the partnership.

The risk-spreading strategy works as a consequence of diminishing marginal utility of wealth. We have seen that a risk-averse individual always prefers smaller gambles if expected value is held constant. For example, the risk-averse person prefers a fair coin flip with $1 at stake to the same coin flip with $2 at stake. The larger gamble represents not only a larger total but also a larger marginal risk cost. The expected utility gain from winning the second dollar is less than that from winning the first, and the expected utility loss from losing a second dollar exceeds that of losing the first—simply because of the diminishing marginal utility of wealth. Thus, the marginal risk cost increases as the stakes increase. Two similar individuals each bearing half the risk from one risky event have lower total risk costs than one individual facing the risk alone.

Another institution which facilitates risk spreading is the futures market. For example, a crop grower may not wish to bear the full risk of planting a crop now to receive an uncertain return when it ripens next year. In the futures market the farmer can sell part of the future crop at a price specified now. Thus the crop grower, in selling now, gives up the possible gains and losses if next year's price turns out to be different. In return, certainty of income is achieved by the sale of the futures contract.

All these examples of insurance, futures contracts, and stock shares can be thought of as *contingent commodities;* their values depend upon which state of the world arises. The theft insurance contract pays nothing if the state turns out to be no theft and pays the value of the insured article if there is theft. The buyer of crop futures faces a loss if next year's price turns out to be low, and a gain if it is high. A share of common stock can be thought of as a claim on the future value of the firm, and its value depends on which states of profitability arise.[21]

In theory, markets for a wide variety of contingent commodities are required to ensure optimal resource allocation in the presence of uncertainty. Yet we actually have very few of those markets developed. I might like to insure the value of my income against inflation, but there are as yet no futures contracts based on the level of the consumer price index. There are many reasons why such markets have not developed, but one reason relevant to policy analysis is that collective action may be required to create them, and we simply have not thought enough about how to do it. But because uncertainty is so pervasive and costly, it is worth a great deal of time and effort to create efficient mechanisms for reducing risk costs.

Policy Aspects of Risk Shifting and Risk Control

In this section we give some brief examples of policies which have important effects on risk costs and their distribution. To do so, it is useful first to mention

---

[21] A nice survey of the analytics of uncertainty and contingent commodities is contained in J. Hirshleifer and J. Riley, "The Analytics of Uncertainty and Information—An Expository Survey," *Journal of Economic Literature, 57,* No. 4, December 1979, pp. 1375–1421.

one important dimension of the relation between risk and resource allocation which we have so far ignored: Risk costs affect the amount of resources allocated to risk-taking situations.

In the pooling and spreading illustrations we accepted the total amount of risk as a given: The risk-creating events would be undertaken regardless of the risk-bearing arrangements. That is, the jewlery and other "unsafe" property would be bought whether or not insurance was available, and the risky high-technology firm would operate whether or not it was owned by a partnership. Those simplifying assumptions were made in order to emphasize this point: The risk costs of random events are not inherently determined by the events themselves; they depend importantly on the institutional arrangements which allow the risks to be moved from one economic agent to another. To be efficient, risks should be allocated in order to minimize their costs; otherwise, there will be room for deals like the ones illustrated. Institutions like insurance and the stock market serve to reduce the risk costs from the initial allocation by allowing them to be pooled and spread.

However, another important aspect of risk-cost-reducing mechanisms is that they increase resource allocation to the risk-creating events. If no theft insurance were available, there would be less demand at any given prices for goods subject to theft. If firms were not allowed to spread their risks through the issuance of stock, the size of firms might be uneconomically restricted (e.g., that might prevent taking advantage of certain economies of scale). If people cannot insure against inflation, they will allocate fewer resources to activities whose value depends upon it (most notably investment).

The policy examples mentioned below are illustrative of other institutional ways in which risk costs are affected. These policies, like the pooling and spreading mechanisms, can have important effects on resource allocation. We note some of the effects, but our primary emphasis continues to be on increasing awareness of social mechanisms used to respond to risk.

An interesting risk-shifting mechanism created through public policy is *limited corporate liability*. That is, a corporation may be held liable only for amounts up to the net worth of the assets it owns. The assets of the corporation's owners, the shareholders, are not at risk. This limitation does not apply to unincorporated businesses, e.g., a partner in an unincorporated business could be forced to sell his or her home to pay business debts. The limit on liability provides a strong incentive for firms to incorporate.

By making the liability of firm owners limited, part of the burden of the risks taken by the firm is shifted to others. In particular circumstances this may foster or hinder the efficient allocation of resources. For example, it may encourage new product development which has positive expected return but high attendant risk depending on sales. Socially, such projects are desirable: Even though some may not work out, the average returns are positive and the aggregate risk from many such projects is negligible from the social point of view. However, those with the new idea may not think it worth their time if the profits must be spread through increased selling of stock. Limited liability combined with debt financing (borrowing) may provide the right mixture of expected private return and risk to make the undertaking privately desirable.

On the other hand, liability that is too limited may encourage excessive risk taking. That happens when the firm does the equivalent of operating the St. Petersburg game while knowing full well that it may not be able to pay as promised. In that case the firm considers taking a risk, such as building a nuclear reactor, which may have catastrophic consequences for others. Decisions of that kind are made in light of the expected benefits and costs to the firm. The firm may know that there is some nontrivial probability of a catastrophic accident, but in that event it cannot be held liable for more than its own assets. Thus, the expected loss in the firm's calculation is less than the actual expected social loss, and the firm may cheerfully undertake risks which have negative expected social returns.[22]

In addition to risk-shifting mechanisms, risk creation can be and often is regulated through a variety of other controls. To take one simple example, legalized gambling on horse races is so designed that there is never any risk in the aggregate. Only individual bettors take risks. The track keeps a fixed percentage of the total funds bet and distributes the balance to the winners of each race in accordance with standard formulas. Thus there is no risk to the track whatsoever.[23]

A related form of aggregate risk control which brings us back to public policy concerns crime and *deterrence*. In our earlier example of theft insurance we took the probability of theft as given exogenously. But it may well be that the resources allocated to criminal justice activities in any area have an influence on the probability of theft. That is, the degree of street lighting, the frequency of police patrol, and the extent of citizen cooperation (as in the prompt reporting of suspected crimes) may influence the likelihood that potential thieves will actually attempt thefts.[24]

To continue with the crime example, individuals may influence the probability of their own victimization by such related resource allocation decisions as to install burglar alarms to protect households and to take taxis rather than walk to reduce exposure to street assault. Thus the decisions about how best to reduce risks are interrelated. That is, the least-cost way of achieving a given reduction in risk will typically involve a combination of public expenditure, private protective expenditure, and insurance.[25] In the example of health

---

[22] This problem is compounded by the Price-Anderson Act, which limits the liability from nuclear reactor accidents to $50 million.

[23] This is a slight exaggeration. In most states the tracks are required to make a payoff of at least $0.05 on each winning $1.00. Occasionally, when a heavy favorite wins, there are not enough losing dollars to make the minimum payment and the track owners must make up the difference. That does not happen very often, however.

[24] For a general discussion see Lee S. Friedman, *The Economics of Crime and Justice* (Morristown, N.J.: General Learning Press, 1976). See also Philip J. Cook, "Punishment and Crime: A Critique of Current Findings Concerning the Preventive Effects of Punishment," *Law and Contemporary Problems, 41*, No. 1, winter 1977, pp. 164–204.

[25] This is discussed generally in I. Ehrlich and G. Becker, "Market Insurance, Self-Insurance, and Self-Protection," *Journal of Political Economy, 80*, No. 4, July/August 1972, pp. 623–648.

insurance to be presented, we will analyze some of the problems that arise from such interrelations.

Another policy form of risk control is *quality certification*. Imagine, for example, the medical care profession without licensing requirements. Anyone who wanted to be a doctor would simply hang out a shingle and offer medical services. An individual seeking services would then be very uncertain about the quality of care that might be received. Society imposes licensing requirements which require a demonstration of at least some medical training. That reduces the consumer's uncertainty in a particular way. It leaves some uncertainty about the quality of care received, but it probably does have the effect of raising the average level of care by eliminating those who would be least competent to provide it.

Whether such licensing requirements have benefits greater than costs is another issue. Milton Friedman argues that they are inefficient.[26] Licensing requirements create a barrier to entry, which gives the suppliers of service some monopoly power and leads to higher prices and lower quantities than in an unregulated market. He further argues that competitive forces in an unregulated market would drive out the least competent suppliers, so that only competent ones would continue to have patients seeking their services.

Kenneth Arrow, on the other hand, suggests that the uncertainty costs of an unregulated regime may be great.[27] Because the primary method of consumer learning about quality is trial and error and because each consumer purchases medical services infrequently and often for different reasons each time, the competitive mechanism may be a very imperfect safeguard. Thus, substantial incompetence could persist, which would turn each decision to seek medical services into a risky lottery from the uninformed consumer's perspective.

These theoretical arguments do not resolve what is essentially an empirical question: whether the benefits of the reduction of uncertainty outweigh the costs of the supply restrictions.[28] Nor does actual policy debate about the medical care industry consider this question in such a broad form. The licensing issues that do receive serious consideration are more narrowly defined. For example, should licenses be required for the performance of specific kinds of surgery, or should the medical knowledge of licensed doctors be periodically reexamined to ensure that physicians keep their knowledge current, or should certain kinds of minor medical treatments be delicensed, or relicensed to include paramedics and nurses as well as physicians?

These same issues can be raised with respect to all occupational licensure requirements: automobile mechanics, real estate agents, dentists, and teachers. They can also be applied to safety requirements for products such as paint and

---

[26] See M. Friedman, *Capitalism and Freedom* (Chicago: University of Chicago Press, 1962), chap. IX, pp. 137–160.

[27] See Arrow, op. cit., chap. 8.

[28] For an example of an empirical study of this issue, see W. D. White, "The Impact of Occupational Licensure of Clinical Laboratory Personnel," *Journal of Human Resources, 13*, No. 1, spring 1978, pp. 91–102.

microwave ovens. In each case it is not sufficient to analyze the number of substandard transactions that occur. One must remember to consider, for example, the pure risk costs that consumers bear because of the possibility of undesirable outcomes.[29]

The above is a point worth emphasizing because ignoring it is a common error. Standards might raise the expected value of a service in a clear way. For example, suppose that certain automobile safety standards reduce automobile accidents. The quantitative reduction in accidents is a readily comprehended benefit, but the standard achieves far more: For *all* of us who drive, the pure risk cost of driving has been reduced. This latter benefit can be substantial.

Another issue to consider generally is that alternative policies can vary greatly in the extent of their coverage. A specific service can be restricted by licensure to a broad or narrow range of suppliers. Certification can be used as an alternative to licensure; it need not be required to supply the service (e.g., an accountant need not be a certified public accountant).

To get a better understanding of the analytic issues involved in considering policies like these, we must broaden our own understanding about individual behavior under uncertainty. Until now, we have simply examined the idea that individuals so behave as to maximize expected utility; however, the extent to which actual behavior may be approximated by this model is disputed.

ALTERNATIVE MODELS OF INDIVIDUAL BEHAVIOR UNDER UNCERTAINTY

The Slumlord's Dilemma[30] and Strategic Behavior

Most of the examples of uncertainty that we have mentioned so far are of the type Knight called "risky," i.e., the probabilities of the different possible states of the world are assumed to be known. However, in many uncertain situations that arise the probabilities are not known. One class of these situations may be referred to as *strategic games against other persons,* like chess playing or even nuclear weapons strategies. (In the latter case countries are viewed as one-minded "persons" who attempt to deter nuclear attacks by choosing defensive capabilities which guarantee the attacker's destruction.)[31]

An interesting game of this type is known as the Slumlord's Dilemma. Imagine that two slum owners, Slumlady Sally and Slumlord Larry, have adjacent tenements. Each owner knows the following: If both invest in improving their tenements, they will have the nicest low-rent apartments in the

---

[29] This is sometimes referred to as the *ex ante, ex post* distinction. *Ex post* one can see the outcomes, but the risk is gone by that time. Social costs include the *ex ante* risk costs.

[30] This version of the Prisoner's Dilemma was first proposed by O. Davis and A. Whinston, "Externalities, Welfare, and the Theory of Games," *Journal of Political Economy, 70,* June 1962, pp. 241–262.

[31] For general reading on game theory and strategic reasoning, see R. D. Luce and H. Raiffa, *Games and Decisions* (New York: John Wiley & Sons, Inc., 1957), and Thomas C. Schelling, *The Strategy of Conflict* (Cambridge, Mass.: Harvard University Press, 1960).

city and will earn high returns on their investments (say an extra profit of $5000 each). On the other hand, if, say, Slumlord Larry invests but Slumlady Sally does not, then Larry will lose his shirt but Sally will make out like a bandit.

The latter may happen because of externalities. That is, Larry will realize only a slight increase in the demand for his apartments because of a negative externality: His apartments are right next door to a slum. The increased rent is more than offset by the renovation costs, and Larry finds his net profit decreased by $4000. But Sally now finds her apartments in much greater demand, without having invested a penny, because of an external benefit: They are now in a nice neighborhood. Her profits go up by $6000. The opposite would be true if Sally were the only one to invest.

The situation is like that shown in the matrix in Figure 6-5. The question is, what will they do? Slumlord Larry might reason as follows: "If Sally invests, then I am better off not to invest ($6000 > $5000). If Sally does not invest, then I am better off not to invest ($0 > −$4000). Since I am better off not to invest in either case, I will not invest." Thus for Larry the strategy of not investing is *dominant:* It gives the best outcome in each possible state of the world. Sally goes through the same reasoning. She considers what will make her best off, and she concludes that the strategy of not investing is dominant for her.

Therefore, Sally and Larry end up with no change in profits, but they have obviously missed a golden opportunity to increase their profits by $5000 each. Why does this happen? Why do they not simply cooperate with each other and both invest?

The problem is that each owner has an incentive to be misleading, and the other knows it. If you were considering investing, say, $20,000 in renovating an urban slum but your success depended on what happened next door, would you trust that slumlord? That is, each player is *uncertain* about whether the other will really invest even if each agrees to do so. Imagine a more realistic example involving 10 to 20 tenements owned by different individuals in which success

FIGURE 6-5
The slumlord's dilemma. The expressions in the matrix ($A, $B) may be interpreted as the change in net profits to Larry and Sally, respectively.

		Slumlady Sally	
		Invest	Do not invest
Slumlord Larry	Invest	($5000, $5000)	(−$4000, $6000)
	Do not invest	($6000, −$4000)	($0, $0)

depends on each owner making the investment. The inability to trust one another can lead to the uneconomic perpetuation of slums.

How can this problem be solved? Like all problems that arise from external effects, the solution involves internalizing the effects in some way. But how can the uncertainty due to lack of trust be overcome? If there were only one owner of the adjacent tenements, then it is clear that the investment would be made. It is possible that one of the two original owners could be persuaded to sell to the other (there is, of course, room for such a deal). However, the more owners that must be coordinated, the smaller the likelihood that one owner will be able to buy out all the others. In these cases the government may wish to exercise its power of eminent domain and buy up all of the property. Then it can redevelop the property as a whole either itself or by selling it to a developer who will do so. The process is more commonly referred to as *urban renewal*.

Note that, in this game, no one is maximizing expected utility. No player knows the probability of each outcome. The analogous situation can be seen to arise in many different circumstances. When the game was first described, it was referred to as the Prisoner's Dilemma. A sheriff arrests two suspects of a crime, separates them, and urges each to confess. Each prisoner has a choice of two strategies: confess or do not confess. If neither confesses, each will get off with a light sentence for a minor offense. If both confess, each will get a medium-length sentence. But if one confesses and the other does not, the one who confesses will be let off on probation and the other will be sent away for life. Not trusting each other, each suspect is led by these incentives to confess.

As a last example of this game consider what happens when a group of people go to a restaurant and agree in advance to divide the bill evenly. Then all participants have incentives to order more expensive meals than if each paid for his or her own. You may order chateaubriand, since your share of the bill will go up by only a fraction of the cost of the expensive steak. Furthermore, your bill is going to be big anyway, because you have no control over the costs that will arise from the orders of the others. Thus the ordering strategy of choosing expensive dishes dominates the strategy of ordering normally, and the whole group ends up with a feast and a bill that nobody except the restaurant owner thinks is worth it.[32] We will see shortly that this identical dilemma is created by health insurance coverage and poses one of the most serious policy problems in the provision of health care.

To highlight the differences between games against persons and those against "nature," we assume a new set of possible outcomes for Larry in Figure 6-6. In a moment, we will discuss the "opponent." But first let us point out that Larry no longer has a dominant strategy. He is better off investing if state A occurs and not investing if state B occurs.

---

[32] Not all people that agree to such bill splitting think the results are suboptimal. Some may think the fun of the process is worth it; others may have a group relationship in which trust keeps all ordering normally. But the beauty of the example lies in recognizing the pressure that comes from the changed incentives and knowing full well that many people do become victims of this dilemma.

		State A	State B
Larry	Invest	$5000	−$1000
	Do not invest	$2000	$0

FIGURE 6-6
The possible outcomes from a decision.

Consider how Larry might reason if state A or state B is to be consciously chosen by another person, the payoffs to the other person are identical with those to Larry, but the two people are not allowed to communicate.[33] Reasoning strategically, Larry will realize that the *other* person has a dominant strategy: State A is superior to state B no matter which strategy Larry chooses. The other person will choose A, and therefore Larry will decide to invest.

Now let us change the opponent from a person to nature: State A or state B will be selected after Larry's choice of strategy and without regard to it. For example, state B could be an earthquake which damaged Larry's building, and state A could be no earthquake. Or we could have states A and B determined by human events not directly related to Larry; e.g., state B could represent a strike by public employees. The strike would interfere with refuse pickup whether or not Larry invested. That would impose greater cleanup costs on Larry and would also delay rental of the renovated units until city building inspectors returned to work. How would Larry behave in those situations?

One decision rule proposed for these situations is the *maximin rule: Choose the strategy which maximizes the payoff in the worst possible state of the world.* Since the worst payoff is $0 if Larry does not invest, and −$1000 if he does, the strategy of not investing maximizes the minimum that Larry could experience.

The maximin strategy is one of extreme risk aversion; it is a strategy which does not depend in any way on Larry's subjective estimate of the probability that each state will occur. Suppose, for example, that Larry thinks the probability of no earthquake or no strike is .9. Then his expected profit from investing is

$$E(\Pi) = .9(\$5000) + .1(-\$1000)$$
$$= \$4400$$

His expected profit if he does not invest is substantially lower:

$$E(\Pi) = .9(\$2000) + .1(0)$$
$$= \$1800$$

---

[33] This may occur when Larry and the other person each represent one of two firms in an oligopoly market and they are prevented by law from conspiring to act jointly as a monopolist would.

As we have already seen, even a risk-averse expected utility maximizer could easily prefer the strategy of investing.

Let us consider one other strategy that might be available: the strategic decision to gather more information. We take a simple example. Suppose Larry, with time and effort, could find out with certainty whether the public employees will go on strike. How much would that information be worth? To an expected utility maximizer, *the utility value of perfect information is the difference between the expected utility of the current situation (with imperfect knowledge) and the expected utility of being able to choose the best strategy in whatever state arises. The monetary value of that information is simply the difference between the certain-wealth equivalents of the two expected utility levels.*

To illustrate, suppose Larry currently has $45,000 in wealth and the risk-averse utility function we have used previously:

$$U = -e^{-0.0002W}$$

With imperfect knowledge, Larry will prefer to invest. The expected utility from this strategy is[34]

$$E(U) = .9U(\$50,000) + .1U(\$44,000)$$
$$= -0.0000559332$$

The certain-wealth equivalent of this is $48,956.76.

If Larry finds out whether there will be a strike, he can either invest or not invest accordingly. The expected utility from finding out is then

$$E(U) = .9U(\$50,000) + .1U(\$45,000)$$
$$= -0.0000532009$$

The certain-wealth equivalent of this is $49,207.17. In other words, Larry should be willing to spend up to $250.41 (= $49,207.17 − $48,956.76) to find out with certainty whether there will be a strike.

To follow the expected utility-maximizing strategy in the above example, Larry must have subjective perceptions of the probability of each state. Whether individuals have these perceptions, how the perceptions are formed, and whether the perceptions are acted upon are critical issues which we have not yet discussed. We will turn to them in the following section.

---

[34] The expected utility from not investing is

$$E(U) = .9U(\$47,000) + .1U(\$45,000)$$
$$= -0.0000867926$$

The certain-wealth equivalent of this strategy is $46,759.94.

Bounded Rationality[35]

When common decisions involving easily understood risks such as a simple coin flip game are considered, it is certainly plausible to entertain the notion that behavior is consistent with expected utility maximization. But as decision situations become more complex and are encountered only infrequently, actual behavior begins to take on quite a different cast. One way to explain this is to recognize that decision making is itself a costly process and that individuals will allocate only a limited amount of their own resources, including time, to the activity of deciding. A somewhat different but related explanation is that there are bounds or limits to human rationality.

To illustrate this with a transparent example, let us consider the differences in decision making that characterize playing the games of tic-tac-toe and chess. In tic-tac-toe it is not hard to become an expert player. Simply by playing the game a few times, it becomes apparent which strategies prevent losing and which do not. That is, a player becomes an expert by trial and error. The optimal choice of moves is not accomplished by mentally considering all the alternatives and their possible consequences (9 possible openings × 8 possible responses × 7 possible next moves, etc.) and seeing which current move is best. Individuals do not have the mental capacity to make such calculations. Rather, a small set of routine offensive and defensive ploys must be *learned*.

For example, of the nine possible opening moves, it does not take long for the novice to realize that there are only three really different ones: the middle, a corner, or a side. Routine responses are developed as well: "If my opponent opens in the center, I will respond with a corner." Tic-tac-toe is simple enough that almost all people learn unbeatable strategies. Because virtually everyone can quickly become an expert at tic-tac-toe, observed behavior will correspond closely with the assumption that each player acts *as if* all possible alternatives have been considered and the optimal one chosen. For all intents and purposes, the players of this game may be thought of as maximizers or optimizers of their chances of winning.

The same limited calculating ability which prevents systematic consideration of all alternatives in tic-tac-toe applies *a fortiori* to the game of chess. No individual (nor as yet even our largest computer) is capable of thinking through all possible consequences of alternative chess moves in order to select the best one. People play chess the same way they play tic-tac-toe: by using routine offensive and defensive ploys which are learned primarily through the trials and errors of playing. That is, the same problem-solving procedure of trying to take a very complicated problem and breaking it down into manageable pieces (the standard routines) is followed.

However, an important difference between the two games is readily apparent. Although almost everyone finds optimal strategies for tic-tac-toe, no

---

[35] Many of the ideas in this section are associated with the work of Herbert Simon. See, for example, Simon's "Theories of Decision-Making in Economics and Behavioral Science," in *Surveys of Economic Theory,* vol. III (New York: St. Martin's Press, 1967), pp. 1–28.

individual has ever found an optimal (unbeatable) strategy for chess.[36] Instead, individuals develop routines that *satisfice*. That is, they are satisfactory only when they are the best known to a player at a given time and do not seem to be the cause of losses. However, it is recognized that better routines can be discovered, and indeed most players strive to improve their routines over time.

Economic decisions run the spectrum of choice situations from those in which we as individuals have optimizing routines to others in which we have satisficing routines, and still others with which we are unfamiliar and for which we have no routines. When we buy meat, for example, it is not too difficult to discover whether the meat selections wrapped in a particular supermarket tend to have less desirable aspects (e.g., fat) hidden from view. And we have the opportunity to make frequent trials. Thus consumers may do pretty well at choosing their meat purchases from the alternative price-quality combinations available in their neighborhoods. To the extent that this is true, the meat choice game is like tic-tac-toe. There is no explicit calculation of all meat purchase alternatives every time one goes to shop; rather, a set of simplified routines for shopping becomes established. But the results may be the same as if an optimizing procedure had been followed.

On the other hand, certain aspects of meat choices may be relevant to consumers but very difficult to perceive when the choice is made. For example, the freshness of the meat may not be apparent. One could rely on competitive forces to keep unfresh meats off the market or to keep meats separated by their relative freshness. But competitive forces respond only to consumer choices. Consumer choice routines might be quite adequate to recognize and cause the failure of any supplier who systematically and frequently attempts to sell unfresh meat. But it is quite plausible that more clever suppliers would be able to get away with such abuses if they are not attempted too often.

In circumstances like this it may be possible for public policy to improve the workings of the market. A regulation requiring that all meat be labeled with a last legal day of sale, for example, might have benefits greater than its costs. For this to work, it is important that the regulation makers have better routines for evaluating freshness than consumers generally have. If the regulator thinks no meat should be sold after it has been cut and wrapped for two days but almost all consumers think that meat bought on the third day is fine, then the regulation can make consumers worse off. The gains from the reduction of unfresh meat sales can be outweighed by the losses from a reduced (and more expensive) supply of fresh meat.

Why not just have the labeling requirement in the above example but leave out the part about a last legal day of sale? This depends upon the sophistication and diversity of consumer choices. If consumers *only lack knowledge* about any specific piece of meat, or *vary widely in their informed choices* about the time within which each would use it, *then the pure information policy may be*

---

[36] It has been shown mathematically that such strategies must exist. See, for example, Herbert Simon, *The Sciences of the Artificial* (Cambridge, Mass.: The M.I.T. Press, 1969), p. 63.

best. Since regulators lack information about individual consumer preferences, there is an efficiency gain from informing them but not restricting choice. On the other hand, consumers may have difficulty processing the information, i.e., using it to make the decision. If many consumers simply do not develop their own standards for freshness (because they do not encounter substandard meat often enough), the legal-last-day-of-sale aspect could have net benefits rather than net costs.

One last meat example might be instructive. Suppose certain color-enhancing or taste-enhancing chemicals have been added to the meat and suppose further that they are carcinogenic, that there is some small probability that the intake of a given quantity will result in cancer in 20 or 30 years. This attribute is like freshness in that it is difficult if not impossible to perceive at the time of sale. But unlike freshness, individual consumers would not observe the consequences in time to consider different routines for making decisions. Even if informed about the facts in a dispassionate way, consumers have no experience in making such choices and may make them poorly.

It may be analogous to hearing a brilliant lecture by Bobby Fisher on how to play chess and then having your first and only opportunity to play. You are not likely to do well, particularly if you are facing a seasoned opponent. If the stakes of the game are important, the novice might well prefer to have Bobby Fisher play as his or her proxy. Similarly, potential consumers of food additives might prefer to have an expert make the decision for them. In this case a regulatory agency with the power to ban certain products may improve efficiency.

To the extent that rationality is bounded, the bounds are themselves the cause of uncertainty. In the last examples, often the consumer has all the information a supercomputer would need to solve for the optimum. The problem is that the consumer has not developed routines or programs which can process the information in order to identify the optimum. In such situations regulatory policies may have the potential to improve consumer satisfaction.

Of course, it is an empirical question whether actual consumer decision making in any particular situation is improvable by public policy (and again this depends not only on there being some deviation from the consumer's optimum but also on the prospects for regulation actually reducing it). However, the existing empirical evidence on *individual* consumer choice suggests that actual behavior, even in simple choice situations, is often grossly inconsistent with expected utility maximization.[37]

In one interesting study a household survey of consumer purchases of disaster insurance was conducted.[38] Approximately 3000 households in disaster-prone areas, half of them uninsured, were asked a variety of questions

---

[37] See David M. Grether and Charles R. Plott, "Economic Theory of Choice and the Preference Reversal Phenomenon," *The American Economic Review, 69,* No. 4, September 1979, pp. 623–638. The experiments in this paper reveal behavior inconsistent with preference theory in general, and not just expected utility maximization.

[38] See Howard Kunreuther, "Limited Knowledge and Insurance Protection," *Public Policy, 24,* No. 2, spring 1976, pp. 227–261.

designed to find out their subjective estimates of the probabilities of a disaster, the resulting loss that they might experience in that event, and their knowledge of available insurance. While a large number of people indicated that they did not have the information, those offering the information appeared to deviate substantially from expected utility maximization. In this group 39 percent of the uninsured should have bought insurance (in order to maximize expected utility), whereas about the same percentage of the insured should not have bought insurance.

To give some policy perspective to the study's findings, less than 10 percent of the entire uninsured sample could be said to have rationally chosen to remain uninsured while living in the disaster-prone area. Over half of this group simply did not know about the availability of insurance, let alone that their flood insurance would be 90 percent federally subsidized. Many of the rest appeared to have unrealistically low expectations of the damage that would occur in the event of a disaster. Is there any policy problem here? If one simply takes the expected utility model on faith, then there is certainly no reason to subsidize the insurance. In fact, the model suggests a good reason not to provide the subsidy: If individuals do not bear the true costs of their locational choices, then they will overlocate in the subsidized areas.

But this model ignores a problem which the model of bounded rationality reveals. There may be many people living in these areas, because they do not have or cannot process the information about possible disaster, who will suffer serious loss in that event. Subsidized insurance probably does alleviate this problem to a small degree (depending on the price elasticity of its demand), but it can simultaneously cause the locational problem mentioned above.

A policy of compulsory unsubsidized insurance might be better. It solves the problem of the unprotected and provides essentially correct locational signals, except for the risk takers who really would prefer no insurance. The best policies may be ones of information or even help with information processing, if consumer choice can be preserved but made more rational. This is not the kind of implication that comes from a traditional economic model, and it should serve as a reminder that it is healthy to remain open-minded about the models to be used in policy analyses.

MORAL HAZARD AND MEDICAL CARE INSURANCE

One of the more serious risky contingencies that each of us faces is the possibility of requiring expensive medical care. It is therefore not surprising that many people choose to purchase health insurance, which is so universal that it is usually provided as a fringe benefit of employment.[39] Medical care is

---

[39] We noted earlier the tax advantages of receiving part of the wage in this form. The employer's contribution is nontaxable; but if the same money were included in the wage, the recipient would have to pay income taxes on it. Thus the public policy is similar to offering individuals (through their employers) a matching grant for medical care insurance when higher-income people receive more generous matches (the tax savings are greater).

also one of those goods of which many people feel a universal minimum should be guaranteed to all; thus it is not surprising that the government Medicare and Medicaid programs provide insurance for the elderly and lower-income individuals (primarily those on welfare). However, many people still "fall through the cracks" of these programs (e.g., the self-employed and the marginally employed), and legislation to provide universal national health insurance has been introduced in virtually every one of the past 10 years. It seems inevitable that some form of national health insurance will eventually be adopted, although exactly what that form will be still appears to be up for grabs.

A factor that has undeniably slowed the movement toward national health insurance has been the dramatic increase in the costs of medical care. From 1965, when Medicare was getting started, to 1976 medical expenditures went from $39 billion to $139 billion, or from 5.6 percent of GNP to 8.6 percent.[40] At first, analysts thought that the cost increase was due almost entirely to the new demand from Medicare and Medicaid patients. But gradually, as medical inflation continued unabated and more data became available, the recognition grew that medical insurance coverage was itself the culprit. It was not simply that more people were being covered by a relatively inelastic supply; the level of real resources (labor and capital inputs) per patient day increased by approximately 80 percent over the period.

To understand why medical insurance has caused this problem, we return to fairly simple and traditional models of economic behavior. As we have already seen, the advantage of insurance is that, through risk shifting and pooling, the cost of risk is reduced. But in our earliest examples of theft insurance we assumed that the insurance company offered insurance at a premium approximately equal to the expected loss without insurance. This turns out to be a false proposition for medical insurance, as another version of the Slumlord's Dilemma makes its impact felt.[41] *The insurance changes the economic incentives that each individual faces, and thus causes behavior to be different.*

The problem arises because medical care expenses, perhaps unlike the events of illness or injury themselves, are not random events. The quantity of medical care demanded by an individual depends, to be sure, on the random event of a medical problem. But it also depends on the income and tastes of the individual (or his or her doctor) and the price of the services. If I must be hospitalized, my decision to have a private or semiprivate room depends on the price. I may stay an "extra day" to be on the safe side if it is cheap enough, or I may be particularly anxious to leave because of the high cost. If I am poor, the doctor may provide only the services which are essential to help keep my bill down; if I am well off, the doctor may provide "Cadillac quality" care.

How does this connect to insurance? The effect of full-coverage insurance is

---

[40] Louise R. Russell, "Medical Care Costs," in *Setting National Priorities: 1978* (Washington, D.C.: The Brookings Institution, 1977), chap. 6, pp. 177–206.

[41] Mark Pauly was the first to point this out. See his "The Economics of Moral Hazard," *The American Economic Review, 58,* 1968, pp. 531–537.

to reduce the price an individual is charged at the point of service from the ordinary market price to zero. Once insured, an individual receives all covered services "for free." Therefore, more medical expenses will be incurred by an insured person than would be incurred by the same person without insurance. A hospital, knowing most of its patients are insured, can buy any medical equipment no matter how expensive, use it as the doctor finds appropriate, and get reimbursed for the "necessary" expenses by the insurance company. Full-coverage insurance leaves the medical care industry without the usual mechanism of consumer demand as a cost control; in fact, it leaves the industry with virtually no method of cost control at all.

Full-coverage insurance can be offered only when the demand for the covered services is inelastic. To see this, let us look at Figure 6-7. Imagine that there are two states of the world: An individual is healthy or ill. If illness strikes (let us say with $\Pi = .5$) and the individual is uninsured, we might observe that 50 units of medical care are bought at the market price of $1.00 per unit. The expected cost to the individual is thus $25. Suppose that the demand for these services is completely inelastic (in this state), as if for every illness there is a unique, unvariable treatment. Then the expected cost of insuring many individuals like this one is also $25, and every risk-averse individual will prefer to purchase the insurance that would be offered at this actuarially fair premium.

Now let us relax the assumption that the demand is inelastic; suppose the actual demand is as drawn in Figure 6-7. The uninsured ill person behaves as before. But because the ill person with insurance faces a zero price at the point of service, *100* units of medical care will be demanded. The insurance company will receive a bill for $100, and thus its expected cost of insuring many people like this is $50 each $[= \frac{1}{2}(0) + \frac{1}{2}(100)]$. Thus the choice that the individual faces is to bear the risk and go uninsured with expected loss of $25 or to give up $50 with certainty in order to shift the risk. In this case, the individual might well prefer to remain uninsured.[42]

---

[42] When the ill and uninsured individual purchases 50 units of medical care, there is a consumer surplus shown in the diagram. Obviously, the individual does not now have more utility than when healthy $[\equiv U(W)]$. The increase in consumer surplus shown is from a base which is substantially lower than when healthy. We should assume that the total utility level of the individual when restored to health (point A in Figure 6-7) is $< U(W - 50)$. That is, the individual is worse off than if merely $50 poorer. Let us call this utility level $U(W - 50 - X)$, where $X > 0$.

It can be shown that, as the example is drawn, the individual's decision about purchasing insurance depends on just how much worse off he or she is when restored to health compared to not being ill at all. If the only loss is the $50 in medical expenses $(X = 0)$, then the individual will self-insure: The certain utility loss from the cost of the insurance policy exceeds any conceivable gains from reduced risk costs and receiving "free" excess medical services. Mathematically, when $X = 0$ (and remembering the insured individual receives a consumer surplus of $25 from the *excess* services when ill):

$$EU(\text{not insured}) > EU(\text{insured})$$
$$.5U(W) + .5U(W - 50) > .5U(W - 50) + .5U(W - 50 + 25)$$

The above inequality holds because the equation simplifies to an obvious truth:

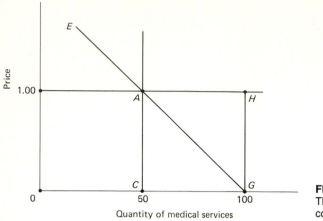

FIGURE 6-7
The moral hazard of full-coverage medical insurance.

Note the presence of the Slumlord's Dilemma here. The insurance company is still charging an actuarially fair premium; it breaks even. Every individual could perceive that his or her own excess use contributes to the rise in premium (from the inelastic case). Nevertheless, each individual controls only a negligible fraction of the premium costs. If I become ill and consider restraining my demands, the savings will not accrue to me but will be spread evenly over the entire insured population. And I will still be charged my share of the excess use by all the others. If I do purchase the excess units, the extra costs are spread evenly over the insured population and I pay only a tiny fraction. Thus I am better off to follow the strategy of demanding the "excess" services, even though everyone would be better off if we all did not demand them!

To make sure that this last point is clear, let us return to Figure 6-7. Under full-coverage insurance, the social costs of units 51 to 100 can be seen to exceed

$$U(W) > U(W - 25)$$

However, if the illness imposes substantial other costs on the individual (e.g., loss of pay because of inability to work), the marginal risk cost from the threat of illness increases. Then the marginal reduction in risk cost due to insurance plus the free excess medical services can lead to a gain in expected utility which outweighs the loss from the premium.

That is, it is possible that

$$EU(\text{insured}) > EU(\text{not insured})$$
$$.5U(W - 50) + .5U(W - 25 - X) > .5U(W) + .5U(W - 50 - X)$$

For example, if $U(W) = -e^{-0.03W}$, $W = \$5000$, and $X = \$50$,

$$-5.01(0.1^{65}) > -7.56(0.1^{65})$$

or in terms of the certain-wealth equivalents:

$$\$4935.20 > \$4921.49$$

their benefits. The area *CAHG* indicates their cost of $50 (paid for through the insurance premiums) and the area under the demand curve ACG measures their value to the consumer of $25. Thus a risk-averse individual will purchase insurance only if the expected utility loss from consuming these marginal services, valued at $12.50 [$= \frac{1}{2}(25)$], is less than the value of the utility gain from the overall risk reduction; otherwise, he or she is better off remaining uninsured. On the other hand, we know that insurance with excess use forbidden would have the greatest value because it would provide the full risk-reduction benefits but *no* expected loss from the consumption of excess services. Thus, all risk-averse people would most prefer an insurance plan with some social mechanism to prevent excess use.

This problem of excess use is known in the insurance literature as *moral hazard*. A typical example used to illustrate the problem is arson: If the owner of a building could insure the property for any desired value, then he or she might buy a policy for twice the market value of the building and secretly arrange to have it "torched"! This example clearly identifies a moral hazard, but it is misleading in the sense that it downplays the pure role of economic incentives, morality aside. That is, we usually think it is quite rational for individuals to increase consumption or investment in response to a lower price, and that is the temptation perceived by both those with medical insurance and the insured potential arsonist.

Is there any way to solve the medical insurance problem? One method that can mitigate the problem, if not solve it, is the use of *deductibles* and *coinsurance*. A deductible requires the individual to pay for a certain amount of medical services before the insurance coverage goes into effect; it is designed to deter reliance on insurance to pay for "minor" illnesses. Coinsurance requires the individual to pay a certain fraction of each dollar spent; the coinsurance rate refers to the percentage paid by the individual. (For example, a coinsurance rate of 25 percent means that, for each dollar spent, the individual must pay 25 percent and the insurance company 75 percent.)

We can see the effect of each in Figure 6-8*a*. Suppose the deductible is for the first 60 units and the insured individual becomes ill. It is not obvious whether the person will file a claim or not. One choice is simply to purchase the 50 units as would be done without insurance. The other choice is to file a claim, pay the full cost of the first 60 units, and consume the rest of the excess units (61 to 100) free.

Triangle *AEF* measures the net cost to the consumer of having to pay for the first 10 excess units, and triangle *FGJ* measures the net benefits of consuming the next 40 free. If *FGJ* > *AEF*, the individual will file the claim. In this particular example, $FGJ = \frac{1}{2}(0.80)(40) = \$16.00$ and $AEF = \frac{1}{2}(0.20)(10) = \$1.00$, so the individual's behavior is unaltered by the deductible.

To understand the effects of deductibles in a more general way, imagine many possible states of illness from mild to severe, and associate with each a demand curve that progressively shifts to the right as we consider more severe illnesses. This is illustrated in Figure 6-8*b*. Since the deductible remains as a

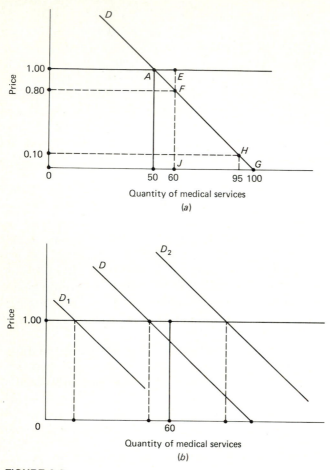

FIGURE 6-8
(a) The effects of deductibles and coinsurance; (b) a deductible
deters filing small insurance claims.

fixed rectangle, it can be seen that one is least likely to file for the less serious
illnesses and that the deductible no longer deters filing past some point.

To see the effect of coinsurance, suppose the coinsurance rate for the
individual represented in Figure 6-8a is 10 percent. If ill, the individual will then
purchase 95 units of medical services (at point H). The smaller the price
elasticity of demand, the smaller the restraining effect of coinsurance (and the
less the moral hazard in the first place). Note that the existence of coinsurance
can make a policy attractive to someone who finds full coverage unattractive.
Although it only partially shifts the risk (the amount depends upon the
coinsurance rate), it does shift the more expensive portion (i.e., it prevents the
losses where the marginal utility of wealth is greatest). Furthermore, it reduces

the consumption of the least-valued of the excess units.[43] So it is quite possible that the risk-saving gains of partial coverage will exceed the expected costs from "excess" use, even if that is not true of full coverage.

The above analysis suggests that one direction to explore in an attempt to solve the medical cost problem is increased reliance on deductibles and coinsurance. When those ideas are integrated into national health insurance proposals, they are typically modified to be income-contingent. That is, it is recognized that lower-income families have limited ability to meet even these partial payments.

However, this section is not intended as a recommendation of what to do; it is intended only to help clarify the nature of the medical cost explosion we have all been experiencing. Although a full discussion of the normative implications that could be explored is beyond our scope, mentioning at least a few of them should help to keep this analysis in perspective.

First, the social benefits and costs referred to in the diagrams of this analysis cannot be easily estimated from observable data for a variety of reasons. Social cost, for example, is the value of what society gives up by allocating a resource to the provision of medical care. In perfectly competitive industries we can often approximate it by the market price. But in the medical care sector, unwarranted entry restrictions (like limiting entrants to medical schools to a number less than the number of qualified applicants) may make observed cost greater than social costs. To the extent that is true, the optimal quantity of medical care should be greater than that which uninsured people choose. In our diagram this might be equivalent to drawing the social marginal cost line at $0.80 rather than the $1.00 observed price and calculating social benefits and costs on the basis of its relation to the demand curve.

But then the demand curves themselves are unreliable guides for social welfare. For one thing, very little is known about the relation between medical care and health; presumably it is health that people seek. This makes it extremely difficult to know whether delivered medical services are excessive. Disagreement among physicians about the appropriate care for a given patient is common. In addition, the specific equity concerns about medical care suggest caution in the use of compensation tests here; to the extent that a patient's income influences the location of the demand curve, the benefits and costs to people of different income groups might require separate analytic treatment.

Finally, much of the problem we have been discussing is exacerbated by the fee-for-service method of organizing the supply of medical services. A physician is supposed to be the consumer's agent and provide expert advice on how to further the consumer's medical interests. The need for an agent arises

---

[43] As drawn, for example, the coinsurance deters purchase of units 96 to 100. This reduces the expected cost of illness by $2.50, and reduces the expected consumer surplus from "subsidized" excess consumption by only $0.125 [$=(0.5)(0.5)(0.10)5$]. So the consumer has an expected gain of $2.375, which is offset to some degree by the increased risk due to having only partial insurance coverage.

because of the generally accepted wisdom that consumers are not competent to choose their own medical treatments. But this puts the fee-for-service physician in an awkward position, because he or she is simultaneously a supplier of services to the patient and a receiver of income in proportion to the amount of services sold. There is a conflict of interest which may cause overpurchasing without insurance; the presence of insurance only exacerbates the tendency.

As an alternative to the fee-for-service system, many analysts have argued for a system of health maintenance organizations to which consumers pay annual fees and by which physicians are employed on a salary basis. That would give the suppliers incentive to conserve on their use of resources, and the forces of competition, as well as physician norms, would work to ensure that appropriate treatments were supplied as required.[44] Still another alternative, much less politically feasible here, would be a national health service like that in Sweden or England.

These cautions about making normative inferences from the moral hazard analysis only hint at some of the complexities which are relevant to health policy. But the complexity does not make the achievement of the analysis presented here any less worthwhile. The medical cost problem continues to be of widespread concern, and the clarification of its source is an important contribution. Furthermore, the same model generated some useful insights (the role of deductibles and coinsurance) for achieving policy improvement.

▽ASSESSING THE COSTS OF UNCERTAINTY

In this chapter we have emphasized that uncertainty is costly. In this section we consider a method, albeit highly simplified, for estimating the order of magnitude of that cost in a policy situation. In particular, the exercise is intended to suggest that plausible boundaries can be placed on the increase in risk costs borne by the population because of an increase in the average medical coinsurance rate. This exercise could be useful in the design of national health insurance.[45]

To begin with, we define two ways of measuring the degree of risk aversion:

1 *Absolute risk aversion:* $a(W) = -U''(W)/U'(W)$
2 *Relative risk aversion:* $r(W) = -WU''(W)/U'(W)$

Note that whenever an individual has a utility-of-wealth function characterized by risk aversion, $U''(W) < 0$ and, of course, $U'(W) > 0$. Thus, both measures of risk are positive when there is risk aversion. Also, the second measure $r(W)$ is simply the elasticity of the marginal utility of wealth. This corresponds to greater risk aversion when marginal utility is changing rapidly or, equivalently,

---

[44] An excellent analysis of this proposal is given by Alain Enthoven, "Consumer Choice Health Plan," *New England Journal of Medicine, 298*, March 23 and 28, 1978, pp. 650–658, 709–720.

[45] This exercise is a simplification of an actual one done by Martin Feldstein and described in his article, "The Welfare Loss of Excess Health Insurance," *Journal of Political Economy, 81*, No. 2, part I, March/April 1973, pp. 251–280.

when the utility function is more concave. A straight-line utility function, on the other hand, scores a zero on both measures ($U'' = 0$) and indicates risk neutrality.

To get a feel for the interpretation of these measures, we use an approximation suggested by Pratt.[46] Recall the risk cost: the difference between the expected wealth in a risky situation and its certain-wealth equivalent. Pratt shows that the risk cost C can be approximated by the following formula, which is derived from a Taylor series expansion:

$$C = \tfrac{1}{2}a(\overline{W})\sigma_W^2$$

where $\overline{W}$ is the expected wealth and σ_W^2 is the variance of wealth.[47] Thus for individuals who have the same expected wealth and are faced with the same uncertainties, those with greater absolute risk aversion will pay more to avoid the risk. The absolute risk aversion is proportional to the absolute amount of money an individual will pay to avoid a fair gamble. Similarly, we can express the relative risk cost as the ratio of the risk cost to expected wealth:

$$\frac{C}{\overline{W}} = \tfrac{1}{2}a(\overline{W})\frac{\sigma_W^2}{\overline{W}}$$

or

$$\frac{C}{\overline{W}} = \tfrac{1}{2}r(\overline{W})\left(\frac{\sigma_W^2}{\overline{W}^2}\right)$$

where the term in parentheses on the right has a standard statistical interpretation: the coefficient of variation squared. This last equation shows that the share of wealth an individual will give up to avoid a certain risk is proportional to his or her relative risk aversion.

As we have seen in earlier chapters, simulation techniques may be profitably used when we do not have precise knowledge of certain parameter values but have some reason to believe the values are likely to lie within a given range. In this case we do not know the values of the risk aversion measures for particular individuals. Nevertheless, common sense can be a useful guide.

Two parametric utility functions have been found to be useful for empirical exercises involving risk aversion. One of them is the function

$$U(W) = -e^{-aW}$$

where $a > 0$, which is characterized by constant absolute risk aversion equal to a. To see this we take the first and second derivatives:

$$U'(W) = ae^{-aW}$$
$$U''(W) = -a^2 e^{-aW}$$

[46] J. W. Pratt, "Risk Aversion in the Small and in the Large," *Econometrica, 32,* 1964, pp. 122–136.

[47] The variance of a random variable W is defined as $\sigma_W^2 = \sum_{i=1}^{n} \Pi_i(W_i - \overline{W})^2$, where $i = 1, 2, \ldots, n$ states of the world, W_i is the value of W in each state, and Π_i is the probability of that state.

Therefore, applying the definition of absolute risk aversion,

$$a(W) = \frac{a^2 e^{-aW}}{a e^{-aW}} = a$$

The other function of interest displays constant relative risk aversion equal to r:

$$U(W) = \frac{W^{1-r}}{1 - r}$$

where $r > 0$, $r \neq 1$. To show this, we again take derivatives:

$$U'(W) = \frac{(1 - r)W^{-r}}{1 - r} = W^{-r}$$
$$U''(W) = -rW^{-r-1}$$

By applying the definition of relative risk aversion, we get

$$r(W) = \frac{rW^{-r}}{W^{-r}} = r$$

Now let us work with the constant absolute risk aversion function and ask what values are reasonable for a. Imagine asking people what entry price they would require in order to make (be indifferent to) a bet with an even chance of winning or losing \$1000. Casual observation suggests that a practical lower bound might be \$50, in the sense that very few people would accept the bet for anything lower and the vast majority of people would demand more.

To see what degree of absolute risk aversion a this implies, we must solve the equations that indicate the utility equivalence of current wealth W with the gamble:

$$U(W) = \tfrac{1}{2}U(W + 1050) + \tfrac{1}{2}U(W - 950)$$

For the constant absolute risk aversion case:

$$-e^{-aW} = -\tfrac{1}{2}e^{-a(W+1050)} - \tfrac{1}{2}e^{-a(W-950)}$$

The initial wealth level drops out, and on simplifying we have

$$2 = e^{-1050a} + e^{950a}$$

This equation can be solved on a calculator, and we find $a \simeq 0.0001$.[48]

---

[48] For those not familiar with inelegant but remarkably practical ways of solving many problems by trial and error, here is how one might proceed for the above. Since we know a is positive when there is risk aversion, the answer will be >0. The first term must be a fraction because of the

Suppose for an upper bound we use an entry price of $333; this makes a 50-50 chance of winning $1333 or losing $667 and is probably sufficient to attract most investors. Solving as above, this implies $a \simeq 0.0007$.

To show how one could use these boundaries in a simulation of the effects of coinsurance on medical care insurance, a highly simplified illustrative calculation is made below. The major simplification is to assume that each household only faces two possible states of the world: healthy with $\Pi_H = .9$, and ill with $\Pi_I = .1$. In an actual simulation, one would use a standard statistical distribution to model the many real contingencies that households face.[49] We assume that the uninsured household would purchase $5600 worth of medical services if ill and that the price elasticity of demand is -0.5; these numbers are within the bounds of plausibility for expected medical expenditures and price elasticity.

Let W_c be the certain-wealth equivalent which makes the "average" household indifferent to its current uninsured and risky state. That is:

$$U(W_c) = EU(W) = .9U(W) + .1U(W - 5600)$$

or for the specific utility function

$$-e^{-aW_c} = .9(-e^{-aW}) + .1(-e^{-a(W-5600)})$$

which can be simplified as follows:

$$e^{a(W-W_c)} = .9 + .1e^{a(5600)}$$

and, taking logs,

$$W - W_c = \frac{1}{a} \ln (.9 + .1e^{a(5600)})$$

By using our two bounds for a in the above equation, we find that

$$W - W_c = \begin{cases} \$723.83 & a = 0.0001 \\ \$2545.31 & a = 0.0007 \end{cases}$$

Since the risk cost of being completely uninsured is $W - W_c$ minus the

---

negative sign in the exponent (the bigger a is, the smaller the fraction). Since $e \simeq 2.72$, any exponent >1 makes the second term too big, or $a > 1/950 = 0.001$. Therefore, we have quickly realized that $0 > a > 0.001$. From here, one can achieve accuracy to any decimal point by trial and error. Take the halfway point in this interval, 0.0005, and try it on the right-hand-side terms. $0.59 + 1.61 = 2.20$, so 0.0005 is too big, and $0 > a > 0.0005$. Proceed in this manner until the difference between the two boundaries is negligible for your purposes.

[49] In the actual Feldstein simulation, the number of hospitalizations per household is assumed to resemble a Poisson distribution and the duration per hospitalization is assumed to resemble the gamma distribution.

expected medical care cost [$560 = .1($5600)], we see it is between $163.83 and $1985.31 per household.

Now, if each household purchased an insurance policy with a coinsurance provision of 50 percent, its members, when ill, would purchase more medical services. We have assumed $Q = 5600P^{-0.5}$, where $P = \$1.00$ initially. With coinsurance, P drops to $0.50 and $Q = 7920$ (the moral hazard factor). Thus, in the event of illness, the insurance company and the household will each pay $3960 to the hospital. The insurance company will charge $396 for each policy, which the household loses in all states. To find the residual cost of risk to the household, we ask what certain wealth W_c^* would bring the same utility as is now expected:

$$U(W_c^*) = .9U(W - 396) + .1U(W - 396 - 3960)$$

or, using the same algebra as above

$$W - 396 - W_c^* = \frac{1}{a} \ln (.9 + .1e^{a(3960)})$$

Using our two bounds for a, we calculate:

$$W - 396 - W_c^* = \begin{cases} \$\ 474.43 & a = 0.0001 \\ \$1308.44 & a = 0.0007 \end{cases}$$

As before, the residual risk cost is the difference between these figures and the household's expected out-of-pocket medical costs of $396, so it is between $78 and $912.45. Therefore, the risk saving from taking out partial insurance coverage is between $85.40 and $1072.87 per household (the difference between the total and residual risk costs).

We emphasize that this exercise is intended to demonstrate a procedure for using risk-aversion measures in a simulation. To present an actual simulation would require more detail and more sensitivity testing than is appropriate for the purpose of this book. However, studying and understanding exercises like this one should provide the necessary courage to grapple with the existing work of this type, and perhaps improve upon it.

SUMMARY

Uncertainty is a pervasive phenomenon; it is present to some degree in virtually all economic choice situations. The sources of uncertainty are varied and many: nature, human interaction, lack of information, or complexity. Although different situations may not fit neatly into any one of these categories, the following examples should illustrate the sources of difference: the weather, labor-management bargaining tactics, buying a used car, and defending yourself against a lawsuit.

The presence of uncertainty is generally considered costly. As a matter of preference, most people simply dislike uncertainty and are willing to pay in order to avoid or reduce it. We call this *risk aversion*. As a consequence of it, resource allocation to activities which generate risk can be profoundly affected. A good example of this is the impact of a high and uncertain inflation rate on the nation's aggregate savings and investment; because this kind of inflation makes the real return from savings and investment more uncertain, it works to reduce them.

It is important to understand how people respond to the uncertainties they perceive, as well as how public policy can affect those perceptions. *The most widely used model of behavior under uncertainty is the model of expected utility maximization:* Individuals, when confronted with risky choice situations, will attempt to make the decisions that maximize their expected utilities. To understand that, we reviewed the concepts of probability and expected value.

Several examples of simple coin-flipping games were given to demonstrate that expected value is not a sufficient predictor of choice making. The St. Petersburg Paradox, which is often used incorrectly for this purpose, was shown to be resolved by a quite different rationale: Practical and realistic perceptions of the maximum prize to be awarded make the actual expected value substantially lower than its theoretical limit. However, other examples easily illustrate that many people will refuse to take risks even when the entry price is fair. Such risk aversion is implied by a diminishing marginal utility of wealth, which leads naturally to the idea that people care about expected utility.

Because risk is costly, social mechanisms which can shift risk to where it is less costly are of great importance. Two methods of doing this are risk pooling and risk spreading. Risk pooling is the essence of insurance; as a consequence of the law of large numbers, the aggregate risk cost to the insurance company from possible claims is much lower than the sum of risk costs when each individual bears his or her own. Risk spreading, on the other hand, derives its advantage from the fact that one risky event has a lower total risk cost if different individuals share the risk. Dividing the ownership of a company among several partners or among many owners through the sale of stock is a good example of risk spreading. Individuals also use futures markets for this purpose; e.g., a farmer may not wish to bear the full risk of growing crops to be harvested in the future and sold at some unknown price and so may sell the rights to some of that crop now at a known price through the futures market.

The ability of insurance, stock, and futures markets to reduce risk costs is limited to coverage of only a few of the many risky phenomena. In later chapters we will see that other mechanisms of risk reduction are used in private markets; e.g., the desire to be an employee rather than an entrepreneur can be understood as a way to reduce the risk. But in addition, many public rules and regulations can be understood as collective attempts to reduce risk costs.

Through the legal system we have the concept of limited liability, which forces certain risks to be shifted. This may not be desirable when the risks taken can have catastrophic consequences; a controversial example that exacerbates this problem is the Price-Anderson Act, which specially limits the liability of private producers from nuclear reactor accidents. Part of the function of the criminal justice system is to deter potential offenders from committing crimes and thus limit the risks of that type to be faced by the population. A whole variety of regulations involving product or service quality can be thought of in terms of risk-reduction benefits; examples are occupational licensure or certification, labeling requirements, and safety standards.

When we shift to policy considerations, it is important to recognize that risk is like other undesirable phenomena which we seek to avoid; the willingness to avoid them depends upon what we must give up to do so. A riskless society would probably be desired by no one, once it is recognized that either crossing the street or driving would have to be banned.

General cost considerations will be explored more fully in later chapters. In this part of the book we are concentrating on models of individual decision making. Thus the next point emphasized in this chapter is that policy analysts must consider critically whether particular choice situations can be modeled successfully by the expected utility maximization hypothesis. Some situations, like that of the Slumlord's (or Prisoner's) Dilemma, may be perceived as uncertain rather than risky. Choice making may result from strategic reasoning rather than estimating probabilities of the various possible states. To the extent that this game-theoretic model applies to urban housing decisions, it may provide a rationale for policies involving urban renewal.

A more general alternative to expected utility maximization is the model of bounded rationality. This model recognizes that there are limits to human information-processing abilities, such that the calculations required to maximize expected utility may be beyond them in some situations. This is not a statement that applies only to some people; it applies to all of us. No one in history has yet discovered an optimal chess strategy, even though we know that at least one exists. It is an empirical question whether particular decision situations we face are ones in which we are likely to find the optimum, or put differently, whether they are more like chess or tic-tac-toe. Most empirical evidence, however, suggests that people do not maximize expected utility in situations perceived as unfamiliar, even if they are quite simple.

The model of bounded rationality emphasizes that people learn by trial and error and often develop strategies of problem solving (or decision making) that satisfice even if they do not optimize. With enough trials and errors, learning and ingenuity, people can solve incredibly complex problems. But in other situations, either because of complexity or the lack of trials to allow trial and error learning, human choice may be very poor. It is recognition that people can make quite serious mistakes which provides a potentially powerful rationale for many regulatory standards and other public policies.

The example of the purchase of disaster insurance in flood- and earthquake-prone locations illustrates this nicely. If people behave according to the expected utility maximization hypothesis, there is no public policy problem except possibly the lack of objective information. But the survey evidence suggests that people do not make the coverage decision in that manner, that many people seem to choose purchase strategies which are inferior given their own preferences, and that public policies designed to take account of the bounded rationality in this situation may lead to better decision making. One of the most important areas of policy-analytic research concerns more careful exploration of the differences in policy evaluations that arise from these alternative models of decision making.

Mechanisms to reduce risk can have adverse side effects, as the moral hazard problem of medical insurance illustrates. In this case, the presence of insurance changes the incentives each individual faces when deciding on the purchase of medical services. Full-coverage insurance reduces the price at the point of service to zero, leading to a Prisoner's Dilemma in which everyone overconsumes medical services. As a by-product of the desirable growth of medical care insurance coverage for the population, we have created a system of medical care that is undesirable because there are no effective mechanisms of cost control. Several strategies have the potential for solving the problem: encouraging the development of health maintenance organizations, a national health service, or increasing the amount of coinsurance and deductibles in the context of a national health insurance plan.

In the optional section several measures of risk aversion are introduced and their use in estimating risk costs empirically is illustrated. In the prior section on moral hazard, we identified a trade-off between the amount of risk reduction and the amount of overconsumption of medical services. The calculation of the risk-reduction part of this trade-off is simulated in the optional section, albeit with a highly simplified model. By using boundaries for risk aversion derived by common sense and past experience, one can begin to get a feel for the magnitudes involved. Such an exercise can be very useful in policy analysis, as in the design of a national health insurance plan.

EXERCISE

6-1 A consumer has a Von Neumann–Morgenstern utility index for income Y:

$$U(Y) = 10Y - \frac{Y^2}{100,000}$$

Furthermore, if she becomes ill, her demand for medical care Q is

$$Q = 200 - 4P$$

where P = dollar price per unit of medical care

The current price is $P = \$25$. The probability that she will become ill is .15. Her current income is $10,000.

To simplify this problem, assume that 100 units of medical care when the consumer is "ill" just restore the consumer to "healthy." Any medical care above that is considered like consumption of any ordinary good or service. Thus, the utility level in each state depends on the income level *after* medical expenses and premiums supplemented by any consumer surplus from medical care *above* the "healthy" point. (In this problem, the consumer will always choose at least enough medical care to restore her health.)

a What is the consumer's expected utility with no insurance? (Answer: $U = 95,316$)

b Political candidate A proposes that fully comprehensive health insurance be provided to everyone. The proposed premium would be 10 percent above the actuarially fair level for this consumer (to cover transaction costs). What premium would be charged for this plan, and what expected utility level would it yield? (Answers: $825; $U = 92,746$)

c Political candidate B proposes a catastrophic insurance plan. It would cover all expenses above $2750, but the consumer would pay for all medical expenditures up to $2750. Again, the proposed premium would be 10 percent above the actuarially fair level. What premium would be charged for plan B, and what expected utility level would it yield? (Answers: Approximately $371; $U = 93,153$) *Note:* Is there any difference in the medical service that would be received by this consumer under plan A or plan B? What causes the difference in expected utility?

d Political candidate C proposes a comprehensive plan with no deductibles but a 60 percent coinsurance rate (the consumer would pay $0.60 for each $1.00 of medical expenditure). The proposed premium would also be 10 percent above the actuarially fair level. What premium would be charged for plan C, and what expected utility level would it yield? (Answers: $231; $U = 94,822$)

e Suppose a $50 preventive visit to the doctor lowered the probability of illness to .075. Would the consumer purchase a preventive visit when she is not covered by insurance? (Answer: Yes) If covered by plan C, would the consumer purchase the preventive visit if the premium were adjusted to reflect the new expected costs plus 10 percent? (Answer: Yes)

PART **THREE**

POLICY ASPECTS OF PRODUCTION, COST, AND ORGANIZATIONAL DECISION MAKING

TECHNICAL POSSIBILITIES AND COSTS IN POLICY ANALYSIS

In this chapter we examine concepts from the economic theories of production and costs. These theories are useful in deducing policy-relevant consequences from observable supply activities. First, they are crucial components of *predictive* models of producer behavior: understanding what outputs will be supplied by these organizations and what resources will be used to make the outputs. Second, they are important for the *normative* purpose of evaluating the efficiency consequences of supply activities. After presenting an overview of these uses below, we explain how the chapter is organized to develop skills by using several fundamental concepts from these theories.

In order to predict the behavior of a supplier organization, economic models provide specifications of the organization's objectives, capabilities, and environmental constraints. The latter are factors which are exogenous to the organization or outside its direct control: demand for its product, the technological possibilities for producing the product, and the costs of the resource inputs used with alternative production methods. In this chapter we will develop familiarity with the supply constraints of technology and costs. In later chapters we will focus more explicitly on analytic issues involved in specifying the objectives and capabilities of an organization and then linking them with the environmental constraints to predict the organization's behavioral response to proposed policies. However, we wish to clarify in advance that making deductions about technology and costs from empirical observations cannot be done in isolation from organizational objectives and capabilities.

Consider first the constraint of *technology*, the methods available for converting inputs into outputs. Obviously, one cannot expect an organization to produce more output than is technologically possible given the inputs it uses;

therefore, understanding the constraint is useful for predictive purposes. Technologies which are efficient in an engineering sense (the maximum output for given inputs) are sometimes represented in models by a *production function*. Estimated production functions, based upon observations of supplier inputs and outputs, are used commonly in analytic work.

Understanding technological possibilities is easier for some activities than others. In agriculture, for example, it might be clear that one particular output is corn and that the inputs used to produce it are land, labor, fertilizer, capital equipment, weather, etc. Even in this relatively clear case there are difficulties in establishing the relation betwen inputs and outputs. Suppose, for example, that less fertilizer does not reduce the amount of corn produced but does reduce its sweetness. Then it would be a mistake to compare only the quantity and not the quality of the output and conclude that the process with less fertilizer is technologically superior. To corn lovers this is like comparing apples and oranges.

Imagine the difficulty of trying to understand the technology constraining some other important supply organizations. How does one define the outputs of a school, police force, or mental hospital, and what are the inputs which determine the outputs? One might think, for example, that the verbal and mathematical skills of children are intended as the outputs of schools and furthermore that they can be measured by scores on standardized tests. However, one community might emphasize learning about civic responsibilities as an important schooling objective, and that output would not necessarily be reflected in the standardized scores. Its schools might have smaller increases in the standardized scores of their pupils, but it would be wrong to conclude they were technologically inefficient compared with other schools with similar resource inputs: It is the objectives which differ, not the technological efficiency.

The other environmental constraint focused on in this chapter is *cost*. The supplier organization's choice of technology will depend upon its perception of costs. The monetary costs of inputs which we observe in the marketplace may or may not fully represent that perception. In the standard example of a profit-maximizing firm, the monetary costs are those perceived by the firm. For example, the firm will produce any level of output with whatever technology minimizes the monetary cost of its required inputs. In this case a relation known as the *cost function* can be used to predict the total costs of producing alternative output levels for any given input prices. Knowledge of the cost function can be useful for predicting how supplier organizations will respond to various policy changes such as those involving taxes or regulatory rules.

However, suppose the supplier organization is a public agency with a mandate to employ the hard-to-employ. It may prefer a labor-intensive technology to a capital-intensive one with lower monetary costs. That is, it may perceive foregone employment oportunities as a cost of using capital in addition to its monetary cost.

Some supplier organizations may produce in environments in which political costs are major expenses. A district attorney's office, for example, may require police assistance to obtain certain evidence. But the police have many important matters on their agenda and establish their own priorities. The district attorney's office may have to pay a political cost, like agreeing to prosecute promptly some other individuals arrested by the police, in order to gain police cooperation in gathering the evidence.

The above examples demonstrate that understanding technological possibilities and costs is important for predicting the behavior of supply organizations; however, one must consider carefully how these constraints apply in specific situations. Now let us turn briefly to the normative use of concepts from the theories of production and cost. We discuss their relevance to the concepts of Pareto optimality and the compensation principle.

We have not yet considered how the concept of Pareto optimality applies to a complicated economy in which decisions must be made about the outputs to be produced and the resource inputs to be used in making each output. Indeed, we defer most of this discussion until Chapter 10. Nevertheless, we shall sometimes point out when there is room for a deal. For example, efficiency requires that each output be produced by a method that is technologically efficient; i.e. one that achieves the maximum possible output with the inputs used. Otherwise, one could use the same inputs with an efficient technology and have more of that output with no less of anything else. The incremental output could be given to anyone and someone would be made better off with no one else worse off. Thus a necessary condition for Pareto optimality is that outputs be produced with technologically efficient methods.

Knowledge of the production function is useful for judging the technical efficiency of supplier organizations. We will illustrate this with an example from an evaluation of a public employment program. Partial knowledge of the production function is developed from empirical observations and used to judge changes in the technological efficiency of production over time.

All of the other normative illustrations in this chapter are applications of the compensation principle (and are subject to all the caveats of interpretation discussed in Chapter 5). The essential point is to demonstrate that knowledge of costs can provide a great deal of the information used to conduct a compensation test. Once that is clear, we illustrate how the knowledge is obtained through techniques like benefit-cost analysis and the use of cost functions. We use examples from a public employment program, trucking deregulation, and peak-load pricing for public utilities.

The chapter is organized as follows: We begin with a review of the relation between technological possibilities and the concept of a production function. Both predictive and normative uses of the production function approach in a policy setting are illustrated from an analysis of a public employment program. We also provide an example to suggest how cross-sectional empirical data are often used to make inferences about a production function, and we warn of a pitfall to avoid when the method is used.

Following the section on technological constraints, we compare and contrast concepts of cost: accounting cost, private opportunity cost, and social opportunity cost. We show how knowledge of the social opportunity cost can be used to test for relative efficiency by the compensation principle. The use of these different cost concepts is illustrated by benefit-cost calculations used in the analysis of the public employment program. The calculations illustrate both predictive and normative analytic tasks.

After reviewing cost concepts, we explore the relations between costs and outputs. The concept of a cost function is explained, and use of the function is illustrated in the evaluation of a regulatory reform concerning interstate trucking firms. Another type of cost-output relation known as the *joint cost problem* is discussed, together with its application to peak-load pricing of public utility services. In an optional section we use the mathematics of duality to clarify some of the relations between technology and cost functions and introduce some of the cost functions commonly used in empirical analysis.

TECHNICAL POSSIBILITIES AND THE PRODUCTION FUNCTION

The notion of a production function is usually introduced as a way to summarize the various technical possibilities for converting inputs, or factors of production, into outputs. For example, if Q represents output, K capital, and L labor, the production function may be expressed as

$$Q = F(K, L)$$

The idea is that output may be produced by various combinations of the two inputs, and knowledge of the production function and specific quantities K_0 and L_0 allows one to infer that Q_0 is the *maximum* output which can be produced with that combination. Usually, more output can be produced if more of one of the inputs is available. In mathematical notation, $\Delta Q/\Delta K > 0$ and $\Delta Q/\Delta L > 0$.

Let us think of a single technology as a set of instructions for converting specified inputs into some output, exactly like the instructions that come with a model airplane kit, where the various parts are inputs and the model airplane is the output. Note that the economic meaning of "technology" is broader than its common interpretation as a type of machine; there can be technologies in which the only inputs are labor, and more generally, the variations in possible instructions to laborers can be an important source of technological change.

For example, suppose we imagine alternative processes of developing computer programs Q to sell to other firms (e.g., to keep track of their accounts receivable) and there are ten computer programmers L and five computer terminals K as the inputs available during a specified production period. There are many ways in which one could imagine organizing these inputs for production: Perhaps some programmers should specialize in drafting the program and others in debugging the drafts. We might instruct each programmer to develop a program from start to finish or perhaps some programmers should specialize in developing financial programs and others in inventory control. Two time shifts of labor might be developed to allow full utilization of the terminals. Each of these is a way to vary the technology of production.

If the production function for this example is represented as above, $Q = F(K, L)$, then the only information we have is on the maximum output that can be attained with the two types of inputs. On the other hand, we might consider the ten units of labor as divided into two different types of labor, e.g., six programmers who make the program plan L_P and four who debug L_D, and represent the production function as follows:

$$Q = F(L_P, L_D, K)$$

We could extend this to consider the morning M and evening E programmers:

$$Q = F(L_{PM}, L_{PE}, L_{DM}, L_{DE}, K)$$

Thus whether the effect of a technological variation can be identified from knowledge of the production function depends upon how the function is defined; the more aggregated the input definitions, the less information is revealed about technical variations.

Often an analyst is expected to be able to determine empirically some aspect of the technology of an actual production process. This typically requires statistical estimation of the production function. Although the statistical procedures are beyond the scope of this text, the theoretical and practical considerations that underlie the analysis can be illustrated.

One example arose in regard to the evaluation of the 1972 New York Supported Work experiment, a public employment program which hired ex-addicts and ex-offenders to deliver a wide variety of public services in the city. One group of the employees was engaged in cleaning the exteriors of fire stations around the city, and the crews had been working for approximately 6 months. The question raised was whether the productivity of the workers had been improving.

Answering this specific question actually had only a latent role in the overall evaluation of the experiment. This particular project was started before the formal experiment, and its participants were not randomly selected. However, the analyst hired to undertake the formal economic evaluation was not well known to the officials operating or funding the program, and they sought some early assurance that his work would be useful.[1] This project provided a low-risk opportunity to get some indication of the quality of the evaluation to come. That is, the resolution of the issue was to some degree a test of the analyst's skill and would be a determinant of the seriousness with which his future analyses and recommendations would be taken.

Accurate data were attainable on the inputs used to clean each building. This does not mean that the mass of data was all prepared, sitting and gathering dust

---

[1] All this is known to the author because he was the analyst.

on some desk while waiting for an analyst to walk in and have use for it. But the project managers, in the course of conducting routine activities, had maintained various records which the analyst could use in constructing a data set appropriate for this task. The project had several crews which allowed them to work at different sites simultaneously. They kept track daily of attendance on each site for payroll purposes. For inventory control they kept daily track of the number of water-blasting machines assigned to each crew and the amount of chemicals used by the crew. Furthermore, precise output data on the square footage of surface cleaned, verified by site visits, were also available.

Let us consider for a moment what is meant by a productivity increase. Imagine a production process in which Q is produced with inputs K and L. The average product of labor AP_L is defined by

$$AP_L = \frac{Q}{L}$$

This measure, output per worker, is what is usually referred to when productivity is discussed. Mayors often seek ways of raising the productivity of city employees. On a larger scale this measure applied to the aggregate private economy has recently been a source of great concern. For the 27-year period 1947 to 1973, real productivity in the private business sector increased every single year. The rate of productivity increase averaged 2.91 percent per year. But from 1973 to 1980, average real productivity growth was only 0.58 percent per year, and in 1974 and 1978 to 1980[2] it was negative.

If we look at standard diagrams of the total, average, and marginal product-of-labor curves, it becomes clear that maximizing productivity is not necessarily a wise or efficient strategy to follow. The curves are shown in Figure 7-1a and b.[3] Recall that these curves are defined for a fixed level of all the *other* inputs and that they show how output (total, average, and marginal) varies as the amount of *labor* is changed. If, for example, the capital inputs increase, all three of the labor product curves will presumably shift upwards. (For example, the more capital each worker has available, the greater the output per worker.)

Recall also that the MP_L reaches is maximum before AP_L and always passes

[2] *Economic Report of the President*, February 1982 (Washington, D.C.: U.S. Government Printing Office, 1982), p. 278, table B-40. Aggregate output in the table is measured by the sum of each output produced weighted by its price. The total is adjusted for inflation by a price deflator using 1972 as a base.

[3] This note reviews the concepts of TP, AP, and MP and their relations. The total product-of-labor curve TP_L is drawn in Figure 7-1a to increase rapidly at first (as enough laborers become available to use the capital stock) and then more slowly until L_T, where it actually begins to decline. (Too many workers jammed into one plant can become counterproductive.) The slowdown in the growth of total product is a consequence of diminishing marginal productivity. The marginal product of labor MP_L is the change in output that results from adding one more unit of labor. In Figure 7-1a it is equal to the slope of TP_L ($= \Delta TP_L/\Delta L$) and reaches a maximum at L_M. The AP_L in Figure 7-1a is the slope of the line drawn from the origin to any point on the TP_L curve (slope = height/base = total product/labor = AP_L); it reaches its maximum at L_A. In Figure 7-1b the AP_L and MP_L curves are constructed from the TP_L curve in Figure 7-1a.

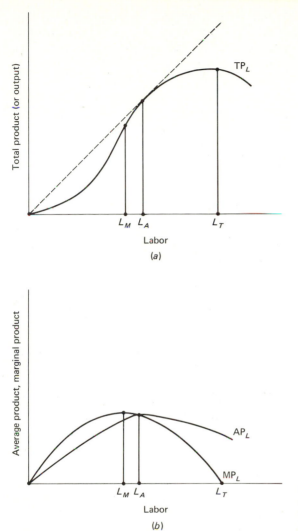

Labor

(a)

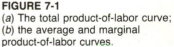

Labor

(b)

FIGURE 7-1
(a) The total product-of-labor curve;
(b) the average and marginal
product-of-labor curves.

through the maximum AP_L. This is shown in Figure 7-1b. That is, the marginal product pulls the average product up whenever it is greater ($MP_L > AP_L$), and pulls it down whenever it is lower ($MP_L < AP_L$). When they are the same, the AP_L is neither rising nor falling; the slope of the AP_L at this point is thus zero and the AP_L is at a maximum.

In other words, maximizing productivity for a given stock of nonlabor inputs implies that the quantity of labor used should be L_A. But is that desirable? In general, the answer is no. Imagine that the MP_L at L_A is 3 per hour, that labor can be hired at $6.00 per hour, and output sells at $3.00 each. Then hiring one more hour's worth of labor will cost $6.00 but result in $9.00 worth of extra output. It would be inefficient to forego this opportunity, since there is clearly room for a deal. It does not matter whether productivity is decreasing; the relevant consideration is whether the value of the *marginal* product exceeds its cost. In this example, labor should be hired until the MP_L declines to 2. That will be to the right of L_A, in general.[4]

One reason for pointing out the inefficiency of maximizing productivity (aside from its relevance to the supported work problem, to be discussed shortly) is that it can be a tempting mistake to make. Public managers, responding to their mayors' pleas to increase productivity, could decrease efficiency by utilizing too little labor with the available capital stock. Two people and a truck on a refuse collection route may collect 2 tons per day; three people on the same truck may collect $2\frac{1}{2}$ tons per day and thereby cause "productivity" to decrease. But the relevant issue is whether the extra cleanliness (resulting from the marginal $\frac{1}{2}$ ton of removed refuse per collection cycle) is worth more than the cost of achieving it.

There are, of course, other ways to change the level of productivity: One can add to the nonlabor inputs like capital stock, or one can make technological progress (i.e., use a new technology which generates more output from a given set of inputs than the old technology). Like changes in labor quantities, neither method can be utilized for free. To generate an increase in the capital stock requires that people save more (defer current consumption), and technical progress is usually a consequence of devoting resources to research and development. Like all economic activities, these methods should be pursued only to the extent that we (individually and collectively) are willing to pay the bills for doing so. Thus the general concern about aggregate productivity in the economy reflects unhappiness about departing from our "usual" level, and it requires further study to uncover whether this is because we have made "errors" in resource allocation, or have been "unlucky" in our research and development efforts, or are simply living in a world in which it has become "more expensive" to buy increases in productivity.[5]

To apply this discussion to the supported work problem, increased productivity of the workers should not therefore be defined by the AP_L; this can change for too many reasons irrelevant to the spirit of the question. One way to pose the question is to ask whether the supported workers, when utilizing any given quantity of nonlabor inputs, produce more output over time. One might think of this as an increase in "human capital": over time, each worker represents more labor. Alternatively, one could think of this as technical progress: The same inputs produce more output because the production

---

[4] Take the case in which inputs and outputs have constant prices. To the left of L_A, where AP_L is increasing, average output cost is decreasing and profits per unit are increasing. Therefore, there is still room for a deal by employing more labor and expanding output. To the right of L_A, profits per unit begin to decrease, but very slowly at first while quantity is increasing at a constant clip. Thus total profits are still increasing. Eventually, profits per unit will decline enough that total profits do not increase; that will be the efficient production point.

[5] For an excellent review of this general problem, see Edward F. Denison, *Accounting for Slower Economic Growth* (Washington, D.C.: The Brookings Institution, 1979).

process is becoming more refined. This case would be one of labor augmenting technical progress.

Letting $a(t)$ represent a technical progress function (where t is time), we might hypothesize:[6]

$$Q = F(K, a(t)L)$$

The term $a(t)$ can be thought of as an adjustment to the nominal quantity of labor in order to account for changes in the effectiveness of labor over time. Now if we can estimate the production function, it may be possible to see if labor inputs produce more output over time, other things being equal. That is, we want to know, for $t_1 > t_0$, whether $Q_1/L_1 > Q_0/L_0$ for constant K and L. If so, it must be that $\Delta a/\Delta t > 0$.

It is necessary to choose some specific empirical form for the production function. Theoretical considerations provide some guidance about the general shape of the function, but the specific numerical equation selected is then a matter of which fits the data the best. Recall that two general characteristics of production functions are the returns to scale and elasticity of substitution. The returns-to-scale characteristic is whether a proportionate change applied to *all* inputs leads to an output change that is proportionately greater, the same, or smaller (corresponding to increasing, constant, or decreasing returns to scale, respectively).[7]

The elasticity of substitution is a measure of the curvature of an isoquant (the locus of input combinations which yield a given output level), as illustrated in Figure 7-2; flat isoquants have an infinite elasticity, whereas right-angle

---

[6] Capital augmenting technical progress is represented as $F(a(t)K, L)$ and neutral technological progress as $a(t)F(K, L)$.

[7] A production function $F(K, L)$ may be partially characterized by its scale coefficient ϕ, where returns are decreasing, constant, or increasing if $\phi < 1$, $\phi = 1$, and $\phi > 1$, respectively. ϕ is equal to the sum of the elasticities of output with respect to each input.

$$\phi = \varepsilon_{QL} + \varepsilon_{QK}$$

A quick derivation of this is possible with some calculus. Consider the total differential of the production function:

$$dQ = \frac{\partial Q}{\partial L} \, dL + \frac{\partial Q}{\partial K} \, dK$$

Divide both sides by Q:

$$\frac{dQ}{Q} = \frac{\partial Q}{\partial L} \frac{1}{Q} \, dL + \frac{\partial Q}{\partial K} \frac{1}{Q} \, dK$$

Note that the term on the left-hand side is the proportionate change in output. Now consider changes that are brought about by increasing all inputs by the same proportion α:

$$\alpha = \frac{dL}{L} = \frac{dK}{K}$$

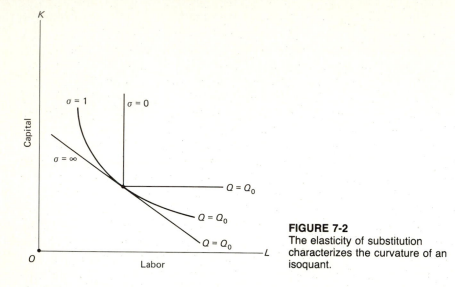

FIGURE 7-2
The elasticity of substitution characterizes the curvature of an isoquant.

isoquants have zero elasticity. The greater this elasticity, the easier it is to substitute one type of input for another. While theoretically the substitution elasticity can change values at different production points, in most empirical work it is assumed that constant elasticity of substitution (CES) production functions can adequately approximate a broad range of production processes.[8]

Divide both sides of the preceding equation by α or its equivalent:

$$\frac{dQ/Q}{\alpha} = \frac{\partial Q}{\partial L}\frac{1}{Q}L + \frac{\partial Q}{\partial K}\frac{1}{Q}K$$

But the term on the left is just the proportionate increase in output over the proportionate increase in input, or ϕ. And the terms on the right are the input elasticities. Therefore,

$$\phi = \varepsilon_{QL} + \varepsilon_{QK}$$

[8] The elasticity of substitution σ is defined by:

$$\sigma = \frac{\%\Delta(K/L)}{\%\Delta RTS_{L,K}}$$

where $RTS_{L,K}$ is the slope of an isoquant ($= -MP_L/MP_K$). CES production functions have the form

$$Q = A[\delta K^{-\rho} + (1 - \delta)L^{-\rho}]^{-1/\rho}$$

where $\sigma = 1/(1 + \rho)$, A is a positive constant, and $0 < \sigma < 1$. For more explanation of the CES function and empirical studies of it, see the following two references: K. J. Arrow, et al., "Capital Labor Substitution and Economic Efficiency," *Review of Economics and Statistics, 43,* August 1961, pp. 225–250, and M. Nerlove, "Recent Studies of the CES and Related Production Functions," in M. Brown (ed.), *The Theory and Empirical Analysis of Production* (New York: Columbia University Press, 1967).

Site inspection of the supported work operations provided some basis for judging an appropriate form. Neither of the extreme elasticities of substitution σ seemed appropriate: The water-blasting machines could not operate themselves ($\sigma \neq \infty$), and there was substitutability between the factors because increased scrubbing of some areas could substitute for more water blasting ($\sigma \neq 0$). In terms of returns to scale, it would be surprising if the data revealed any large differences from the constant-returns case. Buildings large enough to use two crews simultaneously were not cleaned by following procedures very different from those for one crew buildings.

The production function used to approximate the described features was the Cobb-Douglas:

$$Q = AK^\alpha L^\beta \qquad A > 0, 0 < \alpha, \beta < 1$$

The returns to scale of this function always equal $\alpha + \beta$, and it is often used in a more restricted form where $\beta = 1 - \alpha$ (i.e., constant returns). It has an elasticity of substitution $= 1$. (Use of a CES function did not provide significantly different results.[9])

At this point it might seem fairly easy to apply standard statistical methods to determine A, α, and β by substituting the values of Q (the square feet of

---

[9] To see these two points, note the equations for the marginal products in calculus form:

$$\frac{\partial Q}{\partial K} = MP_K = \alpha AK^{\alpha-1}L^\beta$$

$$\frac{\partial Q}{\partial L} = MP_L = \beta AK^\alpha L^{\beta-1}$$

We can use these equations to find the input elasticities:

$$\varepsilon_{QK} = \frac{\partial Q}{\partial K}\frac{K}{Q} = \alpha AK^{\alpha-1}L^\beta \frac{K}{Q} = \frac{\alpha Q}{Q} = \alpha$$

$$\varepsilon_{QL} = \frac{\partial Q}{\partial L}\frac{L}{Q} = \beta AK^\alpha L^{\beta-1} \frac{L}{Q} = \frac{\beta Q}{Q} = \beta$$

Since an earlier note showed that the scale coefficient ϕ is the sum of the input elasticities,

$$\phi = \alpha + \beta$$

Going back to the marginal product equations, let us divide the second one by the first:

$$\frac{\partial Q/\partial L}{\partial Q/\partial K} = RTS_{L,K} = \frac{\beta}{\alpha}\frac{K}{L}$$

Substituting this in the definition of σ gives us

$$\sigma = \frac{\Delta(K/L)/(K/L)}{\Delta RTS_{L,K}/RTS_{L,K}} = \frac{\Delta(K/L)/(K/L)}{(\beta/\alpha)\Delta(K/L)/(\beta/\alpha)(K/L)} = 1$$

building cleaned), K (the number of machine-hours used in cleaning the building), and L (the number of worker-hours) observed for many buildings cleaned by the project. However, the most significant problem in applying that to the supported work setting was that not all buildings were equally easy to clean. Simply knowing the square footage cleaned did not reflect the difficulty of the task. The buildings varied in height from one to four stories, and the taller buildings required either extensive scaffolding to be erected or the rental of a large "cherrypicker" to carry the workers to the higher parts. Some of the buildings had a great deal of limestone surface, which was more difficult to clean and required special chemical treatment.

To get around the difference problem, it was hypothesized first that *standardized* (but unobservable) output Q^S was produced with Cobb-Douglas technology:

$$Q^S = AK^\alpha L^\beta$$

Then it was assumed that the standardized output Q^S was a product of the observed output Q, in square feet, multiplied by several factors to correct for the degree of job difficulty.[10] The idea can be illustrated by assuming there is only one such factor D:

$$Q^S = Q(D)^{-\omega}$$

where ω is an unknown constant presumed < 0 (the bigger D for a given Q, the higher Q^S should be).

Now the two equations can be combined to give an expression which is entirely in observable variables but which, when estimated statistically, will reveal the parameters of the production function (as well as some measures of how well the hypothesized form fits the data):

$$Q = AK^\alpha L^\beta D^\omega$$

Finally, recall that the motivation for undertaking this analysis was to see if the workers were improving over time. A convenient way to hypothesize a time factor t on labor is

$$Q = AK^\alpha L^{\beta + \delta t} D^\omega$$

where δ is the increment to β (the elasticity of output with respect to labor) per unit of time. If δ is positive, labor is becoming more productive over time.

---

[10] A function like this is sometimes referred to as *hedonic*, which implies that the ordinary (output) measure may have a range of attributes about it which must be known to know its "value."

We will not go into the details of estimation, but note what happens when the above equation is put in logarithmic form:

$$\ln Q = \ln A + \alpha \ln K + (\beta + \delta t) \ln L + \omega \ln D$$

The equation is linear. That allows it to be estimated by standard computer programs for multiple regression analysis simply by entering the logarithms of all the variables as the observations. In the actual estimation, there were 25 observations (buildings cleaned) and each was defined to be in one of two periods: $t = 0$ if the building was cleaned in the first 3 months of the project and $t = 1$ if in the second 3 months. The standardized production function was estimated as

$$Q = 50.217 K^{0.60} L^{0.45-0.07t}$$

where K was defined as machine-hours and L as labor-hours. The estimated returns to scale were close to 1, as expected. Note that the coefficient of t is *negative;* in the second time period, labor was *less* productive.[11]

This result did not come completely as a surprise. The raw data had revealed that the unadjusted AP_L had declined, but it was thought possible that the decline was due to taking on tasks of increasing difficulty. However, the production function analysis ruled that out by controlling for the effects of job difficulty: *Other things equal,* labor was less productive.

In the discussion of these results, two kinds of questions were asked of the analyst: (1) Does the equation predict realistically? (2) Could there be real job-difficulty factors which were omitted from the equation and cause distortion of the results? To answer the first question, sample predictions were made, and they satisfied the project supervisor that each factor was predicted to have a reasonable (in his experience) effect. And as for the second question, the project supervisor again played a key role: He could think of no other job-difficulty factors which were not included in the equation. Thus, the result was accepted in the sense that the decision makers were persuaded that the analytic work revealed to them something that had not been known before and which was of concern to them.[12] The analyst had passed the test.[13]

---

[11] All signs were as expected on the equation actually estimated. The R^2 was 0.81. There were three measures of job difficulty (per building): the number of stories high, the cherrypicker rental charge, and the proportion of limestone cleaning solvent to all solvents used. Of these, the cherrypicker variable had a significant coefficient (Student's t statistic >2). The two input variables and the time variable also were significant.

[12] Later it was discovered that not all of the crew members of the masonry cleaning project were receiving the same pay, and that had caused a morale problem during the second period. More careful hiring and promotion policies were instituted as a result.

[13] The clients of the analyst also passed a test by their acceptance of negative program results. Most public officials who operate programs or who have recommended funding for such programs wish the programs to be successful. Policy evaluation is not intended to suggest their wishes have been fulfilled; it is intended to tell them the truth as best as can be determined. Sometimes officials will resist this, which is one reason why good analysts follow this maxim: "Keep your bags packed!"

One of the obvious lessons from the supported work case is that the success or failure of the analytic task can depend crucially on the ability to take a neat concept from theory and figure out how to apply it in a meaningful way to a messy world. Theory can be credited with rejecting the typical productivity measures as unsuitable in this case and for pointing the way toward a form of input-output relation which allowed some substitution among the inputs. But to implement these concepts by taking the path from Cobb-Douglas functions to cherrypicker expenditures per building required learning in some detail about the nitty-gritty of the actual operations being studied.

Often the linkages assumed in ordinary uses of theory do not apply to empirical applications, and one must be careful to interpret the results accordingly. For example, the production function used in theory is one which summarizes all of the technologies which are efficient in the engineering sense (maximum output for the given inputs). But the function we estimated describes the relation between *actual* output and the inputs used. We have no reason to believe that the actual output is the maximum possible output. Nevertheless, we can make an inference about the technical efficiency of the program.

How do we make this inference? The observations during the first period ($t = 0$) give a lower-bound estimate of the true production function: maximum possible output must be at least as large as actual output. It is reasonable to assume that the actual skills of workers are not decreasing over time. Had the coefficient on labor increased during the second period ($t = 1$), there would be some ambiguity about whether the actual worker skills had increased or the program managers simply were able to increase the technical efficiency of the cleaning operations. However, the observed decrease in labor productivity must be due to lower technical efficiency, since skills are at least the same.[14]

In the above example the observations used to study technology came from one organization with considerable detail about the inputs and outputs. It is much more common to have observations derived from a cross section of organizations producing the same good and with less detailed knowledge about the inputs and outputs. For example, one might obtain data from the *Annual Survey of Manufactures* undertaken by the U.S. Census Bureau, where output is reported as the annual dollar value per industry and an input like labor is measured by the annual number of production worker hours in the industry. Even with these aggregated and less detailed data it is often possible to make

---

[14] It might be argued that current program output (in terms of buildings cleaned) is not the only objective of the program, and what appears as reduced labor productivity might simply represent increased and deliberate program efforts to teach the participants skills which will have a future payoff. This argument is only partially correct. It certainly is true that the program is intended to produce both current and future benefits. However, the analysis above counts only the hours the participants were actually at work cleaning the buildings; furthermore, it controls for the amount of supervision given during those hours. Therefore, the conclusion that the reduced labor productivity is due to lower technical efficiency withstands this criticism. Later in this chapter we will discuss the future benefits as additional outputs of the program.

TABLE 7-1
INDUSTRY PRODUCTION DATA

	Output	Capital	Labor
Technically efficient suppliers			
Unobserved but factual:			
Supplier 1	80	20	20
Supplier 2	160	40	40
Observed:			
Industry	240	60	60
Technically inefficient suppliers			
Unobserved but factual:			
Supplier 1	40	20	20
Supplier 2	200	40	40
Observed:			
Industry	240	60	60

inferences about the technology that constrains supplier behavior.[15] However, caution similar to that in the supported work example must be exercised.

For example, a common assumption made when using aggregate (industry-wide) observations is that each organization comprising the aggregate is technically efficient. If that is not true, the estimated relation cannot be interpreted as the production function. To illustrate this concern, Table 7-1 presents two matrices containing data from two industries using highly simplified production processes. In each case we will accept as a given that the true production function is constant returns to scale with fixed coefficients (zero elasticity of substitution), sometimes referred to as Leontif technology.[16]

$$Q = \min\ (aK,\ bL)\qquad a,\ b > 0$$

This function is for processes in which the inputs are always used in fixed proportion ($= b/a$), such as one operator per tractor. Suppose, for example, that $a = 4$ and $b = 4$, so that

$$Q = \min\ (4K, 4L)$$

---

[15] An example of such a study is J. R. Moroney and J. M. Trapani, "Factor Demand and Substitution in Mineral-Intensive Industries," *The Bell Journal of Economics, 12,* No. 1, spring 1981, pp. 272–284. The authors report, on the basis of their study of the technology in several industries using exhaustible resources, that it may be more difficult to substitute other inputs for the exhaustible resources than previously thought.

[16] Wassily Leontif created an economywide model of production showing the flows of resources and goods across each industry. This has become known as input-output analysis. A characteristic of the model is that it assumes that inputs in each industry are always used in fixed proportions to one another (at the angle of a right-angle isoquant like that shown in Figure 7-2). See Wassily Leontif, *The Structure of the American Economy, 1919–1929* (New York: Oxford University Press, 1951).

Then if $K = 20$ and $L = 10$, the output is the minimum of (80, 40), or $Q = 40$. In this case we would say that labor is "binding": more capital would not increase output, but each extra unit of labor from 10 to 20 would add 4 more to output. Note that a technically efficient organization will use inputs in only a 1:1 proportion with this technology; otherwise, it could produce the same output level with fewer resources. One could reduce K from 20 to 10 in the above example and maintain $Q = 40$.

Returning to Table 7-1, imagine that the only data available for analysis are the industry totals and we are trying to deduce the unknown coefficients a and b of the Leontif technologies used by each industry. The example is so designed that the industry totals are identical for each industry, but the underlying production functions are not the same. In the top part of Table 7-1 we assume correctly that each of the two supplier organizations is operating at a point on its production function. This means that for each supplier (represented by subscripts 1 and 2),

$$aK_1 = bL_1 = Q_1$$
$$aK_2 = bL_2 = Q_2$$

and by addition we get the industry totals:

$$a(K_1 + K_2) = b(L_1 + L_2) = Q_1 + Q_2$$

Since we observe that $K_1 + K_2 = 60$ and $Q_1 + Q_2 = 240$, it must be that $a = 4$. By analogous reasoning, $b = 4$. Therefore, the production function is $Q = \min(4K, 4L)$, deduced from industry-level data and the assumptions we made.

If we apply the same reasoning to the suppliers in the lower part of Table 7-1, we reach the same conclusion. But in this case it is false. The truth (let us say) is that supplier 2 is operating on the production frontier with an actual production function of

$$Q = \min(5K, 5L)$$

Supplier 1 is simply operating with technologically inefficient procedures. If it were operating efficiently with inputs $K = 20$ and $L = 20$, it would produce 100 units. Thus the industry as a whole is producing only 80 percent of the output it could produce with the given inputs (240/300).

The aggregate data reveal only the *average* relations between inputs and outputs of the units comprising the aggregate. In the technically efficient case the average corresponds to the maximal output because each unit is attaining the maximum. But when the units are not operating at technically efficient levels, the aggregate data do not reveal the production function.

It is not easy to determine whether supplier organizations are technically efficient in actuality. The strongest arguments for assuming efficiency are generally made with reference to firms in competitive, private industries. In this environment, it is argued, the only firms which can survive are those which produce at the least possible cost, and thus they must be technically efficient. However, not all economists think actual competitive pressures are strong enough to force this behavior or that firms have the capabilities to reach and maintain technically efficient production over time.[17] When one turns to different settings, like production by public agencies, there is even less generalizable guidance. Thus, it can be difficult to determine the production function referred to in ordinary theory.[18]

Nevertheless, it still can be useful to identify the actual average relations between inputs and outputs. The supported work example provides one illustration. If estimated with industrywide observations, the average relations may be used to predict the output effects of a proportionate increase or decrease in resources to each supplier in the sector. But keep in mind that it also might be useful to try to improve the operating efficiency of the organizations, which is something one might overlook if a leap is made too quickly from knowing the inputs to inferring the production function.

COSTS

The concepts of cost are absolutely fundamental to the comparison of alternatives; indeed, *the* most fundamental concept of an action, decision, or allocation being "costly" is that there *are* alternative uses of the resources. ("There is no such thing as a free lunch.") In this section we will review different definitions of cost that the policy analyst encounters and must understand and illustrate their use in a variety of predictive and normative applications.

In the first part of this section we introduce the normative concept of social opportunity cost and show how the concept is applied to the measurement of relative efficiency in benefit-cost analysis. In the second part of the section we introduce the concepts of accounting cost and private opportunity cost and compare and contrast them with social opportunity cost. In the third part we demonstrate both positive and normative application of these concepts in the benefit-cost analyses of the supported work program. In the fourth part we demonstrate some linkages between cost concepts and technology. One type of linkage is in the form of a cost function, and we illustrate the use of a cost function in an analysis of regulated trucking firms. Another type of linkage occurs when two or more outputs are produced with some shared input, and we

[17] See, for example, Richard Nelson and Sidney Winter, *An Evolutionary Theory of Economic Change* (Cambridge, Mass.: Harvard University Press, 1982); see also the debate between George Stigler and Harvey Leibenstein: G. Stigler, "The Xistence of X-Efficiency," *The American Economic Review, 66,* March 1976, pp. 213–216 and H. Leibenstein, "X-Inefficiency Xists—Reply to an Xorcist," *The American Review, 68,* March 1978, pp. 203–211.

[18] For a recent review of techniques for measuring productive efficiency, see Raymond J. Kopp, "The Measurement of Productive Efficiency: A Reconsideration," *The Quarterly Journal of Economics, 96,* No. 3, August 1981, pp. 477–503.

illustrate how benefit-cost reasoning can be applied to this joint cost problem to identify the most efficient allocation of resources. In a final optional section we illustrate the relations between production functions and cost functions by using the mathematics of duality and introduce some of the cost functions commonly used in empirical analyses.

Social Opportunity Cost and Benefit-Cost Analysis

The social opportunity cost of using resources in one activity is the value foregone by not using them in the best alternative activity. In Figure 7-3a we draw a production-possibilities curve for a simple society with a fixed amount of resources which can be devoted to producing two outputs: food F and shelter S. If all resources are devoted to shelter production and the best technology is used, S_M will be the maximum possible shelter output. The *social opportunity cost*[19] of producing S_m is F_m, the alternative output foregone. More typically, we think of smaller changes. If we are currently at point A (with outputs F_A, S_A), the opportunity cost of increasing shelter production by ΔS units of S is ΔF units of F. Thus, the opportunity cost per unit increase in S is simply $\Delta F/\Delta S$, and for a small enough change this can be interpreted as the negative of the slope of the production-possibilities curve at the current allocation. This number is commonly referred to as the rate of product transformation ($\text{RPT}_{S,F}$).

The bowed-out shape of the production-possibilities curve can be explained intuitively as follows. The economy is endowed with a stock of factors in a certain proportion K_0/L_0. The technically best proportion to use with each good is unlikely to coincide with the endowment. Let's say that food is best produced with a relatively labor-intensive technology (low K/L) and shelter with a relatively capital-intensive technology (high K/L). Then at each end point of the production-possibilities curve (F_M and S_M), an "inferior" K/L ratio ($= K_0/L_0$) is being employed. If we insisted that each product be produced by using the ratio K_0/L_0, and assumed constant returns to scale, the production-possibility frontier would be the straight line connecting the extreme points.[20] However, we know we can do better than the straight line by allowing each industry to use a capital-labor ratio closer to its technically best one: Only the weighted average of both has to equal K_0/L_0. Thus the frontier will be bowed outward.

An interesting interpretive point arises if we are currently at point C and ask, "What is the social opportunity cost of increasing shelter production by ΔS?" Point C is productively inefficient, either because some resources are currently unemployed or because the resources in production are not being used to

---

[19] This is often referred to simply as the *social cost*.

[20] If there were continuing economies of scale without limit, under these assumptions the frontier would be bowed inward, since we lose the economies as we move away from the extreme points. However, constant or decreasing returns to scale are empirically much more likely at these (imagined) extreme uses of society's resources.

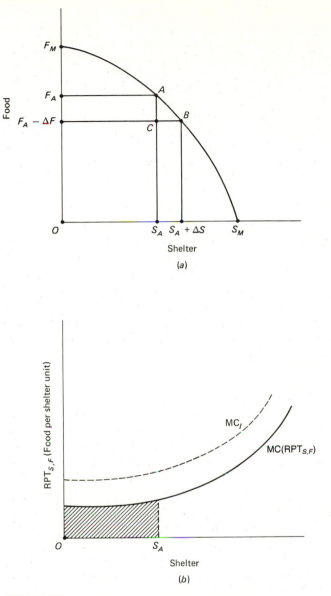

FIGURE 7-3
(a) Social opportunity costs and production possibilities; (b) the
rate of product transformation (RPT) is the social marginal cost
(MC).

produce the maximum possible output (for reason of technological inefficiency
or input-mix inefficiency). The common interpretation is that there is zero
social opportunity cost: Society need give up no unit of F, since it can move

from point C to point B. However, the social opportunity cost concept seems to ask about the *best* use of the resources other than to increase S by ΔS. The best alternative is the one in the preceding example: to increase F by ΔF.

Both interpretations are correct; they simply answer slightly different questions. The first one answers the question "What is the *change* in social cost associated with the resources used for S production at point C and point B, respectively?" Since the same $F_M - (F_A - \Delta F)$ units are foregone by being at either C or B, the change in social cost is zero. There is no increase in social cost because at C we have already paid for the ΔS units even though we do not receive them. The second answer is a correct response to the question "What is the social cost of those ΔS units?" However, it is not a new cost caused by the move from C to B.

Another way to express the social cost is shown geometrically in Figure 7-3b. We keep the quantity of shelter as the horizontal axis, but the vertical axis measures the $RPT_{S,F}$: the number of units of food given up to obtain each additional unit of shelter. Thus the solid curve drawn can be thought of as the least social *marginal cost* of each unit of shelter (in terms of food foregone). The area under the marginal cost curve up to a given quantity is the total social cost of that quantity, since it is simply the sum of the marginal costs of the units of shelter produced. For example, the shaded area in the diagram is the social cost of S_A units, which we know equals $F_M - F_A$ from Figure 7-3a. It might also be noted that if inefficient production methods are used, so that the economy is at an allocation like point C in Figure 7-3a, the observed marginal social costs (MC_I in Figure 7-3b, for example) would be above the least marginal social costs.

Now we wish to show how knowledge of the social costs can be used in making a compensation test. In Chapter 5 we demonstrated that calculating the net change in *consumer* surplus is one way to make the test. This is the appropriate concept, but to calculate it requires taking account of any changes in budget constraints which may be caused by the policy change. Until now, the illustrative examples were designed to hold budget constraints constant (except for offsetting transfers). We relax this restriction by accounting for changes in the *producers' surplus*. A simple way to restate the compensation principle which automatically includes both consumer and producer surplus is this: *A change in allocation is relatively efficient if its social benefits exceed its social costs.* In the simple model below we attempt to explain and clarify these concepts.

Figure 7-4a and b is identical with Figure 7-3a and b except for the addition of a *demand side*. Imagine that we have a Robinson Crusoe economy with no Friday (i.e., a one-person economy). This allows us to draw Crusoe's indifference curves in Figure 7-4a. The highest utility that Crusoe can attain is U_{max}, where the indifference curve is just tangent to the production-possibilities frontier. His optimal production and consumption are F_C and S_C.

Since the two curves are tangent at that point, their slopes are equal and thus $RPT_{S,F} = MRS_{S,F}$ at Crusoe's utility maximum. This feature is often used in the

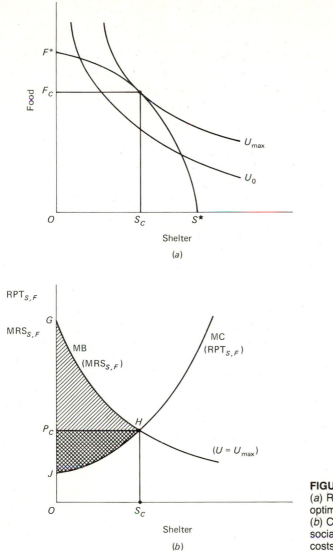

FIGURE 7-4
(a) Robinson Crusoe's Pareto-optimal allocation of resources; (b) Crusoe's maximization of social benefits minus social costs.

many-person economy to identify how much of each good to produce. (It is sometimes referred to as the condition for product-mix efficiency, and it is another necessary condition for Pareto optimality which we review more carefully in Chapter 10.) We show here that the rule is essentially identical with choosing the allocation whereby the marginal social benefit equals the marginal social cost (or, equivalently, maximizes net social benefits by the compensation principle).

In Figure 7-4*b* we graph the $RPT_{S,F}$ as before. It has a clear interpretation as the marginal cost to Crusoe of each unit of shelter. To put this in the context of a compensation test, we need a measure of the marginal benefit of each unit of shelter to Crusoe. Let us graph Crusoe's $MRS_{S,F}$ by using as a base his utility at the maximum level.[21] That is, for each quantity of S, we look on the U_{max} indifference curve to find the $MRS_{S,F}$ at that quantity and plot it in Figure 7-4b. This tells us the amount of food Crusoe would have to forego for each additional shelter unit in order to hold his utility constant. In other words, it is the marginal benefit MB to Crusoe measured in terms of food. In fact, this new curve is just a familiar friend, the compensated demand curve with price expressed in food per unit of shelter.

It is no accident that the demand curve crosses the marginal cost curve at S_C, since that is the point at which $RPT_{S,F} = MRS_{S,F}$.[22] Let us consider how Crusoe would reason as the sole recipient of benefits and bearer of costs. For each unit of shelter he would ask if the marginal benefit (food he is willing to forego) exceeds the marginal cost (food he would have to forego). He will choose to produce and consume each unit of shelter for which the marginal benefit exceeds the marginal cost and thus choose S_C units of shelter. Thus, the marginal benefit–marginal cost reasoning simply reveals utility-increasing changes and leads to the utility maximum (which, in this economy, is the Pareto-optimal allocation).

Let us extend this reasoning, by a two-step process, to the many-person economy. First, we stick with Crusoe to introduce the concept of the producer's surplus. Imagine that the goods must be bought or sold in the marketplace, where shelter has a price of P_C (even though Crusoe is the only trader). Crusoe the producer will produce and sell to the "market" all the units which have opportunity costs below the market price: S_C units. This is the quantity which maximizes his budget constraint (which is necessary for maximizing utility).[23] Then Crusoe the consumer buys from the market all units the marginal benefit of which exceeds the market price: S_C units.

His consumer surplus is the single-lined area, P_CGH. But the point of this illustration is that these are not the only net benefits Crusoe receives. As a producer, he also receives *producer's surplus, or economic rent, defined as payments to the producer above opportunity costs.* This is shown as the cross-hatched area JP_CH. It can be thought of as the increase in his budget constraint that results from producing in the shelter market instead of the next best alternative. *The net social benefit is the sum of the consumer and producer surpluses.*

---

[21] For the reasons discussed in Chapter 5, the choice of the base affects the solution through income effects. We ignore this issue here in order to simplify the exposition.

[22] This holds independently of the base if there are zero income effects (the MRS along a vertical line is constant). If we allowed income effects, the arguments would have to be recast by using approximation reasoning.

[23] The price P_C determines the slope of the budget constraint, which, we know, equals the slope of the production-possibilities frontier at (F_C, S_C). The location of the budget constraint depends on the production point Crusoe chooses; it is the line through that point with the given slope. Thus (F_C, S_C) is the production choice leading to the highest budget constraint.

Of course, Crusoe could not care less about the classification system used by analysts for his benefits, as long as he gets the benefits. But now let us move to step 2, where the people in each category are generally (but not necessarily or totally) different. Here we simply reinterpret the demand and cost curves as those applying to the many-person market and assume there are no aggregation problems of the kind discussed in Chapter 5. The point to emphasize is that the compensation test for a policy change requires the aggregation of the hypothetical compensations necessary to keep each person indifferent without regard to why the policy is affecting the person (i.e., whether the individual is a demander or a supplier in the affected market). The net social benefit is still the sum of the producer and consumer surpluses.

Suppose one thought the only social benefits were in the form of consumer surplus. Let us use the compensation principle to judge whether society is indifferent between having no shelter or having S_C units of shelter *with the consumer surplus removed*. People as consumers would be indifferent, but the producers (who may or may not be the same people) are not indifferent. Without producing shelter, they will receive (by definition) only the opportunity costs of their resources—the area under the marginal cost curve. However, the same resources used in shelter production would yield their opportunity costs *plus* the producer surplus. Thus society as a whole is not indifferent to the two alternatives; the compensation test favors production of the S_C units even with the consumer surplus removed (producers can be made better off with consumers no worse off).

In the above example with only two goods, the social cost of shelter is expressed in terms of food foregone. To apply the concept in a multiproduct economy, we measure the costs and benefits in terms of money (purchasing power). If all the nonanalyzed markets are assumed to be in competitive equilibrium (supply and demand in balance), the marginal value of a resource used in several markets, like homogeneous labor, must be the same in each and equal to its price (otherwise, resources would be bid away from the less valuable to more valuable uses including leisure). Thus *the* opportunity cost of using the resource in the analyzed market, measured in money, is of consistent value. In virtually all applications of benefit-cost analysis this assumption is made. We shall see in Chapter 11 that the consistency is less clear in a more realistic world of the second best, where the assumption is relaxed.

The introduction of explicit accounting for social costs in the framework for compensation testing does not in any way alter the qualifications about its meaning introduced in Chapter 5. The same questions about the meaning of this aggregated definition of efficiency, as well as the equity implications of using it as a criterion in analysis, remain. All that we have done here is show how a compensation test is conducted when resource suppliers receive payments other than their opportunity costs. Each person in the society is a resource supplier as well as a consumer, and we must consider the effects on each side to know how any individual is affected by a change or how society in the aggregate is affected.

Accounting Cost and Private Opportunity Cost

All of the discussion to this point in the section has been about the concept of social cost. This is the concept of most evaluative use to the analyst, but do the available data on costs correspond to it? Often, recorded costs will differ from social costs because a different concept underlies each. *The accounting concept of cost is the bookkeeper's view: that which gets recorded on the financial statements and budgets of firms and agencies.* It is based on the actual price, sometimes modified by various conventions for depreciation (of durable goods). A number of examples illustrate important differences between the concepts.

When the nation switched to an all-volunteer army in the 1970s, it was recognized that higher wages and salaries would have to be offered in order to attract volunteers. Some people, thinking of the impact that would have on the government's budget, argued against the concept because it was "too expensive." But the change in accounting costs is in the direction opposite that of the change in social costs. The social costs of the army personnel are what the personnel could earn in their best alternatives (reflecting the value of the foregone outputs) and foregone psychic incomes (the best alternatives may offer satisfaction in addition to pay). For draftees, the opportunity costs often exceeded their military wages by substantial amounts. Because many draftees would not choose to volunteer even at the higher wages of the voluntary army, it must be that the social cost of using a given number of draftees in the military *exceeds* the social cost of using the same number of volunteers. For volunteers, the total social cost cannot exceed the benefits to them of military employment: If a volunteer had a better alternative, he or she presumably would not have volunteered.

There are advantages to having military wage rates set at the social cost rather than below it: (1) The nation now has a more accurate picture of the true resource cost of providing national defense, which usually influences the amount of it sought. (2) The input mix used in the production of national defense has been biased in the direction of too much labor relative to capital, because labor appeared to be so cheap. That source of distortion has been eliminated. Of course, there are many other issues to consider in conjunction with the draftee-volunteer debate. For example, is it equitable for higher-income people to be more easily able to avoid the risk to life that might arise in the military, or is military service more properly viewed as a civic obligation that all citizens should have?

Other examples of differences in social costs and accounting costs involving labor abound. Jury duty, for example, is similar in this respect to the military draft: The social opportunity costs are greater than the wages paid jurors. Volunteers in hospitals, election campaigns, and other nonprofit activities may receive no wages, but that does not mean there is no social cost of using their services. In the same vein, an entrepreneur who could earn $20,000 elsewhere may draw no salary while operating a business that ends up with a $15,000 accounting profit. The economist, who defines economic profit as revenues above opportunity costs, would count this as a $5000 loss.[24]

The third cost concept, *private opportunity cost, is defined as the payment necessary to keep a resource in its current use.* This is very similar to and often identical with the social cost. Differences between private and social opportunity costs can arise when the prices of resources do not reflect the social costs. In the above examples of the army the private opportunity cost to the draftee is the same as the social opportunity cost. But the private opportunity cost of a draftee to the army equals the accounting cost. If the entrepreneur in the above example produces chemicals but pollutes the neighborhood while doing so (an externality), the social cost of the production exceeds the private cost to the entrepreneur (society not only foregoes alternative uses of the regular inputs to the firm; it also foregoes having the clean air it used to have).

In the above two examples the private opportunity cost to the organization equals the accounting cost even though there is a divergence from the social cost. However, the private cost often diverges from the accounting cost; e.g., the divergence occurs in the example of the entrepreneur with a $20,000 alternative employment opportunity. Another very important example, because it is quite general, is the treatment of capital resources like machinery. The accountant uses the historical purchase price minus a certain amount of depreciation each year calculated according to a formula.[25] However, the historical purchase price is a *sunk cost,* and it is irrelevant to decision making. The opportunity cost of employing a machine for a year is what is given up by not selling it now to the highest bidder (alternative user of the machine).

There are two components of this opportunity cost. One is the true economic depreciation, which is the decrement in the selling price of the machine over one year. This reduction occurs because there is "less" machine (it wears out over time). Sometimes the true economic depreciation can be roughly approximated by the accountant's method of depreciation. The second component is the foregone interest that could have been earned on the money from the sale; this is the opportunity cost of the capital in the machine at the start of the period.[26] (Together, these components are also the rental value of the machine: what someone would have to pay to rent the machine for a year.)

---

[24] To the extent that these costs are borne voluntarily, they must have benefits to the participants which are at least as great. The hospital volunteer, for example, must consider the benefits of volunteering to outweigh the costs. If the entrepreneur claims to prefer operating the business to a higher-salaried opportunity, there must be nonmonetary benefits which more than offset the financial loss (e.g., pleasure from being the boss).

[25] Depreciation rules are somewhat arbitrary. For example, straight-line depreciation is one common method by which a reasonable life span of n years is estimated for a machine and then a fixed percentage equal to $1/n$ of the total cost is deducted each year until the cost has been fully deducted.

[26] The foregone interest is actually a monetary measure of what is being given up. The real change in resource use is that consumers give up current consumption in order to make the machine. This will be discussed more carefully in Chapter 14.

The second component is not taken into account by the bookkeepers, although it is both a private opportunity cost of the firm using the machine and a social cost.

The latter point is of particular importance to policy analysts who use program budgets as one source of information about the costs of a government program. Unless the government agency actually rents (from other firms) all the capital it uses, the social costs of its capital resources will not appear in the budget. They must be imputed by the analyst.

To summarize this discussion, the accountant's concept of cost is largely historical. It often differs sharply from the opportunity cost concepts, which refer to the value of the resource in its best alternative use. The difference between social and private opportunity costs is one of perspective. The social cost concept treats the whole society as if it were one large family, so that everything given up by the employment of a resource is counted as part of the cost. The private opportunity cost, the payment necessary to keep a resource in its current use, is the value in its next best alternative use from the perspective of the resource employer. Analysts are most interested in the opportunity cost concepts, because individual decision makers are thought to act on their perception of cost (the private opportunity cost), and the social costs are most relevant to efficiency considerations.

An Application in a Benefit-Cost Analysis[27]

The interim evaluation of the New York Supported Work experiment can be used to illustrate a number of points about the use of cost concepts. Four different organizational perspectives on costs (and benefits) are shown to have policy relevance. In Table 7-2 *the social costs and benefits* of the program (those known by the end of the second year of the experiment) are summarized. This social benefit–cost calculation is equivalent to a compensation test; benefits and costs are simply a convenient way to organize and then summarize a variety of the effects due to the program (the policy change). In making a social benefit–cost calculation, we are asking whether the gains to the gainers (benefits) outweigh the losses to the losers (costs).

The benefits in Table 7-2 can be thought of as the value of the output of the program. The output consists of the goods and services actually produced as part of the program and the external effects of production. The measured external effects consist of the increase in the future (out-of-program) earnings stream of participants, the reduction in crime by participants, the reduction in drug treatment, and the change in health of the participants. In all cases the existence of the effects is measured by comparison with the control group: individuals who were found qualified to be participants in the experiment but by lottery were chosen not to participate. Without the control group it would be virtually impossible to know if the program was having any effect at all.

---

[27] The material in this section is drawn from Lee S. Friedman, "An Interim Evaluation of the Supported Work Experiment," *Policy Analysis, 3*, No. 2, spring 1977, pp. 147–170.

TABLE 7-2
THE NEW YORK SUPPORTED WORK EXPERIMENT
SOCIAL BENEFITS AND COSTS
Per Year in the Experiment per Person

Benefits	
Value added by program to public goods and services	$4519
Post-program experimental earnings	1154
Savings from crime-connected costs	
System	86
Crime reduction	207
Drug program participation	—
Health	(285)
Total social benefits	$5681
Costs	
Opportunity costs of supported work employees	$1112
Staff and nonpersonnel expenses	2362
Total social costs	$3474
Net benefits	$2207

Source: Lee S. Friedman, "An Interim Evaluation of the Supported Work Experiment," *Policy Analysis, 3,* No. 2, spring 1977, p. 165.

The listed benefits were measured in such a way as to underestimate their magnitude. For example, the out-of-program earnings increases included only the difference between the experimentals and controls within the first calendar year from entrance to the experiment. Presumably this difference will persist at least to some extent in the future, and thus the true benefit is higher than measured. The reason for underestimating the benefits results from analytic judgment about how to handle the *uncertainty* of the exact level of benefits. If there were no uncertainty, there would be no need for this procedure.

Since the analysis indicates that the benefits outweigh the costs, confidence in this conclusion can be tested by deliberately making assumptions conservative (less favorable) to it. Since it still holds, confidence that it is correct increases. Sometimes, small changes in the assumptions may lead to opposite conclusions, and then the analyst must report that it is really ambiguous whether the benefits outweigh the costs. Of course, an important part of analytic skill is learning how to convert available data into information which minimizes the range of uncertainty about the truth.

In Table 7-2 the costs are shown to be substantially less than the benefits. The component of the cost calculation relevant to the earlier discussion in the chapter is the opportunity cost to society of employing the participants in the program. The actual wages received were substantially higher than the $1112 opportunity cost. But that is irrelevant to the opportunity cost; we wish to know the value of whatever is foregone by the employment of participants in supported work. The traditional measure of this value, and the one used in this study, is the earnings that would have been received otherwise. (They are measured quite precisely by the actual earnings of the control group.) The measure presumably reflects the value of the marginal product which would be added by this labor. In other words, one reason why the benefits easily outweigh the costs is that the costs are low: The control group members remain unemployed for most of the time, so society gives up little by employing them in supported work.[28]

It should be pointed out that a summary of the measurable social benefits and costs is generally thought inadequate as a basis for understanding or presenting the social effects of the program. Some decision makers might be more interested in one component than another and wish more detail. For example, the value of goods and services is discussed at length in the main analytic reports, and it might be of use to explore whether there are trade-offs between future earnings and in-program output. Or it might be interesting to find out if the participants are really more ill than the controls, or if they just consume more medical services in response to a given illness.[29] Other effects may be important but impossible to value in a meaningful way; an example is the effect of the program on the family lives of participants. However, the only purpose here is to emphasize the effects of different perspectives on the costs and benefits.

Recall that the preceding calculation of social benefits and costs reflects indifference in dollar terms of who is gaining or losing. However, society is not all one big family, and the costs and benefits to particular subsets of society's members can take on special importance. Through the political system, taxpayers have considerable influence on the spending decisions of government. Thus we can ask, from the persective of taxpayers, how does the supported work program look?

Table 7-3 shows the *major benefits and costs to taxpayers*. The primary difference between this perspective and the social perspective is that certain transfers which cancel out in the latter must be made explicit here. On the benefit side, the taxpayer will experience a reduction in welfare payments and a wider sharing of the tax burden. These are not included in the social calculation

---

[28] This issue is more complicated than the above discussion reveals. There is another part to the opportunity cost: Participants forego not only their alternative earnings but their leisure as well, which must have some value to them. If the unemployment of controls were voluntary, it could be argued that their wage rate (when actually working) applied to the time equivalent of full-time employment is the social opportunity cost. (Controls are making an optimal labor-leisure trade-off.) However, most analysts accept the idea that much unemployment is involuntary because of imperfections in the labor market. Still, the analysis would be improved by an explicit accounting of that effect. Most evaluations of similar programs also have ignored the value of foregone leisure.

In this particular case, accounting for the value of foregone leisure is extremely unlikely to affect the conclusion. All the controls were revealed to prefer program participation to nonpartici-pation, implying that they would forego their leisure for *less* than their net increase in tangible first-year benefits of $1703. Although this excludes the fact that future earnings increases are part of the inducement, those must add more to benefits than to costs; furthermore, the participant is also foregoing the private returns to crime and perhaps better health (so all of the $1703 cannot be simply leisure's opportunity cost).

[29] The study assumes conservatively that the participants are more ill, based on data that indicate they average slightly more time in the hospital per year. However, this average was based on relatively few hospitalizations.

TABLE 7-3
THE NEW YORK SUPPORTED WORK EXPERIMENT
TAXPAYER BENEFITS AND COSTS
Per Year in the Experiment per Person

Benefits	
Public goods and services	$4519
Welfare reduction	1797
Increased income taxes collected	311
Savings from crime reduction	
System	86
Crime	207
Total taxpayer benefits	$6920
Costs	
Supported work costs	$6131
Net benefits	$ 789

Source: Lee S. Friedman, "An Interim Evaluation of the Supported Work Experiment," *Policy Analysis, 3,* No. 2, spring 1977, p. 167.

because, at least as a first approximation, the payments are simply transfers of purchasing power (a dollar lost by the participant is offset by the dollar gained by the taxpayer). On the cost side, the actual wages paid the supported work employees are relevant to the taxpayer.

The taxpayer perspective is sometimes represented as the impact on the government budget. There is, of course, a slight difference between the concepts: The taxpayer perspective reveals private opportunity costs, whereas the impact on the government budget is measured by accounting costs. In this case, because capital assets of the program are very small, there is little difference. A more important simplification is treating taxpayers as a homogeneous group: Federal taxpayers in Ohio do not receive the public goods and services that accrue to the residents of New York City. One could further disaggregate the effects into New York taxpayers and other taxpayers; this might be useful in deciding how to share the costs of the program.

A specific example of *the perspective of a particular agency was offered as the third benefit-cost perspective in the analysis.* The New York City welfare department was one source of program funds. It provided $1.19 per participant-hour in supported work on the theory that this represented a payment it would have to make (to the participants) if the program did not exist. This added up to $1237 per year, and the department also provided certain direct benefits to the participants valued at $842 for a total of $2079. However, the welfare department had to pay out $2639 in benefits to the average control during the same period. Thus the department was getting a bargain: For every $1.00 put into supported work, it received $1.27 in reduced claims for welfare.

Finally, *a fourth important perspective on benefits and costs is that of the participant.* The change in disposable income was calculated. The average experimental received $3769 in program wages and fringe benefits and $1154 in out-of-program earnings, for a total of $4923. To receive this, he or she accepted a welfare reduction of $1797, increased taxes of $311, and foregone earnings of $1112, or $3220 total cost. Thus the increase in disposable income was $1703. This figure is relevant to determining supported work wages. If it is large, taxpayers may be asked to transfer more than necessary to achieve the net social benefits. If the net benefit to participants is small or negative, then it will be difficult to induce program eligibles to apply.

Note that of the four benefit-cost calculations presented, only one has a specific normative purpose: The social benefit–cost analysis reveals whether the economy is made relatively more efficient by the program. The other three calculations can be thought of as summarizing the program effects from the perspective of various constituent groups. By calculating the benefits and costs from the perspectives of different constituencies, one can, for example, predict whether these groups will favor the program. Or one might use calculations in evaluating the equity of the program. The calculations also can suggest whether certain changes in the program will increase or reduce support from the various constituencies. In general, these benefit-cost calculations can be made for any program; they require judgment about which groups are the important constituencies.[30]

In this application, no linkage between the cost concepts and a production function need be made. But in other applications, understanding such linkages can be a key point. In the next section, we illustrate this point.

Cost-Output Relations

In this section we will consider how opportunity costs (with private equal to social) vary as a function of the output level. Both producing agencies and analysts are often interested in least-cost production, and most of the standard cost curves are drawn on the assumption that production is or will be at least cost. However, it is important to recognize that actual observed costs in many situations are not the minimum possible.

Nevertheless, the attempt to identify consistent relations between observed costs and the production function is extremely useful. The primary reason is that it may be much easier to obtain data on costs than on all the different input quantities. We give two examples of decisions which depend on determining aspects of the returns-to-scale characteristic of the production function. The first case involves trucking deregulation, and the second case involves the national supported work program. In both cases inferences about scale are made by estimating cost functions rather than production functions.

In the case of trucking the nature of scale economies in the industry bears on

---

[30] One top analyst in the federal government during the 1970s is reported to have directed all his associates to make at least two benefit-cost calculations: one from the social perspective, and the other from the perspective of those living in Louisiana. The analyst was from the north, but the powerful Chairman of the Senate Finance Committee from 1965 to 1980, Russell Long, was from Louisiana.

whether the industry will be regulated or not.[31] If there are increasing returns to scale over a large portion of the total demand for trucking services, then the way to meet that demand and give up the fewest resources in doing so is to have only a few firms or agencies as supply agents. However, if the supply were by private profit-maximizing firms, there would be little effective competition to ensure that the prices charged are close to the opportunity costs or that enough services are actually provided. The typical response to situations like this has been to regulate the prices charged by the firms, as with utility companies. The Interstate Commerce Commission has been regulating the prices of (interstate) trucking companies in this manner.

However, under regulation there are a large number of interstate trucking firms, not the small number associated with large economies of scale.[32] Proponents of regulation argue that the ICC has maintained prices just high enough for many firms to survive and compete, and that without regulation the industry would become extremely concentrated (i.e., have only a few firms) and would present the problems mentioned above. Opponents of regulation argue that there are no significant economies of scale, that a large number of competing firms would therefore continue to exist without price regulation, and that the result would be lower prices to consumers and services essentially unchanged. Under the assumption that these firms operate on their production frontiers (i.e., are technically efficient), knowledge of the returns to scale of the production function would reveal the expected degree of concentration. This knowledge can be obtained without ever estimating the production function, simply by studying the cost functions of the firms.

Let us illustrate this point. Suppose we have a very simple production function $Q = F(L)$; that is, labor is the only type of input. Let us also assume that a firm can hire all the labor it wishes at the current wage rate w. Then the total cost TC of producing any quantity is wL, and the average cost AC is simply total cost divided by the quantity of output:

$$AC = \frac{TC}{Q} = \frac{wL}{Q} = w\frac{1}{AP_L}$$

If the firm is technically efficient, this can be rewritten

$$AC = \frac{wL}{F(L)}$$

[31] The behavior of monopolies will be treated in the next chapter, and public policy with respect to natural monopolies will be treated in Chapter 15. Here we present only a bare-bones summary in order to motivate the cost analyst.

[32] According to Thomas Moore, there were 14,648 regulated trucking firms in 1974. See p. 340 in T. Moore, "The Beneficiaries of Trucking Regulation," *The Journal of Law and Economics, 21,* October 1978, pp. 327–343.

In this formulation the firm's average cost clearly varies inversely with the average productivity of the one and only factor. The quantity of output where the AP_L is at a maximum must also be the quantity at which the average cost is a minimum. This illustrates that the output quantity at which the firm's average cost is minimized depends upon the shape of the production function (and technical efficiency).

The relation between a firm's average cost curve and the production function is more complicated when there is more than one input. However, the fact that there is a relation extends to the general case of many inputs. Suppose the inputs used are $X_1, X_2, \ldots, X_n$ with associated prices $P_1, P_2, \ldots, P_n$. Imagine three possible production functions which vary in their respective returns to scale. Using superscripts I, C, and D to indicate increasing, constant, and decreasing returns to scale and m to represent some positive constant, let us suppose the functions are represented by

$$m^2 Q = F^I(mX_1, mX_2, \ldots, mX_n)$$
$$mQ = F^C(mX_1, mX_2, \ldots, mX_n)$$
$$\sqrt{mQ} = F^D(mX_1, mX_2, \ldots, mX_n)$$

When $m = 1$, all three functions have the same output level. Since the inputs are the same, they have the same total cost (TC_0) and the same average cost (AC_0):

$$AC_0 = \frac{TC_0}{Q} = \frac{\displaystyle\sum_{i=1}^{n} P_i X_i}{Q}$$

But now let us ask what happens to AC if we expand production by multiplying all inputs by some $m > 1$. Then,

$$AC^I = \frac{TC}{m^2 Q} = \frac{\displaystyle\sum_{i=1}^{n} P_i m X_i}{m^2 Q}$$

$$= \frac{M\left(\displaystyle\sum_{i=1}^{n} P_i X_i\right)}{m^2 Q} = \frac{AC_0}{m} < AC_0$$

Similarly,

$$AC^C = \frac{TC}{mQ} = \frac{\displaystyle\sum_{i=1}^{n} P_i m X_i}{mQ} = AC_0$$

and

$$AC^D = \frac{TC}{\sqrt{m}} = \frac{\displaystyle\sum_{i=1}^{n} P_i m X_1}{\sqrt{m}\, Q} = \sqrt{m}\, AC_0 > AC_0$$

Thus for a firm or agency that would produce at least cost, as the scale of operations increases, the AC increases, stays the same, or decreases depending on whether the production function is decreasing, constant, or increasing returns to scale.

To relate this to the trucking issue, we have argued that the size of the firm (measured by the quantity of output it produces) necessary for least-cost production depends on the returns to scale of the production function: The greater the returns to scale, the larger the firms in the industry should be. Furthermore, the observed relation between average cost and output level (for an organization that produces at least cost) reveals the returns to scale: As firm quantity increases, the change in AC will vary inversely with the returns to scale. Therefore, we can look for evidence about the returns to scale by examining the cost-output relationship.

This is precisely what is done in a study by Spady and Friedlaender of the regulated trucking industry.[33] There are some problems in measuring the output of each firm; they are similar to those of the supported work example. The number of ton-miles carried is the unadjusted measure, but it must be converted into standardized ton-miles which account for the length of haul, the shipment size, and other quality factors which cause differences in the effective output. For example, one firm may make one trip of 1000 miles on open highway, and another firm may make 1000 trips of 1 mile each. The ton-miles are the same, but the outputs are really quite different, and they should not be expected to have either the same value to consumers or the same costs. Similarly, a firm which handles shipment sizes that fill up the truck is producing a different output than one which picks up many small loads to fill the truck. Since these factors vary continuously, rather than each firm producing a small discrete set of different output types, an appropriate way to account for them is to create a continuously adjusted effective output measure.

The results of the Spady-Friedlaender analysis are shown graphically in Figure 7-5. The figure shows two alternative specifications of the AC function: one assuming that the output is hedonic (quality variable) and that its quality attributes must be included in the estimation procedure, the other assuming that the unadjusted ton-miles measure is sufficient (the output is nonhedonic). The results of testing them statistically indicate that the nonhedonic specification is erroneous.

One of the crucial insights from the analysis is the importance of not making this specification error. Under the erroneous specification, it appears that there are significant economies of scale: The AC declines as firm size increases from its current average level to that of the largest firm. But under the maintained hypothesis (not rejected statistically as false) of the hedonic specification, the average-size firm is currently very close to the minimum AC and the lack of further scale economies would discourage expansion of firm size.

---

[33] See Richard H. Spady and Ann F. Friedlaender, "Hedonic Cost Functions for the Regulated Trucking Industry," *The Bell Journal of Economics*, 9, No. 1, spring 1978, pp. 159–179.

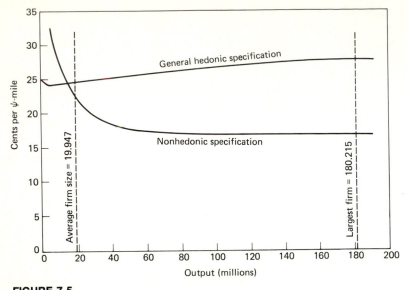

FIGURE 7-5
Average cost functions. (From Richard H. Spady and Ann F. Friedlaender, "Hedonic Cost Functions for the Regulated Trucking Industry," *The Bell Journal of Economics, 9,* No. 1, spring 1978, p. 172.)

The Spady-Friedlaender analysis supports the policy arguments in favor of trucking deregulation. Of course, there are many other aspects of this policy which should be considered; our purpose was simply to illustrate the relevance of the cost-output relation to a policy decision. That decision, by the way, has been made: In 1980, Congress passed and the president signed the Motor Carrier Act, which removed regulatory entry barriers to the trucking industry and significantly reduced the rate-making (price-fixing) authority of the ICC.

A second interesting application of a cost function bears on the supported work experiment and can be explained briefly. On the basis of the interim success of the New York program, a consortium of federal agencies decided to sponsor an expansion to 15 cities. After the second year of the national program (when start-up costs were not a factor), the average cost per participant-year was significantly greater than in New York alone ($13,562 versus $9853). This was puzzling until analysts decided to look at annual costs in relation to the scale of each site as measured by annual participant-years.[34]

There turned out to be a clear cost advantage for larger sites, primarily because management expenses of a relatively "fixed" nature could be spread over the larger number of participants. Annual management expenses ranged from over $6000 per participant-year at smaller sites to under $3000 at the larger

[34] See David A. Long and others, *An Analysis of Expenditures in the National Supported Work Demonstration* (Princeton, N.J.: Mathematica Policy Research, Inc., March 6, 1980).

ones. Thus, many of the sites were not operating at the minimum of the average-cost curve.

In this example the analysts recognized that there are no obvious policy conclusions without further information. Perhaps most importantly, the output of supported work is not measured by the participant-years, and it is possible that the social value of a participant-year at one site is quite different from that at another. This is simply another illustration of the need to control for quality when measuring output. Second, the number of participants desirable in each program is best thought of as determined by marginal benefit–marginal cost considerations. Even so, the analysis is useful because it provides some information on the cost side of this calculation and, more importantly, calls attention to the issue.

To make sure this last point is clear, in Figure 7-6a and b we contrast the supported work example with the trucking discussion. In both cases it is desirable that each unit of output be produced if its marginal benefit (the height of the demand curve) exceeds its marginal cost. The optimal levels of output are denoted as Q_E in each diagram. In Figure 7-6a, representing supported work, the assumption as drawn is that it is more efficient for one agency to supply the demand in any location (a natural monopoly). Given that one agency has a cost structure like AC and MC, the correct level of output is determined by the intersection of the demand curve with the marginal cost curve.[35] Like our earlier productivity example of crew size on sanitation trucks, it does not matter whether AC could be improved by a different quantity: The value of any change in output level from Q_E would not exceed its marginal cost.

In Figure 7-6b, representing trucking, the assumption is that many firms should supply the demand for trucks. Each U-shaped curve represents the AC over the quantity of output one firm can supply. As drawn, one firm would encounter significant diseconomies of scale well before it reached output levels that satisfied market demand. On the other hand, the industry can expand at constant AC simply by adding identical firms. Obviously the least-cost way of producing in this situation is for each firm to operate at the minimum of its AC curve. At the risk of oversimplification, the Spady-Friedlaender analysis was attempting to find out if the trucking cost structure looked more like Figure 7-6a or b.

An additional cost-output relation that arises frequently in public policy analysis is that of *joint costs*. It occurs when two or more discrete outputs are made from some of the same inputs, and the problem is deducing whether the marginal cost of an output is greater or less than its marginal benefit. A standard example is that both wool and mutton are obtained from lambs. One may know precisely the marginal benefit of additional wool, but how is one to decide on the division of the marginal cost of a lamb between wool and mutton?

---

[35] This is a simplification by which it is assumed that the total benefits outweigh the total costs and second-best arguments are ignored. The latter are discussed in Chapters 9 (Ramsey optimal pricing) and 11.

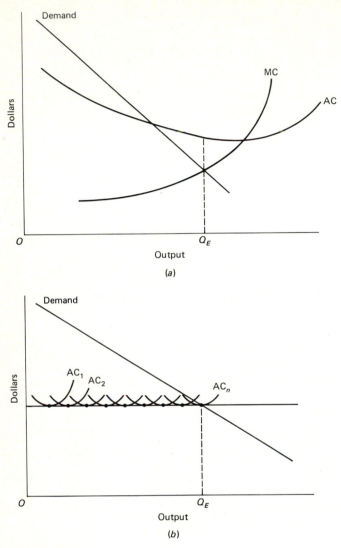

FIGURE 7-6
(a) Supported work may be a natural monopoly; (b) trucking may
be naturally competitive.

From a public policy perspective, a more interesting example of the same problem is often referred to as *peak-load pricing*. We may consider as our joint input an electricity generating plant, and we have two discrete outputs: day electricity (the peak) and night electricity. Given the demand for each and the costs of building and operating the generating plant, what should we supply of each to make marginal benefits equal marginal costs?

Let us assume that the (separable) operating costs per kilowatthour are 3 cents and the joint cost of providing each kilowatthour of capacity is 4 cents per day (the capital costs spread out over the life of the plant). The principle we follow is to provide to consumers all units of capacity the marginal benefits of which outweigh the marginal costs. To identify them, we must add the incremental net operating benefits from each of the joint products to see if the total exceeds the marginal cost of providing additional capacity. We illustrate this in Figure 7-7a and b by using the following two half-day-each demand curves for day D and night N electricity:[36]

$$P_D = 10 - \tfrac{1}{250}D \qquad 0 \le D \le 2500$$
$$P_N = 8 - \tfrac{1}{250}N \qquad 0 \le N \le 2000$$

In Figure 7-7a we graph the demand curves and the marginal operating costs (but not yet the joint capital costs). The consumer willingness to pay over and above the operating cost of 3 cents is shown by the areas between each demand curve and the operating cost: ABG for night demanders and AEF for day demanders. For each unit of capacity that we provide, the market willingness to pay (above operating costs) is the *sum* of what each of the two consumer groups will pay (since they share the use of the capacity).

In Figure 7-7b we graph the demands for capacity (demand minus operating costs) of each group (D_C and N_C). We also graph the *vertical* sum of those two curves to show the total market demand M_C for each unit of capacity. The amount of capacity to provide is thus found where market demand intersects the 4-cent capital cost per unit of capacity, or 1000 kilowatthours. We can find the same solution numerically. The demand-for-capacity equations are

$$P_{D_C} = \begin{cases} 7 - \tfrac{1}{250}D_C & 0 \le D_C \le 1750 \\ 0 & \text{Otherwise} \end{cases}$$

$$P_{N_C} = \begin{cases} 5 - \tfrac{1}{250}N_C & 0 \le N_C \le 1250 \\ 0 & \text{Otherwise} \end{cases}$$

We then sum them, to find the total willingness to pay for each unit of capacity.[37]

$$P_{M_C} = \begin{cases} 12 - \tfrac{2}{250}M_C & 0 \le M_C \le 1250 \\ 7 - \tfrac{1}{250}M_C & 1250 \le M_C \le 1750 \\ 0 & \text{Otherwise} \end{cases}$$

To find the quantity of capacity at which marginal benefit P_{M_C} equals marginal cost, we use the part of the expression relevant for $P_{M_C} = 4$ cents:[38]

---

[36] For simplicity, we make the unrealistic assumption that the demand during either time period is independent of the price in the other time period. This eases the exposition but is not necessary to illustrate how joint costs bear on allocative decisions.

[37] Note that, to add demand curves in the usual horizontal way, we have quantity on the left of the equation and a price expression on the right. We add to find total quantity for a given price. To find the vertical sum, however, we write the equation so that price is on the left and a quantity expression is on the right. This gives us the total willingness to pay for an incremental unit at any given quantity. We do this only when different consumers receive benefits from the same resource.

[38] If one substitutes $P_{M_C} = 4$ and uses the other line segment $= 7 - \tfrac{1}{250}M_C$, one finds $M_C = 750$. But this quantity is not in the range $1250 \le M_C \le 1750$ where the segment applies. Thus, it is not a valid solution.

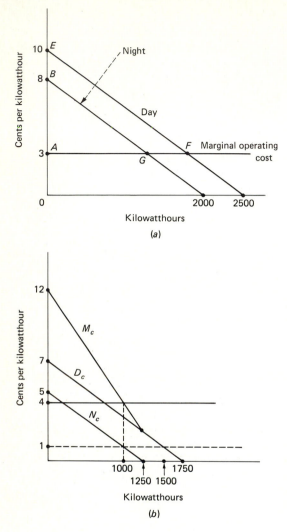

FIGURE 7-7
(a) Marginal benefits of day and night electricity; (b) the demand for capacity of day and night electricity.

$$P_{M_C} = 12 - \tfrac{2}{250}M_C = 4$$

whence

$$M_C = 1000$$

On substituting this capacity in the separate demand-for-capacity equations, we find that

$$P_{D_C} = 7 - \tfrac{1}{250}(1000) = 3$$
$$P_{N_C} = 5 - \tfrac{1}{250}(1000) = 1$$

Thus the incremental 4-cent cost of capacity is allocated 1 cent to the night demanders and 3 cents to the day demanders. The capacity is fully utilized both day and night, with day demanders being charged 6 cents per unit and night demanders being charged 4 cents per unit (the marginal capacity cost share plus the unshared 3-cent marginal operating cost).

An interesting insight can be had if we make a minor change in the problem. Suppose that the marginal cost of a unit of capacity is only 1 cent rather than 4 cents. Then the relevant part of the market willingness-to-pay equation is the one in which night demanders have zero marginal willingness to pay:

$$P_{M_C} = 7 - \tfrac{1}{250}M_C = 1$$

whence
$$M_C = 1500$$
and
$$P_{N_C} = 0$$

That is, night demanders do not get allocated any portion of the capacity costs: The marginal capacity is there only because the day demanders are willing to pay for it. Of course, both groups must pay the marginal operating costs they impose, so $P_D = 4$ cents and $P_N = 3$ cents. Thus, the capacity is fully utilized during the day ($D = 1500$), but at night there is unused capacity ($N = 1250$).

This concludes the discussion in this section. In the following optional section we look more formally at the dual approach to cost-output relations.

∇Duality: Some Mathematical Relations between Production and Cost Functions

In this section we examine briefly some of the mathematical relations between production functions and costs when it can be assumed that the supplier will operate at least cost. Much of this material is just now emerging from the theoretical literature, and it has not yet been widely applied to policy analysis. However, it is likely to be used with increasing frequency, and it is very helpful for understanding (and undertaking!) work like the Spady-Friedlaender analysis.

The problem of choosing the cost-minimizing inputs given a certain production function is usually explained by a diagram much like Figure 7-8. Given a production function $Q = F(K,L)$ and input prices P_K and P_L, suppose we are told to produce an output of $Q = 30$ at the least cost. The isoquant for $Q = 30$ is shown in the figure. An isocost line is a locus of inputs such that $P_K K + P_L L$ is constant. This line has slope $= -P_L/P_K$. Thus, geometrically we wish to be on the lowest possible isocost line which reaches the isoquant where $Q = 30$. This occurs where the isocost line is just tangent to the isoquant. At that point the marginal rate of technical substitution ($\text{RTS}_{L,K}$, the negative of the slope of the isoquant) equals the input price ratio P_L/P_K.

Recall that the RTS is equal to the ratio of the marginal products at any point. To see this, remember that the change in output dQ along an isoquant is zero. That is,

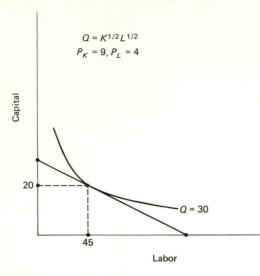

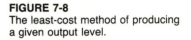

FIGURE 7-8
The least-cost method of producing
a given output level.

$$Q = F(K,L)$$

and along an isoquant (taking the total differential)

$$dQ = \frac{\partial F}{\partial K}dK + \frac{\partial F}{\partial L}dL = 0$$

These terms can be so rearranged that

$$-\left(\frac{dK}{dL}\right)_{Q = \text{const}} = \frac{\partial F/\partial L}{\partial F/\partial K} = \frac{\text{MP}_L}{\text{MP}_K}$$

The term on the left-hand side is the negative of the slope of an isoquant, and thus it is by definition equal to $\text{RTS}_{L,K}$. Thus,

$$\text{RTS}_{L,K} = \frac{\text{MP}_L}{\text{MP}_K}$$

For the general problem of least-cost C input choice for the production of Q units of output, we may formulate it in calculus terms as

$$C = P_K K + P_L L + \lambda[Q - F(K,L)]$$

Thus, the first-order conditions for a cost minimum are

$$\frac{\partial C}{\partial K} = P_K - \lambda\frac{\partial F}{\partial K} = 0 \qquad\qquad \text{(i)}$$

$$\frac{\partial C}{\partial L} = P_L - \lambda \frac{\partial F}{\partial L} = 0 \qquad \text{(ii)}$$

$$\frac{\partial C}{\partial \lambda} = Q - F(K,L) = 0 \qquad \text{(iii)}$$

Dividing the second equation by the first after rearranging slightly gives us the calculus proof of the geometric argument:

$$\frac{P_L}{P_K} = \frac{\partial F/\partial L}{\partial F/\partial K} = \frac{MP_L}{MP_K} = RTS_{L,K}$$

This simply reiterates that the least-cost input choice will be the point on the isoquant whose slope is minus the ratio of the input prices.

This reasoning allows us to find the cost-minimizing input choice given a specific production function, input prices, and a desired output level. For example, suppose the production function is Cobb-Douglas:

$$Q = K^{1/2}L^{1/2}$$

and $P_K = 9$, $P_L = 4$, and the desired output is 30.

We know the correct point on the isoquant will have slope $= -4/9$. To find an expression for the isoquant slope in terms of K and L, let us find the marginal productivity equations directly from the production function and then combine them:

$$MP_L = \frac{\partial Q}{\partial L} = \tfrac{1}{2}K^{1/2}L^{-1/2}$$

$$MP_K = \frac{\partial Q}{\partial K} = \tfrac{1}{2}K^{-1/2}L^{1/2}$$

$$RTS_{L,K} = \frac{MP_L}{MP_K} = \frac{K}{L}$$

Thus K/L must equal 4/9, or $K = 4L/9$. Now we can substitute directly into the production function and solve for $Q = 30$:

$$30 = K^{1/2}L^{1/2}$$

$$30 = \left(\frac{4L}{9}\right)^{1/2} L^{1/2}$$

$$30 = \tfrac{2}{3}L$$

$$45 = L$$

$$20 = K$$

$$360 = C = P_K K + P_L L$$

Refer back to the general calculus formulation of this problem:

$$C = P_K K + P_L L + \lambda[Q - F(K,L)]$$

Note that $\partial C/\partial Q = \lambda$; that is, λ can be interpreted as the marginal cost of increasing the output level by one unit. We know from the first (or second) equation of the first-order conditions:

$$\lambda = \frac{P_K}{\partial F/\partial K}$$

Thus in our specific problem we can identify the marginal cost by substituting the correct expressions:

$$\lambda = \frac{9}{\frac{1}{2}(20^{-1/2})(45^{1/2})}$$

$$= \frac{9}{\frac{1}{2}(1.5)}$$

$$= 12$$

That is, it would cost $12 to expand output by one more unit (in the least-cost way).

Now, one of the problems with the above method of solution, simply a calculus version of the usual geometric argument, is that it can be somewhat tedious. It certainly would be nice if there were a simpler way to find the answers. In recent years economists using the mathematics of duality have increasingly recognized that associated with each "well-behaved" production function is a cost function. From the cost function, it is often much simpler to find the answers to problems like the one just solved.

Of course, if one had to derive (as we will shortly) the cost function from the production function each time, there would be no gain. But the general equation for the cost function can be expressed just like the general equation for a production function. For example, it is no more difficult to remember (or look up) the Cobb-Douglas cost function than the Cobb-Douglas production function. And since cost functions provide answers to standard problems more readily, as we will illustrate, one should expect to see growing use of them in analyses.[39]

Let us first give the general definition of a cost function: *A cost function*

[39] This development on the supply side is analogous to the development to consumer demand reviewed in the optional section of Chapter 5. The textbook by Hal R. Varian, *Microeconomic Analysis* (New York: W. W. Norton Co., Inc., 1978) provides a good introductory approach. A more advanced reference is M. Fuss and D. McFadden (eds.), *Production Economics: A Dual Approach to Theory and Applications* (Amsterdam: North Holland, 1978).

$C(Q, P_1, P_2, \ldots, P_n)$ *is a relation which associates for each output level and input prices the least total cost of producing that output level.*

Once a cost function is known, it is easy to derive the standard cost curves from it. For example:

$$MC(Q) = \frac{\partial C}{\partial Q}$$

and

$$AC(Q) = \frac{C(Q, P_1 P_2, \ldots, P_n)}{Q}$$

To get a better understanding of the cost function, let us derive it for Cobb-Douglas production technology:

$$Q = K^\alpha L^{1-\alpha}$$

To find the cost function, we must solve for the cost minimum in the general problem:[40]

$$C = P_K K + P_L L + \lambda(Q - K^\alpha L^{1-\alpha})$$

The first-order conditions are:

$$\frac{\partial C}{\partial K} = P_K - \alpha\lambda K^{\alpha-1}L^{1-\alpha} = 0 \tag{i}$$

$$\frac{\partial C}{\partial L} = P_L - (1 - \alpha)\lambda K^\alpha L^{-\alpha} = 0 \tag{ii}$$

$$\frac{\partial C}{\partial \lambda} = Q - K^\alpha L^{1-\alpha} = 0 \tag{iii}$$

The solution requires that we express the cost C as a function of only the output level and the input prices (and the fixed parameters). Since $C = P_K K + P_L L$, we will use the first-order conditions to substitute for K and L in this equation.

By dividing (i) by (ii) after rearranging, we see that

$$\frac{P_K}{P_L} = \frac{[\alpha/(1 - \alpha)]L}{K}$$

or $\qquad P_K K = \dfrac{\alpha}{1 - \alpha}P_L L \qquad$ or $\qquad K = \dfrac{[\alpha/(1 - \alpha)]P_L L}{P_K}$

---

[40] Note that this is the same formulation one would use to find the expenditure function associated with a Cobb-Douglas utility function.

Therefore,

$$C = P_K K + P_L L = P_L L \left(1 + \frac{\alpha}{1 - \alpha}\right) = P_L L \frac{1}{1 - \alpha}$$

Now we have only to rid ourselves of the L in the above expression. To do so, we use condition (iii), $Q = K^\alpha L^{1-\alpha}$. On substituting in it our expression for K derived from (i) and (ii), we have

$$Q = \left(\frac{\alpha}{1 - \alpha}\right)^\alpha \left(\frac{P_L}{P_K}\right)^\alpha L^\alpha L^{1-\alpha}$$

$$Q = \left(\frac{\alpha}{1 - \alpha}\right)^\alpha \left(\frac{P_L}{P_K}\right)^\alpha L$$

or

$$L = Q\left(\frac{\alpha}{1 - \alpha}\right)^{-\alpha} \left(\frac{P_L}{P_K}\right)^{-\alpha}$$

Now we may substitute this in the expression for the cost:

$$C = P_L L \frac{1}{1 - \alpha}$$

$$= P_L \left(\frac{P_L}{P_K}\right)^{-\alpha} \left(\frac{\alpha}{1 - \alpha}\right)^{-\alpha} \left(\frac{1}{1 - \alpha}\right) Q$$

$$= P_L^{1-\alpha} P_K^\alpha \alpha^{-\alpha} (1 - \alpha)^{\alpha-1} Q$$

or, letting $\delta = \alpha^{-\alpha}(1 - \alpha)^{\alpha-1}$,

$$C = \delta P_L^{1-\alpha} P_K^\alpha Q$$

Of course, this was tedious to derive, but the point is that the derivation need not be repeated: This expression is no more difficult to remember (or refer to) than the production function itself.

Now let us resolve our problem, where we are given $Q = 30$, $P_K = 9$, $P_L = 4$, and $\alpha = \frac{1}{2}$ (or $\delta = 2$). The least cost is obtained by simply plugging in the formula

$$C = 2(4^{1/2})(9^{1/2})(30)$$
$$= 360$$

But what are the inputs? They are simply the value of the partial derivatives of the cost function with respect to prices! That is, if we let $X_i(Q, P_1, P_2, \ldots, P_n)$ denote generally the optimal level of the ith input given output Q and input prices, we have *Shephard's lemma*.[41]

---

[41] A proof of Shephard's lemma offered by Varian, op. cit., p. 32, is instructive. Let $\hat{X}$ be the vector of inputs which is cost-minimizing at prices $\hat{P}$ and output level Q. Now imagine considering other cost-minimizing input vectors X that are associated with different prices P but the same

$$\frac{\partial C(Q, P_1, P_2, \ldots, P_n)}{\partial P_i} = X_i(Q, P_1, P_2, \ldots, P_n)$$

In other words, this simple derivative property of the cost function can be used to reveal the derived demand curve for any factor holding the output level and other prices constant (i.e., it is a "compensated" derived demand curve).

To make this more concrete, let us apply Shephard's lemma to the Cobb-Douglas case:

$$L = \frac{\partial C}{\partial P_L} = (1 - \alpha)\delta P_L^{-\alpha} P_K^\alpha Q$$

$$K = \frac{\partial C}{\partial P_K} = \alpha\delta P_L^{1-\alpha} P_K^{\alpha-1} Q$$

These functions are the equations for optimal input demand conditional on the level of Q. For our specific example, assume everything is given but P_L. Then the derived demand curve (holding Q at 30 and P_K at 9) is

$$L = \tfrac{1}{2}(2)P_L^{-1/2}(9^{1/2})(30)$$
$$= 90P_L^{-1/2}$$

This tells us the optimal level of L for any price P_L (conditional on the other factors). Thus, when $P_L = 4$, $L = 45$.

Similarly, we find the optimal K in our problem:

$$K = \tfrac{1}{2}(2)(4^{1/2})(9^{-1/2})(30)$$
$$= 20$$

We can also derive the standard cost curves for the Cobb-Douglas with about as little effort:

$$\mathrm{MC}(Q) = \frac{\partial C}{\partial Q} = \delta P_L^{1-\alpha} P_K^\alpha$$

---

output level. Define the cost difference between the X and $\hat{X}$ input vectors at prices P as CD(P):

$$CD(P) = C(P,Q) - P\hat{X}$$

Since C is the minimum cost at prices P, C is less than $P\hat{X}$ for all P except $\hat{P}$ (where they are equal). Thus this function CD(P) attains its maximum value (of zero) at $\hat{P}$, and its partial derivatives must all be equal to zero at that point (the ordinary first-order conditions for optimization). Thus,

$$\frac{\partial CD(\hat{P})}{P_i} = \frac{\partial C(\hat{P},Q)}{P_i} - X_i = 0$$

$$\frac{\partial C(\hat{P},Q)}{\partial P_i} = X_i$$

or for our specific function:

$$MC(Q) = 2(4^{1/2})(9^{1/2})$$
$$= 12$$

That is, the marginal cost curve associated with Cobb-Douglas technology is constant. Of course, this is always true for constant returns to scale production functions. The average cost must thus have the same equation:

$$AC(Q) = \frac{C}{Q} = \delta P_L^{1-\alpha} P_K^\alpha$$

In the main part of the text it was mentioned that most empirical studies of production assume Cobb-Douglas or CES technology. While these may often be good approximations, their use is due more to their ease of statistical estimation than to any strong belief that technology has constant elasticity of substitution. However, a new freedom arises with the cost function approach: Several functional forms that have been discovered are easily estimable statistically but are less restrictive in terms of the type of production function which might underlie them. Two will be mentioned briefly here. The first is the *generalized Leontif cost function:*[42]

$$C(Q, P_1, \ldots, P_n) = Q \sum_{i=1}^{n} \sum_{j=1}^{n} a_{ij} P_i^{1/2} P_j^{1/2}$$

where $a_{ij} = a_{ji}$. The a_{ij}'s are fixed parameters of the function.

For a two-factor technology this may be written:

$$C(Q, P_K, P_L) = Q(a_K P_K + a_L P_L + 2a_{LK} P_L^{1/2} P_K^{1/2})$$

This generalized function is linear in the parameters, so it could easily be tested by statistical methods. It corresponds to the fixed-proportions Leontif technology when $a_{ij} = 0$ for $i \neq j$.[43]

The second cost function of quite general use is the *translog cost function*. It was used by Spady and Friedlaender in their study of trucking:

$$\ln C(Q, P_1, \ldots, P_n) = Q\left(a_0 + \sum_{i=1}^{n} a_i \ln P_i + \frac{1}{2} \sum_{i=1}^{n} \sum_{j=1}^{n} a_{ij} \ln P_i \ln P_j \right)$$

---

[42] This was derived by W. Diewert, "An Application of the Shephard Duality Theorem: A Generalized Leontif Production Function," *Journal of Political Economy*, 79, No. 3, May/June 1971, pp. 481–507.

[43] The reader may wish to prove this as an exercise. It can be done by finding the two derived demand curves and using them to identify the relation between L and K. This is an isoquant, since the level of Q is constant and the same for each derived demand curve. The isoquant collapses to a right angle when $a_{LK} = 0$.

where all the a's are parameters and have the following restrictions:

$$\sum_{i=1}^{n} a_i = 1 \qquad \sum_{i=1}^{n} a_{ij} = 0 \qquad \text{and} \qquad a_{ij} = a_{ji}$$

If it turns out that all $a_{ij} = 0$, the translog function collapses to the Cobb-Douglas.

SUMMARY

In this chapter we examined the role of technology and costs as constraints on an organization's supply decisions. Policy analysts use these concepts in a variety of predictive and evaluative ways. One important way arises in considering technical efficiency in the public sector. For example, to discover if the skills or productivity of participants in a job-training program are improving, it may be necessary to estimate the observed technical relation between inputs and outputs in order to isolate the changing contribution of the trainee. To do this requires a theoretical understanding of production functions, a good working knowledge of the operations being studied, and certain statistical skills (not covered here). At a purely theoretical level it is helpful to understand differences between concepts of efficiency and productivity; we illustrated this by examining the tempting mistake of maximizing productivity that a city manager or mayor might make.

Numerous practical difficulties stand in the way of discovering the empirical truth about input-output relations. One of these, discussed in the examples of masonry cleaning and trucking, is the importance of accounting for quality variations in the output. The hedonic method of accounting for these variations was illustrated at a simplified level. Another difficulty, common in the public sector, is having any good measure of output; we illustrated this with education but could raise the same question in other areas (e.g., how should we measure the output of public fire protection?). In looking at the relation between costs and participant-years in the national supported work program, analysts were able to identify the possibility of substantial managerial scale economies while being sensitive to the inadequacy of participant-years as an output measure.

The concepts of cost are fundamental to economic choice. They are used in virtually every policy analysis which considers alternatives. We explained how social costs are relevant to the concept of a compensation test (Chapter 5) as embodied in social benefit–cost analysis. The important distinctions among social opportunity costs, private opportunity costs, and accounting costs were reviewed. The use of the different cost concepts was illustrated in the analysis of the New York Supported Work experiment; these included the normative social benefit–cost calculation and other calculations from the perspective of different constituent groups which could be used to predict their responses to the program.

The opportunity cost concepts can have very important linkages to production functions. These linkages are most likely in environments where the supply organization produces at a technically efficient level. They are often assumed to hold for private, profit-making firms, like those in the regulated trucking industry. Then the duality relation between a firm's cost function and its production function can simplify certain analytic tasks.

We illustrated this, at a simplified level, by showing how the Spady-Friedlaender study inferred the technical returns to scale of trucking firms from an analysis of their cost functions. The analysis, indicating that no significant scale economies are available by expansion of the average firm, lends support to the arguments in favor of trucking deregulation. In the optional section, we provided more technical details about this duality relation.

We also examined one other type of cost-output relation: the joint cost problem. We illustrated the most efficient solution to joint costs in the context of peak-load pricing problems, as might arise in utility pricing, bridge crossings, or commuter railroads.

EXERCISES

7-1 The director of public service employment for a small city funded two different programs last year, each with a different constant-returns-to-scale production function. The director was not sure of the specification of the production functions last year but hopes to allocate resources more wisely this year.

Production data were gathered for each program during three periods last year; they are listed in the accompanying table.

	Program A			Program B		
	K_A	L_A	Q_A	K_B	L_B	Q_B
1	24	26	48	25	25	50
2	24	28	48	25	36	60
3	24	22	44	25	16	40

a Program A operates with a fixed proportions production function. What is it? [Answer: $Q = \min(2K, 2L)$]

In period 3 what are the marginal products of capital and labor, respectively?

In period 2 what is the elasticity of output with respect to labor? (Answer: 0)

b Program B operates with a Cobb-Douglas production function. What is it? (Answer: $Q = 2K^{1/2}L^{1/2}$)

In period 3 what are the marginal products of capital and labor?

In period 3 what is the elasticity of output with respect to capital?

c∇ Suppose in the third period that the capital was fixed in each program but you were free to allocate the 38 labor units between the two programs any way you wished. If each unit of Q_B is equal in value to each unit of Q_A, how would you allocate labor to maximize the total value of outputs? (Answer: $L_A = 24$; $L_B = 14$)

d▽Suppose you could use two Cobb-Douglas production processes (C and D) to produce the same output:

$$Q_C = K_C^{1/3}L_C^{2/3} \qquad Q_D = K_D^{1/2}L_D^{1/2}$$

If you had 100 units of capital and 105 units of labor, how would you allocate them between the two processes to maximize total output? (Answer: $K_C = 47$, $L_C = 67$, $K_D = 53$, $L_D = 38$)

e▽ Suppose your budget were large enough to employ 100 units of either labor or capital, the cost of a unit of labor being the same as a unit of capital. The production function is $Q_D = K_D^{1/2}L_D^{1/2}$. Given that output must be at least 20, what is the maximum number of people you could employ? (Answer: $L = 90$)

7-2 You are an analyst for a metropolitan transportation authority. You are asked if it would improve efficiency to buy more buses, and if so, how many more should be bought. Currently, there are 80 buses. The operating cost of a bus is $30 during the day and $60 during the night, when higher wages must be paid to drivers and other workers. The daily capital cost of a bus, whether or not it is used, is $10.

The demands for buses aggregated over persons and stops during the 12 hours of day and night, respectively D and N, are

$$Q_D = 160 - P_D$$

$$Q_N = 80 - P_N$$

What is the efficient number of buses? What prices should be charged to induce efficient ridership of them? Will all the buses be in use at night? (Answers: 120 buses; $P_D = \$140$, $P_N = \$60$, no)

PRIVATE PROFIT-MAKING ORGANIZATIONS: OBJECTIVES, CAPABILITIES, AND POLICY IMPLICATIONS

This chapter and the following one are about the organizations which convert inputs into outputs: firms in the private profit-making sector, private nonprofit organizations like certain hospitals and schools, public bureaus like fire and sanitation departments, and public enterprises like mass transit systems.[1] Each of these organizations must decide what outputs to produce, the level of each, and the technologies with which to make them. In the preceding chapter we reviewed the concepts of technological possibilities and their associated costs. These serve to constrain the organization's decisions. Similarly, the organization is constrained by the factors that influence its revenues: sales, voluntary donations, or government funding. For the most part we shall defer an examination of the sources of these latter constraints; they arise in part from consumer (including government) demand for the outputs and in part from the behavior of other producer organizations that supply the same or very similar outputs.

---

[1] The distinction between a public bureau and public enterprise is that the bureau receives its funds from government revenues and the enterprise receives its funds from sale of the output. In actuality most public supply organizations receive some user fees as well as government subsidies, so the distinction is really a matter of degree.

If we simply refer to all the external constraints on the organization as its environment, then we can say that the organization's behavior is a function of its objectives, capabilities, and environment. In this chapter our purpose is to examine the role of analytic assumptions about objectives and capabilities in modeling the behavior of the private, profit-making firm. We begin with models of the private firm because they have received the most attention in the professional literature and are more highly developed and tested than the models of other supplier organizations. The models of behavior we review here are useful for predicting the organization's response to such policy changes as taxes, subsidy plans, regulations, and other legal requirements. Since our standard of living depends to a great extent on what these organizations do and how well they do it, it should be clear that the effects of policies on their behavior are of the utmost importance to understand.

We begin with a discussion of the concept of a firm and emphasize the importance of uncertainty, information costs, and transaction costs to explain the formation of firms. Then we review the standard model of a firm: an organization whose objective is profit maximization and whose capabilities are sufficient to achieve that objective, subject to the environmental constraints. It can be difficult to predict the behavior of this standard firm, which we illustrate with an extended discussion of the firm's choice to price-discriminate. We consider different types of price discrimination, the normative consequences of them, public policy concerning price discrimination, and behavioral factors which determine when price discrimination will occur. In connection with the latter we emphasize the role of information flows and transactions between the firm and its customers.

Next we turn to models which consider different firm objectives and capabilities. Holding the capabilities constant, we consider the effect of alternative objectives. A model of revenue (or sales) maximization is discussed, and other objectives that may apply in particular situations are mentioned. We illustrate the policy relevance of these behaviors in the areas of taxation and antitrust and with regard to information disclosure requirements. Finally, we turn to capabilities and consider the idea that an organization may be boundedly rational: a satisficer rather than a maximizer. A simple rule-of-thumb behavioral model of markup pricing is presented. With it, we illustrate that in certain environments a satisficing firm may behave identically to a profit-maximizing one. However, this will not always be true, as we illustrate in the following chapter in regard to hospital behavior.

Each of these models may apply in particular circumstances, and there are some settings in which analysts are particularly uncertain about which, if any, of them can approximate actual behavior. It would be nice if we could honestly conclude by reporting which models work in which environments. However, that is an unresolved matter which requires considerable additional empirical research. For now we must be content with the conclusion that an analyst who is aware of these competing models will be considerably more sensitive about making policy inferences which depend on any one of them.

THE CONCEPT OF A FIRM

When the workings of a market economy are discussed, it is implicit that individuals own all the resources that are potentially available for use in production and have legal authority over their use. We do not often ask, although it turns out to be a most interesting question, why control over these resources frequently gets formally delegated to some impersonal, intermediary institutions called firms which convert the inputs into outputs and array them in the marketplace for sale. Analogously, we do not often question why, on the demand side, such formal delegations of authority to intermediary institutions rarely exist.

Each individual as a consumer is generally assumed to make perfectly decentralized decisions, i.e., decide on his or her own which goods to purchase and make the purchases from suppliers. We rarely take part of our consumption budget, voluntarily give up authority over it to some central consumption organization which makes purchase decisions for the members, and then receive our share of the purchased goods.[2] Why then is it so normal for us to give up some control over the use of our labor by becoming an employee or give up control over the use of our capital by giving it to a firm in return for stock certificates or bonds? Why do we not supply as we buy, in a decentralized manner? Why do we voluntarily agree to more centralized decision making by centralizing control in the institution known as the firm?

The answer that first comes to mind is economies of scale. Indeed, before the industrial revolution, we did supply as we buy. Many families were self-contained economic units that produced primarily for their own consumption. There was some specialization, of course, because some people were hunters, others dressmakers, etc. But it was not until the development of the factory that individuals began leaving their homes in large numbers to work in groups or teams elsewhere during the day. Much of this economic phenomenon was understood at the time. Adam Smith, writing in the eighteenth century, understood with remarkable clarity the advantages that could be had through the specializations made possible by large-scale enterprise.[3] For a given amount of labor and capital, total output is often greater if produced by assembly line rather than by many small shops.

Yet in an important way, this answer begs the question. To operate a large-scale enterprise, it may be that many individual resource units must be coordinated. But why is it common for this coordination to take place inside one firm rather than through arrangements made across firms? As a simple illustrative example, many firms use legal services from law firms. If one firm is

---

[2] There are, in fact, many instances in which we do allow organizations to spend part of our budgets for us. Governments are an obvious one. Families may be thought of as organizations the members of which pool their resources and make joint consumption decisions (although for most purposes, economic theory treats the family as an individual). Other voluntary institutions—churches, consumer cooperatives, and social clubs—sometimes have these functions.

[3] See his description of the pin factory in *The Wealth of Nations* (New York: The Modern Library, 1937).

assembling an airplane engine, different firms can assemble various components of it, or one firm can do the whole thing. These are alternative ways of organizing to carry out the same physical tasks. So the fact that resources need to be coordinated to produce the final output does not imply that the coordination should be accomplished within one firm.

At one extreme one could imagine that all parts of a production process are accomplished by single-individual "firms" controlling only that individual's resources: complete decentralization of decision making for production. All coordination would take place through arrangements across firms. At the other extreme one could imagine that all the labor and capital resources of society are employed by one gigantic firm coordinating all activities internally: complete centralization of productive economic activities.[4] The common firm simply represents a voluntary choice about the degree to which production decisions should be centralized rather than decentralized.

The key explanatory variables which explain these choices have to do with the information, transaction, and uncertainty costs that would arise under alternative organizational arrangements. One may choose to become an employee rather than a self-employed contractor because of preference for greater certainty of income. An individual may delegate control over capital assets to a firm because it is too expensive for the individual to acquire the information necessary to direct the use of the assets in the most profitable manner. If a firm desires to have certain intermediate products delivered on a variable but precisely timed schedule (e.g., engines to be installed in automobiles), the transaction costs may be cheaper if the intermediate products are made internally than if frequent new contracts have to be negotiated and arranged with an outside supplier. All of these examples remind us that market transactions are not costless. It is the economies of scale from these sources which help explain why individuals choose to delegate some control over their resources to the centralized contracting agent known as the firm; it is also the diseconomies that arise from these factors (past some point of internal growth) that serve to limit the size of the firm.[5]

One interesting point that can be made clearer through the realization that a firm is only an intermediary is that the concepts of outcome equity are not generally applied to firms. That is, firms do not enter as arguments in social welfare functions; only individuals count. The only concern for firm "welfare" arises indirectly through its effects on consumers and on the incomes derived by the individuals supplying resources to the firm. That is also why, in Chapter 5, we described the concept of a compensation test without reference to firms;

[4] In Chapter 15 we point out that there can be considerable decentralization within a firm and discuss the reasons why.

[5] These issues have been pointedly raised by R. Coase, "The Nature of the Firm," *Economica, 4,* November 1937, pp. 386–405; O. Williamson, *Markets and Hierarchies: Analysis and Antitrust Implications* (New York: The Free Press, 1975); and A. Alchian and H. Demsetz, "Production, Information Costs, and Economic Organization," *The American Economic Review, 62,* No. 5, December 1972, pp. 777–795.

all the relevant effects are counted by knowing (in each state) the available goods and each individual's budget constraint. Thus when we discuss the effect of a policy on a firm's behavior, we must be able to trace the consequences through to individuals before the policy can be properly evaluated.

Additional importance to policy analysis of understanding the concept of a firm will become increasingly clear as the successive chapters in Parts IV and V unfold. At this stage let us simply point out that the role of policy in influencing economic organization is large and that deducing the consequences of alternative policies often requires perceiving the "transactional" impacts. We will illustrate, for example, that the design of policy to protect the environment from air and water pollution depends crucially on these concepts, and that can be said for the regulation of natural monopolies also. But before we develop these applications, we must build up a number of other concepts relevant to understanding the production side of the economy. With this brief introduction to the nature of a firm, let us consider how the firm's behavior can be modeled in terms of its objectives and capabilities.

THE PRIVATE PROFIT-MAXIMIZING FIRM

Profit Maximization Requires that Marginal Revenue Equal Marginal Cost

In standard uses of microeconomic theory, a firm in a private market is modeled simply by the objective function of profit maximization. That is, the firm is nothing more than a supercompetent clerk. It considers all production alternatives and chooses the one which will maximize its profit, subject to the constraints of factor prices and the demand for its output. Demand is modeled by a revenue function, $R(Q)$, which indicates what revenue will be brought in by an output level of Q. Costs are represented by the cost function $C(Q)$. Profits $\Pi(Q)$ are defined as the difference between revenues and costs, and the firm is assumed to pick the Q which maximizes

$$\Pi(Q) = R(Q) - C(Q)$$

At the optimal level of output it must be true that the change in profit $\Delta\Pi$ for a very small increase in output is zero. Below the optimal level, increases in output yield positive incremental profits. Past the optimal level, output increases yield negative incremental profits. So exactly at the optimal level, profits are neither increasing nor decreasing:

$$\Delta\Pi = \Delta R - \Delta C = 0$$

or

$$\Delta R = \Delta C$$

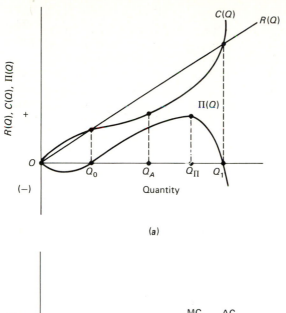

(a)

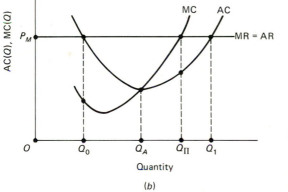

FIGURE 8-1
(a) The firm's revenue, cost, and profit functions; (b) profit maximization occurs when marginal revenue equals marginal cost.

In other words, *marginal revenue must equal marginal cost at the profit-maximizing level of output.*[6]

Graphically, this is illustrated in Figure 8-1a and b. The revenue function is drawn as a straight line (Figure 8-1a), which is equivalent to assuming the firm will sell each unit of output at the prevailing market price. This implies that marginal revenue MR is constant, and therefore average revenue AR is equal to it (Figure 8-1b). The cost function is drawn to reflect economies of scale up to a certain output level Q_A but diseconomies thereafter. Thus the range of output

---

[6] Marginal revenue is the change in total revenue that results from the sale of one more unit of output. Average revenue is the total revenue divided by the quantity produced.

levels in which profits are positive $(R > C)$ is from Q_0 to Q_1. Profits at each output level are the vertical distance between $R(Q)$ and $C(Q)$, shown as the profit function $\Pi(Q)$ in Figure 8-1a. The maximum profit is at Q_Π, where the slope of the profit function $\Pi(Q)$ is zero (Figure 8-1a) and MC = MR (Figure 8-1b).

The Profit-Maximizing Monopolist

In many applications of this standard model of firm behavior, the insights are derived by varying the external or environmental constraints on the firm's actions. For example, the predicted harm from monopoly can be easily illustrated through a simple extension of the analysis above. To see this, let us recognize that the demand curve for the *firm's* output[7] is simply the average revenue function: For any quantity produced, the average revenue is simply the price per unit. Thus the straight-line revenue function corresponds to the horizontal demand curve that each firm in a perfectly competitive market is assumed to face: If the firm charged a price lower than the prevailing market price P_M, it would capture the entire industry demand; if it tried to charge a price higher than P_M, the demand would be zero, since consumers would buy the product from the competitors charging P_M.[8]

In the case of a monopoly the firm faces the entire downward-sloping market demand curve. To keep the example as simple as possible, Figure 8-2 illustrates the monopolist's choice assuming a linear demand (average revenue) curve and constant-returns-to-scale technology, so that the marginal cost is constant and the average cost is thus equal to it. The marginal revenue curve is lower than the demand curve, since to induce consumers to buy an additional unit requires lowering the price for all units.[9] Profit maximization implies that the monopolist will choose quantity Q_M (where MR = MC). The product will be sold at price P_M, and the monopolist's profits are shown by the rectangle $P_E P_M AB$ (the quantity sold times the difference between the price per unit sold and the average cost per unit).

The most efficient quantity to provide, however, is Q_E.[10] That is, assuming

---

[7] Note that this is not equivalent to consumer demand for the product generally; the consumer can buy the same product from other firms.

[8] It is sometimes easier to understand the geometry by first imagining that the firm's demand curve is not perfectly flat but is slightly downward sloping: A small price increase from P_M leads to a large reduction in demand, and a small price decrease from P_M causes a large increase in demand. The more competitive the industry, the flatter the firm's demand curve. The demand does not actually become infinite for prices below P_M; it is just that the entire market quantity at that price is so great relative to the quantities shown that the curve is effectively flat over the diagram's range. The actual firm's demand curve in the perfectly competitive case equals the market demand curve for prices below P_M, is horizontal at P_M, and is zero above P_M.

[9] MR $= \partial TR/\partial Q = \partial PQ/\partial Q = P + Q(\partial P/\partial Q)$. The first term, P, equals the height of the demand curve. The second term is negative whenever the demand curve facing the firm is downward-sloping $(\partial P/\partial Q < 0)$. The second term can be thought of as the reduced revenues on the first Q units caused by the price reduction necessary to sell one additional unit.

[10] Keep in mind that the distribution of resource ownership (wealth) influences the identification of the most efficient quantity by influencing both the demand and cost curves. We discuss this more explicitly in Chapter 10, on general equilibrium. Also, we ignore the general problem of the second best until Chapter 11; this problem bears on determination of efficient levels of output.

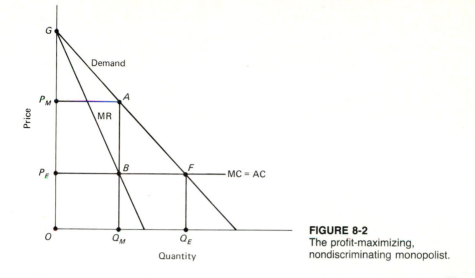

FIGURE 8-2
The profit-maximizing,
nondiscriminating monopolist.

that the marginal cost curve measures the marginal social opportunity cost of production, units should be produced as long as the height of the demand curve exceeds the marginal cost. We have already seen that the height of the demand curve is a monetary measure of the benefit to the consumer of one additional unit: the maximum that someone will pay for that unit. The social opportunity cost of the resources used to make that unit is the maximum that anyone will pay to use the resources *in some other way*. Thus there is room for a deal if any output less than Q_E is produced, and therefore such an output level would be inefficient.

For example, consider the resources that could be used to produce one more unit of output above the Q_M level. In their alternative uses, they are worth only BQ_M (the marginal social cost). But there is a consumer willing to pay AQ_M for the additional unit of output in this market. This consumer will offer an amount greater than BQ_M; the resource suppliers would be better off to accept the offer; and the alternative user is left indifferent (neither receiving the alternative output nor paying its cost). A similar argument can be made about any incremental output levels greater than Q_E; in this case the alternative user values the resources more highly than the consumer in this market. Only at the output level Q_E is there no further room for a deal.

Thus this type of monopoly behavior causes an inefficient allocation of resources: The quantity of the monopoly good that gets produced is too small. The deadweight loss from this misallocation is the triangle *ABF*. The prediction follows simply from the assumptions about the objectives, capabilities, and demand curve the organization faces.

"Not so fast!", the experienced industrial organization analyst might cry out. There is a wrinkle (perhaps a gaping hole) in the above standard description of monopoly behavior. It can be understood from the earlier discussion of the concept of the firm involving information and transaction costs. The conclusions about the firm's behavior, as well as the inefficiency of the allocation, depend on assumptions about the organizational costs. The most typical assumptions are that there are zero transaction costs and perfect information. Under those assumptions, however, the monopolist will not behave as suggested. The reason is that, under these conditions, the monopolist can do best by perfectly price-discriminating among the consumers.[11] Put differently, it is in the monopolist's interest to exploit the room for a deal we have just identified.

Types of Monopolistic Price Discrimination

A perfectly price-discriminating monopolist could charge each consumer the maximum that consumer is willing to pay and thus extract the full area under the demand curve, produce Q_E, and make as profit the entire triangle P_EGF (Figure 8-2). Resource allocation would be efficient, although the monopolist would be hogging all of the gains from trade. Consumers buy the output, but their utility levels remain approximately unchanged;[12] the resource suppliers receive their opportunity costs so their income levels are constant; and the monopolist who costlessly organized these deals walks away with all the surplus. Note the consistency of this behavior with the MR = MC rule; we are simply asserting that the marginal revenue equals the height of the demand curve.

Of course, a more plausible model involves the recognition that information is not perfect and is costly to obtain. The costs can deter the monopolist from discriminating. However, the profit-maximizing monopolist should be expected to price-discriminate whenever the costs of doing so are less than the incremental profits to be derived. Rather than hope to discriminate perfectly, the monopolist can capture some additional profits simply by segmenting customers into groups that have differing elasticities of demand.

To see this, consider the monopolist's problem of how to select an output level and whether to divide it between two groups and charge each group a different price. To maximize profit, the monopolist must choose an output level and so divide it that marginal revenue in each group is the same ($MR_1 = MR_2$) and equal to the common MC. If $MR_1 \neq MR_2$, more revenue (for the same cost) could be generated by moving some of the output to where the marginal revenue is highest. To see the implications of this, first we must derive a more general result which is itself of interest:

$$\mathrm{MR} = P\left(1 + \frac{1}{\varepsilon}\right)$$

where P is the price per unit and ε is the price elasticity of demand.

---

[11] We interpret these conditions to mean that the monopolist, through the exercise of monopoly power at the time of sale, can costlessly bar resales of the good among consumers.

[12] This assumes the consumer surplus under the ordinary demand curve is close to the compensating and equivalent compensations (Chapter 5).

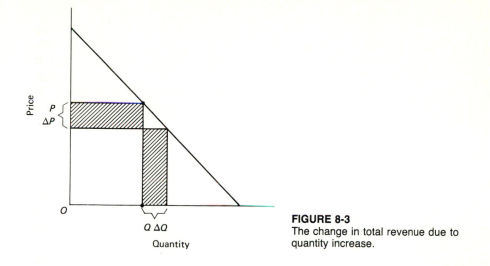

FIGURE 8-3
The change in total revenue due to
quantity increase.

   This equation is important in empirical work because it allows estimation of
the MR from knowledge of the current price and the demand elasticity. Its
derivation is fairly simple. In Figure 8-3 we show a demand curve with initial
price of P and quantity Q. If we increase the quantity by ΔQ (and therefore
price must decrease by ΔP), the change in total revenue ΔR is simply the
difference between the two shaded rectangles:[13]

$$\Delta R = \Delta Q P - \Delta P Q$$

Dividing both sides by ΔQ, the left-hand side is then equal (by definition) to the
marginal revenue:

$$\frac{\Delta R}{\Delta Q} \equiv MR = P - \frac{\Delta P}{\Delta Q} Q$$

This can be rewritten:

$$MR = P\left(1 - \frac{\Delta P}{\Delta Q} \frac{Q}{P}\right)$$

---

[13] This derivation is an approximation. The first term on the left-hand side is actually $\Delta Q(P -$
$\Delta P)$, and we are assuming that $\Delta Q \, \Delta P$ is approximately zero. This approximation is not necessary
for the calculus derivation:

$$\frac{\partial TR}{\partial Q} \equiv MR = \frac{\partial(P \cdot Q)}{\partial Q} = P + \frac{\partial P}{\partial Q} Q = P\left(1 + \frac{1}{\varepsilon}\right)$$

or, recalling that the price elasticity is defined as negative,

$$MR = P\left(1 + \frac{1}{\varepsilon}\right)$$

Now, to return to the discriminating monopolist, profit maximization requires that $MR_1 = MR_2 = MC$, or equivalently,

$$P_1\left(1 + \frac{1}{\varepsilon_1}\right) = P_2\left(1 + \frac{1}{\varepsilon_2}\right) = MC$$

Thus, the monopolist would charge the same price to each group only if $\varepsilon_1 = \varepsilon_2$. Total revenues (for a given output level) can be increased whenever the entire market can be segmented into groups which have differing elasticities of demand. The higher price will be charged to the segment that has the most inelastic demand. The monopolist should be expected to do this whenever the increase in total revenues from the segmentation exceeds the cost of achieving the segmentation. Of course, by the same principle the monopolist could find it profitable to further segment the market, and in the limit this would be the perfectly discriminating monopolist.

Normative Consequences of Price Discrimination

To put these examples into a policy context, let us briefly explain some of the conventional normative reactions to price discrimination by organizations with monopoly power. Basically, price discrimination can occur in many different situations and there is no general conclusion about its effects in terms of equity or efficiency (compared to monopoly with no price discrimination). We illustrate the reasons for this ambiguity below.

First let us consider equity. Price discrimination results in a transfer of income away from consumers to the owners of the monopoly; this is as we suggested in Figure 8-2, where the perfectly discriminating monopolist captures the entire consumer surplus. Furthermore, even the imperfect discriminator must capture more than the nondiscriminating monopolist; otherwise, it would not discriminate. If the discrimination has negligible allocative effects (i.e., essentially the same consumers end up with the same quantity of goods), the equity of the outcome depends on who the monopoly owners are compared to the consumers with inelastic demand. For example, suppose a public utility providing electricity and heat charges residential consumers substantially more than the marginal cost of the service; this type of transfer is unlikely to be viewed as socially desirable. (The average utility shareholder is generally wealthier than the average household.)

On the other hand, often the group of consumers who are most price-inelastic are the relatively wealthy. For example, some airlines may have monopolies over certain routes. Business users of these airline routes may have relatively inelastic demands; that would explain why airlines rarely offer them attractive discounts. But leisure travelers may have relatively elastic demands, and to attract them to fly the same route may require lower fares. These may be achieved by designing rules like those of "supersaver" travel: restrictions which are easy for leisure travelers to meet but difficult for business travelers. (There are no commensurate cost differences to the airlines between these two types of travel.) If the route would be profitable to fly even if the discount fares applied uniformly to all passengers, then the actual fare structure simply extracts some of the consumer surplus from business users. In this case there might be a more neutral social judgment of the income redistribution caused by price discrimination. (That is, profits are being redistributed from one corporation to another.[14])

If one considers cases in which price discrimination does have allocative effects (i.e., changes the quantity of the good purchased by consumers), society might actually favor the redistribution that occurs. Suppose, for example, that a physician in a rural town provides below-cost services to the poor (not covered by Medicaid) by charging fees above costs to the wealthier residents. If it were not for this price discrimination, the poor might not receive the medical services at all.

Let us turn to the efficiency consequences of price discrimination. In connection with Figure 8-2 we pointed out that in a monopoly setting perfect price discrimination improves resource allocation. A more interesting case with a similar result is shown in Figure 8-4. This situation is referred to as *the problem of increasing returns to scale,* because it arises when the AC curve is declining over the range of output relevant to demand.

As drawn, the market demand curve for this product intersects the marginal cost curve at a quantity well below the minimum average cost level. This can happen when there is a large demand and a broad range of output over which AC declines, as when a utility company serves a significant portion of a state. But it also happens with a small demand and a narrow range of output over which AC declines, as when a bridge over a stream is infrequently (but "sufficiently") crossed. In both cases high costs are required initially (e.g., for laying gas pipes in the region and building the bridge), but then the marginal costs of operation are low. In either situation, *producing the output improves relative efficiency if the total benefits minus total costs are positive, and the most efficient output level is the one which maximizes net benefits.* The latter is shown here as Q_E, where the demand curve and marginal cost curve intersect. For convenience, we shall assume that the net benefits are positive over the range of output shown under the demand curve.

---

[14] The demand curve of one firm for another firm's product is a *derived* demand curve and not exactly the same as ordinary consumer demand. The profit-maximizing firm often requires intermediate goods to produce its product, and its demand for those goods is derived from the profitability of selling its own output. Its willingness to pay for one unit of an intermediate good can be thought of as the marginal revenue expected to result from its use.

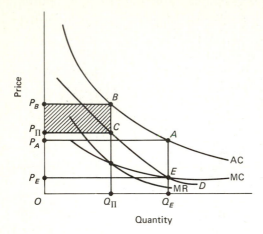

FIGURE 8-4
The problem of increasing returns to scale.

Note that if price equals P_E at Q_E, the price necessary to induce consumers to purchase exactly Q_E, the private firm would be unprofitable. The negative profits, or loss, would equal the area $P_E P_A AE$. If the firm chose the quantity Q_Π, where MC = MR and profits without price discrimination are thus maximized, the firm would still be unprofitable.[15] That is, the maximum profit is really the minimum loss given that the firm operates: the shaded area $P_\Pi P_B BC$. If this is the best operating alternative open to it, the firm will, of course, choose not to produce at all; zero profit is better than a loss. *Thus the private nondiscriminating firm will not supply any of this output despite the fact that the social benefits of its provision exceed the social costs.*

In this situation price discrimination can lead to an improvement in the allocation of resources. For example, if the firm can perfectly price-discriminate, it will produce Q_E. Even if the firm can only imperfectly discriminate, it may be able to extract enough from consumers with inelastic demand to make the operation profitable.

For example, the owner of a monopoly ferry company providing river crossings (where there is no bridge) might charge commercial passengers (e.g., trucks) more per square foot of space occupied than noncommercial users of the service (even if each type of passenger imposes no cost other than the opportunity cost of space utilization). There may be no single price per square foot occupied that makes the enterprise profitable. That is, suppose only commercial users are willing to pay a higher price but that doesn't provide enough revenue to cover the costs. At a lower price, noncommercial types will become users but the revenue gain from the additional demand may be offset by the revenue loss from lowering the price to commercial users. The only profitable way to provide the service may be by price discriminating. And in

---

[15] This is not always the case with increasing returns; indeed most utility companies can and do operate profitably. This is discussed further in Chapter 15.

this situation, all parties—the ferry owner, commercial users, and noncommercial users—consider themselves better off than if there were no service at all.[16]

In the examples of allocative effects given so far, monopolistic price discrimination leads to more efficient resource allocation than monopoly without discrimination. However, this is not always the case; even if we continue to ignore the cost to the monopolist of discriminating, there are demand and cost conditions which lead the discriminator to produce the same or less output than without discrimination. Furthermore, the discrimination will usually result in an inefficient allocation among consumers of whatever quantity is produced.

A simple empirical example may help to clarify the logic used in describing the possible allocative effects. Suppose that the market demand for a product can be divided into two submarkets each characterized by a different linear demand curve. These demand curves are shown in Figure 8-5a and b, and they have equations

$$Q_1 = 12 - P_1 \quad \text{or} \quad P_1 = 12 - Q_1$$
and
$$Q_2 = 18 - P_2 \quad \text{or} \quad P_2 = 18 - Q_2$$

If the marginal cost of the product is constant and equal to \$4, then the most efficient output level is $Q = 22$ and the most efficient allocation among consumers is where $Q_1 = 8$ and $Q_2 = 14$. At that allocation there is no further room for a deal. According to the demand schedule, the most any consumer is willing to pay for an extra unit of output is just under \$4, but no extra unit of output can be produced at opportunity cost below \$4. Furthermore, each of the 22 units produced is allocated to a consumer who values it at \$4 or more, so there is no room for a profitable exchange among consumers.

One way for the economy to achieve the most efficient allocation is by marginal cost pricing: If the price equals \$4, consumers will demand precisely 22 units with $Q_1 = 8$ and $Q_2 = 14$. From the diagrams one can see that the shaded consumer surplus CS of each group is

$$CS_1 = \tfrac{1}{2}(12 - 4)(8) = \$32$$
$$CS_2 = \tfrac{1}{2}(18 - 4)(14) = \$98$$

There is zero producer surplus, since total revenues to producers equal total cost. So the net benefits associated with the most efficient allocation are \$130 = \$32 + \$98 + \$0. These calculations are summarized in the first column of Table 8-1.

The above allocation is not the one which would result if this good were produced by a profit-maximizing monopolist. With no discrimination, the monopolist faces the entire market demand curve shown in Figure 8-6. Its

---

[16] In Chapter 9 we will consider other organizational ways to provide services characterized by increasing returns, including delivery by public enterprises and public subsidies to private firms.

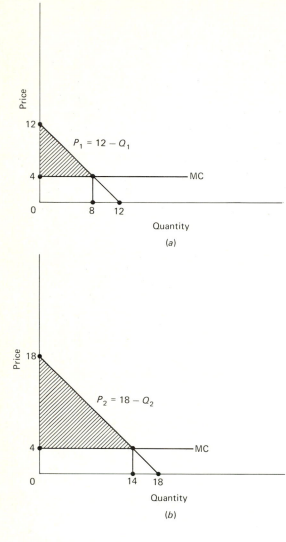

FIGURE 8-5
(a) Allocative effects of marginal cost pricing on consumer group 1; (b) allocative effects of marginal cost pricing on consumer group 2.

equation is in two segments, since above a price of $12 only the consumers in group 2 will make purchases:

$$Q_M = \begin{cases} 30 - 2P & 0 \le P \le 12 \\ 18 - P & 12 < P \le 18 \end{cases}$$

To maximize profits, the monopolist must find the output quantity at which marginal revenue equals marginal cost. The marginal revenue curve also is shown in Figure 8-6. It may be derived from the demand curves:[17]

---

[17] For any linear demand curve $P = a - bQ$, the marginal revenue curve has the equation MR = $a - 2bQ$. This can be derived easily with calculus:

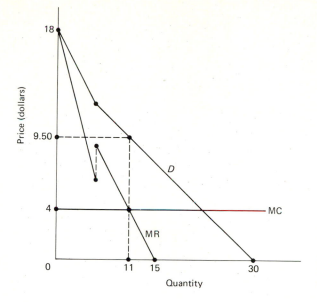

FIGURE 8-6
Monopoly profit maximization
with no price discrimination.

$$MR = \begin{cases} 18 - 2Q_M & 0 \le Q_M \le 6 \\ 15 - Q_M & 6 < Q_M \le 30 \end{cases}$$

In order to set MR = MC = \$4, the monopolist must produce $Q_M = 11$. This implies (from the demand curves) that $P = \$9.50$ with $Q_1 = 2.5$ and $Q_2 = 8.5$. The consumer and producer surpluses are shown as the cross-hatched and shaded areas, respectively, in Figure 8-7a and b:

$$TR = PQ = aQ - bQ^2$$

$$MR = \frac{\partial PQ}{\partial Q} = a - 2bQ$$

The group demand curves in our example are $P_1 = 12 - Q_1$ and $P_2 = 18 - Q_2$. For the first group, 12 corresponds to a in our general linear formula and 1 corresponds to b. Therefore, the marginal revenue curve for this group is $MR_1 = 12 - 2Q_1$. This applies over the range for Q_1 equal to that of the demand curve ($0 \le Q_1 \le 12$). Similarly, $MR_2 = 18 - 2Q_2$ (for $0 \le Q_2 \le 18$). The marginal revenue in the market as a whole can be found analogously by using the market demand function. That is, the market demand function may be written

$$P = \begin{cases} 18 - 2Q_M & 0 \le Q_M \le 6 \\ 15 - Q_M/2 & 6 < Q_M \le 30 \end{cases}$$

and then applying the marginal revenue formula

$$MR = \begin{cases} 18 - 2Q_M & 0 \le Q_M \le 6 \\ 15 - Q_M & 6 < Q_M \le 30 \end{cases}$$

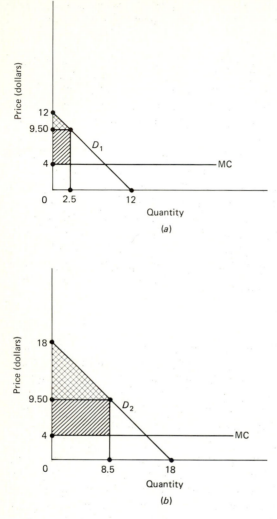

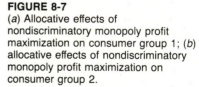

FIGURE 8-7
(a) Allocative effects of nondiscriminatory monopoly profit maximization on consumer group 1; (b) allocative effects of nondiscriminatory monopoly profit maximization on consumer group 2.

$$CS = CS_1 + CS_2$$
$$= \tfrac{1}{2}(12 - 9.50)(2.5) + \tfrac{1}{2}(18 - 9.50)(8.5)$$
$$= 3.125 + 36.125$$
$$= \$39.25$$
$$\Pi = \Pi_1 + \Pi_2$$
$$= (9.50 - 4)(2.5) + (9.50 - 4)(8.5)$$
$$= \$60.50$$

Thus the net benefit from the allocation resulting from this monopoly is only $99.75 (= $39.25 + $60.50), which is less than the $130 net benefit from the efficient solution. The consumers have lost a total of $90.75, of which $60.50 is transferred to the monopolist and the remaining $30.25 is deadweight loss. The main effects of the nondiscriminating monopolist are summarized in column 2 of Table 8-1.

Now, however, let us suppose that the monopolist is able to price-discriminate by charging one price to group 1 and another to group 2. Then profit maximization implies that quantities be so selected that $MC = MR_1 = \$4$ and $MC = MR_2 = \$4$. This is shown in Figure 8-8a and b. Using the marginal revenue formulas derived in footnote 17:

$$4 = MR_1 = 12 - 2Q_1$$

or $\qquad Q_1 = 4 \qquad$ and therefore $\qquad P_1 = \$8$

$$4 = MR_2 = 18 - 2Q_2$$

or $\qquad Q_2 = 7 \qquad$ and therefore $\qquad P_2 = \$11$

The consumer and producer surpluses are again shown as the cross-hatched and shaded areas, respectively, and are calculated by

$$
\begin{aligned}
CS &= CS_1 + CS_2 \\
&= \tfrac{1}{2}\,(12 - 8)\,(4) + \tfrac{1}{2}\,(18 - 11)\,(7) \\
&= 8.00 + 24.50 \\
&= \$32.50 \\
\Pi &= \Pi_1 + \Pi_2 \\
&= (8 - 4)\,(4) + (11 - 4)(7) \\
&= 16 + 49 \\
&= \$65
\end{aligned}
$$

Note in this example that the total quantity of the good produced in the market is the same as with the nondiscriminating monopolist: $Q_M = 11$. However, the net benefits are only $97.50 (= 32.50 + 65)$, which is less than the $99.75 of ordinary monopoly. Why is relative efficiency reduced if the same quantity of the good is being supplied? The available goods are less efficiently allocated among consumers! The marginal consumer in group 2 is willing to pay $11 for an additional unit of the good, while the marginal consumer in group 1 considers the last unit consumed to be worth only $8. There is room for a deal, which the price-discriminating monopolist must prevent. (Otherwise, the consumer in group 2 will buy from a consumer in group 1 instead of from the monopolist.)

The monopolist has incentive to price-discriminate because to do so increases profits from $60.50 to $65.00. In this particular example consumers in group 1 benefit from the discrimination; their surplus is increased by $4.875 $(= 8.00 - 3.125)$. Thus, the losers are the consumers in group 2; they lose $11.50, of which $9.375 is transferred to the monopolist and group 1 consumers and $2.125 is increased deadweight loss. The main effects of this price discrimination are summarized in column 3 of Table 8-1.

For completeness we have also summarized the effects of perfect price

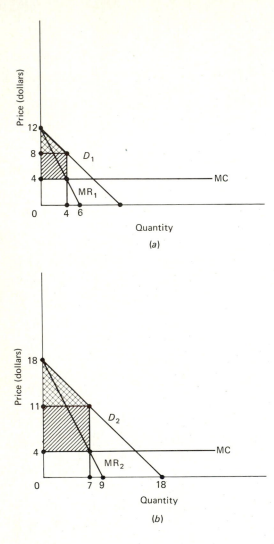

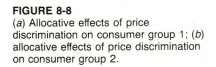

FIGURE 8-8
(a) Allocative effects of price discrimination on consumer group 1; (b) allocative effects of price discrimination on consumer group 2.

discrimination in column 4 of Table 8-1. In this case the net benefits are again at their maximum of $130. Allocation in this market is as efficient as possible (and identical with the allocation from MC pricing). Of course, all the benefits in this case are expropriated by the monopolist; consumers end up with no surplus at all.

In a moment we will offer a variety of actual situations in which price discrimination is observed in order to suggest some of the subtleness with which it occurs. But first let us emphasize a main analytic theme motivating this analysis. Predicting the actual behavior of an organization, even with total certainty about its objectives and capabilities and its market demand curve, is not simple. Major differences in behavior can arise because of variations in

TABLE 8-1
THE EFFECTS OF ALTERNATIVE SUPPLIER BEHAVIOR ON CONSUMERS AND THE
SUPPLIER

	Marginal cost pricing (1)	Profit-maximizing monopolist		
		No price discrimination (2)	Group price discrimination (3)	Perfect price discrimination (4)
Output level	22	11	11	22
Surplus: consumer group 1	32	3.125	8.00	0
Surplus: consumer group 2	98	36.125	24.50	0
Surplus: producer	0	60.50	65.00	130
Total surplus	130	99.75	97.50	130

information and transactions costs under alternative marketing arrangements, and the latter are not easy to understand or recognize in advance. Nevertheless, the effects of policies (and therefore their design and desirability) can depend on them. We are using an organization's decision about whether to price-discriminate as an example of this.

To clarify that it is information and transaction costs which are key determinants of the monopolist's decision about price discrimination, let us work through an additional example. In Figure 8-9 we replicate Figure 8-2 with one change: The cost of identifying each consumer's evaluation and preventing resale to the other consumers (to be discussed further shortly) is constant per unit of output and raises the marginal cost curve to MC'. The monopolist will discriminate as long as it is profitable to do so, i.e., if the profits with discrimination $P_D GH$ exceed the profits without discrimination $P_E P_M AB$:

$$P_D GH - P_E P_M AB > 0$$

Since these areas have the rectangle $P_D P_M AI$ in common, we can subtract it from both areas to get an equivalent expression:

$$P_M GA + IAH - P_E P_D IB > 0$$

Now let us compare this with the deadweight losses in each situation. We have already seen that BAF is the deadweight loss from a nondiscriminating monopoly. The deadweight loss from the discriminating monopolist is $P_E P_D HF$, assuming that MC reflects the least-cost method of production.[18] Thus, purely from the standpoint of relative efficiency, discrimination is preferable if it has a smaller deadweight loss:

[18] Society used to receive alternative outputs from the resources now being devoted to achieving the price discrimination. This use of them adds nothing of social value, and it is the bulk of the social loss.

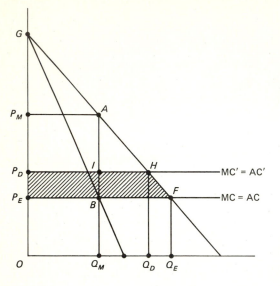

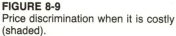

FIGURE 8-9
Price discrimination when it is costly
(shaded).

$$BAF - P_E P_D HF > 0$$

Since these areas have *BIHF* in common, we can subtract it from both to derive an equivalent expression:

$$IAH - P_E P_D IB > 0$$

Comparing this expression with that the monopolist uses in deciding whether to discriminate, we see that they are different by only one term, $P_M GA$. The monopolist may choose to discriminate even though resource allocation may be more efficient under the nondiscriminating monopolist. This further illustrates why the efficiency effects of price discrimination (compared to a nondiscriminating monopoly) are ambiguous.[19]

[19] In the empirical example used earlier, suppose the information and transaction costs of price discriminating are $2 per unit of output. With marginal cost per unit now at $6 rather than $4 (in Figure 8-9, P_D rather than P_E), the perfectly discriminating monopolist with produce only 18 units rather than 22 (Q_D rather than Q_E). The reduced profit is thus

$$\$2 \, (18) + \tfrac{1}{2}(\$2)(4) = \$40$$

The first term is the reduced profit on the units still sold, and the second term is the profit reduction because units 19 to 22 are now unprofitable to sell. Since consumers continue to receive zero surplus, the total surplus is only $106 (= $146 − $40). This is socially less efficient than the nondiscriminating monopolist's strategy ($106 < $115.75 from column 2 of Table 8-1), although the monopolist would choose to discriminate ($106 > $60.50, the monopolist's profits shown in column 2 of Table 8-1).

The Robinson-Patman Act of 1936

With these theoretical examples in mind, let us consider public policy with respect to price discrimination. In Chapter 2 we mentioned that the Robinson-Patman Act of 1936 prohibits certain price discrimination. The Act prohibits charging different prices to different purchasers for "goods of like grade and quality" where the effect may be to "lessen competition." The latter clause means this Act does not usually apply to the natural monopoly situations of increasing returns. For example, generally local gas and electric companies do have rate structures characterized by price discrimination, but they are subjected to review by regulatory commissions and not challenged under Robinson-Patman.

The Robinson-Patman Act had its origins during the Great Depression, when skepticism about the effects of competition was particularly high. This was a time in which large retail chain stores were expanding, entering new markets, and underselling the existing small and independent stores. The intent of the legislation was really to protect the small firms from competition. A standard complaint of the small businesses was that suppliers would sell to the chain at a lower per unit price, which enabled the chains to undersell the independents. However, to the extent that the lower prices were associated with reduced costs of supplying larger and perhaps more stable orders, preventing the lower prices would reduce efficiency.

Let us clarify this. We have been referring to price discrimination as charging different prices for the same good or service. In the models we have been using so far this definition has been satisfactory. But in the more complicated real world *a variety of situations may arise in which the prices a company charges for similar units of a good vary disproportionately to the marginal costs of supplying them. Analysts generally refer to all of these situations as price discrimination.*

In the chain store example above, lower prices due to lower costs would not be discriminatory by the definition. Indeed, producing any given output level at a lower cost is an efficiency improvement. However, Robinson-Patman has often been applied to prevent these benefits from competition.[20]

Let us consider another example. Suppose a company charges two customers a different price for the same item because the shipping costs to the customer farther away are greater than those to the customer nearby. This is not considered price discrimination by the analytic definition, nor is it a violation of Robinson-Patman. (The latter specifically exempts price differ-

---

[20] In a Federal Trade Commission opinion, cited by F. M. Scherer, the Dean Milk Company was found in violation of Robinson-Patman because it tried to enter a new geographical market by charging lower prices in that area than it did elsewhere. What it was actually doing was trying to bring more competition into that area. The FTC found the company guilty of causing economic loss to its competitors and failed to recognize the crucial distinction between harm to *competition* and harm to a *competitor*. For a more extensive discussion of this and other aspects of price discrimination, see F. M. Scherer, *Industrial Market Structure and Economic Performance* (Chicago: Rand McNally and Co., 1970), chaps. 10 and 21.

ences due to delivery cost differences.) However, if the company charges these two consumers the same price despite the delivery cost differences, that is price discrimination by the analytic definition. However, this practice also would fail to violate Robinson-Patman: One must first show a price *difference* before the claim of price discrimination will be heard.

Another situation which is considered price discrimination by the analytic definition but not by Robinson-Patman concerns quality differences. Suppose one company tries to segment its market by creating two slightly different products: a "premium brand" (perhaps heavily advertised) and a "regular brand." A standard example is hardbound and paperbound editions of the same book. If the price differential is proportionate to the marginal cost differences of producing the two editions, there is no discrimination by our analytic definition. But if one edition is priced proportionately greater than its marginal cost compared to the other—as is often alleged for hardbound books—the publisher is trying to exploit the elasticity difference between the market segments by price discriminating. However, this is unlikely to be viewed as a violation of Robinson-Patman because the law applies only to "goods of like grade and quality."

Predicting Price Discrimination

Let us turn to predictive matters. Where and how does price discrimination arise? First of all, a producing organization must have *market power:* some ability to control the price in the market. That is why we discuss this in connection with monopoly; a firm in a perfectly competitive environment (i.e., one facing a horizontal demand curve) does not control the market price and therefore cannot price-discriminate. Lerner has suggested market power M be measured as the following:[21]

$$M = \frac{P - MC}{P}$$

For the firm in a perfectly competitive environment, $P = MC$ (as in Figure 8-1*b*) and therefore $M = 0$. For the monopolist in Figure 8-2, $P > MC$. The measure has an upper bound of $M = 1$ unless some organization finds a way to produce at negative marginal cost. If the firm has constant-returns-to-scale technology, so that $MC = AC$, then this measure is simply profits as a percent of sales. For a profit-maximizing firm, $MR = MC$, and since $MR = P(1 + 1/\epsilon)$:

$$M = \frac{P - MR}{P} = -\frac{1}{\epsilon}$$

[21] Abba P. Lerner, "The Concept of Monopoly and the Measurement of Monopoly Power," *Review of Economic Studies, 1,* June 1934, pp. 157–175.

This suggests that the more inelastic the demand, the greater the market power. Recall that this demand elasticity is for the demand curve facing the firm, not necessarily the whole market. Note also that, since $M \le 1$, the $\epsilon <$ -1. That is, the monopolist must choose to operate on an elastic portion of the demand curve. This may be seen another way. The profit maximum cannot be on the inelastic portion. On that portion, one can raise price and increase revenues while reducing output and costs and thereby increase profit.

Two other conditions, in addition to market power, help explain when price discrimination may arise: the cost of segmenting the market in the first place and the cost of keeping it segmented (preventing resales from customers who buy at a low price to those willing to pay a higher price). These are the information and transaction costs to which we referred earlier.

One group of commodities which are not easily resaleable are services: health care, legal advice, accounting, taxi rides, restaurant meals, automobile fuel and servicing stations, etc. From the health insurance discussion in Chapter 6 it should be apparent that insured patients may be charged more than others for essentially the same services. As another example, compare the price of gasoline along limited-access highways with the price in suburban or urban areas (where there is more competition). Sometimes there is an interesting policy twist to this opportunity for price discrimination; the government may sell the right to operate a service station on its highway by competitive bid. What it is doing, in effect, is extracting from the supplier the value of the profits that will be made from the price discrimination. The consumers suffer either way. Of course, these government arrangements are more likely to arise when the motorists are not voting residents of the jurisdiction and do not have attractive alternative routes.

Another group of commodities which are not easily resaleable are utilities: telephone, electricity, water, etc. Large industrial users of electricity, for example, may receive lower rates not because it is cheaper to serve them, but because they are able to use substitute sources of power and they have a more elastic demand. An interesting variant of this group might be the recipients of such local government goods and services as police and fire protection, which are paid for through taxes. The tax assessor may charge industrial users less (i.e., assess the property at a relatively low proportion of its true market value) not because they use less nor because it is a principle of just taxation, but simply because these users have more elastic demand for the services (i.e., are more likely to relocate elsewhere).

Ordinary durable goods are much easier to resell, so price discrimination is likely to be tied to something associated with the good. For example, in recent years some automobile manufacturers have offered interest rebates to consumers who finance their purchases through loans; this lowers the price for one segment of the market demand. Some very clever schemes for price discriminating and simultaneously obtaining the information about the consumer's demand curve have been concocted. Xerox copying machines, at one time, were leased rather than sold; that avoided the resale problem. Furthermore, the monthly charge was based on the number of copies made (far in excess of the actual marginal costs of the copies); and that allowed the company to extract more of the surplus from consumers with high willingness to pay. A similar result can be achieved with a tie-in sale if, as a condition of the lease, all copying paper must be bought from the same company. The Polaroid Corporation, when its cameras were novel, could effectively price-discriminate as the exclusive supplier of film for the cameras.[22]

In the discussion to this point we have assumed that the organization both seeks and is able to maximize its profits. We have illustrated that some of the insights about such a firm's behavior are derived from very simple changes in the constraints of the model: The ordinary predicted monopoly behavior follows from a change in the shape of the demand constraint the firm faces (from horizontal in the competitive case to downward-sloping in the monopoly case). This leads to the conclusion that monopoly is inefficient. However, the very concepts which are used to understand why firms exist also indicate that predicting actual behavior is more complex than the simple model suggests. If there were no information or transaction costs, all monopolists would be perfect price discriminators. The fact that they are not suggests that the organizational costs are nontrivial, and it is closer examination of them which helps explain some of the variations in monopoly behavior that we observe (e.g., the extent of price discrimination). By developing this understanding, we increase our capacity to design policies that account for the behavior. Now let us turn to another source of variation in organizational behavior: the objectives.

ALTERNATIVE MODELS OF ORGANIZATIONAL OBJECTIVES AND CAPABILITIES

In the preceding section we made the assumption that a firm's objective is to maximize profits. However, we did not include any discussion of why that should be. The simplest reason is that the firm is run in the interests of its owners. The owners are attempting to maximize their own budget constraints because that is what allows them to achieve the highest consumption and thus the highest utility levels. Therefore, the owners are best served by operating the firm in such a way as to maximize profits.

However, this simple reasoning ignores a number of fundamental points, which we discuss below: (1) Because of information and transaction costs, the owners of a firm may not be able to exert perfect control over the behavior of its managers and other employees. Thus the firm's behavior may be influenced by the objectives of this latter group. (2) The owners of a firm may receive utility directly from operating the firm rather than purely from the dollar profit

---

[22] Tie-in sales may be prevented under Section 3 of the 1914 Clayton Act. For example, IBM once required those using its key-punch and card-sorting equipment to purchase IBM cards. However, the Supreme Court in 1936, ruled this a violation of Section 3.

derived from it (e.g., pride in being the first with a new product). If that is so, the owners may seek to operate the firm in a way which trades off dollar profits for the activities that give them utility directly. (3) Because of organizational bounded rationality, which includes the limits of individual information-processing abilities as well as the information and transaction costs of communicating and coordinating within a firm, the actions of a firm may not be those required for profit maximization even if every participant in the firm strives for it.

Few students of organizations doubt the validity of this complexity of motivations and capabilities. The crux of the controversy within the economics profession over the acceptability of the profit maximization assumption concerns the range and accuracy of the predictions that can be made with it (compared with alternative models). The most powerful argument in its favor appears to be that it generates good predictions for firms in a competitive environment. The best explanation for why it makes good predictions is that the survival of a firm in that environment requires that the firm make decisions consistent with profit maximization.

However, many producing organizations are not in very competitive environments and therefore may have considerable degrees of freedom in making choices which allow them to survive. Thus, at a minimum, discussion of organizational intentions and capabilities enhances analytic skill in predicting behavior in these latter environments. We reinforce this in the next chapter with some examples of the behavior of nonprofit organizations and public bureaucracies.

Objectives Other than Profit Maximization

The first point made above which might cause behavior other than profit maximization has to do with the control of the organization. The control problem becomes significant in the larger firms, e.g., firms where there is separation between the owners (stockholders) and managers. Stockholders are often widely dispersed, and each may hold only a very small percent of the firm's total equity. This makes it difficult for stockholders to be knowledgeable about the firm's alternative strategies, to express their desires about the firm's direction, or to build a sufficient coalition of owners in order to exercise effective command over management.[23]

That is not to say that it cannot be done. Dissident stockholders have been known to wage battles with management in solicitation of proxies from all shareholders to elect members of the board of directors. Furthermore, stockholders do observe the results (profits) from the firm's decisions, if not the reasons underlying them. Even if a stockholder cannot use *voice* effectively,

---

[23] As a general reference on managerial control, see Oliver Williamson, *The Economics of Discretionary Behavior: Managerial Objectives in a Theory of the Firm* (Englewood Cliffs, N.J.: Prentice-Hall, Inc., 1964).

management will be pressured by too much *exit,* i.e., sale of stock by unhappy shareholders.[24] Exit puts downward pressure on the price of the stock, which makes it more difficult for management to raise new capital (e.g., from the issuance of additional stock) and easier for others to take over the company by purchasing stock.

Nevertheless, these mechanisms of stockholder control are imperfect at best, and it should not be surprising to find management's objectives receiving attention at the expense of some profit. When asked, management personnel readily admit to other goals: maximizing revenues, market share (percent of total industry output it provides), growth, and anything else that sounds reasonable. The logical impossibility of maximizing these variables simultaneously does not faze them.[25] A number of scholars have noted that managerial salaries tend to rise with the total revenues of the firm, and they have therefore suggested that revenue maximization may be the goal that best serves managerial interests. We illustrate the implications of this goal, as well as its inconsistency with the rival goal of profit maximization, for behavior of a firm facing a downward-sloping demand curve for its product.

In Figure 8-10a we assume a nondiscriminating monopolist is a revenue maximizer. If there were no profit constraint on its behavior, then it would increase quantity until $MR = 0$, shown as Q_R. This is clearly more output than the profit-maximizing monopolist would produce (shown as Q_Π). However, it is unrealistic to think that a private profit-making firm could not be held to some account by its stockholders. Therefore, we assume the firm maximizes revenue subject to earning at least some minimum amount of profit (greater than at Q_R but less than at Q_Π).

Under these conditions, it is still unambiguous that the firm will produce more output than the profit maximizer. At Q_Π the marginal revenue is still positive, so total revenue can be increased by expanding output. This will reduce profit from its maximum level, and the firm will travel as far down the marginal revenue curve as it can until profits are reduced to the constraint level. This will occur somewhere between Q_Π and Q_R, shown as $Q_{R\Pi}$ in the diagrams. The shaded area shows the total profits, which are equal to the constraint level.

Can we say anything about the allocative efficiency of the sales maximizer? As illustrated, the sales-maximizing monopolist is more efficient than the profit maximizer: The deadweight loss is smaller (*BAE* is less than *FCE*). However, perhaps the sales maximizer may produce too much output, i.e., a quantity greater than Q_E. With constant-returns-to-scale technology, this is not possi-

---

[24] The terms *exit* and *voice* were first used by Albert Hirschman. We will discuss them in a later chapter; the basic reference to them is Hirschman's *Exit, Voice, and Loyalty: Response to Decline in Firms, Organizations and States* (Cambridge, Mass.: Harvard University Press, 1970).

[25] This is demonstrated shortly. A common phrase which is also a logical impossibility is "getting the maximum output for the minimum cost." You can produce a *given* output at minimum cost or you can maximize output for a *given* cost, but you cannot maximize and minimize simultaneously. It is always possible, for example, to reduce costs by reducing output.

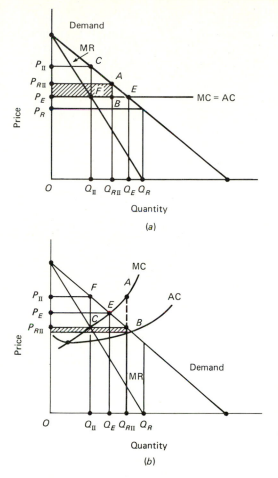

FIGURE 8-10
(a) Revenue maximization subject to the profit constraint of the constant returns to scale; (b) revenue maximization subject to the profit constraint of a natural monopoly. (The size of the shaded area equals the minimum profit requirement.)

ble: Profits are down to zero at Q_E, so the profit constraint keeps output less than Q_E. But in Figure 8-10b a natural monopoly case[26] is illustrated: The sales maximizer will produce too much output, and the deadweight loss EAB is greater than that of the profit maximizer CFE. Therefore, nothing in general can be said about the relative allocative efficiency of these two behaviors.

When we compare the equity of the two behaviors, it appears that consumers are better off if the monopolist is a sales maximizer. This happens because the sale of output levels greater than Q_{Π} requires that the price be lowered (from P_{Π}). Thus the total consumer surplus grows as quantity expands. The monopoly owners are being made worse off simultaneously, of course, but they are receiving economic profits in all cases.

---

[26] As drawn there are increasing returns to scale over virtually the whole range of output, which creates a barrier to the entry of a second firm.

Although managerial control may get exercised in ways other than the pursuit of sales maximization, any deviation from profit maximization should show up in reduced profitability of these firms compared to others. What evidence is there concerning variation in firm behavior under managerial versus owner control? The empirical evidence is somewhat mixed, although the bulk of it supports the idea that firm performance *is* affected by the degree of managerial control. Palmer, for example, finds that, among firms with significant monopoly power in the form of barriers to entry, those in which no single party owns more than 10 percent of the common stock have significantly lower profit rates (other things equal) than other firms.[27] Thus while the last word in terms of empirical research is hardly in, it does seem that the plausibility of other-than-profit-maximizing behavior should be taken seriously.

What relevance has this to public policy and its analysis? Let us suggest briefly three types of application. First and quite broadly, the antitrust laws of the nation—the Sherman Antitrust Act of 1908, the Clayton Act of 1914, and the Federal Trade Commission Act of 1914—are generally designed to promote competition and prevent monopoly and monopolistic practices. Considerable resources are spent every year by the government, and by firms, in the attempt to enforce these laws. In directing the enforcement efforts, it would seem sensible to allocate effort where it yields the greatest social return. By naively accepting one model of behavior when the empirical evidence is inconclusive, the enforcement efforts can be misdirected. Enforcement is not going to wait for analysis to become definitive, but it is sensible to recognize that the social returns from one area of enforcement may be more uncertain than those in another (because of uncertainty about actual firm behavior) and to allow this uncertainty to affect the priorities of different enforcement possibilities.

A second area of policy that may be affected by these behavioral considerations is taxation. Figure 8-11 illustrates this point with a simple partial equilibrium analysis of the effects of a profit tax on the firm's output level. As before, we let Q_Π and $Q_{R\Pi}$ denote the profit-maximizing and sales-maximizing (with profit constraint) output levels, respectively (pretax). Now we imagine imposing a percentage tax (e.g., 50 percent) on the firm's profit. The after-tax profits curve is shown as $\Pi_T(Q)$. The tax does not change the quantity at which profits are maximized, so the behavior of the profit-maximizing firm is not affected (important general equilibrium effects are mentioned below). However, the revenue maximizer is no longer meeting its profit constraint at $Q_{R\Pi}$,

---

[27] He reports a difference of about 3 percentage points on the rate of return on net worth (11.4 percent for management-controlled versus 14.6 percent for owner-controlled). He also includes a critique of earlier empirical studies. See J. Palmer, "The Profit-Performance Effects of the Separation of Ownership from Control in Large U.S. Corporations," *The Bell Journal of Economics and Management Science, 4*, No. 1, spring 1973, pp. 293–303. A more recent empirical test by Stano, using a somewhat different methodology and sample, reports the identical finding of a 3.2 percentage point difference in profitability. See M. Stano, "Monopoly Power, Ownership Control, and Corporate Performance," *The Bell Journal of Economics, 7*, No. 2, autumn 1976, pp. 672–679.

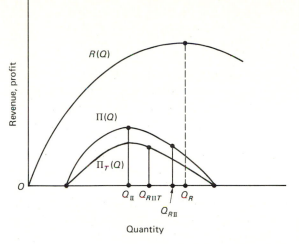

FIGURE 8-11
Firm response to a profits tax.

since net profits have been reduced by the tax. Therefore, it will cut back on the output level until net profits once again satisfy the constraint, shown as $Q_{R\Pi T}$.

This partial equilibrium analysis is not the end of the story about the effects of such a tax; it is only the beginning. In a general equilibrium model, we would, for example, consider investor reaction in terms of the supply of capital resources to the profit-maximizing firms. These investors might now prefer holding land to business equity and withdraw capital from the business sector. That, in turn, would raise the cost of capital to business, which would change cost curves and therefore choices of production techniques and levels. However, our purpose at this point is not to go into an in-depth analysis of taxation, but only to point out that the desirability of any particular tax policy can depend upon the firm's objectives.

These first two areas of policy relevance are potentially of great significance, but simple, pragmatic applications of how and when to use the behavioral uncertainty about firm objectives in analysis are not yet apparent. A third area is mentioned here because its practical significance for regulation can readily be identified. Some analysts have argued that the manager-controlled firm has greater incentive to misrepresent the firm's true economic performance to its stockholders (in the attempt to keep dissidence to a minimum and reduce the probability of takeover by others).[28] The owner-controlled firm has less incentive because the owners already know the truth and are less concerned (not unconcerned) about what others think.

A recent empirical test of this hypothesis lends some support to it.[29] The

---

[28] See M. Jensen and W. Meckling, "Theory of the Firm: Managerial Behavior, Agency Costs, and Ownership Structure," *Journal of Financial Economics,* October 1976, pp. 305–360.

[29] See G. Salamon and E. Smith, "Corporate Control and Managerial Misrepresentation of Firm Performance," *The Bell Journal of Economics, 10,* No. 1, spring 1979, pp. 319–328.

researchers examined the decisions of firms to implement accounting changes in the ways profits or losses are calculated. Often the motive is that the firm derives real economic benefits from the change, regardless of its control. But other changes, like the decision to report an "extraordinary" gain or loss, have more potential for hiding true performance. Assuming that the stock market as a whole ferrets out the truth, which then gets reflected in the stock price and thus the actual returns to investors, the researchers looked for patterns in the differences between the actual stock returns and the reported returns.[30]

In the years in which accounting policy changes were made, the researchers correlated the estimated real returns with the reported results. They found less correlation between the two measures in management-controlled firms compared with owner-controlled firms, which supported the hypothesis that the former are more likely to attempt to misrepresent the truth. The second test was to examine the timing of accounting policy changes. They found that management-controlled firms were more likely to institute such changes in years of below-average stock performance, whereas owner-controlled firms were just as likely to make them in good years as in bad. This also supports the hypothesis of information misrepresentation, since the probability of stockholder dissidence and takeover is higher in below-average years.

This evidence is limited and should be subjected to further investigation, but it does have relevance to the efforts of the Securities and Exchange Commission to ensure accuracy in the reporting of firm financial data. Not only does it tell the Commission where to look for likely abuses; it also offers guidance on how to sample the financial returns for more intensive scrutiny.

In the beginning of this section, three reasons why firms might deviate from profit maximization were offered. We have discussed the first, the exercise of managerial interests, primarily through the sales maximization hypothesis. The second reason, that owners may receive utility directly from operating the firm, can be applied to the exercise of managerial control as well; either group may perceive its self-interest as affected directly by the firm's actions.

For example, newspaper firms, which often operate in environments of imperfect competition, may use their market power not to create additional profits but instead to pursue journalistic goals (like allocating more resources to investigative reporting). To the extent that is true and corresponds with a positive externality (a better-informed citizenry), professional norms may serve as a countervailing power against the profit motive and in favor of efficient allocation.

Similarly, in the discussion of health care (Chapter 6), we suggested that prepaid health maintenance organizations (HMOs) may control the moral hazard problem better than the currently dominant fee-for-service arrangements. Under the latter arrangements both economic incentives and profes-

---

[30] For the stock market to price the security correctly, only some investors must be well informed. But to change management of the firm requires the support of a majority of the common stock votes.

sional norms push inefficiently for Cadillac-quality care, and the abuses tend to be in the form of unnecessary operations. Under the HMO systems, the economic incentives would be to conserve on health resources while the professional norms of doctors would still push toward high-quality care. If one gave no credence to the effect of professional norms on HMO operations (e.g., assume it acts like a profit maximizer), that in conjunction with consumer ignorance could lead to a system no better than the current one. The influence of these professional norms is an empirical question, but the point of the illustration is that the norms may affect firm behavior and may be relevant to public policy formation.

In these two examples the utility that individual members of the firm's team derive from adherence to and furtherance of professional norms may be a positive feature. But it is unlikely that private utility seeking within a firm would generally lead to benevolent outcomes. For example, managerial control of an ordinary firm may lead to the firm's using resources in a socially wasteful way. Just as the price-discriminating firm may waste resources in creating and maintaining price discrimination per se, so a managerial firm can (with market power) produce at greater than least cost in order to pay for various perquisites, more leisurely workdays, etc. This is sometimes referred to as *X-inefficiency*. That is the name given it by Leibenstein, who is credited with highlighting its possible importance.[31]

Some analysts believe that X-inefficiency is one of the most seriously underestimated harms from monopoly power. To see why, refer to Figure 8-12. Line *LAC* represents the least average cost of production. *OAC* represents the observed average cost of production, assumed higher because of management's use of monopoly power to purchase inputs which do not contribute to output but make working conditions more sybaritic.[32] The height of *OAC* compared with that of *LAC* is assumed limited by a "visibility" constraint: too much opulence in relation to output will not go unnoticed.[33] Management is assumed interested in choosing the quantity of observed average cost that maximizes the area of its excess benefits, and we assume that, without further constraint, the maximum would be at Q_{MG} with area $P_E CAB$.[34]

However, management is also assumed to be subject to a profit constraint as before. Since the owners receive no profit at Q_{MG}, this clearly does not meet

---

[31] See Harvey Leibenstein, *Beyond Economic Man* (Cambridge, Mass.: Harvard University Press, 1976).

[32] It should be pointed out that certain managerial perquisites, which some might consider sybaritic, may also be consistent with least-cost production. A corporate jet, for example, may actually produce returns in the form of profits from increased business greater than its costs. Thus, above we are referring only to the cost of inputs above those consistent with least-cost production.

[33] Without this constraint, management would simply go to the profit-maximizing solution and then convert part of the profits into perquisites.

[34] In some circumstances it is possible that the area could increase by continuing to expand output, even though this requires management to lower its excess benefit per unit. For that to happen, the marginal revenue must exceed the least average cost per unit. That is not the case as we have drawn it.

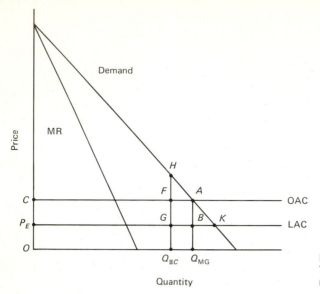

FIGURE 8-12
The social loss from excess-cost
monopoly.

the constraint. We assume that the profit-constrained managerial maximum is
at Q_{IIC} with managerial benefits area P_ECFG.[35]
   The actual social loss in this situation cannot be identified precisely. There
are two areas in the diagram which involve social losses. The first is the triangle
GHK, which has the usual interpretation of deadweight loss and can be
identified. The second is the rectangle P_ECFG, but only part of it is a loss. As
far as consumers and the firm owners are concerned, the use of these resources
in production contributes nothing and the full value equal to their opportunity
costs is lost. But this is offset to some unknown extent by the value of the
resources to the managers (in terms of willingness to pay for them from
personal, not corporate, budgets). For the fun of a crude calculation that we
will make shortly, let us assume that one-half the area is a social loss.
   Now let us consider what happens if one assumes that the observed average
costs are the least costs. Then one would incorrectly measure the deadweight
loss as triangle *HFA*. This is one of the criticisms made of empirical studies of
the harm from monopoly.[36] At least as drawn, it appears that this can be quite a
substantial error.

---

   [35] As in footnote 34 there are some circumstances in which management could increase its
profit-constrained maximum by lowering its per unit excess benefit and expanding output. The
conditions are identical with those in footnote 34 if marginal revenue exceeds the least average cost
per unit. Again, that is not the case as we have drawn it.
   [36] The best known of these heroic efforts is by A. Harberger, "Monopoly and Resource
Allocation," *The American Economic Review, 44,* May 1954, pp. 77–87. Harberger estimated that
the loss from monopolistic restrictions in 73 manufacturing industries from 1924 to 1928 was under
0.1 percent of total sales, a surprisingly low figure. Scherer, op. cit., chap. 17, criticizes the method
of analysis used and, on grounds *other* than those we are discussing above, makes a best-guess
estimate that 1.05 percent of GNP is the total deadweight loss.

To get a feel for the magnitude of the possible error, an illustrative calculation can be made. It is based on assumptions similar to those criticized in the actual studies. However, we simplify even further by treating the goods and services in the measured economy as if they were one product produced by a single, constant-returns-to-scale firm. This unrealistic simplification keeps the exercise simple; its true value is in demonstrating how actual estimates may be made with knowledge of a firm's revenues and elasticity of demand.

The 1979 GNP was approximately \$2.4 trillion. Since that includes almost all goods, we can reasonably assume the price elasticity of demand for the aggregate is -1. If we imagine GNP as the product being produced, the average monopolistic price distortion of the order of 10 percent and the aggregate technology as constant returns to scale, the loss L can be estimated by using the linear approximation

$$L = \tfrac{1}{2}\, \Delta P\, \Delta Q \qquad \text{or} \qquad L = \tfrac{1}{2}(HF)(FA)$$

The derivation that follows is particularly useful for empirical work because it allows L to be estimated with knowledge only of initial expenditures, the demand elasticity, and the price change. Since the price distortion α can be thought of as $\Delta P/P$,

$$\Delta P = \alpha P$$

From the elasticity definition,

$$\varepsilon = \frac{\Delta Q/Q}{\Delta P/P}$$

or

$$\varepsilon = \frac{\Delta Q/Q}{\alpha}$$

and using the absolute value[37] of ε we have

$$\Delta Q = \alpha |\varepsilon| Q$$

Therefore, on replacing ΔP and ΔQ with their equivalent expressions in the equation for L we have

$$
\begin{aligned}
L &= \tfrac{1}{2}\alpha^2 \varepsilon P Q \\
&= \tfrac{1}{2}(0.1^2)\ (1)(\$2.4 \text{ trillion}) \\
&= 0.005\ (\$2.4 \text{ trillion}) \\
&= \$12 \text{ billion}
\end{aligned}
$$

---

[37] The lines around the ε in the formula stand for absolute value.

As can be seen, this calculation leads to a loss estimate of 0.5 percent of GNP.[38] Now let us assume, alternatively, that the true waste arises from inefficient production of a comparable order of magnitude of 10 percent. Then for the triangular portion of the loss *GHK,* we approximate the price distortion as $2 \Delta P/P = 0.2$. Simply substituting this in the *L* formula gives us

$$L_T = \tfrac{1}{2}(0.2^2) \ (1)(\$2.4 \text{ trillion})$$
$$= \$48 \text{ billion}$$

or about 2 percent of GNP. But the major source of loss is from the rectangular portion P_ECFG. By using our assumption that only 50 percent of the area is loss L_R, we get

$$L_R = \tfrac{1}{2}(0.1)(\$2.4 \text{ trillion})$$
$$= \$120 \text{ billion}$$

Therefore, our crude calculation puts the social loss from monopoly power at $168 billion, or 7 percent of GNP—14 times as great as our initial misestimate of 0.5 percent.[39] Percentage variations of this magnitude could be expected as a consequence of using this range of assumptions when applied to any single monopoly.

Limited Maximization Capabilities

In discussing the first two reasons why firms might be expected to deviate from profit-maximizing behavior, we highlighted the difficulty of evaluating firm performance without knowing the behavior that leads to it. For example, observed firm costs may be least costs if firms maximize profits or sales, but the same observations can represent considerably more inefficiency if monopoly power is exercised on firm input selections. This makes the study of actual organizational behavior take on more importance if economic implications are to be drawn accurately. Among the researchers who have undertaken detailed studies of individual firms, there seems to be a near consensus that firm decisions are made primarily by rules of thumb rather than careful optimization calculations on the part of anyone.[40] That is, our third reason why firms might be expected to deviate from profit maximization is that, like individuals, they are boundedly rational.

[38] This is higher than the under 0.1 percent reported in the empirical studies but lower than the 1 percent that critics think more appropriate even when the least-cost assumptions are accepted.

[39] As an exercise, the reader may wish to redo this calculation by choosing the monopolistic distortion to make the initial misestimate be 0.1 or 1 percent of GNP and assuming the cost distortion is of similar magnitude. The revised social loss calculation should come out to approximately 2.6 percent of GNP on the low side and 11.1 percent on the high side.

[40] See, for example, R. Cyert and J. March, *A Behavioral Theory of the Firm* (Englewood Cliffs, N.J.: Prentice-Hall, Inc., 1963); W. Baumol and M. Stewart, "On the Behavioral Theory of the Firm," in R. Marris and A. Wood (eds.), *The Corporate Economy: Growth, Competition, and Innovation Potential* (Cambridge, Mass.: Harvard University Press, 1971), pp. 118–143; Oliver Williamson, *Markets and Hierarchies: Analysis and Antitrust Implications* (New York: The Free Press, 1975).

What does it mean to say that a firm is boundedly rational? It is certainly no insult if we recall the discussion of individual bounded rationality. It is simply a recognition that the circumstances in which decisions are made are more like those in chess than in tic-tac-toe. (The author, at least, has more admiration for the winning chess player than the winning tac-tac-toe player.)

Firm decisions are typically made under conditions of uncertainty. When a firm decides to expand and build a new plant which will take years to complete, it is guessing that the future demand for its products will be large enough to make the investment profitable (let alone optimal). In a world in which inflation might vary anywhere from 5 to 25 percent over the period, that is a considerable risk. A superior technology might become available if the firm delays two years, but then again it might not. Competitors may or may not engage in a similar undertaking. If there is enough certainty about the possible states of the world, the firm may be maximizing expected profit. But given all the choices about the size, location, and technology of the investment, the firm may be like the chess player encountering a new situation in which the actual response is the player's best attempt to muddle ahead.

Not only is the external environment of the firm characterized by uncertainty about future factor prices, technological advances, demand, and competition, but there can be considerable uncertainty internal to the firm because of the costliness of communication and coordination among the members. The sales department of the firm, which generally is paid in accordance with sales, naturally goes full speed ahead for sales maximization. When production cannot keep up with sales, the sales division has fits. Conflict arises over the issue, and the firm must decide whether to speed up production or slow down sales. It can be difficult to know which decision is right. As a way to reduce this uncertainty and avoid some conflict, the firm creates inventories.

Although holding inventory is costly, it is less costly than miscoordination and continual conflict among the firm's divisions. There may be an optimal level of inventory to hold, but it can be difficult to know what that is; and the people in charge of inventory control receive salaries in proportion to the average inventory. If the optimal average is consistent enough over time, other members of the firm may notice excessive inventory costs on their profit and loss statements. The inventory people may claim the fault lies with the firm's shipping department, not them. The firm may hire other people to check periodically on the inventory-level-setting procedures. Rules of thumb tend to develop, such as that inventory should be kept at a fixed percentage of last year's sales during the coming period. The rule of thumb may be close to what is optimal for the firm, but it may also simply represent conflict and uncertainty avoidance which allows the firm to satisfice.

Let us summarize the gist of this discussion. Not all the different members of the firm's team have the same goal. Those with the best information cannot always be counted upon to use it for firm profit maximization, which creates internal uncertainty and the need for costly communication and coordination to reduce it. That in turn creates standard rules of thumb, such as "inventory should be about 5 percent of last year's sales," to which the inventory control manager must justify making exceptions. Everyone tends to work by standard operating rules rather than global optimization calculations for the firm as a whole, and it is only if one part of the firm begins to stand out in some way that the firm initiates search procedures which may lead to a change in the routines. At least as far as the members of the firm are concerned, the firm's performance either satisfices or it does not. Firm profit maximization is too complex to be an operational goal for the firm to pursue. That most firms try to follow the rule that profits should be higher this year than last year, nobody denies.

What does this behavioral model imply about the firm's performance? Given an environment that permits the firm to survive under a broad range of behaviors, as firms with monopoly power have, the behavior is a product of the goals of each firm member and the various communicating, coordinating, and incentive devices that constrain each member's behavior. Presumably, power within the firm has something to do with how these constraints evolve. To the extent that firm members share an important goal such as those on a newspaper may share, the firm as a whole may be understood as acting primarily to further that goal. As a firm grows in size and the shared goals become only a minor portion of each member's goals, one might expect production costs to rise above least costs as in the managerially controlled firm.

But then the same boundedly rational large firm in another environment may behave exactly like the profit maximizer, its denials to the contrary. This is a key concept which is convenient to introduce here in a simple model of a behavioral firm. Let us assume that our behavioral firm follows a rule-of-thumb pricing strategy: It chooses the price that is simply a fixed percentage greater than its average costs. Practically all major firms claim to price that way. They are not sure what marginal revenues or marginal costs are anyway; and even if they did know the revenues and costs, they would not be sure about the location of the demand curve. The system of markup pricing is much simpler, and the firms seem satisfied with it.

Let us define the markup m as

$$m = \frac{P - AC}{P} \qquad 0 \le m < 1$$

It is written that way for convenience, and it is easy to see, by the rewriting, that it is a fixed percentage markup of average costs:

$$P = \frac{1}{1 - m} \, AC$$

How can such simplistic behavior be consistent with profit maximization? Recall that the marginal revenue always has this relation with the price and elasticity of demand:

$$MR = P\left(1 + \frac{1}{\varepsilon}\right)$$

Since the profit maximizer always equates MR = MC, we can substitute

$$MC = P\left(1 + \frac{1}{\varepsilon}\right)$$

or, rewriting,

$$P = \frac{MC}{1 + 1/\varepsilon}$$

If a firm has constant-returns-to-scale technology, *or* if it is operating at the minimum point of its average-cost curve, then MC = AC. When we make the substitution, the profit maximizer can be seen to have this price:

$$P = \frac{AC}{1 + 1/\varepsilon}$$

For this to be identical with that of our boundedly rational markup firm, all that is required is that

$$m = -\frac{1}{\varepsilon}$$

Let us try to summarize the substance of this result. Large firms are virtually unanimous in reporting a pricing procedure that is in the spirit of our markup model. However, every price, no matter how it is derived, will represent some percentage markup over average costs. A profit-maximizing firm with constant-returns-to-scale technology or at its average-cost minimum will have a markup that is the inverse of its demand elasticity: The more inelastic the demand, the greater the markup. How then do the markup firms determine the markups? Empirical observation generally confirms that the markups on the outputs of any single multiproduct firm do differ and do vary as the profit maximization hypothesis suggests: inversely with the product's demand elasticity.[41] The most likely explanation for this is that demand conditions do influence the markup and the profit maximization model can predict them, at least to some extent.

Let us conclude this section with a reminder about models and their purposes. Profit maximization as a model assumption is not the same thing as an assertion that firms have that motivation. Rather, it reflects the belief that, by using the assumption, certain aspects of firm behavior can be predicted accurately enough for the purpose at hand. What makes for enough can be determined only in comparison with alternative models.

The strongest argument for maintaining the profit maximization assumption

---

[41] See A. Kaplan, J. Dirham, and R. Lanzillotti, *Pricing in Big Business: A Case Approach* (Washington, D.C.: The Brookings Institution, 1958).

is that in many situations there do not appear to be alternative models that are "better." The complex behavioral models may be more accurate for individual firm decision making, but so far their construction seems to require a tremendous amount of analytic effort for each occasion. And not every problem requires understanding the response of a specific firm as opposed to the industry as a whole. In this chapter we have reviewed the behavior of firms in an environment in which profit maximization is generally thought weakest, the noncompetitive environment. All the alternative models we have reviewed are included because they may be the best models for particular analytic purposes.

SUMMARY

In this chapter we examine the use of microeconomic models as aids to understanding the behavior of private, profit-making supply organizations. All the models are constructed by assumptions about the objectives of the organization, its capabilities, and its environmental constraints. We emphasize alternative assumptions about objectives and capabilities and leave the determinants of environmental constraints (those external to the organization) for later chapters. Because some environments may be very constraining on the firm's behavior (e.g., a perfectly competitive environment), most of the discussion assumes the organizations are in settings which allow discretionary behavior: private firms with some degree of monopoly power.

The discussion begins by calling attention to the obvious differences in the way demand and supply are organized in our economic system. Individuals typically bring their demands directly to the marketplace, whereas they give their supply resources to intermediary organizations, known as firms, that, in turn, produce and bring finished goods to the marketplace. *This voluntary centralization of decision making (from the individual to the firm) occurs primarily because of economies of scale in handling uncertainty, information, and transaction costs.* Understanding that is fundamental to public policy questions which involve the design or evaluation of economic organization. Examples are offered throughout the chapter, but many more implications of the importance of these phenomena will become apparent in later chapters.

The first model of the firm we review is the standard one: an organization which seeks to maximize profits and has capabilities which allow it to do so. Two principal implications of the model are that the firm will equate its marginal revenue to its marginal cost and will use resources in production efficiently. However, given some degree of monopoly power, the assumptions are not enough to derive an empirical prediction of the firm's behavior.

The example we use to illustrate this is *price discrimination*. Analytically, we define price discrimination as charging, for similar units of a good, prices that vary disproportionately to the marginal costs of supplying the units. This practice can have large effects on the firm's output choice and the prices its consumers face. *Whether it occurs, however, depends on the information costs of finding which consumers have differing elasticities of demand and the transaction costs of segregating the consumers and preventing resales among them.* To the extent that the firm chooses to price-discriminate and incurs costs to do so, this invalidates the implication of production efficiency. It remains true that the firm equates marginal revenues and marginal costs, although these functions are different from those in the nondiscriminatory regime.

The efficiency and equity consequences of price discrimination depend upon the specific circumstances. Except for the empirically unlikely case of perfect and costless price discrimination (in which the firm captures the entire consumer surplus), price discrimination is unlikely to result in efficient allocations. However, the more relevant question is whether price discrimination improves the outcome from what it would be otherwise. It may often do so in the case of goods and services the production levels of which would be in the range of increasing returns to scale; these outputs might not be produced at all without price discrimination.

The Robinson-Patman Act of 1936 forbids price discrimination for "goods of like grade and quality" when the effects may be to "lessen competition." However, the Act is easily evaded even if the behavior reduces competition. The law requires that a price *difference* exist to trigger scrutiny by Robinson-Patman; a firm may discriminate, for example, by charging the same price to two different customers even though the shipping costs to each (included in the price) vary substantially. Similarly, a firm can segment its market by producing similar goods of different quality levels and charging a price disproportionately higher than marginal cost in the market segment with more inelastic demand. Finally, a firm which is not price discriminating in the analytic sense may be found in violation of Robinson-Patman; e.g., it may charge one customer less than another because of cost differences in filling the orders but be unable to document the source of cost savings specifically enough to satisfy a court.

Information and transaction costs also explain why some analysts think firms might have the objective of sales maximization rather than profit maximization. Once the decision-making unit is a team rather than an individual, the goal that the team as a whole pursues can be unclear. The different team members have different individual interests (e.g., the income each derives from the firm), and there is no particular reason why being on the same team must lead to harmony (as on a basketball team perhaps) as opposed to the lack of it (traditional antagonism between management and labor).

The attempt of some team members to control others explains much about the incentive systems set up within firms (e.g., management bonuses as a function of firm profits). The power relations that determine who creates incentives for whom are an additional factor. Those with claim to the economic profit of the firm usually have the legal power to control the firm's contracts. (Usually they are the suppliers of capital in the United States, but that need not be so. In countries like Yugoslavia the labor-owned firm is common.) The sales maximization hypothesis arises from the idea that many dispersed owners (common stockholders) cannot effectively control management because of the high information and transaction costs that would be involved. Thus, much of the power of ownership gets effectively delegated to management, which runs the firm in its own interests. Since managerial salaries are observed to correlate with the size of a firm, size (total revenue) maximization (subject to a profit constraint) becomes the goal.

A closely related hypothesis is that the firm will maximize some weighted average of the utilities of its members. This is a more general version of sales maximization: The same problems of controlling firm members are assumed to exist, but the objectives of each member are thought of more broadly than sales. In particular, each member may wish the firm to purchase inputs which make his or her own job more enjoyable, which leads to inefficient use of resources in production. Owners may view the firm as their personal toy with which to play; managers may seek various perquisites such as oversized offices; and workers may seek more on-the-job "leisure." The waste of resources in this manner is known as *X-inefficiency.*

Sometimes the pursuit of utility through a firm can lead to social benefits rather than social costs. That is the case when journalistic norms correlate with positive information externalities from newspaper reporting, doctors place a patient's interest above that of the medical firm's profits, and day care centers are run with staffs who have the childrens' interests in mind more than the firm's profits.

The problem of organizational control, arising from information and transactional costs, may also be thought of as causing *bounded rationality of firms.* This can explain why a firm may pursue no single goal or even a consistent goal. It also explains why the firm may not be capable of achieving a certain goal even if all the members agree on it. Because it may be difficult for the "left arm" of a firm to coordinate, communicate with, or control the "right arm," the total result may at best be satisficing rather than optimizing.

Before one gets carried away with all the possibilities for understanding and predicting a firm's behavior, it is good to remember that *remarkably simple models sometimes do very well at explaining complex behavior.* Assuming markup pricing behavior of a boundedly rational firm is the "truth," we demonstrated that behavior may be perfectly consistent with what is predicted by profit maximization. The reason is that the firm's environment may be constraining enough that its survival depends upon taking actions like those a profit maximizer would take. Thus another analytic avenue, which we explore in later chapters, is to model the environments of firms rather than the firms themselves. However, the array of behavioral possibilities should be kept in mind when the environment is not so constraining.

EXERCISE

8-1[42] Suppose that daily airline service between two cities can be provided by only one of two types of airplane. Type 1 has a seat capacity of 80 passengers and costs

---

[42] This problem was motivated by an example given in an article by Robert Frank, "When Are Price Differentials Discriminatory," *Journal of Policy Analysis and Management, 2,* No. 2, winter 1983, pp. 238–255.

$3600 for each one-way trip. Type 2 is larger, with a capacity of 110 passengers, and costs $3900 for each one-way trip.

The demand for air travel between the two cities has two components: business and leisure travel. There are 75 business travelers whose demand for daily trips, for our purposes, is perfectly inelastic. (They will fly at the lowest price available to them, no matter how high it is.) Leisure travelers are price-sensitive and have a demand curve

$$Q_L = 50 - P$$

Note: After answering the questions below, you may wish to use the example to think about the desirability of airline deregulation.

a Calculate the average cost of providing service to 80 passengers and to 110 passengers. What is the marginal cost per passenger of the increase in service from 80 to 110 passengers? Would you say that the technology in this range is one of increasing, decreasing, or constant returns? (Answer: Increasing)

b Any firm which wishes to enter this market can do so with no special entry costs (e.g., airlines can shift planes now used on other routes to this route). This means that any firm actually providing service in this market must have zero economic profit. (Otherwise, another firm could enter and undersell it.) If a uniform price is charged per passenger, what will it be, what plane will be used, and how many passengers will travel? (Answer: Type 1)

c How much are the social benefits associated with trips 81 to 110? The social costs? On social efficiency grounds, should these trips be provided? (Answer: Yes)

d Suppose firms did not have to charge a uniform price and could charge a different price to each of the two groups (business and leisure travelers). Given entry conditions as in part (b), could a firm enter the market, offer each group of passengers a better deal than they have in part (b), and still break even? Illustrate with an example. Would this be more efficient? (Answer: This is feasible, and it would be more efficient.)

e▽The threat of competition (through entry) does not lead to a unique fare structure. For example, here are two possible outcomes which cannot be beaten by new entrants: (1) Use type 1 plane; charge 75 business travelers $48.00 per trip; and let 5 leisure travelers fly for free. (2) Use type 2 plane; charge business travelers $46.00; and let 35 leisure travelers fly for $12.86. Neither of these is an efficient outcome. Other outcomes are possible, where the price to business travelers can decline to a minimum of $43.67 (and the corresponding price to leisure travelers is higher than that in the above examples). Can you identify the range of fare structures which are possible market outcomes?

f▽Of the range of possible market outcomes, there is only one fare structure which leads to an efficient solution. The other structures either involve wasteful excess capacity or are characterized by excess demand for leisure travel which causes exchange inefficiency. What is the efficient fare structure? (Answer: Business price = $45.00)

CHAPTER **9**

PUBLIC AND NONPROFIT ORGANIZATIONS: OBJECTIVES, CAPABILITIES, AND POLICY IMPLICATIONS

Much of public policy and its analysis concerns, quite naturally, the organizations which receive government funds. These organizations are often private but not for profit; examples are some hospitals, nursing homes, foster care agencies, and educational institutions. They also include public-service-providing bureaus or enterprises such as fire and police departments, mass transit systems, and highway departments. The general growth in government expenditures that we reviewed in Chapter 1 correlates with increased control over resources by these agencies. In this chapter we consider how analysis may be used to predict the behavior of public and nonprofit agencies and link the behavior to its efficiency consequences.

The type of analysis presented here relies on microeconomic models similar to those of the firm, but work of this kind is still in its infancy. In particular, the models developed have not yet been subjected to thorough empirical testing. Without the testing, confidence in the accuracy of predictions by the models must be severely limited. One should not expect to leap to convincing policy recommendations by use of them, although occasionally alternative models will point toward the same policy conclusion.

Nevertheless, the process of refining the models in light of empirical testing is probably one of the more important tasks for policy research. Normative analyses about how public and nonprofit agencies *should* behave have been

334

much more common than studies of how the agencies *actually do* behave and the reasons for the actual behavior. Unless the actual behavior is serendipitous, the normative recommendations are not likely to have much impact. That is, to induce desired changes in actual behavior requires understanding the political, economic, and organizational forces which determine an agency's objectives, perceived production possibilities, and incentives for making particular choices.[1]

For example, suppose as a policy matter that we are concerned about growing Medicare and Medicaid expenditures. Furthermore, we might learn that hospital services are produced inefficiently; e.g., too many physician inputs are used relative to nonphysican inputs in providing the necessary treatments. If hospital administrators are made aware of this and are motivated to reduce hospital costs and have the power to do so, they will respond in the appropriate way. But if hospitals are controlled by physicians who use them to maximize their own incomes, the findings of production inefficiency will fall on deaf ears. To induce more efficient delivery of hospital services, analysts must understand not only what is inefficient about the services, but why the hospital selects the procedures it uses.

A better understanding of actual agency behavior can have substantial implications for public policy. Services can be delivered through alternative types of agencies, e.g., public, nonprofit, or private profit-making organizations. Our expectations about the efficiency of each type should influence the choice. Or it may be possible to make great improvements in the efficiency of the public and not-for-profit sectors by restructuring the environments (i.e., externally determined incentives) in which they operate.

For example, suppose we find that one public agency currently produces less efficiently than a comparable private agency, as when elementary education is provided by both types of organization. This does not imply that such relative performance is inherent. It may be that we have created an incentive system for the public agency which unnecessarily causes inefficiency; an example could be mandatory enrollment by geographic location of the child's residence, which gives each neighborhood school a captive audience. Through the analysis of organizational behavior we may learn to improve organizational performance.

The models presented in this chapter, like those of the preceding chapter, focus on the objectives and capabilities of the producer agency (rather than the determinants of the agency's environment). We show how one can deduce contradictory and empirically testable implications from alternative models of the same agency. It is through careful empirical analysis of those predictions that we learn which models are more accurate. Empirical testing also reveals

---

[1] Normative conclusions may also depend on recognition of these forces. For example, political constraints of democratic decision making may cause an inefficient allocation of one good, but the inefficiency may be a small cost relative to larger benefits in terms of the maintenance of democracy.

areas in which no model makes good predictions and points the way toward the construction of new models to remedy the deficiencies. It is through the process of continual model improvement that we begin to understand how agencies in fact behave and why they behave that way, and we begin to develop predictive ability about how they will respond to proposed policy changes.

We also demonstrate how one can use models for normative purposes. Consider how public and nonprofit agencies ought to set prices for their services, since that will determine service allocation. Public and nonprofit agencies may be subject to constraints which prevent them from achieving efficient allocations. For example, we saw in the preceding chapter that organizations which produce in the region of increasing returns to scale may be unable to recover their costs. Public enterprises are often in this situation and receive costly subsidies from government sources to supplement revenues raised from the users of the services provided. We will present models which show how to identify the most efficient allocations for enterprises subject to subsidy constraints and the prices that they ought to set in order to achieve these allocations.

The chapter begins with an analysis of nonprofit hospitals. We review the construction of three different models of hospital behavior. In the first two we focus on the objectives of the hospital; in the third we concentrate on the hospital's capabilities. We show how comparison of the models reveals contradictory predictions which can be examined through empirical research. We also illustrate how the models can be linked to policy implications by using the proposed Hospital Cost Containment Act of 1977 as an example.

After reviewing the analyses of nonprofit hospitals, we turn to models of public bureaus and public enterprises. We review the model of a budget-maximizing bureau. Then we consider an empirical test. The model is used to predict the pricing decisions of a public enterprise responsible for rail mass transit services in an urban area. The predictions are compared with those from two alternative models which emphasize the importance of external political influences; then all the predictions are compared with the actual pricing decisions.

Finally, we consider a normative model for the pricing of rail mass transit services. Given a passenger capacity constraint and a subsidy constraint, we derive the prices which will lead to the most efficient feasible allocation of the transit services. The pricing solution when there are subsidy constraints is referred to generally as *Ramsey optimal pricing,* and it has important implications in other policy areas, notably optimal taxation. The mathematical derivation of the Ramsey solution is contained in an optional section.

NONPROFIT ORGANIZATIONS: MODELS OF HOSPITAL RESOURCE ALLOCATION

The nonprofit (and nongovernmental) sector of the economy consists of a wide variety of organizations: charitable, educational, scientific and community service agencies, and associations like labor unions, lobby groups, and organized religions. The most general definition of a nonprofit organization is one which is barred by law from distributing profits to the individuals that control the organization. Public policies affect the formation, size, and performance of these organizations. For example, the nonprofit agency is generally exempt from federal (and usually other governmental) taxes.[2] Furthermore, many nonprofit organizations—the performing arts, for example, or hospitals— are heavily dependent on governmental subsidies. Government regulations often constrain the use of nonprofit resources; e.g., a university's eligibility for federal subsidies depends on maintaining an appropriate affirmative action hiring program.

Our interest is in nonprofit agencies which are substantially involved in service provision or production; i.e., we are focusing on schools, hospitals, and day care agencies rather than charitable foundations or trade associations. We wish to understand such matters as how effectively they use public funds and how to improve their effectiveness. But then we must understand something about their behavior and the motivations which explain the behavior. If the motivation for their existence is not profit, then what objectives guide their decision making?

Before turning to analysis of this issue, it may be helpful to point out several dimensions of the size of the nonprofit sector. One recent paper reports an estimate that nonprofits employ just over 5 percent of all workers employed in the United States.[3] It also reports that the sector accounts for 3 to 5 percent of the GNP, or roughly $79 to $131 billion in 1980. To some extent, these figures are underestimates of the real resources used by nonprofits in their productive activities. For example, they do not include volunteer labor (which is often a substantial part of a nonprofit organization's workforce) or other donated resources. Nor do they include most physician inputs to hospitals, because physicians usually bill patients directly rather than through the hospital. Thus, by any measure, the nonprofit sector uses a significant amount of the nation's resources in the production of its various goods and services.

The nonprofit sector has only recently begun to receive attention from analysts. One area of nonprofit activity which has been the subject of several modeling efforts concerns hospital behavior.[4] Approximately 73 percent of all expenditures on hospitals goes to those which are nonprofit.[5] Given the large

---

[2] One type of exception affects nonprofit agencies which participate in partisan political lobbying; they do not qualify for federal tax exemption.

[3] See Christopher D. Stone, "Large Organizations and the Law at the Pass: Toward a General Theory of Compliance Strategy," *Wisconsin Law Review, 1981*, No. 5, pp. 861–890.

[4] There are some other areas in which interesting work has been done. In Chapter 15, we discuss nonprofit day care centers. Other examples of work on nonprofits are B. Weisbrod, J. Handler, and N. Komesar, *Public Interest Law: An Economic and Institutional Analysis* (Berkeley, Calif.: University of California Press, 1978), and H. Hansmann, "Non-profit Enterprise in the Performing Arts," *The Bell Journal of Economics, 12*, No. 2, autumn 1981, pp. 341–361.

[5] This estimate is cited in B. Weisbrod, *The Voluntary Nonprofit Sector* (Lexington, Mass.: D. C. Heath and Co., 1977), p. 87.

federal role in the financing of growing national health expenditures, it is not surprising that this area has attracted some attention.[6]

Below we review some of the theoretical models proposed by analysts as predictors of nonprofit hospital behavior. In the first two we focus on the objectives of the hospital; in the third we concentrate on the hospital's capabilities. We illustrate some of the contradictory and testable implications of these models, as well as their bearing on some issues of policy with respect to hospitals.

One of the earliest economic models of a nonprofit hospital was constructed by Newhouse,[7] who reasoned that hospital decisions are made by its administrator in consultation with the staff. The principal decisions involve the quantity and quality of medical services to be provided.[8] The administrator prefers more quantity to less because that enhances his or her own sphere of responsibility. Furthermore, higher quality is preferred to lower quality because of the prestige it wins for the hospital. Therefore, we can assume that the hospital is trying to maximize an objective function that consists of both quantity and quality of the outputs. This part of the model substitutes for the profit maximization assumption in the standard firm model.

The model also has these familiar constraints: demand, assumed to be downward-sloping (thus the hospital has some monopoly power), and technological possibilities with their associated costs. The remaining constraints follow from the nonprofit status: The hospital is not allowed to make a profit; and if it is to cover its costs, it must charge price equal to average cost.

Two implications of this model can be derived easily. First, the hospital will use inputs efficiently: For any given quality level, the hospital maximizes its objective function by producing the maximum quantity possible given demand. Or, put differently, it will produce any quality-quantity combination at least cost. (Otherwise, it could achieve a higher level of its objective function.) Second, the hospital will not provide all the services that are efficient to provide; it will be biased against "economy" care.

To see this, let us refer to Figure 9-1a. Each of the average-cost curves drawn is associated with a different quality level: The higher the cost curve, the higher the quality. Also, the higher the quality, the more will be demanded of it at any given price; thus the demand curves shift upward and to the right as quality increases. The zero-profit quantity for each quality is shown by the intersection of the demand curve with the average-cost curve (assuming no price discrimination). Presumably, there is some range of quality over which the break-even quantity increases, as in the movement from AC_1 to AC_2.

[6] In 1979, for example, federal health expenditures were $68 billion and equaled 28 percent of national health expenditures. Hospital costs are the largest component of health care costs. See *The Budget of the United States Government*, fiscal year 1981, pp.242–243.

[7] See Joseph P. Newhouse, "Toward a Theory of Nonprofit Institutions: An Economic Model of a Hospital," *The American Economic Review, 60*, No. 1, March 1970, pp. 64–74.

[8] For simplicity, think of the quantity of care as patient-days and the quality of care as the type of room, e.g., a ward, semiprivate room, or private room.

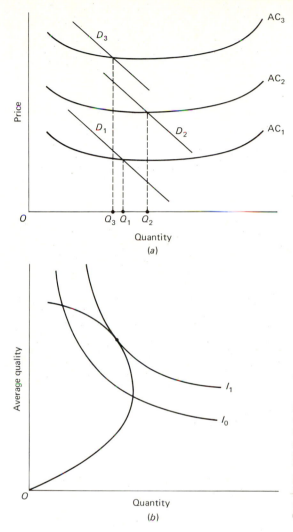

FIGURE 9-1
(a) Quality-variable hospital services;
(b) the hospital quality-quantity trade-off. (Both drawings are similar to those presented by Joseph P. Newhouse, "Toward a Theory of Nonprofit Institutions: An Economic Model of a Hospital," *The American Economic Review, 60,* No. 1, March 1970, p. 68.)

However, past some quality level, demand begins to taper off and the break-even quantity starts to decrease, as in the movement from AC_2 to AC_3.

The hospital can, of course, produce several different quality levels in response to demand. Let us think of aggregate quantity as the sum, in terms of a constant unit (e.g., patient-days), of the quantities associated with the quality levels produced. Then the administrator perceives a quantity-quality frontier that is backward-bending, as shown in Figure 9-1b. If we draw in the indifference curves from the hospital's objective function—the combinations of average quality and quantity which produce the same satisfaction to the hospital—it is clear that, to maximize satisfaction, the administrator will choose the point on the frontier that is tangent to the indifference curve. Thus the hospital is productively efficient.

The second implication is that the nonprofit hospital will be biased against economy care. Efficient resource allocation requires that *all* qualities be produced up to the point at which the willingness to pay for a marginal unit just equals its marginal cost. But consider the hospital's perspective on this. Imagine an individual who is willing to pay the marginal cost of an additional unit of economy care. This expands quantity, which is a plus for the hospital, but it reduces the average quality. At some point along the quality spectrum, the hospital will not consider the unit quantity increase worth the cost in average quality reduction. Thus, some hospital care that can be provided efficiently will not be provided, and the foregone hospital care will be restricted to the lower quality ranges. This latter implication is important because it predicts a difference in the behavior of a nonprofit hospital relative to a profit-maximizing one. The latter would produce all qualities, including lower ones, as long as they were profitable. Thus, there is some opportunity to test the model empirically.

Newhouse cites some evidence that the predicted quality bias is consistent with reality. For example, he points out that the nonprofit hospitals are much more likely than the proprietary hospitals to be accredited.[9] He also suggests that the tax laws favoring nonprofits and philanthropic contributions serve as barriers to the entry of proprietary firms which might attempt to fill the service gap. If the nonprofit is allowed to run a deficit (made up by philanthropic contributions), it simply will provide greater quantity at each quality level, charge price below average cost, and shift its quality-quantity frontier outward to the right. This puts the nonsubsidized profit-making hospital at a disadvantage.

A different model of the hospital has been proposed by Pauly and Redisch,[10] who argue that hospital administrators are primarily figureheads and that real control over the hospital's decision making is in the hands of the staff physicians. Furthermore, staff physicians have the same economic motives as other people, and they will therefore operate the hospital in order to maximize their own net incomes.[11]

In Figure 9-2 we illustrate the physician staff size which maximizes the net income per physician. It is assumed that the hospital faces a downward-sloping demand curve and can purchase nonphysician inputs at given prices. Physicians divide up whatever is left over from the total revenues after paying for

[9] 62 percent of all short-term hospitals listed with the American Hospital Association in 1965 were accredited, but only 34 percent of the proprietary hospitals were accredited. See Newhouse, op. cit., pp. 69, 70.

[10] M. Pauly and M. Redisch, "The Not-for-Profit Hospital as a Physician's Cooperative," *The American Economic Review, 63,* No. 1, March 1973, pp. 87–99.

[11] An important general insight that follows from this reasoning is that nonprofit organizations, which most of us associate with benevolent undertakings, do not have to behave in an altruistic fashion. Although specific institutions with long histories of service may continue to operate in their customary manner, policy changes designed to encourage formation of new nonprofits may not elicit solely altruistic responses.

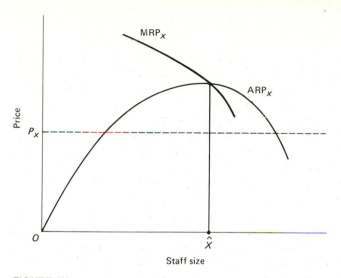

FIGURE 9-2
The hospital as a physicians' cooperative. (From M. Pauly and
M. Redisch, "The Not-for-Profit Hospital as a Physicians'
Cooperative," *The American Economic Review, 63,* No. 1, March
1973, p. 92, fig. 1.)

nonphysician inputs. For each possible physician staff size, there is an optimal
amount of nonphysician inputs to use. Each nonphysician input will be bought
until its marginal revenue product equals its cost.[12] Otherwise, the physicians
could increase the income pie by buying more (or less) of the nonphysician
inputs.

As physician staff size increases, presumably the hospital can take advantage of scale economies and elastic demand to increase average physician
income ARP_X up to some point. This depends, of course, on the supply of
physicians; it is assumed that, in an urban area, physicians have opportunity
costs of P_X and are plentiful from the hospital's perspective. That is, the
hospital can attract the number of physicians it wishes for any net income share
above or equal to P_X. Past the staff size shown as $\hat{X}$ on the horizontal axis,
average physician income begins to decrease. Thus, assuming the current staff
controls its own size, it will not allow that size to exceed $\hat{X}$.[13]

---

[12] The marginal revenue product of a factor is the change in marginal revenue caused by using
one more unit of that factor. The factor results in more output, and selling the additional output
results in marginal revenue. In formula, using capital to illustrate,

$$MRP_K = MR_Q \, MP_K^Q$$

[13] This is very similar to maximizing productivity, as explained in Chapter 7. It is also the way
one would expect a labor-owned firm like the firms common in Yugoslavia to behave. See, for
example, B. Ward, "The Firm in Illyria: Market Cyndicalism," *The American Economic Review,
48,* No. 4, September 1958, pp. 566–589.

Note that the output of this organization is *less* than that which the ordinary monopolist (who hired physicians at their opportunity costs) would produce. *Total* hospital income could be increased by expanding staff size—the marginal revenue product of another member must equal the average at its maximum, and therefore it exceeds P_X at that point. On the other hand, the administrator-controlled model predicts behavior to be more like a sales maximizer for a given demand curve; it will produce more than the ordinary monopolist. Thus the staff-controlled hospital will produce less output than the administrator-controlled one, at least as predicted by these models. Furthermore, the staff-controlled hospital is not producing at least cost: More output could be produced for the same cost by buying slightly fewer nonphysician inputs and using the released funds to add to the physician inputs. Thus, there are at least two predictions different from the Newhouse model. These examples of contradictory predictions are crucial to empirical testing of the two theories; it gives researchers an opportunity to find out if one theory predicts actual behavior better than another.[14]

A third and more recent model of the hospital has been proposed by Harris.[15] He argues that a hospital's behavior cannot be understood without more explicit consideration of the information and transaction costs of its operations—just as whether the monopolist will behave as a price discriminator cannot be understood without those considerations. In other words, Harris emphasizes the capabilities of the organization to produce, given the technical possibilities. He proceeds to the analysis and concludes that a hospital is really two firms in one: a physician firm and an administrator firm which are continually at war with one another.

Before explaining his reasoning, let us mention two implications of the analysis. First, the resolution of particular issues is often accomplished by letting the hospital get bigger and more complicated; this seems more like the size prediction of Newhouse than of Pauly-Redisch. Second, however, Harris predicts that policies like the Carter administration's proposed Hospital Cost Containment Act of 1977 will be ineffective. This policy is designed to put a

---

[14] A recent article indirectly provides some empirical evidence relevant to these models. The evidence suggests that the degree of physician control varies from hospital to hospital and does have effects consistent with the Pauly-Redisch model and possibly the Newhouse model. Hospitals which have greater physician control (measured by physician control over the Blue Shield insurance plan which reimburses the hospital) are found to have lower administrative costs, other things equal. Thus the "residual" (for given demand) to staff physicians is greater with greater physician control, as Pauly and Redisch predict.

If the Newhouse model is correct, the increased physician "profit" comes at the expense of valuable nonphysician inputs (administrative expenses which improve the quality of service from the patient's perspective, such as prompt checking out and checking in). However, if the administrative cost reductions do not lead to lower quality from the patient's perspective, the administrator-controlled hospital must not be behaving like Newhouse's "quantity-quality" maximizer. (There must be waste, such as unproductive managerial perquisites.) See D. Eisenstadt and T. Kennedy, "Control and Behavior of Non-profit Firms: the Case of Blue Shield," *Southern Economic Journal, 48,* No. 1, July 1981, pp. 26–36.

[15] Jeffrey E. Harris, "The Internal Organization of Hospitals: Some Economic Implications," *The Bell Journal of Economics, 8,* No. 2, autumn 1977, pp. 467–482.

limit on the annual increase in hospital expenditures. Harris points out the expenditures result primarily from the short-run decisions of doctors ordering various tests and treatments for all patients, and a hospital administrator "responsible" for overall expenditures has no power to overrule specific physician decisions.[16] Thus the Harris model is more like the Pauly-Redisch model in terms of recognizing the important role physicians play in the allocation of hospital resources.

The meat of the Harris model is not in the assumptions about the general objectives of the hospital decision makers; it is in Harris' explanation of why certain standard procedural routines for decision making arise in the hospital. The hosital is designed to solve a complicated decision problem: the diagnosis and treatment of illness. This requires an organization which can adapt rapidly to changing circumstances and new information. Suppose for each patient's current state of illness there is a minimal acceptable level of various medical inputs; above that minimum may be considered higher quality.[17] But exceeding the minimum is not of the same concern as failure to reach it. In a world in which many of these decisions have to be made almost instantly, the doctor is the only one qualified to decide the minimal level quickly enough. Then production in the hospital must be organized as if every input received by the patient were potentially an absolute necessity.

To ensure that the inputs are available at the physician's command, hospitals develop split organizations. On the supply side the administrator oversees the ancillary services such as the blood supply and the number of operating rooms. On the demand side the medical staff has responsibility for ordering the ancillary services for their patients. The process of caring for a patient can be seen as a series of demands and supply responses, or transactions, between the physician as patient agent and the suppliers of ancillary services.

Why does this split arise? The doctor must maintain considerable independence from the hospital in order to be free to act in the patient's best interest. But the doctor must also be closely linked to the supplies in order to make sure they are available when demanded. The solution is for the patient to have independent contracts with both physicians and hospital. The physicians and hospital administrators work out a set of rules and procedures for sharing the

---

[16] In almost all hospitals a patient receives two bills: one from the hospital and the other from the physician. A simple way to evade the intent of hospital expenditure regulations is to have the doctor's bill include more of the test and treatment charges; this reduces (on paper only) the "hospital" expenditures. Another reason why such regulations are unlikely to work is political; in the one proposed above, for example, the Carter Administration responded to employee pressure and exempted the wages of hospital employees. Since those wages are the bulk of what might really be controllable, the exemption emasculated the proposal. It never reached the floor of either house, but a new and perhaps tougher proposal was contained in the 1980 budget. For a review, see Henry Aaron, "The Domestic Budget," in Joseph Pechman (ed.), *Setting National Priorities: the 1980 Budget* (Washington, D.C.: The Brookings Institution, 1979), pp. 99–159, espec. pp. 106–112.

[17] Note that the patient's state of illness can change in a moment. Typically the patient does go through a number of states: initial diagnosis, treatment during an operation, post-operation recovery, etc.

hospital facilities and directing the internal resource allocations, which is like having two firms in one.

Why does this split arrangement encourage continual expansion of capacity? Each doctor always wants assurance that inputs are available for his or her patients. The hospital administrator won't add such new capital inputs as beds and test machinery unless the existing ones are in use up to capacity. But as the hospital approaches capacity, each doctor becomes more protective of his or her share of the inputs. Standard routines for giving priority—emergency requests for hospital services such as x-rays are filled before routine ones— break down as the doctors specify higher and higher proportions of requests as emergency, and it is virtually impossible to interfere with the doctor's spot judgment. The easiest way out is to add capacity. Once available, it will be utilized as doctors exercise their discretion in giving their patients the "best" care. That sets off the protective instincts of each doctor over the remaining capacity and continues the spiral of increasing capacity.

Regulations which attempt to limit hospital expenditures, like the proposed Cost Containment Act, can set off this kind of mad scramble for the resources. And the hospital administrator, who must enforce the regulations, cannot control the physicians who insist they need a series of x-rays right away. The result could be an *increase* in resources used per case and a "need" for new hospitals as all existing ones are used to capacity with fewer patients. More likely, the regulations will be evaded in one way or the other. In either event there is little reason, in the Harris model, to think that they would achieve their intended purpose.

This review of nonprofit hospital models is intended to illustrate how the logic of microeconomic analysis can be used to understand the behavior of producing organizations which do not operate in ordinary markets. The insights come from applying the basic determinants of organizational behavior— objectives, capabilities, and constraints—to the new setting. Although all of the models have some intuitive plausibility about them, the strength of the methodology is that the models are explicit and empirically testable, or falsifiable. If, by contrast, one simply interviewed hospital administrators and physicians, any story that sounded plausible might be accepted as the "truth." But how would one know there is any general truth unless the story is used to predict something successfully in a different situation? One also might not see the implications of the story for other situations or see that a simplification of complex reality (e.g., physician income maximization) can be useful for predictive purposes.

The range and accuracy of the above hospital models have not as yet been tested. Nevertheless, the few shreds of empirical evidence that we have suggest the models are better than no model (i.e., that hospital behavior is random). Furthermore, something is gained by going through the logic of the models in addition to deducing their implications. Perhaps it is best described as disciplined common sense. It is a way of achieving a heightened appreciation of how and why hospitals work as they do.

PUBLIC BUREAUS AND ENTERPRISES

The application of economic decision–making models to public producing agencies, like that of the nonprofit models, is in its infancy. The best known theory of the type is Niskanen's budget-maximizing bureau.[18] This model assumes that the motivations of upper-level bureaucrats are like those of the sales-maximizing private-firm managers. That is, the bigger the bureau's budget, the higher the salaries of its top-level bureaucrats. If bureaucrats are interested in maximizing their salaries and prestige, one way to do so is to maximize the budgets of their bureaus.

Niskanen makes the further assumption that the bureau has the power of perfect price discrimination, argued in a novel way. There is a "public" demand curve for the output of the bureau; the height of it at any point shows the maximum willingness to pay for that unit. The legislature, which decides on the budget level, is assumed to know this demand curve and therefore the public's maximum willingness to pay for any given output level. However, it is assumed that only the bureau knows the curves of least-cost production. Therefore, the legislature is at the mercy of the bureau: The legislature will be led to accept any budget as long as the area under the demand curve for the promised output quantity is no less than the cost. The bureau will find that output level where the maximum it can extract—the area under the demand curve—just equals the least total cost of production. In other words, the Niskanen model predicts behavior equivalent to that of the perfectly price-discriminating sales maximizer with a break-even constraint.

To see this, let us look at Figure 9-3. We have drawn a linear demand curve and a constant marginal cost curve for simplicity. The economically efficient output level is denoted by Q_E. Clearly, the bureau will produce more than Q_E if it receives a budget equal to the area under the demand curve. At Q_E there will be a surplus of budget over least total cost equal to the triangle P_EAB; the bureau can get a bigger budget by expanding output and still stay within the break-even constraint. Since the budget keeps increasing as output expands, the bureau will expand until it bumps into the break-even constraint. For the linear demand, constant-cost case, this will be exactly twice the efficient output level, shown as Q_M.[19]

The same kind of reservation can be expressed about this model as we expressed earlier by developing alternative models. We will simply summarize them here and then look at an application to the pricing decisions of a public

[18] William A. Niskanen, Jr., *Bureaucracy and Representative Government* (Chicago, Ill.: Aldine-Atherton, Inc., 1971).

[19] This is true only if the demand curve is still positive in the range of Q_M. Should the demand curve hit the axis before reaching the break-even point (empirically unlikely), the budget is at its absolute maximum there and the bureau would not expand output further. Rather, it would use the excess budgetary resources inefficiently, departing from the least-cost production.

To see that the break-even point at Q_M is twice Q_E, note that the loss ΔBCF from the additional units past Q_E must equal the surplus ΔP_EAB from the first Q_E units. With a linear demand curve, these are similar triangles for any $Q > Q_E$. To be equal in area, they must have $P_EB = BC$ or $OQ_E = \frac{1}{2}OQ_M$.

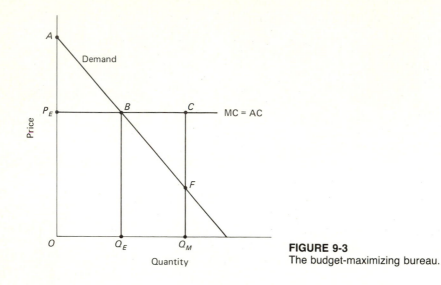

FIGURE 9-3
The budget-maximizing bureau.

enterprise. One type of reservation is that the underlying conception of self-interest which leads to the objective function is too much of a caricature of reality. Expressed in mild form, it can be argued that the bureaucrat might get more pleasure from inefficient production than from large budgets. That is, the bureaucrat might produce Q_E at a cost equal to the whole area under the demand curve, where bureaucratic benefits are garnered at the cost of excess resources $P_E AB$. That would result in the correct quantity being produced, but the consumer loss in each case is the same.[20]

The same reservation expressed in stronger form is simply that the utility that individuals receive is influenced much more strongly by social norms of "doing a good job," or "behaving professionally," or "being honest" than those simple proxies for utility like "salary" suggest.[21] That is, people for the most part behave in a socially responsible manner rather than an exploitative one because they receive more pleasure from living that way. This is not to deny that *some* people would try to exploit others maximally, and perhaps most people would engage in some selfish exploitation if they could get away with it. But social forces, in terms of families, schools, religion, etc., act as very powerful constraints against exploitative urges. The bureau might seek to

---

[20] BCF is the consumer loss in the Niskanen model, compared to producing the efficient quantity Q_E and pricing at marginal cost P_E. $P_E AB$ is the consumer loss in this one, because it measures the opportunity cost of the excess resources. The losses are equal, since the triangles are similar and have equal sides ($P_E B = BC$). The social loss is the consumer loss minus the value of bureaucratic gains.

[21] See, for example, the theory and empirical work of D. McFadden, "Revealed Preferences of a Government Bureaucracy, Parts I and II," *The Bell Journal of Economics*, 6, autumn 1976, pp. 401–416, and 7, spring 1977, pp. 52–72. McFadden concludes that the routing decisions of the California Division of Highways are primarily explained by their net social benefits.

produce much more closely to Q_E and to minimum cost than the Niskanen model suggests.[22]

A second type of reservation about this bureaucratic model concerns the nature of the legislative constraints. A good argument can be made that the legislature knows far more about the cost curves than it does about the location of the demand curves (in terms of the population's true willingness to pay for additional outputs). Generally, there is no market mechanism for goods supplied by the federal and state governments which causes demand to be revealed. The main sources of information about demand are elections, which express voter demand in a very crude aggregate manner, and special interest groups, which by definition represent special rather than general interests.

Records of expenditures and their purposes must be kept by the bureaus, and their procedures for making expenditures are constantly being examined. For example, most bureaus are required to obtain competitive bids from potential factor suppliers, and this bidding process is subject to regular scrutiny by watchdog agencies like the federal Office of Management and Budget (OMB) and the General Accounting Office (GAO). Again, this is not to suggest that oversight committees have as much knowledge about costs as the agency has. But the difference may be of no greater consequence than is the differential knowledge of inventory costs possessed by a firm's inventory specialist and the rest of the firm: One side knows more of the details, but the other side can tell if costs get too far out of line.

Some bureaus, such as public schools, are controlled more directly by local voters. Although state legislators generally do play an important role in the funding of the schools, localities provide almost half of the school revenues and their citizens determine the budget by voting. It could be argued, within the bureau budget maximization framework, that these voters are as ill-informed as the legislature is assumed to be about the least-cost production possibilities. If that is so, the bureau may be able to extract the surplus of the median voter (Chapter 4). On the other hand, the Tiebout model suggests that public producing organizations such as schools are subject to competition from neighboring localities, which may be another way in which the constraint on the organization deviates from the basic Niskanen model to limit the extraction of consumer surplus.

These latter reservations concerning the legislative and voter constraints do not involve alternative assumptions about the motivations or objectives of a bureau. Rather, in the extreme they suggest that the environment in which a bureau operates may be so constraining that the bureaucratic objectives

[22] Note that these forces are often ignored by economists without harm to predictions. That is because, for so many proposed economic changes, social forces are constant, i.e., they exert approximately the same influence with or without the economic change. It also occurs because economic constraints often limit discretionary behavior. In the Niskanen model, in which there are few external economic constraints on behavior and the prediction involves the desired equilibrium (rather than, say, the response to a price increase), it is more important to consider the other social forces.

become moot: The bureau must behave exactly as the legislature or the median voter wishes. In a less extreme version these reservations imply that there are constraints which limit the exercise of bureaucratic discretion substantially more than the Niskanen model suggests.

EMPIRICAL PREDICTION OF PUBLIC ENTERPRISE BEHAVIOR: THE PRICING DECISIONS OF BART

To demonstrate that the alternative theories of public supply organizations can be tested empirically, Cooter and Topakian analyzed the pricing decisions of a public enterprise.[23] They studied the Bay Area Rapid Transit District (BART), which operates the rail mass transit of the San Francisco Bay area. BART is subsidized by both federal grants and funds earmarked from local sales and property taxes; the rest of its costs must be covered by charging passengers fares, a break-even constraint.

Imagine a rail line with one end in the city center and the other in a distant suburb and with a number of stations for pickups and departures spread out along the way. BART must establish fares between all possible origin-destination pairs along the route. The question Cooter and Topakian consider is whether they can predict the fares that BART will set by using some of the theories we have discussed about decision making in public supply organizations. The predicted (or actual) fares in relation to trip costs reveal which passengers (by station) receive the greatest subsidies.

One hypothesis that they use to formulate fare prediction is the bureaucratic one: The fare structure chosen will be the one which maximizes bureaucratic interests, and those interests are best achieved by maximizing the size of the enterprise. They suggest two measures of size: farebox revenues and total passenger-miles. Given their estimates of the elasticity of demand, they calculate the fares which maximize each of the alternative size measures.

Cooter and Topakian note that BART has a nine-member board of directors elected by the voters in each of the nine subdistricts of BART. As an alternative to the bureaucratic view, they hypothesize that BART pricing decisions are effectively dictated by the political process. They suggest two versions of political control: (1) Subsidies will be distributed to maximize electoral votes, which implies maximizing the benefit of the median voter. (2) Subsidies will be distributed in accordance with the political power of various *interest groups*, whose identities are assumed to correlate with socioeconomic characteristics of the people in areas served by BART.

Because the actual Cooter and Topakian study is empirically quite complex, it may be useful to illustrate the different predictions of each model in a highly artificial but numerically simple setting. To do this, we use a setting similar to that we used for the price discrimination example in Chapter 8. We will assume

---

[23] R. Cooter and G. Topakian, "Political Economy of a Public Corporation: Pricing Objectives of BART," *Journal of Public Economics, 13,* No. 3, June 1980, pp. 299–318.

BART consumers may be separated into two groups (stations) with demand curves for passenger-miles as follows:

$$Q_1 = 10 - P_1 \quad \text{or} \quad P_1 = 10 - Q_1$$
$$Q_2 = 20 - P_2 \quad \text{or} \quad P_2 = 20 - Q_2$$

We also assume that the marginal cost per passenger-mile is constant and equal to $4, although BART incurred substantial initial costs to lay the track.

Let us first consider the two alternative bureaucratic objectives: farebox revenue maximization and passenger-mile maximization. If BART seeks to set prices which would maximize farebox revenues, it will, like a discriminating sales maximizer, identify the Q_1 with $MR_1 = 0$ and the Q_2 with $MR_2 = 0$. The marginal revenue curves for these demand curves (derived like those in Chapter 8) are

$$MR_1 = 10 - 2Q_1 = 0 \rightarrow Q_1 = 5$$
$$MR_2 = 20 - 2Q_2 = 0 \rightarrow Q_2 = 10$$

Then the prices charged are found by substituting in the demand curves:

$$5 = 10 - P_1 \rightarrow P_1 = \$5$$
$$10 = 20 - P_2 \rightarrow P_2 = \$10$$

Thus BART charges district 1 commuters $5 and district 2 commuters $10 and collects the maximum farebox revenues of $125 = $5(5) + $10(10).

The above objective is quite different from maximizing passenger-miles ($Q_1 + Q_2$). With unlimited government subsidy, BART would simply set $P_1 = P_2 = 0$, and then $Q_1 = 10$ and $Q_2 = 20$. However, BART may at least be required to cover its operating costs of $4 per passenger-mile. With that constraint, it can be shown that BART would (approximately) set $P_1 = \$1$ and $P_2 = \$6$, which would lead to $Q_1 = 9$, $Q_2 = 14$, and BART revenues of $93.[24]

---

[24] The solution equalizes the marginal revenue for an additional passenger-mile in each group. Otherwise, BART could get more total revenue for the same passenger-miles (and same operating costs). This would give it revenues above those required to meet the operating costs constraint, and it could subsidize additional passenger-miles.

Let us look at the problem in calculus form. In order to maximize $Q_1 + Q_2$ subject to the constraint, we form the Lagrangian expression

$$L = Q_1 + Q_2 + \lambda[P_1 Q_1 + P_2 Q_2 - 4(Q_1 + Q_2)]$$

Then the first-order conditions are

$$\frac{\partial L}{\partial Q_1} = 1 + \lambda\left(P_1 + Q_1 \frac{\partial P_1}{\partial Q_1} - 4\right) = 0 \tag{i}$$

$$\frac{\partial L}{\partial Q_2} = 1 + \lambda\left(P_2 + Q_2 \frac{\partial P_2}{\partial Q_2} - 4\right) = 0 \tag{ii}$$

$$\frac{\partial L}{\partial \lambda} = P_1 Q_1 + P_2 Q_2 - 4(Q_1 + Q_2) = 0 \tag{iii}$$

To understand how the political models would imply different solutions, suppose that the fares (P_1 and P_2) were determined by majority vote, that the number of voters equaled 10 in district 1 and 20 in district 2, and that the voters in each district represented the interests of their commuters. Of course, all voters could then agree to set $P_1 = P_2 = 0$ if there were no subsidy constraint (and the subsidy were provided by the federal government, not the taxpayers in each district!). But suppose BART had to cover its operating costs. That is, voters could approve any P_1 and P_2 as long as total revenues equaled total operating costs:

$$P_1Q_1 + P_2Q_2 = 4(Q_1 + Q_2)$$

Substituting $Q_1 = 10 - P_1$ and $Q_2 = 20 - P_2$, we rewrite this as

$$P_1(10 - P_1) + P_2(20 - P_2) = 4(10 - P_1 + 20 - P_2)$$

On simplifying, we have

$$10P_1 - P_1^2 + 20P_2 - P_2^2 = 120 - 4P_1 - 4P_2$$
or
$$14P_1 - P_1^2 + 24P_2 - P_2^2 = 120$$

This equation is the locus of all P_1 and P_2 combinations which satisfy the constraint. It is shown in Figure 9-4. Note that the equation applies only over the range of prices valid for the demand curves: $P_1 \leq \$10$ and $P_2 \leq \$20$. For $P_1 > \$10$, $Q_1 = 0$ and the constraint becomes $P_2Q_2 = 4Q_2$, or P_2 must equal the marginal cost of \$4. Similarly, for $P_2 > \$20$, $Q_2 = 0$ and P_1 must equal \$4. The fare combinations which satisfy the constraint are shown by the solid lines in Figure 9-4.

Naturally, the voters in district 1 prefer the lowest feasible P_1 (and therefore a relatively high P_2), and the voters in district 2 prefer the opposite. If possible, the voters in district 1 would prefer that $P_1 = 0$. This would imply that

$$24P_2 - P_2^2 = 120$$

This has the two solutions shown below with the associated output levels and BART revenues (equal to the operating costs):

$P_2 = \$16.90$	$Q_2 = 3.1$	$Q_1 = 10$	TR = \$52.39
$P_2 = \$7.10$	$Q_2 = 12.9$	$Q_1 = 10$	TR = \$91.59

We solve these equations simultaneously for Q_1, Q_2, and λ by substituting $P_1 = 10 - Q_1$ and $P_2 = 20 - Q_2$ and noting that $\partial P_1/\partial Q_1 = -1$ and $\partial P_2/\partial Q_2 = -1$. Q_1 is approximately 9.042, and Q_2 is approximately 14.042.

Note that the expressions in equations (i) and (ii) following the λ are simply MR minus MC. Since both these expressions equal $-1/\lambda$, they are equal to one another. And since MC = 4 in both cases, $MR_1 = MR_2$.

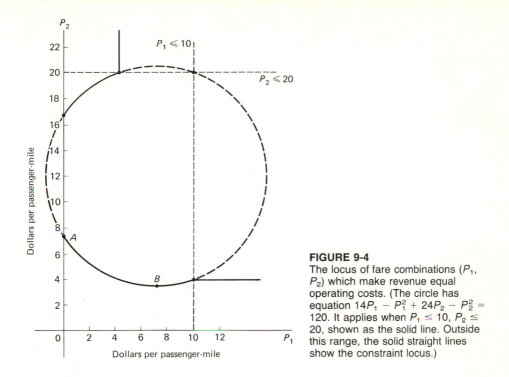

FIGURE 9-4
The locus of fare combinations (P_1, P_2) which make revenue equal operating costs. (The circle has equation $14P_1 - P_1^2 + 24P_2 - P_2^2 = 120$. It applies when $P_1 \leq 10$, $P_2 \leq 20$, shown as the solid line. Outside this range, the solid straight lines show the constraint locus.)

Obviously, of the two solutions district 2 would prefer $P_2 = \$7.10$ (as would BART management from the perspective of either revenues or passenger-miles). District 1 voters, hoping for the best, propose $P_1 = 0$ and $P_2 = \$7.10$ (shown as point A in Figure 9-4).

Of course, district 2 voters must prefer that $P_2 = 0$, which implies that

$$14P_1 - P_1^2 = 120$$

This is not feasible, however. As can be seen from Figure 9-4, there is no P_1 which could be charged district 1 commuters that would raise enough revenue to cover the operating costs of both the district 1 commuters and the 20 passenger-miles that are free to district 2 commuters.[25] Thus the best feasible plan from the perspective of district 2 voters will involve some $P_2 > 0$. It can be shown that the lowest feasible $P_2 = \$3.46$ with $Q_2 = 16.54$; this implies that $P_1 = \$7.00$ and $Q_1 = 3$.[26] This solution has BART revenues (equal to operating

---

[25] The quadratic equation $P_1^2 - 14P_1 + 120 = 0$ has the nonreal solutions:

$$\frac{14 \pm \sqrt{14^2 - 4(120)}}{2} = \frac{14 \pm \sqrt{-284}}{2}$$

[26] We wish to choose P_1, P_2, and λ to minimize P_2 subject to the constraint that TR = TC. We formulate the Lagrangian

$$L = P_2 + \lambda(14P_1 - P_1^2 + 24P_2 - P_2^2 - 120)$$

costs) of $78.23. Thus district 2 voters have a preferred solution of $P_1 = \$7.00$ and $P_2 = \$3.46$ (point B in Figure 9-4).

In this simple problem it is obvious that the voters in district 2 have a majority and can elect their preferred solution; then $P_1 = \$7.00$ with $Q_1 = 3$, $P_2 = \$3.46$ with $Q_2 = 16.54$, and BART revenues are $78.23. Note that this median voter solution differs substantially from either of the two solutions proposed to meet bureaucratic objectives. (BART could achieve $125 in revenues or 23 passenger-miles of service if not constrained by the voters.)[27]

Finally, a simple interest group model might be as follows: If district 1 residents are rich, powerful and well-connected and district 2 residents are not, district 1 residents may be able to impose their preferred solution. Discreetly, they back a candidate to run as the head of BART's board of directors. The candidate makes campaign promises which appeal to everyone: e.g., to keep BART safe, swift, sparkling clean, and subsidized. When elected, the candidate quietly imposes the fare structure preferred by district 1 residents.

These very simple examples are intended to illustrate why the four different models considered by Cooter and Topakian have different predictions. The authors tackled the difficult question of numerically predicting the fares that BART would set if it behaved according to each model. Then they compared those predictions with the actual BART fares.

To test their hypotheses, the authors undertook a careful empirical study. They had survey data indicating the average trip length of riders originating at each of 33 stations along BART routes. The existing fares were, of course, known. Independent studies of the price elasticity of demand for BART riders

---

and take the partial derivatives for the first-order conditions:

$$\frac{\partial L}{\partial P_1} = \lambda(14 - 2P_1) = 0 \tag{i}$$

$$\frac{\partial L}{\partial P_2} = 1 + \lambda(24 - 2P_2) = 0 \tag{ii}$$

$$\frac{\partial L}{\partial \lambda} = 14P_1 - P_1^2 + 24P_2 - P_2^2 - 120 = 0 \tag{iii}$$

From equation (i) we can see that $P_1 = \$7$ as long as $\lambda \neq 0$ (i.e., the constraint is binding). Equation (iii) then reduces to a simple quadratic:

$$14(7.00) - (7.00^2) + 24P_2 - P_2^2 - 120 = 0$$

or

$$P_2^2 - 24P_2 + 71 = 0$$

By use of the quadratic formula, this has the solution

$$P_2 = \$3.456$$

[27] This is a median voter solution in the following sense. We can describe the preferences of the voters in terms of the lowest P_1 they are willing to approve (since a relatively low P_1 corresponds to a relatively high P_2). If we order the 30 voters in terms of those preferences, 10 will approve $P_1 = 0$ and the next 20 will require $P_1 \leq \$7$ for approval. If we imagine starting with $P_1 = 0$, voting on it, and raising it incrementally until 16 voters (a majority) approve the plan, then no plan will be approved until $P_1 = \$7$.

had been calculated elsewhere, and the authors used a range of those elasticity estimates to predict how ridership would change in response to various fare changes.[28]

To calculate the subsidy received by the average rider at each station, one needs to know not only the fare charged but also the costs of the service. In a separate model Cooter and Topakian estimated the costs per mile from each station, again under a range of assumptions. Their methods led to a "best" estimate whereby the cost per passenger-mile is an increasing function of distance from the city center. This occurs primarily because the trains are more fully loaded nearer the center, and the fixed costs per person are therefore lower. With these estimates, they calculated the actual subsidies received by the average passengers at each station.

Figure 9-5 is a reconstruction of a diagram in the Cooter-Topakian article which displays the subsidy possibilities, the observed subsidies, and the ones predicted by the alternative models (except the interest group model, explained below). The subsidy possibilities are directly analogous to the locus of feasible P_1 and P_2 fare combinations in our simple illustrative example. Each subsidy possibility represents a set of fares (one for each station) minus the corresponding cost of service (from each station) which meets BART's break-even constraint.

This representation of the subsidy possibilities involves the following simplification. From each station there are actually numerous fares (and corresponding costs), one for each possible destination. However, Cooter and Topakian found that the fares could be approximated by a simple linear function of average trip length. That is, they calculated that a passenger from station j pays an average of P_j per passenger-mile and imposes average costs of C_j per passenger-mile, or therefore receives an average subsidy per passenger-mile of S_j (= $P_j - C_j$). They also calculated the average trip length t_j from station j. They then found that this subsidy system (all S_j for $j = 1, 2, \ldots, 33$ stations) could be approximated accurately by a linear equation (with coefficients a_0 and a_1):

$$S_j = a_0 + a_1 t_j$$

They then suggested that alternative subsidy systems can be approximated with this equation by varying the coefficients a_0 and a_1. A positive a_1, for example, implies that stations with passengers taking the longest trips get the largest subsidies. For a fixed total subsidy, a higher a_1 implies larger subsidies to passengers with the longest trips, and lower subsidies to those with shorter trips. In Figure 9-5, the vertical axis measures a_1 and the horizontal axis a_0.

---

[28] Over the whole system, the price elasticity estimate used was $-.3$. The authors also had separate estimates of the price elasticities from each station, which averaged about $-.15$. The second estimates were more inelastic because they were based on data from both BART *and* bus riders, so the only transportation alternative was automobile commuting.

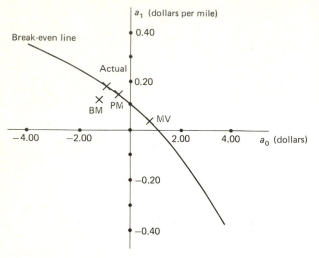

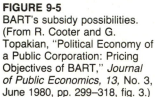

FIGURE 9-5
BART's subsidy possibilities.
(From R. Cooter and G.
Topakian, "Political Economy of
a Public Corporation: Pricing
Objectives of BART," *Journal
of Public Economics, 13,* No. 3,
June 1980, pp. 299–318, fig. 3.)

The solid line in Figure 9-5 shows all possible (linear) subsidy schemes which satisfy BART's break-even constraint. The actual subsidy is seen to favor riders with longer average trips. The budget maximization hypothesis implies that the coefficients on the subsidy equation should be those at BM; this is off the constraint on the assumption that the excess revenues would be converted into increased management expenses of one form or another. The alternative measure of size used was passenger-miles; it would be maximized at the point shown as PM. Both bureaucratic hypotheses are reasonably close to the actual subsidy system.

The median voter model, shown as MV, implies a subsidy structure quite different from the others. Although subsidies still increase slightly with average trip distance, those with shorter average distances are treated relatively more generously. The reason is not complicated. Voters have interests similar to those of the BART riders in their areas: The bigger the subsidies, the greater the number of BART riders and the less the pollution and congestion on the roads in the area. A high a_0 and a low a_1 favor the minority with the shortest trips and displease everyone else. It would be easy to oust the incumbents with a new subsidy proposal. Similarly, a low a_0 and a high a_1 favor the minority with the longest trips and displease everyone else. The only subsidy system which can't be beaten by the formation of a new majority is the one in the middle.

However, the fact that the actual subsidy system does not look like the one predicted by the median voter model suggests that, in this case, there is no effective democratic voting control. If any control were exercised by this method, one would at least expect the actual system to lie between the bureaucratic preferences and voter preferences in Figure 9-5. Instead, the actual system deviates from the bureaucratic preferences in a direction opposite to that which could be explained by pressure from the median voter. The median voter hypothesis is rejected in this context.

The other theory of political control, the interest group model, cannot be represented on the diagram. If some people have more clout than others, the areas in which they are concentrated would benefit relatively more than other areas. There is no reason to assume these areas are geographically linear. The authors, by using regression analysis, attempted to see if they could explain the average subsidy at each station on the basis of the characteristics of people living there—average incomes, education, percent of riders who use BART regularly during the week, etc. The results did not provide much independent support for the hypothesis: The characteristics had little ability to predict the subsidy, except for those correlated with trip length.

Thus we are left with these conclusions: The median voter model is rejected. The bureaucratic models are "close" to the observed subsidies; but under the range of estimates used in their modeling, the bureaucratic predictions are not quite close enough to accept (or strongly reject) the hypothesis that bureaucratic objectives explain the actual subsidies. Furthermore, the bureaucratic interests correlate to some extent with the interest group characteristics correlated with trip length: income and education. Therefore, we cannot be certain about the extent to which these models explain the observed fare structure.

Of course, it is always possible that an untested model would be a better predictor than any of the models tested. Perhaps BART's objectives were to set the most efficient fares, for example. All the tested models focused on differing objectives or constraints that might be driving the system, and none of them considered the capabilities of BART to choose subsidies which meet any given set of objectives. It is possible, for example, that bounded rationality led BART to set its fares to be competitive with those on the existing bus routes, without thinking about which passengers get subsidies.

The above exercise illustrates a methodology for learning how to predict the behavior of a public supply organization. One should not respond negatively to it because the results are somewhat ambiguous. Rather, one should recognize that this work is only in its infancy and requires patient development.

Suppose, for example, that, with some additional research, models which predict more successfully are developed. If we understood the pricing decisions of BART (and perhaps similar mass transit enterprises), we could predict the effects of changing subsidies (perhaps changing federal subsidies to many mass transit systems) on the fare structure and in turn on the usage of the system. Or we could predict how required subsidies would change in response to proposed standards for fare setting. Or we might learn what inducement would be necessary to cause BART to allocate resources efficiently (and how this compares with other institutional forms). Such predictions, derived by a systematic, testable, and improvable methodology, would be substantially more reliable than those based on the untested impressions one might glean from direct observation alone.

A NORMATIVE MODEL OF PUBLIC ENTERPRISE PRICING: THE EFFICIENT FARE STRUCTURE

One question which the BART case study might raise is this: How should BART set its fares if its objective is to be socially efficient? Since prices determine the level of use, this is equivalent to seeking the optimal allocation of resources. The usual answer to such a question is to charge price equal to marginal cost, but that fails to illuminate the reason why BART is a public enterprise in the first place. Rail systems, bridges, utilities, and certain other segments of the economy are characterized by very high fixed or indivisible costs (e.g., laying the track, building the bridge) and low marginal costs. If these increasing returns industries priced at marginal cost, as we saw in Chapter 8, they would be unprofitable to operate.

A review of this problem is illustrated in Figure 9-6. As drawn, the marginal benefit of each unit up to Q_E exceeds its marginal cost; therefore, efficiency seems to require that Q_E units be produced. However, charging price equal to marginal cost implies the enterprise will have *negative* profits equal to $P_E P_A AE$. No private firm would provide efficient service in those circumstances, and, in some cases, there might be no quantity at which operation without price discrimination is privately profitable. (This depends on whether the demand curve is higher than average cost at the quantity where MR = MC, the profit maximum.)

Given this failure of the private market, what kind of organization should provide the service? One suggestion is to have a regulated private firm do it. This could be made possible by a state-supplied *per unit subsidy* of $P_A - P_E$ (in Figure 9-6), with a requirement that the firm charge a price P_E. Another suggestion is to create a public enterprise, charge P_E, and let the government make up losses out of general tax revenues. The preferred organizational form depends upon the difficulty of controlling the behavior of each form. The considerations raised throughout this and the preceding chapter can be helpful in designing and evaluating specific organizational forms to fit specific problems.

But at this point, to get into the pricing question, we must introduce a new issue. It is that the government revenues raised to make up the deficit impose social costs elsewhere in the economy; therefore, the output level Q_E is not optimal after all. We will explore this second-best problem in more detail in Chapter 11, but the idea is to allocate resources such that the net benefits of one additional unit of resource in every controllable sector are equalized. The first-best solution is to have the marginal net benefits be zero everywhere, but this turns out to be an impossibility. If they are zero in this sector (at Q_E) and nonzero for the activities taxed to provide the subsidy, the resources are not optimally allocated. We will not go into the problem of identifying the optimal level here, but we remark that the government's determination of the subsidy level is an important part of solving the larger problem.

The problem we examine is a smaller one. We assume that the government has already set up BART as a public enterprise and announced the subsidy

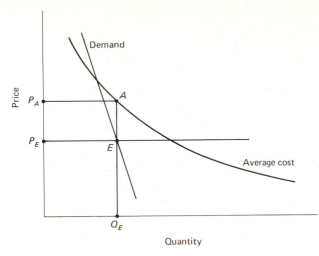

FIGURE 9-6
The problem of increasing returns to scale.

level. The tracks are laid, and the capital equipment is purchased; in other
words, the capacity of the system is "fixed" for the time period we are
imagining.[29] All we want to know is *what prices will lead to the most efficient
resource allocation, given the capacity, the break-even constraint (revenues
must equal costs minus government subsidies), and demand for BART services.* This problem is sometimes referred to as the *Ramsey pricing problem,*
after the man who posed and solved it in 1927.[30]

In the optional section we derive Ramsey's results and mention some other
applications. Here we try to offer a more intuitive understanding of them and
their implications for public enterprise pricing. To simplify matters, let us
imagine that there is a BART line with only three stations: the Business
District, One-Mile Island, and Two-Mile Island. (Three-Mile Island, of course,
is shut down.) Demand is smooth all day (no peak-level problem), and it is the
same coming in to the city as going back. (All passengers are round-trippers.)
We will refer to the daily demand for seats without worrying about the number
of seats per car or scheduling problems. (The BART rolling stock is flexible
enough to handle these matters.) The marginal cost of operating the train is a
constant $1 per person per mile. In addition, we assume there are substantial
"fixed" costs of an unspecified amount. A main constraint is capacity: If
BART stock rolls all the time, it can carry a maximum of 272 passenger-miles.

---

[29] Alchian has pointed out that nothing is ever "fixed." The expression implies that the cost of
altering capacity (by any significant amount) within the time period being considered is too great to
be economical. See A. Alchian, "Costs and Outputs," in W. Breit and H. Hochman (eds.),
Readings in Microeconomics (New York: Holt, Rinehart & Winston, Inc., 1971), pp. 159–171.

[30] F. P. Ramsey, "A Contribution to the Theory of Taxation," *Economic Journal, 37,* March
1927, pp. 47–61.

To make sure this model is clear, suppose that 40 people from Two-Mile Island wanted to ride; this would take up 160 passenger-miles (2 miles each way per person). If 100 people also wanted to ride from One-Mile Island, this would require another 200 passenger-miles and the total of 360 exceeds BART's capacity; there is no way that BART can provide this service. If only 50 people wanted to ride from One-Mile Island, total demand would be 260 passenger-miles and within BART's capacity.

We are not worrying here about the details of assigning the number of rail cars on each run, the number of One-Mile Island runs, etc. We assume that any enterprise smart enough to price efficiently is also smart enough to schedule trains properly. For example, BART might have two trains with a seat capacity of 25 each go to One-Mile Island only and one larger train with a seat capacity of 40 be an express from Two-Mile Island. That would leave BART with 12 passenger-miles of unused capacity, and our assumption implies that the $12 marginal operating cost of the remaining capacity has been avoided. (One car sits idle all day, which saves the labor of moving and cleaning it.)

Now let us suppose that the demand curves for passenger-miles of One-Mile Islanders Q_1 and Two-Mile Islanders Q_2, respectively, are

$$Q_1 = 100 - 4P_1 \qquad 0 \le P_1 \le 25$$
$$Q_2 = 280 - 32P_2 \qquad 0 \le P_2 \le 8.75$$

In Figure 9-7a we illustrate these demand curves as well as their sum when prices are the same, the market demand Q_M:

$$Q_M = \begin{cases} 380 - 36P_M & 0 \le P \le 8.75 \\ 100 - 4P_M & 8.75 \le P \le 25 \end{cases}$$

We have also drawn in the line indicating constant marginal cost of $1. It is clear that the first-best solution is simply to have $P = P_1 = P_2 = \$1$, where $Q_1 = 96$ and $Q_2 = 248$. This can also be interpreted as 48 round trips for One-Mile Islanders (2 passenger-miles each) and 63 round trips for Two-Mile Islanders (4 passenger-miles each). There are two problems with this solution, which we deal with in the following order: (1) The "solution" provides 344 passenger-miles, which, given BART's capacity of 272, is impossible. (2) BART is extremely unprofitable; it covers only its marginal costs and thus does not contribute a cent toward the payment of fixed costs. It is the second problem which raises the Ramsey issue.

Under "first-best" rules, we could point out that BART has the wrong capacity: it "should" choose the capacity which will provide service to all persons who are willing to pay at least the marginal cost (i.e., capacity "should" be 344). This is the long-run marginal cost solution shown in Figure 9-7a. The quotation marks are used to indicate that, because of the second problem, it is erroneous to apply first-best rules. There is an "optimal" capacity which would not turn out to be 344; however, its magnitude is hidden

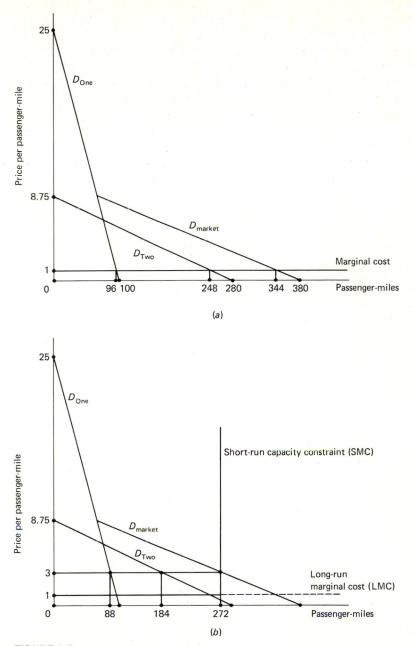

FIGURE 9-7
(a) The marginal cost long-run solution to BART resource allocation; (b) the marginal cost short-run solution for BART with capacity constraint.

by a maze of "second-best" calculating requirements that are necessary to determine the efficiency cost of providing a government subsidy, discussed below. Given the current state of the art, these requirements may exceed our own analytic capacity to clear them away. Fortunately, we are going to duck this issue for the moment and accept BART's current capacity of 272 as a constraint. How should BART price to ration the 272 available passenger-miles if it wishes to be efficient (still ignoring the second problem)?

It can be seen from Figure 9-7*b* that the price at which the market demand equals 272 is $3. At this price $Q_1 = 88$ and $Q_2 = 184$, or One-Mile Islanders get 44 round-trips and Two-Mile Islanders get 46. Two-Mile Islanders have reduced their use of BART by a proportionately greater amount because their demand is more elastic. This is the short-run marginal cost solution, so named because the marginal cost becomes vertical at the capacity constraint. But why should this be the best way to ration the capacity? Perhaps charging each group a different price per passenger-mile would be better?

At this stage of the problem, a $3 price for all does lead to the "most efficient" allocation. Since we are at capacity, the only way to improve the allocation is if there is some nonrider who values riding more than some current rider does. Look at each of the demand curves in Figure 9-7*b*. The marginal riders from each island value the ride *identically* at $3 per passenger-mile. All other riders value it by more and all nonriders by less. There is no room for a deal; the allocation is most efficient given the capacity.

But we still have the Ramsey issue. BART's total revenues are $816, which exceed its operating costs of $272 by $544. The government insists that this is not a large enough contribution to meeting the fixed costs. And it is probably correct: Since taxpayers are making up the difference, the taxes used to raise the subsidy cause a wedge between the supply price and demand price of each taxed commodity. For example, a sales tax T results in the consumer's marginal value of the taxed commodity being $P + T$, whereas the marginal opportunity cost of the resources used to supply it are only P. Being "myopically efficient" by marginal cost pricing in the BART sector causes an inefficiency in the taxed sector (in either the short or long run).

Since all taxes create such wedges (as discussed in Chapter 10), any increasing returns activity which has deficits must balance its efficiency gains against the tax efficiency losses it creates. Thus there is an optimal deficit level, assuming optimal second-best pricing is followed everywhere. As we indicated earlier, a more careful discussion of the general second-best problem is in Chapter 11. For purposes here we assume the government in its wisdom requires BART to contribute $1206. Whether or not this is the correct level for optimal resource allocation, BART is stuck with it and must do the best it can from here.

This raises the Ramsey problem: *How should an enterprise price its products when it is subject to an overall budget constraint?* An analytically identical problem, by the way, is how to select tax rates for taxable goods and services in the economy given that total revenues of a certain amount are to be raised.[31] Thus, solving the optimal enterprise pricing problem involves the same reasoning as solving for the optimal set of taxes. One version of the Ramsey solution, which applies to both, is known as the inverse elasticities rule:

$$\frac{P_i - MC_i}{P_i} = \frac{k}{\varepsilon_i} \qquad i = 1, 2, \ldots, n \text{ commodities}$$

where k is a negative constant (since ε_i is negative). In English, this says that *the percentage deviation of the price of a good from its marginal cost should be inversely related to its elasticity of demand.* This solution applies when the cross elasticities of demand among the goods subject to the budget constraint are zero.[32]

The solution to BART's problem, derived in the optional section, assuming no cross price effects between stations, is to set $P_1 = \$10.00$ and $P_2 = \$3.91$. These prices imply by the demand functions $Q_1 = 60$, $Q_2 = 155$, and $\Sigma P_i Q_i = \$1206$. To show that this obeys Ramsey's rule, we calculate k based on One-Mile Islanders and see if the same k makes Ramsey's equation hold for Two-Mile Islanders. First, it is easy to calculate:

$$\frac{P_1 - MC_1}{P_1} = \frac{10 - 1}{10} = 0.9$$

We know that ε_1 by definition is

$$\varepsilon_1 = \frac{\Delta Q_1}{\Delta P_1} \frac{P_1}{Q_1}$$

For a linear demand curve, $Q = a - bP$. If we increase P by ΔP, then Q changes by $-b \, \Delta P$, or

$$\Delta Q = -b \, \Delta P$$
$$\frac{\Delta Q}{\Delta P} = -b$$

Therefore, substituting in the definition of elasticity (for One-Mile Islanders) gives us

---

[31] In fact, Ramsey actually solved the tax problem. Boiteux is generally credited with seeing the parallel to public enterprise pricing. See M. Boiteux, "On the Management of Public Monopolies Subject to Budget Constraints," *Journal of Economic Theory, 3,* 1971, pp. 219–242.

[32] When one takes account of cross effects, the solution is more complicated but it retains the same pricing tendency as the simpler case. This is shown in the optional section.

$$\varepsilon_1 = -b_1 \frac{P_1}{Q_1}$$

$$= -4 \frac{10}{60}$$

$$= -\tfrac{2}{3}$$

Finally, substituting in the equation for Ramsey's rule gives us

$$0.9 = \frac{k}{\varepsilon_1}$$

$$= \frac{k}{-\tfrac{2}{3}}$$

or $$k = -0.6$$

To see if the same k works for the Two-Mile Islanders, we first calculate ε_2:

$$\varepsilon_2 = -b \frac{P_2}{Q_2}$$

$$= -32 \frac{3.91}{155}$$

$$= -0.807$$

Then our question is

$$k \overset{?}{=} \frac{\varepsilon_2(P_2 - MC_2)}{P_2}$$

$$= \frac{-0.807(3.91 - 1)}{3.91}$$

$$= -0.6$$

Thus our solution does indeed obey Ramsey's rule.

Note that the solution is to charge the One-Mile Islanders substantially more per passenger-mile than the Two-Mile Islanders. This follows from the assumption (implicit in the demand curves) that One-Mile Islanders have a more inelastic demand. We chose this assumption to fit with the directions of the actual elasticities as reported by Cooter and Topakian: The farther out from the city, the more elastic the demand for BART services (because such alternatives as driving become more attractive).

The reasoning underlying Ramsey's rule, and therefore the above result, can be understood intuitively. If we cannot have the first-best allocation of resources because of a profit constraint that must be met, then presumably we wish to be as close as possible to first-best when we satisfy the constraint.

Therefore, we raise the prices more on goods which are inelastically demanded because their allocations are least affected by the price increase.

We may be able to clarify this reasoning more precisely by looking at an equivalent expression of Ramsey's rule:[33]

$$(P_i - MC_i) \frac{\Delta Q_i}{\Delta P_i} = \delta \left[(P_i - MC_i) \frac{\Delta Q_i}{\Delta P_i} + Q_i \right] \qquad \delta = \text{const}$$

On the left-hand side, the first term in parentheses is the net benefit from consuming a marginal unit of Q_i. (P_i is the height of the demand curve and MC_i is the opportunity cost of the resources used to produce the unit.) The second term tells us by how many units Q_i decreases in response to a small price increase. So the whole left-hand side can be thought of as the dollar loss in benefits per unit increase in price.

On the right-hand side, ignoring the constant δ for the moment, we have the increase in "profit" (ignoring fixed costs) per unit increase in price. There are two components to it. The terms in parentheses are identical with those on the left-hand side. They represent the loss in net revenue to the enterprise from the demand reduction due to the unit price increase. But this is offset by the per unit increase in revenue on all the Q_i units that are sold. So the sum of everything between the brackets is the net increase in "profit" for a one-unit increase in price.

Therefore, the whole equation says the net loss in benefits for a unit price increase should be proportional to the net profit gained by it, or *the net loss in benefits for an extra dollar of profit should be the same for all commodities produced by the enterprise.* This is only logical. If social losses must be

---

[33] It is easy to show the equivalence of the two expressions. Let us start with

$$(P_i - MC_i) \frac{\Delta Q_i}{\Delta P_i} = \delta \left[(P_i - MC_i) \frac{\Delta Q_i}{\Delta P_i} + Q_i \right]$$

Noting that the terms in parentheses on the right-hand side are identical with those on the left-hand side, we move them over:

$$(P_i - MC_i) \frac{\Delta Q_i}{\Delta P_i} (1 - \delta) = \delta Q_i$$

or
$$P_i - MC_i = \frac{\delta}{1 - \delta} Q_i \frac{1}{\Delta Q_i / \Delta P_i}$$

Dividing both sides by P_i gives us

$$\frac{P_i - MC_i}{P_i} = \frac{\delta}{1 - \delta} \frac{1}{(\Delta Q_i / \Delta P_i)/(P_i / Q_i)}$$

And by letting $k = \delta/(1 - \delta)$, we get

$$\frac{P_i - MC_i}{P_i} = \frac{k}{\varepsilon_i}$$

imposed (and they must), then they ought to be minimized. If the marginal costs of obtaining an extra dollar of profit from any of the enterprise's products are not the same, then one could reduce the social loss by "giving back" one dollar of profit where the loss is high and making it up where the loss is low.

Note that efficiency in the BART case, as implied by our model, is to have the subsidies increasing as stations get farther away from the central business district.[34] Of course, our solution assumed no cross effects, and we have not considered equity. Let us mention a few considerations that are real, although outside our illustration.

There is good reason to think that One-Mile Islanders are relatively insensitive to changes in fares to Two-Mile Island. But Two-Mile Islanders may not be so insensitive to One-Mile Island fares. If, for example, fares were expensive from Two-Mile Island but cheap from One-Mile island, Two-Mile Islanders might drive halfway and take the train downtown. Furthermore, if automobile congestion and pollution is an unpriced negative externality concentrated in the downtown area, then second-best pricing requires that its substitute (One-Mile Island rail trips) be made cheaper. If it is thought appropriate to charge those with lower incomes less and those groups are concentrated close to downtown, that may be another argument to reduce (relatively) One-Mile Island fares. Since the actual differences in fare elasticity by station do not appear great, it is quite plausible that these additional considerations could reverse the direction of the subsidies implied by our illustrative model.

∇THE MATHEMATICS OF RAMSEY PRICING

In this section we show how the usual Lagrangian techniques of calculus maximization can be used to see the structure of the Ramsey problem, as well as be used to provide specific empirical solutions. It is useful to begin with the "first-best" problem of allocating BART resources subject to the capacity constraint of 272.

The expression "maximize social efficiency" generally refers to maximizing the net benefits, or benefits minus costs, of the economic activities under consideration. It is equivalent to making a compensation test of all alternative resource allocations within the scope of the problem and choosing the alternative which scores highest. The calculus techniques help to identify the best alternative with minimal effort. If we refer to Figure 9-8, the benefits are the area under the demand curve and the opportunity costs are the area under the marginal cost curve for the quantity of the good produced. Thus our problem is to choose quantities Q_1 and Q_2 that maximize the sum of the net benefits under each Islander's demand curve, subject to the capacity constraint that $Q_1 + Q_2 = 272$.

Let us solve the problem for any two linear demand functions:

$$Q_i = a_i - b_i P_i \qquad i = 1, 2$$

---

[34] Since prices are closer to marginal cost farther out, they are farther from average cost and thus the subsidy is increasing.

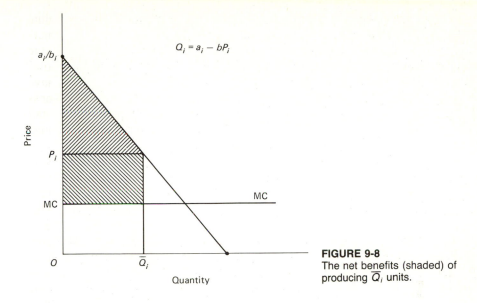

FIGURE 9-8
The net benefits (shaded) of producing $\overline{Q}_i$ units.

We shall substitute later the a_i's and b_i's from our specific demand curves. It is convenient to note that the above equation can be rewritten:

$$P_i = \frac{a_i}{b_i} - \frac{Q_i}{b_i}$$

The term a_i/b_i is the value of P_i where the demand curve intersects the vertical axis (Figure 9-8). We also know that the marginal cost MC is constant. Then, for any level of Q_i, the net benefit NB can be written as the sum of the consumer surplus (a triangle) plus BART "profit" (a rectangle)[35]

$$\text{NB}_i = \tfrac{1}{2}\left(\frac{a_i}{b_i} - P_i\right) Q_i + (P_i - \text{MC})Q_i$$

This can be rewritten as

$$\text{NB}_i = \tfrac{1}{2}Q_i\left(\frac{a_i}{b_i} + P_i\right) - \text{MC}\,(Q_i)$$

Or substituting for P_i from the demand equation, we have

$$\text{NB}_i = \tfrac{1}{2}Q_i\left(\frac{2a_i}{b_i} - \frac{Q_i}{b_i}\right) - \text{MC}\,(Q_i)$$

---

[35] "Profit" is in quotes because we are ignoring the fixed costs. We refer to revenues above marginal costs as "profit" for purposes of this example.

Now we wish to maximize net benefits subject to the constraint. We form the Lagrangian

$$L = NB_1 + NB_2 - \lambda(Q_1 + Q_2 - 272)$$

The partial derivative of L with respect to Q_i is (assuming no cross effects on demand):

$$\frac{\partial L}{\partial Q_i} = \frac{a_i}{b_i} - \frac{Q_i}{b_i} - MC - \lambda = 0$$

Note that this is simply

$$P_i - MC = \lambda$$

In other words, the maximization requirement is that the price of each commodity minus its marginal cost be equal to the same number λ. This number is also interpreted as the marginal net benefit. The condition implies that each commodity has the same price (since each has the same MC in this case). If the two commodities in our problem have the same price, we can equate them:

$$P_1 = \frac{a_1}{b_1} - \frac{Q_1}{b_1} = \frac{a_2}{b_2} - \frac{Q_2}{b_2} = P_2$$

The values of the relevant parameters are in our two specific demand equations:

$$Q_1 = 100 - 4P_1$$
$$Q_2 = 280 - 32P_2$$

On substituting values from the above, we have

$$\frac{100}{4} - \frac{Q_1}{4} = \frac{280}{32} - \frac{Q_2}{32}$$

and on simplifying we have

$$Q_2 = 8Q_1 - 520$$

The remaining partial derivative of the optimization is the constraint equation

$$\frac{\partial L}{\partial \lambda} = Q_1 + Q_2 - 272 = 0$$

Now we have reduced the problem to two equations in two unknowns and can solve

or

$$Q_2 = 8Q_1 - 520 = 8(272 - Q_2) - 520$$
$$Q_2 = 184, P_2 = 3 \qquad Q_1 = 88, P_1 = 3$$

This solved, let us now turn to the Ramsey problem. The government insists that BART have "profit" of $1206, and we wish to know how to maximize social benefits subject to that constraint. (To simplify the mathematics, this problem was selected to ensure the solution is within the capacity constraint.)

After a moment's thought it should be recognized that this problem looks very similar to the last one. Only the constraint is different. The new constraint is that total BART revenues minus operating costs equal $1206. In other words, we wish to maximize

$$L = NB_1 + NB_2 - \lambda[P_1Q_1 + P_2Q_2 - MC(Q_1 + Q_2) - 1206]$$

The partial derivative of this equation with respect to Q_i is (again, assuming no cross effects on demand):

$$\frac{\partial L}{\partial Q_i} = P_i - MC - \lambda\left(P_i + Q_i \frac{\partial P_i}{\partial Q_i} - MC\right) = 0$$

Note that the first two terms in parentheses are simply the marginal revenue from an increase in Q_i: The price P_i of the marginal unit plus the current quantity times the amount price on them is reduced. Therefore,

$$P_i - MC = \lambda(MR_i - MC)$$

which is one way to write Ramsey's result. Note that we can interpret the left-hand side as the marginal net benefit from an additional Q_i and the terms in parentheses on the right-hand side as the marginal "profit" to BART. Therefore, Ramsey's rule states: *The net social benefit foregone to obtain an incremental dollar of profit should be identical for each commodity produced by the enterprise.*

It is easy to show that this version of the rule is equivalent to the other versions we have seen. Recall that

$$MR = P\left(1 + \frac{1}{\varepsilon}\right)$$

We simply substitute in our last equation:

$$P_i - MC = \lambda\left(P_i - MC + \frac{P_i}{\varepsilon}\right)$$

Now we move a few things around:

$$(P_i - MC)(1 - \lambda) = \frac{P_i\lambda}{\varepsilon_i}$$

or

$$\frac{P_i - MC}{P_i} = \frac{\lambda}{1 - \lambda} \frac{1}{\varepsilon_i}$$

Since $\lambda/(1 - \lambda)$ is a number, we can call it k, and therefore

$$\frac{P_i - MC}{P_i} = \frac{k}{\varepsilon_i}$$

The numbers given in the text were already shown to satisfy Ramsey's pricing rule and the constraint, so there is no reason to solve the equations explicitly here.

One last Ramsey result to show is when we allow cross effects among the commodities (i.e., they are substitutes or complements). The objective function and constraints are identical; it is only the partial derivatives which change. They change because now we assume:

$$\frac{\partial Q_j}{\partial Q_i} \neq 0$$

Thus the expanded partial derivative (with two commodities) yields this equation when set to zero:

$$(P_i - MC) + (P_j - MC)\frac{\partial Q_j}{\partial Q_i} = \lambda\left[(MR_i - MC) + (P_j - MC)\frac{\partial Q_j}{\partial Q_i}\right]$$

Note that the last term of the expression on the right-hand side is not exactly analogous to the first term (P_j rather than MR_j). The reason is that, in taking the partial derivative of the constraint, a part of the calculation is as follows:

$$\frac{\partial(P_jQ_j)}{\partial Q_i} = \frac{\partial P_j}{\partial Q_i} Q_j + \frac{\partial Q_j}{\partial Q_i} P_j$$

The first term on the right-hand side, $\partial P_j/\partial Q_i$, is zero: Price in the j market is constant; it is the demand curve which is shifting.

Going back to the full expression, we can substitute $P_i + P_i/\varepsilon_i = MR_i$ and combine terms as before:

$$P_i - MC + (P_j - MC)\frac{\partial Q_j}{\partial Q_i} = \lambda\left[(P_i - MC) + \frac{P_i}{\varepsilon_i} + (P_j - MC)\frac{\partial Q_j}{\partial Q_i}\right]$$

$$(P_i - MC)(1 - \lambda) = \frac{P_i\lambda}{\varepsilon_i} + (\lambda - 1)(P_j - MC)\frac{\partial Q_j}{\partial Q_i}$$

and, using $k = \lambda/(1 - \lambda)$

$$\frac{P_i - MC}{P_i} = \frac{k}{\varepsilon_i} - \frac{(P_j - MC)(\partial Q_j/\partial Q_i)}{P_i}$$

Thus the Ramsey rule with cross effects is similar to the less complicated rule. Note that $(P_j - MC)/P_i$ is always positive. Therefore, the Ramsey rule is as before, modified by the degree of substitutability or complementarity of the two goods. If good j is a substitute for good i ($\partial Q_j/\partial Q_i < 0$), then the price of i should be higher than if there were no cross effects.

Suppose some of our BART riders live on houseboats between One- and Two-Mile Islands and are relatively indifferent to which station they use to board. BART increases its price for One-Mile Island fares, and we have already estimated the drop in demand at One-Mile Island. But now we must include the fact that demand increases at Two-Mile Island: We have lost fewer passengers and gained more revenues than we thought. This makes us favor greater price increases for One-Mile Island than we would without cross effects.

As we mentioned in the preceding section, this analysis does not take into account the unpriced negative externalities of pollution and congestion from automobile commuting, nor does it consider the equity effects. However, those effects can be integrated into the formal analysis. A recent example, for a different type of enterprise, is offered by Harris.[36] He considers how hospitals should price their products, given the distortion and inequities that exist in existing health insurance coverage. His conclusion, which is counter to the conventional wisdom, is that hospital prices "should" involve significant degrees of cross subsidization (some products above marginal costs, some below them) because to do so would improve social welfare. Another empirical application of the Ramsey principles has been by Littlechild and Rousseau for a telephone company.[37] And for those who are groaning about the complications of it all, Manski reports on procedures that boundedly rational people can follow to find prices which achieve various objectives; work of this type may lead to the discovery of simple procedures for identifying the Ramsey optimal prices![38]

SUMMARY

Two areas in which supply organizations may have degrees of freedom for discretionary behavior, aside from noncompetitive settings for profit-making firms, are the nonprofit and public sectors. These areas are just beginning to be

[36] J. Harris, "Pricing Rules for Hospitals," *The Bell Journal of Economics, 10,* No. 1, spring 1979, pp. 224–243.

[37] S. C. Littlechild and J. J. Rousseau, "Pricing Policy of a U.S. Telephone Company," *Journal of Public Economics, 4,* No. 1, February 1975, pp. 35–56.

[38] C. Manski, "The Zero Elasticity Rule for Pricing a Government Service: A Summary of Findings," *The Bell Journal of Economics, 10,* No. 1, spring 1979, pp. 211–223.

explored by economists. We reviewed several studies which develop models to use for predicting and evaluating the behavior of these organizations.

First, we examined three alternative models of nonprofit hospital behavior. The differences in model assumptions appear both in terms of objectives (e.g., whether doctors or administrators control the hospital's decision making) as well as capabilities (e.g., the rapid life and death decision making by physicians explains why hospitals are split organizations and why administrators may be unable to control hospital expenses as proposed in Hospital Cost Containment legislation). The implications of these models often differ, e.g., in terms of hospital size or efficiency of input use, and it is these differences which empirical studies should focus upon to test whether one model is more accurate than another.

Models of public bureaucracies and enterprises have also been constructed as a way to predict their behavior. The bureau budget maximization hypothesis assumes that bureaucrats have a great deal of discretion and behave like sales maximizers. Other conceptions of the bureaucrat's self-interest, such as equating doing a good job with maximizing net social benefits, lead to quite different predictions. We also pointed out that the political environment may severely constrain bureaucratic objectives, no matter what they are.

The empirical work on BART (mass transit) pricing of Cooter and Topakian pits the predictions of a bureaucratic model against those which assume the bureaucracy is controlled by political forces (either the median voter or the interest group theory). The authors conclude that the prices predicted by the bureaucratic model come closer than those predicted by the other models to observed BART prices, although not close enough to make the size maximization hypothesis statistically acceptable. The median voter hypothesis is rejected in this context. We mentioned briefly two other models which might explain BART behavior: one of boundedly rational pricing (e.g. imitating bus fares) and another of pricing for social efficiency. Although empirical model construction and testing of this type is in its infancy, we emphasized that the future payoffs of continued modeling efforts can be great in terms of confidence in the design and evaluation of policy changes affecting these organizations.

To explain efficiency in the mass transit context (or increasing returns to scale), we develop the principles of *Ramsey optimal pricing*. These apply when a public enterprise must price its product to reach an overall profit (or maximum loss) constraint. First we review the effect of capacity constraints on pricing, and then we turn to the Ramsey principle. The best known version of this principle is the *inverse elasticities rule*, which states that the optimal deviation of price from the marginal cost of each good produced by the enterprise should be proportional to the elasticity of demand. This version does not consider the effects of cross elasticity of demand, nor does it consider distributional effects or the unpriced externalities of pollution and congestion from automobile commuting. More sophisticated versions do account for them. In the optional section we develop some of the mathematics necessary to calculate Ramsey optimal prices.

EXERCISES

9-1 The questions below are designed to provide practice in deducing the implications of alternative producer objectives.

A very small country has an economy consisting of 100 farms on which food is grown to support the population. Each farm owner can hire as much labor as she or he wants at a cost of $3000 per person per year, constrained only by the total labor force (= population) of 1000. The yearly crops are sold at the world price of $25 per bushel. The minimum level of food required per person for subsistence is 100 bushels per year. The farm owner is the first hired on each farm.

For any one farm, the yearly crop depends only upon the amount of labor used as shown in the accompanying table. *Note:* There is no simple function relating labor inputs to output levels.

Labor quantity	1	2	3	4	5	6	7	8	9	10
Bushels per year	125	300	500	725	925	1105	1225	1275	1175	1000

a If all farms are owned by profit maximizers, how many bushels will be produced in the economy as a whole? What will total employment be? (Other things equal, farm owners prefer more workers to less.) (Answer: 122,500 bushels)

b If all farms are owned by revenue maximizers, what will total output and employment be? Are wages a larger or smaller proportion of total income (wages plus profits) under this regime compared with (*a*).

c Suppose farms are owned collectively by the country as a whole and the government directs each farm manager to hire labor in order to maximize productivity (output per worker). What are total output and employment? Do they reduce the starvation that has plagued the country under regimes (*a*) and (*b*)? (Answer: Starvation increases)

d Suppose the farms are run as communes in which no wages are paid but output is divided equally among the workers.

1 If each commune admits members only if it is to the other members' advantage, how many members will each commune have?

2 Suppose members of communes were required to let other people join as long as the output shares did not fall below the subsistence level. How many members would each commune have, and how much starvation would there be? (Answer: No starvation)

9-2 ▽A utility company is a monopolistic supplier of energy to two types of customers: residential and commercial. Their demands for energy Q_R and Q_C, respectively, are

$$Q_R = 90 - \tfrac{1}{2}P$$
$$Q_C = 200 - P$$

The marginal cost of supplying energy is constant and equal to $20; however, the utility company must first incur substantial fixed costs equal to $6000.

a A profit-maximizing and price discriminating utility would produce what output, charge what prices, and make what profit? (Answer: $\Pi = \$5300$)

b An attorney for the government has informed the utility company that its price discrimination was illegal, and the company has agreed to a cease-and-desist order. What uniform price will it charge now? Will the social benefits of this action outweigh the social costs? (Answer: $P = \$106.67$; no)

c The community in which the utility company provided service has been upset by the price gouging it perceives under both (a) and (b). It decides to turn the utility into a public enterprise. As a public enterprise, it can charge different prices to the two consumer groups. The public enterprise maximizes total sales, subject to a break-even constraint. What prices and quantities result? Will the social benefits of this change from (b) outweigh the social costs? Will either consumer group be better off or will both groups be better off? (Answer: $P_R = \$90$, $P_C = \$100$; yes; both)

d Newly elected officials in the community vow to institute fair prices and efficient service. If they are successful at making the public enterprise charge Ramsey-optimal prices, provide the service demanded at those prices, and still break even, what prices and quantities will result? Will either consumer group be better off compared with (c) or will both groups be better off? (Answer: $P_R \approx \$45.21$, $P_C \approx \$48.36$; both)

FOUR

POLICY EFFECTS
ON THE INTERACTION
OF SUPPLY AND DEMAND

GENERAL COMPETITIVE ANALYSIS OF MARKET ORGANIZATION, WITH APPLICATION TO TAXATION

The most common model of economic governance used by analysts is the perfectly competitive market. In this chapter we examine this model and distinguish sharply between its normative and predictive uses. For analytic purposes the predictive uses of such models have substantially firmer foundations.

Perhaps the two best known theorems of modern microeconomics, reviewed here, emphasize normative consequences of competition: (1) A perfectly competitive market allocation is Pareto-optimal. (2) Every Pareto-optimal allocation can be achieved by perfectly competitive markets, as long as costless redistribution of endowments is possible. These theorems suggest that there is something desirable about organizing economic activity through a system of perfectly competitive markets: With perfect information and costless transactions, such a system generates an *incentive structure* which leads economic agents to allocate resources optimally. We will show in this chapter that, because of taxation, the opposite result holds: Perfectly competitive markets in an economy with taxation generate incorrect incentives which lead economic agents to allocate resources nonoptimally.

Does the above nonoptimality conclusion imply that it is undesirable for an economy to utilize competitive markets? The appropriate analytic response is to ask, "Compared to what?" In later chapters we will emphasize that the assumption of perfect information and costless transactions must be relaxed to analyze these issues. There are many governance structures which can lead to optimal allocations (of those feasible) under these assumptions. The real analytic issues involve recognition that information is costly to produce, communicate, and process and that transactions are costly to organize and enforce; alternative governance structures (including the use of competitive markets) must be evaluated by the efficiency with which they perform these tasks. Thus the well-known twin theorems do not provide much normative insight about the desirability of competitive markets in an actual economy.

However, we do wish to show that the theory of competitive markets can be very useful as a predictive tool. With respect to taxation, we take note of Ben Franklin's remark: "In this world, nothing is certain but death and taxes." Taxation is an inevitable consequence of the wide variety of activities carried out by governments at all levels. Approximately one-third of the GNP is collected in taxes each year. Who bears the burden of a tax? We use the theory of competitive markets to predict tax incidence, and we show the difference between using models of partial and general equilibrium to analyze it.

We proceed as follows. First, we review the process and characteristics of resource allocation as they occur in a single competitive market. Then we step back to review the necessary conditions for efficiency in an economy as a whole (exchange, production, and product-mix efficiency). Next we turn to general equilibrium in markets and review the twin theorems which relate perfect competition and Pareto optimality.

Before turning to additional normative thought about general equilibrium, we consider how the models can be used in a predictive sense. We introduce concepts of tax incidence and contrast the analyses suggested by a partial and a general equilibrium model of an excise tax. We suggest that policies with large economic effects, like taxes, are better modeled in a general equilibrium framework. However, for small sectors of the economy, partial equilibrium analysis may be sufficient.

We consider the efficiency of taxes briefly, primarily to point out that all main taxes in use have distortionary allocative effects. This means that if an economy with taxation is characterized by markets which are perfectly competitive, it will generate incorrect incentives which will lead to inefficient resource allocation. Thus, although we can accept the predictive power of competitive models in certain situations, we have not yet established any normative conclusions concerning the desirability of competitive markets. To do so, we must first develop insight about how to compare alternative governance structures, a task we leave for the remaining chapters.

COMPETITIVE EQUILIBRIUM IN ONE INDUSTRY

In this section we review the conditions which result in competitive equilibrium in one market and the characteristics of that equilibrium. First, we make a number of assumptions about the trading conditions in this market. One is that we are discussing a *homogeneous* good: Each firm produces the identical product. On both the demand and supply side we assume that consumers and firms are *price takers*: Each economic agent is too small (relative to the total number of agents in the whole market) to affect the market price by its own actions. (This rules out, for example, firms characterized by increasing returns to scale.) Each consumer is a utility maximizer, and each firm is a profit maximizer. We assume *perfect knowledge* and *costless transactions*. These assumptions imply that the *law of one price* will hold: All trades between buyers and sellers will be conducted at the market price. (Otherwise, all buyers would flock to the seller offering the lowest price.) We assume there are *no barriers to the entry of firms to the industry or their exit from it.*

Under those conditions, how are quantity and price determined? The answer is usually divided into two cases by time: the short run, in which it is assumed that the number of firms and their plant sizes are fixed, and the long run, in which all factors are variable and the number of firms varies in response to market forces.

Let us consider the short-run case first. In Figure 10-1a we represent the short-run marginal, average variable, and average total cost curves of a representative firm (denoted MC, AVC, and ATC respectively). We have already seen (Chapter 8) that the firm in a competitive market faces a demand curve for its output perceived to be horizontal at the market price, and profit maximization therefore requires that the firm choose the quantity at which its MC = P (since P = MR in the competitive case). If $P = P_1$, for example, the firm will supply q_1 (Figure 10-1a). The firm's short-run supply curve thus corresponds to the upward-sloping portion of its MC cost, beginning at the point at which P = AVC.[1]

In Figure 10-1b we depict the market demand curve and the industry supply curve. Market demand, it will be recalled, is simply the sum of each individual's demand at each possible price. The market supply is derived similarly, but not exactly analogously. Market supply is defined as the sum of each firm's supply at a given price.[2] If the supply of factors to the industry is perfectly elastic, the analogy is exact. However, it may be that additional factors to the industry as a whole can be obtained only by bidding up their prices and thus shifting all the cost curves of firms in this industry. The market supply curve is upward-sloping in both cases. However, market supply cannot be derived solely from knowledge about each individual firm's supply curve;

---

[1] For $P <$ AVC, the firm is better off not to produce. As an exercise, the reader should explain why the firms will produce at a price like P_2 even though the firm is experiencing losses at that point.

[2] Some authors prefer to define the market supply curves in both the short run and the long run as the partial relations between the output quantity and its own price, input prices constant. With those definitions, the changes in input prices caused by changes in the industry output quantity are treated differently than we treat them below. They would cause shifts in the supply curves rather than movements along them. That is purely a descriptive difference; actual supply is the same function of input and output prices in either case.

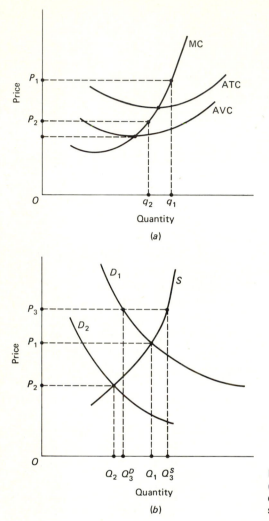

(a)

(b)

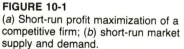

FIGURE 10-1
(a) Short-run profit maximization of a competitive firm; (b) short-run market supply and demand.

one must also know about the effects of changes in industry output levels on factor prices.

Figure 10-1*b* shows the equilibrium point, which is defined as a situation in which the market quantity demanded equals the market quantity supplied. This occurs where the demand and supply curves cross, at price P_1 and quantity Q_1. At any other price-quantity combination, the market forces that would be set in motion would return the market to its equilibrium. If the price were $P_3 > P_1$, for example, the quantity supplied would exceed the quantity demanded ($Q_3^S > Q_3^D$). Suppliers would observe their outputs going unsold, and lowering the price would be the only way to sell the outputs. As the market price lowers, each firm adjusts its supply downward until all firms are in market equilibrium.

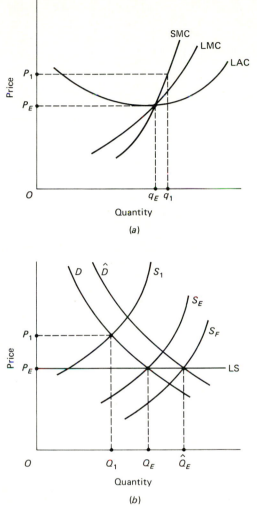

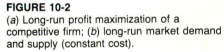

FIGURE 10-2
(a) Long-run profit maximization of a competitive firm; (b) long-run market demand and supply (constant cost).

Note that the equilibrium may or may not be profitable in the short run. As we have drawn it, the representative firm is making economic profits at (P_1, q_1). However, if the demand curve were D_2, crossing the supply curve at (P_2, Q_2), each firm would be in equilibrium at (P_2, q_2) and would be experiencing economic losses.

In the long run, neither allocation would be an equilibrium. To see this, let us turn to Figure 10-2a and b, where we have drawn the long-run marginal (LMC) and average cost (LAC) curves. Recall that, in the long run, all factors are freely variable and firms are free to enter or exit the industry.

Suppose that we are initially at (P_1, q_1), the short-run equilibrium where the representative firm is making a profit. Each firm in the industry will realize that it can increase profits by changing its plant and expanding output (since LMC < SMC at q_1); other firms will enter the industry in response to the existence of profits. Then the short-run supply curve will shift outward, which will cause the market price to fall until there are no profits left to be made by industry expansion. If the representative firm is making zero profit, it must be that $P =$ LAC. Since each firm is assumed to be maximizing profit, it must be that $P =$ LMC. Therefore, LAC = LMC, which occurs when the representative firm is at the minimum of its long-run average cost curve. It is only at this allocation, labeled (P_E, Q_E) in Figure 10-2b, that long-run equilibrium is attained.

What does the long-run supply (LS) curve look like? With perfectly elastic factor supplies it is simply the horizontal line at height P_E. That is, in the long run the market supply will be met by firms identical with the representative one shown, each operating at the minimum of its LAC curve. The number of firms (Q_E/q_E) is determined by where the market demand curve crosses the P_E line. If, for example, demand shifted to $\hat{D}$, the firms would adjust to produce total quantity $\hat{Q}_E$. Each firm would continue to produce q_E; price would remain at P_E; but the short-run supply curve S_E would shift out because of the entry of new firms. This is the case of the *constant cost industry*.

If, because of economies of scale in their production, factors become cheaper as the industry expands, the LS curve will slope downward. That is shown in Figure 10-3b. The expansion will represent an external economy for all firms, because all firms will have their cost curves lowered as shown in Figure 10-3a. Such a situation is described as a *decreasing cost industry*. An example might be electronic calculators; they have come down in price as the market has expanded, in part because of economies of scale in producing the semiconductor components. The last possible case is that of the *increasing cost industry*, the LS curve of which slopes upward (not drawn). But in all cases the conditions for long-run equilibrium are the same: zero profit and profit maximization, which together imply that the representative firm produces at the minimum of its LAC curve.

A number of important insights arise from applying the logic of competitive analysis in various policy settings. To take an unusual example let us consider a policy, pursued under the Nixon administration, to reduce the illegal use of heroin. Drug enforcement officials knew that Turkey was a main source of the illegal U.S. heroin supply, and an arrangement was made with Turkish officials to ban the growing of the opium poppy from which the heroin was derived.

In the short run the heroin supply in the United States was indeed reduced, but then the prospect of abnormally high profits enticed potential suppliers from elsewhere. A large number of countries have climates favorable to the cultivation of opium, and within a year several new countries were reported as the source of "major supplies" of heroin to the United States. The point is that it is silly to think that a long-run solution to the heroin problem can be attained by a narrowly targeted supply strategy. Furthermore, the United States is not

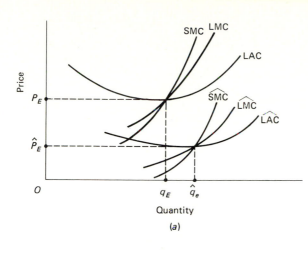

Quantity

(a)

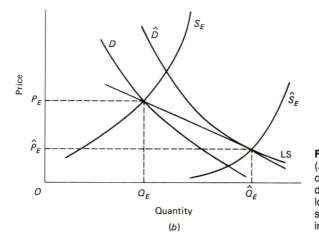

Quantity

(b)

FIGURE 10-3
(a) Long-run profit maximization of a competitive firm in a decreasing-cost industry; (b) long-run market demand and supply in a decreasing-cost industry.

capable of persuading all countries to ban (effectively) opium cultivation.[3] If there are opportunities for profits in a market, the competitive model indicates that new firms should be expected to enter.

Before concluding this section, let us note the important roles of the price in a competitive market. First, price is created through the interaction of demand and supply in the market. It is *information* which all economic agents use in making their decisions. The price serves to *ration* the available supply among

---

[3] There may be circumstances in which a series of short-run disruptions add up to a long-run solution. In this case the strategy did not work, as was predicted by analysts before the Turkish policy was adopted. See John Holahan, with the assistance of Paul Henningsen, "The Economics of Heroin," *Dealing with Drug Abuse* (New York: Praeger Publishers, 1972), pp. 255–299.

consumers. It also serves as a *signal* to producers, who use it in determining the output levels. In the short run, producer responsiveness to price is determined by the elasticity of the short-run supply curve. In the long run, price affects industry profitability which in turn affects firm entry, exit, and investment decisions. The supply elasticity is greater in the long run than in the short run because of the greater time flexibility for adjustments.[4]

ECONOMIC EFFICIENCY AND GENERAL COMPETITIVE EQUILIBRIUM

In this section we first review the three basic necessary conditions for Pareto optimality in an economy with many people and goods. We assume that the satisfaction of those conditions is sufficient to ensure Pareto optimality.[5] The conditions are completely independent of the type of economy; they are required for efficiency in capitalist, socialist, or any other economic organization.[6] Then we turn to a second question: whether the characteristics of a general competitive equilibrium in a market economy satisfy the necessary conditions for Pareto optimality.

Note that we are not making any organizational comparisons at this point. That is, we do not ask the equivalent questions about the efficiency of other than competitive organizations. The reasons for not asking those questions will become more apparent as we go on, but they can be previewed briefly. There are no economies which are perfectly competitive or perfectly anything else; all economies are mixed. The policy questions most relevant for organizations in a mixed economy have to do with determining the mixture. It is skill in answering the latter question, case by case, which we seek to build in the remainder of the text.

In Chapter 2 we reviewed the general definition of efficiency or Pareto optimality: An allocation is efficient (Pareto-optimal) if and only if no person can be made better off without making another person worse off. Logically, Pareto optimality in a many-person, many-good economy can be shown to require that certain relations hold among all the economic agents (individuals and firms). We have already seen some of those requirements, but we gather them here for general reference.

1 *Efficiency in exchange.* An economy is efficient in exchange if it is impossible to so reallocate the available goods that one person is better off and

---

[4] Actually, there are not two distinct elasticities. Rather, the supply elasticity is an increasing function of the time allowed for industry response.

[5] Establishing this result is complicated. For an excellent in-depth exposition of the issues involved in this section, see the first essay in T. Koopmans, *Three Essays on the State of Economic Science* (New York: McGraw-Hill Book Company, 1957).

[6] In the discussion below we assume that preferences are those of the individuals in the economy. However, as a logical matter, one could imagine alternative mechanisms for deciding preferences, and then the conditions described here would remain necessary and sufficient for achieving efficiency.

no one else is worse off. For any two goods this requires that each consumer of both goods have the same MRS for the two.[7] This was proved in Chapter 2.

2 *Efficiency in production.* An economy is efficient in production if and only if it is impossible to increase one output quantity without decreasing any other output quantity. There are four requirements that producers must meet for this to hold.[8]

a Technological efficiency. The maximum possible output is achieved with the inputs used by each producer.

b All producers using both of any two factors must have the same RTS for the two.

The proof of this is identical with the exchange efficiency proof that equal marginal rates of substitution are required. Suppose producer X has $RTS_{K,L}^X = 3$ (3 units of labor can be given up in return for 1 unit of capital without affecting the output level). Let producer Y have any different value, for example, $RTS_{K,L}^Y = 2$. Have X release 3 units of labor, and give 2 of them to Y. Take 1 unit of capital away from Y; thus, Y's output level is unaffected on balance. Give the 1 unit of capital to X and so restore X to the original output level. Both producers are at their initial levels, but we have one unused unit of labor left over which we can give to either. By doing so it is possible to increase one output without decreasing any other; therefore, the economy could not have been productively efficient initially. Productive efficiency requires that the rates be equalized. Note that this condition applies regardless of whether X and Y are producing the same or different outputs.

The above requirement is often the only one mentioned for production efficiency. It seems geometrically analogous to exchange efficiency; indeed, for a fixed supply of inputs, an Edgeworth box can be constructed for production, isoquants drawn in for two goods, and the tangency conditions used to define a production "contract curve" which is equivalent to the production possibilities frontier. However, this construction is based on the assumption that society so arranges its producing units (i.e., for a particular good) that resources cannot be reallocated within the industry to increase output. The following two conditions are necessary for efficient resource allocation within industries:

c The marginal product of any single factor used by firms producing the same output must be identical in each of the firms.

The proof of this is trivial. Suppose firm X has $MP_L = 2$ and firm Y has $MP_L = 3$. Then, by taking one unit of labor away from X and giving it to Y, we can increase the total output.

---

[7] This assumes that there are no consumption interdependencies, which would require the modifications discussed in Chapter 3. In addition, note that most individuals consume only a small fraction of the types of goods and services available. Let Q be a good that individual A does not consume but individual B does consume. If Z is any good that both A and B consume, efficiency requires $MRS_{Q,Z}^A < MRS_{Q,Z}^B$. This corner solution was demonstrated in Chapter 2.

[8] The assumption is that there are no technological externalities, which would have effects directly analogous to those of consumer interdependency. We discuss them later in the book.

d When multiple-product firms produce at least two of the same outputs, the RPT of those outputs must be identical in each firm.

Suppose firm X has $\text{RPT}_{Q_1, Q_2} = 4$ and firm Y has $\text{RPT}_{Q_1, Q_2} = 2$. Then have firm X reduce its Q_1 output unit by 1 and use the freed-up resources to produce 4 additional units of Q_2. Then have firm Y increase its production of Q_1 by 1 unit and thereby cause it to reduce Q_2 production by 2. Each firm is still using the same resources; total Q_1 production is unaffected; but there are now 2 more units of Q_2 than before.[9]

The conditions in **2** are designed to ensure that society is on its production-possibilities frontier. But it may not be on the right point of the frontier. For this, we need condition **3**:

3 *Efficiency of the product mix.* An economy has an efficient product mix if and only if it is impossible to choose an alternative product mix on the production-possibilities frontier (or transformation surface) and so distribute the new mix that one person is made better off and no one else is worse off. For any two goods this requires that the MRS among consumers equal the RPT of the transformation surface.

The proof is analogous to the preceding proofs. Suppose the condition is violated; for example, $\text{MRS}_{X, Y} = 3$ and $\text{RPT}_{X, Y} = 2$. Let a consumer give up 3 units of Y. Let a producer convert 2 units into one more X and so restore the consumer to the initial utility level. An extra Y is left over, and we can give it to anyone and thereby increase one person's utility without decreasing the utility of another. Thus, the initial product mix could not have been efficient.

These conditions have a simplicity that may belie their importance. They apply to every sector of the economy, whether public, private, nonprofit, or anything else. They are necessary conditions: If there is a violation of them anywhere (and, of course, there always are violations), then resource allocation in the economy is not efficient. The conditions are based purely on technical possibilities and consumer tastes; we have no need to refer to prices, wages, incomes, or profits. To suggest the breadth of the requirements, and at the same time introduce a dimension convenient for the discussion in the next section, let us suggest how the conditions determine the *level* of resource availability at any point in time.

Given the number of people in the economy, the supply of labor depends on how individuals make the labor-leisure trade-off discussed in Chapter 3. The efficiency conditions apply to this as well. They require that the rate of product transformation between leisure and any other good equal the marginal rate of substitution between leisure and that good. If there is involuntary unemployment in an economy (above the amount necessary for efficient job searching), then the efficiency conditions are violated.

---

[9] This rule, incidentally, is referred to as the theory of *comparative advantage* when the "firms" are countries. It is used as an argument for specialization by country combined with free trade among countries.

The labor-leisure trade-off is assumed to take place within a specified time period. Society also faces resource allocation trade-offs that go across time periods. They are the subject of more careful discussion later in the text, but we can plant the idea now. Society begins with a natural endowment of land, minerals, etc. which can be converted into consumption. Consumers have a marginal rate of substitution for a good today versus the same good tomorrow. That is sometimes referred to as the *marginal rate of time preference,* although it need not be the same for different goods. As long as the economy does not spend all of its resources that are available today on today's consumption, it is saving some (often referred to as *capital*) for tomorrow.

Like all economic activities, the amount of savings required by the efficiency rules depends not only on preferences but also on the technical possibilities for converting consumption deferred today into consumption tomorrow. Demand for snow skiing in the Vermont summers may be great, but few Vermont resort operators would keep skiers off the winter snow in order to try and preserve it until summer. On the other hand, young trees can produce a large increase in tomorrow's lumber supply, although they are only a small amount of lumber today. Efficiency requires that, for every good and every time period, the MRS between time periods equal the RPT for those periods.

With the above review of requirements for economic efficiency in an economy, it is easy to suggest why *any general competitive equilibrium is Pareto-optimal.* This proposition is the first of the well-known twin theorems relating efficiency and competition. The second theorem addresses distributional considerations: Assuming economic agents have well-behaved preferences and production technologies,[10] *any Pareto-optimal allocation of resources can be achieved as a general competitive equilibrium, as long as costless transfers of initial endowments are allowed.* It will be recalled from Chapter 2 that there are many possible Pareto-optimal allocations in an economy; and as long as society can choose among them, (outcome) equity does not require the sacrifice of efficiency.

We shall not attempt to prove either of the two theorems rigorously, but simply review the logic behind them. A simple way to summarize the proof of the first is that (1) all traders (individuals and firms) face the same prices in competitive equilibrium for the available factors and goods, which ensures that the required equality of all the marginal rates is satisfied (provided supply equals demand), and (2) market equilibrium ensures that supply equals demand. We clarify this below.

First, we must emphasize what we mean by a general competitive equilibrium: that a full set of markets exists (for every good, including future goods), that each of these markets is characterized by the conditions we described for one competitive industry, and that each market is in long-run equilibrium. This

---

[10] The phrase "well-behaved" is used to refer to the convexity requirements, which rule out such problems as increasing returns to scale. For a rigorous review and proof of the theorems, see the essay by Koopmans cited earlier in the chapter.

implies that supply equals demand for all goods. Now all we have to do is show that the prices at the equilibrium lead to the correct marginal trade-offs.

First consider efficiency in exchange. For any two goods X and Y with equilibrium prices P_X and P_Y, each consumer of both (in order to maximize utility) will equate $\mathrm{MRS}_{X,Y}$ with P_X/P_Y. Since all consumers face identical prices, all will have the same $\mathrm{MRS}_{X,Y}$ and exchange efficiency will be satisfied.

There are four rules for efficiency in production. The first is technological efficiency. Firm profit maximization requires that this rule be satisfied: If more output can be produced with the same inputs, then more revenue can be produced for the same cost and the firm is not at the profit maximum.

The second rule requires equality of rates of technical substitution among firms using the same inputs, $\mathrm{RTS}_{K,L}^{X} = \mathrm{RTS}_{K,L}^{Y}$. But we know that each firm, to produce at least cost (necessary for profit maximization), must set

$$\mathrm{RTS}_{K,L} = \frac{P_K}{P_L}$$

This is the condition of tangency between a firm's isoquant (the slope of which is $-\mathrm{RTS}_{K,L}$) and an isocost line (the slope of which is $-P_K/P_L$), which is required if the output level represented by the isoquant is to be produced at least cost.[11] Since all firms face the same prices for homogeneous factors, the RTS of all firms using them will be the same.

The third rule for productive efficiency is that the marginal product of a factor must be identical for each firm producing the same output. This can be shown to hold in competitive equilibrium as a consequence of profit maximization. If a firm hires one more factor, say, a unit of labor, the marginal cost of that action is P_L. The marginal revenue to the firm equals the marginal product times the price of the output P_X: $P_X \mathrm{MP}_L^X$. Profit maximization requires the firm to hire the amount of labor that makes

$$P_L = P_X \mathrm{MP}_L^X$$

We rewrite this as

$$\mathrm{MP}_L^X = \frac{P_L}{P_X}$$

Therefore, all firms in industry X will have identical marginal products, since all face the same prices P_X and P_L.

The fourth rule for productive efficiency is that the rate of product transformation between two goods must be identical across firms. In the Robinson Crusoe model of Chapter 7 we demonstrated that the $\mathrm{RPT}_{X,Y}$ can be

---

[11] This is shown graphically in the optional section of Chapter 7.

interpreted as the marginal cost of X in terms of Y foregone. If we wish to express the marginal cost in dollar terms, we have only to multiply by P_Y:

$$MC_X = RPT_{X,Y}\, P_Y$$

Competitive profit-maximizing firms always choose the output level where $MC = P\ (= MR)$; therefore, in competitive equilibrium

$$P_X = RPT_{X,Y}\, P_Y$$

or
$$RPT_{X,Y} = \frac{P_X}{P_Y}$$

Finally, since all producers of X and Y face the same prices P_X and P_Y, the $RPT_{X,Y}$ must be the same for all producers.

So far we have shown that, in the general competitive equilibrium, exchange and production efficiency are satisfied. The final condition, product mix efficiency, follows trivially. We have already shown that $MRS_{X,Y} = P_X/P_Y$ for all consumers and that $RPT_{X,Y} = P_X/P_Y$ for all producers. Therefore, $MRS_{X,Y} = RPT_{X,Y}$ and the last condition is satisfied. A general competitive equilibrium is Pareto-optimal.

The second of the twin theorems states that any Pareto optimum can be achieved by a general competitive equilibrium (assuming preferences and technologies are well-behaved). In other words, suppose we know where we wish to end up; the question is whether a competitive system can take us there. Consider any particular optimum. Since it satisfies all the efficiency requirements, we know the required marginal trade-off for each of them: e.g., all consumers must have $MRS_{X,Y} = \alpha_{X,Y}$, where $\alpha_{X,Y}$ is some number. Therefore, we must choose prices P_X and P_Y such that $P_X/P_Y = \alpha_{X,Y}$.

Note that we have a degree of freedom: the efficiency conditions refer only to *relative* prices, not to each one singly. Therefore, we can pick any good to serve as a reference unit, called the *numéraire*, for expressing the relative values of all other goods. For example, set P_X equal to any number we like. Since there is only one remaining unknown in each of the equations relating good X to every possible other good, this determines the prices of all other goods.[12]

Of course, we have not yet ensured that demand and supply will be in equilibrium at these prices. To achieve the equilibrium, we must assign to each individual an income that exactly equals the value of his or her optimal allocation at the prices identified above. Given that income and facing the specified prices, each consumer will be in equilibrium only when purchasing

---

[12] In macroeconomics, it is often useful to think of the numéraire good as "money" and to consider how macroeconomic forces influence its level.

the bundle of goods and services (including leisure) that we initially identified as the goal. We have simply assigned budget constraints (prices and income levels) that are tangent to each person's indifference curves at the desired allocations. Thus, as long as we can costlessly redistribute income, any Pareto optimum can be achieved through a general competitive equilibrium.

Some economists interpret this second theorem as a reason to avoid equity concerns. That is, as long as any optimal allocation can be achieved, the economist can simply assume that policy makers will assign the incomes to individuals that they think appropriate (e.g., through a progressive tax system, a welfare system, etc.). The economist can restrict his or her concern to the efficiency of the situation. This can have the added advantage of simplifying policy debate over specific issues.[13]

There are numerous counterarguments to this position, and those involving process equity and political limits on the use of a small number of policy instruments were reviewed in Chapters 2 and 5. An additional important argument which will be shown later in the chapter is this: *There is no costless method of redistribution,* and efficiency requires that any given redistribution be achieved through whatever policy instruments achieve it at least cost.[14] In Chapter 13 we review more carefully some basic choices of instruments to achieve specific equity goals in particular markets.

GENERAL COMPETITIVE ANALYSIS WITH A TAX INCIDENCE ILLUSTRATION

Several times in the text we have cautioned that specific analytic effects which appear in *partial* equilibrium models may disappear or be quite different in *general* equilibrium models. In the partial equilibrium model we allow variation in only the prices and quantities of one or several markets and assume all other prices are held constant. But depending on the source of the changes we consider, the assumption that other prices are unaffected may not be tenable. A tax on corporate capital, for example, may not affect only the price and allocation of capital through its direct effect on the corporate sector; it may cause the relative price of capital to change elsewhere in the economy and thereby shift cost curves in other industries, which will affect allocation in them. This may cause further changes in the corporate sector because the other prices have changed.

In this section we attempt to clarify the importance of this difference with an illustration of partial and general equilibrium analyses of *tax incidence:* the changes in the real income of individuals caused by the imposition of a tax.

---

[13] Charles Schultze has expressed concern that "equity" is an argument which can be used by any clever special interest group to tie up, change, or frustrate the attempt to improve the efficiency of the economy in specific areas, even if most people would benefit from the change. See his book, *The Public Uses of Private Interests* (Washington, D.C.: The Brookings Institution, 1977). Policy analysis which includes equity considerations should be able to address such arguments.

[14] See also A. Okun, *Equality and Efficiency: The Big Tradeoff* (Washington, D.C.: The Brookings Institution, 1975).

However, the point we wish to emphasize is not the incidence in the specific illustrative model developed. The more important point is to develop analytic ability in understanding the reasons for differences between the two types of analyses and in beginning to judge the adequacy of one method versus the other in applications.

We begin the analysis with a partial equilibrium model and introduce the concepts of tax incidence and tax shifting. Then we extend the analysis to general equilibrium in a two-sector model. We discuss each part of the general model and then derive the competitive allocation by ensuring that all markets are *simultaneously* in equilibrium. Then we look at the effects of the same tax examined in the partial equilibrium model and contrast the results. We conclude with a brief discussion of lump-sum taxes and efficiency in taxation.

Partial Equilibrium Analysis: The Excise Tax

Suppose, for our partial equilibrium model, that we are producing a product Q in a competitive market. The demand for Q is given as

$$Q = \frac{200}{P}$$

The production function for Q is constant returns to scale:

$$Q = \tfrac{3}{2} L$$

Thus the marginal product of labor is simply $\tfrac{3}{2}$, no matter how many producers there are. We know that each competitive producer will hire labor until the value of the marginal product equals the market price of labor:

$$P_L = \text{VMP}_L^Q = \tfrac{3}{2} P$$

or
$$P = \tfrac{2}{3} P_L$$

In this model we take P_L as a given parameter; only Q and its price P are allowed to vary. This means that the supply curve for Q is perfectly elastic: the horizontal line of height $\tfrac{2}{3} P_L$. We will assume that $P_L = 3$ in the economy; therefore, $P = 2$ is the supply curve. We draw the demand and supply curves in Figure 10-4a. The equilibrium quantity is $Q = 100$ at $P = 2$.

Now suppose we put an excise tax of 0.67 on this industry's produce. *It does not matter whether we put the tax on the manufacturer or the consumer.* The relevant aspect of the tax is that it creates a wedge between what the consumer pays and what the producer receives: There will be a *difference* between the demander's price and the supplier's price for any given quantity. For the excise tax of 0.67, the (partial equilibrium) effect is shown in Figure 10-4a. Producers receive only $2 per unit, although demanders pay $2.67; and the new equilibrium market quantity is shown as $Q_T = 74.91$ units.

In this case, with perfectly elastic supply, the consumers bear the full burden

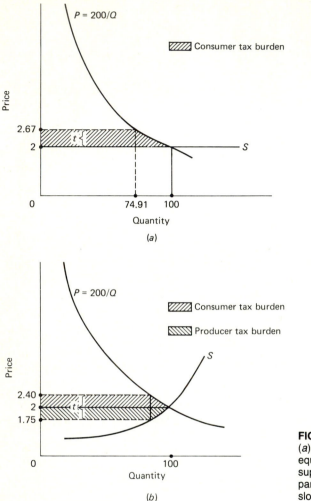

FIGURE 10-4
(a) Excise tax incidence, partial equilibrium with a perfectly elastic supply; (b) excise tax incidence, partial equilibrium with upward-sloping supply.

of the tax. All of the tax payments (as well as all of the deadweight loss) come from a reduction in consumer surplus. If we had a sloping supply curve, as in Figure 10-4b, the incidence of the tax would be partially borne by both consumers (through the loss in consumer surplus) and producers (through the loss of economic rent). Thus, the more elastic the demand curve and the more inelastic the supply curve, the more the incidence of the tax will fall on producers (other things equal). Of course, one cannot evaluate the equity of this unless one knows something about who the consumers and producers are.[15]

---

[15] The market could be for low-rent housing, in which it is likely that tenants are less well off than apartment suppliers and the tax is a property tax. Alternatively, the market could be for expensive jewelry, in which the consumer may be at least as well off as the jewelry suppliers and

Another concept that is often used in the study of tax incidence is called *tax shifting*. As we have already suggested, the economic agents upon whom the tax is levied may not be the full bearers of the tax. When they are not, we say that the tax has been partially shifted. If the tax in Figure 10-4*a* is placed on the manufacturers, the partial equilibrium effect is to shift the tax fully *forward* to consumers. The same tax placed initially on consumers has an identical incidence but would not be considered shifted. Of course, the concept is intended to apply to more interesting cases like that in Figure 10-4*b*: partially shifted *forward* if initially placed on producers or *backwards* if initially placed on consumers. A tax may also be shifted backwards to the factor suppliers (not shown).

General Equilibrium Analysis: Perfect Competition, No Taxation

Let us now look at the shortcomings of this analysis that are due to our considering only the partial equilibrium effects. To do so, we introduce a simple general equilibrium model. We assume that the economy is composed of individuals whose tastes are identical and that there are only two goods (sectors). Keep in mind that our purpose in constructing this simple model is to illustrate the reasons why partial equilibrium analysis can be insufficient or misleading in terms of the conclusions drawn from using it.[16]

More specifically, we assume that each individual has a utility function of the form

$$U = Q_1^{1/2} Q_2^{1/2}$$

As was calculated in the optional section of Chapter 5, this function implies demand curves for a budget of B as follows:

$$D(Q_1) = \frac{\frac{1}{2} B}{P_1}$$

$$D(Q_2) = \frac{\frac{1}{2} B}{P_2}$$

Thus each person will spend one-half of his or her budget B on, say, Q_1 independently of the budget level. This implies that the aggregate expenditure

---

the tax is an excise tax. Even these distinctions refer to specific groups, and there is sure to be variation of individual well-being within each group.

[16] More realistic general equilibrium models, which allow for greater variation in tastes and technologies, are complex to explain and may require computer analysis for making empirical calculations with them. However, powerful techniques are being developed to facilitate this work. One technique is explained in H. Scarf, with the collaboration of T. Hansen, *The Computation of Economic Equilibria* (New Haven, Conn.: Yale University Press, 1973). An empirical application of the technique is offered by J. Shoven and J. Whalley, "Equal Yield Tax Alternatives: General Equilibrium Computational Technique," *Journal of Public Economics, 8*, 1977, pp. 211–224.

for Q_1 will always be one-half of aggregate income, and the aggregate quantity demanded is simply one-half total income divided by price. This means that aggregate demand for each good is not affected by the distribution of income in the economy. (More realistic models would relax that assumption.) It also means that there is zero cross-price elasticity, which keeps the consumption side "simple."

On the production side we also choose assumptions to simplify the analysis. We assume that the economy has a fixed (perfectly inelastic) supply of labor ($L = 100$) and capital ($K = 100$); thus we are ruling out changes in the total quantities of factors which might be caused by policies. (For example, a tax on labor income might in actuality reduce the labor supply, and this model would obviously not be a good one for analysis of that effect.) We also assume that each good has constant returns to scale (CRTS) technology:

$$Q_1 = K_1^{1/2} L_1^{1/2}$$
$$Q_2 = \tfrac{3}{2} L_2$$

Note that the second technology is the one used in the preceding partial equilibrium analysis. At this point all the information necessary to determine the general competitive equilibrium has been given: We know tastes, technologies, and factor endowments. All that remains is to apply the logic of competitive analysis.

We first note one convenient implication of the assumptions we have made. The competitive environment and the CRTS technology imply that the output of each sector can be calculated as if all the factors were used by one big firm which behaves competitively.[17] This simplifies a number of the derivations which follow.

---

[17] We know competition ensures that each firm will choose the same $RTS_{K,L}$. For CRTS this implies that each firm operates at a point on its isoquant that is on the same ray through the origin (capital-labor ratio) as all other firms in the sector. Because there are neither economies nor diseconomies of scale, the sum of the outputs of all firms on this ray is the same as if one firm using the summed inputs produced the output.

To show that all competitive firms operate on the same ray requires use of Euler's theorem for homogeneous functions. A function $Q = F(X_1, X_2, \ldots, X_n)$ is homogeneous of degree s if, for any positive constant m,

$$m^s Q = F(mX_1, mX_2, \ldots, mX_n)$$

Euler's theorem states that, for any homogeneous function of degree s,

$$sQ = \frac{\partial F}{\partial X_1} X_1 + \frac{\partial F}{\partial X_2} X_2 + \cdots + \frac{\partial F}{\partial X_n} X_n$$

Furthermore, the partial derivatives of a homogeneous function of degree s are themselves homogeneous of degree $s - 1$:

We have already established the competitive supply curve for sector 2:

$$P_2 = \tfrac{2}{3} P_L$$

However, it is useful to derive it again by using the cost function approach described in Chapter 7 (with technical details in that chapter's optional section). Recall that the cost function expresses total cost as a function of the output level and input prices. The (total) cost function C_2 associated with sector 2's production function is

$$C_2 = \tfrac{2}{3} P_L Q_2$$

The marginal cost of one more unit of Q_2 is thus

$$\mathrm{MC}_2 = \tfrac{2}{3} P_L$$

Profit maximization requires that the firm produce where marginal cost equals marginal revenue. Since in the competitive environment MR = P, we have

$$P_2 = \tfrac{2}{3} P_L$$

This is the supply curve for the sector (as we happen to know already).

$$\frac{\partial F(mX_1, mX_2, \ldots, mX_n)}{\partial mX_1} = m^{s-1} \frac{\partial F(X_1, X_2, \ldots, X_n)}{\partial X_1}$$

All CRTS production functions are linearly homogeneous ($s = 1$). Thus, if $Q = F(K,L)$ is CRTS, we have:

$$Q = \frac{\partial F}{\partial K} K + \frac{\partial F}{\partial L} L$$

$$= \mathrm{MP}_K K + \mathrm{MP}_L L$$

Since the marginal products are the partial derivatives of a linear homogeneous function, they are themselves homogeneous functions of degree *zero* (like demand functions). Multiplying K and L by any constant m does not change the value of the marginal products, but multiplying an initial K and L by any positive constant m defines precisely the locus of points along one ray from the origin in an isoquant diagram. Thus, all points on the ray have the same MP_K, MP_L, and $\mathrm{RTS}_{K,L}$.

We have not shown that all points off the ray must have a different $\mathrm{RTS}_{K,L}$, but that is not a problem. For any elasticity of substitution σ strictly within the interval $0 < \sigma < \infty$, the slope of each isoquant becomes continually flatter from left to right, so the locus of points with a constant slope must lie on one ray. (Otherwise, some isoquants would have two points on it with the same slope, which we have ruled out.) For the extreme case of $\sigma = \infty$, the slope of each isoquant is everywhere constant (i.e., the isoquant is a straight line). In this case the factors are perfectly substitutable and the competitive (and efficient) firm will use only one factor or be indifferent to any K/L combination (should the isocost line and isoquant have identical slopes). For the case of $\sigma = 0$, the competitive firm will produce at the right angle of the isoquant as long as factor prices are positive; CRTS implies all these lie on one ray.

What is the derived demand for labor in this sector? In the optional section in Chapter 7 we showed that the change in the cost function for a small (1 unit) change in the input price is the optimal input quantity (Shephard's lemma). That is, consider the change in least total cost caused by a small factor price change while the output level is held constant. In the one-input case it is simply the amount of labor multiplied by the price change, since the same labor is required. If we think of the small change as being a 1-unit price change, the change in total cost is 1 multiplied by the optimal labor input, or simply the optimal labor quantity.

Thus, we use the cost function to identify the quantity of factors demanded. If we ask how sector 2's least total cost changes in response to a small (1-unit) change in the price of labor, the answer is

$$\Delta C_2 = \tfrac{2}{3} Q_2$$

But since that must equal the optimal labor input,

$$L_2 = \tfrac{2}{3} Q_2$$

This equation is the derived demand curve for labor, given any output level. In this case the answer may appear to be a trivial consequence of the production function, and one may wonder why we did not just assert that directly. Do not be misled; the cost function procedure is generally a means of simplification rather than complication.

Let us turn to sector 1, where the power of the cost function approach is more apparent. The cost function C_1 associated with our Cobb-Douglas production function is[18]

$$C_1 = 2P_K^{1/2}P_L^{1/2}Q_1$$

Then the marginal cost per unit of Q_1 is simply

$$MC_1 = 2P_K^{1/2}P_L^{1/2}$$

Note that, from the perspective of a firm, which regards P_K and P_L as fixed parameters, this is simply a constant. Since the competitive firm equates MC to product price, in equilibrium we have

$$P_1 = 2P_K^{1/2}P_L^{1/2}$$

This is the competitive supply curve for sector 1.[19] It is perfectly elastic for fixed factor prices (as expected for CRTS production).

---

[18] This was derived in the optional section of Chapter 7.

[19] Any one skeptical of the usefulness of the cost function approach in deriving the supply curve, and the factor demand curves which follow, is urged to derive the curves directly from the production function.

In this sector both capital and labor are used. The derived demand curves are found by calculating the effect of a small change in the factor's price on the cost function:[20]

$$L_1 = P_K^{1/2} P_L^{-1/2} Q_1$$
$$K_1 = P_K^{-1/2} P_L^{1/2} Q_1$$

We have now described the equations for demand and supply in the product market and calculated the derived factor demands which (summed across sectors) must be equated to the (fixed) factor supplies. There is one last step to take before solving for the equilibrium: What is the budget level that goes in the demand equations?

The aggregate income in this economy is simply the sum of the payments to the factors:

$$B = P_K K + P_L L$$

That is, each person rents out his or her capital and labor, receives the competitive payments, and then uses the income to buy the two products available. We have already indicated that, in this simple model, the distribution of income does not affect the demand. However, how do we ensure that the model's equilibrium is one in which total income equals total spending? After all, it would be embarrassing to discover our model calls for consumers to spend twice as much as they earn.

Fortunately, the competitive assumptions with CRTS technology imply that the factor payments add up to the total value of the output.[21] To show that, we made use of Euler's theorem (see earlier footnote) as it applies to CRTS (= linear homogeneous) technology. It implies that

$$Q_i = MP_K^i K_i + MP_L^i L_i \qquad i = 1, 2$$

Multiply both sides of this equation by P_i, and note that each term on the right-hand side contains the value of the marginal product (P_i MP),

$$P_i Q_i = (P_i\, MP_K^i) K_i + (P_i\, MP_L^i) L_i \qquad i = 1, 2$$

In equilibrium, each firm hires factors until the value of the marginal product

---

[20] These equations are found by taking the partial derivative of the cost function with respect to each factor price:

$$L_1 = \frac{\partial C_1}{\partial P_L} \qquad K_1 = \frac{\partial C_1}{\partial P_K}$$

[21] This would hold for DRTS as well. Competition ensures that each firm will be at the minimum of its average cost curve, and thus all firms are "locally" CRTS. However, the competitive model does not work with IRTS.

(the marginal benefit of an additional factor) equals the factor price (the marginal cost of the factor). Thus, we can rewrite the above equation by substituting P_K and P_L:

$$P_i Q_i = P_K K_i + P_L L_i \qquad i = 1, 2$$

If we sum across both sectors,

$$\Sigma P_i Q_i = P_K \Sigma K_i + P_L \Sigma L_i$$
or
$$\Sigma P_i Q_i = P_K K + P_L L$$

In other words, aggregate consumer spending equals aggregate income. With that reassurance, we rewrite the product demand equations:

$$Q_i = \frac{\frac{1}{2}(P_L L + P_K K)}{P_i} \qquad i = 1, 2$$

Now we are ready to solve for the equilibrium. Table 10-1 summarizes all the equations that we have used to characterize the competitive equilibrium in this economy. We have eight equations with eight unknowns: P_K, P_L, P_1, P_2, K, L, Q_1, and Q_2.[22]

However, we know from theoretical considerations that only *relative* prices matter. That is, we must pick one good as numéraire and measure all other prices relative to it. That will give us only seven real unknowns but eight equations. Does that mean there will be an infinite number of solutions to our problem? No, because *Walras' law* tells us that one of the equations is redundant anyway.

Walras' law states that the price-weighted sum of demands minus supplies for all quantities must be equal to zero, whether or not the economy is in equilibrium; therefore, if demand equals supply in $n - 1$ of n markets, Walras' law implies that demand equals supply in the nth market as well.[23] In our model let us say we make sure the solution equates supply and demand in the first three markets of Table 10-1. Then we do not have to bother equating the two sides of the labor market; Walras' law assures us that the market will be in equilibrium as a consequence of equating the first three.

Let us solve the system in just that manner. We pick as a convenient numéraire $P_K = 1$, and we note that factor endowments are $K = 100$ and $L = $

---

[22] Consider K and L as trivially unknown.

[23] A proof of this may be found in H. Varian, *Microeconomic Analysis* (New York: W. W. Norton and Co., 1978), pp. 163–164. The idea behind the proof is simple. Remember that firms are merely intermediaries. Each person has an endowment of goods and factors which may be supplied to the marketplace (e.g., through employment, the provision of capital to firms, or garage sales). The income received from these sources (e.g., wages, firm profits, and garage receipts) is the budget constraint, which is then spent entirely in order to maximize utility. Thus, for an individual, the price-weighted sum of demands (over all commodities) minus supplies (over all commodities) equals zero. But then the sum over all persons is zero, and that is Walras' law.

TABLE 10-1
SUMMARY OF THE TWO-SECTOR COMPETITIVE
ECONOMY

Product markets		

Sector 1

Demand	$Q_1 = \dfrac{\frac{1}{2}(P_L L + P_K K)}{P_1}$	(1)
Supply	$P_1 = 2P_K^{1/2} P_L^{1/2}$	(2)

Sector 2

Demand	$Q_2 = \dfrac{\frac{1}{2}(P_L L + P_K K)}{P_2}$	(3)
Supply	$P_2 = \frac{2}{3}P_L$	(4)

Factor markets		

Capital
Demand	$K = K_1 + K_2 = P_K^{-1/2} P_L^{1/2} Q_1$	(5)
Supply	$K = 100$	(6)

Labor
Demand	$L = L_1 + L_2 = P_K^{1/2} P_L^{-1/2} Q_1 + \frac{2}{3}Q_2$	(7)
Supply	$L = 100$	(8)

100. In sector 1 we equate supply and demand by ensuring that P_1 in equation (1) has the value required by (2):

$$Q_1 = \frac{\frac{1}{2}(P_L L + P_K K)}{2P_K^{1/2}P_L^{1/2}}$$

Next we equate supply and demand in the capital market equations (5) and (6) and then use the expression above to substitute for Q_1:

$$100 = P_K^{-1/2}P_L^{1/2}Q_1$$
$$100 = \frac{\frac{1}{2}(P_L L + P_K K)}{2P_K}$$

Or substituting for the endowments and numéraire, we have

$$100 = \frac{\frac{1}{2}(100P_L + 100)}{2}$$

or

$$P_L = 3$$

By substituting this back in equations (2) and then (1), we get

$$P_1 = \sqrt{12} \approx 3.46$$

and

$$Q_1 = \frac{100}{\sqrt{3}} \approx 57.74$$

Now we can complete our solution by noting that the supply equation (4) in sector 2 can be solved for P_2 directly, and using this value in (3) ensures equilibrium in that market:

$$P_2 = 2$$

and
$$Q_2 = 100$$

This completes the solution. Note that we never equated demand and supply in the labor market in order to obtain the solution. Has the promise of Walras' law been kept?

$$\text{Demand} \qquad L = 1^{1/2}(3^{-1/2})\,\frac{100}{\sqrt{3}} + \tfrac{2}{3}(100)$$

$$= 33.333 + 66.667$$

$$= 100$$

Therefore, demand equals supply in the labor market, as expected. Let us note a few other characteristics of the equilibrium:[24]

$$
\begin{array}{ll}
L_1 = 33.333 & \text{share of labor in sector 1} \\
L_2 = 66.667 & \text{share of labor in sector 2} \\
P_L L = 300 & \text{labor's share of total income} \\
P_K K = 100 & \text{capital's share of total income}
\end{array}
$$

[24] In this economy it is particularly simple to illustrate the second of the twin theorems. Because of our assumptions, neither the aggregate supply of factors nor the aggregate demand for products is affected by the distribution of factor ownership. That is, no matter how the ownership of K and L is distributed, the equilibrium market prices and quantities will be as above.

Suppose there are only two people in this economy. Then the locus of Pareto-optimal allocations in the economy is simply any proportionate distribution of the two outputs. That is, for all $0 < \alpha < 1$, allocate αQ_2 and αQ_1 to person R and $(1 - \alpha)Q_2$ and $(1 - \alpha)Q_1$ to person S (Q_2 and Q_1 are the constant market quantities 100 and 57.74, respectively).

To achieve any of these Pareto-optimal allocations, one simply redistributes income to give each person the appropriate budget size. Suppose each person starts with $K = 50$ and $L = 50$; then competitive markets will result in each earning \$200 and will lead to the optimal allocation where $\alpha = 0.5$. If we want to achieve some other efficient allocation, say $\alpha = 0.6$, then we must take away the equivalent of \$40 from S and give it to R. We could do that by taking 40 units of capital away from S and giving it to R. In this example competitive markets would then lead to all the same prices and aggregate quantities; R simply ends up with \$40 more income and thus can purchase more. To make R very much better off than initially ($\alpha > 0.625$), we would have to assign R some of the fruits from the labor of S in addition to redistributing all 50 units of capital from S.

[25] The story would, of course, change if the government used the funds to demand different goods. Since that is what governments normally do with taxes, a word of explanation for our assumption may be helpful. The most common method of tax incidence analysis is called *differential tax incidence*. In this method two or more different taxes designed to be of equal yield are compared, the assumption being that the government's purpose for the funds does not change with the tax method. If we allowed the use of the funds to cause a change in our example equilibrium, the analysis would not capture the pure tax effects. We are implicitly comparing our tax to a perfectly neutral one which changes no allocation decisions and keeps income distribution the same.

General Equilibrium Analysis: The Excise Tax

Now let us turn to the primary purpose for constructing this model: to see how the solution changes in response to some change in the economy and compare the evaluation from a partial equilibrium analysis with that from a general equilibrium analysis. Let us note that the partial equilibrium version of sector 2 is precisely that which we have already analyzed. That is, sector 2's demand and supply curves are treated as partial equilibrium equations when we hold the variables P_L, L, P_K, and K constant at their general equilibrium levels:

$$Q_2 = \frac{\frac{1}{2}(300 + 100)}{P_2} = \frac{200}{P_2}$$

$$P_2 = \tfrac{2}{3}(3) = 2$$

Therefore, let us now impose the $0.67 excise tax on good 2 and see how it affects the economy. We assume that the taxes collected are redistributed to individuals (retirees perhaps) who spend the funds as all other individuals do.[25] For convenience we assume the tax is levied on the consumer at the point of purchase.

Referring to Table 10-1, all factor market equations are unaffected and the supply equations in each product sector are unaffected. However, both demand equations must be changed. In the numerator of each we must take account of the change in aggregate income for the economy:

$$B = P_L L + P_K K + t Q_2$$

where t is the excise tax rate on Q_2. (Tax receipts become income when redistributed.) In sector 2 the demand price (the denominator) becomes $P_2 + t$, since in the new equilibrium consumers must pay t more per unit than the P_2 received by suppliers. Thus our new system of equations is identical with the old except for these changes:

$$\text{Demand} \qquad Q_1 = \frac{\frac{1}{2}(P_L L + P_K K + t Q_2)}{P_1} \qquad (1')$$

$$\text{Demand} \qquad Q_2 = \frac{\frac{1}{2}(P_L L + P_K K + t Q_2)}{P_2 + t} \qquad (3')$$

We can see without making any numerical calculations that the economy will remain productively efficient (factor suppliers face the same factor prices that factor demanders face). However, the economy will not be at the optimal point on the production frontier because

$$\text{RPT}_{Q_1, Q_2} = \frac{P_1}{P_2} \qquad \text{for suppliers}$$

$$\mathrm{MRS}_{Q_1,Q_2} = \frac{P_1}{P_2 + t} \quad \text{for demanders}$$

Therefore $\qquad\qquad \mathrm{RPT} \neq \mathrm{MRS}$

With a bit more manipulation, which may be done as an exercise, the system can be solved as in the preceding example. Using $P_K = 1$ as numéraire and $t = 0.67$, the equilibrium values are

$$
\begin{array}{ll}
P_K = 1 & K = 100 \\
P_L = 2.41 & L = 100 \quad (L_1 = 41.42, \; L_2 = 58.58) \\
P_1 = 3.10 & Q_1 = 64.45 \\
P_2 = 1.61 & Q_2 = 87.87
\end{array}
$$

$$\text{Tax collections } tQ_2 = 58.58$$
$$\text{Labor income } P_L L = 241$$
$$\text{Capital income } P_K K = 100$$
$$\text{Total income} = 399.58 \; (\approx 400)$$

The striking aspect of this result is that the tax is borne fully by labor throughout the economy. Capital income is unchanged, as is total income. Labor income has gone down by the full amount of the tax proceeds. Why did that happen? We have taxed the *labor-intensive industry*. The changes in consumer prices cause Q_2 production to go down (by releasing labor from sector 2) and Q_1 production to go up (by hiring more labor). With more labor per unit of capital in sector 1, the value of labor's marginal product falls. It also falls in sector 2 because of the reduction in P_2 (it is, of course, the same in both sectors). Capital's marginal productivity goes up, but in this case the value of the marginal product remains constant because of the decrease in P_1.

Under less restrictive but still competitive model assumptions, we would find that an excise tax on the labor-intensive industry always makes labor worse off.[26] Capital may or may not be made worse off; that depends on whether the marginal productivity gain outweighs the relative price loss.

We might also note that the consumer with average income is worse off than before the tax even though average income is the same. The reason for that should be obvious: We already know that the product mix under the tax regime differs from the optimal one. Under the tax regime prices, the consumer cannot purchase as attractive a bundle of goods for a given budget. To see that, we have only to calculate the aggregate utility in each regime:[27]

$$U = Q_1^{1/2} \, Q_2^{1/2}$$
$$U_0 = 57.75^{1/2}(100^{1/2}) = 75.987$$
$$U_1 = 64.45^{1/2}(87.87^{1/2}) = 75.254$$

Of course, the utility numbers by themselves have no meaning other than the ordering. To put them in context, we divide the 0.733 loss in utility by the marginal utility of an additional budget unit (0.18996 at the optimum or 0.18833 at the tax equilibrium).[28] The deadweight loss (sometimes called the *excess burden* of the tax) in the economy is 3.9 budget units, or about 1 percent of aggregate income.

To return to the incidence of the tax, note that we cannot evaluate it further without knowledge of the distribution of factor ownership among the population. If each person owned one unit of capital and labor, the equity of labor bearing the full burden would be no different than if labor and capital shared it equally. On the other hand, if the ownership of capital is concentrated among the wealthy few and the labor is that of the poor majority, we say the tax is regressive in its incidence.

Comparing Partial and General Equilibrium Analysis

Now, how does this general equilibrium analysis compare with the partial equilibrium analysis? Certainly the qualitative effect of the excise tax on consumption is the same: It reduces consumption of Q_2. However, the partial model completely fails to predict the backward shifting of the tax to the labor factors of production throughout the economy.

This illustrates, in a simple way, why there has been such a disavowal of old conventional wisdom about the incidence of taxes.[29] Reasoning by partial equilibrium analysis, it appears that consumers bear the burden of the tax. In a tautological way they do. (Who among us is not a consumer?) But it is not the "average" consumer of Q_2 who bears the burden. That is, the fact that Q_2 is a

---

[27] The utility function in our model, like both production functions, is linear homogeneous. This implies that the sum of utilities based on each person's consumption equals the utility assuming that Robinson Crusoe consumes the total output of the economy. Thus, if aggregate utility is higher in one regime, the utility of the consumer with average income must be higher as well.

[28] We have seen that, when utility is maximized, the Lagrangian multiplier λ on the budget constraint may be interpreted as the marginal utility of an additional budget unit (Chapter 2, optional section). We have also seen that, for a Cobb-Douglas utility function, $U = \lambda B$ at the optimum (Chapter 5, optional section). At the optimum here, $U_0 = 75.987$ and $B = 400$, which implies $\lambda = 0.18996$. At the tax optimum here, $U_1 = 75.254$ and $B = 400$, which implies $\lambda = 0.18833$.

[29] A good example of this is the property tax, which had long been considered regressive. Many analysts now feel that it is progressive or proportional, although the issue is unsettled. See, for example, H. Aaron, "A New View of Property Tax Incidence," *American Economic Review, 64,* No. 2, May 1974, pp. 212–221.

good with unitary income elasticity does not identify who the losers are in this case. Net of the tax redistribution, assumed to be the same no matter which tax is used to raise revenues, labor income is reduced by a full 20 percent and capital income is unchanged.

The particular result of this model depends, of course, on the specific assumptions we made. If, for example, we made Q_2 more of a luxury good relative to Q_1 and labor income were used primarily to purchase Q_1, then the burden on labor would be reduced. The point we are trying to emphasize is that reasonable prediction of tax incidence may require a much fuller specification of conditions in the economy than is required for partial equilibrium analysis.

There is another important way, aside from incidence, in which the partial equilibrium analysis is substantially misleading: the prediction of government tax receipts. The partial analysis substantially overestimates the size of the Q_2 reduction. (It predicts 74.91 as the new Q_2 equilibrium, whereas the correct quantity is 87.87.) That leads to a substantial underestimate of tax receipts (50.19 estimated versus 58.87 actual) and an overestimate of the deadweight loss (the partial estimate is 7.60 under the ordinary demand curve, or closer to 2 percent of national income).

The primary reason for the inaccuracy of the partial analysis is that it does not take account of the reduced price of labor at the tax equilibrium. The new supply curve for sector 2 is lower than its initial level. It lowers as labor flows out of the sector, which causes its marginal productivity to fall in the rest of the (more capital-intensive) economy. Consider the perspective of government budget makers who may have relied on the partial estimates in planning expenditures. Our general model suggests revenues will be almost 20 percent greater than expenditures; not many governments can afford errors of that magnitude.

General equilibrium models are increasingly being used for applied problems. Harberger has pioneered the application of a two-sector model to the study of tax incidence.[30] He found, using a model no more complicated than ours, that a tax on corporate goods (the capital-intensive sector) is borne fully by capital. That tax is the corporate income tax. Furthermore, his findings are supported by the more recent work of Shoven and Whalley, which expands the number of sectors considered and the range of demand and supply elasticities considered.[31] In another work Shoven and Whalley compare a uniform tax on capital as a replacement for the existing differential capital taxes that exist in the United Kingdom.[32] Furthermore, they find that the more general model suggests a substantially greater uniform tax would be needed (to replace the differential ones) than cruder calculations suggest.

These applications suggest that general equilibrium models do have substan-

[30] See A. Harberger, "The Incidence of the Corporation Income Tax," *Journal of Political Economy, 70,* 1962, pp. 215–240.

[31] See J. Shoven and J. Whalley, "A General Equilibrium Calculation of the Effects of Differential Taxation of Income from Capital in the U.S.," *Journal of Public Economics, 1,* 1972, pp. 281–321.

[32] Cited earlier in this section.

tial promise for pragmatic applications. Of course, they are not necessary for every problem. If the taxed sector is small, compared to the rest of the economy, it may be that the released resources will have a negligible impact on the rest of the economy.

However, one must be careful about the choice of perspective. For example, the decision of the federal government to bail out the Chrysler Corporation with loan guarantees could have been analyzed as one small project in a large economy. But if your economy is that of Michigan, then you might want to understand the implications for the non-Chrysler Michigan sector as well. That is, thousands of laborers released to the general economy may be a drop in the aggregate bucket of millions, but their concentration in Michigan would mean that the regional economy would have the primary job of absorbing them.

As this example suggests, general equilibrium models are not relevant only to taxation. They may be applied to any large economic change, which might include import restrictions, major changes in unionization or minimum wage laws, national energy subsidies (subsidies are actually negative taxes), and changes in the regulation of large industries.[33] However, it happens that one more tax example with our trusty model will lead nicely to the next chapter on second best; therefore, we stick with it.

Lump-Sum Taxes Are Efficient and Real Taxes Are Inefficient

The tax that we wish to consider is, like Social Security, an employment tax which yields revenue equal to our excise tax. That is, in this regime the new price of labor to producers is $P_L + t$, although labor continues to receive as income only P_L. The striking aspect of this tax is that, in our model, it causes no allocative changes from the untaxed Pareto optimum. (The same thing would be true of a capital tax.)

Referring back to Table 10-1, let us consider the changes that must be made. They can be summarized with one instruction: Everywhere there is a P_L, substitute for it the variable $P_L + t$. There is no distortionary wedge in the model because the labor supply equation is *fixed* at $L = 100$. If there were a variable labor supply, the equilibrium quantity of labor would be affected by any change in the real wage P_L. But since all the payments to labor (and capital) in this model are pure *economic rent* (payments *above* opportunity cost), no labor supply decisions are affected by the tax.

The only equation changes which may need further explanation are for the product demands. The new budget constraint is earned income plus tax proceeds:

$$B = P_L L + P_K K + tL$$
$$= (P_L + t)L + P_K K$$

It therefore comports with our single instruction for the necessary changes.

[33] See, for example, H. G. Johnson and P. Mieszkowski, "The Effects of Unionization on the Distribution of Income: A General Equilibrium Approach," *The Quarterly Journal of Economics, 84,* No. 4, November 1970, pp. 539–561.

Thus we need not go through the solution again; it is essentially identical with our original solution. The only change is that, instead of $P_L = 3$, we have

$$P_L + t = 3$$

What is t? To make the tax have equal yield to the excise tax, we have to collect 58.58:

$$tL = 58.58$$
$$t = \frac{58.58}{L} = \frac{58.58}{100} = 0.5858$$
$$P = 2.4142 \approx 2.41$$

In other words, the tax is fully borne by labor and the after-tax distribution of income is exactly the same as with the excise tax. However, *this tax is efficient:* The allocation of resources in the economy is identical with the no-tax Pareto optimum. The deadweight loss from taxation is zero. The general explanation for this result is as follows: *If there is no substitution effect in the (official) taxpayer's response to the tax, there will be no distortion in the allocation of resources.* Since we have postulated that labor is fixed in supply, the wage earner's labor-leisure trade-off has been assumed away. Furthermore, if the tax does not alter the demands or supplies for other goods (e.g., as it typically would through income effects), the incidence of the tax will be completely on the (official) taxpayer.

The catch to all this is that it is doubtful whether such taxes exist. In the real world, social security taxes and income taxes do affect labor-leisure trade-offs. Product taxes affect consumer purchase decisions. A tax on all consumption distorts the consumption-savings decision. Property taxes affect decisions about the type of structure to build.

A tax (or a subsidy) which does not depend on the taypayer's behavior, called a lump-sum tax (or transfer), is nondistortionary. Although theoretical exercises often make use of the idea of lump-sum transfers—note the importance in the second of the twin theorems of being able to redistribute income costlessly—there is no practical tax proposal, let alone an actual tax, which economists agree is lump sum and which could be used to raise all (or the bulk) of tax revenues. There may be some actual lump-sum taxes, but it is hard to identify any with confidence. Two common suggestions for lump-sum taxes are poll, or head, taxes and pure land taxes. Let us look at each briefly.

For the poll tax to be lump-sum, its magnitude must be totally independent of actions that individuals can take in response to it. Suppose we say that everyone must pay $1000 per year. That, in all probability, would be highly regressive.[34] If we made the tax contingent on income or wealth in any way,

---

[34] The *incidence* of the tax may still be shifted through income effects, for example; thus there is slight uncertainty about its regressivity.

individuals would have incentive to alter their wealth statuses. That is a major pragmatic stumbling block.

Even accepting the regressivity, individuals can still immigrate or emigrate, and they can still control the number of offspring they have. (That is, there is a distortionary wedge between the general supply of people and the demand for them.) If this sounds of no practical concern, think of the arguments about the mobility of the poor from low-subsidy southern states to high-subsidy northern states. (Being poor is an alterable condition, perhaps, but differences in pure poll taxes across areas would induce analogous mobility effects.) Furthermore, what should be done about those who cannot or refuse to pay? The penalty must not be influenced by the behavior of the defaulter; otherwise, it will affect the behavior leading to default. In short, there may not be any socially acceptable way of creating a lump-sum poll tax.

How about the land tax? The idea is that land is fixed in supply, and therefore any tax levied on it will not distort the allocation of resources. (The product mix may change because of income effects, but there will be no distortionary wedges.) Furthermore, since the worst-off people do not own much land, the incidence is likely to be progressive.[35] However, the supply of land is not perfectly fixed, owing to land reclamation activities. Furthermore, the tax cannot have anything to do with the quality of the land, since that is alterable by human efforts. If those obstacles can be overcome, it may be possible to design a tax on acreage which is considered equitable and efficient.

The principal conclusion which we wish to draw from this brief analysis of taxation and efficiency is as follows: All, or virtually all, existing methods of generating tax revenues are distortionary. There is no reasonable hope of replacing the current system of taxes with one that is nondistortionary. In 1979 the portion of our national income that became government receipts through the various taxes in our economy was 32.6 percent.[36] Therefore, the economy is characterized by substantial and essentially unalterable deviations from a first-best Pareto-optimal solution, even ignoring all other possible reasons (for the moment) why the economy deviates from perfect competition. The questions to which we turn in the next chapter are these: (1) Given that we cannot have a first-best solution, what is the second-best solution? (2) How helpful are competitive markets (and limited lump-sum taxes) in achieving the second-best solution?

---

[35] In an interesting article, Feldstein has shown that a pure land tax may be shifted other than through ordinary income effects. Because land is an asset for savings, a reduction in its return will cause savers to increase their demands for produced capital (an alternative savings asset). The expansion of produced capital raises the marginal product of land and thus shifts part of the tax to capital owners. Even if capital were perfectly fixed as well, there would be shifting because of risk aversion: If the returns to land and capital are uncertain, the value of land initially falls in response to the tax. Land becomes a less risky part of the portfolio, and thus its price will rise above the "full burden" level. See M. Feldstein, "The Surprising Incidence of a Tax on Pure Rent: A New Answer to an Old Question," *Journal of Political Economy, 85,* No. 2, April 1977, pp. 349–360.

[36] Tax receipts were $771.9 billion and GNP $2368.5 billion. See the *Economic Report of the President, January 1980* (Washington, D.C.: U.S. Government Printing Office, 1980), pp. 203, 288.

SUMMARY

In this chapter we review some general models of a competitive economy. We first review the standard description of the competitive process in one industry and then extend the model to consider characteristics of general competitive equilibrium, one in which all markets are simultaneously in equilibrium. We summarize the twin optimality theorems of microeconomics: Every perfectly competitive equilibrium is Pareto-optimal, and every Pareto-optimal allocation can be achieved by a perfectly competitive economy with costless transfers of income. The marginal rules that characterize the optimality conditions, like marginal cost pricing, have come to be used as the basis for judging efficiency in most "piecemeal" (single-sector) policy analyses.

We then turn to a predictive task. Competitive models are frequently used in the study of taxation. We examine analytic use of a two-sector general equilibrium model for the study of excise tax incidence, i.e., determining who ends up paying the tax.

When the results are contrasted with the partial equilibrium model, they are seen to be quite different. The general equilibrium model reveals the extent to which a tax will be shifted either forward or backward. Furthermore, the general model can give more accurate estimates of tax revenues. The importance of using a general equilibrium model for predictive purposes depends on the size of the changes to the economy. Because taxes have large impacts on the economy, general equilibrium models are more appropriate for tax analysis.

After looking at tax incidence, we consider the efficiency of taxation. Lump-sum taxes, which do not depend on the taxpayer's behavior, are nondistortionary. However, they are more prevalent in the minds of theorists than in policy use. All major real-world taxes—income, sales, property, excise—do alter the allocative decisions of taxpayers and thus have an efficiency cost, called a deadweight loss, or an excess burden.

The simple fact of the existence of distortionary taxes, which are used to collect over 30 percent of the national income, implies that the economy is not at a first-best allocation (one that meets the conditions for Pareto optimality in all sectors). That is, the use of market governance in an economy with substantial taxation creates price signals which cause economic agents to allocate resources inefficiently. Contrary to the suggestion of the twin theorems, we have not yet uncovered any reasons why competitive markets in an actual economy might be a desirable method of resource allocation.

EXERCISE

10-1 Local education finance equilibrium with interdependency among counties.

A state is composed of two counties. All those who live in county R are rich, and those who live in county N are not rich. Within each county all families are homogeneous. In county R each family owns property assessed at $2000. In county N each family owns property assessed at $1000. There are 100 families in each county, and each family has one school-aged child.

Educational achievements are measured completely and accurately by Q-scores on a standardized test.

The demand for educational achievement as a function of the education expenditure per family is

$$Q_D^R = 150 - E_R \qquad \text{in county R}$$
$$Q_D^N = 100 - E_N \qquad \text{in county N}$$

The supply of educational achievement as a function of expenditure per student is

$$Q_S^R = E_R \qquad \text{in county R}$$
$$Q_S^N = E_N - 10 \qquad \text{in county N}$$

a   Suppose we treat decisions in each county as if they were independent or, equivalently, as if we had two partial equilibrium models. Assume the voters in each county set a property tax rate t to finance education expenditures. For each county what tax rate will the voters select, what expenditure per student will result, and what will be the educational achievement level? Is there any sense in which the families in county N can be said to be making a greater effort to provide education than the families in county R? (Partial answer: $t_R = 0.0375$; $E_R = 75 = Q_R$; yes)

b   A famous court decision allows each county to continue to set its own tax level but orders the state to collect the taxes and so distribute them (administrative costs are zero) that expenditures per pupil are equal throughout the state.

   This system causes demanders and suppliers in each county to perceive different prices for education, as with an excise tax. Furthermore, the interdependence of counties caused by this system makes general equilibrium considerations important.

   For each county what tax rate will be chosen, what will be the expenditure per pupil, and what will be the educational achievement level? (Partial answer: $t_N = 0.045$; $E = 65$; $Q_N = 55$)

c   ▽Suppose expenditures are fixed at $65 per student and are financed as in part (b). The state announces a new open enrollment plan. Assume there are only two schools, one in each county. Collectively, the families in the state are highly rational. Any individual family will always choose to have its child attend the school offering the highest achievement level.

   For each enrolled student in excess of 100 in a school, the achievement level of all students in that school slips down one unit (an overcrowding effect). For each of the first 25 rich students who attend the school in the nonrich county, the educational achievement of all students in that school is raised by one unit (a one-way positive integration effect).

   What educational achievement level do you expect in each county? Does this system improve the solution in any way compared with (b)? Is there a unique solution to the number of rich and nonrich in each school? Explain why the results are like those in the Slumlord's Dilemma of Chapter 6. (Answers: $Q_N = Q_R = 65$; yes; no)

d   ▽Suppose the families in each county are now free to set their own tax rates with both the spending rules from part (b) and the open enrollment plan in effect. Family motivations and capabilities are as assumed in part (c). What tax rates will be chosen; what expenditure level will result; and what achievement level will result in each county? How do these outcomes compare with those of the earlier parts? (Partial answers: $Q_N = Q_R = 62.5$; $t = 0.04375$)

CHAPTER 11

MARKET ALLOCATION IN AN IMPERFECT WORLD

This chapter is about the role of markets in an imperfect world. We begin by probing a normative matter of general equilibrium. Given that a competitive market economy must inevitably have significant distortions (e.g., taxes), what are the most efficient allocations it can achieve? We will see that it cannot in general, even with substantial corrective intervention, achieve allocations which meet the rules required for Pareto optimality (the first-best allocations). The critical questions then are what are the second-best allocations, and can they be achieved through markets? The theory of the second best leads to allocative rules which turn out to be substantially different from those which characterize the unattainable first-best allocations.

At least three important problems for policy analysis are raised by implications of the theory of the second best. First, the prices and quantities determined by competitive markets in an imperfect world do not achieve first- or second-best results. Second, in piecemeal policy analysis—the most common form of analysis, in which one area or sector of the economy is studied while the rest of the economy is taken as a given—we cannot confidently rely upon the first-best rules or observed prices in the rest of the economy to evaluate efficiency consequences in the sector or area under study. Third, the empirical identification of the second-best allocative rules is beyond routine analytic capabilities.

After reviewing these issues, we seek to lay the foundation for another perspective from which to view the efficiency of market organization. Perhaps a simple way to think about it is to suppose we agree that nobody, or no method of organizing economic activity within our current capabilities, can identify efficient, feasible allocations and direct resources to achieve them. Still, we must decide resource allocations in some manner. Given any method of deciding upon target allocations, a method of coordinating economic agents to achieve them is also necessary. Viewed from this satisficing rather than optimizing perspective, market organization may be a very desirable part of the processes for deciding upon allocations and achieving them.

That is, it may be that a viable and relatively efficient economic system is one which relies upon the allocative "judgment" of the marketplace, subject to various political override mechanisms when the market judgments are thought to be unsatisfactory on either efficiency or equity grounds, or on both. The success of the economic system then depends upon the design of the political intervention mechanisms and how well they interact with the allocative mechanisms of the market. In some area of the economy, the intervention may take the form of a simple tax or subsidy which continues substantial reliance upon decentralized market decision making (e.g., investment tax credits). In other areas, more substantial governmental control may be appropriate (e.g., national defense).

In order to develop analytic skills in the design of resource allocation mechanisms, we survey in this chapter the characteristics which are thought to cause market failure. Traditionally, these characteristics have been identified as those which cause deviations from the first-best allocations in specific markets. Although this is true, we do not take it as a sufficient normative basis for preferring some alternative method of resource allocation. We prefer to regard the characteristics as a set of circumstances which identify areas in which the market has serious flaws as a coordinating mechanism. In those areas there is a high probability that some form (not just any form) of policy control can lead to a superior institutional structure or allocative mechanism for guiding the detailed resource allocations within the sector.

The chapter is organized as follows. The first broad part uses a general equilibrium framework to analyze the theory of the second best and its implications. First, we introduce the theory of the second best and show that the second-best solutions in a market economy involve policy intervention. Then we show that the second-best theorem implies that piecemeal policy analysis cannot rely upon first-best rules or observed prices in competitive sectors as guides to evaluating efficiency consequences in the sector under study. Furthermore, empirical identification of the consequences of following the second-best rules is beyond normal analytic capabilities. We consider several analytic paths out of the second-best dilemma, including explicit recognition that our understanding of actual efficiency consequences is based upon satisficing rather than optimizing standards.

The second broad part of the chapter reviews the theory of market failure. The characteristics identified as sources of failure are those which make it difficult for the market to coordinate and guide the decisions of the economic agents who operate within it. *The sources of market failure reviewed and discussed include: (1) increasing-returns-to-scale technology, (2) public goods, (3) externalities, and (4) imperfect information.*

PERFECT COMPETITION IN AN IMPERFECT WORLD

In the preceding chapter we examined a model of a perfectly competitive economy with an excise tax imposed on one commodity. This tax caused a violation of one of the necessary conditions for a Pareto-optimal resource allocation; the result was an inefficient allocation of the economy's resources. Distortionary violations of the necessary conditions for Pareto optimality may arise for many reasons other than taxation.[1] For example, the existence of a monopoly sector can have the same allocative effect as the tax.

To illustrate quickly that monopolistic behavior can lead to analogous distortion, consider this simple example. Recall the two-sector model used in the last section of Chapter 10. Imagine that there are no taxes, but good 2 is produced by a satisficing monopolist who insists upon making a 0.67 profit on each unit sold (or 58.58 total profit). Then the monopolist is behaving exactly like the tax collector, except that the "taxes" (profits) are distributed to the monopoly owners. Since the distribution of income does not affect demand in our model, the solution is identical with the excise tax case.

The Theorem of the Second Best

Let us accept as a fact that many sectors of a large economy will deviate substantially from the first-best allocations (i.e., those implied by the necessary conditions for Pareto optimality). It is not a catastrophe if reality falls short of Utopia; it has consistently done so in the past and the world survives nevertheless. However, we must press on to a next logical question: Given that some imperfections are inherent, do we achieve the second-best allocation (the best feasible one) by following the first-best rules whenever possible? That is exactly what is done by allowing the *unconstrained sectors* to be organized in a perfectly competitive laissez-faire manner. This is also the allocation that would result from following the outcomes of benefit-cost calculations based on observed prices in the economy. Unfortunately, the answer to our question is no. This is the theorem of the second best:[2] *Accept as a constraint that one or more of the necessary conditions for Pareto optimality are violated in an economy. Then meeting the other necessary conditions in the rest of the economy is generally not desirable on efficiency grounds.*

We can illustrate the theorem simply with our trusty two-sector model. In Figure 11-1, we draw the production-possibilities curve for the economy.[3] We

---

[1] Two exceptions to the distorting effects of taxes are for lump-sum taxes and for taxes specifically designed to correct an externality. Externalities are discussed later in the text.

[2] R. Lipsey and K. Lancaster, "The General Theory of the Second Best," *Review of Economic Studies, 24,* 1956–1957, pp. 11–32.

[3] The equation for the production-possibilities curve is

$$Q_2 = 150 - \frac{3Q_1^2}{200}$$

It may be derived as follows. Since all capital ($K = 100$) is allocated to sector 1,

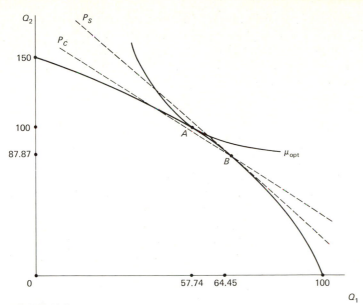

FIGURE 11-1
Misallocation due to a monopoly sector in a two-sector economy.

also draw the indifference curves (as if Robinson Crusoe were the sole consumer). The unconstrained Pareto optimum is point A, where $Q_1 = 57.74$ and $Q_2 = 100$ as in Chapter 10.

The $\text{RPT}_{Q_1, Q_2} = 3Q_1/100$ at any point on the frontier.[4] This equals 1.73 at the

---

Also,
$$Q_1 = K_1^{1/2} L_1^{1/2} = 10L_1^{1/2}$$
$$Q_2 = \tfrac{3}{2} L_2$$

The other resource constraint is that $L_1 + L_2 = 100$. By substituting in the preceding equation, we get

or
$$Q_2 = \tfrac{3}{2}(100 - L_1) = 150 - \tfrac{3}{2} L_1$$
$$L_1 = \tfrac{2}{3}(150 - Q_2)$$

Substituting in the Q_1 equation gives us
$$Q_1 = 10[\tfrac{2}{3}(150 - Q_2)]^{1/2}$$

By squaring both sides and rearranging, we get
$$Q_2 = 150 - \frac{3Q_1^2}{200}$$

[4] The RPT is the negative of the slope of the production-possibilities curve. It is easily found by taking the derivative of its equation:
$$-\frac{\partial Q_2}{\partial Q_1} = \frac{6Q_1}{200} = \frac{3Q_1}{100}$$

optimum. The $\mathrm{MRS}_{Q_1,Q_2} = Q_2/Q_1$ along any indifference curve.[5] This also equals 1.73 at the optimum. Of course, the equilibrium prices $P_1 = 3.46$ and $P_2 = 2.00$ also have the ratio $P_1/P_2 = 1.73$.

Now let the satisficing monopolist replace perfect competition in sector 2. That causes allocation in the economy to shift to point B, where $Q_1 = 64.45$, $Q_2 = 87.87$ (i.e., exactly the same as with the 0.67 excise tax). The marginal costs faced by producers in this model are $P_1 = 3.10$ and $P_2 = 1.61$, and their ratio should equal the negative of the slope of the transformation curve at equilibrium:

$$\frac{P_1}{P_2} = \frac{3.10}{1.61} = 1.93$$

$$\mathrm{RPT}_{Q_1,Q_2} = \frac{3Q_1}{100} = 1.93$$

Consumers, however, face the prices $P_1 = 3.10$, $P_2 + t = 2.28$. In equilibrium, the negative of the slope of the indifference curve must equal the consumer price ratio:

$$\frac{P_1}{P_2 + t} = \frac{3.10}{2.28} = 1.36$$

$$\mathrm{MRS}_{Q_1,Q_2} = \frac{Q_2}{Q_1} = \frac{87.87}{64.45} = 1.36$$

In other words, one can see graphically that this allocation is an equilibrium despite the fact that the MRS $\neq$ RPT. The price lines showing consumer and producer price ratios are drawn in and labeled P_C and P_S respectively.

The Second-Best Solution Involves Policy Intervention in the Market

Note that, in this equilibrium, competitive market forces allocate resources in an unfettered manner everywhere except in sector 2 (where there is a monopolist who, we assume, cannot be controlled). Sector 1 is perfectly

---

[5] For the utility function $U = Q_1^{1/2}Q_2^{1/2}$ the MRS can be found by taking the ratio of the marginal utilities:

$$\frac{\partial U}{\partial Q_1} = \tfrac{1}{2}Q_1^{-1/2}Q_2^{1/2}$$

$$\frac{\partial U}{\partial Q_2} = \tfrac{1}{2}Q_1^{1/2}Q_2^{-1/2}$$

whence
$$\mathrm{MRS} = \frac{Q_2}{Q_1}$$

competitive and in equilibrium with zero profits to firms and consumer price equal to the marginal cost of supply. In sector 1 the necessary conditions for Pareto optimality are satisfied. The second-best question is equivalent to asking whether the allocation resulting overall (at *B*) yields the highest utility possible given the (monopolist's profit) constraint. Put differently, is it best to let perfectly competitive markets allocate resources in all of the "controllable" sectors, given that there are imperfections elsewhere?

The general answer is no. We can do better through policy intervention in the controllable sectors. In this special case, we can achieve the original optimum (point *A*) despite the constraint. We achieve this result by intervention to make *all* consumer prices deviate from marginal costs by the *same* proportion. (We can do that because one constraint on an "absolute" price does not prevent us from keeping relative prices optimal; the general and more realistic cases involve more significant constraints.)

Let us call the monopolist's profit per unit t_2; thus, the constraint is

$$\Pi = t_2 Q_2 = 58.58$$

Let us now consider imposing a corrective tax t_1 on sector 1's product (i.e., altering the price from the consumer's perspective). That is, we are creating a policy instrument with which to alter the equilibrium. We seek to determine the most efficient solution to the demand and supply equations summarized in Table 11-1. When the corrective tax t_1 has been added, consumers will choose a point on their indifference curves where

$$MRS_{Q_1, Q_2} = \frac{P_1 + t_1}{P_2 + t_2}$$

If we wish to be at the Pareto optimum,

$$1.73 = \frac{P_1 + t_1}{P_2 + t_2}$$

Similarly, the marginal costs to producers P_1 and P_2 must have the same ratio

$$1.73 = \frac{P_1}{P_2}$$

On combining these, we see that we require

$$\frac{P_1}{P_2} = \frac{P_1 + t_1}{P_2 + t_2}$$

or, by rearranging,
$$\frac{P_1}{P_2} = \frac{t_1}{t_2} \quad (= 1.73)$$

TABLE 11-1
SUMMARY OF THE TWO-SECTOR SECOND-BEST ECONOMY WITH A SATISFICING
MONOPOLY IN SECTOR 2 AND CORRECTIVE TAXATION IN SECTOR 1

Product markets		

Sector 1

Demand $\quad Q_1 = \dfrac{\frac{1}{2}(P_L L + P_K K + t_1 Q_1 + t_2 Q_2)}{P_1 + t_1}$ (1)

Supply $\quad P_1 = 2P_K^{1/2} P_L^{1/2}$ (2)

Sector 2

Demand $\quad Q_2 = \dfrac{\frac{1}{2}(P_L L + P_K K + t_1 Q_1 + t_2 Q_2)}{P_2 + t_2}$ (3)

Supply $\quad P_2 = \frac{2}{3}P_L$ (4)

Factor markets		

Capital

Demand $\quad K = K_1 + K_2 = P_K^{-1/2} P_L^{1/2} Q_1$ (5)

Supply $\quad K = 100$ (6)

Labor

Demand $\quad L = L_1 + L_2 = P_K^{1/2} P_L^{-1/2} Q_1 + \frac{2}{3}Q_2$ (7)

Supply $\quad L = 100$ (8)

This suggests that if all consumer prices $P_i + t_i$ are the same proportion above marginal costs P_i, equality between the MRS and the RPT can be resurrected despite the constraint.

Since $Q_2 = 100$ at the optimum, we can work backwards and solve for t_2 from the profit constraint:

$$58.58 = t_2(100)$$
and
$$t_2 = 0.5858$$
Since
$$1.73 = \frac{t_1}{0.5858}$$
$$t_1 = 1.0134$$

In the factor markets, the price of labor (and, of course, the numéraire, capital) is unchanged from the unconstrained solution. By using either the capital or the labor market, we find that $P_L = 3.00$ (and $P_K = 1.00$ by definition). Therefore, the supply prices (marginal costs) also are unchanged: $P_1 = 3.46$ and $P_2 = 2.00$.

The income components in the economy (which enter the demand functions) are thus:[6]

---

[6] Computations may not be exact because of rounding errors.

Labor's share	$P_L L = 300$
Capital's share	$P_K K = 100$
Corrective tax proceeds	$t_1 Q_1 = 58.58$
Monopoly profits	$t_2 Q_2 = 58.58$
Total income	517
Spending on Q_1	$(P_1 + t_1)Q_1 = 258.50$
Spending on Q_2	$(P_2 + t_2)Q_2 = 258.50$

Note that, in this solution, we have caused "inflation" with important distributive effects. Labor and capital incomes are nominally the same as in the unconstrained solution, but those incomes cannot buy the same quantity of goods. Put differently, the corrective tax (before distribution of its proceeds) reduces the real income of the monopolist and of capitalists and holds labor's share of total income approximately constant.[7] The tax proceeds represent 11.3 percent of income, and they may be redistributed in any manner deemed appropriate by the government.[8]

Piecemeal Policy Analysis May Not Reveal Efficiency Consequences

This simple model suggests that perfect competition with no policy intervention in the unconstrained sectors generally does not lead to the best feasible allocation. This also means that *piecemeal* (single-sector) *analytic work cannot confidently rely upon the first-best allocative rules or the observed prices in the rest of the economy to evaluate efficiency consequences in the sector or area under study*. To see this, imagine that the satisficing monopolist is in sector 2 (the "rest of the economy") and a bureaucrat is instructed to allocate resources in sector 1 in order to maximize net benefits.

The setting is illustrated in Figure 11-2a. The bureaucrat observes the demand curve for Q_1 ($= 200/P_1$) and also observes that the market prices are 2.41 for labor and 1.00 for capital. At those prices, the least marginal cost of production is 3.10. Therefore, the bureaucrat reasons that all units should be produced where the marginal benefit P_1 exceeds the marginal cost. All units meet this test until

$$P_1 = \frac{200}{Q_1} = 3.10$$

or
$$Q_1 = 64.45$$

---

[7] With no corrective taxes the monopolist receives 14.6 percent of real income (58.58/400). With the tax the monopolist receives only 11.3 percent of real income (58.58/517). The capitalist's share falls from 25 to 19.3 percent. Labor's share is now 58 percent, and with the monopoly it was 60.3 percent.

[8] This may seem like a good way to recapture some monopoly profits. However, recall that the satisficing monopolist may be nobody's fool. As an exercise, show that the monopolist can maintain a steady share of national income by simply raising the profit per unit. (Answer: $t_2 = 0.82$; national income $= 565$.)

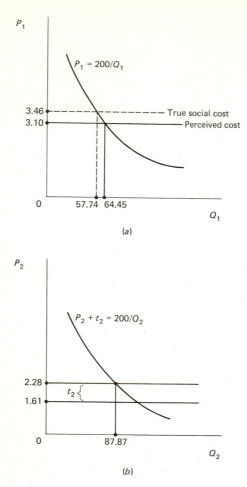

(a)

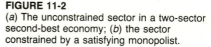

(b)

FIGURE 11-2
(a) The unconstrained sector in a two-sector second-best economy; (b) the sector constrained by a satisfying monopolist.

The serious fallacy in this reasoning, which has essentially nothing to do with the size of sector 1 relative to the rest of the economy, is that the observed market equilibrium prices are not the social costs. The true social costs have little to do with sector 1. They are determined by the value to society of the alternative uses of the resources.

For example, the bureaucrat considers the last $\frac{2}{3}$ unit of labor used in sector 1 to have value equal to its cost of $1.61 = \frac{2}{3}($2.41)$. But if it were released to sector 2, its social value there (where it would produce exactly one more unit of Q_2) would be the height of the sector 2 demand curve, or 2.28 (shown in Figure 11-2b). The bureaucrat, however, does not observe the height of the demand curve in sector 2. The true social cost of producing Q_1 is that associated with the second-best solution: The social marginal cost per unit is 3.46, and the equilibrium quantity is 57.74. In this example the well-intentioned bureaucrat overproduces Q_1 by approximately 12 percent (64.45/57.74).

Because this point—that attempting to achieve first-best conditions in single sectors does not necessarily improve relative efficiency—is so important, let us present a second example. We add a new wrinkle to the illustrative model we have been using. We continue to assume that the monopolist controls sector 2, where the no-intervention output levels are $Q_1 = 64.45$ and $Q_2 = 87.87$. Now, however, we observe the formation of a closed-shop labor union in sector 1. This means that individuals cannot work in sector 1 unless the union admits them as members. We consider whether the closed shop increases or decreases relative efficiency.

The union has incentive to restrict its membership, in order to drive up the wage rate in sector 1. In Figure 11-3 we show the demand for labor in sector 1. Before the union is formed, wages are $2.41 (determined competitively and uniform across both sectors) and the amount of labor employed is 41.42. Suppose that 30 of the laborers agree to form the union and will admit no additional members. What happens?

To answer the above question, we must recalculate the new market prices and quantities subject to the monopoly constraint in sector 2 and the union constraint in sector 1. Perhaps the easiest way to do this is to note that, with the union constraint, it must be that sector 1 has $L_1 = 30$, $K_1 = 100$, and $L_2 = 70$. From the underlying production function, we know that

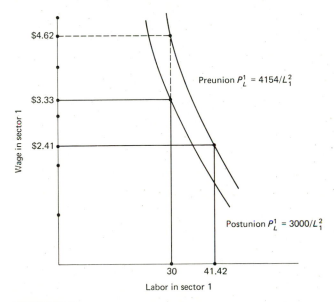

FIGURE 11-3
The closed-shop union and the demand for labor in sector 1 of the two-sector economy. [The demand curves are found by using the general demand curve for sector 1 labor:

$$L_1 = Q_1(P_K)^{1/2}(P_L^1)^{-1/2}$$

In the preunion period, $Q_1 = 64.45$ and $P_K = 1.00$. In the postunion period, $Q_1 = 54.77$ and $P_K = 1.00$.]

TABLE 11-2
SUMMARY OF ALLOCATIVE AND DISTRIBUTIVE OUTCOMES IN THE TWO-SECTOR
ECONOMY UNDER VARIOUS CONDITIONS

	Union and monopoly constraints	Monopoly constraint only	Perfect competition
Sector 1	(Union constraint)	—	—
P_1	$3.56	$3.10	$3.46
Q_1	54.77	64.45	57.74
P_L^1	$3.33	$2.41	$3.00
L_1	30.00	41.42	33.33
P_K	$1.00	$1.00	$1.00
K_1	100.00	100.00	100.00
Sector 2	(Monopoly constraint)	(Monopoly constraint)	—
P_2	$1.35	$1.61	$2.00
t_2	$0.56	$0.67	—
Q_2	105.00	87.87	100.00
P_L^2	$2.02	$2.41	$3.00
L_2	70.00	58.58	66.67
GNP (income)			
$P_L^1 L_1$	$100.00	$100.00	$100.00
$P_L^2 L_2$	$141.00	$141.00	$200.00
$P_K K$	$100.00	$100.00	$100.00
$t Q_2$	$ 59.00	$ 59.00	—
Total GNP	$400.00	$400.00	$400.00
Deadweight loss	$0.81	$3.86	—
Percent of GNP	0.20	0.96	—

$$Q_1 = K_1^{1/2} L_1^{1/2} = 100^{1/2}(30^{1/2}) = 54.77$$
$$Q_2 = \tfrac{3}{2}L_2 = \tfrac{3}{2}(70) = 105.00$$

The prices which sustain this real resource allocation can be found by substituting these quantities in the appropriate equations of Table 11-1, modified for this situation.[9] The outcomes are summarized in Table 11-2. To facilitate comparison, Table 11-2 also includes the Pareto-optimal competitive outcomes and the outcomes with the monopolist but no union.

Let us note first, in Figure 11-3, that the closed-shop union has succeeded in

---

[9] Since this situation does not involve any corrective taxation, $t_1 = 0$. Since the monopolist requires $t_2 Q_2 = \$58.58$ and $Q_2 = 105$, $t_2 = \$0.5579$. The labor market is now divided into two markets, where total labor income is $P_L^1 L_1 + P_L^2 L_2$ and the wages in each sector will be different ($P_L^1 \neq P_L^2$). The demand for labor in sector 1 must be equated to the supply of labor to sector 1 (the latter is fixed at 30):

$$30 = P_K^{1/2}(P_L^1)^{-1/2}Q_1$$

Since P_K is the numéraire and equals 1 and $Q_1 = 54.77$, the above equation implies $P_L^1 = \$3.3333$. This in turn implies from equation (2), Table 10-1, that $P_1 = \$3.65$. That leaves P_L^2 as the only unknown in equation (1), and the equation can be solved to find $P_L^2 = \$2.02$. Then, from equation (4), $P_2 = \$1.3469$.

raising the wages of its members from $2.41 to $3.33, a hefty 38 percent gain. This is not the gain of $4.62 that would be predicted by a partial equilibrium analysis. The market responds to the union constraint by adjusting other prices and quantities, which causes the demand for labor in sector 1 to shift inward and thus partially offsets the unionization. The increase in income to the 30 union members comes, in this model, entirely at the expense of the 70 other laborers in the economy whose wages are reduced from $2.41 to $2.02, a drop of 16 percent. Capital income and monopoly profits are unaffected by the unionization.[10]

Now suppose an analyst were asked to examine the union situation in sector 1 while treating problems in the rest of the economy as outside the scope of the analysis. He or she might observe that the labor used in sector 1 is no different from the labor in the rest of the economy and that the wage differential caused by unionization creates room for a deal. A worker from outside sector 1 would prefer to work in sector 1 at any wage higher than $2.02, and an employer in sector 1 would prefer to hire an additional worker for any wage less than $3.33.

The usual assumption in piecemeal analysis is that prices in the rest of the economy represent social opportunity costs (as if the rest of the economy were at the first-best competitive equilibrium). In this case, the assumption is that the $2.02 wage rate in sector 2 is the social opportunity cost of labor. Thus the social benefits of additional labor to sector 1 (= $3.33) outweigh the social opportunity costs (= $2.02). As long as there is a difference in the wages received by homogeneous labor, the piecemeal analysis would conclude there is room for a deal and the allocation is inefficient. Since the closed-shop union is causing this wage difference, the obvious conclusion is that it creates inefficiency.

However, if we look at Table 11-2, we can see that the allocation with the union constraint is more efficient than the allocation without it (i.e., with the monopoly constraint alone). The deadweight loss in the economy with the union is only 0.2 percent of GNP, whereas without the union it is almost 1 percent of GNP. *The piecemeal analysis comes to the wrong conclusion.* Why? Because the $2.02 wage rate in sector 2 is *not* the social opportunity cost of labor. The true social opportunity cost is the value to consumers in sector 2 of the marginal product of labor. The marginal product equals 1.5 units of Q_2, which has value at the price per unit faced by consumers ($1.91 = $1.35 + $0.56) of $2.87 = 1.5($1.91). Thus, although the union does result in an overallocation of resources to Q_2 production, it is a less serious misallocation than that caused by the monopolist alone.

Both these examples, of the well-intentioned bureaucrat and the analysis of the closed-shop union, suggest the danger of applying first-best rules in an imperfect economy. The example of corrective taxation, given imperfections in the economy, illustrates *a general second-best result: In theory, we can do*

---

[10] This, of course, will not always be true. If a union forms in a sector in which the employers receive monopoly profits, it may be able to capture some of those profits through higher wages.

better by policy intervention in the market price-setting process than the market would do on its own. The example does not reveal, however, the enormous difficulty of the task of finding the second-best rules (even in theory).

Identifying the Second-Best Solution May Be Beyond Current Analytic Abilities

All we had to do in the example was raise all prices to be the same proportion above marginal costs. After our intervention, none of the necessary conditions for (first-best) Pareto optimality was violated. But with more realistic constraints in a many-sector economy, that will not be possible. If there is a consumer good which cannot be taxed (e.g., leisure), or another monopoly sector, we will have fewer policy instruments (controllable prices) than conditions to satisfy with them (relative price requirements). In these more realistic cases, the second-best prices no longer have the property of being the same proportion above respective marginal costs.

Rather than work through more complicated second-best models to illustrate this, we note that we have already done much of this in Chapter 9: the Ramsey pricing models. There we examined the problem of how a public enterprise subject to a budget constraint should price its various products. We also assumed the government would make up the remaining deficit of the public enterprise. Now we restate the same problem from the other direction: The government must raise revenues through taxes to meet the sum of deficits from its enterprises (as well as to perform other functions). But all the possible taxes are distortionary (i.e., we assume there are no feasible lump-sum taxes), so we can ask how government should alter consumer prices (i.e., choose taxes) to meet its revenue constraint in the least distortionary way.

The simplest Ramsey solution for optimal taxation is the inverse-elasticities rule, but this assumes there are no cross effects among the taxed commodities. If we allow (realistically) for cross effects, and try to account for other inherent problems in the economy like monopolistic sectors (e.g., public utilities), the solution for the optimal prices cannot be described by a simple rule.[11]

---

[11] Layard and Walters illustrate the idea with an n-good Robinson Crusoe model in which the problem is to maximize $U(X_1, X_2, \ldots, X_n)$ subject to two constraints: (1) the ordinary one of the production-possibilities frontier $T(X_1, X_2, \ldots, X_n) = 0$ and (2) a fixed relation between marginal benefits and marginal costs in one sector i: $\partial U/\partial X_i = a(\partial T/\partial X_i)$.

We can write this maximization problem by using Lagrange multipliers:

$$L = U(X_1, X_2, \ldots, X_n) + \lambda_1[T(X_1, X_2, \ldots, X_n)] + \lambda_2\left[\frac{\partial U}{\partial X_i} - a\left(\frac{\partial T}{\partial X_i}\right)\right]$$

Then, using subscript notation for first and cross partial derivatives, for any two goods j and k (neither equal to i) the first-order conditions are

$$U_j = - [\lambda_1 T_j + \lambda_2(U_{ij} - aT_{ij})]$$
$$U_k = - [\lambda_1 T_k + \lambda_2(U_{ik} - aT_{ik})]$$

Let us try to get at the crux of the issue. Under realistic assumptions that apply to an imperfect economy, the optimal second-best prices in all sectors deviate from observed marginal costs according to complicated formulas which depend on many empirical facts about the economy: demand and supply elasticities, cross elasticities, and elasticities of factor substitution. Given the current state of the art of general equilibrium analysis and the limitations of our empirical knowledge, we cannot pragmatically determine the direction of the deviations from observed marginal costs, let alone their magnitudes. Thus there does not appear to be any efficiency justification from general equilibrium analysis for using "free markets," which set prices in an economy equal to observed marginal costs. Furthermore, analysts in an imperfect market economy who would like to correct one sector at a time (e.g., through benefit-cost calculations) have only the unreliable market prices to serve as analytic guides. Are we stuck, with no hope of rescue? On what intellectual foundation can we stand if we are claiming to "improve" the allocation of resources?

Some Responses to the Second-Best Dilemma

The situation is not as hopeless as it sounds. The theoretical literature on this subject is burgeoning, and there may well be significant breakthroughs in terms of the empirical requirements for identifying welfare improvements.[12] There may also be breakthroughs in terms of expanding the empirical base that can be considered in analyses, as general equilibrium calculation routines become more accessible with greater flexibility in the underlying model assumptions.

As one example of a simplification from the second-best dilemma, let us illustrate the notion of *separability*. Most commodities fall naturally into groups: food, clothing, energy, etc. Suppose that consumer behavior, roughly speaking, is first to allocate part of the budget to each group and second to decide on specific products within each group. In other words, the intragroup decisions are made independently of intergroup decisions. This implies that the consumer's utility function of n goods which are in one of two groups

$$U = U(X_1, \ldots, X_m, X_{m+1}, \ldots, X_n)$$

and
$$\text{MRS}_{j,k} = \frac{U_j}{U_k} = \frac{\lambda_1 T_j + \lambda_2(U_{ij} - aT_{ij})}{\lambda_1 T_k + \lambda_2(U_{ik} - aT_{ik})}$$

Thus the relative price of good j in terms of good k must be made equal to the expression on the right. If all cross partials were zero, the expression would collapse to the RPT. Without knowing the four cross partials, we don't know if the optimal second-best price is greater or lesser than its first-best counterpart. And, of course, the more second-best constraints there are, the more cross-partial terms enter the expression and the more difficult it is to know the magnitude or the direction of change from ordinary marginal costs. For more discussion of this, see P. R. G. Layard and A. A. Walters, *Microeconomic Theory* (New York: McGraw-Hill Book Company, 1978), pp. 180–188.

[12] For an interesting discussion of this point which brings in process equity considerations, see M. Feldstein, "On the Theory of Tax Reform," *Journal of Public Economics*, 6, 1976, pp. 77–104.

can be written as a function of two functions $A(X_1, \ldots, X_m)$ and $B(X_{m+1}, \ldots, X_n)$:

$$U = U(A,B)$$

The important implication of separability is that the MRS between any two goods in one group is unaffected by a change in the quantity of a good in another group.[13]

The same concept of separability may be applied to the transformation (production-possibilities) curve. That is, the goods in groups A and B are separable in production if the transformation curve:

$$T(X_1, \ldots, X_m, X_{m+1}, \ldots, X_n)$$

can be written

$$T(C, D) = 0$$

where $C = C(X_1, \ldots, X_m)$ and $D = D(X_{m+1}, \ldots, X_n)$.

If it happens that some group of commodities is separable in *both* consumption and production and this group does not contain any inherent distortionary

---

[13] For two goods I and J in group A, the $\text{MRS}_{I,J}$ can be written by using the chain rule:

$$\frac{\partial U/\partial I}{\partial U/\partial J} = \frac{(\partial U/\partial A)(\partial A/\partial I)}{(\partial U/\partial A)(\partial A/\partial J)} = \frac{\partial A/\partial I}{\partial A/\partial J}$$

A change in good K from another group B does not cause any change in group A, and therefore does not affect the $\text{MRS}_{I,J}$. For example, a separable utility function is

$$U = (X_1 X_2)^\alpha (X_3 X_4)^\beta$$

We can separate the function by defining

$$A = (X_1 X_2) \qquad B = (X_3 X_4)$$

Then

$$\frac{\partial U}{\partial X_1} = \frac{\partial U}{\partial A} \frac{\partial A}{\partial X_1}$$

$$= \alpha A^{\alpha-1} B^\beta X_2$$

Similarly,

$$\frac{\partial U}{\partial X_2} = \alpha A^{\alpha-1} B^\beta X_1$$

Therefore,

$$\text{MRS}_{X_1,X_2} = \frac{\partial U/\partial X_1}{\partial U/\partial X_2} = \frac{X_2}{X_1}$$

If a good like X_3 from group B changes, then

$$\frac{\partial \text{MRS}_{X_1,X_2}}{\partial X_3} = 0$$

constraint, then the second-best general equilibrium solution will require that *within* the group MRS = RPT. This does not tell us what the optimal prices are for the group *relative to other goods,* but it does tell us how each commodity in the group should be priced in relation to the others. We may be able to price grains relative to vegetables even if we are uncertain about the average price of food relative to other things.

This suggests another line of thought: that the concept of optimal allocation is too abstract and is not a sufficiently pragmatic short-run goal for policy analysis. As a good colleague once expressed it, ''It is fine to reach for the stars as long as you keep at least one foot on the ground.'' It may be that, as in our discussion of the use of benefit-cost analysis in Chapter 5, the best we can do is muddle through. That is, we rely on the political system to serve as a check on the broad allocative decisions that arise from the market (e.g., between consumption and investment or the general spending level for education). Within those broad parameters, analysts may come up with specific programs or policies that suboptimize, like accepting the public enterprise budget constraint and analyzing how to price optimally within it. Perhaps as important new relations become uncovered in the course of time, our policy agenda adapts to them. The unease over energy pricing during the last decade may be a case in point.

The greatest danger is to fall back on the foolish priority of either doing ''nothing'' or doing ''anything.'' Such a strategy is as sensible as conceding a chess game because you are unable to deduce the optimal strategy. Of course, it would be nice to know the best thing to do; failing that, do your reasoned best! For example, let us consider the arguments *for* marginal cost pricing of electricity made by Kahn in response to a second-best argument.[14]

The argument for below marginal cost pricing (at the time of Kahn's response) was that the prices of both oil and natural gas—substitutes for electricity—were governmentally controlled and were below the marginal costs. Therefore, to keep relative allocation in balance, electricity users should also be charged below marginal cost. Kahn responded with several counterpoints including the following:

1 Second best in general has no more bias against marginal cost as a specific price than any other price; it is a recognition that we do not know the optimal price.

2 Since oil and natural gas are priced below marginal cost because of controls, demand may be great but supply will be below the equilibrium level. The opponents' argument can thus be stood on its head: There will be no large diversion to these artificially cheaper substitutes, since supply will not be forthcoming.

3 Less obvious but important electricity substitutes, like insulation and greater efficiency of such electrical devices as motors, are priced at marginal

---

[14] Alfred E. Kahn, ''Applications of Economics to an Imperfect World,'' *The American Economic Review,* 69, No. 2, May 1979, pp. 1–13.

costs. We have to consider relative allocations among electricity and these as well.

Where does this leave us? Should we pursue marginal cost pricing despite recognizing the theoretical validity of the second-best argument? Kahn's response seems to be yes, with modifications justified by perceived misallocations. If the actual quantities of oil and gas really were in oversupply (relative to perceived marginal costs), Kahn might have been more sympathetic to a second-best pricing argument. A case of this type might be mass transit commuting if automobile commuting is perceived to be priced substantially below its marginal cost (including pollution, congestion, and road maintenance).

Of course, the really big uncertainty may not be with the obvious substitutes for the commodity under discussion. The problems may come from prices of goods that are major sources of second-best distortions: those that are taxed heavily and those which are delivered in other than perfectly competitive settings. Until we know more about these distortions, no one can offer a definitive resolution of the general second-best dilemma.

Nevertheless, the concentration on optimal allocations may be more of a "marginal" task for policy analysts than the creation of a basic organizational framework to make allocations. For example, the author has seen no argument to suggest that the sustained rise in medical care costs relative to other costs is desirable from a second-best viewpoint. No one argues that air and water pollution levels should be uncontrolled (i.e., that the optimal price to charge polluters is zero). As another example, there seems to be substantial sentiment that we must find ways of becoming less vulnerable to foreign control of our energy resources. In all of these examples there is sufficient agreement on the social goals to allow productive discussion and analyses of alternative ways to achieve them. In the final section of this chapter we discuss organizational choice from a perspective which assumes reasonable agreement about the desired allocations.

THE MARKET AS A COORDINATING ORGANIZATION

Within the swirl of general equilibrium analysis it is easy to overlook the economic accomplishments of market-oriented systems. Yet an obvious empirical reality is the enormous economic progress that has occurred throughout our history. Without ever claiming to be in equilibrium, real GNP per capita has multiplied many times over the centuries. Of course, other countries which rely far less on markets also have made substantial progress during this same period. And as Arrow has pointed out, it is difficult to say on purely economic grounds whether one type of system does better than another.[15]

---

[15] Kenneth J. Arrow, "A Cautious Case for Socialism," *Dissent*, fall 1978, pp. 472–480. This article contains an interesting discussion of the relations among values and the methods of economic governance.

Our purpose is not to compare economic systems in the large, but to begin to identify the strengths and weaknesses of various market and government controls as a means of coordinating the economic agents in specific sectors in an economy. Other than the price-setting attribute of markets which we have reviewed, we have not attempted to probe deeply into other aspects of market organization. Consider, for example, the implicit solution to the second-best problem should we learn the optimal prices: Create the prices with taxes and subsidies and *let the market do all the rest of the work*.

By the perfectly competitive model we are using, we would not need to give a centralized directive to anyone for anything. There would be no rules about what to buy, where or when to buy, how to produce, what to produce, or who should produce. Individuals, acting totally out of their own self-interests (i.e., utility maximization), would find themselves coordinated by the impersonal forces of the marketplace. Production costs would be kept at a minimum through competition, and demand would ensure that the best possible products were made with the available resources. If all sectors of the economy met the perfectly competitive conditions, the role of government could be limited to redistributional goals and optimal price setting (i.e., taxation), with the attendant tax collections and distributions.

Obviously, this characterization assumes away many of the real problems of the economy, and these problems are the ones that government is expected to solve. We have mentioned many of them before (e.g., monopoly, increasing returns to scale technology), and in a moment we will summarize them. However, even with all the problems we will identify, it will remain true that the market as a coordinating device is an incredibly effective mechanism. That is one reason why "solutions" to problems often involve the public policy additions and deletions to *parts* of the market mechanism and leave the rest of the task to the same impersonal market forces. This is as true for economies considered broadly as "socialistic" as for those considered "capitalistic."[16]

There is a useful taxonomy of the specific problems that cause *market failure*.[17] Much insight into the economic functions of government has been gained from its use. However, the taxonomy does not go as far as pinpointing satisfactory government responses to the problems identified. Markets cannot be expected to function perfectly under all conditions, but neither do government controls and operations. The real problem may not be in identifying deviations from perfection or optimality; it is identifying the best organizational

---

[16] We discuss this further in Chapter 15. However, let us point out here that there is an important distinction between alternative views of who are the appropriate *owners* of capital (socialist regimes favor more collective ownership of capital than do capitalist regimes), and what mechanisms a society should use to direct its *allocation*. As an illustrative example, pension funds own significant amounts of capital in the U.S. economy even though they rely on the financial markets to decentralize decision making about specific allocations of the funds. One can imagine a pool of government-controlled pension funds owning the bulk of the capital and making allocative decisions in the same manner; this would be an example of market socialism.

[17] A classic reference article on this subject is F. Bator, "The Anatomy of Market Failure," *Quarterly Journal of Economics, 72,* 1958, pp. 351–379.

package from among the real alternative ways to coordinate economic agents in specific situations.

To develop these skills, it is helpful to have an understanding of the sources of problems in using the market as a coordinating device, and we go through the taxonomy briefly for this purpose. For each market failure, we point out why the market deviates from first-best efficiency requirements. However, it is important to recognize that these failures, if not addressed directly, are equally likely to cause deviations from second-best rules. That is, the failures are generally coordinating flaws which should be addressed no matter what the allocative target.

Increasing Returns to Scale over the Relevant Range of Demand[18]   We have already seen (Chapter 9) that increasing returns to scale can lead to unprofitable enterprises despite the allocative efficiency of providing the product. If the market price to consumers does not equal the marginal cost of supplying the output, then the MRS of this good for any other will not equal the corresponding RPT and one of the necessary conditions for Pareto optimality will be violated. The common solution is to subsidize the enterprise; the enterprise itself may be either public (e.g., the Post Office, Amtrak, most subways) or private (e.g., some urban bus companies).

A second version of the problem arises with profitable natural monopolies, like public utility companies.[19] In this case, the monopolist is unlikely to allocate resources "correctly." ($P \neq MR = MC$, so the MRS of this good for another will not equal the corresponding RPT.) In addition, it may be able to charge consumers substantially more than marginal cost by exploiting its monopoly power. The standard solution, which we discuss further in Chapter 15, is rate-of-return regulation.

Public Goods   Until now we have generally assumed that a good is something that is consumed by one person only. Some goods, however, are jointly consumed by "everybody." National defense is the classic example. More common are *local* public goods which are consumed by "everyone in the area"; examples are street lights, lighthouses, police patrols, weather forecasts, flood control projects, parks, and public health activities. Some public goods, like the threat of street crime, are actually public "bads."

Two characteristics are identified with public goods. The goods are *nonrival* in consumption; my consumption of the weather forecast does not decrease the amount of it left for you. Also, most public goods are *nonexclusive:* Once a good is provided to one person, others cannot be prevented from enjoying its benefits (at least, without enormous expense). If I buy streetlights for my street, it is difficult for me to exclude those who use the street from the benefits

---

[18] The qualification is to restrict our attention to cases in which the net benefits from production are positive.

[19] This was mentioned briefly in the discussion of trucking deregulation in Chapter 7.

of lighting. Those who receive the benefits without having to pay for them are called *free-riders*, and they are an important reason why the market fails to provide public goods efficiently. A public good such as a zoo does not pose quite the same problem because individuals can be excluded with admission gates; a movie may be public up to the theater capacity, but there is no problem excluding people.

Efficiency requires, as usual, that we provide each unit of the public good when the marginal benefit exceeds the marginal cost. However, since everyone gets benefits from each unit, we have to *sum* the benefits to see if they outweigh the costs. Of course, not everyone will place the same marginal value on each unit. More formally, the Pareto-optimal allocation to the m consumers of a public good G requires that, for any private good X,[20]

$$\sum_{i=1}^{m} \mathrm{MRS}_{G,X}^{i} = \mathrm{RPT}_{G,X}$$

[20] Recall from our discussion in Chapter 7 that the $\mathrm{MRS}_{G,X}$ can be thought of as the marginal benefit of one more unit of G expressed in terms of units of X. The technical condition can be proved easily with a simple model using calculus. Imagine that we have a two-person economy and that we seek to maximize one person's utility U_1 while holding the other's $\overline{U}_2$ at a constant level. (This will therefore be one of the Pareto-optimal allocations.) There are two goods in the economy, one public G and the other private P. We are subject to a production-possibilities frontier as usual, which we will describe as $F(G) = $ the maximum number of units of the *private* good that society can produce, given that they are producing G units of the public good. Then the derivative $\partial F / \partial G$ is the number of units of the private good which must be foregone for one more unit of G, or $\mathrm{RPT}_{G,P}$. Note also that, for any allocation among the two people

$$P = P_1 + P_2 \qquad G = G_1 = G_2 \qquad \text{(the public good is shared)}$$

Now the problem is to find the optimum of this Lagrangian expression:

$$L = U_1(P_1, G) + \lambda_1[U_2(P_2, G) - \overline{U}_2] + \lambda_2[F(G) - P_1 - P_2]$$

The first-order conditions with respect to P_1, P_2, and G simplify to:

$$\frac{\partial U_1}{\partial P_1} = \lambda_2 \tag{i}$$

$$\lambda_1 \frac{\partial U_2}{\partial P_2} = \lambda_2 \tag{ii}$$

$$\frac{\partial U_1}{\partial G} + \lambda_1 \frac{\partial U_2}{\partial G} = \lambda_2 \frac{\partial F}{\partial G} \tag{iii}$$

Let us divide both sides of equation (iii) by λ_2

$$\frac{\partial U_1/\partial G}{\lambda_2} + \frac{\lambda_1(\partial U_2/\partial G)}{\lambda_2} = \frac{\partial F}{\partial G}$$

For the λ_2 in the first term on the left, substitute from equation (i). For the λ_2 in the second term, substitute from equation (ii).

$$\frac{\partial U_1/\partial G}{\partial U_1/\partial P_1} + \frac{\partial U_2/\partial G}{\partial U_2/\partial P} = \frac{\partial F}{\partial G}$$

But by definition, this is

$$\mathrm{MRS}_{G,P}^{1} + \mathrm{MRS}_{G,P}^{2} = \mathrm{RPT}_{G,P}$$

If their provision were left to the marketplace, public goods would be underallocated. The reason is that individuals have incentives to understate their own preferences in order to avoid paying and free-ride on the demands of others. Thus, public goods provide one of the strongest arguments for government intervention in the marketplace: not only does the market fail, but it can fail miserably.

Even in the case of a public good such that exclusion is possible, e.g., a zoo, the market will not allocate properly. An entrepreneur will provide a zoo if admission fees generate revenues which equal or exceed total costs.[21] But since the marginal cost of admitting an extra person is zero, it is inefficient to deter entrance with admission fees. (This is similar to the pricing problem under increasing returns.)

However, there is also no perfect mechanism for government to use in deciding allocations. One of the most important uses of benefit-cost analysis is to estimate the proper quantity to provide of a public good. But taxpayers cannot be taxed in accordance with their true preference for the good (for the same reason that the market fails to reveal preferences honestly), and an optimal allocation may be disapproved by the voters because of the tax incidence (rather than the allocation).

An important area of public policy research is the design of organizational mechanisms which are "incentive compatible" with the honest revelation of preferences.[22] A fascinating and practical example is the method of selecting programs to produce for viewing on the public broadcasting system (PBS). There are many affiliated PBS stations scattered throughout the country; and once a program is produced for one, it could be shown by all the others at essentially no extra cost. Thus, the consumption of programs by a local station is nonrival.

Originally, the decisions about programs to produce were made by a central PBS authority in Washington, D.C. But the network found its choices subject to *political* pressures. With the avoidance of those pressures as motivation, the network designed a decentralized bidding system. Each affiliate is assigned a certain budgetary power, and it allocates its budget among the hundreds of proposed programs. The allocations are summed across affiliates, through several rounds of bidding, to see which programs have total bids which exceed their costs.

For example, each of 10 stations may bid $5000 for program A on the first round, but the total cost of A is $100,000. The center informs all the affiliates that it "looks like" $10,000 each will be needed, and the affiliates reallocate

---

[21] The entrepreneur may be able to make profits on food concessions and other activities "packaged" with the public good and thus avoid charging entrance fees. However, nonmarginal cost pricing of the concessions is inefficient.

[22] An important theoretical article on this subject is by T. Groves and J. Ledyard, "Optimal Allocation of Public Goods: A Solution to the Free Rider Problem," *Econometrica, 45,* 1977, pp. 783–810. A more comprehensive survey is found in J. Green and J-J. Laffont, *Incentives in Public Decision-Making* (New York: North Holland Publishing Company, 1979).

their budgets among *all* the programs in light of the new information on expected costs. According to the research done on this system, the outcome is not "optimal" but is remarkably close to it. And the discovery of this new relatively efficient mechanism occurred as an unintended consequence of a political maneuver.[23]

Externalities We introduced the concept of an externality in Chapter 3: whenever the actions of one economic agent affect at least one other economic agent other than through prices. Externalities occur among and between consumers and producers. In Chapter 3 we focused on the type of consumption externality which arises simply because one person chooses to "care" about some aspect of another person's activity. In many cases the externality is imposed, as when my neighbor's lawn becomes a junkyard or my house burns down because the house next door catches fire. Obviously, consumption externalities can be either negative or positive; i.e., the external effect can have either net benefits or net costs to its recipients.

Externalities in production are common as well. A chemical plant which pollutes a waterway reduces the productivity of the local fishing industry; if the plant happens to leak fish food, it may bring a positive externality to the local fishing industry. If a glue factory locates in my neighborhood, there is an externality between a producer and many consumers; the same is true of an apartment builder who constructs a 10-story building which blocks views.

There are many other examples of externalities. The Slumlord's Dilemma in Chapter 6 occurs only because of externalities. The victimless crime of prostitution may involve negative externalities for the businesses on the walked streets. All the pollutions are externalities: air, water, noise, and visual. An automobile trip during rush hour imposes congestion costs on others. One of the most important production externalities comes from basic research: When a really new idea is discovered, it often has thousands of applications. An example is Pasteur's discovery of the benefits of inoculation with a weakened agent of disease.

The market fails to allocate resources properly to activities which generate externalities. The reason is that there will be a divergence between the private and social benefits and costs. When the apartment developer considers building a view-blocking structure, the developer weighs the cost of the land and the construction materials against the selling price of the finished product. The costs of blocking the view of others do not enter the developer's calculus. Why not?

Those whose views will be blocked have no right to prevent the construction, unless public policy creates such a right (which is one reason for zoning laws). Nor is there any mechanism for the surrounding inhabitants to "bribe"

---

[23] For more details and excellent analysis, see the work of J. Ferejohn, R. Noll, and R. Forsythe, "An Experimental Analysis of Decision-Making Procedures and Discrete Public Goods: A Case Study of a Problem in Institutional Design," in V. Smith (ed.), *Research in Experimental Economics,* vol. 1 (Chicago: Johnson Publishing Company, Inc.—Book Division, 1978).

the developer to keep the new structure "low." Even if the inhabitants were willing as a group to make such a bribe, there would be the free-rider problem in collecting it. (And think of all the potential developers that would go into the bribe-collecting business.) The market will produce too little of the activities which generate positive externalities (like basic research), and too much of those which generate negative externalities (like pollution).

The rule for efficient allocation of the activities involving externalities is similar to the rule for public goods. (The latter can be thought of as a special case of externality.) For each unit undertaken, the sum of the benefits to each agent affected should exceed the sum of the costs imposed on each agent affected. We explain the market failure for production externalities below.[24]

When there is an externality in production (between goods X and Y), competitive markets lead to inefficient output levels at which $\text{RPT}_{X,Y} \neq P_X/P_Y$. To see this, recall that the $\text{RPT}_{X,Y}$ is the slope of the production-possibilities curve and represents the marginal cost to *society* of X in terms of Y foregone. This can be thought of as the ratio in money terms of the social marginal cost of X to the social marginal cost of Y:

$$\text{RPT}_{X,Y} = \frac{\text{SMC}_X}{\text{SMC}_Y} = \frac{\text{dollars per unit of } X}{\text{dollars per unit of } Y} = Y \text{ per unit of } X$$

When the marginal cost to society equals the marginal cost to each firm, competitive markets lead to $\text{RPT}_{X,Y} = P_X/P_Y$. However, *when there are production externalities, the social marginal costs do not equal the private marginal costs*. Suppose that the production of X (chemicals) has an external effect on the production of Y (fish). That is, the production function for Y is of a form

$$Y = F (K, L, X)$$

In other words, the amount of Y (fish) is a function of the amount of ordinary capital and labor inputs selected by the firm (boats and crew) but is also affected by the amount of X (say, because each unit of chemical produced leaves residual waste which enters the waterway where the fish are). If the externality is positive (the residual waste is fish food), $\text{MP}_X^Y > 0$. If the

---

[24] The exchange efficiency conditions when there are consumption externalities were derived in Chapter 3. Here we simply note that efficiency in the case of a consumption externality associated with good X requires that, for every pair of consumers i and j in an economy with m consumers of X and other goods Y,

$$\sum_{k=1}^{m} \text{MRS}_{X_i, Y}^{k} = \sum_{k=1}^{m} \text{MRS}_{X_j, Y}^{k} = \text{RPT}_{X, Y}$$

In normal market trading each consumer sets his or her own $\text{MRS}_{X,Y} = P_X/P_Y$, and the above condition will not be satisfied.

externality is negative (the residual waste destroys natural fish food), $MP_X^Y < 0$. The social marginal cost of an additional unit of X is thus

$$SMC_X = MC_X + P_Y MP_X^Y$$

The first term on the right is the usual marginal cost of X as perceived by its producer. The second term on the right is the money value per unit of Y times the amount Y changes because of the extra unit of X. Thus, the rate of product transformation is

$$RPT_{X,Y} = \frac{MC_X + P_Y MP_X^Y}{MC_Y}$$

Since competitive firms will choose quantities that equate the private marginal costs to the market prices,

$$RPT_{X,Y} = \frac{P_X + P_Y MP_X^Y}{P_Y} = \frac{P_X}{P_Y} + MP_X^Y \neq \frac{P_X}{P_Y}$$

Since each consumer will have $MRS_{X,Y} = P_X/P_Y$, we see that, when there are production externalities,

$$RPT_{X,Y} \neq MRS_{X,Y}$$

We shall look at some applications of this and focus on how to design solutions in Chapter 15. The solutions proposed for externality problems vary, and here we only try to suggest the types of solutions. For the negative externality of automobile congestion, raise the price by imposing a commuting *tax*. In partial response to the external accident costs to others imposed by poor drivers, it may be efficient to design a uniform bumper height standard for automobile manufacturers. For certain kinds of pollution (e.g., factory air pollution) it may be efficient to assign property rights for the total permissible level and let economic agents trade them in the marketplace. If the externality involves only a few economic agents, as in the Slumlord's Dilemma, having one owner of both properties (merger) would solve the problem.

Every one of these solutions *internalizes* the external benefits or costs. The best way to do this often depends crucially on the *transactions costs* of the alternative remedies. It might be easy to meter and thus tax an automobile's contribution to congestion. Measuring the pollution level of the same car each trip might be difficult, and a pollution standard might be a better policy.

Note the contrast between the perfectly competitive assumption of zero transaction costs and our statement indicating that good solutions often depend on the transaction costs associated with proposed alternatives. The discussion in Chapter 8 suggested that, in the market, transaction costs influence the formation of firms and the centralization of decision making *within* them.

Externalities cause market failure because of the high individual transaction costs of "internalizing" them *across* economic agents. We shall expand this discussion in Chapter 15.

Imperfect Information   The perfect information assumption of the competitive model is one of the least satisfactory aspects of the model. The reason, as we began to emphasize in Chapter 6, is that the presence of significant uncertainties is more characteristic than its absence for a wide range of decisions, and behavior is changed because of it. That does not, by itself, imply any market failure. Suppose we think of uncertainty like hunger and knowledge like food which satisfies our appetites. We produce both food and knowledge in accordance with our preferences and our production possibilities; perhaps there is no problem.

However, we have good reason to believe that market failure occurs both in the production of knowledge and in the allocation of the residual uncertainty. For example, the price of a good has little meaning to a consumer unless the qualities of that good are known as well. The market does produce some information about qualities, as any subscriber to *Consumer Reports* knows. But these information markets fail because information has public good qualities: Many people can "consume" the same information without reducing its supply. Thus the market produces too little information, and that is one reason why government often acts to increase it as by information disclosure requirements and government testing of products.

Similar problems can arise in hiring decisions. An employer may not know which of two potential employees has the higher marginal productivity and therefore may offer each an average wage. The better worker may invest in some signals, like getting a college degree, simply to be identified initially as "better." (Thus, we are ruling out the consumption value of education in this example.) But if the degree does not itself improve productivity, society has lost. It has foregone output to pay for education and received no extra output in return; the distribution of income has also become more unequal.[25]

More problems arise because of imperfect information about future prices. One of the most important social tasks involves the allocation of resources over time. Efficient market allocation requires a full set of futures markets to establish relative prices across time for all commodities. For example, decisions about how much oil to use today relative to electricity and other things depends not only on current relative prices but on future prices relative to today. Oil may be cheap relative to electricity today, but it could be worth saving if its value in the future will be much greater.

Futures markets do not arise for all commodities because of transaction costs. The existing futures markets are limited in the types of commodities

---

[25] See J. Stiglitz, "The Theory of Screening, Education, and the Distribution of Income," *The American Economic Review*, 65, June 1975, pp. 283–300.

included and the span of time. Even when there are partial future markets, a difficulty is that future people are not here to articulate their share of demand.[26] Thus, the longer-term futures markets fail. This opens the door for a government role in preserving some of our important resources (e.g., oil, Yellowstone National Park), as well as influencing the aggregate savings-consumption trade-off. We focus on policy problems involving intertemporal allocation in Chapter 14.

We have already discussed, in Chapter 6, many mechanisms for reducing the risk cost of uncertainty. One of the more important of these mechanisms, insurance, may fail because of moral hazard as well as *adverse selection*. The latter occurs when the insurer cannot separate better and poorer risks. The better risks find that the average premium is too high relative to their own expected costs. Accordingly, they drop out of the insurance market, which causes the premium to rise for everyone else. That, in turn, causes the best of the remaining insured to drop out, which further raises the premium, and so on, until no one has insurance.[27]

If one wishes to consider the implications of imperfect information that is due to bounded rationality, the problems can multiply. Nelson and Winter argue, for example, that the competitive mechanism may sometimes be a very weak instrument for ensuring least-cost production.[28] This is best illustrated when we recognize that economies are not static; they are dynamic and evolve.

If firms are boundedly rational, it will take them time to perceive profit opportunities in markets and more time to figure out by trial and error how to take advantage of the opportunities. For complicated technologies with long production times, as may characterize the airframe industry, the technology may change more rapidly than the ability of firms to keep up with it. There may be progress, but there may also never be least-cost production by any firm. The changes may involve big mistakes, with no competitors standing ready to knock the blunderers out of the business. It is possible that the imperfect knowledge caused by competition (firms protective of their knowledge) is more costly than a regime of less competition and more shared information.

All these examples are intended to illustrate that reconciling many of the standard conclusions of microeconomic theory to account for imperfect information is a large and difficult task. Many of the problems we examine in the following chapters (e.g., rent control, student loans for higher education) involve policy responses to problems of imperfect information, and we will attempt to be sensitive to the efficiency implications.

---

[26] To some extent, families may try to represent the wishes of their future descendants (although their information about the preferences of future descendants is surely imperfect).

[27] See G. Akerlof, "The Market for Lemons: Qualitative Uncertainty and the Market Mechanism," *Quarterly Journal of Economics, 84,* 1970, pp. 488–500.

[28] See Richard R. Nelson and Sidney G. Winter, *An Evolutionary Theory of Economic Change* (Cambridge, Mass.: Harvard University Press, 1982).

SUMMARY

This chapter raises the second-best issue, which is to identify the most efficient feasible allocations in an economy characterized by some inherent distortionary constraints. The second-best allocations, given that the first-best allocations are infeasible, are *not* characterized by following the first-best rules in the unconstrained sectors. Thus, free markets, which lead to allocations following first-best rules in each competitive sector, will not lead to the most efficient allocations of an economy's resources. Nor will the government benefit-cost analyst, who relies for calculations on observed market prices, come to the right conclusion about the optimal allocation for any particular sector.

Although markets and analysts may allocate suboptimally, the requirements for a true second-best solution exceed our empirical, and in all probability our political, abilities. The theoretical solution involves a system of taxes and subsidies on all commodities, but the correct magnitudes require extensive knowledge of demand and supply elasticities and cross elasticities. Therefore, it may be sensible, as a matter of policy, to treat the elusive optimal allocation as the chess player treats the elusive optimal chess strategy: Surely it would be nice to know; but until we do know, we should use the best decision rules at our disposal.

The practice seems to be following the first-best marginal rules except when some visible problem suggests that a second-best strategy, like Ramsey pricing for mass transit, might be more appropriate. To the extent that activities fall naturally into groups that are separable in both production and consumption, this strategy has some support in theory. However, it should be recognized that one cannot have much confidence that this method identifies optimal allocations.

From a normative point of view, the general equilibrium theory does not (at this time) provide much policy guidance. Rather than continue to emphasize price-quantity equilibrium characteristics, there is much of policy relevance to learn about the organizational attributes of markets. That is, an obvious striking characteristic of a market is how it coordinates economic activities with minimal policy directives. We will look more closely, in later chapters, at circumstances which seem to be handled well by this undirected, decentralized process and those in which policy intervention can improve the organizational functioning.

As a start, we review the standard reasons for market failures: public goods, externalities, increasing-returns-to-scale technology, and (a catchall of) imperfect information. These identify situations in which markets do not work well, and our quick review of standard solutions to the problems indicates that analysis of transaction costs often plays a significant role in designing a pragmatic response to them. This theme will continue throughout the remaining chapters.

EXERCISES

11-1 Any firm can produce a service at MC $= \$4$ once it spends \$380 for setup costs.

    a Using first-best rules, explain the efficient quantity of the service to provide if it is demanded by two consumers as follows:

$$Q_A = 40 - 2P$$
$$Q_B = 20 - P \qquad \text{(Answer: 48)}$$

    b Explain the efficient quantity if demands are as follows:

$$Q_A = 30 - 2P$$
$$Q_B = 25 - P \qquad \text{(Answer: Zero)}$$

    c Could firms unable to price-discriminate survive by producing the efficient quantity under the demand conditions in (*a*)? Explain. How many firms are required technically to provide that quantity at the least social cost of production? (Answers: No; one)

    d Suppose the service is a pure public good, demands are as in (*a*), and we ignore second-best considerations. What is the efficient quantity to provide? What if the demands are as in (*b*)? (Answer: 32; 24)

    e Explain how second-best considerations might lead to the conclusion that the public good in (*d*), or the private good in (*a*), should not be provided at all.

    ∇f Suppose the only way to finance the production of public good Q is through a sales tax on private goods. Let X be an aggregate good representing private goods, and suppose good X can be produced at constant marginal cost equal to \$1 per unit. The demand for good X is

$$X = 3000 - 1000P_X$$

Assume for simplicity that the tax does not cause any shifts in the demand or supply curve for either good.

    What is the most efficient quantity of the public good Q to provide in this economy, under the demand conditions in (*a*), and what tax rate is used to finance it? *Note:* Determining the exact answer to this question through Lagrangian techniques involves solving a cubic equation. An approximate answer may be obtained more simply by noting that (1) the tax revenues must equal the cost of providing the public good, and (2) since 4 units of X must be sacrificed for each unit of Q produced, the marginal net benefit of Q must roughly equal 4 times the marginal net benefit of X. (Answer: $Q \approx 30$; $t \approx \$0.29$)

CHAPTER 12

THE CONTROL OF PRICES AND PROFITS TO ACHIEVE EQUITY IN SPECIFIC MARKETS

For a variety of reasons, individuals in an economy will attempt through collective action to alter a specific market's distributional consequences. In earlier discussion (Chapters 2 and 4) we recognized specific egalitarian concerns, i.e., a desire that the distribution of certain things, usually necessities, meet equity standards such as a universal minimum or strict equality (e.g., housing, food, jury duty). A somewhat different concern might be called *specific redistribution:* when consumers in a specific market believe that the payments they make to producers are unfairly high.[1]

Two clear cases evidencing this latter sentiment, discussed in this chapter, are apartment rentals and oil products. Rent control ordinances exist in many cities; they are intended to keep most apartment rental prices below market rates. The federal government has recently passed a windfall profits tax on domestic oil-producing companies; it is intended to take "unfair" profits and convert them into resources for general "public use."

We might think of these policies as reflecting the thirteenth-century concern of St. Thomas Aquinas: Sellers should receive the "just" price. What standard determines the just price? St. Thomas believed that the values of goods and services were divinely determined; he thought, for example, that the just interest rate was zero.

---

[1] A related set of concerns, which we do not discuss here, occurs when workers feel they are being paid an unfairly low wage.

Modifying the general idea slightly, we will refer to the just price as the opportunity cost of supply. Then payments above opportunity costs, or economic rents, are unjust payments. That is, *we pose the general issue of this chapter as a struggle between buyers and sellers over the distribution of economic rent.* We review a number of situations in which the market generates economic rent and consumers attempt to claim at least some rights to it.

Several points specific to these policies are emphasized throughout the discussion. We list them here for convenience:

1 If controls only remove economic rent from sellers, the supply response in the short and long run will be identical with the uncontrolled market.

2 It can be very difficult to limit the effects of controls to economic rent because of the subtlety of some real opportunity costs to sellers and the administrative difficulties of accounting for them.

3 Many of the potential benefits to buyers as a collectivity can dissipate as individual buyers use other resources in the scramble to claim them.

4 Buyers who do end up with benefits may be an arbitrary subset of all buyers, rather than those who correspond to any reasoned definition of equity.

The specific policy problems studied here also help in the development of new and more general skills of policy analysis. The predicted outcomes of the processes we study depend on how individual economic agents are affected by the *joint* forces of the market and public policy and how the nature of the individual responses can lead to a new equilibrium. These responses depend heavily on the information economic agents have and the transaction costs of making and enforcing arrangements between agents. We suggest that the details of the changes in legal specification of property rights and responsibilities associated with a specific policy can have substantial impact on individual behavior and thus also on the new equilibrium and predicted outcome. At a minimum, the analyst interested in the design of policies to alter specific market outcomes should appreciate why basic microeconomic insights about markets must be combined with careful specification of the new policy before the policy's effects can be predicted.

We proceed as follows. First, we discuss policy intervention in specific markets as a response to a sudden change in demand or supply which creates "unusual" *quasi rents*. We use apartment rent control as an example. Then we consider the standard argument which suggests that rent control is inefficient.[2] This argument does not illuminate either the possibilities for or the difficulties of rent control, so more detailed models of economic rent in housing markets are developed.

---

[2] Throughout this and other chapters we define efficient allocations as those which meet the usual first-best rules unless stated otherwise. This use is not essential to the fundamental points of the chapters, although it greatly eases exposition. The analytic principles that we explain and develop about the coordination of economic agents would also apply to allocations defined as efficient by second-best rules.

These more detailed models show the relation between rent control and the capitalized value of the controlled property, and they lead to the conclusion that, for rent controls to avoid adverse housing supply consequences, the capitalized value of the property in apartment rental use must be kept greater than in any other use. The capitalized value depends not only on the formal control price but also, heavily, on how the exchange side of the market (matching tenants with apartments) works. This in turn depends upon specific details of the rent control ordinances and their enforcement. We discuss this and show that the same details also explain why the individuals who receive benefits from the controls may be a fairly arbitrary subset of tenants.

One policy which could have avoided most of the pitfalls of rent control is that which led to the windfall profits tax on oil. We explain the functioning of the OPEC cartel and how the initial U.S. response to it of price controls caused a variety of inefficiencies including the overuse of imported supplies and insufficient conservation incentives for consumers. The newer policies of price decontrol coupled with the windfall profits tax are discussed, and they are shown to remove some of the inefficiencies without necessarily sacrificing distributional concerns.

DISSATISFACTION WITH MARKET PRICING DURING
TEMPORARY SHORTAGE OF A NECESSITY

In this section we examine a special circumstance which causes many people to conclude that certain market prices are unfair. The circumstance occurs when the short-run market equilibrium price of a necessity is temporarily but substantially higher than the usual long-run price. It can arise due to a temporary supply disruption, as during the October 1973 oil embargo. It can also occur when there is a temporary surge in demand, as for apartments in New York City when the soldiers returned at the end of World War II. The feeling of unfairness is generated by the payments of *quasi rents* to suppliers: payments *above* opportunity costs which would not persist in the long run. Such sentiments are a source of demand for policy intervention.

In Figure 12-1 we illustrate this type of market situation. We imagine that initially we observe an equilibrium quantity of housing (standardized to be of constant quality) Q_0 at a price P_0. The long-run supply curve is drawn horizontally; it represents the assumption that housing in the long run is a constant cost industry (to be modified later). In a world in which all population changes occur slowly, the equilibrium quantity would shift only gradually over time in response to demand—and the price to all current households would remain unchanged at P_0.

However, suppose there is a sudden surge in demand, as in New York City at the end of World War II. The demand curve shifts outward to D'. The short-run supply SS of housing is fixed at Q_0. With more apartment seekers ready to pounce upon each vacancy that arises, the market price is driven up to P_S. Landlords raise the rents for existing tenants as well, since there are plenty of

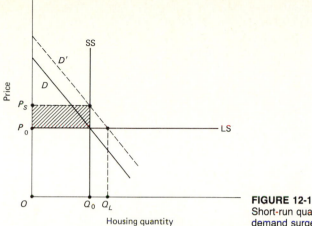

Housing quantity

FIGURE 12-1
Short-run quasi rents in response to a
demand surge.

people who would pay P_S should the existing tenants refuse. In other words, the landlord perceives a private opportunity cost of not raising the rent.

The final short-run allocation is efficient. There are no mutually profitable trades which could be made among any agents in this market. How has the market made room for the extra people, given that supply is fixed? By raising the price, each household is left free to respond in whatever way best suits its taste. Many, who had been receiving a substantial consumer surplus, make no changes and simply pay the higher rent. Others look for smaller apartments, and still others take on roommates or boarders. Premarital engagements may even become shorter if it becomes too expensive to maintain separate apartments! Thus, the density of people per housing unit inceases. Furthermore, the normal vacancy rate goes down: If the average unit used to be vacant 10 days per year, now it may be vacant only 3 or 4 days per year. *In short, each apartment is used more intensively with respect to both time and people.* And in the long run, of course, the supply expands to Q_L and the price returns to P_0.

What is wrong with this system, given that it allocates so well? The problem is the one perceived by the "initial" tenants: Why should they have to pay more when it is obvious that the landlord's operating costs have not increased by one penny? Think of some of the hardships imposed. For example, there are retirees on fixed incomes who have lived in the same apartments for 20 years. Should their lives be radically upset as a by-product of the "market" need for time to supply new housing? Is there no alternative by which the extra people could be housed without charging all the initial tenants more? After all, the short-run housing supply is fixed. A law which freezes rents at P_0 will leave the same total amount of housing available. Find another way of deciding how to house the new people.

In fact, the market might work almost as well under the rent freeze ordinance as under no ordinance; only this time the initial tenants would be the beneficiaries of the demand surge. They would receive offers from others to accept them as roommates or to give up apartments in return for lump sums of money. No initial occupant of an apartment receiving less than an average of $P_S - P_0$ surplus per unit of it would remain in the initial situation, because potential occupants would offer at least $P_S - P_0$ in addition to the controlled rent for it.

People could find each other through rental agencies, where initial tenants could list the "rent" at which they would take on a roommate or the "finder's fee" that they would charge for locating an apartment (their own). If you doubt that all this would happen, ask anyone who has looked for an apartment in New York. The final short-run allocation is the same as under the "free" market.[3] And in the long run, the supply expands to Q_L as before.[4]

Under the two simple alternatives, it should be clear that the majority of voters within one district would favor the latter plan (assuming apartment owners are a smaller percentage of voters than tenants).[5] In Figure 12-1 it can be seen that the net social benefit from housing under either plan is the area above LS and below D' up to the quantity Q_0. In the free-market plan, apartment owners receive the shaded area as quasi rent. Under the rent freeze plan, the shaded area is distributed to tenants.

In this analysis the two alternatives are equal on efficiency grounds and differ in their equity implications. The main theoretical point illustrated is this: *Since economic rent is a payment to a factor above opportunity costs, its removal does not cause any distortions in resource allocation.* But in terms of coming to grips with actual apartment rent control, the model specification—the set of assumptions from which we draw inferences—is, at this stage, overly simplistic.

A STANDARD EXPLANATION OF THE INEFFICIENCY OF RENT CONTROL

The preceding description is not the one that is usually given in explaining rent control policies. The usual one concludes that rent control is inefficient. This is illustrated in Figure 12-2. The only difference from the prior illustration is that

---

[3] This assumes that no difference in D' occurs as a consequence of the changed income effects from the prior example. However, one would expect that some families who would have been forced to move because of higher prices (or who would have taken in roommates) will not do so under rent control.

[4] For convenience, we assume throughout that producers will supply all goods and services for which they break even (zero economic profit). This should be understood as a limiting case. It is the prospect of positive economic profits (even if very small) which attracts more resources into an industry. For example, a very small increase in price may be all that is needed to lure additional single-family homeowners to provide rental space within their homes.

[5] We might note that the population surge would also cause a substantial increase in price for potential home buyers. Similar arguments could be made about the inequity of this windfall gain to existing homeowners at the expense of home buyers. However, the politics of this situation are very different: The number of existing homeowners compared with home buyers in a jurisdiction is large, whereas the number of landlords relative to renters is small. Thus, local control of windfall gains in housing prices is politically unlikely.

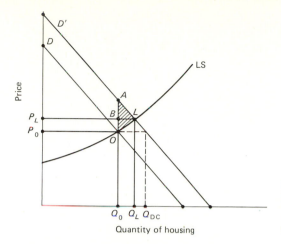

FIGURE 12-2
Standard illustration of the inefficiency of rent control in the long run. (The minimum social loss is shaded.)

the long-run supply curve LS is upward-sloping (an increasing cost industry).

The short-run analysis of this situation is unchanged; it is the long-run effects which are dramatically different. Under the "free-market" policy, long-run equilibrium is at (P_L, Q_L), where both price and quantity are higher than the initial levels (P_0, Q_0). The supply has expanded in response to the increase in demand, and the resulting allocation is optimal. However, the long-run effects of a policy which keeps rent at its initial level are deleterious. Although tenants demand Q_{DC} at the controlled price, suppliers provide only Q_0. The supply does not expand to the efficient quantity Q_L, and there would be a perceived housing "shortage" of $Q_{DC} - Q_0$.

If this model captures the essence of rent control, there is always a net social loss in comparison with the uncontrolled market equilibrium. The long-run deadweight loss is shown as the shaded area OAL in Figure 2-2. Landlords lose the area P_0P_LBO because of lowered rent receipts from tenants, and they lose OBL in economic rent (or producer's surplus) because the units between Q_L and Q_0 are not supplied under rent controls. Thus, landlords are unambiguous losers from this policy (which is, of course, what is intended).

Tenants, on the other hand, may be net gainers or losers. Assuming that the Q_0 housing units are distributed efficiently among consumers (as in our short-run model), they gain rectangle P_0P_LBO but lose the consumer surplus ABL on the $Q_L - Q_0$ units which are not supplied. Tenants gain if $P_0P_LBO > ABL$ and lose if the reverse is true. In either case the rectangle P_0P_LBO is a transfer between tenants and landlords and the area OAL is a deadweight loss (nobody gains it).[6]

---

[6] One empirical study concludes that, in 1968 in New York, the real income of occupants of rent-controlled housing was 3.4 percent higher than if there were no rent control and that poorer families received larger benefits. However, the study also concludes that the cost to landlords was

Many analysts believe that rent control policies have another serious adverse effect: In the long run, rent control causes disinvestment in rental housing. Landlords are faced with rising bills for building maintenance, for example, but are unable to pass the costs on to tenants. So they respond by reducing building maintenance, which lowers the quality of housing and causes the housing stock to deteriorate more rapidly. This, of course, would be an exacerbation of the shortage we have already described.

A RAND Corporation study of rent control in New York City reported these disinvestment effects.[7] From 1960 to 1967 the inventory of sound housing grew by 2.4 percent while the inventory of dilapidated housing grew by 44 percent and deteriorating housing by 37 percent. In the 3 years 1965 to 1967, a total of 114,000 housing units was withdrawn from the market (vacated and boarded up). Thus, it seems clear that if these disinvestment effects are in fact due to rent control policies, they constitute a serious, if not disastrous, problem with the policy.

Several good reasons why rent control might cause the disinvestment effects described above have been put forth in the literature. The problem with them, for our purpose, is that none of them apply analytically when used in conjunction with the standard economic model and the rent control policy we have described. That is, they all make some crucial assumption about behavior which is either not explicitly addressed by the model used in the analysis or is inconsistent with the actual policy. They may be insightful ad hoc rationalizations, but we could not honestly say that they are predictions which an analyst would arrive at naturally by applying the standard models. We seek a method of analysis which leads to insight in advance of actually observing policy consequences. Let us briefly consider three common arguments put forth to explain disinvestment; our effort is to clarify why they are *not* proper deductions from the standard model applied to the rent control policy.

The first argument is that rent controls remove the incentive of owners to maintain their buildings. Without proper maintenance, the quality of the apartments deteriorates, and that leads to fewer units of standardized quality housing over time. Why do the rent controls remove incentives for maintenance? The assumption is that an apartment can continue to be rented at P_0, the legal rent ceiling, even if it is allowed to deteriorate, so that the owner receives the same revenue for lower cost, or at greater profit. Normally, competition would assure adequate maintenance (a tenant could move to an equivalent but maintained apartment at the same price), but under rent control there is excess demand. Owners exploit the fact that potential tenants are willing to pay more per unit than the control price.

This argument depends upon assumptions about the behavior of the rent

twice the benefit to tenants. See E. Olsen, "An Econometric Analysis of Rent Control," *Journal of Political Economy, 80*, No. 6, November/December 1972, pp. 1081–1100.

[7] RAND Corporation, "The Effects of Rent Control on Housing in New York City," *Rental Housing in New York City: Confronting the Crisis*, RM-6190-NYC, February 1970.

control board and other economic agents which have not explicitly been considered. The control price for an apartment is defined in terms of quality-adjusted units, and it should be lowered commensurately with any quality decrease in the unit. If that is so, there is no incentive to forego maintenance. The argument is thus not a deduction of the standard model; it depends crucially on the notion that the rent control board will not adjust the control price as it should.

This is not to suggest that there is no insight here. Perhaps the board will not have the *information* necessary to keep the control price at the appropriate level for each apartment. Tenants, of course, have the incentive to inform the rent control board if maintenance is reduced. Nevertheless, this is an interesting question, and we shall return to the information issue later. Here the important point to note is that the disinvestment deduction depends upon an implicit assumption about imperfect decision making of the rent control board, although the rest of the model assumes (e.g., under no rent control) that other agents have perfect information (and face zero transaction costs). Thus, although it may be true that rent control boards behave in this imperfect manner, it is a far cry from saying that the standard model explains the disinvestment effect.

A second approach used to suggest that rent control causes housing disinvestment is illustrated in Figure 12-3. This approach defines rent control broadly as an attempt to redistribute wealth from landlords to tenants (no surge of demand, or cutoff of supplies, is used to motivate the controls). The control price is drawn *below* the initial equilibrium price, and it is clear that suppliers will respond by withdrawing $Q_0 - Q_{SC}$ units from the market. The problem with this approach, for our purposes, is that it does not model a policy which attempts to control economic rent only (as most rent control policies do). The

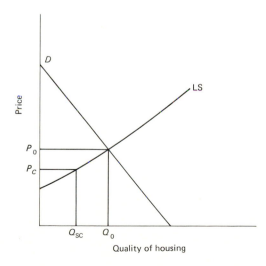

FIGURE 12-3
A controlled price P_C below the opportunity cost of existing housing Q_0 causes disinvestment $Q_0 - Q_{SC}$.

control price is set below the opportunity costs of supplying existing units; this is inconsistent with the rent control policy we are modeling.

In a sense this second approach makes the essential deduction of the standard model crystal clear: *If the control price is set below the opportunity cost, the unit will be withdrawn from the rental market.* However, the standard model provides *no* insight about why the control price might be set at such a level. Let us consider one final argument.

A third approach which leads to the disinvestment conclusion is shown in Figure 12-4. This is like the model in Figure 12-2, except that the long-run supply curve LS' is assumed to shift upward gradually over time. The upward shift is based on the idea that the real opportunity cost per unit of housing rises over time (e.g., the real wage rates paid for building maintenance increase). Then, at the control price P_0, suppliers will respond in the long run by withdrawing $Q_0 - Q_{SC}$ units from the market.

The problem with this approach is similar to that of the second: The policy shown here allows the control price to fall below the opportunity costs of the existing units. This is inconsistent with the policy we said we are modeling. It equates rent *control* to a rent *freeze,* but actual rent control policies do allow periodic rent increases based upon increases in opportunity costs.

Do these long-run models offer any improvement over the short-run model? If so, by what analytic criteria? The empirical realities of the housing market and rent control administration determine how closely a model comes to identifying important aspects of the policy design. Our purpose is to illuminate those aspects. If we take the New York case as evidence that rent control can cause shortages and disinvestment, the short-run model fails in calling that to our attention. The long-run models are better because they offer explanations for important empirical concerns. They are also better in calling attention to

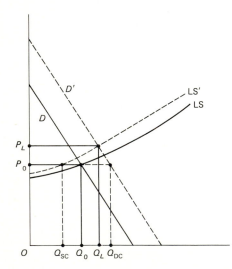

FIGURE 12-4
A rent freeze causes housing disinvestment if the long-run supply curve shifts upward.

this aspect of political economy: Rent control may be introduced as a response to a *short-run* problem, but in New York the policy did continue into the long run. It is in the long run that the problems developed.

However, the long-run models are still too much of an oversimplification for our purposes. There are two significant problems with them. The first is that all of them are inconsistent with actual rent controls. Even the first long-run model (predicting a shortage but no disinvestment) equates rent control to a rent freeze and assumes the frozen price applies to units as yet unbuilt. But most rent control policies, including New York's, specifically exempt new units and allow them to be rented at market-determined rates.

That is, most rent control policies attempt to control *economic rent only*. If successful, they would not affect opportunity costs or, therefore, supply decisions. Thus, the long-run models presented do not really offer a satisfactory explanation for shortages or the observed disinvestment in New York. They may *predict* correctly, but they do not identify the *causal* mechanism. If we wish to know whether the same result should be expected elsewhere, we have to look more carefully at actual behavior.

A second problem with the analyses we have presented so far is that *transactions and their costs* have a much greater role than is yet apparent in determining both the allocative and distributive effects. The transactions among economic agents are a function of the *property rights and responsibilities* associated with the good or service to be traded, and rent control actually changes them. (For example, the landlord has a reduced right to the income generated by the property.) A thorough analysis of rent control must trace through the impacts of the changes, and the design of rent control policies must carefully consider the legal specifications.[8]

In ordinary market analysis we treat the legal specifications as constants and assume that the transactions which follow from them involve negligible costs of deal making among economic agents. For example, we assumed that, under the free-market system, the cost of locating and matching demanders and suppliers (after the demand increase) is negligible. Thus, in the versions of rent control presented, we have made an analogous assumption: The cost of matching incoming demanders with initial tenants as suppliers is assumed to be zero.

But in neither case are transaction costs zero, and they are not likely to be of equal magnitude (with or without rent control). One must consider the legal changes and the transactional responses they induce in order to know how the benefits and burdens will be distributed. One must recognize that the policy problem includes the design of the legal changes. For example, enforced bans on finder's fees for initial tenants may cause benefits to be spread more evenly among all tenants. To understand rent control better, we present a simple but to the point model in the following section.

---

[8] See S. Cheung, "A Theory of Price Control," *The Journal of Law and Economics, 17,* No. 1, April 1974, pp. 53–71, and "Rent Control and Housing Reconstruction: The Postwar Experience of Prewar Premises in Hong Kong," *The Journal of Law and Economics, 22,* No. 1, April 1979, pp. 27–53.

RENT CONTROL AS THE CONTROL OF LONG-RUN ECONOMIC RENT

In this section we first develop an understanding of why economic rent may be a persistent part of total payments for urban apartments. We do this by presenting a very simple model of urban land rents in a special area known as Flat City. This model allows consideration of rent control as a long-run policy.

Flat City is drawn in Figure 12-5. Its downtown area is at the extreme left, where all employment takes place. There is only one road into (and out of) Flat City, and all workers live with families in rental homes spaced at one-mile intervals along the road. Family units have identical preferences and incomes. Sites along the road are restricted to residential use. (We relax this assumption later on; it makes an important difference.)

For a moment let us assume that the homes are costless to build and do not depreciate. They are competitively supplied at the long-run supply price of zero. Their size is determined by the common "satiation" point of all families. (Past some point, for example, the disutility of cleaning a house outweighs the advantages of greater space.) Families would be completely indifferent about residences *except for the location* (the feature we seek to emphasize first). The cost of commuting to Flat City is $1 per mile (which includes the opportunity cost of the individual's time), and each occupied house has one worker who makes the trip each day (Flat City has no day of rest). The commuting cost is the *only* aspect of location that families care about. There are exactly 50 families (and one worker per family) in all. Under these obviously special conditions, what will the prices of the rental homes be to the families?

The landlord at each site would be willing (if necessary) to supply the home for free: the site itself is fixed in supply, and the competitive price of the structure is zero. However, each consumer wishes to pay the minimum cost for a house including its associated commuting cost, and each will bid against the others to obtain the most desired location. Let us note the difference in commuting costs from site to site. A person who commutes from the worst location, the 50th house, travels 50 miles each way and pays $100 in commuting costs. From the 49th house, the commuting cost is only $98, etc., and from the first house it is only $2.

As long as the commuting cost is the only concern about location, no family will bid anything to live in the last house: There are no savings in commuting

FIGURE 12-5
Home rents in Flat City.

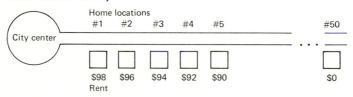

costs from living there. Nevertheless, in equilibrium there must be at least one family content to live there. Since $2 is saved by being in the 49th house (instead), up to $2 will be bid for the right to occupy it. Similarly, $4 is saved from the 48th house, $6 from the 47th, etc., up to $98 for the first house. Thus the competitive rents are, starting from the first site, $98, $96, $94, . . . , $2, $0. A characteristic of these equilibrium rents is that, for each site, the rent plus the commuting cost equals the cost of the *marginal* commute (i.e., the one from the last site, which is $100 in this case).

The rentals paid to live in each house are pure economic rents. They represent payments to the owner above opportunity costs, since the houses and land would be supplied for zero.[9] Note that the landlord can do nothing to influence these rentals, which arise as a consequence of the number of families and from the locational preferences. That is why *economic rent is not a determinant of price; it is the marginal commuting price which determines economic rents*.

It is useful to point out that the landlord is performing two economic roles simultaneously: one as a supplier of a factor, land, to the shelter industry, and the other as a shelter supplier. Since the land at a particular location is fixed in supply, any payment to it is pure economic rent. The landowner will rent the land to the highest bidder from among alternative users of it; this ensures that the land is in its most valuable use. In Flat City we have restricted these bidders to be residential users.

To use the land, *any* shelter supplier would bid up to the value of the profits (before land rental fees) from the home rental business (tenant receipts minus structure costs). Thus, the competitive shelter industry per se receives no net economic rent; it is the landowner who receives it. Even though it is typical for these agents to be the same person (apartment owners usually own the land and the structure), the distinction has allocative importance which will become apparent shortly.

The above model should clarify why economic rent is a persistent component of urban apartment rentals: Each apartment comes with a specific site, fixed in supply, that has a locational "attractiveness" completely determined

---

[9] An important digression from our main purpose is to note that the pattern of urban rents in our model happens to *reflect* a real social cost: the cost of foregone commuting. It is generally true that urban rents will reflect the costs and benefits of all the attributes of that area: the quality of the housing itself, the available public services like schools, the quality of the air, the convenience to employment and shopping, the property tax rates, the view, etc. We would expect a household to pay less rent if, for example, the air were bad, all other things equal. Econometric studies have attempted to derive estimates of these implicit market values for each attribute as a way of isolating willingness to pay for various public goods and services (e.g., the value of making the air 10 percent cleaner).

A good example of this is the article by W. Oates, "The Effects of Property Taxes and Local Public Spending on Property Values: An Empirical Study of Tax Capitalization and the Tiebout Hypothesis," *Journal of Political Economy, 77*, No. 6, November/December 1969, pp. 957–971. For a survey and description of some of the analytic challenges in this area, see John M. Quigley, "What Have We Learned about Urban Housing Markets," in P. Mieszkowski and M. Straszheim (eds.), *Current Issues in Urban Economics* (Baltimore: Johns Hopkins University Press, 1979), pp. 391–429, esp. pp. 401–405.

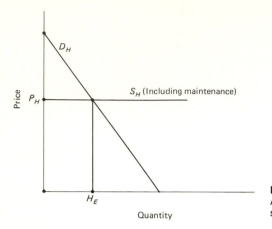

FIGURE 12-6
A Flat City family's demand for home structure size.

by factors external to the landlord (the "attractiveness" of the marginal site). Because families are willing to pay for it, this fixed attribute receives economic rent.

Let us now relax the assumption that houses are costless and do not deteriorate. We assume instead that structures are competitively supplied and maintained at a constant cost of P_H per unit, expressed for convenience in daily terms. By our assumptions about consumer preferences, the demands for structures and location are independent.[10] (Each homogeneous family will end up with the same net income after paying commuting and "location" costs; thus, the demands for structures are identical.) Figure 12-6 can thus depict a family's demand for home rental D_H (in terms of structure size, standardized for quality) exclusive of location. Each family will live in a structure of size H_E which the market supplies and maintains for a daily charge of $P_H H_E$. If for some reason the structure is not maintained, there will be fewer than H_E units of it. (The amount less will depend on the depreciation rate.)

To gain the right to use the house on a particular site, families will bid up the price exactly as before. The total rental on the first site will be $98 + P_H H_E$, on the second site $96 + P_H H_E$, etc., and on the last site just $P_H H_E$. This time, only part of the tenant's payment is economic rent (equal in magnitude to that of the last model). There is no room for a deal among any economic agents, so the allocation is optimal. The allocation is also an equilibrium, since at the market prices no economic agent has any reason to change his or her demand or supply decisions. Each of the homogeneous families would be equally happy at any of the locations, given their respective prices.

Now suppose we pass a rent control ordinance in Flat City. It states that no

---

[10] A more realistic model would allow families to trade off the amount of site space and home size for locational advantages (e.g., more intensive use of the scarce land nearer to the center). However, this aspect of reality is an unnecessary complication in terms of illustrating the effects of rent control.

landlord may charge a tenant more than the competitive price for the structure and its maintenance. All tenant payments are thus reduced (initially) to $P_H H_E$. We know that the initial allocation is Pareto-optimal. *If there is no behavioral response by any agent, the result is just like the quasi-rent model* in the first section: *a transfer of wealth from landlords to tenants with no harmful efficiency consequences. In this case it is long-run economic rent which is being redistributed.* As long as landlords lose the economic rent, the policy transfers \$2450 daily away from landlords to tenants.[11]

THE RELATION BETWEEN RENT CONTROL AND CAPITALIZED PROPERTY VALUES

It is likely that there will be behavioral responses to rent control. In truth, these cannot be predicted without specific knowledge of legal changes, enforcement efforts, and transaction costs faced by the agents in the market. Before we discuss them, we first clarify the important relation between rent control and the change in the value of the landlord's property.

This relation is of general importance because the economic logic applies to *all* policies which affect the earnings of *any* asset; examples are deregulation of trucking (removal of entry restrictions) and its effect on the value of trucking firm *operating rights,* construction of a new bypass road and its effect on the *land values* along the old route and a change in the patent (or copyright) laws and its effects on the values of assets protected by *patents (or copyrights). The changes in value caused by forces external to the owner of the asset (like policy changes) are often referred to as windfall gains or losses.*

In Flat City consider the original landowner who built a rental house on the first site, well before rent control. The (daily) cost of the house was $P_H H_E$ (including maintenance), and the (daily) rent of $P_H H_E + 98$ came in like clockwork. Suppose this owner moved away and sold the property to the highest bidder from among those wishing to be new owners.

With no inkling that rent control was to come to Flat City, each potential bidder expected to receive a stream of \$98 above daily costs in rental payments each day. Naturally, anyone who bid a sum less than the value of that stream (referred to as the *capitalized value* of the property) was outbid by another seeing the chance to make a small profit. The winning bid was therefore the one that exactly equaled the value of the stream and produced zero net profit.[12] To

---

[11] The sum S_n of an arithmetic progression of n terms $a_0, a_1, \ldots, a_n$, where each term differs by a constant, is $(a_0 + a_n)n/2$. In this case, the sum of $0, 2, 4, 6, \ldots, 98 = (0 + 98)50/2 = 2450$.

[12] We have simplified by assuming the future "structure" payments by tenants $P_H H_E$ are exactly offset by daily "construction and maintenance" costs and so do not affect the expected stream of future net benefits. The purpose of this simplification is to keep the economic rent from the land in clear focus. However, it is more realistic to assume that the "construction" part of the "structure" payment (which has a corresponding opportunity cost) is not offset by any *future* cost. Therefore, it enters the expected stream of future net receipts, and increases the capitalized value, and thus the sale price, of the property.

This happens, under our competitive assumptions, because the current owner has already paid the structure costs. The increase in capital value merely repays the current owner for the structural

keep this transparent, let's assume the winning bidder financed the sum (given to the original owner) by a bank mortgage which required no money down and a $98 daily mortgage payment. This is obviously equal in value to the stream of rental payments. We assume for convenience that the current value of this stream, or the capitalized value of the house, is $357,700.[13]

Now let us impose rent control in Flat City. Our initial effect is unchanged: The same amount of money is transferred to tenants, but note that it comes from *current* landlords. We have really devastated the new owner of the first site. If he or she tries to sell the property, the highest bid will be the value of the stream of future economic rents under controls. That is zero, as long as the controls work as intended. (More on this later!) The original owner captured all the profit by taking the expected future stream of economic rents (precontrol) and converting it by sale into cash on the table (the precontrol capitalized value). The new owner, who paid in advance for the privilege of receiving the economic rent, now finds none coming in. All rental property owners at the time of the new policy announcement, whether they are new or old owners, suffer whopping *capital losses*.[14]

Thus the first point we are raising is whether the transfer of wealth from owners to tenants is equitable. It is common for assets (like apartments) to be shifted from one owner to another through financial transactions (which do not necessarily affect the use of the assets). However, *any changes in the expected future earnings of an asset become instantaneously capitalized into the asset's present or current value.* It is the owner at the time a future change becomes perceived who bears any burdens or receives any benefits.

In the initial illustration of this point we assumed that rent control strikes like a totally unexpected thunderbolt. In actuality, many potential changes are considered by investors as possible states of the world, and they affect the calculation of the expected present value and thus the amount bid for the asset. For example, suppose rent control was under discussion in Flat City at the time of the home sale on the first site. With no rent control, we suggested earlier that the house could sell for its capitalized value of $357,700. With rent control, the

---

services he or she has paid for (at the competitive price) but will not receive. The new owner (like the former owner) pays in advance and receives the rights to the remaining structural services which the asset produces in the future. Thus, each owner pays the opportunity costs and receives the benefits for the structural services supplied during the time of his or her ownership; the result is equivalent to our simpler model. This more realistic version does illustrate two important points: *Any durable asset (one that produces services over time) has capital value, and the concepts of capital value and economic rent are distinct.*

[13] In Chapter 14 we will consider how to place a single *present value* on a future stream of payments $X_0, X_1, \ldots, X_n$. For those curious now, if we assume the $35,770 annual economic rent on this home will be paid continually and the annual interest rate is 10 percent (compounded continuously), the present value of the home is $357,700 (annual rent/interest rate). This must be the size of the winning bid.

[14] The new owner may have no means of making the mortgage payments and may declare bankruptcy. In that case the ownership of the property will be assigned to the bank providing the mortgage (or similarly, the bank will foreclose on the mortgage). However, that does not change the zero value of the property, and the bank becomes the loser.

selling price would be zero. If rent control was thought to have a 50-50 chance of passing, the expected value was

$$EV = 0.5(357,700) + 0.5(0) = \$178,850$$

Because of uncertainty and risk aversion, the maximum bid of a single potential investor would be below the expected value.[15]

Obviously there are many sources of change in the expected future earnings from an asset, and investors in such assets may be thought to understand the risks that they take.[16] One can argue, therefore, that it is tough luck on the part of the home purchaser when rent control passes. He or she was aware of the possibility at the time of sale, and the government need not be concerned with which of the two parties (buyer or seller) ends up the real winner. (If rent control were defeated, the original owner would feel that the sale at a price under $200,000 was a big mistake.)

Thus we make these observations. *The longer the time the economic rent has existed, the more unfair its "control" will seem to rent recipients.* That is because, through the transfer of assets, the current recipients of the rent are less likely to be making financial profit from it. (The original owner is the one who profited.[17]) *Conversely, the best time to consider a policy of controlling economic rent is simultaneously with the event that is expected to cause the rent.*

A second consideration reinforces these observations: *It can be difficult, if not impossible, for an administrator or an assessor to determine accurately the amount of economic rent a landlord receives.* In homogeneous Flat City this task may not be overwhelming. However, real cities have virtually infinite quality variation among the apartment buildings in the housing stock and a multitude of factors which determine the attractiveness of the site itself. Furthermore, there may be nonresidential bidders for the land (which we discuss shortly). One must be able to separate the total free-market price into the opportunity cost of all variable inputs (the structure, its maintenance, and any value of the land in an alternative use) and the balance as economic rent.

In practice, virtually none of the rent control ordinances attempt to control old economic rent. Rather, some events (e.g., a rapid population increase) cause unusual and visible increments to economic rent, and these increments

---

[15] Investment syndicates would be expected to form and outbid a single risk-averse investor because of the syndicate's lower risk cost (Chapter 6).

[16] Sometimes public policy action is taken to try to improve the information available to the investment community. This may involve required disclosure of certain information by potential sellers, liability laws in case of failure to disclose certain facts, and the production of certain information which may be relevant to investors (and others) more generally, such as actual and predicted inflation rates and unemployment rates.

[17] Note that the previous owner is not necessarily the original owner. This whole line of argument extends backwards *ad infinitum:* The previous owner had to buy the land from someone, and presumably had to pay a price reflecting the value of expected rents. The first settler is the only one who receives private benefits greater than private costs. All others break even, except for the windfall gains and losses that arise.

trigger a political demand for rent control. Housing is particularly susceptible to these demands because (1) it is a significant part of each consumer's budget, (2) moving to avoid higher monetary rents is itself expensive, both financially and psychologically, (3) land is a scarce input which earns long-run rents, and (4) the housing stock responds slowly to market pressure, which can result in significant quasi rents on structures. *The most common way to implement rent control is to use the market prices existing at the start of the causative event as a base and thus control only part of the economic rent.* Then annual fixed percentage increases are usually allowed automatically (designed for normal increases in operating and maintenance costs), and there is an appeal mechanism for landlords claiming higher cost increases.

THE SUPPLY RESPONSE TO RENT CONTROL

So far we have not considered the behavioral responses of landlords to the imposition of rent control. We have seen that landlords, by making no changes, suffer large capital losses. Is there anything they can do to avoid those losses of economic rent? In particular, since it is now less profitable to supply rental housing, will the supply be reduced? Let us assume for the moment that rent control is administered as it is often intended: Initial control prices are no lower than the supply price (opportunity cost) for shelter, and the allowable annual rent increase is at least as high as the increase in optimal uncontrolled maintenance costs.

Under those circumstances there are reasons to expect a supply reduction. One is condominium conversion (the occupant is an owner rather than a tenant). This is primarily a change in legal contract rather than the actual quantity of housing units; thus, it is more significant to the frustration of the redistributional objectives than to the actual housing supply.

In the simple Flat City model with no rent control, each family is actually indifferent to owning its own home or renting. For example, the family in the first site pays $P_H H_E$ + $98 each day it rents. If it buys the property, it will pay the same amount. (Like our previous purchaser, the $98 becomes a daily mortgage payment, or the family finances the purchase with any other method of equivalent capital value.[18]) Since the rent control ordinance does not change the demand for the first site (or any other site), condominium conversion is a way of making essentially the same deals as would be made without rent control. If that happens, there is no redistribution at all. Thus, most rent control ordinances include bans on condominium conversions.[19]

---

[18] In actuality, imperfections in the capital market (imperfect information) cause ownership to be favored by temporally stable households. (The transaction costs of entering and terminating ownership agreements are high compared with rentals.) We discuss these imperfections in a later chapter. The point here is that unrestricted condominium conversion with rent control can be associated with socioeconomic population change.

[19] Condominium conversion bans generally apply when an owner of one building wishes to subdivide the ownership rights by dwelling units and sell them separately. They do not restrict the sale of the original structure to a new owner who may wish to occupy it rather than rent it. Thus, single-family homes (and duplexes in part) which were rented out can avoid controls by sale to an owner-occupant.

The more general reason for supply reduction (which includes condominium conversion as a special case) is as follows: *If the land has value in an alternative (and thus noncontrolled) use, the landowner may change the use of the land.* Think of rent control as an imperfect attempt to impose a lump-sum (nondistortionary) land tax. Each landowner pays the tax, which then gets redistributed to the landlord's tenants. However, the tax is not lump-sum because it is on one use of the land, rather than the land itself. The land and its location may be fixed, but its use for residential rental purposes can be varied.

The Flat City model assumes this problem away by restricting the land to home rental uses. Zoning laws, if they are perceived as permanent, may justify such an assumption. But if there are alternative legal uses of the land, the alternative uses are an opportunity cost of using the land for apartment provision. Figure 12-7*a* and *b* is an effort to clarify the effect of alternative uses on economic rent.

In Figure 12-7*a* we draw the supply of land as fixed, exactly as we have stated before. Think of this land as the amount that lies on a fat circle of given radius from a city center. (If you insist, Fat City.) The demand curve crosses the fixed supply at P_L; this is the competitive price for the land, and all payments to it are pure economic rents. However, the demand curve is for all potential land users, and so the diagram shows all potential benefits and costs in the land market. If the only demands are for rental housing purposes, then rent control takes away only economic rent. But now let us imagine that some of that demand is from nonapartment land users.

In Figure 12-7*b* we draw the demand and supply of this land *to the apartment industry*. The demand curve is shifted to the left from diagram (*a*) because we have removed all the nonapartment land demanders from it (thus, at any price, less quantity is demanded). However, *the nonapartment demands are the opportunity costs in the supply curve of land to the apartment industry.*[20] As drawn, all land is shown to have some alternative use.[21] However, the value of L_A units in apartment use exceeds the value anywhere else. Thus, L_A units are allocated for apartment rental purposes and $\overline{L} - L_A$ units for other purposes. The economic rent received by the units is shown as the shaded area.

The economic rent in Figure 12-7*b* is considerably smaller than the amount of Figure 12-7*a*, which equals all payments. What explains the difference, and which one is relevant for rent control? One obvious difference is the definition of the market: the top diagram includes rent from both residential and nonresidential land uses. However, even if we eliminated the rent payments of nonresidential users, the remaining rent would exceed that shown in Figure 12-7*b*. That is, the shaded area in Figure 12-7*b* is less than $P_L L_A$. The same units of

---

[20] For any price $\overline{L}$ minus the quantity shown on S_A is the precise demand for land in nonapartment use. That is, the supply curve S_A is also the mirror image of the nonapartment demand curve for land (with price axis as the dashed vertical line and greater demands farther to the left away from $\overline{L}$).

[21] Alternative use may include an owner's personally using a room or unit and the land it is on, rather than renting it out. In some areas this type of apartment makes up an important share of the total rental housing market.

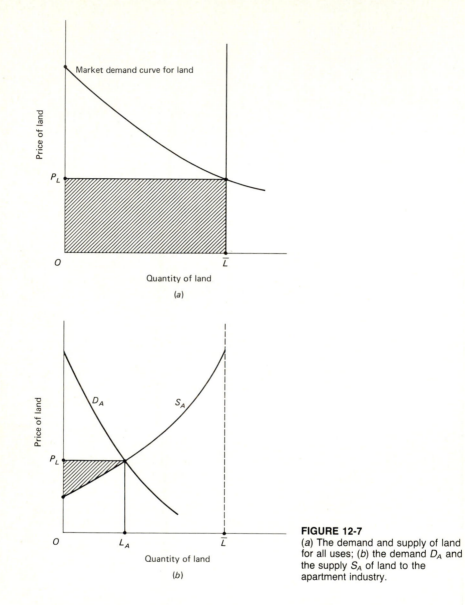

FIGURE 12-7
(a) The demand and supply of land for all uses; (b) the demand D_A and the supply S_A of land to the apartment industry.

land are shown receiving different amounts of rent. How can we reconcile the two diagrams?

Figure 12-7a shows the value of land *in its best productive market use relative to the opportunity cost of allocation off the market.* Figure 12-7b shows the value of land *in its best apartment use relative to the opportunity cost of nonapartment allocation.* These are simply two different ways of dividing the general land allocation issue. The latter is the one of concern to rent control policy, because it divides the land universe into units directly affected by the policy versus all others. To keep land in apartment use, it must receive a payment greater than or equal to its value in alternative uses. One can only "control" the economic rent that *accrues to the apartment sector* without affecting resource allocation *to it*.

To express this point more generally, *economic rent is a relational concept*. It is defined as a payment above the opportunity cost. But "the" opportunity cost depends on how we divide the universe of possible allocations into two exclusive and exhaustive sets of uses and alternative uses. Thus "the" rent also depends on this divisional choice. A resource receives economic rent in use X *relative* to its employment in the best alternative from among the uses in not X. If we change the definition of X, we change the definition of the alternatives, and thus the opportunity cost and economic rent. The employment of the resource is constant; it is only the way we look at it that changes.

For a different example, suppose it is true that everyone will supply their maximum labor if the wage is at least $4 per hour. Then payments above that are economic rents to labor from a social perspective. We could remove them and cause no reduction in the aggregate labor supply. This does not imply that one can pick out a particular occupation, like fire fighting, and reduce the wage from $16 to $4 with no distortionary allocative effects. Such a change alters relative occupational wages *within* the labor market, and society is not indifferent to labor allocation among occupations. The market handles this routinely because fire fighters perceive occupational alternatives as opportunity costs. Each agent defines X in the narrowest possible manner, consisting only of the resource's exact current use. Policies, however, generally affect a broad set of resources, and one must use the definition of rent that corresponds to this set and its alternative uses.

To return to price control of rental housing, we were exploring how the rent control ordinance affects the supply decisions of landlords. The critical feature we have just discussed is that the landlord may find it profitable to change the use of the land, despite a rent control administration which allows all supply costs of housing and its maintenance to be passed along. This can happen if rent control continues into the long run. That is, we have assumed all land uses are optimal right before the event causing rent control, and the base prices are set to correspond with those prevailing in the free market at that time. Thus, problems of land use arise only if the reallocations that occur over time are different from those which would have occurred without rent control.

Imagine the causative event to be a rapid population surge resulting in a permanent increase in land rents as well as short-run quasi rents for housing per se. The growth in population can easily stimulate an increased willingness to pay on the part of retail establishments to service it, e.g., a gasoline station on the first site of Flat City. Suppose that, before the population surge, the station was not willing to offer the $98 land rent (now part of the control price) to obtain the use of the land. After the surge, the station might bid $120 because of the increased business. The true value of the land in housing might be still greater (say, $150), but the controls prevent apartment suppliers from bidding more than the $98 control price. Thus, the landowner will be able to avoid the full capital loss from controls by changing the use of the land. This is a misallocation of resources (which, in this model, results in residential displacement from near the city center to the "suburbs").

The seriousness of this as a problem with long-run rent control is not really known. For one thing, zoning laws which exist independently of rent control may rule out nonresidential uses in many areas. The zoning policies themselves probably improve resource allocation compared to a free market because of the rampant externalities involved in urban land-use decisions. Thus, land in apartment use may be earning substantial economic rent. Nevertheless, on the margins between zoned areas landlords may believe there is a good chance a zoning change or exception will be granted. This chance may be further enhanced if the area becomes run down and the request is presented as part of a revitalization effort.

This suggests one explanation for the disinvestment in housing that can be associated with rent control. The capital value of the property in apartment use is restricted by rent control. Any property owner will seek ways to increase the value. If the restriction is only on economic rent, there will (by definition) be no alternative use which yields a higher value. *Allowed rent increases must be sufficient to keep the capitalized value of the property greater in apartment use than any other use.* If not, the landlord has incentive to change the use. *Rent control ordinances which allow only building costs and maintenance expenses to be passed on to tenants will generally cause inefficiency in the long run.* That is because the opportunity cost of the land in an alternative use may be growing over time as well.[22]

We should also note that rent control will have similar effects on the supply of new housing. As long as uncontrolled (market) rent can initially be charged for them, the supply of new structures will depend on expected future control board decisions analogously to the existing stock. *If the expected net capitalized value of building a new rental housing structure is greater than any alternative, the structure will be built; otherwise, the land will be used for an alternative purpose.* Often, rent control ordinances do not deter the construction of new condominiums (even if they prevent conversion of existing structures). In that case one would expect that the close substitutes with much

---

[22] Several rent control studies have suggested that rent control administrators do not allow increases equal to the maintenance costs, which causes disinvestment. For example, in the RAND study of New York, cited earlier, it was found that, from 1945 to 1968, the rent control board allowed average increases of only 2 percent while the real annual cost of maintaining the apartments rose at 6 percent. The above argument suggests that it is difficult to establish the causes behind these statistics. Some landlords will choose to undermaintain their buildings, even if they can request and receive approval for a higher maintenance level, as a way of converting the property to a more profitable use (without throwing away the "free" benefits from the existing capital structure).

higher capital values would largely displace any new rental units which would have been supplied if no rent controls were in effect.

In the discussion of the response of landlords to rent control we have assumed the policy is successful at reducing the payments from tenants to landlords. That lowers the capital value of the property and causes landlords to seek alternatives to increase it. Nevertheless, "perfect" rent control could, in theory, affect only economic rents and cause no supply inefficiency even in the long run. The models of Flat City and Fat City illustrate the existence of this rent, as well as some of the difficulties of knowing how much of any payment is economic rent. Actual rent controls like those in New York differ from the theoretical ideal and cause inefficient disinvestment in rental units in the controlled area. Now let us turn to the tenant side of this market and, in so doing, reexamine our assumption that rent control reduces tenant payments.

THE EFFECTS OF RENT CONTROL ON APARTMENT EXCHANGE

Rent control may or may not disturb the supply equilibrium (depending on whether only economic rent is controlled), but it *unambiguously creates disequilibrium in exchange*. Consider first the control of all economic rent in Flat City with all land use restricted to home rentals, so that all tenant payments are initially reduced to $P_H H_E$. Before, each family was indifferent to its location. With the rent control prices in effect, each family strictly prefers the first site to the second, the second to the third, and so on. Each family will seek ways of obtaining a closer location and will be willing to pay up to the reduction in its own commuting costs for it.

Suppose for a moment that there is no behavioral response from tenants, and consider the resulting equity implications. The first family now has an increased daily income of $98, the second $96, and so on, and the last family is unaffected. But all these families are homogeneous with identical incomes and utility levels before rent control. Instead of redistributing the total savings equally among the families, the benefits go disproportionately to the families closer to the city center. Since all families are equally deserving of any redistribution, this appears to be a grossly arbitrary and unfair method. This illustrates another reason why the control of old economic rent can be inequitable.

However, the control of new economic rent may be thought more reasonable. To see this, let us assume that the population of Flat City surges from 50 to 60 homogeneous families. The additional 10 families live in homes on sites 51 to 60 (we will not treat the short-run problem of home construction), making the cost of the marginal commute $120. Thus, the land rent on the first site increases to $118, the second $116, and so on; each of the original families must pay $20 more in economic rent. Outraged by this, the original families pass a rent control ordinance which freezes the rents at the level existing before the population surge (with new rental homes uncontrolled). Each of the original families saves $20, and the market rents on the new homes start at $P_H H_E + 18$ for the 51st site and decline to $P_H H_E$ for the 60th site.

In this more reasonable case, there is still disequilibrium in exchange. The first 50 families are content; they see no alternative sites which they would prefer to their current ones (at the control prices). However, the last 10 families strictly prefer any of the first 50 houses to their own and are willing to pay more than the current tenants for the right to occupy them. Each of these families would pay up to its savings in commuting costs. The 60th family, for example, would offer up to $P_H H_E + 118$ for the first site.

The prediction of the behavioral responses to this disequilibrium, and the resulting distribution of benefits and costs, depends on the details of changes in legal specifications and their enforcement which accompany the rent control ordinance. The ordinance reduces the right of the landlord to receive income from the property, but it is not always clear who ends up with the right. Below, we describe a variety of behaviors which are commonly observed in rent-controlled cities.

If the rent controls apply to the rental unit rather than its occupant, then a waiting list system may develop. This will result in the original tenants getting most of the benefits, although new families will capture some benefits through turnovers. Those waiting for vacancies may hire an agent to watch for them—and so spend some of the potential gain in consumer surplus. That can happen for several reasons.

Landlords, for example, have no incentive to spend time tracking down people on the waiting list, and they may quickly cross off names of people who are "hard to locate" (i.e., don't answer the telephone by the second ring) in order to pass it on to someone more favored. An agent with enough clients can afford to monitor the waiting lists continually and be accessible to landlord calls. If waiting lists are not used, and rare vacancies are pounced upon by whomever is there first, potential tenants may prefer to hire agents to search rather than pay the time costs themselves. All this is part of the cost of rent control: an overallocation of resources to the agent industry and other search activities beyond the amount desired at market rental prices.

The above activities are usually legal, but there is also incentive to engage in bribes or side payments which may be illegal. We mentioned in the first section that original tenants can sometimes pass on their apartments to new tenants in return for some sort of finder's fee. A common way in which that occurs is for the original tenant to make a "permanent improvement" in the apartment which is truly valueless and sell it to the new tenant. In the limit the original tenant can capture the full capital value of the future stream of reduced rents.

Of course, landlords do not necessarily have to accept any particular incomers.[23] Thus, they can try to extract the market rent in some other form similar to the sale of the worthless improvement. (When the landlords are

---

[23] This is an important source of racial discrimination in housing. See, for example, George C. Galster, "A Bid-Rent Analysis of Housing Market Discrimination," *The American Economic Review, 67*, No. 2, March 1977, pp. 144–155.

absentee, building managers may get into the act.) Although these payments are almost always illegal, it is difficult to enforce a law against behavior which is engaged in voluntarily by both parties to the transaction. The original tenant has some incentive to prevent these transactions in order to get some of the surplus. The systems may evolve where the accepted practice is to split the gains in some way. On the other hand, one should expect many landlords and tenants to refrain from engaging in illegal side payments simply because they are law-abiding people (or at least are highly price-inelastic with respect to this behavior).

All these behaviors may arise when the rental unit is controlled independently of the occupant. A considerably milder form of rent control is tenancy-specific: Controls are in effect during a tenancy, but the landlord may charge market rates when filling a vacancy. Obviously, this version allows landlords to keep more of the economic rent than the other version does; the expected stream of rental payments is higher. It is thus less likely to interfere with opportunity costs and cause a disinvestment problem, although that still depends on how rates are controlled during a tenancy.

The tenancy-specific version also creates a somewhat different set of exchange incentives. Current occupants receive the same benefits as long as they remain in the apartment, but they no longer have any *transferable* value to their "squatter's rights."[24] An incoming tenant, faced with paying the market rent, will no longer be willing to pay for worthless improvements made by the current occupant. Thus there will be more of a tendency to keep the apartment "in the family," and this can cause increasing exchange inefficiency over time. (Assuming a family's composition and income changes, the family will tend to stay in an apartment that it would leave if charged the market price.)[25] Another change is that the landlord has a large incentive to evict tenants; in fact, it increases with each year of tenancy. Usually, tougher eviction laws accompany this kind of ordinance.

The primary beneficiaries of this type of ordinance are tenants who are occupants from the start and retain the apartment for a long period. Once the control rules are understood, the knowledge will drive up the market rents paid when vacancies are filled. To see this, let us go back to the Flat City model and imagine a steady population growth which would cause regular rent increases. Suppose a vacancy in the first site arises when the uncontrolled economic rent would be $98. Let the expected uncontrolled increase be $10 per time period and the controlled increase be zero.

A student coming to Flat City for a graduate program of two time periods will be willing to bid more than $98 for the apartment. That is, the student knows that offering more now is the way to obtain control benefits next period.

---

[24] Regulations regarding sublease clauses may affect this value. For example, the right to sublease indefinitely is a property right of transferable value.

[25] A similar inhibition to mobility has applied to California homeowners since the passage of Proposition 13 in 1978. Proposition 13 keeps the assessed value of homes below their market value for the current owners. If the homes are sold, they are reassessed at the market value, which can be substantially greater.

Unfortunately for the student, someone who plans to be in the area longer than 2 years will make a higher bid. Thus, *tenants simply bid away their expected control benefits in order to get occupancy rights, and the landlord ends up with close to the equivalent of the uncontrolled market rents*. Because there is uncertainty in advance about the actual length of a tenancy, risk aversion will cause the bids to be somewhat below the uncontrolled market value. This uncertainty is itself an exchange inefficiency caused by rent control. (Both landlord and tenant would prefer a regime of uncontrolled prices with flexibility to recontract each year rather than this system of effectively paying too far in advance.)

In terms of equity, it is hard to argue that the long-term tenants who are here from the start are the people who are most deserving of benefits. For example, why should they pay substantially less than the long-term tenant of comparable income who moves in one period after the start of controls? (That is, why is the initial period an exceptional characteristic?) Why should families that suffer hardships like divorce or death of a family member (events that often motivate changes of dwelling units) be the ones to lose benefits? Why aren't the poorest families made the beneficiaries? The policy seems inequitable by both process and outcome standards.

Let us sum up the discussion. Exchange inefficiencies arise because the controls prevent economic agents from making trades that are mutually beneficial in both the short and long run. Under controls, this is necessary to keep landlord receipts below the market level. Tenants as a group are better off (assuming no supply inefficiency), but *many individual tenants have incentive to bid up prices to obtain another's apartment, and this sets forces in motion which work to reduce the net benefits that accrue to tenants*.

The reduced property right of the landlord to receive income creates a contracting problem. If the occupant were given all property rights except the right to receive controlled income, then tenants would only bid with each other, the rent control benefits would remain in the tenant class, and exchange would be efficient. However, this is a pure transfer of future wealth from landlords to occupants at the time of control, whether or not they remain occupants. Furthermore, no rent control ordinances give occupants these rights. Landlords retain rights of tenant selection and eviction.[26] Thus, potential occupants may make side payments to tenants, landlords, or building managers who influence the choice of new tenants, and they may pay extra search costs in looking for apartments. Of the potential gain in tenant consumer surplus from rent control, some finds its way back to landlords, some gets dissipated by search costs and by tenants remaining in nonoptimal apartments, and some portion becomes actual gain for tenants. The balance among these depends on more detailed aspects of the legal specifications and their enforcement.

We have also suggested that *the equity of rent control often seems arbitrary*. It is not targeted at specific groups identified by income levels, nor are the total benefits likely to be "evenly" distributed among those in the tenant class. We

---

[26] This is subject to tenant sublease rights.

have roughly specified the equity objective for rent control in terms of the "just" price; tenants should not have to pay any "new" economic rents. But we have seen many subtle ways to circumvent this intent, so that only some arbitrary subset of tenants will make payments in accordance with it.

In the next chapter we will discuss alternative policies to pure price controls which appear generally more attractive in both equity and efficiency terms. Nevertheless, one must keep in mind that apartment rent control is often a quick political response of a democratic electorate to a perceived problem. A stark example of this followed the passage, by statewide referendum, of California's Proposition 13 in June 1978. This proposition, known as the Jarvis-Gann amendment after its authors, rolled back all property taxes to 1 percent of the 1975–1976 level of assessed valuation in each local district. Furthermore, it limited annual increases to a small percentage of the base.

A fascinating aspect of this amendment is that many renters evidently expected to receive rebates from their landlords commensurate with the property tax savings. Perhaps this expectation came about because it was asserted repeatedly by Howard Jarvis during the campaign. Anyone with a modicum of training in microeconomics would realize that *Proposition 13 has no effect on the market equilibrium price for rentals in the very short run: with a fixed supply, demand determines price.*

In another culture, perhaps, landlords might be severely dishonored for not providing rebates, and a very small minority did provide rebates in the "spirit" of the Proposition. But the overwhelming majority of landlords provided no rebates and continued business as usual. Therefore, it is not surprising that outraged renters responded by passing rent control ordinances in many California cities, including Los Angeles, San Francisco, Santa Monica, Berkeley, and even Beverly Hills. One should wonder about the structure of these political processes, in terms of the room for analytic thought in the design of the measures and consideration of alternatives.[27]

A WINDFALL PROFITS TAX AS RENT CONTROL[28]

An example of an economic situation which comes close to meeting the "ideal" condition for a feasible "rent control" policy is in the energy field: the

---

[27] There are other issues concerning rent control which we do not analyze here but wish to mention. All the models in this section are within the context of one housing market, but there are often many political jurisdictions within one region. If one jurisdiction passes an effective rent control, tenants in the neighboring jurisdictions may bear part of the costs. See R. Albon, "Rent Control, A Costly Redistributive Device? The Case of Canberra," *The Economic Record, 54,* No. 147, December 1978, pp. 303–313.

Similar effects arise when only some apartments within a jurisdiction are controlled but others are not (e.g., exempted buildings with three or fewer rental units). In Glasgow, unfurnished apartments were controlled before furnished apartments. Then control was extended to the furnished sector, which has its own special problems. See D. MacLennan, "The 1974 Rent Act—Some Short Run Supply Effects," *The Economic Journal, 88,* July 1978, pp. 331–340; see also the comment by C. Jones and MacLennan's response in the same journal, *90,* March 1980, pp. 157–160.

[28] This tax raises several issues concerning the intertemporal allocation of oil. These issues are discussed in Chapter 14; they do not affect the major points of this section.

decontrol of oil prices and the simultaneous imposition of a windfall profits tax. Some background information on oil prices is useful.

Throughout the 1970s the OPEC cartel of major oil-exporting nations exercised its monopoly power to raise substantially the world price of oil.[29] The short-run response of this country, a large importer of foreign oil, was to "insulate" the American consumer from the unexpected price increases by controlling domestic oil prices. The effect was to keep consumer prices at close to the weighted average of domestic and foreign supply prices rather than at the high marginal price of foreign oil that the market would set.

Let us quickly review the operation of a *cartel, an association of independent producers who agree to coordinate activities in order to exploit the collective monopoly power*. Typically, this means restricting joint output below the competitive level to the reduced level of the profit-maximizing monopolist in order to raise price and create monopoly profits. The economic problem a cartel faces is in assigning and enforcing the output quantities (and thus shares of the monopoly profit) among the members.[30] Each member naturally wants as large a share of the total quantity as possible.

Assuming an initial agreement, each member is still in a Slumlord's Dilemma. Given the restricted industry output, any single member can increase its profits by cheating the cartel: cutting price slightly and selling a quantity beyond its cartel limit. But if all members do this, output expands, price falls, and the cartel collapses to the competitive solution. That is why cartels are notoriously unstable.

In the case of OPEC it is countries rather than producers who are the cartel members. The OPEC countries agree on a price which they achieve by taxing all their oil exports at the necessary rate; as long as all OPEC members sell at the agreed-upon price, the total quantity is restricted by demand. At first the U.S. reaction was that the cartel agreements would soon collapse. That belief is some defense for the policy we adopted, as a short-run strategy. The consumers of OPEC oil were already jarred by the sudden transfer of wealth from them to the OPEC countries. For U.S. consumers, the transfer to OPEC would seem small in comparison with the transfer to domestic oil concerns if the world price were allowed to prevail. If the cartel is to collapse soon anyway, why not preserve the distribution of income at its "normal" level?

Of course, at the time this book was published, the OPEC cartel had been operating aggressively and with success for almost 10 years. Over anything but a short time period, the U.S. domestic price controls create allocative problems. These include excess demand satisfied by excess OPEC imports *subsidized* through the control process and insufficient incentive to expand

---

[29] OPEC is the Organization of Petroleum Exporting Countries, 13 nations, concentrated in the Middle East, with approximately two-thirds of the world's known oil reserves among them. They supply about 85 percent of the oil for world trade. Europe and Japan are essentially totally dependent on them. The United States receives approximately one-third of its oil from OPEC.

[30] Domestically, a cartel would also have a legal problem, since price-fixing behaviors violate the antitrust laws.

domestic energy sources. We illustrate that in a simplified way in Figure 12-8a and b.

Figure 12-8a shows the effect of the OPEC cartel on an uncontrolled U.S. market. Initially we imagine that, from the perspective of U.S. oil consumers, the world market (domestic plus OPEC imports) supplies all that is wanted at a price P_0 and consumption is Q_0. In the short run the domestic supply is limited as shown. When OPEC suddenly raises the price of imported oil, the market responds by reducing consumption from Q_0 to Q_1 with a new and higher equilibrium price of P_1. The reduction comes about entirely through import reduction, and domestic suppliers experience large windfall gains.

Rather than allowing that "temporary" transfer to occur, the United States controlled prices. Basically, domestic producer prices were frozen at P_0. Refiners had to charge the weighted average of total domestic oil Q_{DM} and imported oil Q_I:[31]

$$P_C = \frac{P_0 Q_{DM} + P_1 Q_I}{Q_{DM} + Q_I}$$

This leads to a supply curve of oil to consumers which slopes slowly upward from the limit of domestic supply, as drawn in Figure 12-8b. Since the marginal cost to consumers under controls is less than the actual marginal cost paid to OPEC, consumers buy more oil than they would under a free market arrangement ($Q_C > Q_1$). This is still less than before the OPEC cartel raised import prices ($Q_C < Q_0$); nevertheless, OPEC does even better than it expected.

We should note that the welfare economics of oil pricing is a difficult issue, primarily in terms of identifying the true social cost of oil at the margin. On the one hand, the OPEC cartel is clearly using monopoly power to raise the world price above the competitive level. On the other hand, oil must be allocated over time and we have seen that a full set of properly working futures markets does not exist. Therefore, the competitive world price is not necessarily the price required to induce an efficient supply.[32] Within this uncertainty about the optimal world price, there are numerous issues for domestic policy. Examples are the response to OPEC and the distributional issues between consumers and producers.

Suppose we take the OPEC price as a fact and consider the interests of the U.S. citizens as both oil consumers and income earners. As a group, the United States should not consume more than Q_1. Past that point, the marginal cost to the United States ($= P_1$) exceeds the U.S. marginal benefit. The reasoning

---

[31] To make individual refiners indifferent to the source of their oil, an entitlements program was included as part of the controls. This essentially taxed each refinery per unit of domestic oil in order to provide rebates to refiners for each unit of imported oil.

[32] It is reputed that when one U.S. President was asked about the kind of economist he sought as an adviser, he replied, "Find a one-handed one." We consider the problem of pricing oil over time more explicitly in Chapter 14.

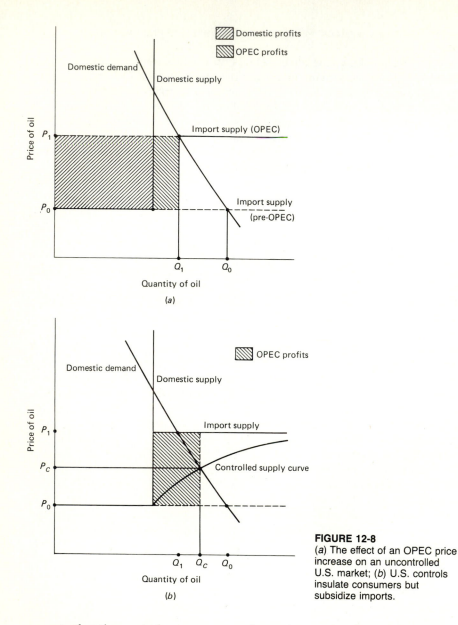

FIGURE 12-8
(a) The effect of an OPEC price increase on an uncontrolled U.S. market; (b) U.S. controls insulate consumers but subsidize imports.

suggests that the controls cause excess demand which is supplied with excess imports.[33]

---

[33] Do not be misled by calculating benefits and costs with the controlled supply curve. It hides the fact that the marginal cost of the last unit includes the increased consumer costs on all other units, with no offsetting income benefits. That is, in normal compensation testing, we ignore this

Not only do consumers have too little incentive to conserve (in order to reduce demand to Q_1), but domestic producers and alternative energy suppliers have no incentive to expand their supply. In the very short run, supply may be fixed, but in the longer run new and more expensive wells replace the older wells. Furthermore, additional oil can be obtained from old wells by using more expensive tertiary production techniques. Sources of additional oil and alternative energy sources that can be profitably utilized at or below the price of P_1 (for the energy equivalent) should be brought into production. Consumers may be indifferent to the source, but this would raise the aggregate U.S. budget constraint (income) at the expense of OPEC.

Decontrol would help solve all of these problems except for the large transfer of wealth that would occur on the old oil.[34] And that reason alone is enough to cause consumers to be against it. The United States as a whole is better off, but the gains are concentrated among those who earn incomes from the domestic oil industry and the losses are dispersed among all consumers.

Therefore, we consider the idea of the windfall profits tax coupled with decontrol. Suppose it is designed as follows. For all the wells in production before the OPEC price increase, a tax of $P_1 - P_0$ per unit of oil is imposed. There is no tax on any new wells or alternative energy sources that come into production. Finally, to assure consumers that they will be the beneficiaries of the tax, the design includes reductions in individual income taxes commensurate with the tax revenues from the windfall profits. This leaves consumers with better incentives to conserve and suppliers with better incentives to bring new energy sources into production; it removes the subsidy to OPEC and reduces dependence on foreign oil; and it essentially preserves the status quo distribution of income.[35]

Of course, it is always easier to illustrate a design in theory than it is to implement one in practice. In actuality, old oil wells vary in their marginal production costs, and it is not so simple to assign a base price per unit of oil above which is the windfall profit. For example, it becomes increasingly expensive to get oil out of any given well over time. The actual legislation sets base prices by year of discovery of the well and lowers the tax rates when certain expensive tertiary techniques are used. These broad categorizations are sure to cause some supply inefficiency, though its extent should be limited.

---

pecuniary externality because the extra consumer cost is exactly offset by extra producer surplus. However, in these calculations, OPEC receives the external gains, which are net losses to the United States.

[34] Predicting the size of the transfer is problematic. Garber and Nagin suggest, for example, that U.S. decontrol can cause a substantial reduction in the *world* price of oil, with magnitude estimated roughly between 12 and 27 percent. That is, OPEC may respond to U.S. policy changes. See Steven Garber and Daniel Nagin, "U.S. Energy Policy and the World Price of Oil: Some Theoretical and Empirical Considerations," typescript, School of Urban and Public Affairs, Carnegie-Mellon University, January 1980.

[35] Problems still remain because of the uncertainty about OPEC behavior. For example, relatively expensive synthetic fuels may be efficient if recent price trends continue, but investors may be reluctant to commit large amounts of capital to developing them since OPEC can moderate its prices at any time. Thus, some policy protection (e.g., price guarantees) may be appropriate.

Probably the most important safeguard against taxing anything but economic rent on these wells is that the windfall tax rates are designed to capture only 60 to 70 percent of the extra revenues these producers will receive through decontrol.[36]

The actual tax does contain an important violation of the principles for successful "rent control." It includes a tax on oil from new wells: 30 percent of revenues (per barrel) over a base price of $16.55. This provision discourages the expansion of the domestic oil supply.[37]

Another issue is that the windfall taxes will accrue to the U.S. Treasury, and so they can be used to make tax cuts or to increase government spending. Again, only time will tell if the public is satisfied by the distributional effects of the proceeds. As with rent control in housing, political pressures may demand that a certain group (landlords, oil producers) not receive "unfair profits," but these pressures do not seem to lead to much control over who should receive them. In the next chapter, we consider policy methods that exercise more explicit control over who will benefit.

SUMMARY

This chapter presents analyses of the effect of price and profit controls on market processes. We suggest the use of these controls stems from a concern among consumers over an unfair redistribution of income in a specific market, as when apartment renters in California did not receive any rent rebates after the 1978 passage of the property tax reduction amendment, Proposition 13. Seen as a struggle over economic rent, there is no inherent allocative reason to determine who should receive the rent. In theory, economic rent may be redistributed without causing any allocative efficiency in the short or long run; any further changes in resource allocation are due only to the income effects of the distribution.

Of course, it is a practical matter whether particular methods of intervention can achieve equity goals without adverse efficiency consequences. The standard supply and demand analysis of rent control suggests it is inefficient in the long run because it prevents landlords from receiving payments equal to (or greater than) their opportunity costs. But this analysis is really of a rent freeze, and it does not identify the possible aim of the policy as the control of economic rent or the reasons why control might be difficult to accomplish.

We use the models of Flat City and Fat City to demonstrate that economic rent is a long-run as well as a short-run phenomenon in urban housing markets. The short-run rents are quasi rents which exist because the supply of structures responds only slowly to demand pressure; they disappear in the long run as

---

[36] Government estimates are that about $440 billion would accrue to domestic oil producers through 1980 because of decontrol (after all normal taxes). However, some of those revenues are from new oil. The windfall profits tax is designed to yield $220 billion over that period. See *The Wall Street Journal*, February 22, 1980, p. 3, col. 1.

[37] Another violation occurs because the tax on all oil is temporary; we show in Chapter 14 that this discourages the provision of domestic supply during the period of taxation.

price settles to its long-run level. The long-run rents are primarily on the land when its long-run supply is inelastic to the rental housing industry (perhaps because of zoning laws). In all cases in which there is economic rent, it is important to remember that price determines economic rent and not vice versa. This is seen clearly in the Flat City model; the cost of commuting from the farthest dwelling unit in use determines the economic rent on all other dwelling units.

To understand the effects of rent controls on allocation, we first consider the landlord's position and how rent controls affect the *capitalized value* of the property. The capitalized value is the current worth of the asset based upon the stream of benefits and costs it is expected to bear in the future. Any policy which reduces the returns on a durable asset (like housing) will create windfall losses for the owner and reduce the capitalized value correspondingly. However, if the reductions are only economic rent, then the capitalized value of the assets in their current use remains greater than in any alternative use. Thus, there will be no allocative changes that result.

When economic rent has been a significant part of the returns to an asset which has changed ownership, the current owner makes no profit because the purchase price included the economic rent. Therefore, it may not be considered equitable to control old economic rent; the best time to consider controlling it is simultaneously with the event that causes it. This is reinforced by the administrative difficulties of determining the amount of old economic rent. Thus, in practice, most apartment rent control attempts only to control the increment to economic rent associated with some change such as a population surge.

For rent control to avoid adverse supply consequences (reductions in housing supply), the capitalized value of the property must be kept greater in its rental use than in any other use. If condominium conversion is allowed, many landlords will be able to evade the controls by making the legal change. (For stable households with access to the credit markets, ownership may be essentially equivalent to renting the same structure at competitive rates.) In other words, the building stays the same but the tenant becomes an owner. If there is an alternative use of the land which has greater capitalized value than the rent-controlled apartments, the landlord will allow the building to deteriorate and eventually rebuild to undertake the new use (e.g., as a new condominium or as retail stores). Thus, rent control ordinances which allow only current building costs and maintenance expenses to be passed on to tenants will generally be insufficient to prevent the change to an alternate use in the long run.

The degree to which rent control reduces the capitalized value of the building depends not only on the base level and the allowed annual increases but also on how the market for apartment exchange is affected. Since rent control does not affect demand, potential tenants will eagerly seek the benefits of controlled apartments. This may lead to side payments to current tenants or the landlord or both, depending on particular specifications of the rent control ordinance and its enforcement. For example, rent control which is tenancy-specific (uncontrolled rates may be charged to fill a vacancy) will lead to rents almost the same as without controls: Tenants simply bid away their future control benefits in attempting to obtain the apartment. If the controls apply to the rental unit regardless of tenant, the incomers may bribe the landlord and the current tenant to gain the occupancy right.

To the extent that the landlord receives them, the extra payments keep the capitalized value up but only by defeating the distributive purpose of the controls. The distributive purpose is also defeated by the extra costs tenants bear in terms of searching for controlled apartments (e.g., hiring rental agents). To the extent that extra benefits do accrue without dissipation to the tenant group, the distribution of them can be quite arbitrary (e.g., the side payments to the initial occupants). There is little in the control process to lead one to think that the benefits are spread evenly among tenants or are targeted to particularly deserving groups.

In the final section of the chapter we look at another example of controlling economic rent: the windfall profits tax on domestic oil. The oil pricing problem arises because of the exercise of monopoly power by the OPEC cartel to raise the world price of oil above its competitive level. Although the United States must pay the OPEC price for imported oil, it is not necessary to allow domestic producers to charge the same price and receive large windfall profits.

The initial U.S. response to OPEC was essentially to freeze domestic prices and charge U.S. consumers the weighted average of the import plus domestic supply prices. This kept the price to consumers below its marginal cost (in terms of imported oil), which led to overconsumption of oil satisfied by OPEC imports subsidized through the control process. It also gave domestic suppliers of oil and alternative energy sources no particular incentive to increase supply of their products. Decontrol of prices, currently being implemented, solves all these efficiency problems but not the distributional one.

A windfall profits tax on domestic oil could be a reasonable solution to this issue. On the domestic wells operating profitably before decontrol, the establishment of base prices (to use in calculating the windfall profit) at this level should not cause important supply inefficiencies. The actual 1980 legislation includes provisions to lower the tax on old wells when more expensive tertiary techniques are used to pump the oil at the bottom. These provisions also help to ensure against the legislation causing supply inefficiency.

However, the actual windfall profits tax also taxes new oil, which discourages the expansion of the domestic oil supply. In addition, consumers do not get the tax receipts directly; the government receives the revenues. Thus, only time will tell if consumers are satisfied (or even aware) of the net distributional impact.

EXERCISES

12-1 Solaria is a small country where people have been totally dependent on imported oil for an energy source. They used 15 megaunits of oil when its price was 4 megabucks per megaunit, but when the price doubled to 8, they used only 14 megaunits. (The demand curve is assumed to be linear.)

Four industrialists in Solaria have been building solar energy plants in the hope that energy prices will keep rising. Each plant can produce at most 2 megaunits of energy; the AC of operation at each is constant up to capacity. However, each plant represents a slightly different technology and the AC varies; from cheapest to most expensive, AC is 10, 12, 14, 16. The plants are ready to operate, but they have not been operating because it would be unprofitable for them to do so.

a The oil-producing nations announce that the price of oil is trebled to 24, effective immediately. The rest of the world is outraged, but the Solarians are ready. They ban all oil imports. How much energy is used in Solaria now; what is its price; and what is the loss of consumer surplus? How much of this loss is profit to the domestic producers? (Partial answer: $\Pi = 152$)

b The Solarians are ready to revolt. Although they continue to believe in energy independence, they see no reason why they should have to pay so much for energy. They know that, in the long run, when more plants can be built, the energy price will be 10. But now, in the short run, it seems the four industrialists are making "obscene" profits.

   The Solarian government responds and imposes price controls. Each industrialist is allowed to charge only AC + 2, where the 2 is the government's conception of a generous profit. All the energy is funneled through a costless and profitless government distributor who buys from the industrialists and charges all consumers the same price. (The distributor comes out even.)

   What is the price of energy under controls? What is the consumer surplus? What is the producer surplus? (Partial answer: $\Pi = 16$)

12-2 An administrator of a city's apartment rent control bureau wishes to determine initial control prices which remove all economic rent. Two landlords come in to the office to register. Both charge the same market rents, have the same mortgage payments, and have the same annual maintenance expenses. Does this imply that both should have the same control price? Explain.

12-3 This problem is an exercise involving rents, externalities, and information in land values.

   The scene of the exercise is Flat City. Now there are 100 homogeneous two-person families who live in rental homes spaced one mile apart along the one road leading into and out of the city. All the homes are identical except for two characteristics: their distances from the center and the amount of pollution which envelops them.

   Each day, one member of each family leaves home to work in the center and returns later that day. The other member stays at home. Workers are paid the competitive wage of $6 per hour in Flat City. Each worker drives the family car and travels at 2 miles per minute. Each car emits one pollutant per mile. The pollutant lingers for several hours, and it is unpleasant wherever it is emitted.

   Assume that the only commuting costs are the time values involved and that the only other real cost is from the pollution externality. (The houses are costless to build and are nondeteriorating.)

a If there were no pollution, what numerical pattern of rents would you expect to observe? Explain by assuming constant marginal values of travel time equal to the wage rate. (Also explain why the value of travel time might be related to wage.)

b Suppose there is constant marginal harm whenever a family member is exposed to a unit increase in the average daily pollution level. The observed pattern of rents and pollution in Flat City is shown in the accompanying table.

	City	House 1	House 2	House 3	House 99	House 100
Round-trip time, minutes		1	2	3	99	100
Average daily pollution level	100	100	99	98	2	1
Daily rent, $		0.00	0.05	0.10	4.90	4.95

Explain the observed pattern of rents. Why is the rent on the first house zero and that on the 100th house $4.95?

What would be the value of totally eliminating air pollution? In what way is the calculation different for the city center pollution as opposed to the residential pollution?

Note: The sum of a series $1 + 2 + 3 + \cdots + n = (1 + n)(n)/2$. (Partial answer: Eliminating air pollution is worth $2257.50 per day.)

c Someone has suggested that automobiles be banned and a large nonpolluting bus be put on the road to pick up each commuter. The bus could travel at only half the speed of cars. Would the people of Flat City as a group regard that as an efficient change? Would any families be made worse off? (Partial answer: The change would be efficient.)

DISTRIBUTIONAL
CONTROL WITH RATIONS
AND VOUCHERS

In Chapter 12 we examined the use of price controls and profit taxes as instruments to achieve redistributive goals in a market. A weakness of those instruments, aside from the difficulty of avoiding adverse efficiency consequences, is the lack of control over the benefit distribution. In this chapter we consider additional methods (ration coupons and vouchers) which allow more explicit distributional control.[1] Then we compare the various methods as they might apply to the rationing of gasoline during a shortage. During the Carter administration, the president was congressionally mandated to devise a plan precisely for that contingency.

While the chapter builds up substantive knowledge about these new rationing instruments, we are also integrating the skills of analysis covered in earlier chapters into a problem-solving approach. The ability to design alternatives and evaluate their effects depends on understanding and applying the concepts reviewed earlier, e.g., transactions and their costs, equilibrium, and the efficiency and equity criteria. We use each of these skills in our consideration of alternative strategies for rationing gasoline.

The chapter is organized in the following manner. First, we introduce the method of ration coupons as a policy instrument to achieve specific equity and consider how it affects market functioning. Then we discuss the use of an

---

[1] This chapter owes much to the general discussion of the instruments provided in James Tobin, "On Limiting the Domain of Inequality," *The Journal of Law and Economics, 13,* October 1970, pp. 263–277.

alternative instrument, vouchers, to achieve similar goals. These two instruments may be used together as a combined ration-voucher ticket, which we also discuss.

After the general discussion, we turn to the problem of rationing gasoline during a shortage. We evaluate the price freeze method that was adopted after the OPEC embargo of 1973, a nontransferable ration coupon plan, transferable rations, and an excise tax plan with rebates or vouchers. To help clarify the differences among these plans, we use a pedagogical two-person model to illustrate the effects. We also discuss the actual Carter administration plan, which indicates the political pressures on policy design and suggests why awareness of those pressures should influence the analytic work.

RATION COUPONS

Ration coupons are likely to be used when the good being allocated is in short and *inelastic* supply: water during a shortage, food during wartime, or parking in a congested city (e.g., required residential permits). The only way to ensure a minimum to some or all in these situations is to prevent consumers who would exercise greater purchasing power in the marketplace from doing so. *A ration coupon has this crucial feature: Its presentation is a necessary condition for receiving the good.* The government controls equity by the initial distribution of ration coupons to consumers. The coupons may or may not be transferable among consumers.

Generally, individuals will still have to pay a money price to receive the rationed good. *If the rationing is at all effective, the money price (with competitive supply of the good) will be lower than with no rationing.* Consider first the nontransferable case. The demand at any given price is lower because some consumers who are willing to pay will not have a coupon that allows them to enter a bid. For example, someone willing to buy 8 units at a price of $2 per unit may only have coupons authorizing the purchase of 5 units; thus this individual's demand at a $2 price drops from 8 units (before rationing) to 5 units (when coupons are required for purchase).

Figure 13-1*a* illustrates an example of this. The effective demand curve shifts downward and to the left (from D to D_{NT}), with the exact nature of the shift a function of the total number of coupons Q_C and how they are distributed. As drawn, demand is reduced from Q_0 to Q_C, price is reduced from P_0 to P_R, and all the coupons are used.

In Figure 13-1*b* is drawn an example of some of the coupons going unused. In this case we do not reach the aggregate coupon limit Q_C along the ration demand curve D_{NT} until *after* D_{NT} crosses the supply curve. Price is still reduced ($P_{NT} < P_0$), and the equilibrium quantity Q_R is less than the total number of coupons issued. The unused coupons $Q_C - Q_R$ are owned by individuals whose marginal value of one more unit of the rationed good is less then P_{NT}.

Nontransferable ration coupons usually cause inefficiency in exchange: The

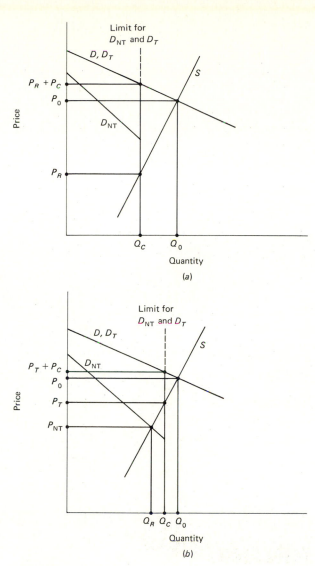

FIGURE 13-1
The effects of ration coupons with (a) binding and (b)
nonbinding nontransferable coupon constraints.

rationed supplies are not allocated to the consumers willing to pay the most for
them. If the coupons are *transferable,* however, the resulting allocation will be
exchange-efficient. "High" consumers simply purchase the coupons from
those willing to part with them. *The total price for the rationed good is the*

money price for it plus the opportunity cost of not selling the transferable ration coupon.

In Figure 13-1*a* the demand curve under transferable rationing D_T is shown as coincident with the ordinary demand curve until it becomes vertical at the aggregate coupon limit Q_C.[2] The money price of the good P_R is unaffected by the transfer option, but the total price of the good $P_R + P_C$ includes the coupon price P_C.[3] In Figure 13-1*b* the effect of making the rations transferable is slightly different. There will no longer be any unused coupons, and the money price of the good rises from the nontransferable level P_{NT} to P_T, where the supply curve crosses D_T. Thus, when the coupon limit of the nontransferable solution is not binding, a switch to the transferable option causes increased consumption of the rationed good at a higher money price.

It is also important to note that the change in *individual* consumption caused by ration coupons (compared to no rationing) can be very substantial. This is true even when the coupons are transferable. Consider the case when our supply of oil imports is suddenly cut off, which can easily lead to a doubling of the U.S. gasoline price.[4] How might this affect a low-income family?

The pure income effect of the change may be great even if the pure price effect is highly inelastic. This is illustrated in Figure 13-2. That is, with no rationing and an unchanged budget level the family has constraint B_M and chooses to cut back on gasoline; the dollars required for minimum food and shelter are unchanged. Given a quantity of transferable ration coupons equal to prior consumption and an unraised money price of gasoline, the real price of gasoline (which includes the market coupon price) is close to the free-market level. However, in this case the family has constraint B_{TR} and can and will consume essentially the same goods as before, because its pure price elasticity is assumed low.

---

[2] This ignores income effects. Actually, positive income effects arise in the aggregate from the receipt of the coupons: Less money income is spent on acquiring the rationed good up to the quantity of the individual's coupon allocation. Thus, the demand curve with transferable rations would actually lie slightly above the ordinary demand curve (until the coupon limit is reached).

[3] These examples assume that supply of the good is competitive. A monopolist supplying the rationed good could charge $P_R + P_C$ and get away with it. Since the coupons are fixed in supply, their price is determined by the difference between demand for the good and the supply price at the margin. The coupon price is P_C under competitive supply of the good and zero under monopolistic supply.

[4] The short-run (one-year) price elasticity of demand for gasoline is thought to be in the range of $-.2$ to $-.4$ [*Economic Report of the President, January 1980* (Washington, D.C.: U.S. Government Printing Office), p. 108]. Using the midpoint of $-.3$, and assuming the cutoff reduces gasoline supplies by 30 percent, a back-of-the-envelope calculation can be made as follows:

$$\varepsilon = \frac{\Delta G/G}{\Delta P/P}$$

$$-.3 = \frac{-.3}{\Delta P/P}$$

$$1 = \frac{P}{\Delta P}$$

Therefore,
$$\Delta P = P$$

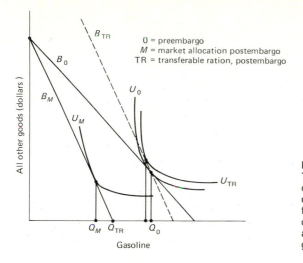

FIGURE 13-2
The effect of transferable rations on a low-income family. (For convenience, we assume that the family receives just enough ration coupons to consume its original, and probably low, quantity of gasoline.)

Another way to state this point is as follows: *If there were zero income effects from the coupon distribution, each individual would have consumption identical with that of the free-market solution.* The only effect of the coupons would be pure income redistribution. The actual change in individual consumption which occurs (compared with the free market) is due purely to the income effects on demand of the income redistribution. The change in an individual's income depends on the number of coupons received in the initial distribution and their value in the market. For a low-income family, the income effects on demand can be substantial if the rationed good is a necessity.

Transferable rations have an administrative advantage when variation in individual consumption is permitted and is difficult to monitor. Not knowing which consumers will have high or low demand, administrators may issue too many nontransferable coupons in the aggregate and cause the rationed demand curve to cross the supply curve at a high price. With transferable coupons, however, one can simply issue the number of coupons equal to the available supply. The money price of the rationed good will always equal the supply price for that quantity.

To illustrate this advantage, first imagine rationing gasoline. This is a case in which consumers have diverse demands and administrators prefer a system which allows for the diversity. However, the administrators do not know which individual motorists (e.g., owners of all registered passenger vehicles) have high or low demands. Coupons are issued in equal amounts to all motorists, at least within broad categories. If they are nontransferable, the administrator must issue a high average share to enable those with high inelastic demands to obtain a reasonable portion. But this can cause effective demand to approximate ordinary demand, with the resulting high price.

Other goods may also be characterized by very diverse demands, but monitoring them may be easy. For example, residential heating oil or water use is metered and records of past consumption are available. It is much more feasible in these cases to issue nontransferable coupons as a fixed proportion (perhaps above some minimum) of past individual demand. There is still the exchange efficiency advantage of transferable rations, but it is not as severe as with gasoline because the initial distribution leaves individuals closer to their optimal quantities. Whether one uses the transferable option may depend upon the transaction costs of creating and operating the coupon market.

Finally, in some cases of rationing, the supply may be so scarce that diverse market demands must be ignored. If there is only just enough food or water for everyone to survive, the nontransferable rations will lead to the same outcome as transferable rations. (Presumably no one would sell his or her ration.) It might be better to ban transfers to protect against consumer ignorance. ("I sold them because I thought I could always get more.")

Since transferable rations are more efficient and often have administrative advantages, one might wonder about reasons other than strict scarcity why nontransferable rations are used. One reason is *external effects*.[5] For example, special medical examinations (the rationed good) may be intended only for a population possibly exposed to an infectious disease (the "coupon" recipients), and not their hypochondriac neighbors. That is, a voluntary exchange between the coupon recipient and the hypochondriac does not take into account the social interest in ensuring that the coupon recipient specifically is examined. As another example, in the British Navy each sailor received one tot of grog which had to be consumed immediately. This was a strict way of precluding any transfers that might give rise to drunkenness (a negative externality).

A second reason is significant transaction costs of coupon trading. A water company, we suggested above, may be able to monitor each metered user's consumption very easily to see whether it is within the ration allotment. However, the cost of keeping track of *traded* allotment rights may be prohibitive relative to the potential exchange benefits. A crucial part of a water-rationing policy analysis would be to try to design a simple, pragmatic method for accomplishing such transfers.

A third reason for using nontransferable rations involves a political judgment about equity: In some situations the redistribution may be thought fair only if it is in kind. Put differently, visible coupon selling may lead to charges that government coupon distribution is arbitrary (i.e., not according to need) and provides undeserved and unearned windfall gains to the recipients.

The examples used suggest that one should not be myopic in terms of recognizing situations that in effect are coupon rationing. Similarly, one should be broad-minded about the market purchasing power that is being restrained by the coupons. For example, goods like parking spaces in a company lot are normally allocated on a first-come, first-served principle. Special parking rights (coupons) may be issued to a privileged few, who can then arrive late and still

---

[5] These are discussed generally in Chapter 11.

be assured of a reserved and desirable space. One can imagine many methods of identifying the reserved spaces (e.g., painting them a special color, having a special entry) and the rights bearer (e.g., a special permit, the license plate). Again we see that the rationed exchange need not involve coupons literally. In this example, ordinary parking space consumers exercise purchasing power in the form of *time*. That is, one buys a better space by arriving early and paying the price of time wasted (or spent nonoptimally) before paid hours begin. The ration coupons alter the outcomes of the allocation-by-time process.

Recall that we have stated that ration coupons are used when the supply is relatively inelastic. They cause a redistribution of the rationed good away from some consumers to those who receive the coupons. Because this lowers the money price, producers may not be getting the correct signals to expand supply. If the supply is elastic, then vouchers may be the more appropriate instrument.

VOUCHERS AND RATION-VOUCHERS

A voucher is a grant that has value only for the purchase of a specific good; it is not necessary to have one in order to purchase the good. Again, the government controls equity through the initial distribution to consumers, and the vouchers may or may not be transferable among individuals. The effects of vouchers on individuals, depending on the rules for obtaining and using them, are simply the various grant effects that we have already analyzed in Chapters 3 and 4. They increase consumption of the good at least through a pure income effect, and often through substitution effects or choice restrictions. Food stamps and Medicaid are examples of vouchers.

An interesting proposal is to use vouchers for elementary and secondary education.[6] Under the current monopolistic system of public education, a minimum is provided but each child is a captive of the school to which he or she is assigned.[7] There do not appear to be particularly strong incentives to improve the quality of education, particularly if diverse approaches are best suited for the diversity of students. If the state instead gave each child a voucher of a fixed dollar amount (or allowed the purchase of education stamps by family power-equalizing formulas analogous to the district power equalizing discussed in Chapter 4) and allowed the family to choose any licensed school it wished, this would create keener competition among schools and thus create incentives to improve quality.[8]

---

[6] See, for example, John E. Coons and Stephen D. Sugarman, *Education by Choice: The Case for Family Control* (Berkeley, Calif.: University of California Press, 1978).

[7] One can escape only by expensive routes: private schools or residential relocation.

[8] Voucher proposals are controversial, and for good reason. In the first place, they may not work as intended because organized interest groups in the school systems will not let them; the voucher experiment in Alum Rock, California, was not successful for that reason. Various interest groups within the organization (e.g., teachers, principals) were successful at preserving enough of their traditional powers to prevent some of the most important competitive mechanisms from working. For example, teachers insisted that there be no threat of firing under the voucher plan;

Another use of vouchers is in the form of housing allowances for low-income families. Such allowances have recently been the focus of major social experimentation at the national level.[9] One interesting part of these experiments was that the vouchers were made conditional upon the household living in units which met minimum quality standards. This constraint, if effective, would cause housing consumption to be different from a pure cash transfer of the equivalent size. Analysis of the data so far suggests that the constraint had only a minor effect on housing: In Pittsburgh and Phoenix, housing expenditures under the constraint averaged 9 and 27 cents, respectively, out of each subsidy dollar, compared with 6 and 9 cents out of each subsidy dollar with no constraint.[10] This suggests that the housing allowance in these programs worked primarily like income maintenance.[11]

The *aggregate* effect of adding vouchers to a particular market is to increase

this made it difficult for educational "firms" to improve their productive efficiency. See Elliott Levinson, *The Alum Rock Voucher Demonstration: Three Years of Implementation* (Santa Monica, Calif.; Rand Paper Series P-5631, April 1976).

Another argument against vouchers is that school officials and teachers are better motivated now by their professional interests in child development. Under a system of financial incentives (and very limited ones, since high profits are unlikely to be tolerable politically), more attention may be paid to gimmicks which create the appearance of educational success by taking advantage of consumer ignorance and less attention to achieving real success. A still different argument is that public schools produce an important sense of community (local, state, and national) which would be absent in a voucher system.

[9] See K. Bradbury and A. Downs (eds.), *Do Housing Allowances Work?* (Washington, D.C.: The Brookings Institution, 1982).

[10] See H. Aaron, "Policy Implications of the Housing Allowance Experiments: A Progress Report," in Bradbury and Downs, op. cit., pp. 67–112.

The figures above and those from other parts of the experiment led to a surprising but relatively unambiguous conclusion: The price and income elasticities of demand for these households are much lower (in absolute value) than had previously been thought. Based on earlier studies, it was thought that reasonable values for the price and income elasticities were -1 and 1, respectively. But according to the experimental data, the income elasticity is only .2 in the short run and .4 in the long run. Similarly, the price elasticity is only $-.2$ in the short run and between $-.5$ and $-.6$ in the long run. Thus, neither price subsidies nor income subsidies should be expected to influence housing consumption greatly; they will primarily be used as rent relief. See E. Hanushek and J. Quigley, "Complex Public Subsidies and Complex Household Behavior: Consumption Aspects of Housing Allowances," in Bradbury and Downs, op. cit., pp. 185–246.

[11] Housing vouchers can also be considered as an alternative to rent control. From an efficiency perspective, this proposal probably has advantages on the exchange side: It does not reduce the apartment owner's legal entitlements to rental income as rent control does, and thus it does not set off the inefficient scramble among market participants to claim (or reclaim) the entitlements. However, housing vouchers may also create exchange inefficiencies such as the illegal markets for food stamps.

Whether vouchers have an advantage in terms of long-run housing supply effects depends on the method of financing them. For example, financing through a property tax (which may be likely on equity grounds) can induce a net reduction in the housing stock. This reduction could be greater or smaller than that caused by rent control; the latter depends on the degree of imperfection in administration.

The relative merits of the two proposals depend importantly on the equity objectives. If the objective is, for example, to target aid selectively to low-income families, housing vouchers given through an existing welfare agency may be a relatively easy way to ensure that the intended beneficiaries are the actual beneficiaries. If, however, the objective is to prevent tenants from paying and owners from receiving quasi rents in the short run, then housing vouchers are probably counterproductive. (They increase demand, which raises price with a fixed short-run supply.)

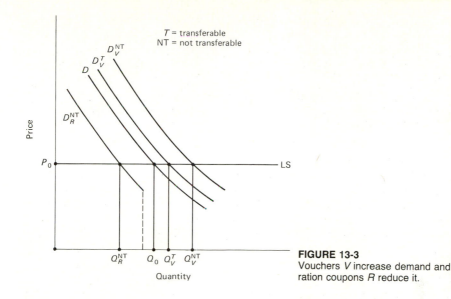

FIGURE 13-3
Vouchers *V* increase demand and
ration coupons *R* reduce it.

the equilibrium quantity and perhaps to increase the price. (If in a constant cost industry, no price increase will result.) We illustrate this in Figure 13-3, which contrasts the aggregate effects of nontransferable ration coupons R and vouchers V. Nontransferable ration coupons dampen demand (shown as D_R^{NT}) and vouchers enhance it. Transferable vouchers D_V^T compared to the same quantity of nontransferable vouchers D_V^{NT} result in a smaller increase in demand: They will be transferred until each person is affected only by a pure income effect, as in our earlier analysis of food stamps in Chapter 3.

It should be clear that, when vouchers are used to ensure a minimum, the extra quantity of the good comes from expanding supply. When ration coupons are used, the intended additional consumption for some comes by taking the same good away from others. We argued in Chapter 4 (see footnote 21) that vouchers are more efficient when the supply is elastic. As Tobin points out, in that situation vouchers may be considered more equitable as well.

Consider the example of providing medical care to the poor when the long-run supply is elastic. If done by rationing, the effect will be, illustratively, to reduce the number of physicians who would become plastic surgeons in order to increase the number of general practitioners. But there are many other places from which the extra resources for general practice can be drawn. Why should consumers who desire cosmetic surgery like facelifts and eye-tucks bear the main burden of supplying the poor, when the burden can be spread easily among the rich consumers of other things like furs, yachts, and caviar?

Sometimes the two instruments may be used together, to form a *combined ration-voucher ticket*. This means the ticket is necessary to obtain the good, and it also represents purchasing power. Depending on the number issued, their distribution, and the amount of purchasing power, the effect could be to move the equilibrium in any direction. Policy uses of the instrument are often associated with civic rights and responsibilities. The right to vote, for example, is a nontransferable ration-voucher distributed to each citizen 18 years of age and older. This ensures a perfectly equal distribution of voting rights and prohibits voluntary sales of votes for the good of the overall political process. As another example, we assign those of school age ration-vouchers which enable them to attend the public schools in their areas.

An interesting example mentioned by Tobin of the combined ration-voucher concerns conscription policy. To provide military labor, we now rely upon a voluntary system. This provides correct signals to the government, as the employer, about the cost of labor. However, the volunteers have disproportionately poor socioeconomic backgrounds. That offends people who feel that military service is a civic obligation in which all should share equally, particularly during wartime when lives are at risk. In the past we have treated it more as a civic obligation and used a variety of other systems that often involved ration-vouchers.

The most egalitarian system is one we have never used: complete selection by a nontransferable lottery (since not all individuals are needed to serve). This means that every eligible person has precisely the same chance of serving. Those with ration "coupons" are the ones who are eligible for lottery selection, and the "voucher" is for a contingent commodity with value either zero (if not selected) or negative (if selected, one must pay the tax of time in service). If each eligible is to share equally in the civic obligation, volunteers must be forbidden just as voluntary vote buying must be forbidden. This has the interestingly perverse effect of denying income-earning opportunities to those who may have few alternatives—the volunteers.

In the Civil War a partial lottery was used with transferable vouchers: Anyone drafted was free to pay another eligible to take his place. Although it hardly seems attractive to observe the rich bribing the poor to serve for them, the equity may be thought to have one advantage over our current system. Now the general taxpayer bears the burden of the army, and those who choose to avoid the civic obligation do so for free. Lest one feel too offended at this inequity, recall that the current system does force the government to face more of the true costs of having a military as compared with the Civil War system.

RATIONING GASOLINE DURING A SHORTAGE

Let us turn now to a discussion of gasoline rationing in response to a sudden and large reduction in the short-run supply exactly like the one that occurred in October 1973 when OPEC ordered an oil embargo. The purpose of the discussion is to illustrate the effect of alternative responses to one situation. We begin with a summary of the criteria. Then we present our actual policy response at the time, consider some alternative strategies, and include a discussion of the plan designed by the Carter administration. We make use of some simple mathematical models to illustrate some of the differences among the policies considered.

It is helpful to clarify in advance specific criteria to keep in mind for evaluating these options. It is useful to decompose efficiency into five mutually exclusive and together exhaustive categories: exchange, production, product mix, market transaction costs, and administrative transaction costs. Among the three usual components, we emphasize exchange (i.e., goods are allocated to those most willing to pay for them) with some attention to product mix. We ignore production efficiency only because none of the alternatives discussed cause any deviation from least-cost production. Product mix efficiency (i.e., an additional unit of gasoline is valued by consumers at its marginal cost) is treated as less important than exchange because the inelasticity of short-run supply makes only small product mix changes possible.

The two transaction cost categories capture other resource allocations which do not fit easily into the three usual ones. Market transaction costs take account of costs to the agents in a market which are not included in price (e.g., waiting in long lines to buy gasoline and restricted selling hours). Administrative transaction costs refer to the government costs of administering and enforcing the policy (e.g., printing and distributing coupons and enforcing coupon use).

Equity concerns involve both the distribution of gasoline and the "after gas" incomes of individuals. Since Congress actually mandated the president to prepare a rationing plan, we make the presumption that quasi rents should not accrue primarily to suppliers through high prices. A succinct but somewhat flexible way to summarize equity concerns which incorporate this aspect might be as follows: Each individual should be able to purchase a minimum share of gasoline at a price approximately equal to long-run rather than short-run marginal cost (i.e., eliminate quasi rents to suppliers).

The flexibility comes in defining the ideal minimum share. One candidate, more likely in the event of a severe shortage, is to define the minimum as the same for all. An alternative definition of each person's minimum is some fixed proportion of past use. Mixtures of the two are possible. For example, the first 25 percent of supply could be allocated as a "lifeline" share to everyone and the rest be allocated in proportion to past use. Or the federal government could allot shares to the states in proportion to past use and let the states make their own decisions about intrastate allocation (and some might choose equality).

There are many other equity issues which we do not treat here but which would be treated in a fuller analysis. One is the definition of the potential recipients: registered motor vehicles, licensed drivers, or some other category. Should two-car families receive twice the share of a one-car family, for example? Another concerns exceptional characteristics: the vehicle is an ambulance, police car, fire truck, etc. Although these are important issues, for the sake of brevity we restrict our attention to the capability of a proposed plan to meet the broader equity standard above.

Another two criteria might be thought of as implementation considerations.

One is the speed with which a plan can be put into effect. If it would take a year to print and distribute coupons, that would be a serious disadvantage. A second is the certainty that the plan will work at some tolerable or satisficing level. We take this to mean that we have the knowledge to set parameters so that the outcome is reasonably equitable and efficient; e.g., if coupons are issued, we are reasonably certain about the number which will restrain demand to a quantity that approximates the available supply at a money price near the supply price. This keeps us from choosing an alternative which in theory could work beautifully but which, to implement, requires empirical knowledge that is not available.

Comments relevant to other important criteria such as political and organizational feasibility will occasionally be offered. These sparse thoughts should not be taken as a substitute for the more careful attention such criteria deserve in a full analysis. Let us now turn to the discussion of alternatives.

The initial U.S. response to the shock of the embargo was to *freeze the price of gasoline*. That is illustrated in Figure 13-4. The domestic supply curve of oil is assumed to be elastic at low quantities, but it becomes very inelastic past the point of current domestic production. The preembargo equilibrium is at price P_0 and quantity Q_0. After the embargo, the price freeze is announced. Demand remains at Q_0, but the available supply falls to Q_F; thus consumers perceive a shortage.

Long lines developed at gasoline stations, and the available supply was rationed primarily through time. Those gasoline consumers who valued their time the least had an advantage. For others, much of any potential consumer surplus (above the money price) was used up in waiting. Various regulations were passed in order to assert some priorities other than time. For example, weekend hours of service stations were severely restricted in order to reduce "unnecessary" pleasure driving. Also, a 10-gallon limit was placed on each purchase in order to increase the probability that everyone would get a minimum. These regulations imposed social costs because they reduced the flexibility of purchasing which consumers valued; e.g., not only did the consumers have to wait, but for some it was more expensive (in terms of the opportunity cost of time) to wait during the week rather than on a weekend. Those with a willingness to pay that was high in cash but low in time would hire people to buy gas for them and thus partially evade the time-rationing system.

We can compare this briefly with the *hypothetical laissez-faire response*. The market-clearing price is P_S in the short run, and the allocation of gasoline is efficient.[12] Gasoline suppliers have a producer's surplus of $P_S - P_0$ on each of

---

[12] Sometimes an argument is made that *short-run* willingness to pay is not a reliable indicator of social value. For example, small businesses may operate profitably in the long run but be unable to absorb short-run losses because of the temporary high price. That may be true, but no social costs are incurred by shutting down the business *except* the transaction costs of reallocating the resources to their best short-run uses. If the owner had to bear them, the owner's decision on whether or not to close would still be the efficient one. However, the owner does not bear the social cost of the unemployed labor created by closing. Labor might be willing to work for a reduced

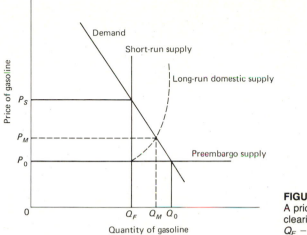

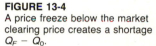

FIGURE 13-4
A price freeze below the market clearing price creates a shortage $Q_F - Q_0$.

the Q_F units. We have already suggested that much of this pure transfer turns into a net cost under time rationing: Consumers pay more than P_0 because of the time cost of waiting and restrictions on the choice of when to wait, but producers receive only P_0. We think of this as a *market transaction inefficiency.*

There is another efficiency disadvantage of the actual policy. Under the price freeze with time rationing, some of the demands from the portion of the demand curve between Q_F and Q_0 may be provided while other, "higher" demands (between 0 and Q_F) are not. Thus, the price freeze causes *exchange inefficiency.* Another way to illustrate this is to point out that some consumers (e.g., busy executives) who do not get "enough" gas under the price freeze could (in theory) make a deal to buy gas from other consumers who get "too much" (e.g., low-income retirees) so that both would consider themselves better off. Of course, the laissez-faire method would not make the compensation: The higher willingness of the busy executives to pay becomes profit to the service station, and the retiree gets neither gas nor compensation.

The price freeze with time rationing, for all its inefficiency, does generally help the lower-income segments of the population. As an immediate and temporary response to an unexpected but urgent situation, it should not be judged too harshly. However, if the government were sufficiently prepared to

---

short-run wage in order to prevent unemployment, but it is not clear whether labor markets work well in making such unexpected, short-run arrangements. In sum, the argument is that there are external costs to the short-run disruptions that might be caused by a large but temporary price increase. It follows that there is the potential for efficiency improvement by policy intervention which causes the externalities to be internalized (e.g., a special penalty related to the wage savings from firing labor during the period).

have contingency plans ready to implement should a crisis arise, it is unlikely that a price freeze would be seen as the optimal policy. Let us review some additional short-run alternatives.[13]

Another strategy would be to issue *nontransferable ration coupons*. These could be issued to the registered owners of every licensed vehicle. The initial distribution could be made in any of a variety of ways: equal coupons to all, more to commercial vehicles than passenger vehicles, more to states with heavier driving patterns (i.e., equiproportional coupons), etc.

One large advantage of this plan over the price freeze is that it would remove the excess demand which causes large lines and the attendant transaction inefficiency. It would also remove some of the arbitrariness over who ends up with the available gasoline.[14] Furthermore, it would keep the price low, although not necessarily as low as the frozen price. This is illustrated in Figure 13-5, where Q_C is the quantity of coupons issued and P_{NT} is the price of gasoline under nontransferable rationing.

However, there are a number of disadvantages to this plan. One is that it is administratively costly; it involves a bureaucracy to print and distribute the coupons. In itself, that is probably a small transaction inefficiency relative to the cost of the queues that would result from a price freeze. Another disadvantage is that there will still be exchange inefficiency: Some consumers who do not receive enough coupons would be willing to pay for more, and others who use their coupons would be willing to sell them. This can be seen in Figure 13-5. The value of gasoline to the marginal coupon user at Q_F is P_{NT}, but some other consumer values it at a minimum of P_S (the height of the ordinary demand curve at Q_F).

A third disadvantage, and an important one, is the uncertainty about how many coupons to issue in the aggregate. If too few are issued, the demand curve can cross P_0 before quantity Q_F, like D_F in Figure 13-5. This means that some of the available supply will go unused, and the public is not likely to be tolerant of such governmental bungling. If too many ration coupons are issued, the price and allocation will approach the free-market level and therefore fail to meet the distributional objectives which motivate the policy. Other than making the number of coupons greater than Q_F, there is no obvious procedure (besides trial-and-error learning, which should not be sneered at) for determining the right number of coupons.

To make sure this is clear, we give a simple numerical example involving a two-person economy. It will be convenient to express quantity Q in gallons and

---

[13] In all these cases we are not particularly concerned with the long-run effects because the policy is intended to be temporary and the short-run supply is inelastic. However, it is critical for analysts to be aware of how policies will affect the long-run supply response. A long-run price freeze, just as with apartments, would cause seriously deleterious supply reductions compared to the market-clearing price. Historically, unlike apartments, gasoline price controls have not been allowed to continue indefinitely (an interesting difference in political economy).

[14] Inevitable deviations from the equity standards are caused by the administrative need to classify diverse individuals into a limited number of categories for coupon distribution. We discuss that under transferable rationing.

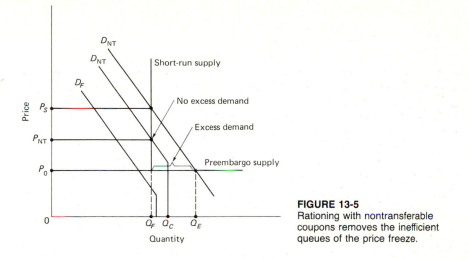

FIGURE 13-5
Rationing with nontransferable coupons removes the inefficient queues of the price freeze.

price P in cents. Unbeknown to policy makers, the demand curves of the rich R and the waif W are respectively

$$Q_R = \begin{cases} 1000 - P & P \leq 1000 \\ 0 & P > 1000 \end{cases}$$

$$Q_W = \begin{cases} 500 - P & P \leq 500 \\ 0 & P > 500 \end{cases}$$

Therefore, the market demand curve, being careful to match the segments correctly, is

$$Q_M = \begin{cases} 1500 - 2P & P \leq 500 \\ 1000 - P & 500 < P \leq 1000 \\ 0 & P > 1000 \end{cases}$$

Suppose there are 700 gallons to ration, provided price is above the marginal supply cost of 200 cents (or \$2) per gallon. The market-clearing price is simply 400 cents:[15]

$$Q_M = 700 = 1500 - 2(400)$$

This is illustrated in Figure 13-6a. At this equilibrium the rich person gets 600 gallons and the waif gets 100.

---

[15] Note that if one equates the 700 supply with the middle segment of the demand curve, the solution $P = 300$ is inconsistent with the valid price range for that segment. That is how we know it is an incorrect answer.

Suppose the policy makers want the outcome to be more equal in terms of gasoline distribution, as well as at a lower price, and issue 500 ration coupons to each person. We know in general that nontransferable rations reduce demand. The ration-restricted demand curves are

$$Q_R = \begin{cases} 500 & P \le 500 \\ 1000 - P & 500 < P \le 1000 \\ 0 & P > 1000 \end{cases}$$

$$Q_W = \begin{cases} 500 - P & P \le 500 \\ 0 & P > 500 \end{cases}$$

and therefore

$$Q_M = \begin{cases} 1000 - P & P \le 1000 \\ 0 & P > 1000 \end{cases}$$

The market demand curve under rationing is shown in Figure 13-6a; it is under the ordinary demand curve as expected. With the supply of 700, the equilibrium price with rationing is 300 cents:

$$700 = 1000 - 300$$

At this price, the rich person gets 500 gallons and the waif gets 200.

The policy makers did not know in advance what the outcome of the above plan (500 coupons per person) would be. If instead they had issued 375 coupons per person, or 750 in total, they would have found that too few coupons were issued. The new ration-restricted market demand curve is as follows:[16]

$$Q_M = \begin{cases} 750 & P \le 125 \\ 875 - P & 125 < P \le 500 \\ 375 & 500 < P \le 625 \\ 1000 - P & 625 < P \le 1000 \\ 0 & P > 1000 \end{cases}$$

We have drawn this in Figure 13-6b. As can be seen, the supply curve intersects the demand curve at 675, the equilibrium price is 200 cents, and 25 gallons of gasoline which could be supplied is not because of insufficient demand. From the individual demand curves, we see the rich person gets 375 gallons and the waif gets 300.

Note that with fewer coupons distributed equally, the resulting gasoline distribution becomes more equal. The final result is always somewhere between the market solution as one boundary (too many coupons) and perfect equality as the other, with price lower toward the equality boundary. Why is this? It should be clear that a reduced number of coupons restricts market demand and thereby causes a lowering of price. In Figure 13-7 we illustrate

---

[16] It can be derived from the individual curves as an exercise.

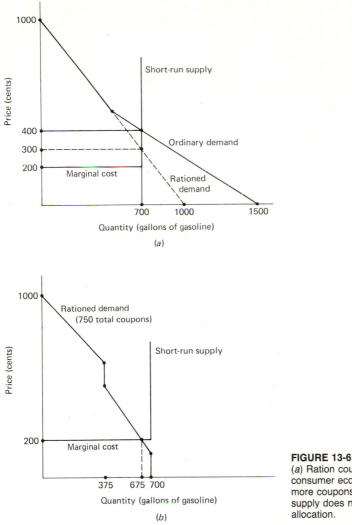

FIGURE 13-6
(a) Ration coupons in a two-consumer economy; (b) issuing more coupons than the available supply does not ensure full allocation.

that, for any given price, a lower coupon quantity tends to equalize consumption of the rationed good.

Consumption of the rationed good is measured along the horizontal axis, and consumption of all other goods (measured in dollars) along the vertical axis. Two budget constraints are drawn, one for the rich person B_R and one for the waif B_W. The optimal choices of both individuals with no rationing are shown as points R and W. When a high number of coupons C_H are issued to each, both

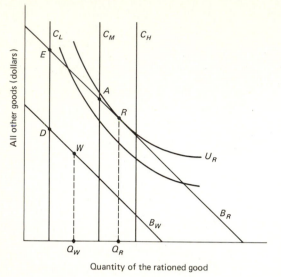

FIGURE 13-7
Lower ration coupon allotments result in more equal consumption.

Quantity of the rationed good

can and do continue to consume the unrestricted optimum (the market solution).

When a medium number of coupons C_M are issued, the rich person can no longer attain point R; the effective budget constraint drops vertically down at point A. Point A, the kink of the budget constraint, yields more utility than any other feasible point. That is, point A has higher utility than any point on the original constraint to its left because utility along the constraint systematically decreases as we move away from the optimum at R. (We have drawn in some indifference curves to illustrate this.) Point A also has more utility than any point directly under it, because more is better. Thus, the rich person with C_M ration coupons will choose point A. Since the waif still chooses point W, consumption is less unequal.

Now let the coupon limit C_L be low enough to restrict both individuals. By the same reasoning as above, both will choose the kink points on the respective budget constraints—point D for the waif and point E for the rich person. They use all their ration coupons C_L and have the same consumption level of the rationed good. Thus, as the number of ration coupons alloted to each person is reduced, we see two effects: Price is reduced, and consumption becomes more equal.[17]

The specific numerical examples above illustrate how and why the equilibrium changes with the number of ration coupons issued. But it is also important to recognize that, for the same number of coupons, the outcome changes if the

---

[17] The example we gave is for a normal good, but it holds true for an inferior good also. The only difference is that initially the waif would be consuming more than the rich person and would be the first to feel the effects of lowering the coupon quantity.

individual demands are distributed differently (even though aggregate demand is the same) or if the distribution of the coupons among individuals changes. If all people were homogeneous in their demands, there would not be nearly as much uncertainty about the effects of any specific ration plan. But if all people were homogeneous, the ration coupon solution would be identical with the free-market solution and the policy would achieve nothing but administrative waste.[18] It is precisely because people differ in their incomes and tastes that concern about how to ration arises in the first place. It is also those differences which create the inherent uncertainty about equilibrium in a nontransferable rationing plan.

To sum up, we have said that, compared with the price freeze, the nontransferable plan has these advantages: less transactions inefficiency and less arbitrariness about who ends up with available gasoline. Both plans cause exchange inefficiency. However, the nontransferable coupon plan involves substantial initial uncertainty about the number of coupons to issue and the price that will result. We should also point out that it would take longer to implement.

Another problem which arises when exchange inefficiency is caused by policy intervention is the potential for illegal markets. Under the price freeze plan, this is not a serious problem because the transaction costs of having an illegal market are high. Even if one consumer were willing to sell gas to another who would pay more for it, neither can get it without waiting in the queue, filling the tank to the regulated limit, and transferring the gasoline.

Under coupon rationing, however, all one has to do to make an illegitimate transaction is buy the coupons from another. This is illegal, but it is very difficult to prevent. It could be prohibitively costly to print coupons which are personalized, e.g., prestamped with the license plate number. One could issue a coupon book to each consumer and require the whole book to be presented each time, but the station operator would still need to loosen and collect the coupons as proof that gas was sold only to those with coupons. Since the station operator has no particular incentive to hassle the customers about the validity of their coupons, it would be difficult to prevent illegal coupon sales.

Of course, this discussion forces us to ask what objectives we serve by preventing people from doing what they wish to do. Why not *allow the ration coupons to be transferable?* The exchange inefficiency disappears and the price at the service station remains low. The true price that each consumer faces (including the opportunity cost of foregone coupon sales) provides appropriate

---

[18] For any coupon quantity greater than the available supply. This can be checked in our two examples by assuming each person has the "average" demand curve $Q = 750 - P$. For coupon quantities below the available supply, naturally the policy would cause underconsumption. In the case of a coupon quantity exactly equal to the available supply, the solution with perfectly fixed supply is indeterminate but between the marginal supply cost and the free-market price. However, this is more of a mathematical quirk than a real economic problem. Given any positive elasticity of supply at all, the solution is determinate. However, a real problem is price instability: Price can change very rapidly for coupon amounts in the neighborhood of the available supply.

incentives to conserve. Perhaps most importantly, the uncertainties about both the number of coupons to issue and the resulting price level disappear. One simply issues the number of coupons equal to the available supply; all will be used. The initial distribution of coupons can be proportionately the same as in the nontransferable case. In fact, none of the three reasons given in our general discussion for preferring the nontransferable option—externalities, transaction costs of transfers, and a sense of equity among citizens that the redistribution can only be in kind—seem to be present here.

We can illustrate the redistributive effect of the transfer option in our two-person model. To keep this simple, we ignore any income effects of the transfer on demand. In order to get a determinate solution for a coupon price and a gasoline price, we postulate a supply curve of gasoline which has a nonzero (but small) elasticity past the "available supply" of 700:

$$Q_S^G = \begin{cases} 680 + .1P_G & P \geq 200 \\ 0 & P < 200 \end{cases} \qquad (1)$$

The market demand curve for gasoline is just like the free-market demand (since we ignore income effects) except that the price now has two components: the price of gasoline at the station P_G and the opportunity cost of the coupon P_C:

$$Q_D^G = \begin{cases} 1500 - 2(P_G + P_C) & P_G + P_C \leq 500 \\ 1000 - (P_G + P_C) & 500 < P_G + P_C \leq 1000 \\ 0 & P_G + P_C > 1000 \end{cases} \qquad (2)$$

In equilibrium, we know that

$$Q_S^G = G_D^G \qquad (3)$$

These three relations will ensure equilibrium in the gasoline market, but we have three relations and four unknowns: Q_S^G, Q_D^G, P_C, and P_G. *We also have to ensure that there is equilibrium in the coupon market.* Suppose we issue 350 coupons to each person. Then each person must demand one coupon *in the market* for each gallon consumed over 350. That is, for gallon demand > coupon allotment,

Coupon demand = gallon demand − coupon allotment

The rich person, for example, will have a coupon demand of

$$Q_D^{C,R} = [1000 - (P_G + P_C)] - 350$$
$$= 650 - (P_G + P_C)$$

which applies only in the price range which makes the right-hand side positive:

$$650 - (P_G + P_C) > 0$$

or

$$P_G + P_C < 650$$

At any price at which $P_G + P_C > 650$, the rich person will demand zero coupons (and become a coupon supplier instead). Thus, we can write the rich person's demand for coupons in the market as follows:

$$Q_D^{C,R} = \begin{cases} 650 - (P_G + P_C) & P_G + P_C \leq 650 \\ 0 & P_G + P_C > 650 \end{cases} \quad \text{rich}$$

Similarly, we find the waif's demand for coupons in the market:

$$Q_D^{C,W} = \begin{cases} 150 - (P_G + P_C) & P_G + P_C \leq 150 \\ 0 & P_G + P_C > 150 \end{cases} \quad \text{waif}$$

Then the total demand for coupons to be purchased is the sum:

$$Q_D^C = \begin{cases} 800 - 2(P_G + P_C) & P_G + P_C \leq 150 \\ 650 - (P_G + P_C) & 150 < P_G + P_C \leq 650 \\ 0 & P_G + P_C > 650 \end{cases} \quad \begin{matrix} \text{coupon} \\ \text{demand} \end{matrix} \quad (4)$$

Similarly, the supply of coupons for trade equals the number that each person will not use of the initial allocation (350 minus gasoline demand). That is, for coupon allotment > gallon demand,

$$\text{Coupon supply} = \text{coupon allotment} - \text{gallon demand}$$

The rich person, for example, will supply this number of coupons to the market:

$$Q_R^C = 350 - [1000 - (P_G + P_C)]$$
$$= P_G + P_C - 650$$

This applies only in the range in which $0 \leq 1000 - (P_G + P_C) \leq 350$. The left-hand side of this boundary is to account for prices at which the gallon demand is zero ($P_G + P_C > 1000$); at such prices the person can supply no more than the initial allotment ($Q_R^C = 350$). The right-hand side of the boundary is for cases when the gallon demand exceeds the initial allotment ($P_G + P_C \leq 650$); at those prices the person uses the entire allotment for personal gas consumption and supplies none of it to the market. (The person becomes a demander rather than a supplier of coupons.) Thus, the full expression for the rich person's supply of coupons to the market is

$$Q_S^{C,R} = \begin{cases} 0 & P_G + P_C \le 650 \\ (P_G + P_C) - 650 & 650 < P_G + P_C \le 1000 \\ 350 & P_G + P_C > 1000 \end{cases} \quad \text{rich}$$

Similarly, we derive the waif's supply of coupons to the market:

$$Q_S^{C,W} = \begin{cases} 0 & P_G + P_C \le 150 \\ P_G + P_C - 150 & 150 < P_G + P_C \le 500 \\ 350 & P_G + P_C > 500 \end{cases} \quad \text{waif}$$

Then the total supply of coupons for purchase is the sum:

$$Q_S^C = \begin{cases} 0 & P_G + P_C \le 150 \\ (P_G + P_C) - 150 & 150 < P_G + P_C \le 500 \\ 350 & 500 < P_G + P_C \le 650 \\ P_G + P_C - 300 & 650 < P_G + P_C \le 1000 \\ 700 & 1000 < P_G + P_C \end{cases} \quad \begin{matrix} \text{coupon} \\ \text{supply} \end{matrix} \quad (5)$$

The last relation is that coupon supply equal coupon demand:

$$Q_S^C = Q_D^C \tag{6}$$

Now we have six relations and six unknowns (adding Q_S^C and Q_D^C to the four before), and we can solve. Inspection of the segments quickly eliminates many of them. Suppose, for example, that $P_G + P_C > 650$. In equation (4) this means coupon demand is zero. But in equation (5) this means the coupon supply is a positive number. Together these imply that supply does not equal demand in equilibrium, which is a contradiction. So we eliminate from consideration all segments in the relations at which $P_G + P_C > 650$. Similarly, from equations (1) and (2) we eliminate the range $P_G + P_C < 200$. The correct segments turn out to be the following:

$$Q_S^G = 680 + .1P_G \tag{1}$$
$$Q_D^G = 1500 - 2(P_G + P_C) \tag{2}$$
$$Q_D^C = 650 - (P_G + P_C) \tag{4}$$
$$Q_S^C = P_G = P_G + P_C - 150 \tag{5}$$

By equating (1) and (2) by (3), and (4) and (5) by (6), we get

$$820 = 2.1P_G + 2P_C \qquad (1), (2), (3)$$
$$800 = 2P_G + 2P_C \qquad (4), (5), (6)$$

By subtracting the bottom equation from the top, we get

$$20 = .1P_G$$
$$P_G = 200 \text{ cents}$$
$$P_C = 200 \text{ cents}$$
$$Q^G = 700 \text{ gallons purchased in the market}$$
$$Q^C = 250 \text{ coupons exchanged in the market}$$

Looking back at the individual equations, we see that the rich person buys 250 coupons from the waif. The final allocation of gasoline is 600 to the rich person (who uses the 350-coupon allotment plus 250 coupons bought in the market to achieve the necessary 600 coupons), and 100 to the waif (who has sold 250 coupons from the initial allotment of 350, leaving the 100 coupons necessary for this purchase). That is exactly the same as the free market. But compared with the free market, both the waif and the rich person are $700 richer and the service station is $1400 poorer. These are simply the values of the initial coupon distribution; the economic rent gets distributed in proportion to the coupons received.

Before leaping to the conclusion that transferable rationing accomplishes nothing but income redistribution, recall that we have left the income effects out of our numerical example. During the preembargo period when the total price was 200 cents, the waif used to consume the meager amount of 300 gallons. If that amount is important to the waif, as we suggest in Figure 13-2, then we should expect the waif's demand to shift out considerably under transferable rationing (compared to the laissez-faire solution). A beauty of the transferable rationing plan is that policy makers can attempt to distribute a fair share of coupons to each person initially and the market automatically corrects for exchange inefficiencies by compensating those who prefer to conserve (by more than their fair shares dictate) and use the coupon values for other things.

Before we conclude that the transferable ration plan is ideal, recall that it does require an administrative bureaucracy and it may not be so simple to get legislative agreement on the coupon allocation.[19] Another proposal which could achieve an identical result is an *excise tax plan*. Imagine passing an excise tax of $2 per gallon of gasoline in our model. That will lead to the free-market equilibrium of 700 gallons purchased. As before, the rich person buys 600 gallons and pays a total cost of $2400. The waif buys 100 gallons at a total cost of $400. The service station receives $1400, just as under transferable rationing. But what does the government do with its $1400 in tax revenues? Suppose it redistributes the proceeds equally among consumers: $700 to rich and waif alike. Then the excise tax solution with this rebate is identical with

---

[19] Achieving legislative agreement under nontransferable rationing would presumably be more difficult because Congress would have responsibility for the greater constraints imposed. (For example, each lobby group cares more about its allocation when the coupons are nontransferable.)

transferable rationing. *It is always possible to design the two plans to have identical equilibrium.*

There is one clear advantage of the excise tax plan with rebate over transferable rationing. We can dispense with the entire administrative bureaucracy that would be needed to oversee coupon printing, distribution, and enforcement of coupon use at gasoline stations. To be sure, the excise tax plan would cause additional administrative costs, but they would occur as small parts of existing operations. For example, there is already a federal excise tax on gasoline, and the machinery to collect the tax is in place whether or not we increase it.

Another difference between the two plans concerns the net redistribution that is likely to arise from each plan: Although it is possible to design the plans to be identical, political pressures will likely cause differences in the redistribution. Put simply, the transferable ration plan will give greater weight to gasoline "need" or past use in determining the redistribution, whereas the tax rebate plan will put more emphasis on ability to pay. However, the gainers and losers are not clearly predictable. This needs a little explanation.

When rations are transferable, the redistribution is not explicit but is proportional to the number of coupons received. All the political pressure for determining the initial distribution is based on perceived gasoline need, or past use. Commercial consumers can be expected to receive a large share of coupons, and passenger vehicles are likely to receive the same coupons regardless of the incomes of their owners. Consumers in states with heavier driving patterns will receive proportionately more coupons than other states.

One important inequity is involved in transferable rationing: Coupons will be allocated by broad classes, and within each broad class those who ordinarily use little gasoline will receive undeserved windfall gains. In our numerical example we have categorized the two consumers as "rich" and "waif." The waif has a low demand presumably because of a low income. But all the results are the same no matter what the reason for the different demands. The high demander could be a person who ekes out a living by delivering milk by truck, and the low demander could be a wealthy individual who commutes to work by train. The low demander, whether rich or poor, ends up better off than before the oil embargo (in our example). We illustrate this in Table 13-1, in which the distributional impacts of all the programs except the excise tax are compared. Thus, another blemish on the transferable rationing plan is that distributional benefits will accrue to many who do not deserve them on grounds of either high gasoline usage *or* ability to pay.

The excise tax rebates force policy makers to redistribute cash, and the political pressures here involve more attention to ability to pay rather than gasoline usage.[20] It is unlikely that commercial users will do as well, although certain deductions might be written into business income taxes. Individuals

---

[20] Note that a policy to rebate the tax precisely according to usage is equivalent to the price freeze. In the transferable ration case, one receives cash in proportion to the coupons *not* used.

TABLE 13-1
THE DISTRIBUTIONAL EFFECTS OF ALTERNATIVE RATIONING PLANS IN THE TWO-PERSON EXAMPLE*

Alternatives	Consumer and producer surpluses ($)				
	High demander	Low demander	Gasoline sellers	Deadweight loss†	Total
Preembargo (P = $2) market (long-run equilibrium)	3200	450	0	0	3650
Postembargo market (short-run equilibrium)	1800	50	1400	400	3650
500 nontransferable rations	2250	200	700	500	3650
375 nontransferable rations	2296.875	450	0	903.125	3650
Transferable rations (350)	2500	750	0	400	3650

* All figures are calculated for the surplus areas under the individual demand curves which correspond to the equilibrium price and quantity of each alternative, plus income from the sale of coupons.
† We use the long-run equilibrium (preembargo) as the efficient reference point against which other allocations are compared; that is why the postembargo market solution has a positive deadweight loss even though it is the most efficient short-run allocation (tied with transferable rationing).

might receive rebates through income tax reductions. These could take so many forms that it is impossible to predict how the benefits would be spread, except again many low users of gasoline could receive large benefits. Deductions are of most benefit to the wealthy, who save the deductible amount times their high marginal tax rates. Refundable credits would give the same to every taxpayer whether a driver or not. Another possibility is to give special fuel assistance payments through the welfare system, or some combination of these proposals.[21] In terms of redistributing a fixed total, it is difficult to see a clear equity advantage of either plan; all depends on how one wants to weight gasoline usage versus ability to pay.

There is one advantage of the transferable ration plan over the excise tax with rebates. Consumers are more certain of avoiding the payment of quasi rent. *For the excise tax plan to operate correctly, policy makers must set the correct excise tax rate.* But because the aggregate demand reduction is a large amount, there is a large uncertainty about what the correct rate is. Even the best demand elasticity estimates are reliable only in the neighborhood of the consumption observed. Although the total price will be that of the free market, the taxes may represent only a small portion of the quasi rent. Political pressure to keep tax rates down works to reinforce this possibility. With *transferable ration coupons, policy makers only have to know the right coupon quantity; the market will determine price on its own.* This may be an important advantage.[22]

[21] Note that the fuel assistance payment can be in the form of vouchers. If the vouchers are given in proportion to usage, they tend to nullify or offset the price change caused by the tax.
[22] For more theoretical reading about circumstances which cause quantity rationing to be preferred to price rationing, see the interesting article by M. Weitzman, "Prices vs. Quantities," *Review of Economic Studies, 41,* October 1974, pp. 477–491.

In Table 13-2 are summarized the evaluative (and partially subjective) comments we have made on each of the plans discussed. The actual Carter administration plan was one of transferable rationing. It was intended to go into effect if the nation experienced a 20 percent or greater supply cutoff. Its initial design, rejected by Congress, was to give the same basic allotment to each registered vehicle in the country. This is the transferable plan that can be implemented most swiftly and with the fewest administrative errors.

To gain Senate approval, the plan had to be redesigned to base allotments on state driving patterns and give extra allotments to farmers and energy companies. The House demanded more special-interest categories and killed the Senate-approved version. To gain approval of the full Congress, the final plan had to allow for "supplemental" allotments to businesses based on past gasoline use, priority status for taxis, car rental companies, and certain other businesses, and 5 percent of each state's allocation to be at the discretion of the governor in order to handle certain "hardship" cases (e.g., handicapped drivers).

Each one of these exceptions causes additional delay from the time of the shortage until the plan can operate, and each will lead to more errors, complaints, and confusion in the coupon distribution process because individuals will claim they have not been categorized properly. Since the coupons are transferable, the extra allotments to most businesses that Congress required are windfall gains that will have little allocative function. These provisions may reflect the congressional sense of what is equitable. They may also represent the clout that special-interest groups have in the political process.

This case is another illustration of the importance of political feasibility to policy analysis. The designers of the plan should be able to anticipate the pressures that are likely to arise in gaining legislative approval and consider their worthiness and the best realistic design that can gain approval. It is the latter—the best politically feasible transferable rationing plan—which should be compared with the best politically feasible versions of the other alternatives in making a recommendation. Thus, the basic design skills that come from microeconomics must be combined with other skills of policy analysis if one wishes to seek effective policy change.

SUMMARY

To achieve redistributive goals in a specific market, the policy instruments of ration coupons, vouchers, or their combination may be appropriate. The resulting equity with all of these instruments is controlled by the initial distribution, which makes it less arbitrary than direct control of market price as in apartment rent control.

When ration coupons are used, they are necessary to purchase the good. They are most likely to be used when there is a shortage of an essential good in inelastic supply. The only way to guarantee a minimum for some or all is to forbid the exercise of the purchasing power which would result in an excessive

TABLE 13-2
SUMMARY OF (SUBJECTIVE) EVALUATIVE COMMENTS ON FIVE GASOLINE-RATIONING STRATEGIES

Criteria			Alternatives		
	Free market	Price freeze	Nontransferable rations	Transferable rations	Excise tax with rebate
Exchange efficiency*	Good	Poor	Poor	Good	Good
Incentives for long-run product mix efficiency (output level)	Good	Poor	Fair to poor	Poor	Fair to poor
Production efficiency (least-cost production)	Good	Good	Good	Good	Good
Market transaction efficiency	Good	Poor	Good to fair	Good	Good
Administrative transaction efficiency	Good	Good to fair	Poor	Fair to poor	Fair
Equity* (minimum share with no rent)	Poor	Fair	Good to fair	Good	Good to fair
Speed of implementation	Good	Good	Fair	Fair	Good to fair
Certainty of satisficing	Poor	Fair to poor	Fair to poor	Good	Good to fair

* Most heavily weighted in judging certainty of satisficing.

497

share. Nontransferable rations restrict an individual's demand to the coupon allotment and thus cause market demand to shift inward and price to fall. This can allow those with coupons to obtain the good at a price near the supply price.

Transferable ration coupons also allow each bearer to purchase the good at a money price near the supply price. However, in this case use of the coupon entails the opportunity cost of not selling the right in the marketplace. Since an individual could sell all the coupons, the initial receipt of them is equivalent to an income grant. This grant can have a substantial positive income effect on the purchases of the rationed necessity by low-income families. The resulting allocation of the good is efficient in exchange; it differs from the free-market allocation only by the income effects. The other main difference from the free market is that suppliers receive no quasi rent; it all accrues to the coupon recipients in proportion to their initial allotments.

Nontransferable rations are favored over transferable ones when the available supply is only enough to provide minimum essential quantities to each, if positive external effects are associated with the coupon recipient's consumption, if there are significant (external) transaction costs of coupon transfers, or if a prevailing equity judgment is that the redistribution must be in kind. Transferable rations are favored if there is a diversity of individual demands which administrators cannot easily know and the supply is sufficient to permit the exercise of the diversity.

There are many markets in which supply is elastic, but it is nevertheless important to ensure a minimum consumption to all. This might characterize food, education, and medical care. In these cases use might be made of vouchers: individual grants that have purchasing power only for a specific good but are not necessary to purchase the good. Their effects on individuals have been analyzed in Chapters 3 and 4; their market effect is to increase the equilibrium quantity and perhaps increase price if supply is less than perfectly elastic. When supply is elastic, it is both more efficient and more equitable to use vouchers rather than ration coupons.

The two instruments are sometimes used together in a combined ration-voucher ticket, which has purchasing power and also is necessary to receive the good. Civic rights and obligations like voting and jury duty may be seen as goods which are rationed in that manner. An interesting case of the type is military service. Although it is now supplied through the free market (all volunteers), many people feel it is a civic obligation in which all should participate equally: a lottery in which all eligibles are the coupon holders and the voucher is zero if not selected and time in service otherwise.

We introduce a problem-solving approach by considering which of a variety of rationing plans might be used to ration gasoline during a shortage. The criteria used account for efficiency, equity, and some implementation concerns. The free market is used as a benchmark, but it is not seriously considered in light of the actual congressional mandate to find a more equitable alternative. A price freeze fails on almost all grounds except for speed of implementation; it may be a better response than doing nothing in the very short run because its equity is better than that of the free market. Nontransferable rationing would satisfy the basic equity objective, but it is cumbersome and causes unnecessarily large exchange inefficiency.

The two plans that are most capable of meeting the policy objectives are transferable rationing and an excise tax with rebate. In theory these two can always be designed to have identical equilibria. The differences between them are administrative and political. Transferable rationing requires greater administrative cost because of the coupons. The excise tax plan has an important administrative uncertainty: It can distribute the rent fully to consumers only if the administrator knows the correct tax rate to set.

Transferable rationing redistributes by classification of individuals into broad categories of prior use. Political pressures will be exerted on the definitions of these categories, as in the Carter administration plan. The excise tax is subject to political pressures to keep the tax rate low, and the funds that are rebated will be distributed in accordance with the special tax provisions made. A thorough political analysis is required to predict those pressures with any accuracy, which suggests why economic skills are only part of the skills needed by the working policy analyst.

EXERCISES

13-1 There is a drought, and the Hudson–Orlando Water District (H2O) has determined that only 50 percent of the available reservoir water should be consumed this year and the other 50 percent be saved for next year. The aggregate consumption will be 75 percent less than consumption in a normal year. Although that allows an average quantity per household above the life-essential level, the situation is nevertheless severe and it is very important that the targeted consumption level not be exceeded.

a In theory, any given quantity of water can be rationed efficiently among consumers by charging the correct price. Yet in this situation a serious problem could arise from trying to use this method. Leaving issues of equity aside, what is the problem with price rationing in this situation?

b One proposal is that H2O set a strict quantity limit per household (e.g., 20 gallons per household per day). Any household violating the limit would have a flow restrictor installed on its main water line. How would you evaluate this method as a means of meeting the aggregate objective and ensuring the efficient allocation of water among consumers?

c Another proposal is to use the method in (*b*) with one important change: The rights to each household's ration quantity are to be transferable. (For example, each household is to receive coupons for 20 gallons per day, is to be free to trade them, and must turn in enough coupons to cover its actual consumption.)

   Under this plan the price of a gallon of water to a household consists of more than the money price paid to H2O. Explain.

   Answer the same questions as are asked in (*b*).

   If there are no income effects of this rationing plan, the equilibrium price of water in the plan is the same as the equilibrium price in plan (a). Explain.

   Thinking of your answer to (a), does plan (c) have any comparative advantage?

13-2 Last spring the university experienced a severe parking shortage. The university had 50 parking spaces offered at $10 each, but the students S needed 40 and the faculty F needed 20. What to do? After carefully considering the needs of each group, the university decided students should get 34 spaces and the faculty should get 16. The university recognizes that needs are diverse because of a study which indicated differing group price elasticities: $\varepsilon_S = -.5$ and $\varepsilon_F = -.25$.

a Even if the parking permits are allocated within each group to those who value them the most, the allocation is still inefficient. Prove this. *Hint:* Recall $\varepsilon \equiv (\Delta Q/Q)(\Delta P/P)$.

b Give a minimum estimate of the maximum expense worth incurring to change the situation and make it efficient. (Answer: $5, approximately)

POLICY PROBLEMS
OF ALLOCATING
RESOURCES OVER TIME

Current economic decisions often have extremely important consequences for the future well-being of both individuals and society as a whole. For example, the decision of an individual to invest in schooling today can have a large impact on his or her future earnings profile. The amount someone chooses to save from current earnings greatly influences the amount of retirement income available in the future. The amount of oil used by the current generation determines how much, if any, oil will be left over for use by future generations. Clearly, an important task of any economic system is to enable these decisions to be made wisely.

One can describe how a perfect market system must operate to lead to optimal decision making over time. Such a description is contained in the first section of this chapter, and the concepts reviewed there, as well as the mathematics in the second appendix, are a prerequisite to a good understanding of the policy issues addressed herein. Essentially, the section reviews how perfect capital markets (for the borrowing and lending of purchasing power, or claims to the use of real resources) allow an economy to achieve an efficient allocation of resources between use for current consumption and investment.

An investment is an increment to the *stock of a durable resource* (capital) which will be available to produce a *flow of consumption* in the future. For example, raw materials, land, and labor can be allocated this year to the construction of a new factory which will be used to make clothing in the future. The creation of the factory is an investment which increases our total capital stock and also increases the future flow of clothes available for consumption.

Similarly, one can invest in humans and increase the stock of "human capital." For example, an additional student in medical school is an investment which adds to the stock of physicians and increases the flow of future medical services.

When a society invests, it is giving up current consumption in order to obtain future consumption. The medical student, for example, could be working in a shoe factory instead of attending school. Any individual, in deciding whether to invest, must consider the current and future effects on both income and consumption. The medical student must be able to pay tuition and have enough left over for room and board.

Thus, some investments will be undertaken only if the investor can today *borrow* purchasing power which can be repaid with postinvestment earnings in the future. This means that others must be willing to *lend* or *save* some of their current purchasing power. Investment demands are bids to use real resources for future rather than current consumption, and savings supplies are offers to forego the use of real resources for current consumption. We will show that the interest rate is the price which equilibrates the investment demand (a declining function of the interest rate) with the savings supply (an increasing function of the interest rate). *In equilibrium, savings equals investment, and with perfect capital markets all investments whose net present values are greater than zero (at the market rate of interest) are undertaken.*

There is wide agreement among economists that private capital markets are imperfect. For a variety of reasons they do not coordinate economic agents in the manner required for efficiency. Thus, it may be possible to improve resource allocation through carefully designed public policies. In this chapter we focus on two sources of capital market imperfections and the policy problems that are associated with them. These investigations are not meant to be exhaustive, but they are representative of the types of skills required for policy analyses involving resource allocation over time.

The first imperfection we consider is that private markets lead to underinvestment in higher education by potential undergraduates. This productive opportunity is one of the more important ways to enhance human potential, or human capital. There are two different reasons for the underinvestment: (1) Society may receive significant positive external benefits from an individual's undergraduate education. (2) For investments in human capital generally, there is substantial uncertainty in the loans market concerning the repayment of funds. These market failures can be used as reasons for public policies which involve tuition subsidization as well as government-guaranteed student loans. We examine some of the problems that are perceived with these policies currently.

The second imperfection we consider is an intergenerational one: the inadequate representation of future consumer claims. We examine this in the specific context of the allocation of oil, a resource that is nonrenewable, at least with current technological knowledge. When a resource is expected to be rationed over a considerable span of time involving multiple generations, today's marketing decisions may not adequately represent the interests of the future generations. Even speculators, who are popularly thought of as evil exploiters but often serve the useful social function of representing future interests, are likely to be too myopic to represent those interests optimally.

We begin examining the allocation of natural resources by looking at models of a renewable resource, trees. Then we turn to an exhaustible resource, oil. We review how a perfect market would ration oil, and we consider briefly the use of a simulation model to aid in the design of current energy policy. We also consider, as a simple extension, the effect of a windfall profits tax on the intertemporal allocation of oil.

One problem which is not inherent in intertemporal allocation but which greatly affects all intertemporal decisions is inflation. An analysis of the causes of inflation is beyond the scope of this book. However, in the first appendix to this chapter we explain how various indexing mechanisms are used to adapt to inflation. After reviewing some principles of index construction, we consider a number of practical problems that arise in constructing and implementing the necessary indices. These problems have obvious relevance in a number of policy areas like government bond issuance, Social Security payments, and school financing. They may also be thought of as a special subset of the more general problem of linking decision making to any social indicator (crime rates, health statistics, etc.).

We proceed with the analyses in the order described.

INTERTEMPORAL ALLOCATION AND CAPITAL MARKETS

For most people the timing of the receipts of income from their wealth does not match perfectly the desired timing of their expenditures, or consumption. Although one could consider this problem over any period of time, it is most useful to think first about an average lifetime or life cycle. In Figure 14-1 we draw a picture of a representative family's income over a period of approximately 60 years and its consumption pattern over the same period. The most important feature to notice is the evenness of the consumption pattern as contrasted to the unevenness of income.

The patterns in Figure 14-1 approximate facts we can observe. Incomes are typically low when the adult family members are in their 20s and may be in school or just starting their careers. Then income usually rises fairly steadily until it peaks somewhere in the late 50s or early 60s, and shortly thereafter it plummets sharply because of retirement. Meanwhile, consumption is likely to outpace income in the earlier stages: home-occupancy and child-rearing expenses, for example, are usually financed by borrowing which is paid back out of the savings that occur during the middle stages of the family's life cycle. Similarly, the savings are used to help finance consumption during the low-income years of retirement. In other words, these facts suggest that a family

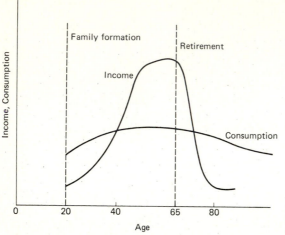

FIGURE 14-1
Typical life-style pattern of family income and consumption.

prefers to consume at its permanent income level—roughly the average income over a lifetime—rather than have to alter consumption to fit the pattern of transitory annual income.[1]

Individual Consumption Choice with Savings Opportunities

What we wish to do now is build up a more systematic model of individual desires to allocate resources over time and examine the extent to which capital

[1] The difference between permanent and transitory income can often have a profound analytic impact on the evaluation of policies by equity standards. As one example, consider the degree of progressivity (or regressivity) of a tax like the property tax. (This example is given in Henry Aaron, "A New View of Property Tax Incidence," *The American Economic Review, 64,* No. 2, May 1974, pp. 212–221.) If the tax dollars paid by homeowners are compared with their annual incomes, a regressive bias results.

To see this, recognize that many families living in homes with tax bills that are high compared with their low current incomes are either at the beginning or end of their lifetime income stream; The tax bill as a proportion of permanent income for these families is much lower. Similarly, people in the equivalent homes but in the high-income stages of the life cycle will pay only a small portion of their high current incomes in taxes, even though their taxes are a much higher proportion of their permanent incomes. In other words, a tax which is proportional to home value is also approximately proportional to permanent income but will appear to be regressive in relation to current income. Thus, whatever the true incidence of the property tax, it appears more regressive if measured by using current income as a base.

This does not mean that property taxes are no more of a burden to low-current-income families than to high-current-income families with the same permanent incomes. However, differences in burden are due to imperfections in the capital market. For example, an elderly couple may own a home the value of which has greatly appreciated and the mortgage on which has long been paid off. This can leave them in the awkward position of being wealthy but with little liquid income. They might wish to pay their property taxes by giving up some of the equity in their home, but few banks have methods of lending to facilitate that.

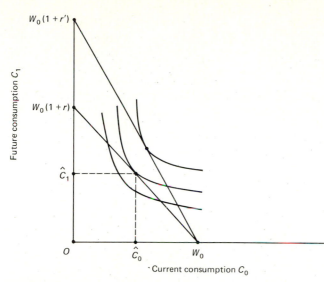

FIGURE 14-2
Savings $W_0 - C_0$ in a two-period model with interest rate r.

markets can and do facilitate that. We begin by imagining a consumer to have a fixed wealth endowment which can be allocated for consumption in one of two time periods.

In Figure 14-2 we have drawn some indifference curves to represent the preferences of an individual for current consumption C_0 versus future consumption C_1. The units of consumption are homogeneous except for time, and both are normal goods. The curves are drawn more bent than straight, with the corner near an imaginary 45° line from the origin. This is to reflect the observation that many individuals have a preference for reasonably even consumption over time. (That is, over a wide range of possible slopes for the budget constraint, the tangency will be near the 45° line.) The slope of the indifference curve is sometimes referred to as the *marginal rate of time preference,* but it is nothing more than an ordinary marginal rate of substitution and varies along any indifference curve. There is no reason why the time indifference curves for more specific commodities, like food or water skiing, cannot have quite different shapes from each other and from the ones drawn.

The wealth endowment is shown as W_0, where each unit of wealth can be used to purchase a unit of consumption today. However, we must determine the rest of the budget constraint; W_0 is only one extreme point of it. An alternative to consuming all the wealth today is to defer consumption completely and save all the wealth for future consumption. If that is done, the wealth can be put in a bank or in government bonds or other savings instruments, where it will earn the market rate of interest r.[2] Thus the maximum future consumption that is possible is $W_0(1 + r)$. Of course, the individual could choose any of the combinations on the line connecting the two extreme points, and that locus is the budget constraint. At each point on the locus, *savings is simply the amount of deferred consumption* $W_0 - C_0$.

As usual, to maximize utility, the individual will choose the point on the budget constraint which is just tangent to an indifference curve. In Figure 14-2 the individual consume*s* $\hat{C}_0$ in the current period and saves $W_0 - \hat{C}_0$, which becomes $\hat{C}_1 = (W_0 - \hat{C}_0)(1 + r)$ units of future consumption. Thus, the choice of how much to save depends not only on the initial wealth endowment and preferences but also on the slope of the budget constraint. This brings us to the next important point of this illustration: to *interpret the interest rate as a relative price*. That is, the slope of the budget constraint is

$$\frac{-W_0(1 + r)}{W_0} = \frac{-1 + r}{1}$$

Since we know the slope of an ordinary budget constraint for two goods is minus the ratio of the two prices, it is only natural to interpret this slope similarly. If we give up one unit of consumption today, we can buy $1 + r$ units of consumption tomorrow; or the price of a unit of consumption tomorrow is $1/1 + r$ units of consumption today. This latter number is sometimes referred to as the *present value*, or *present discounted value*, of future consumption. The rate r is then referred to as the *discount rate*. If the discount rate is 0.10, it means \$0.91 of consumption today must be foregone to get \$1.00 worth of future consumption.

An alternative way to see the same point is to rewrite the budget constraint as

$$W_0 = 1C_0 + \frac{1}{1 + r}C_1$$

This looks like any ordinary budget constraint:

$$W = P_X X + P_Y Y$$

where the prices and quantities in the time equation correspond as follows:

$$P_X = 1 \qquad X = C_0$$
and
$$P_Y = \frac{1}{1 + r} \qquad Y = C_1$$

---

[2] We are ignoring regulatory constraints that may prevent banks from offering the market rate of interest. We are also referring to the "riskless" rate of interest; a range of interest rates exist at any one time in part because some vehicles for saving and borrowing are riskier than others.

Note that in this model an increase in the interest rate unambiguously makes the individual better off. It is equivalent to reducing the price of the future good, all other prices being constant. The budget constraint rotates outward from W_0, as shown in Figure 14-2, which means the individual can reach a higher indifference curve. This result is due purely to the fact that the individual can only be a *saver* in this model: There are no opportunities for borrowing. C_0 must be less than or equal to W_0. It is clear that an increase in the interest rate will increase C_1; both substitution and income effects are positive. However, we do not know if savings will increase. The income effect on C_0 is positive, but the substitution effect is negative.

Individual Consumption Choice with Borrowing and Savings Opportunities

The unambiguous welfare effect of an interest rate increase disappears as we make the model more realistic and allow borrowing. To do so, we replace the wealth endowment by an income stream. The individual owns a *stock* of real resources which we refer to as *capital*. The capital produces a *flow* of services which earn income Y_0 in the current period and Y_1 in the future. Constrained by the value of those income flows, the individual must decide on a consumption pattern. We assume for now that current borrowing or lending (saving) of capital resources can be done at the market rate of interest.

Figure 14-3 shows this slightly more sophisticated model graphically. The individual is initially at the point (Y_0, Y_1) and of course, could choose $C_0 = Y_0$ and $C_1 = Y_1$. But what does the budget constraint look like? At one extreme, the individual could save every penny of Y_0 (i.e., choose $C_0 = 0$), put it in the bank where it returns $Y_0(1 + r)$ in the future period, and have $C_1 = Y_1 + Y_0(1 + r)$. At the other extreme, the bank will lend $Y_1/(1 + r)$ today in return for being paid back Y_1 next period. Current consumption can be made equal to the present value of the income stream. So when $C_1 = 0$, $C_0 = Y_0 + Y_1/(1 + r)$. The budget constraint is thus the line which connects those two points:[3]

$$C_1 = Y_1 + (Y_0 - C_0)(1 + r)$$

The second term on the right-hand side represents the future value of savings if $Y_0 > C_0$ and the cost of borrowing (in terms of foregone future consumption) if $Y_0 < C_0$. The slope of the budget constraint is $-(1 + r)$, as before.[4]

---

[3] Let $C_1 = mC_0 + b$, where m and b are respectively the unknown slope and intercept of the budget constraint. From the point where $C_0 = 0$ and $C_1 = Y_1 + Y_0(1 + r)$, we know $b = Y_1 + Y_0(1 + r)$. From the point where $C_0 = Y_0 + Y_1/(1 + r)$ and $C_1 = 0$ we know $m = -b/C_0 = -[Y_1 + Y_0(1 + r)]/[Y_0 + Y_1/(1 + r)] = -(1 + r)$. Therefore, $C_1 = b + mC_0 = Y_1 + (Y_0 - C_0)(1 + r)$.

[4] We check this by taking the partial derivative:

$$\frac{\partial C_1}{\partial C_0} = \frac{\partial [Y_1 + (Y_0 - C_0)(1 + r)]}{\partial C_0} = -(1 + r)$$

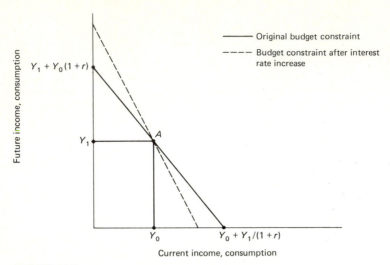

FIGURE 14-3
The budget constraint for allocation between time periods with saving and
borrowing possible.

The budget constraint can be rearranged to show that *the present value of all consumption must equal the present value of all income:*

$$C_0 + \frac{C_1}{1 + r} = Y_0 + \frac{Y_1}{1 + r}$$

The individual may be either a saver or borrower, depending upon personal preferences. Any point on the budget constraint to the right of point A represents borrowing, and any point to the left of point A represents saving. Suppose the interest rate now increases. That causes the budget constraint to rotate clockwise about point A: The present value of future income is lower, and the future value of current income is higher.

If the individual was a saver originally, he or she must be better off, since more of each good can be consumed than previously. However, the person who was a borrower initially may be better off or worse off depending on whether the new savings opportunities outweigh the worsened borrowing prospects. Regardless of whether the person is a borrower or saver, the substitution effect is to increase C_1 and reduce C_0. For the saver, income effects are positive and thus C_1 will increase and C_0 is ambiguous as before. For the borrower, we do not know if real income is increased or decreased and thus cannot predict the income effects.

The Separation Theorem of Individual Investment and Consumption Choices

So far, we have shown that an individual may choose a consumption pattern over time by taking advantage of opportunities for borrowing or saving. Now we wish to add a third alternative: undertaking productive investment. To make this clear, let us go back to the start of the last model: An individual can earn Y_0 in the current period and Y_1 in the future period. Let us say that the source of this income comes partly from labor (a return on human capital) and partly in the form of rent from occupants in an office building owned by the person.

One productive opportunity which might be available is education. Instead of allocating all current labor to employment, the individual can use some of it to enroll in school for the current period. This is an investment in human capital. It reduces current income, but it raises future income because of the better job which can then be obtained. Note that the primary cost of education may be not tuition, but the earnings foregone. The tuition payment further reduces the income available for current consumption. In Figure 14-4 this opportunity might be represented by a change in the income stream (available for consumption) from point A to point B.

A second productive opportunity might be to renovate the office building during the current period in order to make it more attractive to commercial occupants and receive higher rents in the future period. This is an ordinary capital investment. Its cost includes the rent foregone in the current period while the renovation work is being done. It also includes, of course, the cost of the labor and materials that go into the renovation. Since the owner must pay for them, they further reduce the amount of owner income available for current consumption. Graphically, this investment might be thought of as a move from point B to point C.

The idea in both these examples is that the individual controls an endowment of real resources which can be used for current production and earn up to

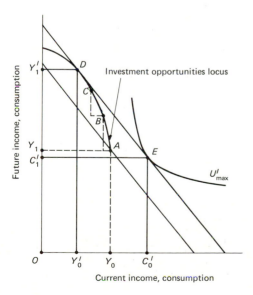

FIGURE 14-4
The effect of investment opportunities on intertemporal consumption choice.

the amount of the endowment flow of Y_0. He or she can also choose to withhold some of them from use in producing current consumption goods and instead convert them to a different productive use for the future period.[5] Investment implies that a real resource spends *time* out of the most profitable use for current consumption and imposes a social opportunity cost equal to the amount of deferred consumption. The investment process is sometimes referred to as *real capital formation,* and the amount of investment is the increment to the existing capital stocks (human skills, buildings, machinery, etc.).

Imagine someone facing a whole array of investment opportunities. For each unit of real resource, the individual considers removing it from production of current consumption (moving one unit to the left starting from Y_0) and allocating it to its best investment use (the largest possible gain to future income). This traces out the investment opportunities path in Figure 14-4, where the slope becomes flatter as we move closer to the future-period axis (the marginal investments are less lucrative).

Consider how these investment alternatives affect the individual's consumption possibilities. Any point on the investment opportunities path can be chosen, and then the budget constraint is determined precisely as in our last model. Naturally, the individual seeks the budget constraint with the best consumption possibilities: the one farthest out from the origin. Since the slope of the budget constraint is determined by the market rate of interest, the individual will choose the investment portfolio such that the budget constraint is just tangent to the investment opportunities path. We label this point D. Note that it is also the choice which intersects the axes at the farthest possible points. Thus we have the following result: *A necessary condition for utility maximization is to undertake the investment opportunities which maximize the present value of income calculated at the market rate of interest.*

The above rule is equivalent to undertaking all investments whose present values are positive at the market rate of interest. At point D, the slope of the investment opportunities locus is $-(1 + r)$. To the right of D the slope is steeper, and to the left it is flatter. If we undertook one additional investment project (and thus moved to the left),

$$\frac{\Delta Y_1}{\Delta Y_0} < 1 + r$$

or, by rearranging,
$$\frac{\Delta Y_1}{1 + r} - \Delta Y_0 < 0$$

Since the expression on the left is the present value of the incremental project, we can see that projects to the left of point D have negative present values and those to the right will have positive present values.

---

[5] In the formal model we use, each unit of real resource is homogeneous and thus there is no need for the individual to buy investment inputs in the market. Our examples add realism by having the individual produce current consumption but spend some of the proceeds on buying investment inputs. The net effect is the same: Equivalent amounts of real resources are withheld from use in current consumption, and equivalent amounts of income are available to purchase current consumption.

Once this is done, the individual may choose any of the consumption possibilities along the constraint by using the capital market to borrow or lend claims to the current use of real resources. We draw the optimal consumption choice as point E, where the individual borrows $C_0^I - Y_0^I$. Note that it is arbitrary to label some portion of this loan for investment and another for consumption; the amount of borrowing or saving is jointly determined by the amount of after-investment income available for current consumption, the present value of future income, and consumption preferences.

In this model, utility maximization is divided into two independent parts: the choice of investments to maximize wealth and then the choice of how to spend it on a consumption path over time. This is sometimes referred to as the *separation property* of perfect capital markets. An important implication of this property is that a hired agent can select and supervise the investments without having to know anything about the personal preferences of the owner: The agent's function is neither more nor less than wealth maximization.

The performance of competitive investment managers is observable in the marketplace. As long as it is competitive, it makes the selection of any particular manager as irrelevant as the choice of which firm to shop at in a perfectly competitive market. The purchase of a share of stock in a firm, for example, can be thought of as a delegation to the firm's managers of specific investment decision-making authority (e.g., which machinery to build). The investor-shareholder only has to look at the results (dividends plus stock price appreciation). A perfectly competitive stock market keeps the share prices of firms at exactly the level required to keep potential investors indifferent among them.[6]

Capital Market Equilibrium

Now let us consider how the capital market determines an equilibrium interest rate and quantity of investment, given the diversity of individual desires for consumption and the productive possibilities for investment. The separation property suggests a convenient way to conceptualize the demand and supply. The demand for investment resources derives from the individual (or firm) wealth maximization decisions about how to allocate the available stock of resources between current productive use and investment. The supply of resources for investment comes from the utility maximization decisions about the current consumption level: Total resources minus the amount required to

---

[6] As part of the perfect-market model, we have been ruling out uncertainty and its effects. Real firms cater to investors with a particular type of risk preference. For example, people generally are not indifferent to investing in a utility company with a long history of uninterrrupted dividend payments or a brand new genetic engineering company whose uncertain future may be to earn either a fortune or nothing. For more discussion of the stock market and its allocative role, see W. Baumol, *The Stock Market and Economic Efficiency* (New York: Fordham University Press, 1965).

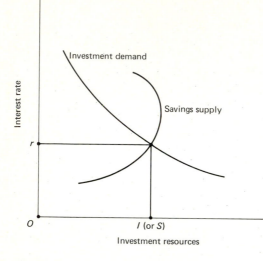

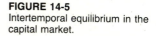

FIGURE 14-5
Intertemporal equilibrium in the capital market.

satisfy current consumption demand equals the supply left over for investment. These are shown in Figure 14-5 and explained below.[7]

It is not hard to see that the demand for investment resources is an inverse function of the interest rate. For any given interest rate, each individual (or firm as the agent) chooses the point on the investment possibilities locus where the present value of an incremental project is zero. A higher interest rate means the slope at the wealth-maximizing point is steeper, or closer to point A in Figure 14-4: less investment. The market demand for investment is simply the sum of all the individual demands at each possible interest rate, and thus it also is downward-sloping.

The supply of investment resources is drawn as rising but backward-bending. As the interest rate rises, each individual perceives current consumption to be relatively more expensive than future consumption. Thus, the substitution effect works to reduce demands for current consumption, or put differently, increase the supply of resources available for investment. By itself, this suggests a normally rising supply curve.

The income effect is ambiguous, however. Although there may be net saving in the economy as a whole, some individuals (those who wish to consume more than their residual current claims after investment) will be made worse off because of the interest rate increase and have income effects which reduce current consumption (i.e., increase aggregate savings). Other individuals

---

[7] An alternative way to conceptualize the market is in terms of the demand and supply of loans, or claims on the current use of real resources. Since loans can be used for either consumption or investment, the equilibrium quantity does not reveal the amount of investment. However, the two conceptualizations are just different ways of representing the same equilibrium.

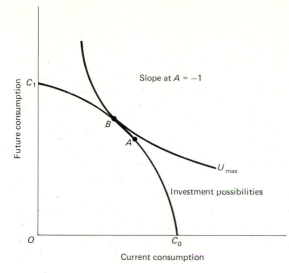

Slope at $A = -1$

U_{max}

Investment possibilities

C_1 — Future consumption

C_0 — Current consumption

O

FIGURE 14-6
The real interest rate may be negative.

(savers) will be made better off; they will have income effects which increase current consumption (i.e., reduce aggregate savings). Recall that the magnitude of an income effect depends on the importance of the good in the overall budget. Then the probability of the investment supply response being negative (to an interest rate increase) is greater when aggregate savings are greater. That is why the supply curve is drawn as rising first and then bending backward, but it is an unresolved empirical question whether and at what point this occurs.[8]

One interesting aspect of capital market equilibrium can be seen more clearly by referring to a Robinson Crusoe economy: *There is no theoretical reason why the interest rate need be positive.* Figure 14-6 shows Crusoe's productive possibilities for current and future consumption. Point A is the allocation where the slope is -1, or the interest rate r is zero. (r is positive to the right and negative to the left as one moves along the frontier.) To maximize utility, Crusoe must choose the point on this frontier which is just tangent to one of his indifference curves. There is no reason why it cannot occur somewhere to the left of point A, as at point B. The likelihood of this occurring depends on Crusoe's preferences and the shape of the transformation curve.

It is often thought that the real interest rate will be positive, and for much of our history that appears to be so. Reasons offered in explanation are that (1) as a matter of preference, consumers are "impatient" and must be offered more than one unit of future consumption before they will defer a unit of current

---

[8] Empirical studies of the interest elasticity of savings find that it is positive, although the estimates range from near zero to as high as .6. For a brief review of these with application to taxation policy, see A. Atkinson and J. Stiglitz, *Lectures on Public Economics* (New York: McGraw-Hill Book Company, 1980), chap. 3, esp. pp. 92–94.

TABLE 14-1
REAL INTEREST RATES (NOMINAL MINUS INFLATION) CAN BE NEGATIVE

	Annual interest rates				
	Before tax		After 25% tax		
Year	T-bills	Aaa bonds*	T-bills†	Aaa bonds*	ΔCPI‡
1971	7.39	4.51	5.54	3.38	4.30
1972	7.21	4.47	5.41	3.35	3.30
1973	7.44	7.18	5.58	5.39	6.23
1974	8.57	7.93	6.43	5.95	10.97
1975	8.83	6.12	6.62	4.59	9.14
1976	8.43	5.27	6.32	3.95	5.77
1977	8.02	5.51	6.02	4.13	6.45
1978	8.73	7.57	6.55	5.68	7.66
1979	9.63	10.02	7.22	7.52	11.26

* Corporate bonds as rated by Moody's Investors Service; data from *Economic Report of the President, January 1980* (Washington, D.C.: U.S. Government Printing Office, 1980), table B-64, p. 279.
† New issues of 6-month Treasury bills; data from ibid.
‡ The change in the Consumer Price Index, where $\Delta CPI_t = (CPI_t - CPI_{t-1})/CPI_{t-1}$. The data are from ibid., table B-49, p. 259.

consumption and (2) the productive possibilities for investments which yield more than what is put into them (in terms of consumption units) are plentiful because time itself allows growth (e.g., the quantity of lumber in a growing tree).[9]

As an empirical matter, however, positive interest rates do not always prevail. The decade of the 1970s was one in which negative real rates of interest on savings instruments were commonly observed. This was primarily a phenomenon explained by inflation.[10] In Table 14-1 we show the nominal interest rates on two low-risk savings instruments: six-month U.S. Treasury Bills and corporate bonds rated Aaa by Moody's. We also include two columns which show the *after-tax* rate of interest calculated with the modest assumption of a 25 percent marginal tax bracket.[11] The latter shows the percentage increase

[9] The first statement should be interpreted to apply to the marginal rate of time preference in the neighborhood of "even" consumption bundles on the indifference curve. If there were a stock of food which had to last for two time periods because the productive possibilities for making more food were scant, people would no doubt prefer to save a sizable portion even if half of the units saved were expected (statistically) to spoil.

[10] With no inflation an individual could simply hold money to avoid a negative interest rate, but not every individual can do that. Suppose there were many individuals identical with the one in our Robinson Crusoe model and that they all thought they could do better than point A by choosing point B for investment and then following a money-holding constraint upward and to the left with a slope of -1 (that is, $r = 0$) for consumption. That in itself would cause inflation in the future, since the actual amount of future consumption per person can be no greater than that shown on the investment possibilities frontier. (The dollars per good available would increase.)

[11] This approximates the tax bracket of the median-income U.S. family. However, savers are likely to be concentrated in the higher income levels. For households in higher brackets, the after-tax return is even lower.

in dollars available for private consumption. But these are only nominal interest rates.

The nominal rates must be compared with the final column: the percentage increase in the Consumer Price Index, which represents the dollars required to purchase a constant basket of private consumer goods.[12] For the real interest rate to be positive, the nominal after-tax rate of interest must exceed the inflation in the price of consumption goods. As can be seen, the real rate of interest for these savings instruments was primarily negative during the 1970s.

Of course, the model we have been using does not account for the effects of taxation policy.[13] Nevertheless, even the before-tax interest rates in the table are sometimes less than the change in the price level. One reason may be the uncertainty about future price levels, which itself is a deviation from the perfect-knowledge assumption of the model. If individuals in the market have incorrect expectations about the rate of inflation during the period, that can explain negative real rates of return on savings.

For example, Treasury bills pay $10,000 to the holder after 6 months, and the competitive bid price for the bond *at its issue* determines the 6-month nominal interest rate r_n. Let us say that the competitive bid price is $9500, which implies a simple 6-month rate of interest of

$$r_n = \frac{10,000}{9500} - 1 = 0.053$$

Since bidders are interested in the real rate of return, they must add the anticipated inflation rate i_e during the period to the demanded real rate r:[14]

$$r_n = r + i_e$$

If the equilibrium real rate in a certain world is 0.015 for 6 months,

$$i_e = r_n - r = 0.053 - 0.015 = 0.038$$

However, the actual inflation rate may turn out to be higher over the period—6 percent, for example. In that case, the real rate of return is negative:

$$r - r_n - i = 0.053 - 0.060 = -0.007$$

Investment and Equilibrium in Multiperiod Models

Let us sketch the extension of the basic model (with no inflation or uncertainty) from the two-period case we have been using to many periods. As long as there

---

[12] This is discussed further in the appendix to this chapter.

[13] For a review of tax effects on intertemporal choice, see Atkinson and Stiglitz, op. cit.

[14] Note that i_e is subjectively determined and can vary among individuals. Note also that this implies that intertemporal decisions are based on the *expected* real interest rate, not the one which is realized *ex post*.

is a perfect capital market, the rule for selecting investment projects (from along the multiperiod investment possibilities surface) applies as in the two-period case: All investments with positive present values should be undertaken (i.e., investments should be chosen in order to maximize wealth). Each independent possibility can be represented by the stream D_i of benefits and costs (net income per period) associated with it:

$$\text{PDV} = D_0 + \frac{D_1}{1 + r_1} + \frac{D_2}{(1 + r_1)(1 + r_2)} + \cdots + \frac{D_n}{(1 + r_1)(1 + r_2) \cdots (1 + r_n)}$$

Note that, in this more general formulation, we allow for the possibility that the market interest rate varies from period to period.[15] There is nothing in the theory of perfect capital markets which requires that the price between periods j and $j + 1$ equal the price between periods $j + 1$ and $j + 2$ (or, for that matter, $j + k$ and $j + k + 1$).

The multiperiod investment equation can be used in the conduct of a Hicks-Kaldor compensation test of a proposed public investment involving benefits and costs which occur at different time periods. For example, suppose the government is considering whether to construct (or approve the private construction of) a hydroelectric facility in a wilderness area. Skipping the hard part, suppose analysis has led to the following estimates of benefits and costs:[16] (1) The social benefits are that $140,000 worth of increased electricity output (above operating costs of production) will be available annually for 48 years starting in the third year from project initiation. (2) The social opportunity costs include $3 million for construction ($1 million in the first year, $2 million in the second year). (3) Social costs also include $80,000 in recreation benefits foregone annually (e.g., the facility interferes with the environment for fishing, hiking, and hunting purposes) for 50 years starting at project initiation. Do the benefits outweigh the costs?

To calculate this, we must convert the stream of benefits and costs into a single present value, as suggested by the equation above. If the social rate of discount is constant and equal to 3 percent per year, then[17]

$$\text{PV (electricity benefits)} = \frac{\$140,000}{1.03^2} + \frac{\$140,000}{1.03^3} + \cdots + \frac{\$140,000}{1.03^{49}}$$

$$= \$3,434,310 \tag{1}$$

---

[15] We adopt the convention that r_i is the interest rate between period $i - 1$ and i.

[16] This example is motivated by a highly regarded study in which considerable effort and ingenuity are used to derive actual estimates of a wide variety of benefits and costs. The study concerns the proposal to build a hydroelectric facility in Hells Canyon of the Snake River. See A. Fisher, J. Krutilla, and C. Cicchetti, "The Economics of Environmental Preservation: A Theoretical and Empirical Analysis," *The American Economic Review, 62,* No. 4, September 1972, pp. 605–619.

[17] In the second appendix to this chapter we review the formulas used to sum these geometric progressions.

$$\text{PV (construction)} = \$1,000,000 + \frac{\$2,000,000}{1.03}$$

$$= \$2,941,748 \tag{2}$$

$$\text{PV (foregone recreation)} = \$80,000 + \frac{\$80,000}{1.03} + \cdots + \frac{\$80,000}{1.03^{49}}$$

$$= \$2,120,133 \tag{3}$$

The net present value of the project is (1) $-$ [(2) + (3)]:

$$\text{PV (net)} = \text{benefits} - \text{costs} = -\$1,627,571$$

Thus, on efficiency grounds, the proposed project is a bad one: The social costs exceed the social benefits by \$1,627,571.

In the above example we assumed the interest rate $r = 0.03$ was constant across all periods. But what are the equilibrium interest rates that would be set by perfect intertemporal markets? The equilibrium prices or interest rates are simply those which equate supply and demand in each period. Their determination is exactly analogous to calculating general equilibrium in the static model, where here we simply call the goods C_0, C_1, . . ., C_n with current prices P_0, P_1, . . ., P_n. The relative price P_0/P_1, for example, is the number of units of C_1 that can be bought for one unit of C_0, or what we have seen earlier is $1 + r_1$.

For each of these periods there is an investment demand function. It is the sum of the wealth-maximizing investment choices of each individual based upon his or her investment possibilities surface. The ordinary investment demand schedule is defined by allowing only that period's price to vary, all other prices being held constant at their equilibrium levels. For general equilibrium, we allow all the prices to vary simultaneously.

The investment supply function for each period can be thought of as the residual from the consumption decision. That is, each person chooses consumption to maximize the intertemporal utility function $U(C_0, C_1, \ldots, C_n)$ given a budget constraint determined by intertemporal prices and after-investment income flows. The difference between the endowment income and the optimal consumption level, summed over all individuals, is the supply of savings for that period. The ordinary savings schedule is defined by allowing only that period's price to vary, all other prices being constant at their equilibrium levels. For general equilibrium, all n prices in the savings function are allowed to vary simultaneously.

Together these give us n supply and demand equations with n unknown prices. Since behavior depends on relative prices, only $n - 1$ of the P_i are needed for a unique solution and the other can be set as the numéraire. Walras' law applies to the n submarkets of the intertemporal economy, so ensuring supply equals demand in $n - 1$ is sufficient. This leaves $n - 1$ unknown relative prices with $n - 1$ equations, which, when solved simultaneously, yield the many-period intertemporal equilibrium.

One could construct an even more general model in which we distinguish among the real goods available within a period. That is, instead of just having one good called "consumption," we have the usual m goods $X_1, X_2, \ldots, X_m$. If these are n time periods, each good must be identified by the time of its consumption; for example, X_{15} is the quantity of the first good that is consumed during the fifth period. Then individuals must maximize the intertemporal utility function:

$$\text{Max } U[X_{10}, X_{20}, \ldots, X_{m0}; X_{11}, X_{21}, \ldots, X_{m1}; \ldots; X_{1n}, X_{2n}, \ldots, X_{mn}]$$

In such a model there is no such thing as "the" interest rate between any specific periods. All goods have their own intertemporal prices as well as intertemporal cross prices with all other goods. There is no theoretical reason why the "own" interest rates should be the same across different goods. Technically, all these intertemporal prices are required to exist for an economy to achieve a first-best Pareto-optimal allocation of resources.[18]

EDUCATION AS A CAPITAL INVESTMENT

Now let us turn to a dimension of intertemporal allocation with important policy implications: the development of human potential through higher education. Virtually everyone agrees that public policies are needed to help finance higher education, although there may be much disagreement about the quantity and form of assistance.

Education is somewhat analogous to making an improvement on a home. It results in a stream of consumption benefits over time: the educated person may derive more enjoyment from reading, skiing, discussing rent control with friends and landlords, or any of a myriad of human activities. In addition, education is an income-generating investment: By allocating one's time to taking courses and studying rather than indulging in leisure or current employment, future earnings can be enhanced. In other words, humans, like homes, can be viewed as durable goods which represent a form of savings and capital assets which may be invested. Education increases the stream of consumption and income benefits from human capital; it is a process of human capital formation.[19]

Of course, human capital differs from other capital in important ways. One of the few public policies which is noncontroversial is the ban on the sale of human capital (i.e., slavery). This creates capital market inefficiency (!) despite the empirical likelihood that few informed adults would choose to sell themselves even if they legally could do so. The more important problem arises in

---

[18] For an overview of some models which look at the efficiency implications of imperfect future markets, see P. S. Dasgupta and G. M. Heal, *Economic Theory and Exhaustible Resources* (Oxford: James Nisbet & Co., Ltd. and Cambridge University Press, 1979), chap. 8.

[19] For a thorough exposition of this view, see G. Becker, *Human Capital,* National Bureau of Economic Research (New York: Columbia University Press, 1964).

financing human capital investments, since the asset invested cannot be used as collateral.

Recall that a perfect capital market will lend the individual up to the present value of the future (investment-enhanced) earnings stream. But the lender is uncertain whether any loan will be repaid: Even with legal rulings that support the lender's right to be repaid, the borrower may have no tangible assets which can ensure the repayment. If one borrows to buy a house, the house can be claimed by the lender in the event of defaut. But if one borrows to finance an education and then spends the next 5 years as a part-time ski instructor in Europe, the lender may be just plain stuck.

Consider the equity implications of this issue. Recall that borrowing is used to buy the services of other inputs for the investment (tuition to pay for faculty, teaching assistants, etc.) *and* to finance the desired level of current consumption. Those who are wealthy may have no need to borrow; they may have endowments with current income sufficient to undertake higher education by self-financing. Even if current income is not high, there may be other assets (e.g., a trust account) which can be used as collateral. But what about the bright individual from a not-so-wealthy family? The investment value may be high, but the imperfect capital market will not provide the necessary current resources. (Note that a loan equal to the tuition costs may not be enough if too much current consumption must be foregone.)

When one considers the imperfect market for human capital and opportunities for higher education, the obvious policy remedies are to provide or encourage some type of loans for students (which we discuss below). But this is not the only imperfection in the higher-education market. Many argue that there are substantial positive external benefits to the rest of society from higher (undergraduate) education. If so, this could be internalized by giving a subsidy such that the cost of a marginal unit of education equals the sum of the private plus the external benefits. It is very difficult to quantify these external benefits (they are usually described as community leadership, increasing social mobility, etc.). Therefore, one of the main policy issues is to decide the extent of tuition subsidization and to treat the residual as a potential capital market problem.

Income-Contingent Loan Plans for Financing Higher Education

One of the more interesting policy options to reduce the capital market imperfections is the *income-contingent loan* introduced by Yale University in 1971.[20] It allows students to convert their uncertain future incomes into current cash. The really novel twist to it is that the amount paid back is an increasing function of actual future income; thus, the loan is also an insurance policy which protects the borrower against the event of a relatively low future income.

[20] This plan is described in Marc Nerlove, "Some Problems in the Use of Income-Contingent Loans for the Finance of Higher Education," *Journal of Political Economy, 83,* No. 1, February 1975, pp. 157–183.

The Yale plan essentially works as follows: Yale, being a credit-worthy institution, borrows money at favorably low rates from banks or other financial institutions. (Presumably, governments could do the same thing.) Students who borrow from the University can repay the loan over a relatively long time period, up to 35 years. Those with higher incomes pay more, and those with lower incomes pay less. The long time period for repayment allows the size of the annual payments to be small; in the Yale plan, payments are 0.4 percent of the individual's adjusted gross income (AGI) per $1000 borrowed. For example, the student who borrows $10,000 will make the following annual repayment for each representative income level shown:

AGI, $	Annual repayment, $
10,000	400
20,000	800
40,000	1600

The length of time that a student will make these payments depends on his or her actual income, the aggregate payments of the cohort to which a student is assigned, and the interest charges. When a student begins repayment, he or she is assigned to a "payment cohort" consisting of all those who begin repayment that year. Yale calculates the aggregate repayments of this group over time, compared with its aggregate debt at the beginning. It discharges the entire cohort as soon as the repayment level reaches the aggregate debt plus interest charges (calculated at a rate set for each 6-month period by a specified formula), up to a maximum of 35 years. Furthermore, the total repayments of any single student are limited to a maximum of 150 percent of the principal and accrued interest, so that those who earn high incomes will not have to pay too high a penalty for doing so.

Thus, if we think of the income figures above as representing the permanent income streams of three different students, it is likely that they will finish repayments at different times. For example, the high earner might reach the individual limit after 15 years and the medium earner after 25. Assuming the cohort continues for the 35-year maximum, the low earner might contribute each year without ever making full repayment. (The present value of the repayment stream at the contracted interest rates is less than the loan value.)

According to some realistic but illustrative calculations made by Nerlove, it is likely that the relatively low earners (from among this generally quite select and high-earning group as a whole) will receive only modest subsidies. Note too that Yale cannot come out ahead: It discharges the whole group if the break-even point is reached. Thus the high and medium earners provide the modest subsidies, or Yale does. It is, however, difficult to predict the amount of relative subsidization in advance; e.g., experience may reveal that there are relatively few low earners in a group and that it is typical to discharge a cohort after 25 years—thus increasing the relative subsidization of low earners.[21]

Tax considerations make the Yale plan even more attractive to students. When the repayments are spread over a relatively long time period (unlike conventional student loans), the value of the tax deductibility of interest payments increases. (Guardians of the U.S. Treasury, take note.) The Internal Revenue Service allows the first payment (when income is low) to be counted as nondeductible return of principal. The later payments increase as income rises, but they are counted as tax-deductible interest charges and the value of the deduction rises with the marginal tax bracket.

We can illustrate this with a simplified example. Suppose someone has to repay $10,000 through either a conventional 10-year student loan or a new, extended 20-year plan. In both cases pretax payments are so scheduled that their present value at 8 percent interest is $10,000. The annual payments (R_c and R_n, respectively) are calculated as follows:

$$\$10,000 = \frac{R_c[1 - (1/1.08)^{10}]}{1 - 1/1.08}$$

whence

$$R_c = \$1379.90$$

$$\$10,000 = \frac{R_n[1 - (1/1.08)^{20}]}{1 - 1/1.08}$$

whence

$$R_n = \$943.08$$

If annual pretax payments were the only consideration, many students would favor the new plan simply because it reduces the annual burden in the years immediately following graduation. But tax considerations are important. For simplicity, let us assume that after graduation a student is in a 25 percent tax bracket for the first 10 years and a 50 percent bracket for the second 10 years. We calculate the present value of the tax deductions of each plan below.

For the conventional plan, all of the first 7 years are nondeductible return of principal ($9659.30). Thus the interest payments are in years 8, 9, and 10: $1039.20, $1379.90, and $1379.90. When they are deducted from income taxes in those years, 25 percent of each amount is the tax savings: $259.80, $344.98, and $344.98. The present value of the savings is

$$PDV = \frac{259.80}{1.08^8} + \frac{344.98}{1.08^9} + \frac{344.98}{1.08^{10}}$$
$$= \$472.73$$

[21] Two interesting articles which grapple with this and related problems are Robert W. Hartman, "Equity Implications of State Tuition Policy and Student Loans," *Journal of Political Economy, 80,* No. 3, part II, May–June 1972, pp. S142–S171, and Stephen P. Dresch and Robert D. Goldberg, "Variable Term Loans for Higher Education: Analytics and Empirics," *Annals of Economic and Social Measurement, 1,* January 1972, pp. 59–92.

For the new extended-payment plan, all of the first 10 payments are return of principal. The 11th payment includes \$373.88 interest, and all succeeding payments (12 to 20) are interest charges only. These interest charges result in tax savings equal to 50 percent of their amounts (\$186.94 in year 11 and \$471.54 in each of the following years). The present value of the tax savings is

$$\text{PDV} = \frac{186.94}{1.08^{11}} + \frac{471.54}{1.08^{12}} + \cdots + \frac{471.54}{1.08^{20}}$$

$$= 80.18 + 1076.02$$

$$= \$1156.20$$

Thus, it is clear that the tax advantage of the new plan is fairly substantial. This advantage can be even greater if the repayments are low initially and gradually rise along with the marginal tax bracket, as in the actual Yale plan.

What determines whether Yale (or some other institution, like a government) will break even in undertaking such a plan? One problem to worry about is adverse selection: The participants may be those most likely to have low earnings profiles or, even worse, to fail to make their obligated repayments. This may be less of a problem at a small institution with a fairly homogeneous student body than if the concept is applied, say, to the U.S. student population as a whole. Assuming the repayment is set to account for the above factors, within any cohort Yale will break even as long as there is a reasonably constant *difference* between interest rates and the growth of money incomes.

To see this, note that Yale must choose the repayment rate γ and the time period for repayments T. Let $L(t)$ = the amount of the original loan which Yale discharges each year. The university will break even if the inflowing repayments equal $L(t)$ plus the accrued interest charges on it (including administrative costs). If we let Y = money income at the start, δ = the one-period growth in money income, and r = the interest rate per period, then $L(t)$ can be defined by this relation:

$$\gamma Y (1 + \delta)^t = L(t)(1 + r)^t$$

The term on the left is the repayment amount in time t, and the term on the right is the amount of the original loan to be discharged plus accumulated interest charges on it. Thus, we can solve for $L(t)$:

$$L(t) = \frac{\gamma Y(1 + \delta)^t}{(1 + r)^t}$$

For small r and δ, this can be approximated:[22]

[22] Nerlove, op. cit., uses this approximation. Approximating $(1 + \delta)/(1 + r) = 1 + \delta - r$ implies by cross multiplication that $1 + \delta = (1 + \delta) + (\delta r - r^2)$. Thus, the second term $\delta r - r^2$ is the error in the approximation, but each term of the error is small (involving only second-order magnitudes), and furthermore, the terms tend to cancel out.

$$L(t) \simeq \gamma Y(1 + \delta - r)^t$$

Note that the approximation is the same even if δ and r vary from period to period as long as the difference between them, $\delta - r$, is constant. Thus we can think of the university's choice of γ as determining $L(t)$, given the parameters Y and $\delta - r$. To break even, the university chooses any γ and T combination which make $\sum_{t=1}^{T} L(t) = $ the original loan.

The main point is that the success of the plan (in terms of breaking even) depends not only on knowing the initial income of the group but also on the differential between money income growth and interest rates being approximately constant (or otherwise predictable in advance). Not knowing what these rates will be, Yale tries to minimize the risk of misestimating the difference by borrowing only for short time periods, knowing that changes in short-term interest rates are unimportant as long as nominal money income growth changes commensurately. However, the recent experience of a decade in which interest rates often changed more rapidly than money income growth may serve to caution against relying too heavily on historical relations.

Higher-Education Subsidies: Proposals for Grants and Tax Credits

In fact, the recent policy emphasis at the federal level has not been to solve the capital market imperfection. Rather, the proposals advanced have been to expand the general taxpayer subsidy.[23] The focus of them has been to reduce the burden on middle-income families with children attending college; this follows a decade in which aid to the worst-off students increased substantially.[24] We comment on them briefly below.

Numerous proposals were introduced in Congress during the late 1970s to provide tuition tax credits. A tax credit is normally an amount that is subtracted from the tax liability. It may or may not be refundable. If it is nonrefundable, the family with no tax liability is not able to benefit from it. A refundable credit means the government owes the tax filer if the net tax liability is negative after subtracting the credit and will, in that case, send a check equal to the liability minus the credit amount. This obviously benefits lower-income families and makes any tax credit proposal less regressive (and more expensive).

To take a specific example, one tax credit proposal called for a nonrefundable amount of $250 per full-time student. Such a proposal would cost about

[23] These are reviewed in David W. Breneman, "Education," in J. Pechman (ed.), *Setting National Priorities: The 1979 Budget* (Washington, D.C.: The Brookings Institution, 1978), pp. 117–125.

[24] Total federal aid to students increased from $1.7 billion in 1969 to $8.1 billion in 1979. About 25 percent of the total in 1979 was for basic educational opportunity grants available only to families with under $16,000 income; the program did not exist (or have close substitutes) in 1969. The data are from Breneman, op. cit., p. 106.

$1.8 billion (1980 dollars). It is regressive in the sense that it concentrates the benefits among the highest-income families, whose children are more likely to attend college. According to Breneman, the poorest 44 percent of families would receive only 8.6 percent of the total benefits and the richest 14 percent of families would receive nearly 45 percent of the total. Even if that were made refundable so that families with little or no tax liability could benefit from it, the richest 14 percent would still get 33 percent of the total benefits (approximately $2.5 billion). Because the benefits are concentrated in the upper-income groups, the proposal is not likely to encourage increased investment in education (demand is thought to be relatively inelastic for these groups).

An alternative method of increasing the taxpayer subsidy to higher education, proposed by the Carter administration and independently in the Senate, involves expanding the basic educational opportunity grants program. In 1978 the existing program provided a $1600 grant per full-time student to families with incomes up to approximately $7000 and proportionately smaller grants to families with up to $15,000 in income.[25] Both the Senate and administration proposals called for increasing the maximum grant to $1800 and extending the eligibility level of family income to $25,000.

However, the administration proposal essentially raises the grant level of all previously eligible by $250 and gives a flat grant of $250 to those in the $16,000 to $25,000 class. This is like a refundable credit with a cap on eligibility at $25,000. Its cost (in 1980 dollars) is approximately $1.2 billion. While it does not give aid to the wealthiest families, it treats the broad class of families in the $16,000 to $25,000 range identically. The Senate proposal, on the other hand, maintains the link between income and size of grant by letting the grant level decline gradually and proportionately from the $8000 to $25,000 income levels. This has the advantage of concentrating the incremental aid to families at the lower part of the "middle income" range. Its cost (in 1980 dollars) is $1.4 billion, slightly higher than that of the administration proposal. Of the different subsidy plans we have mentioned, this is the one most likely to increase educational enrollments.

In this section we have identified two sources of market failure with regard to educational investments: inadequate borrowing opportunities and positive external benefits of the investments. We have looked at two general types of policies (student loans and student subsidies) which can alleviate these imperfections to some extent. However, these are merely examples of the problems and policies involved in the provision of higher education. We have not touched upon the rationale for having a mixed public and private system, the important research roles of higher education institutions, or other aspects of the supply side of this market.[26] Our point is to emphasize the policy

---

[25] Eligibility criteria for the program include both income and assets.

[26] For more reading on these issues, see Marc Nerlove, "On Tuition and the Costs of Higher Education: Prolegoma to a Conceptual Framework," *Journal of Political Economy, 80,* No. 3, part II, May–June 1972, pp. S178–S218; David W. Breneman and Chester E. Finn, Jr. (eds.), *Public Policy and Private Higher Education* (Washington, D.C.: The Brookings Institution, 1978); Fred

relevance of understanding capital formation and capital markets by linking it in this section to problems of educational policy. In the following section, we turn to a quite different policy area—energy—to reinforce the same basic point.

THE ALLOCATION OF NATURAL RESOURCES

The logic of utility maximization, along with the separation theorem of perfect capital markets, implies that investment choices will be made to maximize the present value of income. In this section we apply that logic to an analysis of the markets which allocate natural resources over time. There is a finite amount of oil in the world, for example, and we seek to understand how private markets allocate this oil. Why has it not been used up already? For how much longer can we expect supplies to flow? At what prices? What are the likely effects of policies like price decontrol and the windfall profits tax on intertemporal oil allocation? Although the issues involved in answering such questions and considering policy in relation to them are complex, the analysis reviewed here is basic to an understanding of them.

We begin with a very simple model of a renewable natural resource; when to cut trees in order to maximize the present value of lumber from them. This model reinforces two general points: One of the factors involved in the creation of capital is the time cost of deferred consumption, and the amount of time that will be used varies with the interest rate. No supplier will make the investment without compensation for this cost, and the compensation should not be thought of as economic rent.

Renewable Resources: Tree Models

Imagine that a small amount of labor is used to plant a tree and then to harvest the lumber from it when it is cut down. The price per board-foot of lumber is the same over time. Given that it is planted, when should the tree be cut? Let P be the price per board-foot and $Q(t)$ be the quantity of lumber (which increases over time as the tree grows). If the cost of cutting down the tree is assumed to be zero for the moment, then the net value of the lumber at any time t can be described by the following equation:

$$F(t) = PQ(t)$$

The increase in the value of the tree from one period to the next is

$$\Delta F(t) = P\Delta Q(t)$$

Thompson and Gary Fiske, "One More Solution to the Problems of Higher Education Finance," *Policy Analysis, 4,* No. 4, fall 1978, pp. 577–580; and J. Froomkin, D. Jamison, and R. Radner, *Education as an Industry,* National Bureau of Economic Research (Cambridge, Mass.: Ballinger Publishing Company, 1976).

One way to consider when to cut the tree (or equivalently, how much capital to create) is to think of the alternatives. At any time, one can simply let the tree grow. We have just seen that the increase in net value from this strategy is $\Delta F(t)$. Another alternative would be to cut the tree down, sell the lumber, and put the receipts in the bank where they earn the market rate of interest r. In that case the increase in value is $rF(t)$. When the tree is growing rapidly [$\Delta F(t)$ is big], letting it grow (sometimes called capital deepening) is the better investment. Past a certain point, however, the tree's growth slows down and its natural increase in value will be less than the cut-and-bank strategy. In order to maximize the value of the tree investment, one should let the tree grow until just that point at which[27]

$$\Delta F(t) = rF(t)$$

or
$$r = \frac{\Delta F(t)}{F(t)}$$

Once the tree is planted, in other words, its present value is maximized at a time when the proportional growth in its value $\Delta F(t)/F(t)$ equals the market rate of interest. The initial planting costs are not irrelevant to the decision, however; the maximum present value (given the tree is planted) could be a negative number. Thus, the result must be qualified: One should plant the tree only if there is at least one $t \neq 0$ at which the present value is positive. Provided the planting condition is met, the investment time is determined by the proportional growth rule.

It is easy to extend this model to the case when cut-down costs C are positive and, for simplicity, assumed to be constant.[28] The net value of the tree at any time is then

$$F(t) = PQ(t) - C$$

The increase in the value of the tree from one period to the next is independent of the cut-down and planting costs; it is the same as before:

$$\Delta F(t) = P\Delta Q(t)$$

---

[27] In the calculus version using continuous discounting, the same result is easy to formulate. The present value of the investment at any time t is PV $= F(t)e^{-rt} - C_0$ where C_0 is the initial planting cost. To maximize this, we take the derivative with respect to t and set it equal to zero:

$$\frac{\partial \text{PV}}{\partial t} = \left(\frac{\partial F}{\partial t}\right)e^{-rt} - re^{-rt}F(t) = 0$$

By dividing both sides by e^{-rt} and rearranging, we have

$$r = \frac{\partial F/\partial t}{F(t)}$$

[28] This would not be true if, say, the real wage of labor were increasing over time.

This time the cut-and-bank strategy is not so profitable; after cut-down costs, only $F(t) - C$ can be put in the bank. Thus, the cut-and-bank strategy will yield $r[F(t) - C]$. Whenever $\Delta F(t) > r[F(t) - C]$, it is more profitable to let the tree grow rather than cut it down and bank the proceeds. In order to maximize the value of the tree, one should let it grow until

$$\Delta F(t) = r[F(t) - C]$$

If we divide each side of this equation by $F(t)$, we see that

$$\frac{\Delta F(t)}{F(t)} = \frac{r[F(t) - C]}{F(t)}$$

Since $[F(t) - C]/F(t) < 1$,

$$\frac{\Delta F(t)}{F(t)} < r$$

That is, when there are cut-down costs, the maximum value of the tree occurs when its proportional rate of growth is *less* than the interest rate: One lets the tree grow a little longer in response to an increase in cut-down costs.[29]

---

[29] This can be seen more precisely in the calculus version of this model with positive cut-down costs. The present value of the tree at any time t (with continuous discounting) is

$$PV = F(t)e^{-rt} - Ce^{-rt} - C_0$$

To maximize, we take the partial derivative with respect to t and set it equal to zero and thereby derive the equilibrium condition:

$$\frac{\partial PV}{\partial t} = \left(\frac{\partial F}{\partial t}\right)e^{-rt} - rF(t)e^{-rt} + rCe^{-rt} = 0$$

Dividing both sides by e^{-rt} and simplifying gives us

$$\frac{\partial F}{\partial t} = r[F(t) - C]$$

To see how the optimal t changes as C increases, we differentiate the above equilibrium condition totally:

$$\frac{\partial^2 F}{\partial t^2}\frac{\partial t}{\partial C} = r\left(\frac{\partial F}{\partial t}\frac{\partial t}{\partial C} - 1\right)$$

Solving for $\partial t/\partial C$ gives us

$$\frac{\partial t}{\partial C} = \frac{-r}{(\partial^2 F/\partial t^2) - r(\partial F/\partial t)}$$

Since $r > 0$, the numerator is negative. The denominator also is negative as long as the tree grows ($\partial F/\partial t > 0$), and the tree grows more slowly over time ($\partial^2 F/\partial t^2 < 0$). Thus, the whole fraction is positive; the optimal time to let a tree grow increases in response to increased cut-down costs.

Finally, let us note that, so far, we have ignored *replanting*. The solutions we have discussed for the planting and cutting of trees are correct only if land is not scarce. But if land is scarce, efficiency requires us to use it to maximize the present value of the profits from it over *all* time. This changes the solution by reducing the time each tree grows. Intuitively, the earlier solutions ignored the cost of pushing back the time at which profits from replanting would accrue. When that cost is taken into account, we cut the tree down a bit sooner.[30]

The tree model is an example of a special type of investment sometimes referred to as *point input, point output,* where the terms refer to the technologi-

---

[30] This point and its solution were first recognized by Martin Faustmann in 1849 (cited by Paul Samuelson, "Economics of Forestry in an Evolving Society," *Economic Inquiry, 14,* December 1976, pp. 466–492).

We show the Faustmann solution in a simple model in which we let $G(t)$ be the net value of the tree at time t (i.e., the value after paying cut-down costs). Then we wish to maximize the net present value of the yield from timber production over all time:

$$PV = G(t) \left[e^{-rt} + (e^{-rt})^2 + \cdots + (e^{-rt})^n + \cdots \right]$$

For positive r and t, the expression in brackets is an infinite series with a finite sum $= e^{-rt}/(1 - e^{-rt})$. Thus, we can simplify:

$$PV = \frac{G(t)e^{-rt}}{1 - e^{-rt}}$$

We maximize this by taking the partial derivative with respect to t and setting it equal to zero:

$$\frac{\partial PV}{\partial t} = \frac{[(\partial G/\partial t)e^{-rt} - re^{-rt}G(t)](1 - e^{-rt}) - re^{-rt}[G(t)e^{-rt}]}{(1 - e^{-rt})^2} = 0$$

Since the denominator does not equal zero, the numerator must. We can simplify the numerator by factoring out e^{-rt} from each term and dividing both sides of the equation by it. That leaves us with

$$\left[\frac{\partial G}{\partial t} - rG(t)\right](1 - e^{-rt}) - rG(t)e^{-rt} = 0$$

Moving the terms with $G(t)$ to the right-hand side gives us

$$\frac{\partial G}{\partial t}(1 - e^{-rt}) = rG(t)$$

or, finally,

$$\frac{\partial G/\partial t}{G(t)} = \frac{r}{1 - e^{-rt}}$$

Since the denominator on the right is positive but less than 1,

$$\frac{\partial G/\partial t}{G(t)} > r$$

That is, the optimal time to cut the tree when replanting is considered occurs when the proportional growth in the tree's value is greater than the interest rate (or before the optimal time without considering replanting).

cal fact that an initial outlay of resources is made and the output (and therefore income return) comes in one lump at the end. In such a model there is an important relation between time and the interest rate: The optimal time for the point input, point output investment is reduced by an increase in the interest rate.[31] This accords with the general rule that investment decreases with increases in the interest rate.

A Note on Investment Time and Interest Rates: Switching and Reswitching

However, one cannot generalize about the relation between the length of time of investments and interest rates. Under some circumstances, longer investments may substitute for shorter ones in response to a rise in interest rates. The basic reason for what may seem like a counterintuitive result is that the time cost depends upon the quantity of resources diverted from current consumption, and this quantity can vary during the "life" of an investment.

To understand this, first it is helpful to mention other investments besides the point input, point output ones. Some crops may require continuous attention while growing and then yield output all at once (continuous input, point output). An oil well may have high initial drilling expenses and then return oil output over many periods (point input, continuous output, to an approximation). Many investments, like building an airplane or a new modernized factory, may involve years of construction and provide years of output (continuous input, continuous output). To produce any given future output, there may be alternative investment opportunities of these different types which could be used. We use the criterion of maximizing present value to identify the economically most desirable ones.[32]

---

[31] We assume the technology satisfies the first- and second-order maximization conditions at a market interest rate r. Consider the simplest tree model. The first-order condition, equating the proportional growth in value of the investment to the interest rate, is a necessary one. To be sufficient, the second-order condition must be satisfied: the investment grows at a decreasing rate over time. Define $s(t)$ as the rate of growth at time t:

$$s(t) = \frac{F'(t)}{F(t)}$$

Then the second-order condition requires that $s'(t) < 0$. Otherwise, the investor is at a minimum (or a turning point), but not the maximum present value. Thus, in the neighborhood of the optimum, the rate of growth must be decreasing with time. This means that for a small decrease (increase) in the market interest rate r, the time to hold the investment must increase (decrease) if the first-order condition is to be satisfied.

[32] In the presence of capital market imperfections, the use of this criterion may be difficult or even inappropriate. For example, suppose a firm cannot borrow unlimited funds at the market rate of interest and has a limited amount of capital to ration. The opportunity cost of that capital in one investment use depends upon the alternative internal investment opportunities, and the proper discount rate must be determined simultaneously with the optimal investments. This can be done by methods of integer programming, among others. For a discussion of this, see William J. Baumol, *Economic Theory and Operations Analysis* (Englewood Cliffs, N.J.: Prentice-Hall Inc., 1977), chap. 25. In other situations, e.g., when individuals face different interest rates for borrowing and

TABLE 14-2
TWO TECHNOLOGIES FOR AGING WINE TO BE SOLD AT
TIME t

	Treatment cost in each period		
Years before output	**$t-3$**	**$t-2$**	**$t-1$**
Process 1	0	100	0
Process 2	43	0	58

Suppose, for example, that we have two processes for aging wine quickly. In process 1 the wine is treated after crushing and then left to age for 2 years, at which time it is ready for sale. In process 2 the wine is crushed and aged "naturally" (with no costly treatment) for 2 years and is then processed and aged for 1 more year. Consumers, wine experts, and the FDA all agree that the outputs from the processes are identical. Suppose that the nominal values and times of the resources invested with each process are as shown in Table 14-2. Which process has the least cost (measured in dollars at the time the output is ready for sale)? We know the costs (per unit of output) are calculated as follows:

$$C(1) = 100(1 + r)^2$$
$$C(2) = 43(1 + r)^3 + 58(1 + r)$$

If $r = 0.05$, then $C(1) = \$110.25$ and $C(2) = \$110.68$, and process 1 has the least cost. However, if $r = 0.15$, then $C(1) = \$132.25$ and $C(2) = \$132.10$, and process 2 has the least cost. It can be shown that cost-minimizing investors will switch processes when the interest rate rises above 10.58 percent.[33] But more startling is that they will *reswitch* if the interest rate rises above 21.98 percent. If $r = 0.23$, for example, then $C(1) = \$151.29$ and $C(2) = \$151.36$: the first process is cheaper again!

In this example, process 2 is the longer investment, in the sense that it takes 3 years to produce the output whereas process 1 requires only 2 years. But what is omitted from this usage of length is that the quantity of specific resources and the time they are invested differ in each process. Even though the quantity of physical resources each uses is fixed, we cannot judge which uses "more" resources without an interest rate to account for the time differences. And, we have seen, the judgment varies with the interest rate. Finally, we have seen that there is no simple generalization of how investors

---

lending, the separation property does not hold and they, like Robinson Crusoe, must go back to the basics of maximizing utility subject to the constraints. For some examples of this, see P. R. G. Layard and A. A. Walters, *Microeconomic Theory* (New York: McGraw-Hill Book Company, 1978), chap. 12.

[33] Find the values of r which make $C(1) - C(2) = 0$; the equation can be solved by the quadratic formula.

will change the length of their investments in response to interest rate changes.[34]

The Allocation of Exhaustible Resources: Oil and the Windfall Profits Tax Revisited

With these cautions let us extend the tree analysis to demonstrate the optimal pricing pattern for an exhaustible resource like oil. The first question we will consider is how a perfect market would set prices to allocate the oil.[35] Then we will consider the actual imperfect market, with attention to the effect of a windfall profits tax on the allocation.

Let the unknown price of oil at any time t be denoted $P(t)$. Suppose we start with an exceedingly simple model in which there are no extraction costs of pumping the fixed supply of oil and the market rate of interest is r. Competitive suppliers will allocate their oil reserves in order to maximize present value. This implies, for a given price path, that any supplier is indifferent on the margin between pumping one more unit in the current period instead of in any future period. (The incremental present value must be the same.) In particular, the result we saw in the tree model must hold for this marginal unit:

$$\frac{\Delta P(t)}{P(t)} = r$$

or, equivalently,

$$\Delta P(t) = rP(t)$$

Note that in the bottom equation the term on the right can be thought of as the interest the supplier would earn in return for pumping one more unit of oil today and "banking" the proceeds until tomorrow. The term on the left is the "interest" the supplier earns by leaving the unit in the ground and letting its price appreciate. Suppose the equation did not hold. If, for example, the "banking" strategy were yielding a greater return, suppliers would sell more oil today. That would cause a reduction in the market price today relative to tomorrow and thus raise $P(t)$ until equality between the two terms was reached.

The above condition implies (for discrete time periods) that the price path is a geometric progression. That is, it must have the form

$$P(t) = P_0 (1 + r)^t$$

where P_0 is any constant greater than 0. If that is so,

---

[34] The reswitching phenomenon has caused much discussion in the literature on capital theory. The discussion is sometimes referred to as the Cambridge-Cambridge controversy (involving economists from Cambridge, Massachusetts, and Cambridge, England, although others have participated as well), and bears on, among other matters, the measurement of the capital stock for econometric modeling. For a review, see Paul Samuelson, "A Summing Up," *Quarterly Journal of Economics, 80,* November 1966, pp. 568–583.

[35] This analysis is based largely upon the article by William D. Nordhaus, "The Allocation of Energy Resources," *Brookings Papers on Economic Activity,* No. 3, 1973, pp. 529–570.

$$\Delta P(t) = P_0 (1 + r)^{t+1} - P_0 (1 + r)^t$$
$$= (1 + r) P(t) - P(t)$$
$$= rP(t)$$

In other words, any geometric price path satisfies the one condition we have identified.[36]

The other conditions necessary to achieve the efficient allocation of a perfect market involve accounting for the finite stock of reserves and consumer demand. We handle this in a very simple way. Let $R(t)$ be the amount of oil left in reserve at time t. Suppose we specify (for the moment) that all allocation is to take place within a time horizon of T years. Then we specify that

$$R(t) > 0 \qquad t < T$$
$$R(t) = 0 \qquad t = T$$

In other words, the last unit of oil is not used until the final period.

This terminal condition plays the role of equating demand with supply and establishing a unique price path. If the price path is such that the constant P_0 is too low, demand will be too great in the earlier periods and the oil will run out before $t = T$. If P_0 is too high, $R(T)$ will be positive (there will be unused oil at the end). Thus, only one value for P_0 will satisfy the terminal requirement; our two conditions determine the efficient price path.

Let us illustrate this with a simple example. Suppose there are two periods, the interest rate is 10 percent, and there are available 100 units of oil competitively supplied with zero extraction costs. The demand for oil in each period is

$$Q(1) = 115 - P(1)$$
$$Q(0) = 90 - P(0)$$

The first condition for an efficient allocation is that the price path of oil make suppliers indifferent on the margin between supplying or holding an additional unit of oil in the initial period:

$$P(1) - P(0) = rP(0)$$

Since $r = 0.10$,

$$P(1) = 1.1P(0) \tag{i}$$

---

[36] In continuous time, the price path is exponential where $P(t) = P_0 e^{rt}$ and P_0 is any constant. This follows from the derivative property:

$$P'(t) = rP_0 e^{rt}$$

and therefore

$$\frac{P'(t)}{P(t)} = r$$

The second condition, or terminal condition, is that the sum of demands over time just equals the supply:

$$Q(1) + Q(0) = 100$$

Substituting from the demand equations gives us

$$205 - P(1) - P(0) = 100 \qquad \text{(ii)}$$

On substituting from (i) in (ii), we solve and find

$$2.1P(0) = 105$$
$$P(0) = 50 \rightarrow Q(0) = 40$$
$$P(1) = 55 \rightarrow Q(1) = 60$$

The prices in this model are sometimes called *royalties* because they arise from the scarcity value of the oil resources. All the price *increases* in this model reflect social opportunity costs: payments to oil owners for preserving the oil and thus foregoing the opportunities available from increased current income. However, the *level* of the price path P_0 is an economic rent that arises from rationing a fixed supply to meet the aggregate demand. (The identical intertemporal supply could be induced with any value of $P_0 > 0$.[37]) Now let us add a small wrinkle to this simple model and allow extraction costs to be positive. By using $y(t)$ to denote the scarcity value or royalty (which may or may not result in some economic rent for suppliers) and Z to denote the (constant) marginal extraction cost, we have

$$P(t) = y(t) + Z$$

Again as in the tree model, equilibrium requires that the price increase over time equal the interest that could be earned by the sell-and-bank strategy:

$$\Delta P(t) = r[P(t) - Z]$$
or
$$\Delta P(t) = ry(t)$$

and on dividing both sides by $P(t)$, we have

$$\frac{\Delta P(t)}{P(t)} = \frac{ry(t)}{P(t)} < r$$

The inequality on the right-hand side follows from $y(t) < P(t)$. In English, *the*

[37] This is an oversimplification which ignores initial exploration and drilling costs. Even with no uncertainty as to location, P_0 must be high enough to make the present value of the oil minus drilling costs be positive. Also, costly exploration will not be undertaken unless the costs can be recovered through oil prices.

proportional increase in the price of an exhaustible resource along the efficient path is always less than the interest rate when there are positive extraction costs.

Now let us extend the model to substitute the fascinating prospect of a backstop technology for our fixed-horizon assumption. That is, it should be clear that if exhaustible resources are the only way to provide energy, there is no finite horizon *T* beyond which we need not worry. The potential savior from this plight is what Nordhaus refers to as the backstop technology: a technology like solar, geothermal, or nuclear which is expensive in terms of the capital cost per Btu of safely produced energy but which runs on resources that are for all intents and purposes unlimited and free (e.g., perhaps the sun).

Suppose that, as in our first model, oil is "costless" to produce but finite in quantity. The backstop technology uses *K* units of capital per Btu equivalent, but it can be used to produce unlimited quantities of energy. How should society allocate its energy resources, given consumer demands? Obviously, the free stuff should be used first. Let the switch point, where oil is depleted and the backstop technology is brought into use, be denoted T_s. At that point, efficiency requires that the price of a Btu from oil equal the competitive price of obtaining the Btu with the backstop technology:

$$P(T_s) = (r + \delta)K$$

where δ is the depreciation rate of the capital equipment. The expression on the right-hand side is just the opportunity cost to society of using the backstop technology.

But now that we know the price of oil at one time T_s, we know the price at each time: It is simply the switch price discounted back to the relevant period;

$$P(t) = P(T_s)(1 + r)^{-(T_s - t)}$$

or equivalently, $$P(t) = (r + \delta)K(1 + r)^{-(T_s - t)}$$

The switch date plays the same role as choosing the constant P_0 in the first model: It must be picked to balance the aggregate demand with the available supply of oil. If it is too early, the price path necessary for intertemporal supply equilibrium (discounting backwards from the proposed switch date) will result in too great a price today. Too little oil will be demanded currently and there will be unused oil at the switch point, which is inefficient. If the switch point is too late, the oil will be used up too quickly (before it is reached).

To sum up this analysis, *the efficient price for an exhaustible resource today should consist of its marginal production cost plus a royalty component. The size of the royalty component is determined by the cost of the backstop technology, the interest rate, and the switch date (which ensures the aggregate balancing of demand and supply). The more expensive the backstop and the earlier the switch date, the larger the royalty component of the current price. The effect of an interest rate change on current price is ambiguous.*[38]

Of course, there are many reasons why actual markets for exhaustible resources deviate from the perfect markets required to achieve efficient allocation. One is uncertainty; the backstop technology is not yet known. Another is the absence of long-term future markets and the myopia of economic agents: There is no mechanism, like a global planner, to ensure that the set of demands along the actual price path adds up to the available supplies for any reasonable (or safe) expectation of a switch point. A third reason, which we discussed in Chapter 12, is imperfect competition in some energy sectors like that due to the OPEC cartel.

But this does not mean that nothing can be done. Indeed, Nordhaus went on from his theoretical analysis to construct a large simulation model of the world energy market. One of his objectives was to derive rough estimates for the efficient price of petroleum based on the best available knowledge of resource availability, production costs with currently known technologies (including the cost of meeting all environmental standards), and alternative assumptions about when a backstop technology would be available.

The model was run with alternative assumptions about world trade: one with free trade and the other assuming the United States has to rely entirely upon its own natural resources. He offered two conclusions that seemed to withstand all the sensitivity tests he made: (1) The economy can wait about 100 years before it need get serious about production with nuclear technologies. (Better to worry about synthetic fuels for the rest of this century.) (2) The 1970 prices for petroleum were well above the efficient prices even under the self-sufficiency assumptions, and thus there is no long-term rationale for policy intervention to increase them dramatically.

Of course, this analysis was undertaken before OPEC began to exert the considerable monopoly power of its cartel. Continued analysis in light of the OPEC problem may (or may not) suggest different conclusions.[39] Nevertheless, the study demonstrates that what may seem like esoteric theoretical concepts can be brought to bear on pragmatic and important issues of public policy.

The theoretical oil allocation model can be used to clarify a point raised in Chapter 12 about the windfall profits tax. Because the tax applies to new oil as

---

[38] To see this, we use the continuous time version of the efficient price path $P(t) = (r + \delta)Ke^{-r(T_s - t)}$ and differentiate:

$$\frac{\partial P(0)}{\partial r} = Ke^{-r(T_s)} - (T_s)(r + \delta)Ke^{-r(T_s)} = Ke^{-rT_s}[1 - T_s(r + \delta)]$$

Since K and the exponential term are positive, the whole expression is positive when $T_s(r + \delta) < 1$ and negative when $T_s(r + \delta) > 1$.

[39] In early 1981 Nordhaus released a new study which argues that industrialized countries should place a substantial tax on oil to be implemented by 1990. The tax is intended to minimize the harmful effects of OPEC price racheting, according to the *International Herald Tribune*, January 20, 1982, p. 11, cols. 5, 6.

well as to existing wells, we know it deters exploration and drilling for new sources to some extent. But the question remains whether, if applied only to wells operating before price decontrol, there are any adverse supply effects or the tax captures only economic rent.

Put simply, the flow of oil from existing domestic wells, which typically average from 15 to 20 years of useful production, will change in response to a change in *relative* intertemporal prices. Therefore, we must consider whether a windfall profits tax alters the relative prices from what they would be otherwise (i.e., under pure decontrol). Two extreme cases clarify the possible effects: a permanent windfall profits tax and a short-run temporary one.

Let us take a simple two-period example in which the interest rate is $r = 0.10$, the extraction cost per unit is \$0.50, and the pure decontrol prices are $P_0 = \$2.00$ and $P_1 = \$2.15$. In this initial equilibrium before the windfall profits tax, oil suppliers are indifferent to the pump-now-and-bank strategy and the hold-and-sell-later one. That is,

$$r(P_0 - Z) = P_1 - P_0$$
$$0.10(2.00 - 0.50) = 2.15 - 2.00$$
$$0.15 = 0.15$$

Now impose a 50 percent windfall profits tax on the difference between actual price and the base. Assume the base level (from the controlled period) is \$1.00. After the tax, the supplier has less left over to bank from selling today: The tax is \$0.50, so only \$1.00 rather than \$1.50 can be banked. This reduces the capital value but does not necessarily change the use of the well. Allocation will be unchanged if the after-tax return of the hold-and-sell-later strategy equals the \$0.10 that can be earned by the pump-now-and-bank strategy. If the base remains at \$1.00, the supplier does *worse* by holding: The tax is \$0.575 next period, leaving only \$1.075 after paying extraction costs. This causes an *increase* in the amount of oil pumped today relative to tomorrow. If the base is adjusted upward each period, this distortion can be removed and there will be no effect of the tax on the allocation pattern from existing wells.[40] This is the ideal windfall profits tax.

---

[40] In the simple case of zero extraction costs the base should be adjusted upward by the interest rate for each period. Assume the windfall tax is assessed on prices above the base level B_i defined for the ith period. The after-tax equilibrium condition is

$$r[P_0 - t(P_0 - B_0)] = [P_1 - t(P_1 - B_1)] - [P_0 - t(P_0 - B_0)]$$

We rewrite this slightly to make the next step more transparent:

$$rP_0(1 - t) + rtB_0 = (P_1 - P_0)(1 - t) + t(B_1 - B_0)$$

Recall the pretax equilibrium condition:

$$rP_0 = P_1 - P_0$$

However, suppose the windfall profits tax is only *temporary:* it will be removed after the first period. Then the return from the hold-and-sell-later strategy skyrockets, and the supply of pumped oil for use in the current period will be reduced in order to preserve it for more profitable sale in the future.

It is difficult to judge whether the actual windfall profits tax, designed to last for 10 years, is "permanent" enough to avoid significant adverse intertemporal consequences on oil supply from old wells. If the average well life is normally 15 to 20 years, the tax probably does cover the bulk of the remaining lives of the wells (if pumped as usual). Under any reasonable discount rates, it is certainly not worth shutting the wells down and waiting 10 years. However, the *marginal* unit of oil pumped today is no longer equal in value to the marginal unit pumped in year 11, and one should expect some supply reduction from these sources (negligible at first, more noticeable in year 10). By the time the tax expires, however, the residual stock of old oil will be a much smaller proportion of U.S. consumption.

Although President Carter requested a permanent windfall tax, Congress provided the 10-year design with a gradual phasing out of the tax. This phasing should make the intertemporal allocation smoother than sudden cutoff. The incoming Reagan administration, by announcing that the time period of the tax might be shortened, could have exacerbated the adverse effects of a temporary tax. A better strategy which is consistent with the values of the new administration is simply to ask for the removal of the tax on new oil. However, one should bear in mind that this works against the objective of oil conservation.

SUMMARY

In this chapter we explored policy problems involving resource allocation over time. We first reviewed the theory of perfect capital markets, in which individuals are free to borrow or lend at the market rate of interest. Interest rates play the role of the prices used to determine relative allocations among time periods. These allocative decisions include the investment of resources for

---

Note that if we multiply each side of this equation by $1 - t$, we have terms identical with those in the second equation above (the first term on each side of the equation). Therefore, they cancel out and we are left with

$$rtB_0 = t(B_1 - B_0)$$

On dividing both sides by t and rearranging, we have

$$B_1 = (1 + r)B_0$$

With positive extraction costs, a similar derivation leads to this adjustment condition:

$$B_1 = (1 + r)B_0 - rZ = B_0 + r(B_0 - Z)$$

In other words, the base adjustment, like the price increase, is proportionately less than the interest rate.

wealth accumulation, and the amount of wealth to consume in each time period.

For each individual, utility maximization requires that wealth be maximized. Given an endowment of real resources and a set of investment possibilities, the individual maximizes wealth by undertaking all investments which have a positive present value (evaluated at the market rate of interest). Since this part of utility maximization is independent of the individual's preferences (the separation property), it can be delegated to experts in wealth accumulation. (For example, the individual can buy stock in a corporation or pay taxes to a government and let corporate or government management undertake the real investments in new factories or new roads.) Once wealth is maximized, the individual chooses whatever consumption pattern maximizes utility subject to the constraint that the present value of all consumption (including bequests) equal wealth.

The market rate of interest is determined by equilibrating the aggregate demand for investment with the aggregate supply of saving. The aggregate demand for investment at any interest rate is determined by the initial endowments to each individual and the investment opportunities locus. This can be thought of as the demand to allocate real resources to uses other than current consumption. The aggregate supply of savings at any interest rate is determined by consumption choices; it may be thought of as the residual resources left over after allocating the necessary resources to satisfy current consumption demands. The equilibrium interest rate is the one which equates the investment demand to the savings supply.

There are many reasons relevant to public policy making why private capital markets fail to allocate resources efficiently. The first imperfection the chapter explores is the underinvestment of resources by private markets in the development of human potential, with particular reference to higher education. The market fails because there are positive external benefits from these investments and because there are insufficient loans to finance the investments (as a consequence of the lack of legal collateral). These lead to policies of tuition subsidization and guaranteed loans, respectively, although the proper mix between them is an unsettled and perhaps analytically unsolvable issue. The equity implications of these failures are particularly significant, because individuals from families with relatively low current incomes are most likely to be unable to afford the current burden of investing despite its future payoffs.

A particularly interesting form of student loan is the income-contingent type introduced by Yale University. It differs from conventional loans in that its payback period is quite extensive (up to 35 years rather than 7 to 10 years) and the amount paid back is an increasing function (up to a limit) of actual future income. Thus, the loan is also an insurance policy which protects the borrower against the event of a low future income. The insurance feature and the extended repayment period (with its tax advantages) make this plan attractive to students.

Based on the characteristics of the student group to be covered, the sponsoring government or institution has a wide latitude in choosing repayment rate and payment period combinations which allow it to break even. The primary risk to the sponsor is that the difference between money income growth and the interest costs of the borrowed funds will not be constant over the payback period. Yale tries to minimize the risk by reborrowing every 6 months and assuming money income and interest rates will change commensurately. More experience is needed before the success of this method is known.

In recent years, proposed changes in federal policy have focused on increasing tuition subsidization rather than improving student loan opportunities. The tuition tax credits proposed in many bills are regressive (even if refundable), in the sense that the bulk of the benefits would accrue to students from the wealthiest families. Thus for the total dollars of subsidization offered, relatively few new enrollments would result. The more interested one is in expanding educational opportunities, the more the funds must be targeted at the groups whose investment decision can be altered. Alternative proposals to expand the basic educational opportunity grants program are more oriented toward this objective. (For example, families with incomes above $24,000 are excluded.)

A second imperfection in the markets that allocate resources over time is primarily an intergenerational one: the inadequate representation of the demands of future generations for current resources. We explore this in the context of the intertemporal allocation of oil. First we build up an understanding of the relation between wealth maximization and the supply of natural resources. Using trees as an example of a renewable resource, we show that the time at which trees are cut and replanted (to maximize their present value) depends on the growth rate of the trees, the planting and cut-down costs, and the market rate of interest. We then show that similar relations exist for exhaustible resources like oil.

The efficient price path for the exhaustible resource, oil, should rise over time because its scarcity value increases (or, equivalently, because the compensation for holding it must increase with the length of the holding period). This royalty component, at any given time, is a function that increases with the cost of alternative energy sources and with the nearness of the switch date to an alternate source. It is also affected by changes in the interest rate. (An increase in the interest rate reduces the current royalty if the switch date is far off and increases it otherwise.)

In the actual market for oil, there is no mechanism (like a global planner) to ensure that the price path is one which balances intertemporal demand with the recoverable supply of oil reserves. Simulation models can be used to estimate the optimal price path based on the best knowledge of reserves, estimated future demand, and the costs of alternative energy sources. Then current prices, and policies to affect them, can be considered in terms of the model implications. The work of Nordhaus, as an example, suggests that current efforts should be concentrated on developing synthetic fuels rather than nuclear power.

A simple extension of the oil allocation model is helpful in predicting the intertemporal effects of a windfall profits tax on old oil wells. If the tax causes the after-tax intertemporal rate of return to deviate from its equilibrium level, the time at which oil is pumped will be affected. It is possible to design a permanent windfall profits tax which does not cause distortion from this condition, but a temporary tax inevitably causes some distortion. The actual windfall tax, which will last for approximately 10 years, is unlikely to have any significant impact on the allocation of old oil, although there may be some noticeable hoarding of old oil in the years immediately preceding the expiration of the tax.

EXERCISES

14-1   A house can be rented in an uncontrolled market for a profit of $20,000 this period and $20,000 next period. (There are only two periods.)

    a   If the market interest rate is 10 percent, what is the most you would expect a housing investor to offer for the house? Explain.

    b   Suppose the investor in (*a*) buys the house for his maximum offer and rent controls are then imposed, allowing the new owner to charge in each period only the operating expenses actually incurred plus $5000. Upset by the effect of rent controls on his profits, the new owner considers selling the house. Now what is the maximum a housing investor would bid for it? (Answer: $9545.45)

    c   Is there any economic incentive under this rent control law to alter such expenditures as building maintenance? Explain.

14-2 ∇Suppose a tree costs $300 to plant and has a lumber content the net value of which (excluding planting costs) after t years of growth is described by the following equation:

$$V = 60t - t^2 \qquad 0 \le t \le 30$$

    a   The continuous discount rate is 5 percent. What would you do to maximize the present value? (Answer: $t = 13.94$; PV $= \$19.80$)

    b   How would your decision change if the continuous discount rate were 10 percent? (Answer: $t = 0$, PV $= 0$)

14-3   Suppose 1000 units of oil are competitively allocated over three time periods. The oil is costless to extract. The demand for oil in each period is:

$$
\begin{aligned}
Q_0 &= \ 900 - P_0 \\
Q_1 &= 1000 - P_1 \\
Q_2 &= 1100 - P_2
\end{aligned}
$$

    a   If the interest rate is 8 percent, what are the prices and quantities at the competitive equilibrium? (Partial answer: $Q_2 = 381.42$)

    b   Suppose the government imposes a $200 excess profits tax per unit of oil in the period in which the oil is consumed. Calculate the new equilibrium consumer prices and quantities. What is the efficiency cost (in present value terms) of this tax? (Partial answer: The efficiency cost is $219.21)

    c   Suppose the excess profits tax is $200 in the current period and rises by 8 percent in each of the next two periods. Calculate the equilibrium prices and quantities. What is the efficiency cost of this tax? (Partial answer: $P_0 = \$616.07$)

APPENDIX ONE: Uncertain Future Prices and Index Construction

A major cost involved in intertemporal resource allocation is that of uncertainty concerning future price levels caused by inflation. One may know that a $5000 investment now will return $10,000 in 5 years, but one does not know how much consumption can be bought with $10,000 in 5 years. The uncertainty makes intertemporal resource allocation choices very difficult. How can one decide which investments to undertake if their real returns are highly uncertain or how much to consume rather than save if one is highly uncertain about one's own real wealth level?

One mechanism that is frequently used to respond to this type of uncertainty is *indexation*. Roughly speaking, this is a method of adjusting a nominal amount of dollars over time in order to hold their purchasing power constant. For example, Social Security payments are indexed each year. Many other public and private programs have indexed payments; examples are food stamps, pension plans, labor contracts, and state grants to local public schools (to account for local variation in education costs). In some countries (e.g., England) there are indexed bonds which adjust nominal interest payments to maintain their purchasing power. About 30 percent of all federal expenditures are indexed currently.

All of these indexation plans are intended to make the real level of expected future receipts and expenditures more certain and thereby give individuals a better sense of their own wealth and a clearer picture of the consequences of alternative intertemporal resource allocations. Yet the construction of these indices is often controversial. For example, social security is adjusted in accordance with changes in the Consumer Price Index (CPI). But it is not clear that this index accurately captures the change in the cost of living experienced by retired individuals. In this appendix we review some of the basic principles of index construction and then some of the problems which plague index construction in practice.

A starting point for understanding index construction is to look at the *Laspeyre and Paasche indices* as they apply to one person in a two-good economy whose tastes do not change over time.[41] In Figure 14A1-1 we show at point E an individual's choice of goods X and Y in period 1 at prices P_{X1} and P_{Y1}. In period 2 we observe the individual at point F purchasing X_2 and Y_2 at prices P_{X2} and P_{Y2}. Can we estimate whether the person is better off or worse off in period 2 without knowing the exact location of the indifference curves?

The Laspeyre *quantity index* (price is fixed, quantity varies) can help us to make the comparison. Using period 1 prices as a base we compute

$$L_1 = P_{X1}X_1 + P_{Y1}Y_1$$
$$L_2 = P_{X1}X_2 + P_{Y1}Y_2$$

---

[41] These are also used in empirical work to estimate the "compensation" necessary to keep an individual indifferent to a change (i.e., to keep real income constant, which ideally means on the same indifference curve).

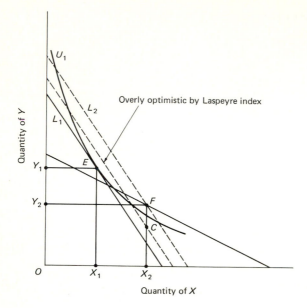

FIGURE 14A1-1
The Laspeyre quantity index.

Then we define the Laspeyre quantity index:

$$L \equiv \frac{L_2}{L_1}$$

In Figure 14A1-1 we see that L_1 is the actual budget constraint when point E is chosen in the base period. L_2 is the budget constraint through point F with the same slope (prices) as in the base period. A change is a welfare improvement by the Laspeyre test if $L = L_2/L_1 > 1$. This is clearly the case at point F, since L_2 is a "higher" budget constraint than L_1. However, Laspeyre indications of welfare improvements are overly optimistic, and they can be wrong. If period 2's consumption were shown at point C (still where $L > 1$), the change would be a welfare reduction (i.e., utility is lower). In the case when $L < 1$ there is no ambiguity: Welfare is unambiguously decreased (the new allocation must be interior to the old budget constraint L_1).

The Paasche quantity index uses current prices (period 2) and has the opposite flaw. Changes that are Paasche improvements are unambiguous improvements; those that indicate a welfare decrease may be overly pessimistic. To see this, we compute:

$$P_1 = P_{X2}X_1 + P_{Y2}Y_1$$
$$P_2 = P_{X2}X_2 + P_{Y2}Y_2$$

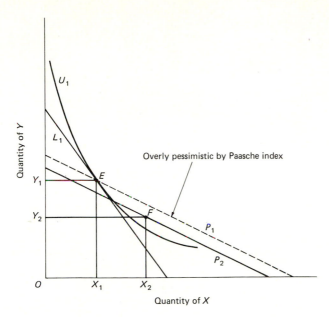

FIGURE 14A1-2
The Paasche quantity index.

and define the Paasche quantity index:

$$P \equiv \frac{P_2}{P_1}$$

This time, $P > 1$ means the old bundle of goods must be interior to the new budget constraint P_2 and welfare must be higher in the current period. If $P < 1$, the Paasche test indicates a welfare decrease. This is the case drawn in Figure 14A1-2. The solid line through point F is the period 2 budget constraint, or P_2. P_1 is the budget constraint through point E with the same slope (prices) as in period 2.

However, since the goods consumed during period 1 were those at point E, the budget constraint for period 2 allows welfare to increase (as at point F) even though $P < 1$. Thus, Paasche indications of welfare decreases are overly pessimistic and can be wrong, as in this case. Note that the change from point E on constraint L_1 to point F on constraint P_2 is judged an improvement by Laspeyre's method (Figure 14A1-1) and a welfare decrease by the Paasche method, so that the "truth" cannot be unambiguously determined in this case without knowledge of the indifference curves.

The same concepts apply in forming and using the Laspeyre and Paasche price indices (quantities are fixed, prices vary). In Figure 14A1-3 let us say a retired individual living on Social Security is initially (period 1) at point A. Price

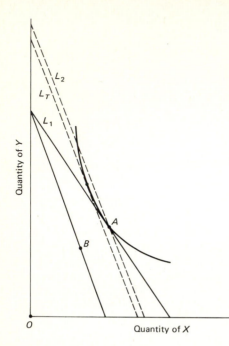

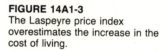

FIGURE 14A1-3
The Laspeyre price index overestimates the increase in the cost of living.

changes in the next period are such that the same nominal income leads to the budget constraint through point *B* (which the retiree would choose if necessary). However, the government wishes to compensate the individual for the increase in the cost of living. Using the period 1 quantities as a base, it calculates:

$$L_1 = P_{X1}X_1 + P_{Y1}Y_1$$
$$L_2 = P_{X2}X_1 + P_{Y2}Y_1$$

and defines the Laspeyre price index:

$$L \equiv \frac{L_2}{L_1}$$

It then gives the retiree a Social Security payment of $L_2 = L \cdot L_1$; just the amount of money which enables the person to buy last period's quantity (point *A*) at the current period's prices.

This is overly generous, of course; the individual is at least as well off as last period and must be better off if he or she chooses to spend the money differently. *A true cost-of-living index measures the percent change in nominal income required to hold utility constant at the base level.* It would give the budget constraint drawn in Figure 14A1-3 as L_T. Thus, the Laspeyre price index overestimates the increase in the cost of living. Similarly, the Paasche price index underestimates the cost-of-living increase.

The theoretical imperfections of these common methods of indexing are probably less significant than the practical problems of defining the goods and services which are included in an index and updating the index over time. We illustrated the method of index construction with just one person, two goods, and two time periods. But most indices are intended to include many people, goods, and time periods.

If the sum of the nominal budget constraints of several individuals is adjusted upward in accordance with the Laspeyre price index, there is no implication that each individual is now better off than initially. The welfare of the individuals within the group depends on how individual budget constraints change over time, how the prices of specific goods in the aggregate bundle change, and the preferences of the individuals for the different goods in the aggregate bundle. When university faculty are told they will receive a 10 percent cost-of-living raise, some of the faculty will have had their apartment rents raised by 20 percent and others by only 5 percent. Senior faculty may have their salaries increased by 12 percent and junior faculty by only 8 percent. Which are the goods that should be used to determine this group's "average" cost-of-living change? How would one decide the components of the cost of living for the "average" retiree on Social Security, or the "average" lower-income family? If one keeps track of the prices of the components over time, how often should their composition be reviewed?

The most familiar price index is the CPI calculated by the Bureau of Labor Statistics by using the Laspeyre method. Legislation at all levels of government ties annual increases in individual grants to the CPI; Social Security, food stamps, welfare payments, and government pensions are examples. Many private labor contracts tie wage increases to the CPI. This makes the details of the CPI computations important. One study reports that during 1979 an alternative index, the personal consumption expenditure (PCE) deflator of the gross national product, rose only 9.5 percent as compared with the 14.3 percent CPI increase. If Social Security payments had been tied to the PCE, government outlays would have been reduced by $5.5 billion.[42]

The CPI is a *fixed-weight index;* the weight on each price included in it is derived from an occasional survey of urban household expenditures. (For example, in 1980, the weights were based on the survey done in 1972 and 1973.) If movie going averaged 2 percent of all expenses in that survey, then the price of movie going is weighted by 0.02 in each year's calculation. One problem with such a fixed-weight index is that the weights become more irrelevant to consumers over time. For example, beef prices may have increased significantly relative to other foods, but consumers respond by spending less on meat and more on poultry. This is an example of what we saw earlier in Figure 14A1-3:

[42] See Joseph J. Minarik, "Does the Consumer Price Index Need Deflating?," *Taxing and Spending, 3,* No. 3, summer 1980, pp. 17–24.

The cost of achieving a fixed utility level never rises as quickly as the cost of achieving it with the original bundle of goods and services. Being faithful to the concept of a *price index* over time works against the accuracy of the figure as a *cost-of-living index*.

One way to make a Laspeyre price index more useful as a measure of the cost of living is to have it *chain-linked*. For example, the current CPI measures the change in prices from 1979 to 1980 by using the 1972 weights, where P_iQ_j is short for the sum over the n goods in the index $\sum\limits_{k=1}^{n} p_{ik}q_{jk}$:

$$L_{80} = \frac{P_{80}Q_{72}}{P_{72}Q_{72}}$$

$$L_{79} = \frac{P_{79}Q_{72}}{P_{72}Q_{72}}$$

$$\frac{L_{80}}{L_{79}} = \frac{P_{80}Q_{72}}{P_{79}Q_{72}}$$

But a chain-linked index would compute:

$$\frac{L_{80}}{L_{79}} = \frac{P_{80}Q_{79}}{P_{79}Q_{79}}$$

$$\vdots \qquad \vdots$$

$$\frac{L_{73}}{L_{72}} = \frac{P_{73}Q_{72}}{P_{72}Q_{72}}$$

This, of course would require a method of identifying the changes in consumption patterns each year (bearing in mind that accurate surveys are expensive).

The PCE index, because it is constructed from the national income accounts calculated each year, does have a changing basket of goods and services. It is a Paasche price index whereby each year's prices are compared with those in 1972. For example, the 1980 and 1979 price deflators are calculated as follows:

$$PCE_{80} = \frac{P_{80}Q_{80}}{P_{72}Q_{80}}$$

$$PCE_{79} = \frac{P_{79}Q_{79}}{P_{72}Q_{79}}$$

Unlike the CPI, the denominators of these deflators do not cancel out when one calculates the annual price level increase (= PCE_{80}/PCE_{79}). Note that the PCE index is not chain-linked either; if it were, the prices in the denominator of each year's deflator would be those from the prior year rather than 1972.

A problem with any index is the difficulty of controlling for quality changes. Although we know inflation was extensive from 1950 to 1980, it is not obvious whether an individual with $1000 would prefer to spend it on the goods available in a 1950 Sears catalog or a 1980 Sears catalog. Minarik cites an example of radial auto tires being more expensive than the older bias-ply style but lasting far longer.[43] Another example is controlling for quality improvements in medical technology, like better surgical tools. Quality also may decrease, as it undoubtedly has on certain airline routes after deregulation.[44] All these quality changes should be taken into account by the index, but it is usually not possible to take them into account.

One of the most controversial items in the CPI is the treatment of housing prices. Housing is the prime example of a consumer durable, and care must be taken in interpreting changes in the prices of durables. Their purchase represents one of the most important forms of consumer saving. (Much current consumption is deferred to make the purchase, which returns a stream of consumption services over time.) Increases in the prices of durables make current owners of them better off and current consumers of them worse off; like homeowners, individuals have both roles simultaneously.

A cost-of-living index is intended to reflect the costs of consuming only. To know whether any person is better off or worse off when the cost of living goes up by a certain amount, we must examine the changes in the budget constraint that occur during the same period (e.g., wage increases). Increases in asset values, whether they are common shares of stock or consumer durables, work to increase the budget constraints of their owners and tend to offset cost-of-living increases.

The CPI, however, is not designed as a cost-of-living index; it is a price index. It counts the housing expenditures of the people in its survey who purchase a home during the survey period (7 to 8 percent of homeowners), as measured by the net cost of the home (purchase price of the new home minus sale price of the old one) plus the value of interest charges on a mortgage for its first 15 years (when the average mortgage is terminated by resale). Many people assume this causes overweighting of housing in terms of annual cost-of-living changes, but that is not necessarily so; the 92 to 93 percent of homeowners not buying homes are treated as spending nothing for home purchase or its financing. However, the CPI housing component is *volatile* because the change in present value of a long stream of services (both the asset price and the interest charge) shows up all at once. According to Minarik, an increase in the mortgage interest rate from 10 to 16 percent causes a 60 percent increase in the interest component of the CPI.[45] (Of course, a decrease similar in size would have the opposite effect.)

The PCE deflator uses an alternative approach, which is simply to estimate

---

[43] Ibid., p. 18

[44] When price competition was prevented by regulation, airlines competed by offering nonprice benefits such as more space, more choice of travel time, and free in-flight movies. They are now able to offer lower prices as a more efficient means of competing.

[45] Minarik, op. cit., p. 20.

the rental value of the home. This is actually done by using the CPI rent index adjusted to reflect the difference in size and quality between the average rental unit and owner-occupied home. In theory, the rental value is the actual cost of "consuming" the house. The competitive rental price equals the opportunity cost of its provision: interest foregone by the house supplier (who could have sold the house and banked the proceeds), plus home depreciation over the period (or minus its appreciation).

Note that the actual mortgage payments are irrelevant to the consumption costs. The homeowner as an investor cares about this: The net return to the investor from "renting out the home" depends on the opportunity cost of his or her equity in the home plus the actual mortgage interest costs. (The mortgage provider may be thought of as gaining or losing depending on the difference between current and contracted mortgage rates.) But current rental value is a function of the current, not historical, rate of interest. If the investment and consumption roles were not separated, homeowners with particularly good investments could end up with negative cost-of-living increases despite general inflation. This violates the idea of the cost of living as a measure of the nominal income required to achieve a given utility level.

Both the CPI and the PCE are very broad indices, and they do not necessarily reflect the change in cost of living experienced by particular groups (e.g., families in a certain state or very low income households). For example, in the last decade, price increases have been concentrated in food, energy, medical care, and housing. One group has called attention to this by publishing a "necessities" index consisting of just those items from the CPI; it has risen more rapidly than the CPI. If a widely shared inflation burden emanates from a few specific sources, one might wish to orient inflation policy around the sources.

However, others point out that these four CPI components should not really be thought of as representative of necessities; they include restaurant meals, expensive foods, and the cost of home purchases, and they exclude clothing and public transportation. An alternative necessities index, which adds in clothing and excludes meals away from home and home purchases, rises more slowly than the CPI as a whole for the period.[46] Thus it is unclear whether average families, and particularly lower-income families, are burdened by sector-specific inflation any more than by general inflation. Nevertheless, the idea that one might wish to use special indices for particular policy purposes is an important one and is worthy of more exploration.

Another example of an area in which special indices have policy use is education. In Chapter 4 we reviewed the problems of achieving equity in school finance. One of the problems mentioned was that nominal dollar expenditures of districts cannot always be compared directly. In California, for example, northern school districts may have to spend considerably more dollars than other districts to provide reasonable temperatures in classrooms.

---

[46] For a capsule discussion of these indices, see *Newsweek*, November 3, 1980, p. 66.

Suppose one is interested in the wealth neutrality of the real educational resources available to each child under a state financing plan. One must adjust the observable nominal dollar relations to account for the cost differences in obtaining real resources. But then one needs to have a comparison basket of educational resources. Furthermore, one must not confuse the observed price of each item in the district with the opportunity cost of the resources. For example, teacher salaries may be high because local demand for teachers is high or because previous grants were converted to higher salaries through the flypaper effect. Untangling these effects poses thorny statistical problems.[47]

One final point about the practical problems of index construction and use should be made: Political pressures to influence the index calculations are enormous. A few analysts arguing for, let us say, the use of the rental concept for housing in the Social Security index, may be no match for the lobbying efforts of the many groups representing interests of the elderly. Rational arguments are unlikely to be persuasive when the 10-year historical record shows that the elderly did better with the ordinary CPI than they would have done with the proposed revision.

Perhaps a better example of the importance of political strength can be seen in the "double-indexing" problem with Social Security.[48] There was a technical error in the 1972 legislation providing for automatic indexation of benefits. An individual's Social Security is calculated on the basis of his or her average monthly earnings over the working years. The 1972 legislation essentially required that the historical earnings data be expressed in current dollars, which would keep current benefits at a fixed percent of real permanent income. But the legislation also required that the benefit schedule associated with each adjusted earnings level be increased; this increases the value of Social Security benefits by more than inflation for those who will retire in the future.

A simple example can illustrate this problem. Suppose an individual works for two periods, earning $400 and $600 respectively, and is then eligible in the third period for social security at 60 percent of average earnings. The CPI is 1.00, 1.10, and 1.21 for each period, respectively. Thus earnings expressed in third-period dollars are:

$$400(1.21) = \$484$$
$$600(1.10) = \$660$$
$$\text{Average} = \$572$$
$$60\% \text{ average} = \$343.20$$

[47] See W. Norton Grubb, "Cost of Education Indices: Issues and Methods," in J. Callahan and W. Wilken (eds.), *School Finance Reform: A Legislator's Handbook* (Washington, D.C.: National Conference of State Legislatures, 1976), pp. 87–93.

[48] See M. Feldstein, "Toward a Reform of Social Security," in R. Haveman and J. Margolis (eds.), *Public Expenditure and Policy Analysis* (Chicago: Rand McNally, 1977), pp. 421–441. See also B. Chiswick and J. O'Neill, *Human Resources and Income Distribution* (New York: W. W. Norton & Co., 1977), pp. 132–136.

This method is sufficient to keep real benefits at a constant proportion of real permanent income, but the legislation had benefits associated with the $572 average level (the $343.20) indexed to increase as well. The replacement rate for those still working (i.e., those who actually earned the same nominal amounts of $400 and $600 in the first two periods but have not yet retired) was indexed to increase above the 60 percent level. Despite the widespread consensus that this double-indexing was a technical error, it took 5 years for Congress to correct it.

APPENDIX TWO: Discounting over Discrete or Continuous Intervals

In this appendix we review some of the mathematics necessary to calculate present or future values under various definitions of the interest rate and assumptions about the stream of payments. We first review calculations involving a discrete stream of payments such as those encountered with home mortgages. Then we review the concept of a continuous stream of payments, which is often used in analytic calculations and requires some knowledge of integral calculus.

A helpful mathematical fact to keep in mind while reviewing calculations over many time periods is this: A finite length of time can always be conceptualized as consisting of *any* number of intervals one wishes simply by choosing the length of the interval. Of course, the definition of the interest rate must change accordingly, even though nothing real has changed. When viewed in that way, a many-period model is just a mathematically finer disaggregation of a "lumpy" two-period model. The behavioral predictions of a perfect market model of many periods, for example, must "add up" to those for the two-period model.[49]

First we review the mathematics of compounding and discounting. Let us define r as the simple interest rate for a 1-year period: $1 saved in the bank now will yield $(1 + r)$ a year from now. Recall that, in the perfect capital market, borrowing and lending are done at the same interest rate r (the law of one price). Thus, a guarantee to repay $1 in 1 year has a current loan value equal to the present discounted value of the future repayment: $1/(1 + r)$.

If the saver leaves the money in the bank for a second year and the interest rate remains constant, the amount A at the end of 2 years is

$$A = 1(1 + r)(1 + r) = (1 + r)^2$$

If the money is left in the bank for n years, the amount at the end is

[49] Note this mathematical fact is distinct from the important idea that actual behavior may have to be modeled differently if one is considering allocation over a year versus over a lifetime. (For example, bounded rationality may cause lifetime choices to deviate substantially from expected utility maximization, whereas annual budgeting decisions may not.)

$$A = (1 + r)^n$$

Similarly, if the borrower is going to repay $1 two years after receiving a loan, the current loan value of that repayment is its present value (PDV):

$$PDV = \frac{1/(1 + r)}{1 + r} = \frac{1}{(1 + r)^2}$$

If the $1 is not repaid until n years, its present value is

$$PDV = \frac{1}{(1 + r)^n}$$

If someone offers a payment of D in n years from now, its present value is

$$PDV = \frac{D}{(1 + r)^n}$$

Finally, if someone offers a stream of payments over the years of D_0 (a down payment), $D_1, D_2, \ldots, D_n$, the present value of that stream is

$$PDV = D_0 + \frac{D_1}{1 + r} + \frac{D_2}{(1 + r)^2} + \cdots + \frac{D_n}{(1 + r)^n}$$

This last equation is very important because it allows us to convert any stream of payments (or, in some applications, social costs or benefits) over time into one present value. For example, suppose someone buys a house and borrows $100,000 from a bank at 10 percent interest for 30 years. If the borrower wishes to make constant annual payments beginning in 1 year, what will they be? We have to find the mortgage payment M which makes[50]

$$100,000 = \frac{M}{1 + 0.10} + \frac{M}{(1 + 0.10)^2} + \cdots + \frac{M}{(1 + 0.10)^{30}}$$

[50] In the calculation we use the formula for the sum of a geometric progression. If the progression is

$$a, ad, ad^2, \ldots, ad^{n-1}$$

then the sum is

$$S = \frac{a(1 - d^n)}{1 - d} \qquad \text{for } 0 < d < 1$$

In the above equation, $a = d = 1/1.1$, and $n = 30$.

$$100,000 = M\left(\frac{1}{1.1} + \frac{1}{1.1^2} + \cdots + \frac{1}{1.1^{30}}\right)$$

$$= M(9.4269)$$

or $$M = \$10,607.92$$

We also use calculations like these in ordinary analytic work. For example, in the beginning of the chapter we discussed the concept of permanent income. Now we can define it precisely: *Permanent income is the stream of constant earnings whose present value is identical with that of the actual earnings stream.*

For example, if someone earns \$10,000 in period 1 and \$20,000 in period 2, the present value at a 10 percent discount rate is

$$PV = 10,000 + \frac{20,000}{1.1} = \$28,181.82$$

To find the permanent income equivalent Y_p, we must have

$$\$28,181.82 = Y_p + \frac{Y_p}{1.1} = 1.909 Y_p$$

$$Y_p = \$14,761.91$$

The calculation of present value extends easily to the case in which the stream of payments continues indefinitely. There are financial instruments which have this feature; perpetual bonds, called consols, are commonly sold in England, for example. If the bond issuer promises to pay \$M each year for perpetuity and the market rate of interest is 10 percent annually, then the current market price of the bond is the present value:[51]

$$PV = \frac{M}{1.1} + \frac{M}{1.1^2} + \cdots + \frac{M}{1.1^n} + \cdots$$

$$= \frac{M/1.1}{1 - (1/1.1)} = \frac{M}{0.1} = 10M$$

The general present-value formula for a perpetuity has this simple form:

$$PV = \frac{M}{r}$$

---

[51] For an infinite geometric progression $a, ad, ad^2, \ldots,$ the sum is

$$S = \frac{a}{1 - d} \qquad 0 < d < 1$$

Suppose the annual payment on the consol is $10,607.92 (a number we use here only because of its relation to the last example). Then the present value of the consol (at 10 percent annual interest) is simply $106,079.20. Notice by how *little* the present value increases when we extend the stream of payments from 30 years in the mortgage example to perpetuity in the consol example. That is because the present discounted value of payments which will not be received (or made) until the distant future is meager. For example, the present value of a payment of $10,607.92 made in the 31st year is only $552.66 and in the 60th year only $34.94.

However, it is also important to note that the discount rate can make a big difference in the calculation of present value for a stream that goes over a lengthy period. For the consol that pays M annually, the present value doubles to $20M$ if the market rate of interest is only 5 percent. At a lower rate of discount, each future dollar payment is worth more currently.

All our examples so far have involved *simple* interest rates, but it is sometimes more convenient to work with *continuously compounded* rates over the same interval. To understand that, first imagine that we deposit P in a bank which pays r percent annual interest compounded semiannually. This is equivalent to keeping the money in the bank for two 6-month periods at a 6-month simple interest rate of $r/2$:

$$A = P\left(1 + \frac{r}{2}\right)^2$$

In other words, compounding holds the simple rate of interest constant but redefines the intervals to be shorter. The difference between this and the simple interest case is that with compounding one earns interest on the interest. The interest earned after 6 months is $Pr/2$, and that is added to the account balance. Thus, during the second 6 months, one earns $Pr/2$ as interest on the original deposit plus interest on the first 6 months' interest $(Pr/2)(r/2) = Pr^2/4$. To check this, note that:

Simple interest $\quad\quad\quad\quad\quad\quad A = P(1 + r) = P + Pr$

Compounded semiannually $\quad A = P\left(1 + \frac{r}{2}\right)^2 = P + Pr + \frac{Pr^2}{4}$

If we let the original deposit of P dollars earn compound interest for t years, we would have

$$A = P\left(1 + \frac{r}{2}\right)^{2t}$$

The saver is better off the more often interest is compounded (for a fixed simple rate). If it is compounded quarterly and held for t years,

$$A = P\left(1 + \frac{r}{4}\right)^{4t}$$

And if the savings is compounded n times per year and held for t years, the amount at the end of the period is

$$A = P\left(1 + \frac{r}{n}\right)^{nt}$$

Now what happens if we let n approach infinity, or compound continuously? To answer that, we first define the number e:[52]

$$e \equiv \lim_{n \to \infty} \left(1 + \frac{1}{n}\right)^n \approx 2.718$$

This number can be interpreted economically as the yield on \$1 invested for one year at a 100 percent interest rate compounded continuously. If the simple interest rate is r rather than 100 percent, one must make use of the following limit to calculate the continuously compounded yield:

$$e^r = \lim_{n \to \infty} \left(1 + \frac{r}{n}\right)^n$$

Table 14A2-1 shows the effect of the frequency of compounding or discounting on savings and borrowings.

Note that if \P is deposited and compounded continuously at annual interest r for a period of t years, the amount at the end is

$$A = P(e^r)^t = Pe^{rt}$$

If one asks about the present discounted value of A dollars in the future, the answer expressed with continuous discounting is

$$\text{PDV} = Ae^{-rt} = P$$

We have already seen that the present value of a stream of payments is the sum of the present value of each payment. If one receives a payment A_t each year for n years, its present value using the continuously discounted rate is:

---

[52] In this definition and the one below, we refer to mathematical limits. If these are not familiar, try taking a calculator and experimenting. Compute the expression $(1 + n)^n$ for $n = 10$ and then $n = 100$ to see that it approaches $e \approx 2.718$. Do likewise for the other expression, using any interest rate you like.

$$\left(1 + \frac{1}{n}\right)^n$$

TABLE 14A2-1
THE EFFECT OF COMPOUNDING ON YIELDS AND PRESENT VALUES

Deposit $1 for 1 year at 10% annual interest	Formula	Yield	Equivalent simple interest*
(a) Simple	$1(1 + 0.10)$	1.1000	10.00
(b) Compounded semi-annually	$1(1 + 0.10/2)^2$	1.1025	10.25
(c) Compounded quarterly	$1(1 + 0.10/4)^4$	1.1038	10.38
(d) Compounded continuously	$1(e^{0.10})$	1.1052	10.52

Repay $1 in 1 year at 10% annual discount rate	Formula	Present value	Equivalent simple discount rate
(a) Simple	$1/(1 + 0.10)$	0.9091	10.00
(b) Discounted semi-annually	$1/(1 + 0.10/2)^2$	0.9070	10.25
(c) Discounted quarterly	$1/(1 + 0.10/4)^4$	0.9060	10.38
(d) Discounted continuously	$1/(e^{0.10})$	0.9048	10.52

* If r_s is the simple interest rate and r is the continuously compounded rate over a given time interval, they are equivalent if their yields are identical:

$$1 + r_s = e^r$$

or

$$\ln (1 + r_s) = r$$

This formula allows conversion from simple to continuous interest rates.

$$\text{PDV} = A_0 + A_1e^{-r} + A_2e^{-2r} + \cdots + A_ne^{-nr}$$

There is one last idea which is important to develop because of its analytic convenience. A payment at the rate of A_t per year could be sent in installments, just as annual rent is usually paid monthly. $100 per year could come in quarterly payments of $25, or weekly payments of $1.92, or at some other frequency. The frequency we wish to focus on is payment at each instant! An example of why we are interested in this may help. Suppose someone owns a tree and wishes to cut it and sell the lumber when its present value is maximized. The tree grows at its natural rate each instant; it adds more lumber as a stream of continuing payments and changes the present value. Or a machine may be thought of as *depreciating* continuously over time, i.e., as generating a stream of instantaneous negative payments. The mathematics below is useful for finding the present value in these and similar cases.

Let us call $A(t)$ the annual dollars that would result if the instantaneous payment at time t continued for exactly 1 year. Let us call Δt the fraction of the year during which the payment actually does continue. Thus, the amount received is $A(t)\Delta t$, and its continuously discounted value is:

$$\text{PDV} = [A(t)\Delta t]e^{-rt}$$

If we have a stream of instantaneous payments for T years, where the annual rate is constant within each small portion of the year Δt, then the present value of the whole stream can be thought of as the discounted sum of the payments during each Δt. The number of intervals being summed is $T/\Delta t$:

$$PDV = \sum_{t=0}^{T} [A(t)\Delta t]e^{-rt}$$

Now if we go to the limit where the size of the interval Δt approaches zero, the above expression becomes an integral:

$$PDV = \lim_{\Delta t \to 0} \sum_{t=0}^{T} [A(t)\Delta t]e^{-rt} = \int_{t=0}^{T} A(t)e^{-rt} \, dt$$

To see what this means, let us use some numerical examples. Let $A(t) = \$100$. If it is paid in a single payment at the end of the year, $\Delta t = 1$. At an annual rate of 10 percent continuously discounted, its present value is:

$$PDV = [A(t)\Delta t]e^{-rt}$$
$$= \$100e^{-0.10} = \$90.48$$

If the $100 is paid in two 6-month installments, $\Delta t = \frac{1}{2}$, so that $A(t)\Delta t = 50$ and there are two components to the present value:

$$PDV = 50e^{-0.10(0.5)} + 50e^{-0.10(1)}$$
$$= 47.56 + 45.24$$
$$= \$92.80$$

We can imagine paying the $100 in an increasing number of installments until the interval size is that of an instant. If the $100 is paid in equal instantaneous installments, its present value is

$$PV = \int_{t=0}^{t=1} 100e^{-0.1t} \, dt$$
$$= \frac{100e^{-0.1(1)}}{-0.1} - \frac{100e^{-1(0)}}{-0.1}$$
$$= -904.84 + 1000$$
$$= \$95.16$$

We show the geometric interpretations of these calculations in Figure 14A2-1. The downward-sloping line shows the present value of $100 (discounted continuously) at any point between the present and 1 year into the future. The single-payment calculation is the area of the rectangle using the height of the curve ($90.48) where $t = 1$ and with length $\Delta t = 1$. The two-payment calculation is the sum of two rectangles: Both have length $\Delta t = 0.5$, and the heights are the discounted values of the payments at $t = 0.5$ and $t = 1$, or $95.12

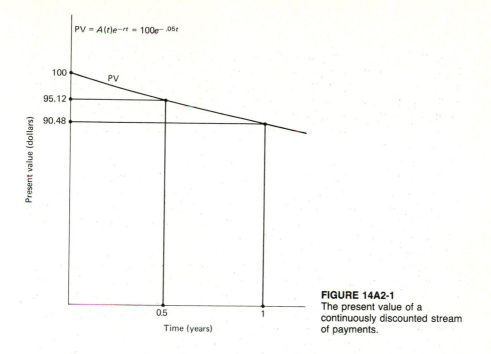

FIGURE 14A2-1
The present value of a
continuously discounted stream
of payments.

and $90.48, respectively. Note that the second calculation comes closer to measuring the whole area under the curve from $t = 0$ to $t = 1$. If we divided the intervals into 4, 8, and 16 payments, we would come even closer to measuring that whole area. In the limit of instantaneous payments at each infinitesimally sized interval, the area is the whole area. The integral is simply the way of calculating the area under the given curve for the relevant period ($t = 0$ to $t = 1$).

THE FRONTIERS OF MICROECONOMIC POLICY ANALYSIS: ORGANIZATIONAL PROCESS AND INSTITUTIONAL CHOICE

DESIGNING GOVERNANCE STRUCTURES FOR ECONOMIC ACTIVITIES

In Part IV we reviewed a number of policy concerns about the functioning of specific markets in the economy. We have seen that information and transaction costs often play an important role in explaining market problems as well as evaluating remedies for them. However, we have not generally considered why or when the decision-making structure for resource allocation should involve market processes at all.

In this chapter we consider market governance in comparison with various alternative control processes such as regulation and public provision. When the market fails, it still may be relatively efficient to allow individual economic agents *some* discretion to influence or to govern partially, through a market process of engaging in voluntary transactions, how resources are allocated. Again, *information and transaction costs play important roles in determining the relative efficiency of any governance structure for a specific activity*.

No single theoretical framework has been accepted as the proper method for analyzing these issues. Therefore, we introduce several approaches which can be demonstrated to yield good insights. Each offers a different way to clarify certain relations between the governance structure and information and transaction costs. First we introduce Arrow's framework of classifying an organization by the kind of operating instructions it issues and its rules for enforcing them. We emphasize the difference between centralized and decentralized control. Then market organization or governance can be seen as a command and control structure which uses a particular form of decentralized decision making.

561

Under the assumptions of perfect information and zero transaction costs, perfectly centralized as well as decentralized structures can lead to a Pareto-optimal allocation of resources. However, these assumptions understate the importance of uncertainty (the absence of information) and its great influence on organizational design. Because economic agents are confronted with much costly uncertainty, they seek a method of organization which efficiently reduces those costs. But that depends on the specific sources of and the ability to reduce uncertainty (as by the creation, transmission, and use of information), or shift it to those best able to bear it. There are no obvious generalizations about the relative efficiency of centralized or decentralized governance structures for such tasks.

To put Arrow's framework in the context of practical policy analysis, we consider alternative methods of air pollution control. Many people have suggested that pollution taxes (a decentralized method) would be more efficient than our actual policy which relies on regulatory standards (a more centralized method). Such reasoning is often based on naive assumptions about the information structure, although the conclusion may be correct in certain circumstances. Reasoning from Arrow's framework, we suggest that a policy of marketable pollution permits (which blends centralized and decentralized processes) is more promising than either taxes or standards.

Another framework has been used by Williamson and Goldberg as a means of considering the governance of natural monopolies. They point out that certain governance structures, like ordinary rate-of-return regulation, may be viewed as a particular form of contract. Insight into a desirable form of governance may then be derived by considering alternative ways in which one could specify and let a contract between the government and a supplier.

Rate-of-return regulation is explained and compared with a suggestion to replace it by a market process: competitive bidding for an exclusive franchise to service an area's consumers. The latter suggestion is motivated in part by the hope that it can avoid the problem of *regulatory capture,* which is a theory that regulatory authorities end up being overly sympathetic to the industry position. The analysis shows that many of the features of ordinary regulation will also appear in the contract used to award the franchise. These features, which result from information and transaction costs present under either method of governance, are essentially those used to explain why capture occurs. Thus, there is little reason to think the franchising method is superior to ordinary regulation.

A case study of franchise bidding to provide CATV services in Oakland, California, supports the above reasoning. Two other examples of this type of analysis, involving performance contracting, are discussed briefly. One involves Amtrak contracting for passenger rail service, and the other involves elementary education.

The final section of this chapter is an analysis of day-care services. Two general analytic procedures are introduced here as a means of identifying the information and transaction costs associated with particular governance structures. One is simply to review the economic history of the activity under consideration. The other is the exit-voice-loyalty framework of Hirschman, which is used to understand organizational responsiveness in markets for goods and services when quality is important.

We present a plausible line of argument, based on insights from these frameworks, which suggests that subsidized day care for low-income families is best provided in established nonprofit community organizations, rather than cooperatives, profit-making firms in a market, or public day-care centers. A key element in this argument is that parental uncertainty about the quality of the day-care service is high, and an efficient way to reduce it is for the service to be provided by someone the parent trusts. Nonprofit community organizations, it is argued, have a relative advantage in the trust dimension.

EFFICIENT ORGANIZATIONAL DESIGN AND THE DEGREE OF CENTRALIZED DECISION MAKING[1]

Striving for efficient resource allocation is often thought of primarily as an investment problem: a matter of choosing the economic activities which yield the greatest net social benefits. Yet the more one focuses on how to make the choices, and appreciates the difficulties involved, the more one is drawn to expand the view of the problem to include organizational as well as investment terms. Rather than consider any specific decision, we focus here on how to organize a process of deciding or how to create an organization to be used for making many decisions of the investment type.

Because information for decision making is costly to produce and to communicate, there are often important economies in breaking up decision problems into pieces and assigning particular individuals (or subgroups) responsibility for each of the pieces. A firm, for example, may continually face the problem of what to do next in order to maximize profits. The large firm typically breaks the profit maximization decision down into pieces by creating separate marketing, sales, production, and planning divisions. Each division has responsibility for developing its own expertise and making resource allocation decisions intended to contribute to the overall firm objective. Yet the attempt to organize in order to take advantage of the economies from specialized decision making creates the problem of organizational control: How does one motivate the individual decision makers in each division to act in the interests of the organization as a whole?

To develop perspective on the problem of organizational design, we introduce the concept of a team. *A team is any organization of individuals sharing a common goal or goals.* The individual team members may have other interests in addition to the team goals, and the other interests may conflict more

---

[1] The following discussion is based primarily on the chapter "Control in Large Organizations" in Kenneth Arrow, *Essays in the Theory of Risk-Bearing* (Chicago: Markham Publishing Co., 1971). Other references include J. Marschak and R. Radner, *The Economic Theory of Teams* (New Haven: Yale University Press, 1971), and R. Radner and C. B. McGuire, *Decision and Organization* (Amsterdam: North Holland Publishing Co., 1972).

or less with the team purposes. To achieve its purposes, the team must solve *the general problem of organization: choosing the operating rules or instructions to command or direct certain behavior of the individuals involved and an enforcement mechanism (some form of incentives, either rewards or penalties) to control or induce the individuals to follow the operating rules.*

The concept of a team is one that should be quite broadly conceived. We could consider the organization of a sports team, school district, naval fleet, or department of motor vehicles. We have already suggested that we could think of a large firm as a team and consider its organization. One particularly important conception is to view the whole economy as a team sharing the common purpose of achieving an efficient and equitable allocation of resources. Then governments are seen as particular subgroups of the team (or smaller teams nested within a larger one). We will explain and apply this latter conception after we have introduced some general ways of thinking about alternative types of operating rules and enforcement mechanisms which can characterize the team organization.

We wish to give particular emphasis to the degree of centralization in the organizational design. *The degree of centralization refers to the amount of decision-making discretion left to the doer of an organizational task.* For example, an instruction to another of the form "do this task in this way," like "tighten one nut to each bolt passing on the assembly line," is a centralized instruction. The recipient of the instruction is given no choice—or very little choice—about how to perform the task. Another instruction may be of the form "do whatever is necessary to maximize this objective function," like "minimize the costs of assembling cars from these components." This is decentralized because it leaves the specific decisions about how to organize the assembly to the recipient of the instruction.

Of course, there are intermediate possibilities like a rule book: "Determine which state of the world we are in, and follow the specific procedures described for that state." Here the instructed person has some freedom to interpret which state of the world is relevant: "If the floor is dirty, mop it." Thus, the instructions which individuals receive may be more or less centralized; that is why we refer to the degree of centralization.

In a moment we will discuss circumstances relevant to the desired degree of centralization in the operating rules. One of the factors concerns which individual has the best information (or can obtain and process the relevant information most easily)—the doer of the task or the assigner of the role. However, these rules should be assigned with forethought to their enforcement as well.

Once an operating instruction is assigned, the organization must be able to identify whether it is obeyed. A centralized operating rule, i.e., "do this specific task," may be relatively easy to monitor because obedience is a *yes or no* determination. Obedience to a decentralized rule, i.e., "maximize this function," is a matter of whether the individual has done *more or less*. The same factors which push toward the use of the decentralized rule (e.g., the center or rule assigner has greater costs of learning how to accomplish the maximization) also imply that the center has a more difficult monitoring task: how does it know how close the observed result is to the maximum? Therefore, use of decentralized operating rules is usually accompanied by enforcement mechanisms which reward team members for more or penalize them for less.

Now let us explore circumstances which explain the degree of centralization associated with the efficient conduct of economic activities. In a sense, it is interdependencies among economic agents which suggest that some degree of centralization may be efficient. We show this below in a very simple model of a team. But there is a caveat: The presence of an interdependency is only a necessary, and not a sufficient, condition for centralization to be relatively efficient. We also illustrate this caveat below.

We start with a simple example of a two-person team whose shared objective is to maximize the team profit. Each team member is given responsibility for, and has relevant knowledge about, one investment decision. Each strives to make the decision which most enhances the team profit. *However, each is uninformed about the other's knowledge unless some costly communication or coordination is undertaken.* Thus, we are assuming there is some division of knowledge; no one person knows everything, and responsibility is allocated to the person with the most appropriate knowledge.

We stylize the individual choices and the possible outcomes in a very simple way. Each of the two team members must decide whether to take some action such as to go forward with an investment or to hold off. If person 1 invests, we represent this as $d_1 = 1$. If person 1 decides not to invest, we present this as $d_1 = 0$. Similarly, $d_2 = 1$ if person 2 invests and $d_2 = 0$ otherwise.

Each individual, when deciding whether to invest, is assumed to have only *incomplete* information about the effect of investing on the team's profits (unless costly communication or coordination is undertaken). The information is incomplete because it ignores possible interdependencies. For simplicity, we assume this incomplete information takes on one of three values (denoted Π_1 for person 1's investment and Π_2 for person 2's investment): \$10 if the investment looks good, \$0 if it looks neutral, and $-\$10$ if it looks bad. Person 1 knows the value of Π_1 when choosing d_1, but does not know d_2 or Π_2. Similarly, person 2 knows the value Π_2 when choosing d_2, but does not know d_1 or Π_1.

Interdependencies in the team's decisions are reflected by the shape of the team profit function Π. Consider the following three possibilities:

$$\Pi = d_1\Pi_1 + d_2\Pi_2 \tag{1}$$
$$\Pi = (d_1 + d_2)(\Pi_1 + \Pi_2) \tag{2}$$
$$\Pi = (d_1 - \tfrac{1}{2})(d_2 - \tfrac{1}{2})(\Pi_1 + \Pi_2) \tag{3}$$

If the profit function is (1), no communication or coordination is necessary to maximize it. Each person has sufficient knowledge to decide which investments are profitable for the team (e.g., if $\Pi_1 = 10$, then person 1 knows to choose $d_1 = 1$) and which to reject as unprofitable ones (e.g., if $\Pi_2 = -10$, then person 2 knows to choose $d_2 = 0$). In fact, there is no reason for the two agents in this example to produce as a team rather than independently; function (1) will be maximized if person 1 acts to maximize $d_1\Pi_1$ and, independently, person 2 acts to maximize $d_2\Pi_2$.

However, the profit functions denoted by (2) and (3) contain interdependencies which the team will have to take into account. If the profit function is (2), then communication between the agents is valuable. Suppose, for example, that $\Pi_1 = 0$ and $\Pi_2 = 10$. Then person 1 should choose $d_1 = 1$ in order to achieve the maximum team profit of $\$20 = (1 + 1)(0 + 10)$. But if person 1 does not know the value of Π_2 and acts only on the knowledge that $\Pi_1 = 0$, he or she may choose $d_1 = 0$ and the team will end up with a profit of only $\$10 = (0 + 1)(0 + 10)$.

A profit function like (3) gives value to both communication and coordination. Communication is valuable for reasons similar to the example in (2). One of the agents needs to know if the sum of Π_1 and Π_2 is positive, negative, or zero. With that knowledge the agents must coordinate their actions appropriately. If the sum is positive, for example, then maximizing team profit requires that both agents take the same action (either both investing or both not investing). If the sum of $\Pi_1 + \Pi_2$ is negative, then the agents must be sure to take different actions (if one invests, the other should not invest). To maximize team profit, communication must be undertaken so that one agent knows the sum of $\Pi_1 + \Pi_2$ and what action the other agent chooses, and the agent so informed must take the action which coordinates the team appropriately.

Consider, as an illustrative example, the mass production of an automobile engine which must fit into the automobile body and then meet given performance standards. There are hundreds of features of both the engine and body which must be designed to perform in harmony with one another. Not only does the engine construction require knowledge (communication) of the body design (and vice versa), but the designs must be chosen to fit each other (coordination). Furthermore, if the team is to do its job properly, the resulting product must be one which meets its performance standards at the least cost.

If the different activities of automobile engine and body construction are organized to take place under one firm, the communication and coordination problems are addressed through some centralization of the decision making. Recall Chapter 8 pointed out that activity within firms (as opposed to across firms) represents a centralization of decision making. Within the firm, some directives of the "do this specifically" type are given (e.g., from managers to other employees). Thus communication and coordination problems can be addressed simply by directing one employee to communicate and (or) to coordinate with another.

On the other hand, the interdependencies involved in communicating and coordinating need not necessarily be addressed by centralizing the decision making within one firm. In the case of the automobile engine and body, it is also possible for separate firms to build each component. That is, *one can communicate and coordinate by contract through the market.* This method is a decentralized market transaction: a priced exchange between units that presumably is undertaken because each unit independently believes the exchange will further its objectives.

Agreement on exactly what is being exchanged requires specification of multidimensional aspects of the transaction: the timing or flow of deliveries, dimensions of all the connecting parts, the strength of various components, etc. If there needs to be some trial and error in construction before all these specifications can be known or agreed upon, it may be impossible to agree on price beforehand; there is too much uncertainty about what is to be produced. But the potential contractee may refuse to incur the costs of trials without a contract. Centralized construction within the firm may be a more adaptable and thus more efficient way to proceed in this case. On the other hand, if it is difficult for one part of the team to monitor or know the least costs of production of the other part, competitive contracting may have the advantage.

Recall that one of the key problems of organization is that the participating individuals do not necessarily share identical objective functions. The standard assumption that each individual is a utility maximizer does not itself imply that team member behavior will be consistent with team objectives. Whatever type of operating instructions are issued, the team must be able to ensure that they are obeyed. Within a firm, it is not always easy to monitor or measure the contribution of each of its subparts. This also makes it difficult to devise a decentralized self-monitoring plan of incentives which establishes an appropriate relation between rewards to the subpart and the subpart's contribution to the firm. In the automobile example, the adaptability advantages of centralized construction may be outweighed by the difficulties of motivating each subpart to attend to the team goals.

One solution may be to decentralize outside the firm (team) in the form of a contract arrangement with another. *Competitive bidding for the contract shifts some of the monitoring functions from the buyer to the competitors, and the latter may have better knowledge about what is least-cost production.* That is, the instruction "minimize the costs of production" may be best enforced by the decentralized monitoring of informed competitors rather than centralized monitoring by another part of the same firm.

Let us now broaden our view of an economic team to encompass more than one or two firms. It is important to be able to see an entire market economy as one large team, with smaller subteams like firms nested inside of it. In the market as an organization the operating rules and the enforcement system are decentralized in a particular way. Consumer demand and competition jointly provide the controls (determine the rewards or penalties) over the firm's choice of behavior. If competitive enforcement is perfect, the observed centralization of decision making within large firms (as well as observed contracting arrangements) must be efficient. Inefficient centralization (or contracting) by a firm would result in production above least cost, and the firm would be undersold by more efficient firms. In other words, when the interdependencies are confined to small subsets of agents in a large market, perfect competition internalizes them efficiently.

However, competition as an enforcement mechanism is not perfect. It is crucially dependent on information, and information can be difficult to come by. We have seen many examples of imperfect consumer control due to a lack of information. Competitor firms also may have imperfect information. This is particularly true when one recognizes that conditions change over time and firms must learn about the new conditions. Some centralized procedure may improve the speed at which the industry learns.

In a competitive market, for example, individual firms may have little incentive to reveal certain (unpatentable) information about a new technique. But information is like a public good: once produced, it is not used up by giving it to others. The speed of diffusion of innovations may be slower than optimal. Thus, the efficiency of competitive enforcement depends on how quickly the "enforcers" receive relevant information. A centralized effort to diffuse new knowledge, perhaps like the USDA efforts to inform farmers of methods to improve productivity, may improve the overall organization for certain sectors. However, the effectiveness of such efforts can vary greatly with the type of economic activity. Both computer and farm technologies may change quickly, but competitors may find it easy to identify and imitate computer advances and the opposite for farming.

Another way to make and extend this focus on information-handling ability is to recall the debate between Lange-Lerner and Hayek over the merits of decentralized socialism.[2] We sketch this in oversimplified terms below. First, note that if all economic agents have perfect knowledge, a perfectly centralized authority can achieve resource allocation identical with perfect competition. (The central authority simply uses perfect knowledge to direct each resource to where it would be in the competitive regime.) Lange and Lerner place less burdensome demands on the central authority, but it is nevertheless their information assumptions which raise Hayek's ire.

In the socialist setting, the property rights to produced capital belong to the state as a whole rather than individual "capitalists." The question naturally arises whether and how socialist economies can achieve an efficient allocation of resources. Lange and Lerner demonstrated that it can be done in theory by having central planners set prices and issue decentralized operating instructions to firm managers. Firms are instructed to produce at least cost and at the level of output where price equals marginal cost (the same task capitalist firms have). They can hire whatever labor and capital they wish at the state-determined prices. A state-operated bank rents out the available capital to firms demanding it. Individuals make consumption purchases and supply labor as in capitalist countries.

---

[2] See, for example, Oskar Lange and Fred Taylor, *On the Economic Theory of Socialism* (New York: McGraw-Hill Book Company, 1964).

If demand exceeds supply for an activity, the central planning board simply raises its relative price (and vice versa if supply exceeds demand) until equilibrium is reached. When the board sets the prices which equate supply and demand in all markets, the allocation is Pareto-optimal. Therefore, Lange and Lerner conclude, decentralized socialism can be just as efficient as competitive capitalism. They have shown that a plausible price adjustment mechanism can be used to reach equilibrium.

The logic of the Lange-Lerner model fully supports its conclusion. Furthermore, the logic is essentially no different than that used to show the optimality of perfect competition. But does that prove the two systems are equally efficient? Hayek's vehement protests concern the information-generating properties of each system. He argues that competitive capitalism is associated with rapid and subtle price adjustments. These efficiently convey the information necessary to allow economic agents to adapt promptly to changing circumstances. He continues by suggesting that socialism, on the other hand, is characterized by sloppy and slothful price adjustments made by a cumbersome central planning board. By the time the board deduces the correct prices for this year, it will already be next year; the economy will be in constant disarray.

Our earlier discussion suggests that Hayek's focus on information is appropriate, although his response is too strong. We do not really have any established theory which evaluates the relative informational efficiency of markets versus other procedures.[3] For specific activities, which is our interest, centralized procedures are often more efficient than decentralized ones. Nevertheless, the Lange-Lerner-Hayek debate does reinforce the importance of considering the learning and coordinating processes associated with any institutional design to guide resource allocations. The method of organization clearly affects the demand and supply of information in both the short run and long run. We shall try to illuminate this more, and show its relevance for policy analysis, in the practical problems considered in the following sections.

ORGANIZING AIR POLLUTION CONTROL EFFORTS

The theoretical considerations of the preceding section can be directly applied to an analysis of air pollution control policy. Air pollution is a case of negative externality in which the interdependency is among many economic agents, and the government is the central authority which must design some institutional way of internalizing it. The predominant form of control used in the United States is to set *regulatory standards*. For example, firms subject to federal requirements must use the "best available technology" to minimize pollution. The Environmental Protection Agency (EPA) then implements this rule by

---

[3] International comparisons are difficult, but Thurow concludes that several countries with substantially more government control of the economy than ours have a larger GNP per capita. West Germany and Sweden fit this category in 1978, for example. See Lester C. Thurow, *The Zero-Sum Society* (New York: Penguin Books, 1981), pp. 3–9.

specifying the required technology for particular firms and inspecting to make sure the firm is using it.

Many economists have attacked regulatory standards for two reasons: (1) The standard requiring use of the "best available technology" implies that the harm from a marginal pollutant is always greater than any finite cost (even if high) of reducing it. (2) The costs of achieving a given aggregate pollution reduction are not minimized. The first criticism is surely just, although there is great uncertainty about what the "optimal" level of pollution should be. (For example, long-run damage may result from pollution levels which do not have deleterious short-run effects.) From any pollution level, the "best available technology" may make it feasible to eliminate more pollution, but the costs of doing so may greatly outweigh the benefits. However, it is the second criticism which is more controversial and ties in directly to the analysis of this chapter.

The usual reasoning behind the second criticism is approximately as follows. If an aggregate pollution reduction has been efficiently achieved, the marginal cost to each polluting firm of the last unit reduced must be the same. Otherwise, there is room for a deal which leaves the aggregate pollution level unchanged. Suppose firm A has a marginal cost of $3.00 and firm B has a marginal cost of only $2.00. Then firm A saves $3.00 by polluting one additional unit, but at the same time persuades firm B to cut back one more unit for a payment of, say, $2.50. Society is indifferent, but the owners of firms A and B are each better off by $0.50.

The next step in the usual reasoning is to argue that regulatory standards do not achieve this equalization of marginal costs. As interpreted by the regulatory agency, the "best available technology" required for one firm has no necessary relation to the requirements for another. One factory, for example, may be required to install and operate smokestack scrubbers. This may leave it in a position analogous to, say, firm B above. Furthermore, unbeknown to the regulatory agency, this same factory could reduce pollution further by substituting a more expensive chemical for one it is currently using. A second firm in the same air basin may be emitting the same pollutant but, because it is a very different type of firm, it receives an order to reduce its pollution by a spraying process. It may be left in a position analogous to firm A above, and thus there is room for a deal between the two firms.[4]

---

[4] In this example we have assumed the regulatory standard is a *technical* one. Another form of regulation is the *performance* standard; e.g., pollution can be no more than 500 particulates per minute. Performance standards have the same type of flaw as technological ones, at least by the reasoning we have been using so far. Assuming that firms have different cost functions for pollution reduction and that the assignment of standards does not take perfect account of the fact, the costs of achieving the aggregate reduction will not be minimized.

According to the same reasoning, however, there is a critical advantage of the performance standard over the technological one: the inefficiency must be of a lower degree. The proof of this is easy. Imagine replacing the technological standards assigned to each firm with the performance standard that requires the same reduction. The firm can certainly achieve it at no greater cost than is required by the technological standard, but it may be able to achieve its performance level more cheaply by using a different technology (e.g., chemical substitution rather than scrubber installation). Performance standards may also have a dynamic advantage over technical ones in terms of encouraging research and development of lower-cost methods to meet the standards.

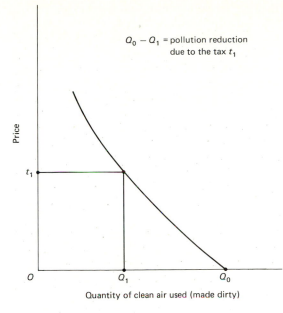

$Q_0 - Q_1$ = pollution reduction
due to the tax t_1

FIGURE 15-1
The effect of a tax on the factor
demand of firms for clean air.

Quantity of clean air used (made dirty)

The final step in the standard critique is to note that there are simple market mechanisms which would automatically eliminate the problem. Rather than rely on standards, a pollution tax could be imposed. In other words, firms could buy as much of the right to pollute as they wished, as long as they paid the tax price. Imagine that within any single air basin there is a spectrum of polluting firms with marginal cost for pollution reduction rising with the aggregate amount reduced. Think of clean air as an input that is demanded and used up (made dirty) by firms in their production processes. Then the factor demand curve for clean air, illustrated in Figure 15-1, depends on firm willingness to pay the marginal cost of pollution reduction avoided.

At the current supply price of clean air (i.e., zero), the firms use up (or dirty) Q_0 quantity of previously clean air. To achieve any desired pollution reduction, all we need do is set a tax rate corresponding to that level on the factor demand curve. For example, if we desire pollution to be reduced from Q_0 to Q_1, we simply impose a tax rate t_1 per unit of polluted air. Every polluting firm now prefers to reduce its pollution whenever its marginal cost of so doing is less than t_1 (otherwise, it would have to pay the tax). Thus we reach the conclusion of the usual reasoning: Taxes are a more efficient method of pollution reduction than regulatory standards because they achieve the reduction at the least social cost.

It is interesting to note this implication of the reasoning so far: A *subsidy* to reduce existing pollution (thus not available to any new pollution sources) has an allocative effect identical with that of the *tax*. That is, suppose each firm were offered t_1 for each unit of pollution reduction. Then for every unit when the marginal firm cost of reducing the pollution was less than the offered subsidy, the firm would increase its profits by choosing to reduce pollution. Since that is true of all the units of air between Q_0 and Q_1, again the result would be to reduce pollution to Q_1![5] In both cases the opportunity cost of polluting is the same: The firm either foregoes a subsidy or pays an equal size tax for each unit of pollution it produces.

The allocative equivalence of the tax and subsidy policies is a special case of *the Coase theorem: With perfect knowledge, zero transaction costs, and well-specified property rights, market allocation is the same no matter which economic agents have initial title to the property rights of the traded goods.*[6] In the above example, the good being traded is clean air. In the tax case the government (as an agent for those harmed by pollution) can be considered to have the property rights to the air. If firms wish to use the air, they must pay its owner (the government) for the privilege of doing so. In the case of the subsidy the polluters can be considered to have the rights to the air. If others (again acting through the government as agent) wish to have more clean air, they must pay the firms to provide it.

The underlying logic of the Coase theorem is that (under the assumptions) the assignment of property rights does not affect the net benefits from any specific allocation. Each agent has the same intrinsic value for consuming a particular quantity of the good, and the cost of doing so is either the price actually paid (if bought from another who holds the initial rights) or the equivalent opportunity cost (if one has the initial rights and foregoes selling them to another). Since the true price per unit of consumption is the same in either case, all agents buy the same quantities (again, assuming no income effects).

An additional implication of the Coase theorem is that the resulting allocation is efficient (even with income effects). As long as the property rights are well-defined, there will be no externalities; all interdependencies get internalized. This result depends crucially on the assumption of zero transaction costs. In the air pollution example, the externality does not get internalized precisely because of high transaction costs. There are several reasons why the transaction costs are high; among them are the institutional specification of property rights and the bargaining costs of securing agreement among many economic agents. These are explained below.

Historically, air has been treated legally as common property. This means that no one has the exclusive rights to control the use of the resource; anyone, including polluters, can use the air for free. At that price, it is not surprising that the property gets overutilized. Since no economic agent has the authority to establish a positive price which others must pay to use the property, the external effects from each user on the others do not get internalized.

---

[5] This assumes there are no income effects on the aggregate demand for pollution reduction. Note the similarity between the equivalence here and those identified for various rationing plans in Chapter 13.

[6] We continue to assume no income effects. See R. Coase, "The Problem of Social Cost," *Journal of Law and Economics, 3*, October 1960, pp. 1–44.

Imagine that those who dislike pollution costlessly band together and offer a subsidy to polluters to reduce emissions. Free entry to use the "commons" would be exploited by new sources as long as such entry was profitable (the marginal cost of making pollution was less than the offered subsidy). This would cause resource misallocation (no social value to the resources used in making the extra pollution), and would likely mean that the group offering subsidies would not be viable. The claimants to the offered subsidies would be essentially unlimited.

One could imagine trying to reduce transaction costs by changing the specification of property rights: making them private rather than common. Suppose each landowner were given the air rights above his or her property and anyone violating them would be liable for damages. Then any one polluter would need to purchase permission to use the air from many independent landowners. But landowners could strategically hold out in order to bargain for a larger payment, and those bargaining costs would prevent any agreement from being reached. The same problem could arise if someone attempted to reduce the bargaining costs by offering to buy up all the land (thus giving one person all the air rights): The many independent landowners would have the same strategic incentives to hold out and would make the success of an attempted buy-out unlikely.[7]

Those bargaining costs could arise in another form if initially the private property rights were given to the polluting firms. The many independent pollution sufferers could in theory be willing to pay collectively an amount which would induce the polluting firm to reduce emissions. But there would be a free-rider problem in trying to organize a collective offer: Each pollution sufferer would have a strategic incentive to deny or understate his or her willingness to pay when contributions were solicited, and then enjoy for free or at low cost the cleaner air purchased by the collectivity.

Thus high transaction costs, relative to achievable allocative gains, explain why the externality of air pollution does not get internalized through voluntary market transactions. The natural question to ask next is whether there is some other institutional structure which could achieve allocative gains that exceed the organizational costs of operating the structure itself. But it is precisely that type of logic which is absent from the usual reasoning about the tax solution that we reviewed earlier. *The key fallacy in the standard reasoning is this: The "solution" is derived without taking explicit account of the transaction costs which create the problem and how to overcome them.* This does not mean the solution is wrong, necessarily; it does mean the analysis is unpersuasive.

Let us reconsider the problem and the proposed tax or subsidy solutions to it by using the framework of operating rules and enforcement mechanisms described in the first section. First, it should be noted that both solutions, as well as the regulatory standards approach, involve the "appointment" of the government as a centralized bargaining agent to represent interests in pollution avoidance. This reflects a trade-off: a loss of allocative efficiency (the bargain-

---

[7] This situation is similar to that of the slumlords in the Slumlord's Dilemma of Chapter 6.

ing agent does not know the exact preferences of individuals for clean air) in order to gain transactional efficiency.

The most interesting aspect of the proposed tax and subsidy solutions is their use of decentralized operating instructions to firms: "Maximize profit, accounting for the tax cost (or subsidy) of pollution that you produce." This stands in contrast to the regulatory standards approach which uses centralized operating rules, e.g., "Install this scrubber in your smokestack."

One factor to consider in comparing the two types of rules is the generation and diffusion of pollution-reducing techniques among the relevant economic agents. Do firms have better information than the central authority about how to control their own pollution? This must be asked not only in the static sense, based on current knowledge, but also in the dynamic sense: how quickly new techniques will be discovered and adopted. Since the use of particular techniques may be different under the centralized and decentralized alternatives, it would not be surprising if the efforts to improve the techniques (i.e., by would-be inventors) also were different.

Arguments can be made on various sides of the technical knowledge aspect. For example, firms ought to know best what substitute materials they can use in order to remain productively efficient under pollution reduction constraints. The central government would have to become an expert on every product in order to possess that information. On the other side, the decentralized adoption of particular techniques to reduce pollution may be invisible to other firms and result in slow diffusion of the techniques. That is, the innovating firm may hoard its knowledge (if not privately marketable) in order to gain a competitive advantage. A centralized authority might achieve a more rapid diffusion.

One might charitably assert that behind the suggestions for the tax (or subsidy) approach lies a belief in the superiority of the decentralized method for generating and diffusing technical knowledge. But that concerns only the operating rules. What about the enforcement side? Is it possible to establish a system of rewards or penalties which leads to the intended result of achieving a given overall air quality at least cost? Therein lie the primary difficulties with the proposals.

In contrast to other inputs like electricity or natural gas, the amount of pollution emitted by specific sources is not routinely metered. A tax on an input (or output) that is routinely metered is relatively easy to assess: one simply multiplies the tax rate by the known quantity. Even in this case one must solve the problem of knowing the right tax rate. (That is, it must give sufficient incentive to firms to achieve the desired aggregate reduction.) But for pollution this may require substantial trial and error, which would be prohibitive politically.

In addition, in the case of pollution, metering would have to be undertaken solely for the purpose of assessing the tax. It is not clear that we have the technology to meter all the different sources of the same pollutant at a reasonable cost; pollution is not as readily meterable as home electricity or gas.

For tax assessments it is important that the quantity of pollution be accurately metered: The tax payments will be more or less, depending on the specific quantity.[8]

But some firms may be metered easily, whereas others cannot be. It may be feasible to sample a firm's pollutant levels randomly, but that must take account of the firm's ability to vary its pollution by time of day. Sampling may not be considered a sufficient legal basis for assessing the firm's average tax for the tax period. Even if it is, there is an unfortunate incentive for corruption between the firm and the pollution level inspector: Who would know if the assessments were lower than the actual pollution level?[9] Thus, the difficulty or costliness of pollution metering may be a severe drawback to the tax approach.

The same problems arise with a subsidy plan. In addition, one has the problem of establishing a base level below which subsidies are offered. Firms have an incentive to jack up pollution levels as soon as they realize subsidies will be available for reductions. One can restrict this problem to the initial subsidy period by establishing a new base each future period based on the prior subsidies awarded. However, one must be careful not to remove the incentive to keep pollution down. That is, what prevents the firm from collecting a subsidy and then promptly returning to its original pollution level? One deterrent would be a combined tax-subsidy plan: let pollution decreases be subsidized and increases be taxed. Even if one avoids the unique problems of the subsidy compared with those of the tax, the basic metering requirements make either approach difficult to implement in practice.

By contrast, enforcing regulatory standards is a much easier task. Compliance is a yes or no rather than a more or less question. If firms are required to operate particular technologies like smokestack scrubbers or cannot exceed certain pollution levels, random site visits are a highly plausible way of enforcing the rules. To be sure, enforcement of standards would also be imperfect; e.g., firms might not provide proper maintenance for the pollution control equipment. Nevertheless, this could be relatively easily observed on a random site visit and a penalty for noncompliance could readily be assessed.[10] The ease of checking compliance also makes it easier to spot-check the

---

[8] The accuracy required would be greater than that for performance standards. The latter involves answering only the yes and no question of whether the pollution level is greater or lower than the standard, and not by how much.

[9] It is easier to prevent corruption in the enforcement of regulatory standards, e.g., it is easier to check up on the inspector if the inspection task is to see if the scrubbers are working. Corruption is influenced by the system for monitoring the inspectorate. For example, inspectors could receive a bounty for each pollutant they catch a source emitting, or one could randomly sample the inspectors' reported levels. But those enforcement systems might be enormously costly. For more on this subject, see Susan Rose-Ackerman, *Corruption: A Study in Political Economy* (New York: Academic Press, 1978). For an interesting example of how an inspectorate for regulatory standards might be used to simulate a tax, see John Mendeloff, *Regulating Safety: A Political and Economic Analysis of OSHA* (Cambridge, Mass.: The M.I.T. Press, 1979).

[10] Note that if penalties are proportional to the seriousness of the violations, this begins to resemble a tax. Recognition of this is a key part of the analysis in Mendeloff, op. cit.

inspectors and reduces the likelihood of corrupt enforcement relative to the tax or subsidy plan.[11]

To sum up this discussion of pollution control, we have considered a market plan which relies on taxes or subsidies to be the price per unit of pollution, and we have compared it with regulatory standards. Analysis of this issue requires that we treat it as an information problem. Under the usual assumptions of perfect information and zero transaction costs, all these systems can be optimal. We must recognize that each method of organization has its own implicit demand and supply structure for the information used in decision making. Using Arrow's theoretical framework of operating and enforcement rules, we consider the information demand and supply under each.

The analysis of the operating rules, or the instructions given to polluting units on how to behave, is inconclusive. We interpret the usual argument for the tax approach as a judgment that the polluting units know best and can learn best how to reduce their own pollution and by how much. Given the subtle substitution possibilities that might characterize input choices of various products, and the incentives of pollution control equipment suppliers to spread information about new marketable control techniques quickly, this judgment is not unreasonable.

It is on the enforcement side that the weakness of the tax or subsidy method becomes apparent. The amount of tax due is a more-or-less question which requires accurate metering of pollution by each source. One must also know what tax rate will lead to the desired aggregate reduction. Both pose very difficult information burdens on the taxing authority; in fact, the cost of meeting minimum legal requirements for taxation, so that the tax is not considered arbitrary or capricious, may be prohibitive.

The enforcement of regulatory standards, on the other hand, is a yes-or-no question which is open to dispute only in marginal cases. The achievment of aggregate reduction targets is more certain, since quantity is being rationed directly. Noncompliance can be penalized by fines. Although the standards themselves are sure to be imperfect, they are at least reasonably enforceable.

The preceding analysis is intended only to provide some insight into the comparison of the two systems, and not to resolve the matter. We have not made any attempt to consider other alternatives, but part of the power of having some framework for thinking about the issues is to generate alternatives. The more one thinks about how to capture the combined strengths of both centralized and decentralized procedures, the more interesting the problem becomes.

For example, perhaps one can use the market and still ration by quantity in

---

[11] Recall the earlier footnote distinguishing technical and performance standards and reviewing the argument for favoring performance standards. Now we can see that this argument is subject to the same flaw as the usual pollution tax argument: It makes implicit assumptions about information and transaction costs which may be quite erroneous in certain circumstances. In particular, the enforcement of a performance standard (even though it is a yes or no question) may be much more difficult than a technical standard; measuring particular pollutants can be more difficult than checking scrubber installation.

the form of transferable ration coupons for pollution. A regulatory authority could declare centralized quantity standards as before but this time issue ration coupons in an amount equal to the applicable standard for each polluting firm. Let the firms trade—indeed, encourage them to trade—these "pollution rights" among themselves. Then define the compliance level for each firm as equal to its after-trading coupon quantities. That still leaves the regulatory agency with a yes-or-no question to answer.

Presumably firms will sell coupons as long as the market-determined price for them is greater than the marginal cost of pollution reduction. Other firms, with high marginal reduction costs, will be the buyers. Assuming the quantity issued is identical with the aggregate target in the tax or subsidy case, the equilibrium coupon price will be the same (assuming no income effects) as the optimal tax rate. But, of course, by this method, the market locates the price and saves the central authority from the task.[12]

In a small way the recently introduced "offset" policy of the EPA uses the above process. Before the policy was introduced, air basins which had not met their pollution reduction targets were forbidden to allow the entry of any new pollution sources. Thus, the nonattainment areas had policies of no growth. That can be a very expensive policy, since the net benefits of new polluters are often greater than the net benefits from older polluters (of equivalent quantity). Under the offset policy, the new source may enter the area if it can induce (through the market) old sources to reduce their pollution by more than the amount the new source will cause. This is equivalent to distributing pollution rights to all the existing sources and allowing them to be transferred only to new sources.

REGULATING A NATURAL MONOPOLY

Another policy problem in which specific attention to the information structure is important concerns the public response to natural monopolies. The cost structure of a natural monopoly was introduced in the discussion of trucking deregulation in Chapter 7. Because of economies of scale over the relevant range of demand, competition can sometimes sustain only one firm in a market. In Figure 15-2 we illustrate such a situation.

The efficient output quantity to produce is Q_E, where the marginal cost curve intersects the demand curve. But a monopolist is unlikely to choose that output level. A profit-maximizing monopolist, for example, will produce at Q_M.[13] At that quantity, price P_M will be substantially above the marginal cost. Thus, consumers are being "exploited" (i.e., by the amount above marginal cost) and the quantity produced is below the optimal level.[14]

---

[12] The principles here are discussed more extensively in Chapter 13.

[13] Barring price discrimination.

[14] Note that the problem of the unprofitable natural monopoly will occur if the demand curve shifts far enough to the left. The usual response to this case, discussed in Chapter 9, is either to have a public enterprise or to subsidize a private firm. Of course, if the demand curve is too far to the left, there may be no positive output level at which the benefits outweigh the costs.

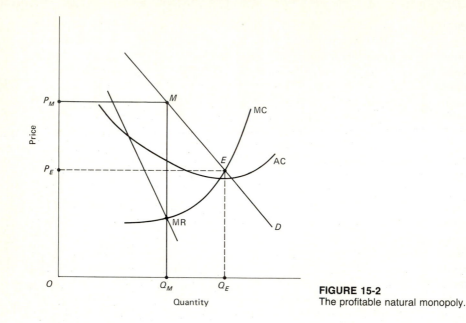

FIGURE 15-2
The profitable natural monopoly.

Historically, this market structure has been thought to characterize such activities as electricity, gas, and telephone services. It would be inefficient, for example, to have two sets of telephone poles when one is bad enough. The predominant response to these natural monopolies has been to subject them to rate-of-return regulation. Under that type of regulation, a regulatory commission determines a "fair" rate of return f on the company's net capital stock K. It then limits the price P charged per unit of service Q such that, after paying the wage bill wL,

$$\frac{PQ - wL}{K} \le f$$

Two quite different types of criticism are often made against this form of regulation. The first one is known as the *Averch-Johnson theorem;* it relies on the ordinary model of firm profit maximization for its proof: *A profit-maximizing monopolist subject to rate-of-return regulation will produce its output with an inefficient combination of inputs. In particular, the firm will use too much capital relative to labor for any given output level.*

The complete proof of this theorem is somewhat tedious, and we present only an abbreviated, simplified version of it.[15] First assume that the firm finds

---

[15] The original proof is in H. Averch and L. Johnson, "Behavior of the Firm under Regulatory Constraints," *The American Economic Review, 52,* December 1962, pp. 1053–1069. A somewhat simpler geometric proof is offered by E. Zajac, "A Geometric Treatment of Averch-Johnson's Behavior of the Firm Model," *The American Economic Review, 60,* March 1970, pp. 117–125.

the regulatory constraint binding (otherwise, it could choose the ordinary profit maximum). With a convex production function, profit levels at production points where the constraint is not fully used up are strictly less than the maximum attainable. Also assume that the allowable rate of return f is greater than the competitive price per unit of capital. (That is, there will be some positive economic profit, as would characterize, for example, the efficient solution at point E in Figure 15-2.) We show below that, under these conditions, the firm cannot have an efficient input combination and simultaneously be at its equilibrium (i.e., constrained profit maximum). It can do better by finding another constraint point where it uses more capital relative to labor.

For convenience, we define the input units such that the price of a unit of capital equals the price of a unit of labor. Then if the firm is using an efficient input combination, $MP_L = MP_K$. If this is also a firm equilibrium, the regulatory constraint must be binding. But we will show a contradiction: The firm can make the same profit without running into its constraint (i.e., when the constraint is not binding), and therefore that profit amount cannot be the maximum.

Imagine that, from this hypothesized efficient equilibrium, we reduce labor and increase capital by one unit each in order to remain on the same isoquant. This marginal change holds output and total cost, and therefore profit, constant. The firm's rate of return, however, is now strictly less than f:

$$\frac{PQ - w(L - 1)}{K + 1} < \frac{PQ - wL}{K} = f$$

How do we know this? We multiply both sides of the claimed inequality by $K(K + 1)$ and cancel like terms:

$$Kw < PQ - wL$$
or
$$0 < PQ - w(L + K)$$

But the right-hand side is simply the firm's profit, which we know is greater than zero from our initial assumptions. Since this shows the firm can achieve the same profit level hypothesized as the maximum without running into the constraint, that profit level cannot be the maximum.[16]

---

[16] An informal calculus argument may be made along the same lines. Along an isoquant,

$$dQ = MP_K \, dK + MP_L \, dL = 0$$

Since the efficient point on that isoquant is one where $MP_K = MP_L$ (given our choice of units), it follows that at it the slope is -1, or

$$-dK = dL$$

A movement from this point along the isoquant has the following effect on the rate of return:

Note that one cannot make the same argument by moving the opposite way along the isoquant, i.e., by increasing labor and reducing capital. That would strictly violate the rate-of-return constraint. An intuitive explanation for this bias toward capital is as follows. Consider expanding output by using either a unit of capital or a unit of labor, either of which would increase profits by the same amount. The unconstrained firm would be indifferent about the input choice, but the regulated firm must consider whether the extra profit will be allowed, given its rate base. The extra unit of labor does not change the base, but the extra unit of capital expands it and thus allows greater profit. Thus, the regulated firm has some bias to favor capital relative to labor. In other words, when seeking marginal revenue, the firm considers both the ordinary marginal costs and the marginal cost of using up some of its scarce constraint.

In an important sense the Averch-Johnson theorem demonstrates government failure analogously to the examples we have seen of market failure. It shows that a particular way of regulating a specific activity (the natural monopoly) is imperfect. It does not say anything about the degree of imperfection; that depends on the actual behavior of the regulatory commission. (For

---

$$df = \frac{\partial f}{\partial K} \, dK + \frac{\partial f}{\partial L} \, dL$$

$$= \left(-\frac{\partial f}{\partial K} + \frac{\partial f}{\partial L} \right) dL$$

Thus our claim that $df < 0$ in response to this change (where $dL < 0$) is equivalent to the claim that

$$0 < \frac{\partial f}{\partial L} - \frac{\partial f}{\partial K}$$

By definition,

$$f = \frac{PQ - wL}{K}$$

We take the partial derivatives, but for simplicity omit writing below the terms associated with the partial changes in the total revenue term PQ which later net out to zero (because we are moving along an isoquant):

$$\frac{\partial f}{\partial L} = -\frac{w}{K}$$

$$\frac{\partial f}{\partial K} = -\frac{PQ - wL}{K^2}$$

On substituting in the claimed inequality above, we have

$$0 < -\frac{w}{K} - \left(-\frac{PQ - wL}{K^2} \right)$$

By multiplying both sides by K^2 and rearranging, we get

$$0 < PQ - w(L + K)$$

Thus, the claim that f decreases is equivalent to the claim that firm profits are positive, and we know by assumption that the latter is true. Q.E.D.

example, will the allowed rate of return be generous or stringent?) Furthermore, it does not say anything about rate-of-return regulation in comparison with other alternatives (e.g., unregulated monopoly, public enterprise, and other forms of regulation).

Indeed, one of the strongest arguments against rate-of-return regulation is offered by those who believe in *the "capture theory": The regulatory commission gets capured by the firms in the industry it is supposed to be regulating.*[17] This can happen in an unsubtle way if the commission members appointed believe that the public interest coincides with unconstrained industry profit maximization. A more subtle method is to dangle the prospect of attractive industry jobs for cooperative commissioners when they leave public service. But the sophisticated version is that fair-minded commission members are subjected to heavily biased information channels, which lead to decisions that are "as if" the commission had been captured.

The last version follows from the assumption that the industry possesses an enormous information advantage. It knows its own cost structure and the demand for its products. Others, including the regulatory commission, must rely on the firms just to obtain basic information about the industry. The industry, however, has strong incentive to release and present only that information which is most favorable to its desired position. Thus, even if commission members truly seek to set a fair rate of return, the information used to determine the rate will be biased.

Commission hearings, in this latter view, are like court cases in which only one side gets to present its arguments (or more realistically, in which only one side has adequate representation). For any given real capital base, for example, the industry will invest considerable resources in maximizing the value of it accepted by the commission (and thus the fair "interest" which it is allowed to earn). Thus, fair-minded commission members, reacting to biased information, make decisions that are overly generous to monopolists.[18]

If the capture theory in any of its versions is correct, fiddling with the formula for the regulatory constraint should not be expected to have great impact. The allowed rate of return, or the constraint under an alternative form of regulation, would always be close to nonbinding. A proposal which purports to do away with the regulatory process altogether is for the government to sell the right to operate the monopoly through a competitive bidding process.[19]

Bidding processes are usually thought of as market arrangements: The transaction is priced, and the price is determined by the competitive bids. The regulatory commission, on the other hand, is a centralized price-setting agent with periodic hearings as an adjustment mechanism to keep the rate of return at

---

[17] Typically one commission regulates several natural monopolies; e.g., a state public utilities commission usually regulates electric companies serving various regions of the state.

[18] For a review of these theories and some proposed reforms, see Roger Noll, *Reforming Regulation* (Washington, D.C.: The Brookings Institution, 1971).

[19] See, for example, H. Demsetz, "Why Regulate Utilities?", *Journal of Law and Economics, 11,* April 1968, pp. 55–66.

its equilibrium ("fair") level. At least in some situations, the bidding procedure has the effect of removing the central agent's demand for information about the eventual supplier.

A simple example of bidding is the federal government's weekly Treasury bill auction, some of the revenue from which is used to finance government expenditure and refinance old debt. A Treasury bill is a promise to pay a certain amount to the holder at a specified future time, such as $10,000 to be paid 6 months from the date of issue. Suppose the government wishes to sell a certain number of these bills. It knows that individuals will be willing to pay only something less than $10,000 at the time of issue (since nominal interest rates are positive). If it sets a price by guessing, demand may not equal supply. In either direction the error is costly; either the government does not raise the revenue it desires (supply exceeds demand), or it foregoes revenue it could have collected (demand exceeds supply). Since interest rates vary substantially over time, there is no reason to think the government can learn the right price after a few trial weeks.

On the other hand, competitive bidding solves the problem of finding the equilibrium price. Each potential buyer submits a bid which is the maximum price that buyer is willing to pay for a desired number of bills. The government orders all bids from highest to lowest and awards the bills to the top bidders. The cutoff point is determined by the total quantity offered, and each winner pays only the price at the cutoff point. Since there is no price discrimination, each bidder has incentive to offer the true maximum willingness to pay. (It costs nothing to be honest; and by understating true willingness to pay, one risks not buying a bill which is truly desired.)

A second bidding example brings us closer to using the process to prevent monopoly exploitation. Periodically, the federal government wishes to allow a small portion of its land to be leased for coal exploration and mining. The value of any particular land tract is very uncertain at the time of leasing, but the government nevertheless wishes to receive revenue near the true value for the use of the land. Furthermore, it wishes the land to be developed in efficient order: the least expensive coal sources first. The problem is how to organize the leasing process to obtain that result.[20]

One centralized way to approach the problem is to let geologists from the U.S. Geological Survey (USGS) examine the tracts in much the same way the geologists of any private mining company would. USGS routinely collects certain basic information relevant to estimating the tract value (e.g., average thickness of coal seams in the county), but it would have to collect a great deal more (e.g., sulfur content of the coal in a specific tract) to replicate private company procedures. If it did, the USGS analysts could estimate the fair market value for each of the tracts to be leased and the government would

---

[20] A description of the problem and its proposed solution is contained in C. B. McGuire, "Intertract Competition and the Design of Lease Sales for Western Coal Lands," presented at the Western Economic Association Conference, Hawaii, June 25, 1978.

simply use the estimates to set the lease prices and identify the efficient tracts to lease (i.e., those with highest value).

The problem with this procedure is that because there are many tracts, many mining firms, and realistic limits on the size of the USGS evaluative staff, the information at the "center" will almost always be worse than the information of some firms for a particular tract. The lease prices for some tracts will be set too high, and the tracts will go unleased. For other tracts, the lease price will be too low and mining firms will receive economic profit at the expense of reduced government revenues.

So far, this does not sound too different from Treasury bills. But there is good reason to believe that competitive bidding for each tract will not solve the problem. That is because the true value of any specific tract will vary from firm to firm, depending on who owns adjacent land, operates a nearby mine, or has surface rights to the tract in question. In other words, the firm already in the area is the only one which can take advantage of these scale economies. Other firms, recognizing this, will not waste their time and exploration resources on preparing bids for such tracts. Thus, there will not be effective competition in the bidding, and the advantaged firms will be able to win at a price substantially below true value.

The ingenious solution to this problem is to have *intertract* competitive bidding. For example, the government announces that it will consider bids received within 6 months of an announcement on any of 100 specified tracts. It selects 100 "homogeneous" tracts to be eligible for bids based on the limited information available from the USGS. Furthermore, it announces that only 10 tracts will be leased: the 10 receiving the highest bids.

Thus, each firm in an advantaged position for a particular tract has incentive to bid the full value for it. That is, each firm recognizes that it is now competing against many other firms in situations similar to its own. The firm physically next to tract 12 may be the only firm which can achieve scale economies by producing on it, but it must bid higher than a similarly advantaged firm bidding on tract 37. Any bid substantially lower than the true value is at the risk of foregoing an opportunity the firm would consider worthwhile.

The most important aspect of the process is the efficiency of its information structure. Economic agents, including the center, need no further information than that they already have. The government not only achieves its revenue objectives but does so in such a way that the most efficient coal sources are utilized first.[21] (The highest bids are made for tracts where the coal extraction costs are lowest.)

Now, with these examples of bidding processes in mind, let us consider how competitive bidding might be used as a replacement for regulating a natural monopoly. One possibility would be to auction off the right to provide service

---

[21] In this bidding process, the government collects all the winning bids as revenues rather than charge the tenth highest bid to each of the winners. This may prevent firms from bidding their true willingness to pay, because they can trade off a reduced probability of winning for increased profit.

in the area to the highest bidder. This has the advantage of allowing the government to collect all of the monopoly profit. (If competitive, any bidder offering less than the present value of expected monopoly profits will be outbid by another seeing the opportunity for gain.) However, this process would force the winner to produce and charge like the profit-maximizing monopolist (it is the only way to recover the purchase price). That is not allocatively desirable and is unlikely to be thought distributively fair.

Another suggestion is to award the franchise to whichever firm agrees to charge consumers the lowest price. That is, the bids are offers to provide service at a certain price to consumers, and the low bid wins. If there are no requirements to serve all who demand at this price, the winning bid is the price corresponding to the minimum of the average cost curve (refer to Figure 15-2). If the supplier must service all demanders at the bid price, then presumably the winning bid will be at the price at which the demand curve intersects the average cost curve (the lowest price at which there is zero profit and no excess demand). Neither of these is allocatively efficient, although both keep the price low (in fact, the price is below the efficient price whenever the demand curve crosses the average cost curve to the right of its minimum).

Since all these bidding proposals are imperfect, it is not obvious whether the (diagrammed) solutions would be more desirable than those achieved through rate-of-return regulation. However, Williamson argues that the consequences of such competitive bidding in practice cannot be accurately deduced from models like those underlying the above analysis.[22] His objections highlight the effect of imperfect information and transaction costs and the importance of designing a natural monopoly solution which creates an efficient information structure. To illustrate these theoretical points, he presents a case study of the competitive bidding approach used by Oakland, California, to grant an exclusive franchise for the right to provide cable television services within the city.

In presenting the franchise bidding idea, we have described it as if there were one auction at which each bid submitted is a simple price per unit and the unit is a well-defined good which would be identical no matter which supplier provided it. This description ignores a number of real problems, e.g. the franchise's duration and provisions to enforce its terms. The implicit assumption of the simplifying description is that these problems are complications which do not affect the essential validity of the model implications. But Williamson argues otherwise. He conducts an analysis by considering how one might specify the contract which the potential bidders are supposed to be seeking. The contract must take account of multidimensional aspects of time, price, and quality in specifying the operating agreement. But those aspects of the transaction are often associated with costly uncertainties to each of the contracting parties, which can be reduced only by costly enforcement mechanisms. The result can easily be a contract with negotiation, arbitration, and

[22] Oliver E. Williamson, "Franchise Bidding for Natural Monopolies: In General and with Respect to CATV," *The Bell Journal of Economics, 7,* spring 1976, pp. 73–104.

inspection provisions that, if called by any other name, would surely be regulation.

In short, the original proposals for franchise bidding solutions to natural monopoly problems have the same analytic flaws as the original pollution tax proposals. When the transaction costs are considered more carefully, Williamson concludes that substantial regulation is likely to be part of the franchise arrangement. Therefore, *the "market" solution and "regulation" are not really substitutes*. In fact, *traditional regulation can be viewed as nothing more than a particular form of contract (whether or not it is let by competitive bidding)*.[23]

To derive these conclusions, Williamson considers whether the contract should be once and for all, long-term, or one in a series of recurrent short-term contracts. In each case, the contract can be complete (if it specifies the response to all future contingencies) or incomplete (if it specifies mechanisms to resolve conflicting claims that may arise among the contracting parties). The complete once-and-for-all contract, for example, would have to specify the prices at which service is to be provided now and under every conceivable future condition. Since firms do not know how their factor prices might change over an indefinite future, they will certainly not agree to a price that is forever constant. Furthermore, since the possible states of the world extending into the indefinite future are infinite, it is too complex for the contracting parties to specify and agree on a price for each of them. Thus complete, once-and-for-all contracts are not written for services which are expected to be provided indefinitely.

Williamson argues that the incomplete once-and-for-all contract has essentially the same flaws as incomplete long-term contracts. With either of these or the complete long-term contract, the initial award criterion is obscure. How does one compare bids which represent different price-quality combinations, let alone bids which specify a whole vector of prices and qualities for the various services a company might provide? A local telephone company, for example, might have a basic monthly rate for one telephone, rates for additional telephones, installation charges, and a special rate for unlimited local calls. Furthermore, the quality of service can vary: The speed of installation, the frequency with which line repairs are needed, and the probability of receiving a busy signal are examples. Even if different companies submit bids specifying their price-quality offerings, it is not obvious how to compare them. Logially, one ought to pick the proposal which maximizes social welfare. But this task is a far cry from the simplicity of the auctioneer's decision rule.

A second series of problems are associated with the execution of a contract. Under incomplete contracts, for example, the parties may agree to some form of price-cost relation instead of price alone (because of the uncertainty of future cost conditions). The kind of incentive problems that arise are familiar to

---

[23] This general point is made in Victor Goldberg, "Regulation and Administered Contracts," *The Bell Journal of Economics, 7,* autumn 1976, pp. 426–448.

students of defense contracting.[24] Cost-plus contracts, for example, give suppliers incentive to maximize their costs. Under any price-cost arrangement, stringent auditing will be required by the government awarding the franchise. Note too that ordinary regulation can be described as a particular form of price-cost relation with attendant auditing procedures.

Another problem arising during contract execution is the enforcement of quality standards; even if the contract specifies exactly what the standards are supposed to be, the supplier may fail to meet them. Simply to inspect quality requires that personnel with relevant technical skills be part of the inspectorate. (Again, this resembles ordinary regulatory staffs.) The value of regular inspection depends, of course, on the technology used to deliver the service, as when continual maintenance is necessary to keep output quality at its contracted level.

It should also be noted that, once a long-term contract is let, it may be virtually impossible to enforce contract provisions strictly. The reason for this limitation is that there are opportunity costs to the government and the public of canceling the contract for reason of franchiser violations. Again, this is familiar from defense contracting, where "renegotiation" is almost standard. Government officials responsible for the contract fear that they will be held responsible for the supplier's failure, and thus they are not anxious to call public attention to any violations. Similarly, the officials will not be anxious to cause any disruptions in the services being rendered. Thus, it is often easier to renegotiate a contract and make its terms more favorable to the supplier.

In fact, the capture theory of regulatory behavior may apply with equal or greater force to the contracting process. Firms with high contracting expertise and low technical performance may be those which do best in this situation. That is, the contract may be awarded to a firm which deliberately bids an unrealistically low price, knowing it has the political skills to renegotiate favorable terms at a later date and the ability to cut corners on its legal obligations. Thus it captures the government contract supervisors at all stages of the contract.

Many of these problems might be avoided if we consider short-term recurrent contracts instead of long-term ones. Such contracting encourages adaptive and sequential decision making rather than complex contingency planning, and it may better suit the bounds of rationality. With short-term contracts, there is no need to create price-cost relations to deal with the various possible future states of the world. Potential suppliers simply take the actual changes into account in making bids during the next contracting period. Similarly, the government is in a stronger position to enforce quality standards: firms which violate them can be barred from the next contracting period.

Gaining these advantages depends crucially on having parity among bidders during contract renewal. However, there are two good reasons why parity is

[24] See, for example, Merton J. Peck and Frederic M. Scherer, *The Weapons Acquisition Process* (Cambridge, Mass.: Harvard University Press, 1962).

elusive. The first concerns procedures to facilitate the transfer of capital assets from the former to the new contractor. The second concerns the unique human capital skills developed in the process of providing the service. These are explained below.

In many of the natural monopolies, efficient service provision is associated with large investments in durable goods such as pipelines and large plants. In order to induce the contracting firm to undertake those investments, given that the contract period is much shorter than the useful lives of the assets, the firm must have assurances that it will receive the true economic value in the event of a change of contractor. But this raises essentially the same issues that are involved in determining the annual rate base of a regulated firm.

The firm that wins the initial contract has incentive to exaggerate the size of its capital assets for the next round of bidding. There are two reasons for this: (1) The more other firms have to pay to take over the fixed assets, the higher will be the prices they propose to charge and the better the chances of the original contractor to have the winning bid. (2) If the original contractor loses the second round, it will naturally seek to receive the largest possible compensation. Therefore, other firms and the government franchisor will employ their own experts to inspect the physical plant and examine the records involving original costs and depreciation write-offs. The various sides will have divergent estimates of the transfer value, and some process will be required to reconcile them.

Since the valuation of these assets is a very uncertain task (unlike valuing goods which are commonly and frequently traded in the marketplace), there is no reason to believe any process will arrive at the correct value with certainty. But a process which is risky to the firm, because it might substantially undervalue the assets, will deter the investments in the first place. And if the process is biased to err in the direction of overvaluation, there may be little difference between it and rate-of-return regulation. In addition, such a process will favor the original contractor during the renewal bidding. (Other firms will have higher cost structures because of the inflated price of the assets they must purchase.)

Human capital can also cause a lack of parity during contract renewal bidding. Although we often think of labor as interchangable, that is a simplification which ignores the development of human capital quite specific to a particular workplace. There may be many idiosyncratic aspects of production within the firm: maintenance of certain machinery, development of informal communication networks across divisions, relations with suppliers, etc. A new firm is at a disadvantage because it does not possess any of these assets.

It can be terribly inefficient for a new firm to start developing the idiosyncratic human capital from scratch. If this is the only alternative open to them, new bidders are unlikely to be able to submit the winning bid (their cost structures are too high). Alternatively, they can try to arrange for the transfer of personnel as well as physical equipment from the original contractor.

In the case of employee transfer, one must consider whether the employees are likely to strike more costly bargains with their original firm or with potential competitors. Again, the cost of dealing with the familiar is generally lower than the cost of the unfamiliar. Informal understandings about wages, promotions, and working conditions are possible in a familiar, established context. But with a potential employer, employees are less likely to be trusting, harder to bargain with, and more demanding of formal guarantees. Thus, one would expect potential entrants to be at a disadvantage because of these human capital elements as well as the problems of transferring durable plant and equipment.

In sum, the low-price, low-cost advantages of competitive franchise bidding over ordinary regulation for a natural monopoly may be an illusion. The weakness of the analysis underlying the bidding suggestion is identical with that in the usual pollution tax argument. Since the problem is inherently caused by information and transaction difficulties, one cannot examine it through a model which assumes information and transaction costs are negligible.

A more detailed analysis of the possible forms for the contractual agreement suggests that under both long- and short-term contracts, the firm receiving the initial franchise has considerable information and bargaining advantages over the government and potential competitors. To counter this, substantial arbitration, negotiation, inspection, and auditing procedures would be necessary. But then the bidding arrangement looks much like ordinary regulation. Furthermore, to the extent that ordinary regulation is thought to fail because the regulators have an information disadvantage, it is possible that competitive franchising can fail for the same reasons. Thus, whether franchise bidding can be used to effect some improvement in natural monopoly supply will depend on the particular service in question. Improvement seems a more likely prospect when the durable assets of the firm are easily valued and transferable and when the amount of idiosyncratic human capital within the firm is low (e.g., local refuse collection).

All of the problems Williamson raised were apparent in his case study of the decision of Oakland, California, to award the right to provide community antenna television (CATV) service by competitive bidding for the franchise. After holding preliminary discussions with interested potential suppliers, the city asked for bids to provide two types of viewer service: service A to consist of cable for local stations and FM radio and service B to include special programming services at the supplier's option. The city assumed that service A would be the predominant service, and the award criterion was therefore the lowest bid for providing it. It turned out that 90 percent of the customers chose service B instead. The price charged for it was requested by the company on one day and approved as requested on the following day.

Construction of the system was due to be completed by December 1973. But it went more slowly than expected; costs were claimed to be higher; and fewer households subscribed than had been anticipated by the company. The company appealed to the city to renegotiate the terms, which it did. The revised agreement allowed the company a reduction in the number of channels it had promised to carry, a reduction in the cable-laying requirement from dual to single cable, and substantially higher prices for providing cable to additional household televisions after the first.

After the service began operating, enough customers complained about its poor quality to make the city hire expert consultants to test for compliance with the quality standards in the contract. In renegotiating the dual-cable requirement, the revised terms also smacked of regulation: The city would require the second cable when the marginal revenues from it would exceed the company's gross investment cost plus 10 percent. In response to all these difficulties with the company, the city did consider contract termination. But it ended up accepting the poorer terms, and Williamson documents the city council's aversion to any service disruption and fears of expensive and extensive litigation.

In short, there is nothing in this case study to suggest that franchise bidding is superior to ordinary regulation. The two main lessons of it are that (1) much of what is normally thought of as ordinary regulation became a part of the franchisee-franchisor relationship, and (2) the same information and bargaining problems which support the capture theory of regulation are evident in this example of franchise bidding as well. Thus, any differences between franchise bidding and ordinary regulation are a matter of degree, and not of kind.

Before concluding this section, we note that this same form of analysis can be applied to *performance contracting*. An alternative way of trying to maintain the quality of supply at a low price is to establish a price-performance, rather than price-cost, contractual relationship. One natural monopoly situation in which this has been suggested and briefly tried is Amtrak's passenger rail service. Another example of a brief trial, although not in the context of a natural monopoly, is OEO's experiment with performance contracting for the education of children. We offer a few comments on these below.

Amtrak is a government corporation which sells rail tickets to passengers, contracts with private railroads to operate the trains, and receives subsidies from the federal government to make up the difference.[25] The traditional form of Amtrak contract with private suppliers is a flat fee derived from cost estimates of providing the service plus a fair return. Once the contract is written, the supplier has no incentive to care about the number of passengers carried or the quality of the service.

An incremental performance contract was tried briefly in the mid-1970s. It made the plus part of the flat fee into a plus-or-minus function dependent upon quality dimensions of actual service (trains on time, heated properly, clean, etc.) and economy (the supplier could keep funds resulting from cost savings). The incremental aspect was due to the uncertainty about how to establish appropriate rewards and penalties under performance criteria; possibly, this

---

[25] Before Amtrak, private suppliers were forced by the regulatory authorities to operate unprofitable passenger routes which were cross-subsidized by the suppliers' more profitable freight service. This is both inefficient (the benefits of the service do not outweigh its costs) and inequitable (the subsidies are paid by users of freight service rather than the general public). The creation of Amtrak is thought to alleviate the inequity.

resulted in insufficient incentives. The initial contracts placed heavy weight on punctuality at the expense of comfort. That might coincide with social value, but it happened because the availability of historical information on timeliness allowed more confidence among the contracting parties in determining a reasonable reward structure. However, Amtrak soon decided to abandon this experiment and reverted to its traditional contracting forms. It is not clear whether the abandonment resulted from inherent difficulties with performance contracting in this situation, implementation difficulties of defining an appropriate reward structure, or impatience.[26]

A brief trial also characterized the attempt at educational performance contracting. The experiment was motivated in part by the concern that ordinary public schools do not have sufficient incentive to improve the education that children receive. The merit of performance contracting, in this context, is to create a profit incentive for improving. To test it, OEO let performance contracts with six firms for 1-year periods. The rewards were made a function of the children's test scores. On average, the test scores of the children subject to this treatment (compared with a control group) did not improve, and the experiment was terminated.[27]

The experiment did not test the long-run aspects of the new organizational relationship which represent its most plausible source of gains. Unlike the railroads, there may be no obvious source for short-run gains in the schools. Ordinary school teachers and principals have a different set of motivations than railroad entrepreneurs. The latter may well know some ways to produce that are socially efficient, and it is not difficult to see how fixed-fee contracts create private incentives for the monopolist to diverge from efficient production. Improving the incentives for railroads can plausibly be expected to lead to observable service improvements in the short run.

But teachers are less likely to choose inferior techniques deliberately: they make no apparent profit by doing so, and it would be contrary to their professional principles. Some inefficiency may arise if teaching effort affects learning and if teachers under the existing systems are not motivated to put forth much effort. However, it would be surprising to observe performance contracting results that are, on average, substantially better than the usual ones, at least in the short run.

However, the long run is another matter. Even if one grants that ordinary teachers and principals are well-motivated, it does not follow that the public educational system is organized in a way that best facilitates achieving educational goals. Consider improvements in teaching techniques that are largely unpatentable; i.e., the source of the improvement is something like a

---

[26] For more information, see W. Baumol, "Payment by Performance in Rail Passenger Transportation: An Innovation in Amtrak's Operations," *The Bell Journal of Economics, 6,* spring 1975, pp. 281–298.

[27] For an account of this experiment, see E. Gramlich and P. Koshel, *Educational Performance Contracting* (Washington, D.C.: The Brookings Institution, 1975).

different way of teaching. Private entrepreneurs might have incentive to develop these techniques if they could market them in a way that prevented imitation (perhaps like private speed-reading courses). But the regular public school system prevents such marketing; once the method is taught to one district's teachers, there is little to prevent free imitation by others. Furthermore, the public school system may not have a very efficient screening mechanism to weed out the bad ideas; the rapid diffusion of the "new math," later discarded, may be an example.

It is at least plausible that, in the long run, performance contracting provides a source of organizational improvement. The idea is to encourage suppliers to learn over time by trial and error in the context of a process which diffuses successes and halts failures. One attains these advantages by allowing the contractor to provide the service directly to the children, thus giving it more opportunity to preserve its valuable "technical" knowledge (perhaps like commercial speed-reading methods, which are largely unpatentable). Other firms will, of course, try to imitate, and improvements come about by the growth of successful firms, the eventual success of imitators, the entry of new firms, and the demise of those unable to produce satisfactorily.

It is unlikely that any of these possible advantages could be observed in the one academic year OEO gave its six contracting firms to perform. It could be that the most important observation about the experiment is that one of the six contractors did appear to have significant success. The average result may not seem very exciting, but a one-out-of-six success rate in the short run could translate into much wider success if the system were allowed to spread its success and weed out its failures. At least this is what one would hope for with performance contracting, but the opportunity to find out was foreclosed by the experiment's termination.

In this section we have tried to show how analytic insight concerning the design of a governance structure can be generated by posing it as a question of choice among alternative contractual forms. This offers a different way of "seeing" information and transaction costs than the framework of operating rules and enforcement methods used in the preceding section. In the final section we consider still other analytic methods for generating these insights.

NONPROFIT ORGANIZATIONS AND THE DELIVERY OF DAY-CARE SERVICES

In thinking about the design of an organizational structure for conducting economic activity, it is important that the analyst not be too limited in the alternatives considered. Most of our examples have concerned governing private profit-making firms, but we have also seen that public bureaus and nonprofit oganizations may be used as agencies of production. In this section we offer an analysis which considers the use of these latter institutions.

The purpose of this section is really twofold. First, we wish to illustrate that there are economic rationales for preferring, in certain situations, nonprofit agencies over the other supply institutions we have discussed.[28] Second, we wish to demonstrate analytic methods that help one to assess the relative strengths of these institutions compared to others. We do this in the context of a specific example: public policy with respect to day care for small children. As in the earlier sections of this chapter, we only wish to establish a plausible argument based on explicit consideration of information and transaction costs; the source literature on day care provides a more appropriate empirical basis for assessing the argument's persuasiveness.[29]

A key part of the argument we present focuses on the demand and supply of information with respect to day care. In this case, the problem is how to obtain reliable indications of the quality of service being provided. Day care poses atypical information problems because it is by definition a service that is rendered when the parent (who acts as the consumer agent for the child) is not present, and its quality level is generally considered quite important. Nursing homes, hospital care, and, to some extent, elementary education pose similar problems.

We use two distinct analytic methods, both of which happen to be useful for this particular illustration. The first can be stated simply: *Review the history of the activity being analyzed from an economic perspective.* Economic theory by itself does not suggest the importance of history. But we have often seen that proper applications of theory require careful tailoring to account for the institutional details relevant to a specific problem. To apply the theory, one must be able to identify the relevant institutional details. One good way to learn about the details is to review the economic history of the activity.

The second point of analysis in the section is to introduce a framework suggested by Hirschman. *His "exit, voice and loyalty" framework provides insight into organizational responsiveness in markets for goods and services when quality is important.* We describe it briefly and then turn to the consideration of day care.[30]

Hirschman asks how suppliers are supposed to learn, or become informed,

---

[28] We do not wish to imply that there are no other economic rationales for nonprofit agencies than the one presented. Indeed, there are other very interesting rationales which have been identified in different settings. See Burton Weisbrod, in collaboration with Joel Handler and Neil Komesar, *Public Interest Law: An Economic and Institutional Analysis* (Berkeley, Calif.: The University of California Press, 1978); see also Burton Weisbrod, *The Voluntary Nonprofit Sector* (Lexington, Mass.: D. C. Heath & Company, 1977).

[29] The day-care analysis presented here is based on two primary sources: Richard R. Nelson and Michael Krashinsky, "Public Control and Economic Organization of Day Care for Young Children," *Public Policy, 22,* winter 1974, pp. 53–75; and Dennis Young and Richard R. Nelson, *Public Policy for Day Care of Young Children* (Lexington, Mass.: Lexington Books, 1973).

[30] See A. Hirschman, *Exit, Voice and Loyalty: Responses to Decline in Firms, Organizations and States* (Cambridge, Mass.: Harvard University Press, 1970). Hirschman's framework has been applied to a variety of problems. See, for example, R. Freeman, "The Exit-Voice Tradeoff in the Labor Market: Unionism, Job Tenure, Quits, and Separations," *The Quarterly Journal of Economics, 94,* June 1980, pp. 643–673; see also the papers under the topic "Some Uses of the Exit-Voice Approach," *The American Economic Review,* May 1976.

about specific mistakes they are making. In most situations we assume consumers will not buy very much of an inferior product. If an automobile company introduces new models which consumers do not like, the company sales will fall. Consumers *exit* from the group of firm customers. But when the product has multidimensional quality attributes, this signal to the supplier is a *noisy* one. The exit decisions could be caused by many factors, and the supplier does not receive the information necessary to pinpoint the problem. The firm can and does learn through marketing research. But the firm's task may be made easier if the consumers exercise *voice:* if, rather than exit, they complain to the company and state directly what improvements they wish.

Exclusive reliance on either exit or voice by itself would not be very effective in most situations. If there is no exit, a firm has little reason to respond to voice. If there is no voice, the response may be extremely sluggish. An extreme case of this is the duopoly, in which customers of firm A exit to firm B while customers of firm B do the reverse; all customers are dissatisfied, but each company has constant sales and receives no signal. In an industry with more suppliers, consumers can still hop from one firm to another without signaling any single firm to change. Eventually consumers may exit from the entire industry (depending on the demand elasticity for the good), but this does not signal potential new firms to enter and correct the problem. Some firm may eventually figure out a way to stop the exiting, but there is no reason to believe that the process is one of efficient adjustment.

Thus, Hirschman suggests that in most situations there is some optimal combination of exit and voice. But how can it be achieved? A certain amount of firm *loyalty* may be a desirable means to that end. That is, the loyal customers accept an inferior product temporarily (rather than exit in the hope of finding a superior one) while they exercise voice and await the company's response. Presumably, the firm can create loyalty to some extent (e.g., through access to special sales or preferred service). Less loyal customers exit from the company and reinforce the voice signals. The combination of the two tells the supplier it ought to change and helps to pinpoint how to change. The net result is that the industry adapts efficiently, assuming that most firms in it adopt the strategy.[31]

We shall draw upon the exit-voice-loyalty framework shortly, when we consider alternative organizational ways of providing day-care services. First, it is helpful to provide some historical background about child care. Looking at its provision over the past 200 years in the United States, Nelson and Krashinsky offer insight into two features of it: (1) When the parents work, most child care is and always has been provided by other family members. (2) Nevertheless, there has been a marked growth in the demand for extra-family child care.

---

[31] Note that in this scenario loyal customers are not the same as uninformed ones. Sometimes the voucher idea for education is criticized on the ground that it will lead to a school system segregated by the degree of parental knowledge. The proposition is that the informed parents will have their childen exit from inferior schools and the uninformed parents will leave their children in them. The inferior schools will then have no informed customer voices offering diagnoses of the problem.

Their interpretation of this economic history suggests a revealed social preference for child care to be undertaken by the most familylike institutions. The key economic reason for this is that trust among agents in these institutions is relatively high, and *trust is an efficient mechanism for reducing the uncertainty costs that the agents would otherwise bear*. We explain this below. Then we consider alternative organizational modes which could be used to provide increased day-care services stimulated by public policy. We sketch the plausible argument that established nonprofit agencies should be preferred, because they embody relatively more trust than the feasible alternatives. This line of reasoning is supported by some insights from the exit-voice-loyalty framework.

Over the past 200 years of U.S. economic history, activities which commonly were undertaken at home have progressively shifted to specialized institutions like the firm. Fewer households grow their own food, make their own clothes, or do their own ironing. This is a quite natural response to technical progress characterized by greater economies of scale (mass production). But child care has been much more resistant to this trend. Compared to the other activities, there has been only a modest movement from at-home child care. What is there about this economic activity which explains its relative resistance?

Nelson and Krashinsky suggest a number of factors. Most obviously, child care is more than an ordinary chore. At least to some degree, it gives pleasure to parents and other family members, like grandparents; it is a labor of love, as some would put it. In addition, there are certain "scale economies" to home care which work in its favor. One is that child care requires the full-time *availability* of an adult but is not necessarily a full-time activity. To some extent, the adult can simultaneously be engaged in cooking, cleaning, studying, or other activity. Thus, the time cost attributable to home child care is low compared with that of many activities which have shifted out of the home. Similarly, the space cost of home child care is relatively low: The family generally consumes housing of the same size even if it gives up home care.

In addition to these preference and economy factors, parents care a great deal about the way in which their child is cared for. Child care does not necessarily require expertise, but it does require a sharp eye to make sure the child is comfortable and not in any danger. To have trust and confidence in the care the child receives, there is nothing like providing it yourself. You simply do not know what happens if you are not there. Put differently, alternatives to family care introduce a good deal of costly uncertainty to the parents about quality of the care. Thus, these three sets of factors (preferences, economy, confidence) help explain why child care has been maintained in the home while so many other activities have been shifting out of it.

Despite the factors which operate to keep child care in the home, there nevertheless has been growth in nonfamily care. This growth includes an increase in the number of larger, more formal day-care centers. Much of the reason for the trend is explained by demographic changes. In more recent years, increased public subsidies have added to the demand. We comment briefly on each.

Compared with families in 1800, today's families are smaller. Of course, out-of-home day care is relatively more affordable when there are fewer children who need minding. But there are accompanying changes to this reduction in family size that also bear importantly on the demand for day care. Child mortality rates are much lower. Those two factors combined help explain why the median age of the wife at last birth has dropped from the late 30s to the late 20s and why, as well, the median age of the wife at first birth has risen. Thus, the number of years of intensive child rearing has decreased while life expectancy has increased. That makes investment in career development much more attractive than it once was. Along with the loss of competitiveness for home-produced goods in general, these factors explain much of the increase in demand for day care.

It is important to recognize that decisions about day care are made under quite different circumstances for families of differing socioeconomic circumstances. For a two-parent, upper-middle-income family with one or two children, choice is made without serious economic pressure. The issues that seem important are the value of career involvements and beliefs about what is best for the child. One- or two-parent families that have very low income opportunities, however, are posed with a serious economic dilemma. The importance of achieving some additional money income is very high. But the only way to free up time in order to increase employment is to purchase day care, and the cost may well exceed the potential income from working. This raises the issue of subsidized day care.

The growth in subsidies is another factor which helps explain the increased reliance upon day care. There is a long history of subsidized day care in the form of settlement houses for children of poor families, particularly for immigrant families whose children receive acculturation benefits. A significant expansion of day-care subsidies starting in the 1960s has been rationalized in part by applying a similar argument: Poor and minority children might receive as well as generate external benefits if they are in socially and economically integrated child-care centers. Another justification offered for subsidies is that of the work ethic: a belief that a welfare parent ought to work.[32]

There are arguments, of course, that subsidized day care should be made available to all families with small children. One line of reasoning is simply that day care is like elementary education: there is a social interest in the development and education of children which exceeds the private interest. A different argument is that it is beneficial to encourage women to work by making it easier and cheaper to find suitable places for the children. Whatever one feels about the merits of these arguments, it is clear that policy has not

---

[32] Note that this can be a very expensive belief if the family size is large. Also, one should carefully consider the merits of the in-kind subsidy versus increased cash support. It is one thing to reduce consumer sovereignty in a simple labor-leisure choice; it is another to reduce it by strong intervention in the parent decision concerning labor versus home care of children.

been formulated with them in mind. Subsidies are generally restricted to lower-income families; they support less than 10 percent of children under 5 who have working mothers.

Even with the growth in demand for non-home care, the predominant form of child care is still in the home. According to surveys cited by Nelson and Krashinsky, about 80 percent of the children of working mothers (both full and part time) are cared for by other members of the immediate family or relatives.[33] In some neighborhoods as many as 10 to 20 percent of children are cared for by sitters either in the home of the child or that of the sitter. These informal methods, clearly the predominant form of day care, are very inexpensive. They avoid the use of professional employees, and they require no new facilities.

Of course the in-home day care does not include the formal education programs offered by some of the larger day-care centers. But it is important to point out that the larger day-care centers are very diverse in the type of care they do offer. Of those serving seven or more children, their costs (in 1970 dollars) ranged from $60 per month (a minimal program) to $200 per month (a strong child development emphasis). About one-third of the centers were run by nonprofit organizations (for example, 18 percent were church-affiliated), 60 percent were proprietary, and only a small fraction were government-operated. The nonproprietary institutions were the principal recipients of the public subsidies.

Now let us use this historical review and the exit-voice-loyalty framework in a consideration of alternative modes of day-care provision. We assume the context is one like the present, in which there is a public interest in the care received by children but only limited public subsidy funds are available to enhance demand. The general question is how to govern a system of day care so that it best satisfies the public interest given the resource constraints. "Govern" is used here to refer to both demand and supply: the blend of consumer (parent), professional, and government control over resource allocation to the agencies of supply. We will discuss four types of day-care supply (cooperatives, proprietary institutions, public provision and nonprofit centers), and the problems of governing each. The point is to illustrate the idea that reliance upon nonprofit sectors may be preferred.

One form of organization which might provide good-quality day care inexpensively is the *cooperative;* an example is to have five families share day care, each family providing one parent to mind all the children one day per week. These groups are voluntarily formed, usually by neighbors known to one another. Their attraction, in addition to the low cost, is that a relatively high degree of parental confidence is a consequence of the extensive family involvement. Public sector involvement is minimal; it is limited to various

---

[33] This figure drops to 53 percent when the group is restricted to mothers who work full time. Nevertheless, it is strikingly large.

kinds of organizational assistance such as information about how to set up a cooperative or a clearinghouse to help families in the same neighborhood identify one another.

Since the parent-suppliers can generally be trusted to act with the children's interest in mind, heavy reliance on either the exit or voice option is not necessary. However, both mechanisms can be used: voice for the minor problems and exit (from the cooperative) if one family has a serious disagreement with the other families about the desired plan of care.

There are two serious drawbacks to relying on the cooperative as a primary method for delivering extra-family day care. First, it requires the families to have jobs with arrangeable hours. (This is one reason why cooperatives are relatively popular in university communities.) Given current employment practices, this severely limits the potential use. The second drawback is that cooperatives are often unstable and unreliable. When one family has an emergency or illness or there is some other reason it cannot take its scheduled turn, one of the other families must be able to substitute or someone must be hired. Similarly, when one family leaves the cooperative, another must be found to take its place. These problems are not easy to solve immediately, and they make the cooperative somewhat unreliable. The care may be fine in cooperatives which are stable, but reliable care for a large proportion of families will require at least some paid employees.

Let us consider another mode of supply: *proprietary institutions*. Perhaps we can rely upon self-interested profit seeking to provide the desired services, as we do elsewhere. In this case we issue vouchers to families with children eligible for the day-care subsidy, and we let them be used wherever the parents wish. However, two problems must be confronted. One, already mentioned, is that the parent is not present and will therefore demand assurance of quality. The second problem, discussed briefly below, is that the parent is not always the best agent for protecting the child's interests.

It is useful to raise more explicitly the issue of who the consumer of day-care services is. For the most part, we have not made a distinction between parent and child. But each receives different benefits and costs from day care. As long as the parent acts in the joint interest of both, the second problem does not arise. But it is often suggested that many parents are not sufficiently concerned about the welfare of their children. To some extent this may be a matter of disinterest or neglect, but it may also be a lack of expertise. For either reason there is some argument for professional as well as parental influence in governing extra-family day care.

Consider how a market might respond to these problems. Leaving the role of professionals aside for a moment, recognize that it is the inherent absence of the parent that creates uncertainty about the quality of the service. Since the firm cannot change that, it might seek to create trust between itself and the parents. But private unregulated firms have a difficult time doing so. Consumers recognize that a firm can increase its profits by not fully providing promised services, as long as the consumers do not know. Given the information structure, the profit motive is itself a barrier to the trust that parents demand.

Note that there is plenty of opportunity for both exit and voice. However, neither is an effective mechanism because the consumer (parent) does not receive the information appropriate to trigger the use of either. That is, the consumer generally does not know whether the service is as desired, and therefore he or she has little basis for making an exit or voice decision.

The market can respond to this quality uncertainty by putting some barrier between the profit motives of firms and the behavior of their employees. The common form of this is *professionalization,* as in the legal and medical services. The idea is that professionals act in the child's best interests even if it works against short-run profitability. This solution has the further advantage of dealing with both of the problems we mentioned: low parental information and motivation concerning the quality of the service. Indeed, the more expensive types of day care currently available are provided on this professional model, e.g., with licensed teachers and child psychologists on the staff. But that is exactly the problem with this solution: It is too expensive. We are considering a context in which the available subsidy levels are not large enough to provide developmental day care.

Suppose we consider a third supply alternative: *direct public provision.* This probably could be made inexpensive by not relying upon the fully professional model. Nevertheless, professionals could be very influential at fairly high levels of the decision-making process, e.g., in setting minimum standards for the government day-care centers. The problem with the alternative is the difficulty of achieving enough consumer sovereignty: parents are unlikely to have sufficient choice about the kind of day care their children receive.

That is not to say parents will have no powers of governance. They may be able to exercise voice through parental boards at each day-care center, or certain decisions could be decided by parental voting. But the exit possibilities, if this public service is like other public services, will be severely limited. As we saw earlier, that acts to mute the effectiveness of voice.

One could consider a voucher system restricted to public day-care centers (like open enrollment). To work, it would require a substantial decentralization of public decision-making power: Each center must have significant authority to determine its own policies. Furthermore, the effectiveness of such a plan would depend on the motivation of centers to attract more children when there are no associated profit increases. Since such a system has not been achieved for any other public service, it seems unlikely to be successful here.

Finally, we come to the use of private, not-for-profit day care sponsored by various established community organizations. In principle, the more serious flaws that we have seen can be avoided. Parents are likely to have a relatively high degree of trust in the centers because the organizational objectives, compared with those of profit-making centers and bureaucratic ones, are more likely to be identified with the interests of children. Day-care professionals can have effective voice in setting standards of eligibility to receive public funds, as well as through advisory roles to particular centers.[34]

There should be a reasonable diversity of day care offered, because the various community organizations within one area are generally independent of one another. Parents will thus have relatively effective exit options, and most established community groups depend heavily on the exercise of voice by their members in making decisions. Budgetary costs can be kept low by reliance in part on parent and community volunteers and in part on salaried employees.

Reliance upon the network of established community organizations is not without its problems. One problem is the question whether those with religious auspices will be legally excluded from eligibility for public subsidy in order to maintain the separation of church and state. In addition, there is a resource allocation problem among centers: By what process will successful centers be allowed to expand, and unsuccessful ones contract, so that the total supply balances with demand? If parents are to have choice, the subsidy must be in the form of vouchers. But then parents will require reliable information about each day-care center; perhaps the centers should be open for parental inspection at any time. Some kind of regulatory and planning structure would be needed to resolve these issues, and further thought or experience might reveal important flaws in the overall system.

Nevertheless, the point of this exercise should be clear. It is at least plausible that the preferred way of delivering subsidized extra-family day care is through reliance upon nonprofit community institutions. The essential reason is the peculiar information structure of day care, which prevents the normal consumer-agent (the parent) from knowing the quality of service. Because of the obvious importance of quality to the parent, trust becomes the next best substitute for knowledge.

One can increase the level of trust from that of an ordinary market through professionalization, but that is very expensive. One can generate trust cheaply through reliance on neighborhood cooperatives, but they are difficult to arrange and are unstable. Public provision is usually too bureaucratic with too little parental control to generate high consumer satisfaction, although it might be better than the prior two alternatives. But reliance on established nonprofit community organizations seems a promising way to provide the same economy benefits and public interest guarantees with a higher level of trust and, therefore, greater consumer satisfaction.

We also note that the available supply of trust from established nonprofit agencies is a scarce resource. One should not expect that it is easy to create more trust by, say, encouraging new nonprofit organizations to form. The Pauly-Redisch model of a hospital (Chapter 9) is suggestive of the perverse consequences that could arise from such an attempt. There is nothing about the

---

[34] One might suggest similar use of professionals as a control for private profit-making institutions. This idea has merit, although the profit incentive of the firms might cause substantial resistance to this form of control.

legal form of a nonprofit agency which necessarily creates trust. Rather, trust is associated with some feeling of community within a group, be it a family, or a school team, or a neighborhood organization.

Thus we note another important point from this study. Back in our introductory discussion of values (Chapter 1) we mentioned that the values of "liberty" and "community" are important social ends in and of themselves. But they are important on efficiency grounds as well. It has long been clear to analysts that liberty is associated with efficiency, because it facilitates consumer sovereignty. Now we can see that community is also associated with efficiency, because the trust it engenders facilitates trade.

SUMMARY

The problem of designing an efficient system of governance for particular economic activities is a complex one. No simple theoretical framework has gained acceptance as a procedure for resolving such governance issues. In this chapter we present a variety of analytic approaches which at least yield insight into the problem.

We emphasize a common element important to each of the analytic approaches. Accounting for the information and transaction costs of making resource allocation decisions is often crucial to the identification of an efficient governance structure. These costs depend on the nature of the economic activity and on the governance structure used to guide the decisions of the economic agents. The significance of these costs explains why simple models in which they are assumed to be zero are unsatisfactory for comparing alternatives. With perfect information and no transaction costs, a centralized allocater does at least as well as the decentralized organization of a competitive market. Such a model specification hides the problem the governance structure is supposed to solve.

The trick is to develop a theoretical framework which quickly gets at the essence of information and transaction difficulties and remedies for them. Each of the approaches we review has demonstrated at least some ability to do that in an applied policy context. Arrow suggests that a method of organization can be conceived of as a particular set of operating instructions and enforcement rules. Each may be more or less centralized, which is a matter of the scope of choice available to the agent responsible for doing the task.

We consider how to choose the degree of centralization in the context of air pollution control methods. Actual U.S. policy relies primarily on technical standards. These are a relatively centralized form of operating instruction, since the individual polluter is given little choice about the level of pollution or the control method. It is often suggested that decentralized operating rules in the form of pollution taxes would be more efficient.

We demonstrate the "efficiency" of pollution taxes by using a standard model of economic behavior with perfectly informed agents and zero transaction costs. Using the same assumptions, we also show that the Coase theorem (market allocation of a good is independent of ownership, except for income effects) implies that a subsidy per unit of pollution reduction achieves the same result. But for those solutions to be better than well-intentioned regulation, it must be that the regulatory standards are assumed to be set with imperfect knowledge or are substantially less enforceable. The imperfection of standards may be a valid criticism, but the enforceability argument works strongly in the opposite direction.

To enforce a tax (or subsidy), one must be able to monitor the pollution amounts of each potential taxpayer accurately. This may be prohibitively costly, if not technically impossible in some cases. In general, determining a tax amount is a more-or-less question, which is relatively hard to answer because of the precision involved. Satisfying a standard, on the other hand, is a yes-or-no question whose answer is often easier to determine.

The Arrow framework also helps us to think of alternative pollution control methods which may dominate those we have discussed. The analysis suggests that enforcement is easier if the operating instructions are centralized, although firms may have the better knowledge about how to set the standards to enforce. Marketable pollution rights have this blend of centralized operating rules to enforce with decentralized market allocation of them. The offset policy of the EPA is a governance method which resembles this alternative.

Another framework for analyzing the relation beween a governance structure and the information and transaction costs associated with it has been offered by Williamson and Goldberg. They suggest that certain governance structures can be viewed as a form of contract between the government and a supplier. Insight into the elements of a desirable governance structure may then be derived by considering how one would specify the contract.

A comparison of rate-of-return regulation with competitive bidding for an exclusive franchise is used as an illustration of the analytic method. Rate-of-return regulation is commonly used as a way of preventing consumer exploitation by natural monopolies. It has been criticized because it induces productive inefficiency (the Averch-Johnson theorem) and because it is overly protective of industry rather than consumer interests (the capture theory of regulatory behavior). As a response to the latter criticism, it has been proposed that competitive bidding for the exclusive right to provide services be substituted for regulation. The idea is that the market, through the bidding process, does away with the regulatory institution subject to capture.

Competitive bidding is often an efficient way of decision making. Complex information known only to decentralized economic agents can be neatly summarized in one sufficient statistic—the bid price—and communicated to a central agent who can identify efficient allocations based solely on the ranking of the bids. This is the method used by the government to sell Treasury bills; it is also used as a method of allocating leases for oil and coal mining on government lands.

Williamson points out that it is not the bidding itself but the contract, the object of the bidding, which is to substitute for regulation. However, the services provided by most natural monopolies require a contract that is much more complex than that required to buy a Treasury bill. If the contract is long-term, it will include provisions for arbitration, negotiation, auditing, and inspection. This begins to look quite like ordinary regulation. When one realizes that the supplier retains all the information advantages it has in the regulatory case, the capture theory appears plausible in this context as well. This is supported by the experience from defense contracting, in which cost overruns and contract renegotiation favorable to the supplier are routine.

The parallel of franchising to rate-of-return regulation is just as strong under recurrent short-term contracting. Consider the necessity of asset transfer at a fair price in order to maintain parity among bidders at contract renewal times. The supplier will exaggerate the value of its assets in this case, just as it attempts to inflate estimates of its rate base under ordinary regulation.

In short, competitive bidding in this case is not really a substitute for regulation. The original proponents of the bidding proposal missed this point because they underestimated the importance of information and transaction difficulties which shape the form of the contract to be bid upon. Once one takes explicit account of those difficulties, it is not clear that the competitive bidding method possesses any advantages over ordinary regulation. In both cases the supplier will retain considerable information and bargaining advantages, and the degree of consumer protection from monopoly exploitation will be weaker than intended.

The case study of cable television in Oakland supports these conclusions. Two other cases, those involving performance contracting for passenger rail service and education, are mentioned to suggest other applications of this form of analysis. Each shows a different type of information difficulty. The passenger rail contract may solve a problem such as the timeliness of the trains quickly if rewards and penalties of appropriate magnitude can be identified and specified in the contract provisions. Education contracting has the potential advantage that, over the long term, it may help the sector improve its screening of new methods to weed out the poor ones and diffuse the successes.

In the final section of this chapter we use two additional procedures for identifying the information and transaction costs associated with various governance structures: reviewing the economic history of the activity under consideration and using the exit-voice-loyalty framework of Hirschman. These methods are applied to an analysis of day-care services for small children, based on work by Nelson, Krashinsky, and Young.

The historical review of day-care provision highlights the important role of the family, extended family, and neighbors in the provision of day care. It becomes clear that trust is a key consideration of parents, who generally care a great deal about the quality of service (the degree of attention paid the child) but are by definition not around to verify it. A second point from the historical review is that basic demographic changes in family structure help explain why the demand for day-care centers has grown. We then consider the problem of whether trustworthy centers can be had at a low cost.

We employ Hirschman's framework, which is used generally as a way of understanding organizational responsiveness in markets for goods and services in which quality is important. He suggests that an efficient way of learning usually involves a combination of exit and voice, where the latter is a direct complaint or suggestion for improvement to the firm. Firm loyalty can both induce the use of voice and give a firm time to adjust. This may lead to better industry performance than letting the original firm go bankrupt from exit while consumers wait for a new firm to take up the slack. In applying this framework to the day-care industry, we consider how parents and, to a lesser extent, day-care experts can influence the behavior of day-care institutions. (Experts are given some role on the demand side as insurance for the child, since not all parents always act in the child's best interests.)

Several different supply modes for day care are considered in the context of a public policy which provides limited subsidy funds to help qualifying low-income families pay for day care. The voluntary cooperative is unsuitable because it requires the parents to have jobs with arrangeable hours, and it is often unstable and therefore unreliable. Inexpensive private profit-making institutions are flawed by the lack of consumer trust: the parent knows that it is in the firm's interest to skimp on promised services when the skimping is hard to detect. The mechanisms of exit and voice are not very useful here, because the parent does not have the right information to trigger either one of them.

The market can attempt to remedy this problem by professionalization of the employees, which puts some barrier between the short-run profits of the firm and any behavior of employees which is not in the child's interest. But in this context of limited subsidy funds, the flaw of this response is its expense.

Direct public provision of the service probably could be made inexpensively and still allow for professional influence in setting minimum standards for government day-care centers. However, the degree of consumer sovereignty which can be exercised is likely to be very low. This means the exit option cannot be used effectively, and that in itself tends to mute the effectiveness of voice.

Finally, day-care service could be provided through private nonprofit established community organizations. These have the advantage of having a relatively high degree of consumer trust as compared with profit-making or bureaucratic institutions. Consumer voice is relatively effective here, and parents have some real exit options. Day-care professionals can exercise influence by setting minimum standards of eligibility for receipt of public subsidies; they can also influence the type of day care by serving on advisory boards to each institution. The budgetary costs of these institutions should be low, because the institutions, like cooperatives, can rely in part on parental volunteers and in part on salaried but nonprofessional employees.

This exercise demonstrates a plausible argument leading to the conclusion that the preferred way to deliver a particular service is through nonprofit community organizations. The derivation of this conclusion depends heavily on the peculiar information structure involved with day-care services. This structure leads to an unusually high value placed on trust among the transacting agents. Trust has the effect of reducing the transaction costs. We have suggested that trust is relatively abundant within organizations that value community. We thus conclude by noting that the social ends of liberty and community, for different reasons, foster efficiency: liberty because of the consumer sovereignty it brings and community because the trust it engenders among people facilitates trade.

EXERCISES

15-1 In Exercise 13.1, we posed a problem of how to ration water in the Hudson-Orlando Water District (H2O) during a drought. The exercise involved some analysis of a transferable rationing plan, but it did not consider how a market for the water coupons would actually operate. This exercise is designed to provoke thought about the latter and to encourage the development of organizational design skills.

H2O has already decided on the size of ration allotments to each household, H2O prices, and penalties for water consumption in excess of ration credits. But alternatives to facilitate a well-working exchange process have not been considered.

a Explain how transactional factors could make an ill-designed transferable plan less efficient than a nontransferable one.

b A list of alternative plans for organizing the market follows. Evaluate the pros and cons of each plan. First consider the criteria you think are important, and then note that each alternative is only vaguely identified and that, to evaluate it, you may wish to consider a more specific design. (For example, in each alternative, what form would you choose for the transferable ration?) The alternatives are:

1 Set up conveniently located H2O-staffed exchange booths.

2 Have auctions at regular intervals.

3 Do nothing in the hope that private entrepreneurs will develop an ideal coupon market.

4 Your best idea.

5 Scrap the transferable plan because there is no practical exchange process which will allow efficiency gains.

15-2 For some economic activity, it may be that neither markets with profit-seeking firms nor government bureaus are the best institutional arrangements. Using hospitals as an example, could it be argued that nonprofit, nongovernmental institutions might be the preferred structures for guiding the allocation of medical resources?

NAME INDEX

Aaron, H., 69, 81, 343, 401, 478, 504
Akerlof, G., 433
Albon, R., 461
Alchian, A., 295, 357
Arrow, K., 107, 198, 216, 252, 424, 561, 563, 576, 600, 601
Atkinson, A., 112, 400, 513, 515
Averch, H., 578

Barmack, J., 64
Bator, F., 425
Baumol, W., 50, 200, 326, 511, 529, 590
Becker, G., 215, 518
Bentham, J., 44
Berman, P., 98
Bittner, E., 19
Boiteux, M., 361
Bradbury, K., 478
Braybrooke, D., 9
Break, G., 104
Breit, W., 357
Breneman, D., 523, 524
Brown, M., 252

Calabresi, G., 209
Callahan, J., 129, 549
Cheung, S., 445
Chiswick, B., 549
Cicchetti, C., 516
Clarkson, J., 64
Coase, R., 295, 571
Cook, P., 215
Coons, J., 477
Cooter, R., 348, 352–354
Cyert, R., 326

Daly, G., 69
Dasgupta, P., 210, 518
Davis, O., 217
Demsetz, H., 295, 581
Denison, E., 197, 250

DeSalvo, J., 69
Diamond, P., 198
Diewert, W., 288
Dirham, J., 329
Doolittle, F., 61
Downs, A., 478
Dresch, S., 521
Dreze, J., 198

Ehrlich, I., 215
Eisenstadt, D., 342
Enthoven, A., 232

Faustmann, M., 528
Feldstein, M., 127, 232, 235, 405, 421, 549
Ferejohn, J., 429
Finn, C., 524
Fisher, A., 516
Fiske, G., 525
Forsythe, R., 429
Frank, R., 332
Freeman, R., 592
Friedlaender, A., 275, 276, 281, 290
Friedman, L., 19, 109, 121, 123–125, 129, 215, 268, 269, 271
Friedman, M., 20, 204, 216
Froomkin, J., 525
Fuss, M., 284

Galster, G., 458
Garber, S., 465
Giertz, F., 69
Goldberg, R., 521
Goldberg, V., 562, 585, 601
Gramlich, E., 108, 122, 172, 590
Green, J., 428
Grether, D., 224
Groves, T., 428
Grubb, W., 129, 549

Handler, J., 337, 592
Hansen, T., 391

Hansmann, H., 337
Hanushek, E., 19, 119, 478
Harberger, A., 324, 402
Harris, J., 342, 343, 369
Hartman, R., 521
Hausman, J., 86
Haveman, R., 549
Hayek, F., 568, 569
Heal, G., 210, 518
Heinrich, B., 18
Henderson, J., 53
Henningsen, P., 381
Hicks, J., 163, 164
Hirschman, A., 318, 563, 592, 593, 603
Hirshleifer, J., 213
Hitch, C., 11
Hochman, H., 69, 357
Holahan, J., 381

Inman, R., 122, 129, 130, 137

Jackson, J., 19
Jamison, D., 525
Jensen, M., 321
Johnson, H., 403
Johnson, L., 578
Jones, C., 461

Kahn, A., 423, 424
Kaldor, N., 164
Kaplan, A., 329
Kennedy, T., 342
Kirp, D., 115
Knight, F., 194
Komesar, N., 337, 592
Koopmans, T., 382, 385
Kopp, R., 259
Koshel, P., 590
Krashinsky, M., 592–594, 596, 602
Krutilla, J., 516
Kunreuther, H., 224

Ladd, H., 128, 129
Laffont, J., 428
Lancaster, K., 410
Lange, O., 568, 569
Lanzillotti, R., 329
Layard, P., 420, 421, 530
Ledyard, J., 428
Le Grand, J., 129
Leibenstein, H., 259, 323
Leontif, W., 257
Lerner, A., 314, 568, 569
Levinson, E., 478
Levy, F., 61
Lindblom, C., 9, 10

Lipsey, R., 410
Littlechild, S., 369
Long, D., 276
Luce, R., 217

McFadden, D., 284, 346
McGuire, C., 563, 582
McGuire, M., 69, 106
McGuire, T., 182
McKean, R., 11
McLaughlin, M., 98
MacLennan, D., 461
Manski, C., 369
March, J., 326
Margolis, J., 549
Marris, R., 326
Marschak, J., 563
Meckling, W., 321
Meltsner, A., 13
Mendeloff, J., 575
Messinger, S., 19
Mieszkowski, P., 400, 403, 447
Minarik, J., 545, 547
Moore, T., 273
Morgenstern, O., 198
Moroney, J., 257

Nagin, D., 465
Nelson, R., 11, 182, 259, 433, 592–594, 596, 602
Nerlove, M., 252, 519, 520, 522, 524
Neustadt, R., 36
Newhouse, J., 338, 340, 342
Nicholson, W., 50
Niskanen, W., 345–348
Noll, R., 429, 581
Nordhaus, W., 531, 534, 535

Oates, W., 108, 447
Okun, A., 388
Olsen, E., 442
O'Neill, J., 549

Palmer, J., 320
Pauly, M., 226, 340, 342, 599
Pechman, J., 86, 343, 523
Peck, M., 586
Peltzman, S., 182
Pindyck, R., 19
Plott, C., 224
Pratt, J., 233

Quandt, R., 53
Quigley, J., 447, 478

Radner, R., 525, 563
Raiffa, H., 217
Rainey, R., 18
Ramsey, F., 357, 361
Rawls, J., 44, 45
Redisch, M., 340, 342, 599
Rees, A., 86
Riley, J., 213
Rodgers, J., 69
Rose-Ackerman, S., 575
Rothschild, M., 198
Rousseau, J., 369
Rubinfeld, D., 19, 108
Russell, L., 226

Salamon, G., 321
Samuelson, P., 95, 528, 531
Savage, L., 204
Scarf, H., 391
Schelling, T., 217
Scherer, F., 313, 324, 586
Schultze, C., 10, 11, 388
Scitovsky, T., 167
Shoven, J., 391, 402
Simon, H., 222, 223
Smith, A., 294
Smith, E., 321
Smith, V., 429
Spady, R., 275, 276, 281, 290
Spavins, T., 182
Stano, M., 320
Stern, N., 130, 137
Stewart, M., 326
Stigler, G., 259
Stiglitz, J., 400, 432, 513, 515
Stone, C., 337
Straszheim, M., 447
Sugarman, S., 477

Taylor, F., 568
Thompson, F., 525
Thurow, L., 569
Tiebout, C., 108
Timpane, P., 86
Tobin, J., 110, 471, 479, 480
Topakian, G., 348, 352–354
Trapani, J., 257

Varian, H., 154, 155, 284, 286, 396
von Furstenberg, G., 69, 81
von Neumann, J., 198

Walters, A., 420, 421, 530
Ward, B., 341
Watts, H., 86
Weis-Fogh, T., 18
Weisbrod, B., 337, 592
Weitzman, M., 495
Whalley, J., 391, 402
Whinston, A., 217
White, W., 216
Wildavsky, A., 9, 13
Wilken, W., 129, 549
Williamson, O., 295, 317, 326, 562, 584, 585, 588, 589, 601
Willig, R., 151
Winter, S., 259, 433
Wise, D., 86
Wiseman, M., 61, 109, 121, 123–125, 129
Wood, A., 326

Young, D., 592, 602
Yudof, M., 115

Zajac, E., 578

SUBJECT INDEX

Adverse selection, 433
Aid to Families with Dependent Children, 59, 61, 83–84
Air pollution control, 569–577
  (*See also* Externalities)
Airline Deregulation Act of 1978, 141
Amtrack passenger rail service, 589–590
Auctions:
  involving federal lands, 114n., 582–583
  of U.S. Treasury bills, 582, 583
Automobile congestion, 431
  (*See also* Peak-load pricing)
Automobiles:
  bumper regulations, 431
  insurance for, 7, 209
Averch-Johnson theorem, 578–581

Bay Area Rapid Transit District (BART), 348–355
Benefit-cost analysis, 141–142, 166, 260–265, 268–272
Bonds, 514–515, 541, 552–553
Bounded rationality, 222–225, 238–239
  and disaster insurance, 224–225
  and firm behavior, 317, 326–330
  and food regulation, 223–224
Budget constraint, 30
  segmented or discontinuous, 60, 70–75
  and time, 82–83
  and wealth, 82, 504–508
Budget maximization, 345–349, 354–355
Bureaucracy and resource allocation, 345–348

Cable television, regulation of, 584–589
Capacity constraints on resource allocation, 356–369
Capital, 501–502, 507
  human, 518–525, 587–588
Capital formation (*see* Investment)
Capital markets, 503–518
  equilibrium interest rate, 511–518
Capital stock, 501–502, 509
Capitalized asset values, 449–451
Cartel, 462–463

Centralization and decentralization, 32n., 294–296, 425, 428–429, 561–569
  and air pollution control, 573–577
Chain rule, 53n.
Civil Aeronautics Board, 141
Clayton Act, 316n., 320
Coal mining, leasing federal lands for, 582–583
Coase theorem, 571–573
Cobb-Douglas functions:
  cost function, 285–289
  expenditure function, 155
  production function, 253, 283–284
  utility function, 131, 152–155
Coefficient of variation, 112n.
Collective choice, 4, 8–13, 428–429
  (*See also* Median voter theory)
Communication of analytic work, 35–36
Comparative advantage, 384n.
Compensated price change, 90–94
Compensating variation, 144–148, 150–152, 158–160, 168n.
Compensation principle, 38n., 39n., 74n., 141–143, 160–175
  controversy about, 170–175
  definition of, 164–169, 262
  and market statistics, 175–187
  purpose of, 160–163, 174–175
Competition, perfect:
  in an economy, 382–388
  in an imperfect world, 410–415, 419–421
  in an industry, 376–382
Competitive bidding, 567, 581–589
Compound interest, 553–557
Consols, 552–553
Consumer Price Index (CPI), 515, 541, 545–548
Consumer protection policy:
  and disaster insurance, 224–225
  and food, 223–224
  and prescription drugs, 181–187
Consumer sovereignty, 27–28, 67n.
Consumer surplus:
  aggregate, 175–187
    and market demand curves, 175–179
    and regulation, 179–187
  individual, 147–148, 151–152, 156–158

Contingent commodities, 213
Contract curve, 34
Contracting, 585–591
Cooperatives, 596–597, 599
Corner solutions, 72–73
Cost(s), 243–246, 259–290
  accounting, 266–268
  fixed, 357
  function, 272–277, 281–289
  industry (constant, decreasing, and
    increasing), 380
  information (*see* Information costs)
  joint, 277–281, 290
  long-run versus short-run, 378–380
  marginal, 262
  opportunity, 82
    private, 266–268
    social, 260–265
  political, 244–245
  social, 260–265
  sunk, 267
  transaction (*see* Transaction costs)

Day-care services, 591–600
Deadweight loss, 177
Decentralization (*see* Centralization and
  decentralization)
Defense:
  efficient, 26–28
  spending for, 26n.
Defense contracting, 586
Demand curve:
  compensated, 91, 145–147
  derived, 303n.
  for a firm's output, 298
  market, 175
  Marshallian, 147n.
  ordinary, 91, 147n.
Demand function, 94
Depreciation, 267
Discount rate, 506
Discrimination, racial, 458n.
  and equity, 42–43, 113–116
Distribution of income, 391–398
  (*See also* Equity)
District power equalization, 125–127, 134–136
Diversification, 209–212
Duality, 152–160, 281–289

Economic man (*see* Utility, maximization of)
Economic rent, 264, 440, 446–449, 453–455
Edgeworth box diagram, 32–36
Education:
  loads for, 518–523
  and performance contracting, 590–591
  subsidies for, 523–525
  vouchers for, 477–478, 593n.
  (*See also* School finance equity)

Efficiency, 26–36, 51–54, 382–385
  exchange, 28–36, 382–383
  product-mix, 262–263, 384
  production, 383–384
  relative (*see* Relative efficiency)
  technological, 383
  X-inefficiency, 323–326
  (*See also* Benefit-cost analysis; Compensation
    principle; Pareto-optimality;
    Pareto-superiority; Wealth-maximization)
Elasticity, 89n., 93
  income, 89, 95
  input, 253n.
  price, 91, 95
  of substitution, 251–252
Elementary and Secondary Education Act, 98
Employment contracts, 294–295
Energy price controls, 462–466
  (*See also* Oil prices)
Engel curve, 88–89
Engel-expenditure curve, 88n., 89n.
Environmental Protection Agency, 7, 569–570,
  577
Equality (*see* Equity)
Equilibrium:
  capital market, 511–518
  competitive, 376–388, 391–398
  general, 81, 385–388
  market, 378
  partial, 81, 388
Equilibrium prices, 31, 41–42n., 396–397
Equity, 40–47, 109–129
  and the compensation principle, 170–173
  as equality: of opportunity, 40–41, 114
    of outcome, 42–43, 110–112
  and the just price, 436–437, 460–461
  and market allocation, 387–388
  as neutrality (simple or conditional), 114–116
  outcome concepts of, 109–113, 295–296
  process concepts of, 109, 113–116
  and specific egalitarianism, 110
  and specific redistribution, 436
  as a universal minimum, 110, 112–113
  (*See also* Social welfare function)
Equivalent variation, 145, 148–152, 160
Euler's theorem, 392n.
Exceptional characteristics, 115–116
Excess burden, 177n.
Exit-voice-loyality framework, 317–318, 563,
  592–593
Expected utility theorem, 192, 198, 237
Expected value, 195–196
Expenditure function, 155
Externalities, 4–5, 60, 98, 429–432
  consumption, 68
  interdependent preferences, 60
  production, 429

Fair game, 196
Federal Trade Commission, 313n.

Federal Trade Commission Act, 320
Firms, private:
  bounded rationality of, 326–330
  concept of, 294–296
  management control of, 317–326
  and price discrimination, 298–316
  and profit maximization, 296–298
  and revenue (sales) maximization, 318–322
Fiscal capacity, 128
Flat City model, 446–449
Flood Control Act of 1936, 141
Food, Drug, and Cosmetics Act, 182
Food and Nutrition Assistance, 59
  table, 61
Food Stamp Act of 1964, 65n.
Food Stamp Act of 1977, 77
Food Stamp Program, 60–78, 83, 87, 102
Free-rider problem, 426–428

Game theory, 192, 217–221
Gasoline rationing;
  and consumer surplus, 179–181
  methods of, 480–499
Gasoline tax, 92–94
General Accounting Office, 144
General revenue-sharing program, 99
Giffen goods, 91, 95
Gini coefficient, 110–112
Grants (see Intergovernmental grants)
Gross National Product (GNP), 5, 6

Health insurance (see Insurance, medical)
Health maintenance organizations (HMOs), 232,
    322–323
Heroin supply and law enforcment, 380
Hicks-Kaldor compensation principle (see
    Compensation principle)
History, economic, as an analytic tool, 592–600
Hoffman-Fawell Reform in Illinois, 123–125
Homogeneous functions, 392n.
Hospital Cost Containment Act of 1977
    (proposed), 342–343
Hospitals and resource allocation, 336–344
Housing:
  allowances for, 478
  public, 78–81
  (See also Rent control)
Housing assistance, table, 61
Human capital, 518–525, 587–588

Implementation considerations, 481–482, 590
Implicit form of a function, 52
Incentive structure, 375–376
Income-contingent payments:
  for education loans, 519–523
  for health insurance, 231
Income distribution, 391–398
  (See also Equity)

Income effects, 88–90, 95
Income-expansion path, 101
Income maintenance programs, 43n., 81–86
Increasing returns to scale problem, 303–305,
    426
Indexation, 541–550
  chain-linked, 546
  Consumer Price Index, 515, 541, 545–548
  cost-of-living, 544–547
  Laspeyre, 541–545
  Paasche, 541–545
  personal consumption expenditure deflator,
    545–548
  and school financing, 548–549
Indifference curves, 24, 50–51
Inferior goods, 89, 94–95
Inflation, 503, 513–515, 541–550
Information costs, 75–78
  and air pollution control, 569–577
  and day-care services, 591–600
  and firm behavior, 299–302, 311–312,
    316–318, 321–322
  and food regulation, 223–224
  and governance structure, 561–569
  and hospital behavior, 342–344
  and market failure, 432–433
  and monopoly governance, 584–591
  and ration coupons, 475–477
  and rent control, 443
  and uncertainty, 194, 295
  and value, 221
In-kind transfers, 60–81
Input-output analysis, 257n.
Insurance:
  and adverse selection, 433
  automobile, 7, 209
  and coinsurance, 230–231
  deductibles, 229–230
  disaster, 224–225
  medical, 225–232, 235–236
  and moral hazard, 193, 225–232, 239
  self-, 207–209
Interdependent preferences, 60, 64–70, 74, 76–78
Interest groups, effect of, on public enterprise
    pricing, 348–355
Interest rates:
  compound, 553–557
  equilibrium, 513–515
  as prices, 506–507
  simple, 550–553
Intergovernmental grants, 98–109
  bureaucratic theories of, 108–109
  categorical, 101
  maintenance-of-effort requirement, 104–107
  matching, 102–104
  nonmatching, 99–101
  open-ended versus close-ended, 102–103
  purposes of, 98–99
Internal Revenue Service, 85
Interstate Commerce Commission (ICC), 273

Intertemporal resource allocation, 503–518
  capital market equilibrium, 511–518
  consumption choices, 504–508
  investment choices, 508–511
Inverse elasticities rule, 360–369
Investment, 508–511, 515–518
  in education, 518–525
  timing of, 529–531
Isocost line, 281–282
Isoquants, 251–252, 281–283

Jobs Corps, 174
Just prices, 436–437, 460–461

KISS rule, 36n.

Labor-leisure choice, 81–83
Labor-managed firms, 340–342
Labor unions, closed-shop, 417–420
Lagrange multipliers, 52–53
Land tax, 404–405
Lange-Lerner model of socialism, 568–569
Laspeyre indices, 541–545
Law, public policy and the, 7
Law of one price, 377
Leontif cost function, 288
Leontif technology, 257–258
Life-cycle consumption and income patterns,
      503–504
Locational choices:
  of firms, 128
  and rent controls, 446–449, 455–456
  and the Tiebout hypothesis, 108
Lorenz curve, 110–112
Low-Income Energy Assistance, 59
Luxury goods, 89, 95

Managerial control of a firm, 317–326
Marginal rate:
  of substitution, 24–25, 51
  of technical substitution, 281–283
  of time preference, 385, 505
Marginal revenue product, 341
Market, private, 4
Market coordination, 424–426
Market failures, 408–409, 424–433
Market power, 314
Market socialism, 425n.
Markup pricing, 328–329
Mass transit pricing, 348–369
  BART, 348–355
  Ramsey pricing, 357–369
  (See also Peak-load pricing)
Maximin rule, 220–221
Median voter theory, 107–108
  and public enterprise pricing, 348–355
Medicaid, 8, 31, 59, 61, 83, 226, 335

Medical care:
  and hospitals, 336–344
  and insurance, 225–232, 235–236
  and physician licensing, 216
Medicare, 31, 226, 335
Military, draft versus volunteers, 266, 488
Model specification, 19–21
Modeling, 17–21
Monopoly, 298–312
  auctioning of, 583–589
  and price discrimination, 300–316
  and profit maximization, 298–300
  regulation of, 577–591
  (See also Increasing returns to scale problem)
Moral hazard, 193, 225–232, 239
Motor Carrier Act, 276
Muddling through, 9

Natural resources, 525–537
  exhaustible, 531–537
  renewable, 525–531
Necessity goods, 89, 95
Negative Income Tax, 82, 85–87, 112
Neighborhood Youth Corps, 174
No-fault automobile insurance, 7, 209
Nonprofit suppliers, 334–344, 591–600
Normal goods, 88–89, 94–95
Numéraire, 387

Office of Economic Opportunity, 589–591
Oil and gas exploration, leasing federal lands
      for, 114n.
Oil prices, 531–537
  (See also Energy price controls)
Opportunity costs, 82, 260–268
Organization of Petroleum Exporting Countries
      (OPEC), 462–463
Organizational design, 563–569

Paasche indices, 541–545
Pareto-optimality, 26, 262–263, 382–388
Pareto-superiority, 36–37
Peak-load pricing, 278–281, 290
Performance contracting, 589–591
Permanent income level, 503–504, 552
Pluralism, 9–10
Policy analysis:
  criteria for, 12–13, 335n.
  normative, 12
  positive, 12
  roles of, 11–12
Policy instrument, 19n.
Political feasibility, 12–13, 496
Political process, 8–13
  muddling through, 9
  and policy analysis, 10–13
Poll tax, 404–405

Portfolio choice, 209–212
Preferences, 22–25
  convexity of, 22–23
  and diminishing marginal rates of
      substitution, 24, 25
  and indifference curves, 24, 50–51
  interdependent, 60
  nonsatiation of, 22
  ordering of, 22
  ordinal versus cardinal, 23n.
  revealed, 103–104
  strong monotonicity of, 22, 50
  and time, 504–507, 513–515
Present discounted value (*see* Present value)
Present value, 450n., 506
Price-Anderson Act, 215n., 238
Price change, compensated, 90–94
Price discrimination, 30n., 300–316
  definition of, 313
  and market segmentation, 300–302
  normative consequences of, 302–312
  perfect, 300
  predicting, 314–316
Price taker, 377
Prices:
  equilibrium, 31, 41–42n., 396–397
  intertemporal, 506–507, 517–518
  just, 436–437, 460–461
  oil, 531–537
  relative, 387
  shadow, 55
  uses of, 30, 381–382
  (*See also* Mass transit pricing; Peak-load
      pricing; Ramsey pricing)
Prisoner's Dilemma, 27n., 217n., 219, 238, 239
Producers (*see* Suppliers)
Producer's surplus, 262–265
Product transformation, rate of, 260–264
Production function, 244, 246–259, 281–289
  Cobb-Douglas, 253, 283–284
  constant elasticity of substitution, 252
  elasticity of substitution of the, 251–252
  fixed coefficients, 257–258
  hedonic, 254n.
  returns to scale of the, 251
  scale coefficient of the, 251n.–252n.
Production-possibilities curve, 260–261
Productivity, 248–255
  average, 248–249
  marginal, 248–249
  total, 248–249
Professional incentives:
  and bureaucratic behavior, 346–347
  and day care, 598, 599
  and education, 590
  and medical care, 323
Profit maximization, 296–300
Property rights, 7, 431, 571–573
  and rent control, 437, 445, 459–460

Property tax:
  and fiscal capacity, 128
  incidence of, 401n., 504n.
  limitations of, 459n., 461
Proposition 13 (in California), 459n.,
      461
Public broadcasting system, 428–429
Public bureau, 292, 345–348
Public enterprise, 292, 348–369
  efficient fare structure, 356–369
  pricing decisions of BART, 348–355
Public goods, 426–429

Quasi rent, 438–440

Railroad service, 589–590
Ramsey pricing, 357–369
  mathematics of, 364–369
Rate of product transformation, 260–264
Rate-of-return regulation, 578–581,
      584–589
Ration coupons, 472–477
Redistribution, 8
  (*See also* Equity)
Redwood Employee Protection Program,
      143
Regulation, 6–7
  of air pollution, 569–577
  of apartment rents (*see* Rent control)
  of disaster insurance, 224–225
  of energy prices, 462–466
  of food, 223–224
  of gasoline consumption, 179–181
  of hospital costs, 342–343
  of monopoly, 577–591
  of prescription drugs, 181–187
  rate-of-return, 578–581, 584–589
  of securities, 321–322
  of trucking, 272–277
Regulatory capture, 562, 581, 586–589
Regulatory standards, 569–577
  technical versus performance, 570n.,
      576n.
Relative efficiency, 36–40, 141–143, 160–175,
      262–265
Rent control (of housing), 436–461
  and capitalized values, 449–452
  demand for, 438–440, 461
  and economic rent, 438–440, 446–449
  and exchange, efficiency effects of,
      457–461
  supply effects of, 440–445, 452–457
Resource allocation, 3–4
  and public policy, 5–8
Revealed preferences, 103–104
Revenue, 296–298
  average, 297–298
  marginal, 297, 306–307

Revenue (or sales) maximization, 318–322
Risk, 191–217
    and crime deterrence, 215, 238
    and insurance, 206–209
    and limited liability, 214–215, 237–238
    and quality certification, 216–217, 238
Risk aversion, 196, 200–206, 232–237
Risk cost, 201–202
Risk pooling, 192, 206–212, 237
Risk spreading, 192, 212–213, 237
Robinson-Patman Act, 31, 313, 314
Royalties, 533–535
Roy's identity, 155

St. Petersburg Paradox, 196–197, 237
Sales (or revenue) maximization, 318–322
Satisficing, 222–223
Savings, 506
Scale coefficient, 251n.–252n.
School finance equity, 116–129
    in California (see *Serrano v. Priest*)
    and district cost differences, 128–129
    and district fiscal capacity, 128
    and district power equalizing, 125–127
    and district student variation, 129
    in Hawaii, 120n.
    in Illinois, Hoffman-Fawell Reform, 123–125
    and indexation, 548–549
    long-run versus short-run, 129
Second best, 410–424
    and corrective intervention, 412–415
    identification of the, 420–424
    and piecemeal policy analysis, 415–420
    theorem of the, 410–412
Securities and Exchange Commission, 7, 322
Separability, 421–423
Separation theorem, 508–511
Serrano v. Priest, 99, 109, 116–120, 125, 127, 128,
    138–139
Shadow price, 55
Shephard's lemma, 155, 286–287, 394
Sherman Antitrust Act, 320
Slumlord's Dilemma, 27n., 192, 217–219,
    226–229, 238, 429, 431, 462, 573n.
Slutsky equation, 93–96
Social contract, 65
Social indifference curves (*see* Social welfare
    function)
Social Security, 8, 92, 545, 549–550
Social welfare function, 43–47
    Benthamite, 44
    compensation principle as a, 171–172
    Rawlsian, 44–45
    in school finance, 129–137
Socialist pricing, 568–569
Stock-flow distinction, 501–502, 507–508
Strategic Arms Limitation Treaty, 27, 320n.
Strategic Petroleum Reserve in Louisiana, 191

Suboptimization, 10–11, 423
Substitution effects, 90–91, 95
Supplemental Security Income, 59, 61
Suppliers:
    capability of, 292–293, 326–330
    cooperatives, 596–597
    environment of, 292–293
    nonprofit, 334–344, 591–600
    objectives of, 292–293, 316–317, 322–323
    private (*see* Firms, private)
    public, 334–337, 345–369
Supply curve:
    of labor, 82–83
    long-run versus short-run, 378–380
    market, 377–378
Supported work experiment, 174, 247–248,
    250–256, 268–272, 276–277, 289
Suspect groupings, 114–115

Taxation:
    efficiency of, 403–405
    incidence of, 388–390, 398–403
        differential, 398n.
        the property tax, 401n., 504n.
    lump-sum, 404
    optimal, 360–361
        (*See also* Ramsey pricing)
    and tax credits, 523
    and tax shifting, 391
    of windfall profits, 461–466, 531–537
    (*See also* Gasoline tax; Property tax)
Teams, 563–568
Technology constraints, 243–247
    and technological progress, 250–251
Television:
    cable, 584–589
    public, 428–429
Tiebout hypothesis, 108
Tie-in sales, 316
Transaction costs, 29n., 75–78, 295
    administrative, 481
    and air pollution control, 569–577
    and automobile insurance, 7, 209
    and day-care services, 591–600
    and externalities, 431–432
    and firm behavior, 299–302, 311–312, 316–318
    and governance structure, 561–569
    and hospital decision-making, 342–344
    market, 481
    and monopoly governance, 584–591
    and ration coupons, 476
    and rent control, 445
Transfers, pure, 177
Translog cost function, 288–289
Treasury bills, U.S., 514–515, 582
Tree models, 525–529
Trucking deregulation, 272–276
Trust, 594–600

Uncertainty (*see* Bounded rationality; Expected utility theorem; Expected value; Information costs; Risk; Transaction costs)
United Nations Security Council, 12
U.S. Department of Agriculture, 568
U.S. Department of Health and Human Services, 10
U.S. Department of Labor, 10, 144n., 174
U.S. Geological Survey (USGS), 582–583
Urban renewal, 219
Utility:
  adaptive, 204–205
  expected, 193–206
  maximization of, 21–25, 51–56
  ordinal versus cardinal, 23n.
  Von Neumann-Morgenstern index, 199
  (*See also* Preferences)
Utility function, 21–25
  indirect, 154–155
Utility-possibilities frontier, 37, 162

Variation:
  coefficient of, 112n.
  compensating variation, 144–148, 150–152, 158–160, 168n.
  equivalent, 145, 148–152, 160
Vouchers, 477–480, 593n., 598

Walras' law, 396
Water rationing, 475–476
Wealth maximization, 508–511
Windfall gains and losses, 449
Work experiment (*see* Supported work experiment)

X-inefficiency, 323–326